VOLUME II

LINEAGES

OF THE

National Society of the Sons and Daughters of the Pilgrims

1929–1952

Compiled by

1947 — REGISTRAR GENERAL — 1950

MRS. EDWARD J. MERKLE
and Committee

MRS. EVELYN TRUE BUTTON   MISS ROSALIE HADDOX
MRS. FRED D. COULSON   MRS. W. W. STEARNS
MRS. JOSEPH E. COWAN

ADDENDA

Compiled by

1951 — REGISTRAR GENERAL — 1952

MRS. R. N. BARBER, SR.

GENEALOGICAL PUBLISHING CO., INC.

Baltimore   *1988*

Originally published 1953.
Reprinted with an added index—with the permission of
the National Society of the Sons and Daughters of the Pilgrims—
by Genealogical Publishing Co., Inc.
Baltimore, Maryland, 1988.
Index copyright © 1988 by
Genealogical Publishing Co., Inc.
Baltimore, Maryland
All Rights Reserved
Library of Congress Catalogue Card Number 87-82514
International Standard Book Number, Volume II: 0-8063-1209-2
Set Number: 0-8063-1210-6
Made in the United States of America

Thomas William Bicknell

VOLUME II

Dedicated to our Founder

THOMAS WILLIAM BICKNELL

" To honor a Patriot, Soldier, Christian fine
Whom honor gave Ancestral Line,
Fearless as they and unafraid,
He fought for principles by them laid
Against graft, gambling, greed,
Corruption and vice, some failed to heed.
He, like our oaks, deep-rooted stood,
Firm, patient, working for the good.
With vision clear he looked ahead
Along the path we all must tread.
For well he knew with foresight true,
We everyone have work to do.
And now, Memorial here we place
In honor of our Pilgrim Race
And its great Son and Founder brave."

—AVIS HAWKINS.

NATIONAL OFFICERS

Past Governor General.....................Mrs. Adelbert W. Mears

Past Governor General.....................Miss Helen M. Daggett

Past Governor General......................Mrs. John G. Chappell

Governor General............................Mrs. Therne V. Smith

Deputy Governor General....................Mrs. Alice M. Runyon

Second Deputy Governor General.................Mrs. James W. Knox

Recording Secretary General........ ....Mrs. John L. Harper

Corresponding Secretary General.................Mrs. David R. Smith

Treasurer General...........................Mrs. W. W. Stearns

Registrar General...........................Mrs. R. N. Barber, Sr.

Elder General.............................Dr. Hugh Grant Rowell

Historian General........................Mrs. John Anthony Crook

Captain General...........................Mrs. Joel A. Yarbrough

HONORARY MEMBERS

ANCESTOR INDEX

Gives Initial of Member and National Number

BUNTING, Job. C-5917
BURR, (Jehu) John. P-5882, S-6091
BURT, Henry. K-6299
BUSHNELL, Francis. W-6672
BUTT, Robert. R-6296, R-6273, R-6220, R-6228

— C —

CALVERT, Sir George. M-6006, C-6007, K-6029
CALVERT, Gov. Leonard. S-5953
CAMBERLAIN, Thomas. C-5947
CANFIELD, Thomas. F-6357
CANTEY, George. H-6053
CAPEN, Barnard. C-6531
CAPRON, Banfield. F-6333
CARPENTER, Henry. M-6626
CARPENTER, William. R-6485, B-6569
CARTER, Edward. S-6114
CARVER, Robert. J-6681
CASE, John. K-5868
CHAFFEE, Thomas. S-6465
CHAMBLEN, Nathaniel. R-6302
CHANDLER, William. M-6026, M-6055
CHAPIN, Dea. Samuel. C-6617
CHASE, William. N-6295
CHATFIELD, George. G-6000, M-6026
CHAUNCEY, Rev. Charles. T-5871
CHILTON, John. B-6529
CLAGGETT, Capt. Thomas. B-6086, C-6288
CLARK, Christopher. B-5852
CLARK, Capt. Daniel. C-6068, C-6615
CLARK, Dea. George. A-5950
CLAYE, Capt. John. H-6549
CLEVELAND, Alexander. D-6741
CLIZBE, James. B-6527
CODD, Col. St. Leder. B-6764
COE, Robert. I-5862
COFFYN, Tristram, Sr. G-6728
COGGESHALL, John. W-6619
COLBORNE, Corp. Edward. C-6246, A-6316
COLBY, Anthony. M-5972
COLCARD, Edward. C-6402
COLEMAN, Thomas. W-6405, T-6079
COLLETON, Major James. O-6139, T-6140
COLLIER, Robert. D-5981
COLLINS, Francis. A-6238
COLVER, Edward. C-2024, W-6555
CONANT, Roger. H-6648, B-6730
CONGER, John. B-6141
CONNER, Phillip. S-6623
COOKE, Francis. E-6312, H-6136
COOKE, John. E-6752, R-6753
COTTINGHAM, Thomas. D-5994
CRAM, John. W-6253
CROMWELL, William. S-6232
CURTIS, Richard. K-6203
CUSHMAN, Robert. C-6052, D-6023, F-6445
CUSHMAN, Thomas. B-6084
CUSTIS, John. R-6621
CUTTING, Richard. B-6330

— D —

DARLING, Dennis. D-6364
DARLING, Capt. John. D-6332
DANFORTH, Capt. Jonathan. W-6146
DAVID, Pierre. P-6588
DAVIES, Morgan. A-6178
DAVISON, William. E-6071
DEAN, Walter. T-6103
DE LANCY, Henry M. D-6206
DEMING, John. U-6078
DENNISON, William. D-6209
DENT, Judge Thomas. D-6583
DE PUY, Nicholas. R-6516
DEWEY, Thomas, Sr. P-6556, N-6734
DIGGES, Edward. W-6620, W-6632, Mc-6061
DINGMAN, Adam. F-5925
DISBROW, Henry. G-5838, S-5842, L-5839
DIXSON, Thomas. L-6258
DOANE, John. V-6038, P-6085, W-6115
DODGE, Richard. A-6613, B-6710
DOTY, Edward. H-6675
DOUGLAS, Dea. William. B-6127
DUDLEY, Gov. Thomas. S-6663
DUNHAM, John. B-6429
DYER, William. A-6519, C-5985, R-5883, B-6746

— E —

EASTHAM, George. H-6231, M-6428
EASTLACK, Francis. S-6098, E-6226
EATON, John. E-6011, S-6012, E-6418
EATON, Theophilas. J-5957
EAVENSON, Ralph. H-5828, E-5829, B-5831
EAVENSON, Thomas. B-5945
EDGERTON, Richard. M-6087
ELLIOTT, William. W-6283
ELLIS, Lt. John. G-6328
ELY, Capt. William. P-6384
EMERY, John. F-6484, D-5908
ENDICOTT, Gov. John. O-6419
EPPES, Col. Francis. H-6323
EVEREST, Andrew. E-6431

— F —

FAIRCHILD, Thomas. W-5959
FARNAM, Henry. F-5898, S-5899
FARRAR, David. F-5900, F-6612
FARRAR, William. H-6667
FARRINGTON, Edmund. N-6525
FARWELL, Henry. F-6541
FAUNTLEROY, Col. Moore. M-6534
FAWCETT, John. S-6072
FIELD, Robert. C-5861
FIELD, Zachariah. D-6478, F-6382, R-6400
FISHER, John. D-6039
FISKE, Lt. Nathan. W-6142
FLANDERS, Steven. F-6254, D-6120, D-6150

FLEMING, William. B-6044
FLINT, Thomas. W-6714
FLOOD, Col. John. B-6560, Q-6304
FOOTE, Gov. Nathaniel. W-6433, F-5968
FORD, Dea. Thomas. A-5906
FORMAN, Robert. C-6131
FOWLER, William. W-6610
FOWLKES, Thomas. I-6213
FREEMAN, Lt. Gov. Edmund. W-6343
FRENCH, Lt. William. Y-6614
FROST, Elder Edmund. B-5930
FULLER, Edward. H-6289, R-6290
FULLER, Capt. Matthew. F-6391
FULLER, Samuel. T-6494, B-5940

— G —

GAINES, Thomas. M-6719, B-6738
GALE, Richard. G-6392
GALLUP, John. G-6432, K-6202, H-6175
GEAR, George. C-6005
GIBBES, Robert. S-6082
GIBSON, John. C-6424
GILLIAM, John, Sr. K-6720
GILPIN, Thomas. R-6348
GOADE, John. S-6646
GODFREY, Benjamin. B-5975
GOOCH, Rev. John. W-6199
GOODE, John. B-6600
GORTON, Samuel. L-6629, K-6631, L-6106
GOULD, Nathan. G-6566, M-6458
GRAVES, Capt. Thomas. R-6166
GRAY, William. R-6580, C-6410, H-6581
GREENE, John. B-5830, Q-5850
GREENLEAF, Edmund. S-5894
GREENLEAF, Capt. Stephen. M-6547
GRISWOLD, Edward. S-6081
GRISWOLD, Michael. G-5875
GROESBECK, Nicholas. B-5901

— H —

HALL, John C. M-5923
HALSEY, Thomas. D-0000
HAMLIN, Giles. S-5886
HANCOCK, Richard. C-6059
HARLOW, Lt. William, Sr. D-6676
HARRISON, Benjamin. P-6673
HART, John. R-5884
HATCHER, William. A-6760
HATHAWAY, William. L-6721
HAYDEN, William. G-4820
HAYNIE, Capt. John S. 6088
HELM, Israel. C-6111
HEWES, Joseph. F-5996
HICKS, Robert A. A-5979
HIGGENS, Richard. S-5990
HILLS, Williams. H-5876
HINSKLEY, Gov. Thomas. T-5848
HINMAN, Edward. S-5916
HOLLADAY, Capt. Thomas. H-6043
HOLDEN, Richard, ??-6469
HOLDER, Christopher. P-5834

HOLLISTER, John. H-6470
HOOKER, Rev. Thomas. C-6677, K-6755
HOPKINS, John. H-5881
HOPKINS, Stephen. M-6042
HOTCHKISS, Samuel. K-6729
HOWARD, Capt. Cornelius. R-5910
HOWELL, Edward. C-6147, F-6048
HOWLAND, John. R-6069, P-6016,
    W-5874, C-5877, A-5928, B-5887
HUBBARD, Henry. R-5991
HUDSON, William. W-6388
HUGHES, Orlando. W-6749
HUNT, Enoch. K-6462
HUNT, Ralph. H-5891
HUNTING, Elder John. H-6501
HUNTINGTON, Simon. M-6125

— I —

IRELAND, Thomas. R-5879, P-5966

— J —

JENNEY, Thomas. H-6403
JOHNSON, Isaac. C-5973
JORDAN, Samuel. D-6095
JOSSELYN, Thomas. P-6456
JUNKINS, Robert. H-6135

— K —

KEELER, Ralph. S-6379
KENNON, Richard. G-6707
KEZAR, George. H-6407, K-6497
KIMBALL, Benjamin. S-6453
KINGSLEY, Stephen. M-6486
KORTRIGHT, Jan Bastiansen. G-6489
KUSTER, Paul. E-6077

— L —

LAMBERT, Thomas. C-5977
LAWRENCE, John. A-6417
LeBARON, Francis. J-6406
LEE, Col. Richard. T-6666
LEETS, Gov. William. A-5858
LEVERICH, Sir Sahille. ??-6021
LINDSAY, David. D-5962
LINTHICUM, Thomas, Sr. G-6102,
    T-5844, L-5980, F-5993, D-5931,
    W-5932
LISTON, Morris. S-6426
LITCHFIELD, Josiah. K-5905
LITTLEFIELD, Francis. ??-6047
LOTHROP, Rev. John. L-6398
LUCAS, Robert, Jr. ??-6049
LUDLOW, Roger. R-6073
LUMBERSEN, Frederick. C-5967
LUTEN, Major Thomas. W-5997
LUTHER, Capt. John. N-6063

— M —

MACK, John. F-6415
MANCHESTER, Thomas. H-6129
MARTLING, Abraham. R-6119
MASON, Capt. Hugh. H-6459
MASSIE, Peter. I-6763
MATTHEW, John. ??-5895
MATTOON, Philip. L-6711, L-6713, D-6712
MELYN, Cornelius. D-6768
MERKLE, John C. D-6475
MEYER, Nicholas. G-5951
MINOE, Thomas. L-6017
MIX, Thomas. H-6481
MONNET, Pierre, Sr. M-6025
MOODY, John. B-6708, B-6716
MOORE, Gov. James, Sr. C-5970
MONTAGUE, Peter. W-6393

— Mc —

McKEEL, John. L-6062, D-6745

— N —

NASH, Thomas. B-6446
NASH, Lt. James. H-5944
NEWLIN, Nicholas. L-5984
NICHOLS, Francis. N-6680
NOBLE, Thomas. B-5999
NOELL, Increase. L-5911
NORTON, Rev. William. S-5849
NOYES, Nicholas. D-6449

— O —

OGDEN, Richard, Sr. J-6056
OGDEN, Richard IV. W-5860
OLCOTT, Thomas. R-6099
OLIVER, John. Mc–6020
OP den GRAEF, Herman. B-6076
OPDYCK, Lauris J. H-6116, B-6109 M-6117
OWENS, Joseph. H-5949

— P —

PACE, Col. John. H-6684
PALMER, Walter. C-6893
PARKER, ———. P-6384
PARKHURST, Ebenezer. P-6390, ??-6401
PARSONS, Corp. Joseph. W-6065
PATTERSON, Capt. Thomas. T-5867
PATTON, William. R-6495
PAUL, Philip. P-6101
PEABODY, John. P-5846
PEARSON, Robert. M-5845
PECK, Dea. Paul. N-6019
PECK, William. W-5912
PENNOYER, Robert. P-6399
PHELPS, Nathaniel. K-4995
PIERCE, George. A-5873

— (right column) —

PILLSBURY, William. D-6747
POINDEXTER, George. B-6759, S-6748
POOR, Daniel. R-6404
POPE, Col. Nathaniel. H-6148, H-6149, H-6397, S-6443
PRENCE, Gov. Thomas. Mc-6093
PRICE, George. B-5857
PROSCOTT, Jonathan. T-5872
PROCTOR, Robert. P-6421
PROVOST, David. B-5960
PURDY, Francis. N-6028
PYNCHON, Hon. William. S-6124

— Q —

QUINCY, Hon. Edmund. W-6031

— R —

RANDOLPH, Edward Fitz. Z-6031
RANDOLPH, Col. William. D-6409, C-6442
RAWSON, Edward. A-6461, ?? 6483
RICE, Dea. Edmund. T-5848
RICHARDSON, Es. Mc-6045
RICHARDSON, Samuel. W-6113, B-5933, B-6739
RICHARDSON, William. C-5880
RING, Andrew. C-6027
RISLEY, Richard. C-5878
ROBERTS, John. H-6479
ROBERTS, Thomas. K-6083
ROBSON, John. N-5987
ROGERS, Giles. G-5853
ROGERS, Thomas. B-6411, S-6455, Mc-6476
ROWLETT, Peter. T-6122, P-6725, P-6726, P-6727
RUCKER, Peter. F-6051
RUFFIN, William O. D-6674
RUSH, John. G-6134

— S —

SANDFORD, John. Y-5836
SAYRE, Thomas. M-6434, D-6506, H-5888, P-6509
SCHUYLER, Philip P. M-5889
SEWALL, Hon. Henry. E-5976, W-5992, E-5978
SEYMOUR, Richard. M-6389
SHERMAN, Philip. K-6502
SIMONDS, William. D-6490, S-6503
SLAFTER, John. T-6437
SLAUGHTER, Capt. John. A-6447
SLINGERLAND, Teunise. B-6132
SMITH, Joseph. B-6766
SMITH, Major Lawrence. McA-6472
SMITH, Thomas. E-6444, C-5955, H-5934
SMITH, Hon. Thomas. C-6679
SOMERS, John. G-6498, B-6514
SPICER, Thomas. B-6058
SPRIGG, Thomas. H-6487
STACY, Mahlon. M-6046

STANFIELD, Francis. G-6133
STEELMAN, James. W-6499
STEVENS, John, Sr. P-6075
STOCKTON, Richard. H-6066, P-5865
STOUT, Richard. C-5032
STONE, Gregory. O-6420
STRATTON, Samuel. K-5843
STRONG, Elder John. B-6121
ST. JOHN, Capt. Matthew. K-5895
SUMNER, William. W-6678, D-6750,
  L-6751
SWAN, Richard. S-6511
STACKHOUSE, John. H-5965
STANTON, Thomas. S-5974
SUPPLEE, Andreas. S-5918, F-5919

— T —

TAYLOR, Thomas. C-6491
TELLER, William. T-4966
THELABELL, James. C-6733
THOMPSON, Andrew. L-6440, L-5863
THORNTON, William. L-6074
THOROUGHGOOD, Adam. K-6480
THROCKMORTON, John. ??-6030
TILGMAN, Christopher. P-6756
TOMLINSON, Richard. M-5961
TOWNE, William. L-6074
TRUE, Capt. Henry. F-6496
TUCKER, Robert. S-6474
TURNER, Humphrey. S-6054
TUTTLE, William. G-6493

— V —

VAN SCHAICK, Adrian. G-6040
VAN SCHLECTENHORST, Brant.
  B-6004
VAN KORTRIGHT, Jan B. P-6460
VAN LENT, Harck. F-6104
VER PLANCK, Abraham I. S-6488
VEAZEY, John. Mc-6130
VERNOOY, Johannes. G-6137

— W —

WALBRIDGE, Henry. F-6416
WALDO, Cornelius. B-5988
WALDRON, John. W-6385
WALKER, Capt. Richard. N-6762
WALLACE, William. Mc-5855
WALLIS, Robert. L-6448
WARDER, Willoughby. R-6468
WAREHAM, Rev. John. H-6067
WARING, Capt. Samson. H-5964
WARREN, Richard. W-6089, W-6094,
  J-6213
WASHINGTON, John. S-5921
WATKINS, Henry. H-6744
WEBB, Christopher. W-6112
WEBSTER, Gov. John. C-6018, J-6505
WELLES, Lt. Joshua. W-6423
WELLS, Richard. M-6394
WHARTON, Dr. Jesse. W-5896, C-5915
WHITE, Elder John. F-5837
WHITE, William. H-6464
WHITNEY, Henry. H-6090
WHITNEY, Thomas. D-5989, M-5924,
  H-6041
WIGGLESWORTH, Rev. Michael. H-6500
WILKINSON, Lawrence. F-6683
WILLARD, Major Simon. I-6118
WILLIAMS, Lester J. L-6672
WILLIAMS, Richard. M-6097, T-5848,
  W-6002
WILLIAMS, Roger. W-6036, E-6430,
  B-5954
WILLIAMSON, Daniel, Sr. S-5971
WILLOUGHBY, Gov. Francis. G-6765
WING, Rev. John. S-6010
WINSLOW, Kenelm. C-6422
WOOD, Henry. N-5870
WOODBURY, William. L-6396
WOODSON, Dr. John. H-5998, S-6438,
  E-6682, B-6716, B-6731, C-6715
WORDEN, Peter I. P-5866

DIRECTORY

Should errors be found the members will please take into consideration the difficulty of reading the hand written applications which were not familiar, and, in many cases, the ink of which had been pale when used, and with age, had become almost illegible. As these ancestral lines are being studied by our members, they will undoubtedly rejoice in being able to trace others who have been descended from the same forefathers.

5858 ABBOT, Mrs. George A.,   Recorded 1929, Illinois
         730 N. Grove Ave., Oak Park, Illinois
1. Marie Millage *m.* 1902 George Andrews Abbot
2. Abraham Millage (1839–1912) *m.* 1865 Janette Dillon (1840–1922)
3. William Dillon (1792–1876) *m.* 1835 Thankful Ann Eliza Stone (1807–1861)
4. Ebenezer Stone (1771–1843) *m.* 1806 Clarissa Lobdell (1790–1811)
5. Ebenezer Stone (1752–1803) *m.* 1771 Jerusha
3. Ebenezer Stone (1706–1771) *m.* 1752 Sybil Leets (1724–1803)
7. Samuel Leets *m.* 1677 Margaret de Craves
8. Andrew Leets (1702–) *m.* 1669 Elizabeth Jordan
9. Gov. William Leets (1612–1684) *m.* 1636 Anne Paine (–1668)
Service: Governor of Connecticut, 1676.
Reference: Savage—Dictionary of New England.

6613 ABBOTT, Miss Margaret   Recorded 1949
         24 Marlborough Street, Boston, Massachusetts
1. Margaret Abbott
2. Forrest H. Abbott (1886–1946) *m.* 1908 Mary T. Fraser (1886–)
3. Charles H. Abbott (1859–1935) *m.* 1882 Adelaide L. Burnham (1863–)
4. Simon P. Burnham (1832–) *m.* 1861 Lydia F. Dodge
5. William Dodge (1787–1850) *m.* Lydia Folsom, *d.* 1824
6. John T. Dodge (1764–1851) *m.* 1786 Elizabeth Dodge, *d.* 1851
7. Capt. Richard Dodge (1738–1802) *m.* 1757 Lydia Dodge (1735–1813)
8. Lt. Richard Dodge (1703–1778) *m.* 1724 Mary Thorne
9. Lt. William Dodge (1678–1765) *m.* 1698 Prudence Fairchild, *d.* 1737
10. Richard Dodge (1643–1705) *m.* 1667 Mary Eaton (1641–1716)
11. Richard Dodge (1602–1671) *m.* Edith ——— (1603–1678)
Service: In Salem, Mass., 1638, first on list of 21 subscribers to Harvard College, 1653.
Reference: Genealogy of Dodge Family.

6539 ACKLEY, Mary Louise   Recorded 1946
         11 South State Street, Vineland, New Jersey
1. Mary Louise Ackley
2. John A. Ackley (1854–1933) *m.* 1885 Antha V. Smith (1857–1938)
3. William J. Smith (1833–1913) *m.* 1854 Hannah L. Brown (1833–1899)
4. Elias Smith (1781–1864) *m. ca.* 1812 Janet D. Gates (1796–1855)
5. Ephraim Gates (1760–1852) *m.* 1793 Elizabeth Douglas (1761–1848)
6. Johnathan Gates (1740–1777) *m.*
7. Caleb Gates (after 1692–1774) *m.* 1716 Mary Forbes *ca.* (1695–after 1740)
8. Caleb Forbes *ca.* (1650–1710) *m. ca.* 1677 Mary Huntington (1657–after 1710)
9. Simon Huntington *ca.* (1629–1706) *m.* 1653 Sarah Clarke (1633–1721)
Service: Representative from Norwich, Conn., to Gen. Court of Conn., 1674.
Reference: History of New London, Conn., Gen. and Biog. Record of New London, Conn.

6717 ADAMS, Dr. Arthur (at large)   Recorded 1951
         Trinity College, Hartford 6, Connecticut
         m. Emma Guerin Steelman (no date)
2. James Reading Adams (1835–1890) *m.* 1857 Marietta English (1840–1912)
3. Daniel Adams (1773–1863) *m.* 1818 Elizabeth Good Bartlett (1799–1862)
4. John Adams (1738–1798) *m.* 1763 Margaret Garwood (1740–1825)
5. John Adams (*c.* 1694–*c.* 1771) *m.* Mary Covenover?
6. Jonathan Adams (1668–1727), Barbara * * * ?
7. John Adams (*c.* 1638–1670) *m.* 1657 Abigail Smith
8. Jeremy Adams (1604–1683) *m.* 1636 Rebecca Greenhill, wid. of Sam'l. (–1678)
Service: Served in expedition against the Indians, 1637.
Reference: The pedigree of Jerome Adams, July number of 1905 New England Historical & Genealogical Register & Pedigree Register of Colonial Wars in Conn., pub. in Hartford, 1941.

1

6291   ADAMS, Annetta I. (Junior)   Recorded 1940
          1415 Clearview Street, Philadelphia, Pennsylvania
       1. Annetta I. Adams
       2. Laurence S. Adams, *b.* 1895, *m.* 1919 Ida E. Houghton, *b.* 1894
       3. William L. Houghton, *b.* 1865, *m.* 1889 Elizabeth Kearney, *b.* 1868
       4. Carlos P. Houghton, Jr., (1837–1883) *m.* 1864 Clara L. Hopkins (1842–1916)
       5. Carlos P. Houghton (1816–1883) *m.* 1836 Angelica Taylor (1819–1889)
       6. Abijah Houghton (1792–1855) *m.* Eliza Farrand (1795–1869)
       7. Abijah Houghton, *b.* 1747, *d.* Rev. War, *m.* Mary Sawyer
       8. Abijah Houghton (1723–1802) *m.* 1746 Alice Joslin, *b.* 1802
       9. Benjamin Houghton (1700–1774) *m.* 1720 Ruth Whitlock (1700–1774)
      10. Benjamin Houghton, *b.* 1678, *m.* Zermiah Moore
      11. John Houghton (1651–1737) *m.* 1671 Mary Farrar (1648–1724)
      12. JOHN HOUGHTON (1624–1684) *m.* Beatrice, *d.* 1711
       Service: Settled in Lancaster, Mass., 1635.
       Reference: "Old Families of Concord, Mass.," Potter; "Pioneers of Massachusetts,"
                Pope; Lancaster Records; Woburn Records; New Eng. Hist. & Gen.
                Register, Vol. 79.

6238   ADAMS, Mrs. Harold J.   Recorded 1939
          10 Mayfaire Lane, Buffalo, New York
       1. Laura S. Fortiner (1880) Harold J. Adams
       2. Walter Scott Fortiner (1857–1926) *m.* 1879 Linda Letts (1858–1938)
       3. Daniel Fortiner (1819–1899) *m.* 1854 Eliz. Jane Bates (1826–1899)
       4. Simon Fortiner (1793–1832) *m.* 1815 Martha Thomas (1792–1839)
       5. Daniel Fortiner (1760–1806) *m.* 1785 Elizabeth Ellis (1767–1818)
       6. Simeon Ellis (1738–) *m.* 1760 Priscilla Bates
       7. Simeon Ellis (1699–1773) *m.* 1741 Sarah Collins (1704–1773)
       8. Joseph Collins *m.* 1698 Catharine Huddleton
       9. Francis Collins (1635–1720) *m.* 1663 Sarah Mayham
      10. EDWARD COLLINS
          MARY—
       Services: Justice of Peace, Member of Council of Proprietors of W. J.
       Reference: Gen of Lamb & Rose; Collins Gen.; Fortiner Ellis & Collins Gen.

6483   ADAMS, Jeane F.   Recorded 1945
          Granville, Ohio
       1. Miss Jean Frances Adams
       2. William H. Adams (1888–) *m.* 1922 Marjory Bath (1888–)
       3. John W. Bath (1853–1930) *m.* 1879 Frances Rawson (1860–1932)
       4. Bela Rawson (1824–1876) *m.* 1846 Harriet Nichols (1825–1897)
       5. Bela Rawson (1777–1848) *m.* Polla Cora (1787–1864)
       6. Edmund Rawson (1751–1823) *m.* 1770 Sarah Hull
       7. Edmund Rawson (1718–) *m.* 1743/4 Martha Allen
       8. Edmund Rawson (1689–) *m.* 1717 Elizabeth Howard (–1759)
       9. Grindel Rawson (1659–1715) *m.* 1681 Susannah Wilson (1665–1748)
      10. EDWARD RAWSON (1615–1693) *m.* Rachel Perne
       Service: Secretary of the Massachusetts Bay Colony, 1650–1686.

6577   ADAMS, Katherine Kellogg   Recorded 1948
          1837 Greenleaf Avenue, Chicago, Illinois
       1. Katherine K. Adams
       2. Wm. H. H. Adams (1840–1890) *m.* 1867 Hannah W. Concklin (1842–1932)
       3. Christopher B. Adams (1811–1888) *m.* 1838 Sarah Gannaway (1819–1854)
       3. Eli Adams (1785–1870) *m.* 1810 Elizabeth Beeks (1790–1847)
       5. Eli Adams (1748–1796) *m.* 1770 Sophia Addams (1749–1800)
       6. Isaac Addams (*ca.* 1711–1763) *m.* 1736 Elizabeth Addams *d. aft.* 1760
       7. Thomas Addams (1673–1735) *m.* Anna—
       8. PHILLIP ADDAMS (*ca.* 1650–1696) *m.* 1670 Anna Crewe (1655–1683–91)
       Service: A first settler in Annamessex, Morumsco section, 1663.
       Reference: Adams Family Records, Old Somerset on the Eastern Shore of Maryland.

6461 ADAMS, Mrs. William H.   Recorded 1945
      Granville, Ohio
1. Marjorie Bath *m.* 1922 William H. Adams
2. John W. Bath (1853–1930) *m.* 1879 Frances Rawson (1860–1932)
3. Bela Rawson (1824–1876) *m.* 1846 Harriet Nichols (1825–1897)
4. Bela Rawson (1777–1848) *m.* Polla Cora (1787–1864)
5. Edmund Rawson (1751–1823) *m.* 1770 Sarah Hull
6. Edmund Rawson (1718–) *m.* 1743 Martha Allen (–1781)
7. Edmund Rawson (1689–) *m.* 1717 Elizabeth Howard (–1759)
8. Grindel Rawson (1659–1715) *m.* 1681 Susannah Wilson (1665–1748)
9. EDWARD RAWSON (1615–1693) *m.* Rachel Perne
Service: Secretary Massachusetts Bay Colony in the town of Newbury; 2nd Town
    Clerk; Public Notary and Registrar of Newbury; Selectman.
Reference: Rawson Genealogy 1926 by Family; Rawson Family Memoirs by Crane:
    Savage Dict.

6589 ANDERSON, Mrs. B. T.   Recorded 1948
      123 South Montclair Avenue, Dallas, Texas
1. Florrie Higdon *m.* 1915 Burrell T. Adkerson
2. William P. Higdon (1853–1914) *m.* 1884 Lyde Davis (1856–)
3. William J. Higdon (1816–1862) *m.* 1842 Julie A. Allen (1820–1860)
4. John Higdon (1793–1838) *m.* 1816 Rebecca Reynolds (1791–1867)
5. John Higdon (1757–1816) *m.* 1793 Mary ⸻ (1770–1819)
6. John Higdon (1708–1771) *m. ca.* 1730 Sarah Williams (*ca.* 1713–*ca.* 1757)
7. John Higdon (*ca.* 1677–1720) *m. ca.* (1698 Magdelene ⸻ (*ca.* 1678–*ca.* 1728)
8. John Higdon (*ca.* 1655–1718) m. ⸻
9. Richard Higdon (*ca. 1625–ca.* 1665) *m. ca.* 1651 Jane Brookes (1633–1703)
10. HENRY BROOKES (*ca.* 1590–1663) *m. ca.* 1620 Jane ⸻ (*ca.* 1600–*ca.* 1648)
Service: Colonizer and merchant.
Reference: Westmoreland Wills and Deeds, Cavaliers and Pioneers.

6417 AINSWORTH, Mrs. Harley Enoch   Recorded 1943
      Montpelier, Vermont
1. Lillian M. Pettes *m.* Harley Enoch Ainsworth
2. Cornelius Pettes (1842–1906) *m.* 1864 Marietta Annis Wells (1842–1894)
3. Levi Pettes (1802–1868) *m.* 1826–32 Mrs. Maria (Smith) Rice (1802–1878)
4. John Smith (1756–1822) *m.* 1784 Sarah Lawrence (1759–1843)
5. Bezaleel Lawrence (1736–1796) *m.* 1758 Sarah Muzzy (–1819)
6. Jonathan Lawrence (1706–1773) *m.* 1726 Elizabeth Swain (1707–1790)
7. John Lawrence (1667–1746) *m.* 1687 Anna Tarbell (1670–)
8. Nathaniel Lawrence (1639–) *m.* 1660 Sarah Morse
9. JOHN LAWRENCE (1609–) *m.* Elizabeth ⸻ (–1663)
Service: To America, 1635, and settled at Watertown, Mass.; listed as a proprietor
    there.
Reference: V. R., Williamstown, Chelsea, Newbury, N. H.; V. R., Lexington, Groton,
    Mass.; Gen. John Lawrence of Suffolk, Eng., Wattertown, Mass., by
    John Lawrence.

6276 AKIN, Mabel Carrie   Recorded 1939
      Patterson, Putnam County, New York
1. Mabel Carrie Akin
2. Charles E. Akin (1863–1935) *m.* 1893 Nettie Haviland, *b.* 1873
3. Henry Tudor Haviland (1850–1902) *m.* 1871 Florence Briggs (1852–1895)
4. Israel Haviland (1820–1854) *m.* 1847 Abby Jane Ferris (1819–1908)
5. Zachariah Ferris 5th (1778–1860) *m.* 1802 Hannah Marsh (1784–1867)
6. Joseph Marsh (1754–*c.* 1830) *m.* 1781 Abigail Waldo (1764–1793)
7. Samuel Waldo (Deacon) (1731–1793) *m.* 1754 Hannah Waters Waldo (1730–1818)
8. Shubael Waldo (1707–1776) *m.* 1730 Abigail Allen, *d.* 1799
9. Samuel Allen 3rd, *b.* 1660, *m.* 2nd 1700 Mary Alden
10. Joseph Alden *d.* 1697 *m.* Mary Simmons
11. JOHN ALDEN (1599–1687) *m.* 1622 Priscilla Mullens, *b.* 1600
Service: Member of Mayflower Colony.
Reference: Haviland Genealogy by Josephine Frost; Waldo Genealogy by Waldo
    Lincoln; Waldos of America by J. D. Hall; Alden Family by Frank Wes-
    ley Alden; Descendants of Hon. John Alden by Ebenezer Alden.

6447   ALEXANDER, Mrs. James Willard   Recorded 1949
          Penny Farms, Florida
       1. Sue Paxton *m*. James Willard Alexander
       2. John Richard Paxton (1863–1942) *m*. 1886 Mattie Lee Arnold (1867–)
       3. James Edward Paxton (1834–1921) *m*. 1856 Mary Evelyn Thompson (1834–1883)
       4. Col. Richard Head Paxton (1808–1878) *m*. 1833 Mildred Burrus (1811–1885)
       5. Edmund Burrus (1786–1858) *m*. 1810 Mary Slaughter (1796–1865)
       6. Jesse Slaughter (1768–1824) *m*. Lucy Thornton
       7. Col. Robert Slaughter (1724–1790) *m*. 1750 Susannah Harrison (–1785 aft.)
       8. Col. Robert Slaughter (1702–1768) *m*. 1723 Mary Smith (1706–)
       9. Col. Robert Slaughter (1680–1726) *m*. 1701 Frances Ann Jones
      10. Francis Slaughter (1653–1718) *m*. Margaret Hudson
      11. Capt. Francis Slaughter (1630–1657) *m*. 1652 Elizabeth Underwood
      12. CAPT. JOHN SLAUGHTER (bef. 1600–) *m*. bef. 1630
      Service: Comm. by Sir Thomas Howard, March 17, 1638; died Rappahannock County,
          Virginia.
      Reference: Kerr's Hist. Ky., Vol. 5; Paxton Fam., Wm. Paxton; Va. Mag. Hist. &
          Biog., Vols. 21, 22, 23; Wm. & Mary Quart., Vol. 14.

5906   ALLEN, Frances Strong   Recorded 1930
          73 Fulton Street, Oshkosh, Wisconsin
       1. Frances Isabel Strong (1867–) *m*. 1895 Silas Marsh Allen II
       2. John Owen Strong (1835–1872) *m*. 1865 Mary Isabel Norman (1844–1921)
       3. Cyrus Strong (1796–1891) *m*. 1833 Susan Ann Curtiss (1802–1884)
       4. Uriel Strong (1754–1819) *m*. 179– Phoebe Minor (1767–1825)
       5. Preserved Strong (1712–1800) *m*. 1749 Esther Stoddard (1716–1800)
       6. Adino Strong (1676–1749) *m*. 1702 Eunice (1679–1763)
       7. Thomas Strong (163?–1689) *m*. 1671 Rachel Holton
       8. Elder John Strong (1605–1699) *m*. 1630 Abigail Ford (1619–1688)
       9. DEACON THOMAS FORD (15 –1676) *m*. 1616 Elizabeth Cooke (–1643)
      Service: Deputy to Connecticut General Court, 1637–1643; a Founder of Dorchester,
          Massachusetts.
      Reference: Dorchester, Orcutt, Windsor, Stiles.

5929   ALLEN, Neville Ripley   Recorded 1930
          115 N. Main Street, Charles City, Iowa
       1. Neville Ripley Allen *m*. Bertha H. Campbell
       2. Ethen B. Allen (1859–) *m*. 1884 Mary E. Duffin (1859–1927)
       3. Dr. John H. Allen (1818–1882) *m*. 1857 Nancy Ripley Hall (1829–1881)
       4. Asahel Hall (1799–1877) *m*. 1816 Betsy Wood Ripley (1799–1856)
       5. Hezekiah Ripley (1771–1846) *m*. Priscilla Wood (1776–1843)
       6. Ephraim Wood III (1744–1831) *m*. Sarah French (1753–)
       7. Ephraim Wood II (1715–1781) *m*. 1742 Mary Lazell (–1752)
       8. Ephraim Wood, Sr., (1679–1744) *m*. 1710 Susanna Howland (1690–1743)
       9. Isaac Howland (1659–1723) *m*. 1677 Elizabeth Vaughn (1653–1727)
      10. JOHN HOWLAND (1593–1673) *m*. 1624 Elizabeth Tilley (1609–1697)
      Service: Signer of the Mayflower Compact.
      Reference: Massachusetts Records.

5928   ALLEN, Walter D.   Recorded 1930, Colorado
          115 N. Main Street, Charles City, Iowa
       1. Walter D. Allen *m*. Leulah L. Harrison
       2. Ethen B. Allen (1859–) *m*. Mary G. Duffin (1859–1927)
       3. Dr. John H. Allen (1818–) *m*. 1857 Nancy R. Hall (1829–1881)
       4. Asahel Hall (1799–1877) *m*. 1816 Betsy Wood Ripley (1799–1856)
       5. Hezikiah Ripley (1771–1846) *m*. Priscilla Wood (1776–1843)
       6. Ephraim Wood III (1744–1831) *m*. Sarah French (1753–)
       7. Ephraim Wood II (1715–1781) *m*. 1742 Mary Lazell (–1752)
       8. Ephraim Wood, Sr. (1689–1744) *m*. 1710 Susanna Howland (–1743)
       9. Isaac Howland (1659–1723) *m*. 1677 Elizabeth Vaughn (1653–1727)
      10. JOHN HOWLAND (1593–1673) *m*. 1624 Elizabeth Tilley (1609–1697)
      Service: Signer of the Mayflower Compact.
      Reference: Massachusetts Records.

5969 ALLEN, Mrs. William P.
36 Orange Avenue, Irvington, New Jersey   Recorded 1930, New Jersey
1. Sarah Wilson *m.* 1923 William Porter Allen
2. Minard A. Wilson (1853–1922) *m.* 1877 Cornelia Chatterton (1845–1929)
3. William H. Chatterton (1807–1875) *m.* 1839 Emily Bond (1814–1880)
4. John Bond (1789–1870) *m.* 1813 Mary P. Hand (1798–1870)
5. Aaron Hand (1764–1842) *m.* 1783 Phebe Smith (1767–1845)
6. Walter Smith (1733–1820) *m.* Hannah Baldwin (1735–1812)
7. David Baldwin
8. John Baldwin (1670–)
9. John Baldwin (1640–1706) *m.* 1663 Hannah Bruen (1644–1685)
10. OBADIAH BRUEN (1606–1681) Sarah

Service: Freeman in 1642; appointed Commissioner by the General Court, 1663.
Reference: Baldwin Genealogy, pp. 300, 305; History of New London, by Caulkins, pp. 155, 156; History of Willis Family.

5941 ANABLE, Anna M.
Farrington Avenue, Philipse Manor, New York   Recorded 1930
1. Anna M. Anable
2. Major Samuel L. Anable (1821–1913) *m.* 1844 Sarah R. Babcock (1826–1916)
3. Joseph Anable (1773–1831) *m.* 1814 Alma Sheldon (1785–1875)
4. John Anable (1744–1815) *m.* 1768 Hannah Stewart (1748–1790)
5. Cornelius Anable (1704–) *m.* 1728 Experience
6. John Anable (1673–) *m.* 1692 Experience Taylor (1672–)
7. Samuel Anable (1646–1678) *m.* 1667 Mehitable Allyn (1648–)
8. ANTHONY ANABLE (1599–1673) *m.* 1645 Anna Clark

Service: Representative to General Court from Scituate, 1634–5.
Reference: Anable Genealogy; American Ancestry, Vol. XI, p. 18.

5963 ANABLE, Anthony
Irvington-on-the-Hudson, New York   Recorded 1940, Texas
1. Anthony Anable *m.* 1924 Emily Barton
2. Eliphalet N. Anable (1857–1904) *m.* 1891 Annie S. Horton (1862–)
3. Henry S. Anable (1815–1887) *m.* 1855 Rosanna Frick (1831–)
4. Joseph Anable (1773–1831) *m.* 1814 (2) Alma Sheldon (1785–1875)
5. John Anable (1744–1815) *m.* 1768 Hannah Stewart (1748–1790)
6. Cornelius Anable (1704–) *m.* 1728 Experience
7. John Anable (1673–) *m.* 1692 Experience Taylor (1672–)
8. Samuel Anable (1646–1678) *m.* 1667 Mehitable Allyn (1648–)
9. ANTHONY ANABLE (1599–1673) *m.* 1645 (2) Anna Clark (–1687)

Service: Representative to General Court from Scituate, 1634–5; from Barnstable, 1645–58.
Reference: Anable Genealogy, by Henry S. Anable; Magazine of American Genealogy, 1930. p. 161; Bailie's History of New Plymouth, Vol. I; Savage Dictionary of New England.

5942 ANABLE, Harriet I.
Farrington Avenue, Philipse Manor, New York   Recorded 1930, New York
1. Harriet I. Anable
ANTHONY ANABLE (1599–1673) *m.* 1645 Anna Clark
Lineage same as No. 5941

5943 ANABLE, Sara Alma
Farrington Avenue, Philipse Manor, New York   Recorded 1930, New York
1. Sara Alma Anable
ANTHONY ANABLE (1599–1673) *m.* 1645 Anna Clark
Lineage same as No. 5942

6519   ANDERSON, Mrs. Ida Woodington   Recorded 1946
   1. Ida Woodington *m.* 1889 ―― Anderson
   2. James Woodington (1832–1915) *m.* 1853 Sarah J. Gardner (1833–1909)
   3. William Woodington (1809–1877) *m.* 1827 Rebecca Dyer (1812–1880)
   4. Samuel Dyer (1783–1855/6) *m.* 1808 Elizabeth Keen (1790–1832)
   5. Joseph Dyer (1754–1815) *m.* Mary Ann ――
   6. James Dyer (1727/8–1803) *m.* 1851 Elizabeth
   7. Charles Dyer (1697–) *m.* 1716 Elizabeth Shrief (1698–1778)
   8. James Dyer (1669–1696) *m.* 1680 ――
   9. Charles Dyer (1650–1709) *m.* Mary ――
  10. WILLIAM DYER, *d.* 1677, *m.* Mary ――, *d.* 1660
Service: 1640–1647 Sec. for Portsmouth and Newport, R. I.; 1648 Gen. Recorded;
          1650 Attorney Gen.
Reference: V. R., Newport, R. I.

6760   ANDERSON, Mrs. Walter Edwin   Recorded 1952, Georgia
          3447 Lenox Road N. E., Atlanta, Georgia
   1. Edith May Moore *m.* 1924 W. E. Anderson
   2. Simpson Cortez Moore (1870–1918) *m.* 1892 Josie Estelle Roberts (1876–)
   3. Winfield Taylor Moore (1847–1928) *m.* 1867 Sarah Eugene Hatcher (1845–1907)
   4. John Henry Hatcher (1812–1878) *m.* 1830 Dorcas Ross (1808–1850)
   5. John Hatcher (1781–aft. 1840) *m.* Mary Flippen (1785–aft. 1840)
   6. Major John Hatcher (1756–1837) *m.* 1780 Nancy Gentry (–1845)
   7. Frederick Hatcher (–will 1783) *m.* 1756 Sarah Woodson (1740–1813)
   8. Henry Hatcher (?–will 1743) *m.* Susannah Williamson
   9. Benjamin Hatcher (1644–will 1727) *m.* abt. 1680 Elizabeth Greenhaugh
  10. WILLIAM HATCHER (abt. 1614–abt. 1677)
Service: Came to Virginia, 1635; member of House of Burgesses.
Reference: Bible Records, Wills, Full Family History enclosed with Applications and
          filed.

6321   ANSLEY, Mrs. Francis Wilcox   Recorded 1941
   1. Ellen Whitridge Bennett *m.* 1906 Francis W. Ansley
   2. Samuel Murray Bennett (1854–1933) *m.* 1881 Julia Augusta Bailey (1859–1898)
   3. Isaac Stockton Bennett, Jr. (1822–1878) *m.* 1853 Ellen Cox Murray (1831–1904)
   4. Samuel John Murray (1794–1850) *m.* 2nd 1820 Elizabeth Vander Horst Bonneau
          (1798–1867)
   5. Benjamin Bonneau (1764–1819) *m.* 1795 Martha Hart Screven (1772–1798)
   6. Thomas Smith Screven (1741–1804) *m.* 3rd 1770 Eleanor Hart (1750–1783)
   7. James Witter Screven (1704–1762) *m.* Mary Hyrne Smith (1717–1758)
   8. Thomas Smith (1663–1738) *m.* 1713 Mary Hyrne (1690–1776)
   9. THOMAS SMITH (1638–1694) *m.* 1662 Barbara Schnecking (1648–1687)
Service: Landgrave of Carolina, 1691; member Colonial Council, Governor of Colony,
          1693; received grant of 40,000 acres for services.
Reference: "Ralph Bailey and His Descendants," Bailey; Hist. 1st Baptist Church of
          S. C.," Tupper; "Stateburg and its People," Sumter; "Hist of Williams-
          burg," Boddie; S. C. Hist. & Gen. Mag., Vol. 22, "Hyrne;" "Historic
          Homes of S. C.," Leiding.

6241   APPLEGET, Mrs. Mary Emma Ewing   Recorded 1938
          101 East Avenue, Bridgeton, Cumberland County, New Jersey
   1. May Emma Ewing (1855–) *m.* 1876 ―― Appleget
   2. Samuel Ewing (1822–1893) *m.* 1842 Elizabeth Vanaman (1824–1872)
   3. Thomas Ewing (1780–1867) *m.* 1803 Mihitabel Shaw (1778–1853)
   4. Samuel Ewing (1739–1783) *m.* Mary Miller
   5. Thomas Ewing (1695–1747) *m.* 1720 Mary Maskel (1700–1784)
   6. Thomas Maskell, Jr. (1665–1732) *m.* 1700 Mercy Stathem
   7. THOMAS MASKELL (–1671) *m.* 1662 Bathia Parsons
Services:
Reference: Ewing, by Pobert Patterson, Pa.; Records of Windsor, Conn., by Savage;
          Thomas Maskell of Simsbury, Conn.; "Other Descendants," by Andrews.

5950 ARMSTRONG, Mrs. Lillian C. Recorded 1930, Connecticut
      130 Everitt Street, New Haven, Connecticut
1. Lillian Clark *m.* 1881 ——— Armstrong
2. Henry W. Clark (1834–1919) *m.* 1857 Jane Williamson (1837–1903)
3. Hezekiah Clark (1797–1869) *m.* Jane Fenn (1815–1890)
4. Oliver Clark (1769–1829) *m.* 1790 Sarah Northrup (1773–)
5. Lt. Samuel Clark (1727–1777) *m.* Jane Camp (1735–1809)
6. Samuel Clark (1685–1766) *m.* Mary Andrew (1696–1780)
7. Samuel Clark (1645–1719) *m.* 1673 Mary Clark
8. DEACON GEORGE CLARK (–1690). Sarah (–1689)
Service: A magistrate.
Reference: Pond Records of Milford in New Hampshire Historical Society.

6658 ARNOLD, Mrs. Ruben, Sr. Recorded 1949
      501 S. Central Avenue, Hapeville, Georgia
1. Isabella R. Hope *m.* 1897 Reuben Arnold
2. Samuel Hops (1830–1915) *m.* 1863 Orvilla Rogers (1833–1895)
3. Lemuel S. Rogers (1784–1858) *m.* 1820 Fanny Putnam (1796–1861)
4. Solomon Putnam (1755–1810) *m.* 1779 Miriam Elmer (1755–)
5. Stephen Putnam (1728–1803) *m.* 1754 Mary C. Gebbs (1737–)
6. Dea. Elisha Putnam (1685–1745) *m.* 1715 Susannah Fuller (1695–aft. 1738)
7. Dea. Edward Putnam (1654–1747) *m.* 1681 Mary Hale (1660–aft. 1731)
8. Lt. Thomas Putnam (bapt. 1614–1686) *m.* 1643 Ann Holyoke (1620–1665)
9. EDWARD HOLYOKE *d.* 1660, *m.* 1612 Prudence Stockston
Service: Freeman May 14, 1638, Gen. Court for 10 sessions.
Reference: Hist. of Putnam Family, Vital Records.

6287 ASHLEY, Morgan Recorded 1940
      85 West Street, Rutland, Vermont
1. Rev. Morgan Ashley *m.* 1911 Elizabeth Howell Miller
2. Edward William Ashley (1843–1938) *m.* 1874 Jessie Antoinette Morgan (1846–1912)
3. Francis Morgan (1805–1864) *m.* 1834 Semphronia Antoinette Converse (1811–1879)
4. Archippus Morgan (1772–1857) *m.* 1800 Pamelia Taylor (1779–1867)
5. Titus Morgan (1740–1834) *m.* 1763 Sarah Morgan (cousin) (1742–1819)
6. Joseph Morgan (1702–1773) *m.* 1735 Mary Stebbins (1712–1798)
7. Nathaniel Morgan (1671–1752) *m.* 1691 Hannah Bird, *d.* 1751
8. MILES MORGAN (1615–1699) *m.* 2nd 1669 Elizabeth Bliss (1637–1683)
Service: Early settler of Springfield, Mass.; commanded Blockhouse against Indians in King Phillip's War.
Reference: "History of John Morgan," by Nathaniel Morgan.

6221 ASKEW, Howard Maclin Recorded 1938
      Becatur, Georgia
1. Howard Maclin Askew (1879–) *m.* 1903 Annie Leah Clark
2. John Askew (1845–1907) *m.* 1876 Ida Clara Lundie (1852–1936)
3. James Pender Askew (1809–1893) *m.* 1832 Maria Teresa Connel (1812–1887)
4. Newdigate Connel (1787–1821) *m.* 1809 Polly Simms (1790–1821)
5. Rev. Jesse Connel (1750–1807) *m.* 1780 Penelope Owsley (1760–1807)
6. Newdigate Owsley (1734–1796) *m.* 1760 Mary Ann ———
7. Thos. Owsley, Jr. (1685–1751) *m.* 1720 Ann West
8. THOMAS OWSLEY, SR. (–1700) *m.* Ann
Services: Capt.; Justice of Staffard Co.; Clerk of Courts.
Reference: Virginia Reg., p. 88.

5873 ASKLING, Miss Mary E.   Recorded 1929, Colorado
          1200 Josephine Street, Denver, Colorado
    1. Mary Elizabeth Askling
    2. Gustaf A. Askling (1880–) *m*. 1901 Aimee Blessing (1880–)
    3. Amos T. Blessing (1831–1878) *m*. 1872 Susan D. Pierce (1846–)
    4. Jacob Pierce (1821–1901) *m*. 1843 Marian Chandler (1824–1890)
    5. Jonathan Pierce (1785–1852) *m*. Hannah Darlington (1783–)
    6. Jacob Pierce (1761–1801) *m*. Hannah Buffington
    7. Caleb Pierce (1727–1815) *m*. Hannah Greaves (1763–1790)
    8. Joshua Pierce (1684–1752) *m*. 1729 Rachel Gilpin (1695–1776)
    9. GEORGE PIERCE (1654–1734) *m*. 1679 Ann Gainer
    Service: In the Provincial Assembly for Chester County, Pa., in 1686.
    Reference: Pierce Genealogy in Library of Congress; McKenzie's Colonial Families,
          Vol. I, page 403.

6316 ATKINSON, Mrs. Butler Markham   Recorded 1941
          North Main Street, Madison, Georgia
    1. Mary Morgan *m*. Butler M. Atkinson
    2. J. Hulme Morgan (1863–1927) *m*. 1891 Victoria Gresham (1868–1925)
    3. John Morgan (1830–1896) *m*. 1861 Mary Coburn (1836–1913)
    4. Anson Coburn (1801–1886) *m*. 1831 Celina Osgood (1801–1883)
    5. Asa Coburn (1771–1857) *m*. Mary Gibbs (1783–1808)
    6. Clement Coburn (1749–1814) *m*. 1770 Dorothy Edwards (1745–1826)
    7. Ebenezer Coburn (1711–1759) *m*. 2nd 1737 Phebe Slapleigh
    8. Daniel Coburn (1678–1750) *m*. 1700 Elizabeth Conant, *b*. 1682
    9. Robert Colburn (1647–1701) *m*. 1669 Mary Bishop, *b*. 1651
    10. EDWARD COLBOURN (1618–1712) *m*. 1640 Hannah
    Service: Corporal in King Philip's War, 1675–1677; pioneer settler of Chelmsford,
          Mass.; established town of Dracut, Mass.
    Reference: Directory of Ancestral Heads of New Eng. Families; "Gen of Descendants
          of Edward Colburn (Coburn)," Gordon & Coburn; Waters, "Hist. of
          Chelmsford; J. C. Hooten's Original List.

5979 ATLEE, Mrs. Washington L.   Recorded 1931
          2306 Providence Avenue, Chester, Pennsylvania.
    1. Florence Hicks, (1878–) *m*. 1898 Washington L. Atlee
    2. Napoleon B. Hicks (1841–1896) *m*. 1871 Sophia Ganzhorn (1861–)
    3. Joseph Hicks (–1881) *m*. Elizabeth Dickson (1816–1866)
    4. Charles Hicks (1778–1855) *m*. 1804 Elizabeth Cooper (1780–1858)
    5. Jos. Rodman Hicks (1756–1816) *m*. 1777 Margaret Thomas (1760–1842)
    6. Gilbert Hicks (1720–1786) *m*. 1746 Mary Rodman (1717–1769)
    7. Isaac Hicks (1678–) *m*. Elizabeth Moore
    8. Thomas Hicks *m*. 1677 Mary Doughty
    9. John Hicks (1607–1672) *m*. 1633 Honora Long
    10. ROBERT HICKS (1575–1647) *m*. 1596 Elizabeth Morgan
    Services:
    References: Pioneers of Massachusetts, by Pope, page 233; History of Duxbury, by
          Winsor; Gen. of Benj. Hicks.

6256 ATWOOD, Mr. Howland Fay
          Sanderstead Place, Hartland Four Corners, Vermont
    1. Clarence Fay Atwood (1895–) *m*. 1916 Marjorie Eliz Howland (1892–)
    2. Homer Pratt Atwood (1860–1929) *m*. 1886 Lena Elsie Fay (1868–1933)
    3. Horatis Nelson Atwood (1819–1894) *m*. 1854 Sarah Randella Pratt (1831–1914)
    4. Caleb Atwood (1778–1851) *m*. 1800 Elizabeth Cobb (1776–1854)
    5. Caleb Atwood, Sr. (1749–1835) *m*. 1777 Sarah Shaw (1756–1843)
    6. Nathaniel Shaw (1717–1800) *m*. 1739 Hannah Perkins (1723–1802)
    7. Luke Perkins (1695–) *m*. 1716 Ruth Cushman (1700–)
    8. Robt. Cushman (1665–1757) *m*. 1697 Persia ———
    9. Thomas Cushman (1637–1726) *m*. 1664 Ruth Howland (–1679)
    10. JOHN HOWLAND (1592–1673) *m*. 1623 Elizabeth Tilley (1607–1687)
    Services: Member Gov. Council; Selectman; Deputy; Assessor.
    References:

6436—BADGER, Daniel Graham   Recorded 1944
    10016 Dallas Avenue, Silver Spring, Maryland
    1. Daniel Graham Badger
    2. Walter L. Badger (1904–   ) *m.* 1926 Angeline Bard Skirven (1903–   )
    3. Dr. Augustus P. Badger (1863–   ) *m.* 1886 Matilda Jones (1865–1941)
    4. David Elliott Badger (1834–1886) *m.* 1855 Adelia Ann Lee (1834–1872)
    5. James Badger (1793–   ) *m.* Mary Blaylock Bell
    6. James Badger (1757–1817) *m.* 1786 Elizabeth Swint (1766–   )
    7. Joseph Badger (1736–   ) *m.* 1755 Rhoda Cox
    8. Joseph Badger (1708–1765) *m.* 1730 Mrs. Catherine (Smith) Felch (1693–   )
    9. Stephen Badger (1671–1751) *m.* Marcy Kettell (1679–   )
   10. Sergt. John Badger (1643–1691) *m.* 1670/1 Hannah Swett (1651–1691)
   11. GILES BADGER (–1647) *m. ca.* 1642 Elizabeth Greanleaf (1622–   )
   Service: Settled in Newbury, Mass., 1635
   Reference: Nat. Numbers 5708, 5670, 5600, Pilgrim Index.

6107 BAILEY, Mrs. Benjamin F.   Recorded 1936, Nebraska
    5345 South Street, Lincoln, Nebraska
    1. Minnie Bryant *m.* Benjamin F. Bailey
    2. E. Sumner Bryant (1836–1894) *m.* 1857 Louisa Turner (1839–1863)
    3. Ebenezer Bryant (1811–1881) *m.* 1835 Sophia Sampson (1817–1888)
    4. Sylvanus Sampson (1773–1875) *m.* 1800 Ruth Burgess (1784–1825)
    5. William Burgess (1762–1837) *m.* 1783 Lucia Sampson (1763–   )
    6. Abner Sampson (1726–1780) *m.* 1756 Deborah Bisbee (1726–1780)
    7. Nathaniel Sampson (1682–1749) *m.* 1703 Keturah Chandler (1672–1771)
    8. Abraham Sampson (1658–1727) *m.* Lorah Standish (1701–   )
    9. Alexander Standish (1625–1702) *m.* Sarah Alden (1629–1687)
   10. JOHN ALDEN (1599–1687) *m.* 1623 Priscilla Mullins (–1652)
   Service: Signer of the Mayflower Compact.
   Reference: Mayflower Descendants, Savage I.

6349 BAIRD, Mrs. Samuel Houston   Recorded 1941, Massachusetts
    1. Genevra May Pennoyer *m.* 1908 Henry Harland Smith; *m.* 1936 Samuel Houston
       Baird
    2. Henry Jesse Pennoyer (1835–1911) *m.* 1861/2 Mary Emma Huntington
       (1842–1896)
    3. Seth Huntington (1796–1875) *m.* 1825 Mary Hovey (1803–1879)
    4. Thomas Huntington (1767–1811) *m.* 1795 Submit Huntington (distant cousin),
       1769–1846
    5. Rev. Christopher Huntington (1758–1810) *m.* 1761 Mary (Molly) Dimrock
       (1739–1834)
    6. Thomas Huntington (1688–1755) *m.* 2nd 1733 Mehetable Johnson, *d.* 1740
    7. Capt. Thomas Huntington (1664–1732) *m.* 1686 Elizabeth Backus, *d.* 1728
    8. Christopher Huntington, *d.* 1691, *m.* 1652 Ruth Rockwell
    9. SIMON HUNTINGTON (1582–1633) *m.* 1627 Margaret Baret
   Service: Member First Parish Church, Roxbury, Mass.
   Reference: Huntington Family; Hemenway's "Hist. of Vermont;" Hist. of Norwich,
       Vermont; Hist. of First Parish Unitarian Ch., Roxbury, Mass.

6527 BAKER, Mrs. Charles A.   Recorded 1946, Ohio
    1036 West Elm Street, Lima, Ohio
    1. Charlotte Clizbe *m.* 1916 Charles A. Baker
    2. John A. Clizbe (1853–1918) *m.* 1883 Annie M. Thomas (1857–1940
    3. Ira Clizbe (1822–1901) *m.* 1843 Mary Mahoney (1825–1893)
    4. Jonathan Clizbe (1779–1840) *m.* 1803 Hannah Glass (1784–1865)
    5. Joseph Clizbe (1756–1840) *m.* Hannah Robards (Roberts) (1756–1829)
    6. Samuel Clizbe (1721–1774) *m.* Jane Baldwin (1722–1809)
    7. James Clizbe (1696–   ) *m.*
    8. JAMES CLIZBE (c. 1670–before 1712) *m.* Elizabeth Burrell
   Service: "Plantee."
   Reference: Hudson and Mohawk Valleys.

6537 BAKER, Mrs. L. Warren   Recorded 1946
          4221 Greenbrier Drive, Dallas 5, Texas
   1. Grace Halstead *m.* 1. Warren Baker
   2. James D. Halstead (1860–1931) *m.* 1887 Emma Marshall (1861–)
   3. Seaborn K. Halstead (1824–1901) *m.* 1846 Martha Outlaw (1828–1905)
   4. Daniel N. Halstead (1795–) *m.* 1819 Harriet Tyler (1803–)
   5. Jonathan Halstead (1769–) *m.* Isabella Neil (1771–after 1814)
   6. Caleb Halstead (1721–1784) *m.* 1744 Rebecca Ogden (1729–1806)
   7. Robert Ogden *d.* 1733, *m.* Phoebe Baldwin (1704–)
   8. Jonathan Ogden (1638/9–1732/3) *m.* Rebeckah Wood (1648–1723)
   9. John Ogden (1609–1682) *m.* 1637 Jane Bond
   Service: Dep. to Gen. Court of Conn., 1659; Gen. Ass. N. J., 1665; member Council
          n. j., 1668.
   Reference: Family affidavits, Abstracts of N. J. Wills, Abridged Compendium of
          American Genealogy.

6574 BAKER, Mrs. O. E.   Recorded 1948
          2118 Merchant Street, Abilene, Texas
   1. Helen Kate Dow *m.* 1922 O. E. Baker
   2. Ernest W. Dow (1856–1919) *m.* 1883 Blanche Hinman (1864–1889)
   3. Grove S. Hinman (1835–1890) *m.* 1857 Helen Vedder (1838–1876)
   4. Amadeas Hinman (1812–1907) *m.* 1832 Minerva Snow (1809(10)–1884)
   5. Simeon Snow (1750–1827) *m.* 1779 Priscille Snow (1761–)
   6. Seth Snow (1725–1812) *m. ca.* 1749 Betty Sprague
   7. William Snow (1697–) *m.* 1722 Mary Washburn
   8. William Snow *d.* bef. 1726, *m.* 1686 Naomi Whitman
   9. William Snow (1624–1708) *m.* 1657 Rebecca Brown
  10. Peter Brown, *d.* 1633, *m.* Mrs. Martha Ford
   Service: Mayflower passenger.
   Reference: The Book of Dow, William Snow Family, Mayflower Descendants.

6383 BALCOM, Miss Agnes L.   Recorded 1942
          Attleboro, Massachusetts
   1. Agnes Leonard Balcom (Miss)
   2. Orville Balcom (1840–1928) *m.* 1873 Emma Hodges Grover (1850–1925)
   3. William Todd Balcom (1795–1875) *m.* 1826 Elizabeth Doty Thomas (1809–1885)
   4. William Balcom (1765–1842) *m.* 1791 Nancy Ann Capron (1769–1859)
   5. Lieut. William Balcom (1734–1801) *m.* 1758 Chickering Sheppard (1738–1814)
   6. Alexander Balcom, 3rd (1698–1759) *m.* 1725 Martha Rockinton (–1781)
   7. Alexander Balcom, 2nd (–1728) *m.* Sarah Woodcock (–1725)
   8. Alexander Balcom (–1711) *m.* Jane Leland Holbrook (1601–1677)
   Service: Deputy to General Court, from Providence, R. I., in 1683.
   Reference: V. R. of R. I., Arnold, pages 76–206; Gen. Dic. R. I., Austin, 10–11;
          V. R. of R. I., Vol. I, 261; Starkeys of N. E., p. Families, Wilder, 89–90;
          Hist. of Attleboro, Mass., Daggett.

6076 BALDRIDGE, Mrs. Joseph   Recorded 1934, Pennsylvania
          549 Lincoln Avenue, Pittsburgh, Pennsylvania
   1. Katherine Haldeman *m.* 1914 Dr. Joseph Baldridge
   2. George M. Haldeman (1860–1902) *m.* 1887 Katherine McBurney (1862–)
   3. William Haldeman (1822–1888) *m.* 1849 Sabra Ann Meredith (1831–1893)
   4. Daniel Haldeman (1778–1854) *m.* Susannah O'Neil (1784–1854)
   5. Abraham Haldeman (1746–1827) *m.* Mary Showalter (1755–1843)
   6. Nicholas Haldeman, Jr. (1722–1788) *m.* Elizabeth Cassel (1723–)
   7. Hupert Cassel (–1745) *m.* Stydge Op den Graeff
   8. Herman Op den Graeff (–1708) *m.* Deborah Van Bebber
   Service: First Town President of Germantown, Pa., and a Judge of the Court.
   Reference: History of Washington Co., Pa., by J. H. Beers; McBurney Family;
          Cassel Genealogy.

6329 BALL, Dr. Clarence Franklin   Recorded 1941
         212 Grove Street, Rutland, Vermont
   1. Clarence Franklin Ball *m.* 1902 Mary Olive Marsh
   2. Alonzo Eugene Ball (1855–1924) *m.* 1876 Lizzie Candace Rice (1857–1930)
   3. Benjamin Rice *d.* 1870, *m.* Roxanna Boynton (1833–1907)
   4. William Boynton *m.* Candace Earle
   5. Ebenezer Boynton, *b.* 1742, *m.* Hannah Fay
   6. Jeremiah Boynton, *b.* 1711, *m.* 1736 Patience Sanderson
   7. Ebenezer Boynton (1688–1761) *m.* Sarah Grout
   8. Sergt. Caleb Boynton, *d.* 1708, *m.* 1674 Hannah Harriman (1655–1725/6)
   9. JOHN BOYNTON (1614–1670) *m.* Ellen Pell
   Service: Settled at Rowly, Mass., 1638.
   Reference: "Boynton Family," J. F. Boynton.

6190 BALL, Miss Katherine Alice   Recorded 1938, Mississippi
         1400 Ash Street, Denver, Colorado
   1. Katherine Alice Ball (1879–)
   2. Lewis Henry Ball (1847–1893) *m.* 1873 Jennie Ann Hoffstatter (1849–1928)
   3. Gorham Ehphalet Ball (1819–1854) *m.* 1837 Catherine Terpenning (1820–1901)
   4. Henry Terpenning (1787–1870) *m.* 1810 Sarah Bryam (1792–1846)
   5. George Byram (1767–1830) *m.* 1788 Phoebe Randall (1767–1842)
   6. Enoch Randall (1746–1780) *m.* Phoebe Tinkham (1746–)
   7. Ebenezer Tinkham (1698–) *m.* 1736 Jane Pratt (1710–)
   8. Hezekiah Tinkham (1655–) *m.* Ruth
   9. Ephraim Tinkham (–1683) *m.* 1647 Mary Brown
  10. PETER BROWN (–1633)
   Service: Passenger on the Mayflower; member of The Plymouth Colony and 33rd
         signer of the Compact.
   Reference: Mass. Vital Statistics, Bridgewater, Mass., V. S., pgs. 67–63; Soc. May-
         flower Desc., Vol. 1, pg. 64, Vol. 17, pg. 71, Vol. 14, pg. 157; Vol. 15, pg. 113
         m. v. 26 pg. 86, Vol. 00, pg. 184, Vol. 4, pg. III.

6597 BALLARD, Mrs. Elizabeth H.   Recorded 1948
         219 N. Kensington Ave., LaGrange, Illinois
   1. Elizabeth Hitchcock *m.* 1913 ——— Ballard
   2. Ira P. Hitchcock (1843–1889) *m.* 1869 Agnes Van Brocklin (1847–1934)
   3. Ira S. Hitchcock (1804–1867) *m.* 1829 Abigail M. Schuyler (1806–1869
   4. Philip VC Schuyler (1775–1846) *m.* 1801 Cynthia Carpenter (1782–1857)
   5. Stephanus Schuyler (1737–1820) *m.* 1763 Lena TenEyck (1745–)
   6. JOHANNIS SCHUYLER (1667–1747) *m.* Cornelia Van Cortland
   Service: Capt. in 1690, Mayor of Albany, 1703–6.
   Reference: N. Y. State Archives, Colonial New York.

6294 BARBASH, James Tomlinson, Jr.   Recorded 1940, New Jersey
         1902 Pacific Avenue, Atlantic City, New Jersey
   1. James Tomlinson Barbash, Junior
   2. Samuel Barbash, M.D., *b.* 1884, *m.* 1908 Anna May Tomlinson (1881–1931)
   3. George Tomlinson (1844–1921) *m.* 1874 Mary Augusta Bowen (1849–1928)
   4. James Theodore Tomlinson (1813–1859) *m.* 1841 Margaret Adams (1814–1855)
   5. James Tomlinson (1783–1831) *m.* 1805 Prudence Bowen (1787–1849)
   6. Moses Bowen (bef. 1727–aft. 1778) *m.* Eve Sheppard, *d.* 1765
   7. Samuel Bowen (1687–1727) *m.* Martha Dickson
   8. Samuel Bowen (1650–1729) *m.* Elizabeth Wood (Wheaton)
   9. Obidiah Bowen (1627–1710) *m.* Mary Clifton (1628–1697)
  10. RICHARD BOWEN (1580–1674) *m.* Ann
   Service: Came to America 1630; was Deputy to Court of Plymouth.
   Reference: Town Bk. of Rehoboth; Barbers Col. of Mass.; Plymouth Records 1633–
         1689; Pope's Pioneers of Mass.; Genealogical Dic. of R. I.

6510   BARBASH, Robert William (Junior Member)   Recorded 11-28-1945
          Clinton, Iowa
   1. Robert William Barbash
   2. James T. Barbash (1922-   ) *m.* 1943 Lucille Oekenlander (1923-   )
   3. Samuel Barbash, M.D. (1884-   ) *m.* 1908 Anna M. Tomlinson (1881-1931)
   4. George Tomlinson (1844-1921) *m.* 1864 Mary Agusta Bowen (1849-1928)
   5. James T. Tomlinson (1813-1859) *m.* 1841 Margaret Adams (1814-1855)
   6. James Tomlinson (1783-1831) *m.* 1805 Prudence ——— (1787-1849)
   7. Moses Bowen (*ca.* 1727-   ) *m.* Eva Shepperd (1765)
   8. Samuel Bowen (1687-1727) *m.* Martha Dickson
   9. Samuel Bowen (1650-1729) *m.* 1684 Eliz. Wood Wheaton
  10. Obediah Bowen (1627-1710) *m.* 1647 Mary Clifton (1628-1699)
  11. RICHARD BOWEN (1580-1674) *m.* Aner ——— (-1647)
   Service: Deputy to Court of Plymouth, Mass.

6560   BARBER, Mrs. Richard N.   Recorded 1947
          815 Love Lane, Waynesville, North Carolina
   1. Eva Bell *m.* 1904 Richard Neeley Barber
   2. John J. Bell (1850-1895) *m.* 1869 Mary C. Ashworth (1851-1905)
   3. Joseph T. Bell (1813-1879) *m.* 1849 Martha B. Jones (1825-1879)
   4. Rev. John C. Jones (1795-1863) *m.* 1822 Mary A. Walker (1805-1878)
   5. Capt. John Jones, Jr. (1764-1845) *m.* 1786 Lucy B. Cargill (1769-1823)
   6. John Cargill III (1740-1777) *m.* 1766 Lucy Binns (1745-1773)
   7. John Cargill II (1710-1744) *m.* 1731 Elizabeth Harrison (1712-1753)
   8. Nathaniel Harrison (1677-1727) *m. c.* 1698 Mary Cary (1678-1732)
   9. John Cary (1640-aft. 1701) *m.* 1665 Jane Flood, *ca.* 1647
  10. COL. JOHN FLOOD (1600-1661) *m.* 1646 Fortune Jordan (*ca.* 1627-aft. 1669)
   Service: Burgess 1642-45, 1652-55; Indian interpreter at time of his death.
   Reference: Keith's Hist. of Benjamin Harrison, Wm. and Mary Quarterly.

5999   BARBER, Mrs. William Pond   Recorded 1931
          60 Bainbridge Road, West Hartford, Connecticut
   1. Harrietta M. Tyler (1865-   ) *m.* William Pond Barber
   2. Herman Tyler (1842-1911) *m.* 1865 Harriet A. Noble (1844-1904)
   3. Hiram Noble (1817-1863) *m.* 1840 Lucinda M. House (1815-1900)
   4. John Noble (1776-1849) *m.* 1802 Lucretia Fowler (1782-1867)
   5. Lewis Mathew Noble (1736-1804) *m.* 1758 Lydia Eager (1740-1811)
   6. Matthew Noble (Ensign) (1698-1771) *m.* 1720 Joanna Stebbins (1697-1763)
   7. Matthew Noble (1668-1744) *m.* 1690 Hannah Dewey (1672-1745)
   8. THOMAS NOBLE (1632-1704) *m.* 1660 Hannah Warriner (1643-1725)
   Service:
   Reference: Noble Fam. Gen. by Bottwood.

6174   BARKER, Maria Ely   Recorded 1938
          1038 Farmington, West Hartford, Connecticut
   1. Maria Ely Barker (1854-   ) *m.* 1878 William L. B. Barker
   2. William Brewster Ely (1812-1887) *m.* 1845 Elizabeth Morgan (1821-1896)
   3. Eli Ely (1772-1842) *m.* Bathsheba Blake (1777-1832)
   4. William Ely (1743-   ) *m.* 1766 Deucella Brewster (1745-1825)
   5. William Brewster (1719-   ) *m.* 1737 Damalis Gates (1719-1751)
   6. Benjamin Brewster (1688-   ) *m.* 1714 Elizabeth Willer (1694-1741)
   7. William Brewster (1646-   ) *m.* 1672 Lydia Partridge
   8. Love Brewster *m.* 1672 Laeah Sollier
   9. ELDER WILLIAM BREWSTER *m* Mary
   Service: A member of the Plymouth Colony.
   Reference: Nathaniel Ely & His Desc., pg. 205; No. 3345, pg. 383; No. 3345, pg. 83;
       No. 474, pg. 39, No. 157; Brewster Gen. by E. C. Brewster Jones, Vol. I,
       pgs. 3-7; No. 1, pgs. 26-32; No. 5, pg. 39; No. 8, pg. 57; No. 23, pg. 90;
       No. 62.

6144 BARLOW, Miss Ida   Recorded 1937, Pennsylvania
      6730 N. Broad Street, Philadelphia, Pennsylvania
1. Miss Ida Barlow
2. Owen Evans Barlow (1852–1894) *m.* 1875 Lydia Ann Fox (1854–1936)
3. Mahlon Barlow (1822–1863) *m.* 1848 Hannah Hallman (1828–1903)
4. John Barlow (1790–1847) *m.* 1820 Anna Evans (1798–1871)
5. James Evans, Jr. (1773–1842) *m.* 1798 Charlotte Brooke (1776–1841)
6. Capt. John Brooke (1740–1813) *m.* 1762 Elizabeth May (1740–1786)
7. Robert May (1696–1749) *m.* 1724 Elizabeth Brooke (1705–1777)
8. James Brooke (1678–1720)
9. JOHN BROOKE (1638–1700)   Frances Brooke
Service: Landed Proprietor.
Reference: Penna. Archives, Vol. 13, 2nd Series, p. 66; Records St. Paul's Episcopal Church, Philadelphia, 1771.

6730 BARLOW, Mrs. Stuart   Recorded 1951, Illinois
      4900 Marine Drive, Chicago, Illinois
1. Lena Sage *m.* 1915 Stuart Barlow.
2. Albert Sage (1860–1942) *m.* 1883 Lou Anna Hosmer (1864–1907)
3. Martin J. Hosmer (1830–1904) *m.* 1854 Anna Sophia Parker (1832–1915)
4. Lucius Parker (1797–1879) *m.* 1828 Ann Peirce (–1854)
5. James Parker, Jr. (1764–1851) *m.* 1785 Hannah Knowlton (1764–1836)
6. James Parker (1740–1813) *m.* 1762 Mary Conant (1741–1810)
7. Malachia Conant (1715–1783) *m.* 1738 Sarah Freeman (1720–1791)
8. Caleb Conant (1683–1727) *m.* 1714 Hannah Crane (?–1726)
9. Exercise Conant (1637–1721) *m* Sarah ———
10. ROGER CONANT (1591–1679) *m.* 1618 Sarah Horton
Service: Arrived in Plymouth 1623.
Reference: First five generations photostatic copy; Vital Statistics, Duchess County, Conn., verifies birth of James Parker 1740. History & Genealogy of Conant, pages 197–59, by Frederick Odell Conant; M. A. pgs. 31–36–43.

6640 BARNHARDT, Maggie Harris   Recorded 1949
      Concord, North Carolina
1. Maggie H. Barnhardt
2. John A. Barnhardt (1855–1923) *m.* 1878 Sarah E. McClellan (1857–1945)
3. James H. McClellan (1832–1867) *m.* 1855 Sarah E. Davis (1837–1857)
6. William Davis (1790–1854) *m.* 1831 Margaret Parks (1804–1861)
7. Thomas Davis (1748–1820) *m.* 1769 Mary Newell (1750–)
8. William Davis (1724–1777/80) *m.* 1747 Katherine Pickens (1730–1811)
9. Andrew Pickens (1697–*ca.* 1756) *m.* bef. 1730 Jean Benoit
10. ROBERT PICKENS (*ca.* 1679–*ca.* 1730) *m.* Madam Bonneau
Service: Original settler prior to 1700.
Reference: Annals of Augusta Co., Va., page 26; family records.

6003 BARRETT, Richardson Damon   Recorded 1931
      1911 Pleasant Avenue, Minneapolis, Minnesota
1. Richardson Damon Barrett (1882–) *m.* 1910
2. Brig. Gen. Theo. Harvey Barrett (1834–1900) *m.* 1879 Georgianna Brubaker (1856–1910)
3. George Brubaker (–1856) *m.* Jane R. Richardson
4. Noah F. Richardson (1788–) *m.* Mary Learned
5. Jason Richardson (1761–1805) *m.* 1784 Mary Powers (–1844)
6. Dr. Stephen Powers (1735–1809) *m.* Lydia Drew (1735–1823)
7. John Drew (–1745) *m.* 1727 Susanna Bennett
8. John Drew (1676–1745) *m.* Sarah Dalano
9. Thomas Delane *m.* Mary Alben
10. JOHN ALDEN *m.* Pricella Mullins
Services:
Reference: The Mayflower Desc., Vol. 1; Hardwick, Mass., 455; Powers Family; Richardson Memorial by Rev. John A. Vinton.

6004   BARRETT, Mrs. Richardson Damon   Recorded 1931
            1911 Pleasant Avenue, Minneapolis, Minnesota
     1. Kathryn Spooner (1888–   ) *m.* 1910 Richardson Damon Barrett
     2. Lewis C. Spooner (1850–1928) *m.* 1873 Ella Frances Lord (1852–1930)
     3. Samuel Herkimer Lord (1826–1887) *m.* Catherine Harwick (1830–1896)
     4. Capt. Samuel Lord (1771–1829) *m.* Katherine Herkimer (1780–1846)
     5. Capt. Joseph Herkimer (1751–1817) *m.* 1777 Elizabeth Katherine Schuyler
            (1751–1800)
     6. Peter David Schuyler (1723–1763) *m.* 1743 Elizabeth Barbara Herkimer
            (1726–1800)
     7. David Peter Schuyler (1688–1764) *m.* 1720 Anna Bratt (1692–   )
     8. Hon. Pieter Davidee Schuyler (1659–1696) *m.* 1680 Alyda Van Schlectenhorst
     9. Gerrit Van Schectenhorst (–1684) *m.* ———
    10. BRANT ARENTSE VAN SCHLECTENHORST (–1659) *m.* ———
     Service: Colonial Magistrate; Commissioner of Indian Affairs.
     Reference: Herkimers and Schuylers, by P. S. Cowen; Reg. of Colonial Dames of N. Y.;
            Reg. of Mass. Society of Colonial Dames; Ancestral Tablets, Welles.

6044   BARNETT, Mrs. I. N.   Recorded 1933
            700 East Main Street, Batesville, Arkansas
     1. Lockie Ball (1869–   ) *m.* 1890 ——— Barnett
     2. Geo. Wash. Ball (1844–1918) *m.* 1868 Mary Eliz Huddleston (1846–1915)
     3. Wm. Prior Huddleston (1810–1877) *m.* 1832 Sallie Hodges (1814–1884)
     4. Wiley Bibb Hodges (1792–1861) *m.* 1813 Sallie Brooks (1796–1859)
     5. Jess Hodges (1769–1833) *m.* 1791 Sallie Bibb (1776–1847)
     6. Jas. Bibb (1753–1846) *m.* 1775 Nancy Fleming (1757–1824)
     7. Thos. Bibb (1720–1761) *m.* 1745 Eliz Philips (1725–1803)
     8. Benj. Bibb (1663–1757) *m.* 1698 Temperance Fleming (1680–1760)
     9. WILLIAM FLEMING (1645–1737) *m.* 1666 Nancy Fleming
     Service: Sheriff.
     Reference: Hardy's Col. Fam. of So. States.

5988   BARTLETT, Mrs. G. E.   Recorded 1931
            Marietta, Ohio
     1. Jessie Lyon (1880–   ) *m.* 1909 G. E. Bartlett
     2. Andrew Lyon (1843–1909) *m.* 1865 Henrietta Green (1845–1908)
     3. Richard H. Green (1815–1892) *m.* 1843 Susan Bartlett (1824–1907)
     4. John B. Bartlett (1784–1858) *m.* 1811 Pauline Waldo (1791–1885)
     5. John J. Waldo (1762–1840) *m.* 1786 Peace Bull (1767–1841)
     6. John Waldo (1728–1814) *m.* 1750 Jemima Abbott (1729–1814)
     7. Edward Waldo (1684–1767) *m.* 1706 Thankful Dimmock (1682–1757)
     8. John Waldo (1653–1700) *m.* 1676 Rebecca Adams (–1727)
     9. CORNELIUS WALDO (1624–1700) *m.* 1650 Hannah Cogswell (1624–1704)
     Service:
     Reference: Cogswells in America; History of Chelmsford; History of Old Township of
            Dunstable.

6732   BASKERVILLE, Mrs. William S.   Recorded 1951, North Carolina
            912 W. Tryon Street, Charlotte, North Carolina
     1. Reid Mullen *m.* 1905 William Baskerville
     2. Jonas W. Mullen (1862–1926) *m.* 1885 Virginia Shipp Boyd (1862–living 1951)
     3. Marcus Boyd (1824–1904) *m.* 1851 Mary Elizabeth Reinhardt (1834–1916)
     4. Franklin Reinhardt (1807–1869) *m.* 1834 Sarah Smith (1816–1879)
     5. Christian Reinhardt, Jr. (1786–1837) *m.* 1803 Mary Forney (1785–1867)
     6. Gen Peter Forney (1756–1834) *m.* 1783 Nancy Abernathy (1766–1847)
     7. David Abernathy (1720–Will 1814) *m.* 1738 Ann ——— (c. 1720–after 1814)
     8. Robert Abernathy (c. 1685–Will 1772) *m.* Mary ——— (ca. 1700–ca. 1772)
     9. ROBERT ABERNATHY (ca. 1624–ca 1690) *m.* ca. 1664
     Service: Land Grant in Charles City Co., Va., 1664.
     Reference: Annals of Lincoln Co., N. C., by W. L. Sherrill; Will, 1772, Lincoln Co.;
            Bristol Co., Va., Vestry B, pg. 34; Va. Historical Magazine, Vol. 4,
            pg. 274.

6022   BAUGHAN, Mrs. R. L.   Recorded 1932
          1641 Cresmont Drive, Huntington, West Virginia
       1. Elsie Martin (1897–   ) *m.* 1918 Rob. L. Baughan
       2. Frank H. Martin (1870–1928) *m.* 1896 Edna Frances Robbins (1872–1900)
       3. Ed. Blake Robbins (1838–1890) *m.* 1868 Jennie M. Ashley (1841–1910)
       4. Philander Robbins *m.* 1832 Harriet Hatch Hyde (1805–1888)
       5. Elihu Hyde, Jr. (–1831) *m.* 1798 Mary Hatch (–1842)
       6. Joseph Hatch (1738–1811) *m.* 1773 Hannah Freeman (1740–   )
       7. Jos. Freeman, Jr. (1709–1780) *m.* 1732 Mehitable Tyler (1714–1743)
       8. Jos. Freeman *m.* 1718 Hannah Brewster (1690–1750)
       9. Capt. Daniel Brewster (1666–   ) *m.* Hannah Gajer (or Gager)
      10. Benj. Brewster (1633–1710) *m.* 1659 Ann Addis
      11. Johnathan Brewster (1593–1659) *m.* 1624 Lucretia Oldham (–1678)
      12. ELDER WM. BREWSTER.   Mary ──────
       Service: Political leader; spiritual advisor.
       Reference: History of Norwich, Conn.; Brewster Gen.; Hyde Gen.

5830   BAXTER, Miss Frances   Recorded 1929, Rhode Island
          26 Jefferson Avenue, Warren, Pennsylvania
       1. Frances Baxter
       2. Henry Baxter (1817–1886) *m.* 1853 Julia E. Greene (1835–1910)
       3. Ransom J. Greene (1792–1877) *m.* 1823 Susan B. Gorton (1799–1865)
       4. Hon. John Greene (1742–1796) *m.* 1774 Elizabeth Nichols (1748–1830)
       5. Thomas Nichols (1723–   ) *m.* 1747 Welthian Spencer (1718–   )
       6. John Spencer (1693–   ) *m.* 1716 Mary Fry (1693–   )
       7. John Spencer (1661–1733) *m.* 1692 Audrey Greene (1667–   )
       8. Major John Greene (1620–1708) *m.* Ann Almy
       9. SURGEON JOHN GREENE (1597–1658) *m.* 1619 Jean Tattersall (–1637)
       Service: Member of Rhode Island Assembly.

5831   BEALL Mrs. E. W.   Recorded 1929, Georgia
          912 E. Duffy Street, Savannah, Georgia
       1. Myrtie Strickland Beall (1890–   ) *m.* 1914 Eugene Wilkie Beall
       2. Alexander Hamilton Strickland (1855–1926) *m.* 1889 Sexta Eavenson (1868–   )
       3. Capt. John Wm. Eavenson (1840–   ) *m.* 1865 Jane Josephine Oglesby (1846–   )
       4. George Eavenson, Jr. (1817–1898) *m.* 1830 Sarah Thornton (1824–1863)
       5. George Eavenson, Sr. (1782–1842) *m.* Polly Hilly (1781–1855)
       6. Eli Eavenson (1760–1829) *m.* 1781 Rachael Seal (1760–1830)
       7. George Eavenson (1726–1816) *m.* 1755 Mary Williams (–1828)
       8. Joseph Eavenson (1689–1771) *m.* 1717 Catherine George
       9. Thomas Eavenson (1653–   ) *m.* 1677 Hanna Woodward
      10. RALPH EAVENSON (1625–1665) *m.* 1650 Cicely Orton
       Service: Same at 5228.
       Reference: Eavenson-Thornton Gen., by Mrs. A. H. Sexta Strickland.

5832   BEALL, Eugene Wilkie   Recorded 1929, Georgia
          912 E. Duffy Street, Savannah, Georgia
       1. Eugene Wilkie Beall, Sr., *m.* 1914 Myrtie May Strickland (1890–   )
       2. Alexander Hamilton Strickland (1855–1926) *m.* 1889 Sexta Eavenson (1868–   )
       3. Capt. John Wm. Eavenson (1840–   ) *m.* 1865 Jane Josephine Oglesby (1846–   )
       4. George Eavenson, Jr. (1817–1898) *m.* 1839 Sarah Thornton (1824–1863)
       5. George Eavenson, Sr. (1782–1842) *m.* Polly Hilly (1781–1855)
       6. Eli Eavenson (1760–1829) *m.* 1781 Rachael Seal (1760–   )
       7. George Eavenson (1786–1816) *m.* 1755 Mary Williams (–1828)
       8. Joseph Eavenson (1689–1771) *m.* 1717 Catherine George
       9. Thomas Eavenson (1653–   ) *m.* 1677 Hannah Woodward
      10. RALPH EAVENSON (1625–1665) *m.* 1650 Cicely Orton
       Service: Same as 5228.
       Reference: Eavenson-Thornton Gen. by Sexta Eavenson Strickland.

5833 BEALL, Marion   Recorded 1929, Georgia
         912 E. Duffy Street, Savannah, Georgia
      1. Eugene Wilkie Beall, Sr. *m.* 1914 Martie May Strickland (1890–)
      2. Alexander Hamilton Strickland (1855–1926) *m.* 1889 Sexta Eavenson (1868–)
      3. Capt. John Wm. Eavenson (1840–) *m.* 1865 Jane Josephine Oglesby (1846–)
      4. George Eavenson, Jr. (1817–1898) *m.* 1839 Sarah Thornton (1824–1863)
      5. George Eavenson, Sr. (1782–1842) *m.* Polly Hilly (1781–1855)
      6. Eli Eavenson (1760–1829) *m.* 1781 Rachael Seal (1760–)
      7. George Eavenson (1786–1816) *m.* 1755 Mary Williams (–1828)
      8. Joseph Eavenson (1689–1771) *m.* 1717 Catherine George
      9. Thomas Eavenson (1653–) *m.* 1677 Hannah Woodward
      10. RALPH EAVENSON (1625–1665) *m.* 1650 Cicely Orton
      Service: Same as 5228.
      Reference: Eavenson-Thornton Gen., by Sexta Eavenson Strickland.

5831 BEALL, Mrs. E. W.   Recorded 1929, Georgia
         912 E. Duffy Street, Savannah, Georgia
      1. Myrtie Strickland *m.* 1914 Eugene W. Beall
      2. Alexander H. Strickland (1855–1926) *m.* 1889 Sexta Eavenson (1868–)
      3. John W. Eavenson (1840–) *m.* 1865 Jane J. Oglesby (1846–)
      4. George Eavenson (1817–1898) *m.* 1839 Sarah Thornton (1824–1863)
      5. George Eavenson, Sr. (1782–1842) *m.* Polly Hilly (1781–1855)
      6. Eli Eavenson (1760–1829) *m.* 1781 Rachel Seals (1760–1830)
      7. George Eavenson (1726–1816) *m.* 1755 Mary Williams (–1828)
      8. Joseph Eavenson (1689–1771) *m.* 1717 Catherine George
      9. Thomas Eavenson (1653–) *m.* 1677 Hannah Woodward
      10. RALPH EAVENSON (1625–1665) *m.* 1650 Cicely Orton
      Service: Early settler.
      Reference: Eavenson-Thornton Genealogy, by Sexta E. Strickland.

5832 BEALL, Eugene W.   Recorded 1929, Georgia
         912 E. Duffy Street, Savannah, Georgia
      1. Eugene Wilkie Beall
      2. Eugene W. Beall, Sr., *m.* 1914 Myrtie Strickland (1890–)
      3. Alexander H. Strickland (1855–1926) *m.* 1889 Sexta Eavenson (1868–)
      See National No. 5831.

5833 BEALL, Marian   Recorded 1929, Georgia
         912 E. Duffy Street, Savannah, Georgia
      1. Marian Beall
      2. Eugene Wilke Beall, Sr., *m.* 1914 Myrtie Strickland (1890–)
      3. Alexander H. Strickland (1855–1926) *m.* 1889 Sexta Eavenson (1868–)
      See National No. 5831

6248 BEAN, Rev. Samuel Nelson   Recorded 1939
         North Montpelier Co. of Washington, Vermont
      1. Samuel Nelson Bean (1904–) *m.* 1931 Elisie Maud Gray
      2. Oren Nelson (1871–1918) *m.* 1901 Annie Maria Hathaway (1870–)
      3. William Taylor (1813–1907) *m.* 1870 Nancy Tuck
      4. Jacob Bean (1773–1865) *m.* 1796 Hannah Nelson (–1865)
      5. Samuel Bean, Jr. (1747–1819) *m.* 1768 Dorothy Wells (–1825)
      6. Samuel Bean, Sr. (1710–1800) *m.* 1732 Mary Buzzell (1714–1811)
      7. James Bean (1672–1753) *m.* 1692 Sarah Bradley (1677–)
      8. JOHN BEAN *m.* 1660 Margaret ——
      Service:
      Reference: His. of Sutton, N. H.; Gen. of N. H., by Stearns; Gen. of New Eng., by
         Cutter.

6716 BEAVER, Guy Moody, Sr.   Recorder 1951, North Carolina
         266 N. Union Street, Concord, North Carolina
      1. Guy Moody Beaver, Sr. (1895–1952) *m.* 1919 Elma Crowell Sloop
      2. John David Beaver (1857–1934) *m.* 1885 Jenny Lind Albron (1866–1941)
      3. William Albron Moody (1838–1915) *m.* 1859 Mary Lunda Lyerly (1839–1908)

4. John Moody (1796–) *m.* 1826 Mary McAlpin (1805–1885)
5. Thomas Moody (1755–1817) *m.* 1784 Anna Whitcomb
6. Samuel Moody (1704–) *m.* 1747 Anna Olmstead (1717–)
7. John Moody (1661–1732) *m.* 1700 Sarah Everts (1673–)
8. Samuel Moody (1640–1689) *m.* Sarah Deming (–1717)
9. JOHN MOODY (1593–1655)

Service:
Reference: Family History by H. A. Moody, pg. 32; MMS by Rev. Phinius Moody; N. E. Families Historical & Memorial, by Richard Cutter; Hadley, Mass., Vital Records.

6708 BEAVER, Guy Moody, Jr. Recorded 1951, North Carolina
266 N. Union Street, Concord, North Carolina

1. Guy Moody Beaver, Jr. (1929–)
2. Guy Moody Beaver, Sr. (1895–1952) *m.* 1919 Elma Crowell Sloop (1897–)
3. John David Beaver (1857–1934) *m.* 1885 Jenny Lind A. Moody (1866–1941)
4. Wm. Albron Moody (1838–1915) *m.* 1859 Mary Lunda Lyerly (1839–1908)
5. John Moody (1796–) *m.* 1826 Mary McAlpin (1805–1885)
6. Thomas Moody (1755–1817) *m.* 1784 Anna Whitcomb
7. Samuel Moody (1704–) *m.* 1747 Anna Olmstead (1717–)
8. John Moody (1661–1732) *m.* 1700 Sarah Everts (1673–)
9. Samuel Moody (1640–1689) *m.* Sarah Deming (–1717)
10. JOHN MOODY (bap. 1593–1655)

Service:
Reference: MMS. by Rev. Phinius Moody, by H. H. Moody, pg. 30; N. E. Families & Memorial, by Richard Cutter; Hadley, Mass., Vital Records.

6738 BECK, Mrs. Charles Emmett Recorded 1952, Louisiana
Route 3, Minden, Louisiana

1. Sarah E. Wilthesis
2. George Elam Wilthesis (1875–) *m.* 1915 Nana Thomas (1881–)
3. George L. Wilthesis (1850–) *m.* 1874 Lucy Ann Eliza Johnston (1848–1938)
4. James Henry Johnston (1819–1878) *m.* 1841 Mirium Eliza Johnston (1822–)
5. Thomas Johnston (1789–1849) *m.* 1816 Margaret Cunningham Gaines (1799–1847)
6. Heirome Gaines, Jr. (1758–1815) *m.* 1792 Anne Thompson Adams (1775–1815)
7. Heirome Gaines (abt. 1725–abt. 1786) *m.* 1748 Margaret Taliaferro (abt. 1730– abt. 1784)
8. Col. John Taliaferro, Jr. (1687–1744) *m.* 1708 Mary Gatlett
9. Col. John Catlell, Jr. (1658–) *m.* 1676 Elizabeth Gaines (1660–)
10. Capt. Daniel Gaines (1634–1684) *m.* 1652 Margaret Bernard (1636–abt. 1690)
11. THOMAS GAINES (1605–1667) Margaret

Service: Founder of the Gaines family of America.
Reference: Bible records in family of Heirom Gaines, and papers filed with papers of S. & D. of Pilgrims Lineage Book, one S. & D. of Pilgrims, pg. 506, National No. 6652.

6215 BECKETT, Mrs. H. A. Recorded 1938
1307 Manor Park Avenue, Lakewood, Cleveland, Ohio

1. Mary Maltby (1875–) *m.* 1934 Harry A. Beckett
2. Harrison Maltby (1830–1914) *m.* 1860 Emily Adelia Hough (1839–1922)
3. Thomas Hough (1809–1891) *m.* 1830 Eunice Hinman (1807–1875)
4. Edward W. Hinman (1773–1843) *m.* 1799 Lucy Mather (1781–1861)
5. Abner Mather (1751–1838) *m.* 1775 Lucy Mary Lord (1757–1791)
6. Joseph Mather (1715–1797) *m.* Anna Booth (1718–1798)
7. Lt. Joseph Mather (1686–1749) *m.* 1712 Phoebe ——— (1688–)
8. Richard Mather (1653–1688) *m.* 1680 Catherine Wise (–1710)
9. Timothy Mather (1628–1684) *m.* 1650 Catherine Atherton (–1677)
10. HUMPHREY ATHERTON (1609–1661) *m.* Mary Wales

Service: Speaker of House, Ensign, Capt., Chief Military Officer of New Eng.
Reference: Harrison & Emily Maltby, Mary M. Beckett; Richard & Catherine Mather, by Horace Mather; Timothy & Cath. Eliz. Mather, by Horace Mather; Dames of Am., pg. 91; Beville Fam., by Tedcastle.

6309 BEHRENDS, Earle D.   Recorded 1940
          4943 Victor, Dallas, Texas
     1. Earle D. Behrends *m.* 1909 Daisy Teagarden
     2. Albert Behrends (1859–1902) *m.* 1884 Cora E. Talbot (1865–1938)
     3. John Fletcher Talbot (1827–1888) *m.* 1865 Elinor Ann Derrick (1839–1905)
     4. John Derrick (1794–1858) *m.* 1831 Euphemia Eliz. Walker (1813–1866)
     5. Zachariah Walker (1755/6–aft. 1818) *m.* Ruth DuVall *d. c.* 1844
     6. Gideon Walker (*c.* 1734–1809) *m.* Priscilla DuVall (1737–bef. 1798)
     7. Mareen DuVall III (1702–aft. 1750) *m.* 1724 Ruth Howard (*c.* 1709–1783)
     8. Joseph Howard (*c.* 1676–1730) *m.* 2nd 1708 Margery Reith
     9. Capt. Cornelius Howard (1637/8–1680) *m.* Elizabeth Todd
     Service: Capt. Maryland Militia; House of Burgesses, 1671–75.
     Reference: Maryland archives; "Founders of Anne Arundel and Howard Co.'s" by
          Warfield; Colonial Families of Southern States.

6272 BEHRENDS, Mrs. Earl Derrick   Recorded 1939
          4943 Victor Street, Dallas, Texas
     1. Daisy Teagarden *m.* 1909 Earl Derrick Behrends
     2. Joseph O. Teagarden, *b.* 1861, *m.* 1885 Cornelia R. Birdsong, *b.* 1866
     3. Oswin Teagarden (1812–1887) *m.* 1841 Mehettable Baker (1816–1898)
     4. Artemas Baker (1780–1853) *m.* 1813 Mehettable Conant (1793–1873)
     5. Thatcher Conant (1767–1840) *m.* 1789 Elizabeth Manley (1769–1845)
     6. George Conant (1725–1792) *m.* 1761 Lydia Freeman (1733–1808)
     7. Thatcher Freeman, *b.* 1710, *m.* 1731 Anna Gray
     8. Joseph Freeman (1682/3–1758) *m.* 1707 Lydia Thatcher, *d.* 1724
     9. Thomas Freeman (1653–1715) *m.* Rebecca Sparrow (1655–1740)
    10. Major John Freeman (1627–1719) *m.* 1650 Mercy Prence (1631–1711)
    11. Governor Thomas Prence (1600–1673) *m.* 1624 Patience Brewster (1600–1634)
    12. Elder William Brewster (1566/7–1644) *m.* Mary Wentworth (1569–1627)
     Service: Came on Mayflower, 1620; fifth signer Mayflower Compact; ruling Elder,
          1620–1644; Deputy, 1636; Chaplain of Military Co.
     Reference: "Conant Family in America," by F. O. Conant; Truro-Cape Cod, by
          Sebanah Rich; Mayflower descendants and their marriages.

6587 BENN, Mrs. A. N.   Recorded 1948
          5000 East End Avenue, Chicago 15, Illinois
     1. Harriet Waterbury *m.* 1910 Alonzo Newton Benn
     2. Chas. F. Waterbury (1848–1884) *m.* 1871 Martha J. Johnson (1850–1918)
     3. Ralph P. Waterbury (1823–1885) *m.* Maria A. Fanning (1827–1907)
     4. Hiram Fanning (1799–1868) *m.* 1826 Maria A. Van Schaick (1806–1831)
     5. Elisha Fanning (1756–1818) *m.* Mary Button (1761–1834)
     6. David Fanning (1727–1817) *m.* 1749 Abigail Fish (1731–1771)
     7. Jonathan Fanning (1684–1761) *m.* 1714 Elizabeth Way (1695–1772)
     8. Thomas Way, *d.* 1726, *m.* Ann Lester, *d. aft.* 1745
     9. George Way, *d. ca.* 1690, *m.* Elizabeth Smith
    10. Henry Way (1583–1667) *m.* Elizabeth (1581–1665)
     Service: Came to Dorchester 1630/1.
     Reference: Fanning Genealogy, Hist. of Dorchester.

6739 BENNER, Mrs. Henry Lewis   Recorded 1951, Pennsylvania
          Lake Manor, Willow Avenue, Ambler, Pennsylvania
     1. Frances Alice Vanderslice *m.* 1945 Henry L. Benner
     2. A. Murry Vanderslice (1867–1931) *m.* 1890 Fannie Heckart Fisher (1868–   )
     3. Addison Stahl Vanderslice (1830–1915) *m.* 1857 Caroline Green Murray (1833–1905)
     4. John Vanderslice (1801–1882) *m.* 1825 Elizabeth Custer (1805–1887)
     5. Nicholas Custer (1764–1840) *m.* 1792 Christiana Stahl (1773–1845)
     6. William Stahl *m.* 1769 Mary Lane (1747–1825)
     7. Edward Lane (1721–1799) *m.* Ann Evans (1725–1790)
     8. William Lane (1696–1732) *m.* Abigail ———— (1703–1728)
     9. Edward Lane (–1710) *m.* 1694 Ann Richardson
    10. Samuel Richardson (1643–1719) *m.* Eleanor ————
     Service: Member of Governors Council, 1688, 1695.
     Reference: Bulletin of Montgomery Co. History of Pa., Vol. III, No. 2, April, 1942;
          Penn Society of Colonial Families of Pa.; Jordon, Vol. I, pg. 485; Vander-
          slice & Allied Families, Monnett, pg. 123.

6234 **BENSON, Mrs. Warren Edgar** Recorded 1939, Georgia
Marietta, Georgia
1. Regina Elizabeth Rambo (1887–) *m.* 1917 Warren Edgar Benson, M.D.
2. Samuel Dillard Rambo (1853–1934) *m.* 1881 Emma Haseltine Jones (1854–1933)
3. Marcellus Rambo (1830–1883) *m.* 1850 Elizabeth Caroline Dillard (1828–1906)
4. Daniel Rambo (1785–1862) *m.* 1813 James Williams Fort (1790–1838)
5. Lawrence Rambo, Jr. (1750–1810) *m.* 1783 Mary Jackson
6. Lawrence Rambo, Sr. (1713–1782) *m.* 1745 Mary Adams
7. Swan Rambo (1667–1730) *m.* 1675 Barbara ———
8. Peter Rambo (1653–1729) *m.* 1676 Magdalene Skute (or Schute) 1660–)
9. PETER GUNNARSSON RAMBO (1603–1698) *m.* Britta Bretta ———
Service: Commissioner Magistrate, Justice of Peace, Councillor.
Reference:

6359 **BERGMAN, Mrs. Carl Gustave** Recorded 1941, West Virginia
847 Watts Street, Charleston, West Virginia
1. Cecile Clayton Stone *m.* 1913 Carl Gustave Bergman
2. Solomon W. Stone (1857–1940) *m.* 1882 Hannah Elizabeth Sayre (1859–1924)
3. Alfred Sayre (1826–1888) *m.* 1855 Elizabeth Seckman (1837–1875)
4. Daniel W. Sayre (1800–1877) *m.* 1820 Hepzibah Chapman (1801–1867)
5. John Sayre *b. c* 1781 *m.* Hannah Weaver
6. Daniel Sayre (1760–1824) *m.* Sarah Hall, *b.* 1762
7. David Sayre (1736–1826) *m.* 1758 Hannah Frazier (1741–1826)
8. Daniel Sayre, *d.* 1760, *m.* Rebecca Bond
9. Samuel Sayre, *b.* 1708, *m.* ——— Lyons
10. Daniel Sayre, *d.* 1708, *m.* 1659 Hannah Foster
11. THOMAS SAYRE (1599–1670) *m.* ———
Service: One of 8 original undertakers coming to Southampton, N. Y., from Lynn,
Mass., 1640; settled in Lynn, Mass., 1638; Governor of Southampton,
1657 and 1688; served in the French and Colonial wars.
Reference: Howell's "Hist of Southampton, N. Y."; "Sayre Genealogy," Banta.

6653 **BEZARD, Mrs. C. J.** Recorded 1949
Route 1, Box 100, Baker, Louisiana
1. Mary Lee Golson *m.* (2) Charles J. Bezard, 1941
2. Edwin C. Golson (1877–) *m.* 1898 Loula A. Garrett (1881–)
3. John W. Garrett, M.D. (1851–1895) *m.* 1878 Mattie B. Gaines (1862–1883)
4. James R. Gaines (1828–1896) *m.* 1861 Sarah E. B. Jackson (1835–1903)
5. James H. Gaines (1796–1848) *m.* 1822 Anne A. Henderson, *d.* 1815
6. Heirome Gaines, Jr. (1758–1815) *m.* 1792 Ann T. Adams (1776–1815)
7. Heirome Gaines *d.* aft 1786, *m.* 1750 Margaret Taliaferro, *d.* bef. 1784
8. Col. John Taliaferro (1687–1744) *m.* 1708 Mary Catlett
9. Col. John Catlett, Jr. (1693–1782) *m.* Elizabeth Gaines
10. Capt. Daniel Gaines (aft. 1632–1684) *m.* bef. 1657 Margaret Bernard, *d.* bef. 1690
11. THOMAS GAINES *m.* Margaret ———
Service:
Reference: Gen. of Lewis Family, History of Two Virginia Families, by Strubbs;
Hist. of Gaines Family.

6411 **BICKERS, Thomas Hamilton** Recorded 1943
Westfield, New Jersey
1. Thomas Hamilton Bickers *m.* Muriel Yvonne Staiger
2. Joseph Edward Bickers (1875–) *m.* 1909 May Hamilton (1882–)
3. Sidney E. Hamilton (1856–1910) *m.* 1879 Charlotte B. Dana (1860–1923)
4. Isaac J. Hamilton (1820–1896) *m.* 1844 Charlotte Higgins (1814–1888)
5. Nathanial Higgins (1772–1843) *m.* 1797 Mary Lloyd (Loughead) (1775–1838)
6. Beriah Higgins (1727–) *m.* 1749 Thankful Barnes (1730–)
7. Beriah Higgins (ab. 1692–) *m.* Desire
8. Joseph Higgins (1667–) *m.* abt. 1689 Ruth ———
9. Jonathan Higgins (1637–1711) *m.* 1661 Elizabeth Rogers (1629–1678 abt.)
10. Joseph Rogers (ab. 1607–1678) *m.* 1632 Hannah ———
11. THOMAS ROGERS *m.* abt. 1605 Grace ———
Service: Signer of the Mayflower Compact.
Reference: Mayflower Index; Mayflower Desc., Vols. III, IV, VI, VII, VIII, IX, XV.

5890   BIDDLE, Mrs. Charles H.   Recorded 1929, New Jersey
       1011 Hamilton Avenue, Trenton, New Jersey
       1. Elsie Talman *m*. Charles H. Biddle
       2. Joseph Talman *m*. Anna P. Lloyd (1845–   )
       3. William H. Lloyd (1815–1871) *m*. 1843 Hannah S. Lowden (1822–1887)
       4. Archibald Lloyd (1786–1832) *m*. 1815 Priscilla Hughes (1797–1870)
       5. John Hughes *m*. Sarah Antram (1757–1832)
       6. John Antram (1719–1808) *m*. 1743 Priscilla Haines (1722–1796)
       7. John Antram (1683–1731) *m*. 1714 Amy Andrews (–1730)
       8. JOHN ANTRAM (1657–1719) *m*. 1682 Frances Butcher (1659–1720)
       Service: Early settler in Burlington County, New Jersey.

5901   BIDDLE, Charles H.   Recorded 1930, New Jersey
       1011 Hamilton Avenue, Trenton, New Jersey
       1. Charles H. Biddle *m*. Elsie Tallman
       2. William L. Biddle (1843–1920) *m*. 1866 Sarah Ann Rogers (1846–   )
       3. Charles Biddle (1814–1902) *m*. 1837 Sarah Ann Lee (1814–1901)
       4. Israel Biddle (1788–1858) *m*. 1813 Sarah Tallman
       5. Thomas Biddle (1761–1807) *m*. 1785 Charlotte Butler (–1804)
       6. Thomas Bibble (1734–1793) *m*. 1760 Abigail Scull (–1783)
       7. Thomas Biddle (–1772) *m*. 1728 Mary Antrim
       8. Thomas Biddle *m*. 1702 Rachel Groesbeck (*ca*. 1682–   )
       9. Jacob Groesbeck *m*. Anna Vandergrift
       10. NICHOLAS GROESBECK (1624–1706)
       Nicholas Groesbeck came to America prior to 1662.

5902   BIDDLE, Elizabeth A.   Recorded 1930, New Jersey
       1011 Hamilton Avenue, Trenton, New Jersey
       1. Elizabeth A. Biddle
       2. Charles H. Bibble *m*. Elsie Tallman
       3. William L. Biddle (1843–1920) *m*. 1866 Sarah Ann Rogers (1846–   )
       4. Charles Biddle (1814–1902) *m*. 1837 Sarah Ann Lee (1814–1901)
       5. Israel Biddle (1788–1858) *m*. 1813 Sarah Tallman
       6. Thomas Biddle (1761–1807) *m*. 1785 Charlotte Butler (–1804)
       7. Thomas Biddle (1734–1793) *m*. 1760 Abigail Scull (–1783)
       8. Thomas Biddle (–1772) *m*. 1728 Mary Antrim
       9. Thomas Biddle *m*. 1702 Rachel Groesbeck (*ca*. 1682–   )
       10. Jacob Groesbeck *m*. Anna Vandergrift
       11. NICHOLAS GROESBECK (1624–1706)
       Service: Came to America prior to 1662.

6225   BIEBER, Mrs. Floyd F.   Recorded 1938, Pennsylvania
       314 Case Avenue, Sharon, Pennsylvania
       1. Emma May (1898–   ) *m*. 1920 Floyd F. Bieber
       2. Geo. N. May (1864–   ) *m*. 1895 Virgie Shilling (1866–1928)
       3. Albert L. Shilling (1841–1921) *m*. 1863 Josephine Woodward (1844–1923)
       4. Alden B. Woodward *m*. 1839 Lucy Lothrop (1818–1877)
       5. Hornell Lothrop (1787–1857) *m*. 1809 Sally White (1790–1822
       6. Soloman Lothrop (1761–1843) *m*. 1782 Mehitable White (1759–1832)
       7. Dea Jonathan (1723–1771) *m*. 1746 Susanna Johnson
       8. Mark Lothrop *m*. 1722 Hannah Alden (1696–1777)
       9. Dea. Jos Alden (1667–1747) *m*. 1690 Hannah Dunham
       10. Joseph Alden (1627–1697) *m*. 1657 Mary Simmons
       11. JOHN ALDEN (1599–1687) *m*. 1623 Priscilla Mullins
       Services: Founder of Duxbury, Mass.; singer of Mayflower Compact.

6141   BILES, Miss Lois   Recorded 1937, Georgia
       Jackson, Georgia
       1. Miss Lois Biles
       2. Sherrod A. Biles (1866–1906) *m*. 1887 Lizzie R. Maddux (1864–   )
       3. Jefferson Biles (1838–1890) *m*. 1860 Martha A. Lindsay (1844–1878)
       4. Daniel R. Biles, Jr. (1792–1872) *m*. 1822 Elizabeth Cozart (1802–1878)
       5. Daniel R. Biles, Sr. (1755–1835) *m*. 1790 Jean Conger (1777–1829)
       6. John Conger (1745–1802) *m*. 1769 Mary Ross (1751–1795)
       7. John Conger, Sr. (1710–1784) *m*. 1730 Zipporah (1710–1783)

8. Jonathan Conger (1683–1733) *m.* 1705
9. JOHN CONGER (1640–1712) *m.* 1665 Mary (–1683)
Service: Town Clerk, Constable, Member of Jury.
Reference: "The Ross Family and Descendants," by Anna M. Wright, 1911.

5940 BILLINGS, A. Haskell   Recorded 1930, Iowa
       1091 W. 26th Street, Des Moines, Iowa
1. A. Haskell Billings *m.*
2. William Billings (1862–1917) *m.* Arabella Naylor (1867–)
3. Joshua Billings (1818–1901) *m.* 1858 Anna M. Fuller (1835–1904)
4. Jabez Fuller (1791–1873) *m.* 1815 Sarah Churchill (1797–1877)
5. Dr. Jonathan Fuller (1748–1802) *m.* Lucy Eddy (1758–1840)
6. Dr. Jabez Fuller (1723–1781) *m.* Elizabeth Hilliard (1724–1801)
7. Dr. Isaac Fuller (1675–1727) *m.* Mary Pratt (–1717)
8. Rev. Samuel Fuller (1629–1694) *m.* Elizabeth Brewster
9. DR. SAMUEL FULLER (1568–1633) *m.* Bridget Lee (1617–)
Reference: Fuller Genealogy.

6330 BILLINGS, Mrs. Harold W.   Recorded 1941
       27 Main Street, Morrisville, Vermont
1. Edna Louis Cutting *m.* 1898 Harold William Billings
2. Frank Artemas Cutting (1849–1925) *m.* 1876 Emma Lucia Adams (1857–1916)
3. William Baxter Cutting (1825–1899) *m.* 1846 Louisa Stone (1827–1909)
4. Jonas Cutting (1790–) *m.* 1811 Susan Ashley (1793–1833)
5. Col. Jonas Cutting (1765–1834) *m.* 1785 Sarah Baker
6. Jonas Cutting, *b.* 1746, *m.* Lydia
7. Zachariah Cutting, *b.* 1722, *m.* Elizabeth
8. Jonas Cutting will made 1648, *m.* 1719/20 Dinah S. Smith (1695–1748)
9. Zachariah Cutting, *b.* 1670, *m.* 2nd 1701 Elizabeth Wellington (1685–1714)
10. Zachariah Cutting, *b.* 1645
11. RICHARD Cutting, (bapt. 1621–1695/6) *m.* Sarah ——— (1625–1685)
Reference: "Gazeteer of Vt.," Hemenway; "Settlers of Brownington;" V. R. Vermont; "Ashley Gen.," Trowbridge; "Genealogies of Families of Early Settlers of Watertown, Mass.," Bond; "Gutting Kin," T. A. Cutting.

6608 BIRCH, Mrs. C. F.   Recorded 1948
       508 Lake Street, Oak Park, Illinois
1. Jean Edna Virginia King *m.* 1918 Charley F. Birch
2. Albert H. King (1857–1934) *m.* 1880 Mary E. Boies (1863–1912)
3. Amos E. Boies (1825–1878) *m.* 1857 Roxanna A. Britton Comstock (1833–1895)
4. Squire Edwin Britton, Jr. (1808–1901) *m.* 1832 Keziah L. Edmonds (1814–1875)
5. Squire Edwin Britton, Sr. (1767–1822) *m.* 1798 Mary Houghton (1773–1852)
6. Ebenezer Britton (1715–1788) *m.* 1750 Sarah Bullock (1731–1790)
7. William Britton, Jr., *m.* 1698 Lydia Leonard (1679–1735)
8. William Britton, Sr. *m.* Mary Pendleton
9. JAMES BRITTON (1610–1655) *m.* Jane ———, *d.* 1687
Service:
Reference: State papers of N. H.; Britton Gen.; Charlestown Gen.

6710 BIRT, Mrs. G. Leslie   Recorded 1951, Texas
       3401 Bryn Mawr Drive, Dallas 5, Texas
1. Gladys Myrtella Dodge *m.* 1926 Charles Leslie Birt
2. Milton Hale Dodge (1877–1938) *m.* 1901 Myrtella Pemberton (1883–)
3. Owen Livergood Dodge (1847–1935) *m.* 1874 Nancy Ann Bowman (1852–)
4. Owen Dodge (1818–1912) *m.* 1845 Mary Livergood (1823–1867)
5. Nathanial Dodge (1762–1850) *m.* Polly Hover
6. Caleb Dodge (1726–1798) *m.* 1757 Miriam Gilbert
7. Joshua Dodge (1704–1795) *m.* 1723 Elizabeth Clough
8. Antipas Dodge (1677–1707) *m.* 1699 Johanna Low
9. Samuel Dodge (1645–1705) *m.* Mary Parker (1644–1717)
10. RICHARD DODGE (1602–1671) *m.* Edith (1603–1678)
Service: A founder of the First Church of Beverly, Mass.
Reference: Kent Co. records; Grand Rapids, Mich., Dodge Family, Vol. 3, pgs. 487, pg. 75, pg. 42, pg. 5, 7; Ipswitch, Mar. records, Vol. 89, p. 135; Compendium of American Genealogy, Vol. 46, 1894, pg. 26.

6286 BIVINGS, Mrs. F. Lee   Recorded 1940, Georgia
        3110 Habersham Road N. W., Atlanta, Georgia
   1. Florence Lucille Witt *m*. 1921 F. Lee Bivings, M.D.
   2. John Robert Witt, *b*. 1860, *m*. 1890 Nettie Lou Estes (1870–1908)
   3. Edwin Lyddal Bacon Estes (1843–aft. 1870) *m*. 1867 Lou Bridgeforth (1848–1891)
   4. William Isaac Addison Estes (1812–1893) *m*. 1835 Martha Adeline Gilbert
         (1813–1847)
   5. Lyddal Bacon Estes, M.D. (1775–1814) *m*. 1805 Sarah Alston Hunter (1786–1841)
   6. Benjamin Estes (1736–1811) *m*. 1757 Frances Bacon (1738–1821)
   7. John Bacon III (1711–1758/9) *m*. 1735/6 Frances ———, *b*. c. 1715, *d*. aft. 1752.
   8. John Bacon II, *b*. c. 1675, *d*. aft 1733, *m*. 1710 Susannah Parke, *b*. c. 1680–aft. 1734
   9. Capt. Edmund Bacon (c. 1640–aft 1675) *m*. Ann Lyddall (c. 1650–aft. 1675)
  10 LT. COL. GEORGE LYDDALL (c. 1620–1705)
Service: Patented lands in New Kent Co., Va., 1654, 1657, 1662; commanded Fort on
         Mattaponi River, 1679; commander of Fort Matuxion on Pamunkey River,
         1685, and subsequent years.
Reference: Records of Limestone Co., Alabama; "Estes Genealogy," by Charles
         Estes; Land Patents in Land Office, Richmond, Va.; "Valentine Papers,"
         by Edward Pleasants Valentine, Vol. IV; William & Mary Quar., Vol. X,
         XXIII.

6109 BLACK, Miss Elizabeth S.   Recorded 1936
        4606 Baltimore Avenue, Philadelphia, Pennsylvania
   1. Miss Elizabeth S. Black
   2. John A. Black (1826–1894) *m*. 1870 Ann E. Stewart (1842–)
   3. Thomas C. Black (1816–1871) *m*. 1840 Mary Martin (1817–1889)
   4. Samuel Stewart (1769–1847) *m*. Sarah Drake (1773–1855)
   5. William Stewart (1738–1810) *m*. 1769 Frances Sherred (1737–1803)
   6. Jacob Sherred *m*. 1731 Catherine Anderson (–1765)
   7. Joshua Anderson (1667–1731) *m*. 1695 Engeltie Opdyck
   8. Johannes Opdyck (1604–1729) *m*. Catherine ———
   9. LAURIS JANSEN OPDYCK (1600–1659) *m*. Christian Stenclia (–1660)
Service: Member of Committee of Safety, 1659.
Reference: Early Germans of New Jersey, by Chambers.

5960 BLACKMAN, Edward Hawkins   Recorded 1930, New Jersey
        45 McKinley Avenue, Trenton, New Jersey.
   1. Edward Hawkins Blackman
   2. Leonard T. Blackman (1872–) *m*. 1890 Lillian E. Chapman (1871–1923)
   3. Thomas C. Blackman (1843–1912) *m*. 1867 Mary E. Lane (1844–1927)
   4. Ezra Blackman (1817–1872) *m*. 1843 Leah Mathis (1817–1886)
   5. Thomas Blackman (1790–1857) *m*. 1817 Elizabeth Sooy (1790–1857)
   6. David Blackman (1746–1821) *m*. 1790 Mary Scull (1752–1827)
   7. Joseph Scull (1731–1810) *m*. 1752 Sarah Scull (1734–1819)
   8. Abel Scull (–1762) *m*. 1730 Elizabeth Tonkins (1703–1748)
   9. John Scull (1666–1748) *m*. Mary Soners (–1750)
  10. Peter Janson Schol (1635–1697) *m*. 1661 Margaret Provoost (1641–1688)
  11. DAVID PROVOOST (1608–1656) *m*. 1630 Margaretta Gillis (–1702)
Service: Commander of Good Hope, 1642–47.
Reference: New York Records, Vol. 6, Vol. 25; Clement's "Early Settlers of Newtown;"
         Vital Statistics of New Jersey; Hall's History of Atlantic County.

6155 BLAKE, Dorothy Seymour   Recorded 1937
        151 Palisado Avenue, Windsor, Connecticut
   1. Dorothy Seymour (1896–) *m*. 1922 Charles Edgar Blake
   2. William Alfred Seymour (1860–) *m*. Ella Louisa Rhoades (1863–)
   3. Chester Seymour (1825–1895) *m*. 1849 Sabra Thankful Ensign (1826–1901)
   4. Moses Ensign (1794–1864) *m*. 1816 Martha Tuller Whiting (1797–1853)
   5. Isaac Ensign (1744–1816) *m*. 1771 Truannah Pettibone (1749–1845)
   6. Jacob Pettibone (1708–1771) *m*. Jemiha Cornish (1718–1791)

7. Stephen Pettibone (1669–   ) *m.* 1704 Deborah Bissell (1679–1739)
8. Samuel Bissell *d.* 1697/8) *m.* 1658 Abigail Holcomb (1638–1688)
9. JOHN BISSELL, born in England, *d.* 1677
Service: Deputy from Windsor, Conn., to Conn. Legislature, 1648, '50, '51, '52, '53, '54, '55, '58 and '64.
Reference: Quincy, Mass., Vol. of Births, 1889–1902, pg. 114; Simsbury Vital Stat., Vol. I, pg. 40; Mather Gen., p. 292, Sec. 1027, No. 2332; Bates Gen. 274; Pettibone Family, pgs. 5, 6, 7, 12, 13; Bissell Family Manuscript, Conn. Hist. Soc., pgs. 1–3.

6058 BLAKE, Miss Mida Collins   Recorded 1933, New Jersey
1106 South Shore Road, Pleasantville, New Jersey
1. Mida Collins Blake
2. Charles W. Blake (1868–   ) *m.* 1891 Georgiana Collins (1872–   )
3. Mark W. Blake (1844–1920) *m.* 1865 Phoebe J. Adams (1842–1908)
4. William S. Blake (1818–1899) *m.* 1843 Hannah A. Lake (1826–1874)
5. Daniel Lake (1803–1851) *m.* Sarah A. Tilton (1802–1866)
6. John Lake (1773–1855) *m.* 1796 Abigail Adams (1775–1857)
7. Daniel Lake (1740–1799) *m.* 1764 Sarah Lucas
8. Daniel Lake (1697–1774) *m.* 1730 Gartara Steelman
9. William Lake *m.* Sarah
10. John Lake (–1695) *m.* Anne Spicer (–1710)
11. THOMAS SPICER (–1658) Michal
Service: Treasurer of Portsmouth in 1642; Original Proprietor, Gravesend, L. I.
Reference: Genealogy of the Lake Family, Adams-Risley, 1915.

6757 BLACKSTOCK, Mrs. Hal Weaver   Recorded 1952, North Carolina
3 Wake Drive, Winston Salem, North Carolina
1. Evelyn Jackson *m.* 1948 Hal Weaver Blackstock
2. Marshall Oscar Jackson (1872–1941) *m.* 1899 Alma S. Hough (1875–   )
3. Alverson Sanford Hough (1817–1890) *m.* 1874 2nd Mary Frances Brown (1838–1907)
4. Ephraim Hough III (1789–1876) *m.* 1816 Jerusha Sanford (1793–1870)
5. Ephraim Hough II, Jr. (1745/6–1815) *m.* 1785 Lydia Alling (1754–   )
6. Samuel Alling II (1725/6–   ) *m.* 1752 Mary Leek (1721–   )
7. Nathan Alling (1695–1774) *m.* 1722 Hannah Todd (1702/3–1771)
8. Michael Todd (1653–1713) *m.* Elizabeth Brown (abt. 1670–1740)
9. Eleazer Brown (bap. 1642–1714) *m.* Sarah Bulkeley (1640–1723)
10. Thomas Bulkeley (bap. 1617–1658) *m.* Sarah Jones (abt. 1620–1682)
11. REV. PETER BULKELEY (1582–1658/9) *m.* 1613 Jane Allen (?–1626)
Service: Founder and Minister of Concord, Mass.
Reference: Photostat copy of Family Records, New Haven Gen. Mag., p. 851, Vol. I, pgs. 28, 17; Todd Genealogy (1925), pgs. 34, 24; Bulkley Genealogy, by Jacobus; Life of Peter Bulkeley in "Magnalia," by Cotton Mather.

6132 BLANKENSHIP, Miss Burd   Recorded 1937, Georgia
Atlanta, Georgia
1. Miss Byrd Blankenship
2. Wm. H. Blankenship (1840–1929) *m.* 1863 Martha Hallenbeck (1846–1913)
3. Garret Hallenbeck (1796–1868) *m.* 1838 Martha Trotter (1824–1874)
4. Isaac Hallenbeck (1767–1855) *m.* 1790 Magdalena Slingerland (1769–1838)
5. Gerrit Slingerland (1723–1816) *m.* 1757 Egie Van der Zee (1737–1814)
6. Teunis Slingerland (1694–1746) *m.* 1719 Elizabeth Van der Zee (1698–1724)
7. Arent Slingerland (–1712) *m.* 1688 Gertrude Van Vorst (–1694)
8. TENUSIA CORNELIESE SLINGERLAND (1617–1685) *m.* Engeltje Albertse Bradt (–1684)
Service: Landed Proprietor.
Reference: Records of Albany Co., N. Y.; Records of First Dutch Reformed Church.

6536 BLIVEN, Miss Emma Alma   Recorded 1946
          1 Leighton Avenue, Yonkers 5, New York
  1. Emma Alma Bliven
  2. William W. Bliven (1856–1942) *m.* 1884 Charlotte Adams (1862–1936)
  3. Charles Bliven (1818–1879) *m.* 1843 Louisa Morison (1824–1896)
  4. Joshua Bliven (1790–1849) *n.* 1814 Esther Baker (1796–1883)
  5. Lt. Arnold Bliven (1757–1837) *m.* 1789 Maney Wilcox
  6. Maj. Edward Bliven (1722–   ) *m.* 1743 Ann Ross (1726–   )
  7. Maj. Edward Bliven, Sr. (1694–1775) *m.* 1719 Freelove Swares (1698–   )
  8. SGT. EDWARD BLIVEN, *d.* 1718, *m.* 1691 Isabel Maccourn
  Service: Served 1706 in Westerly Town in Arms, also Town Sergeant.
  Reference: Civil and Military Lists of Rhode Island; Gen. Dictionary of Rhode
          Island.

6759 BLOUNT, Mrs. Gerald Rowden   Recorded 1952, N. C.
          1206 N. Stafford Street, Arlington, Virginia
  1. Elizabeth Rothrock *m.* 1926 G. R. Blount
  2. Parmenio S. Rothrock (1873–   ) *m.* 1903 Jessie Martin (1878–1951)
  3. Leroy A. Martin (1854–1917) *m.* 1877 Cora A. Poindexter
  4. Elizabeth Poindexter (1830–1916) *m.* Reps Martin (1826–1911)
  5. Denson Ashburn Poindexter (1809–1876) *m.* 1822 Sarah Jones (1806–1862)
  6. William Pledge Poindexter (1766–1844) *m.* 1795 Elizabeth A. Ashburn (1778–1849)
  7. Capt. Thomas Poindexter (abt. 1737–1807) *m.* 1760 Elizabeth Pledge (abt. 1740–
          1816)
  8. Thomas Poindexter (abt. 1705–1773/4) *m.* Sarah ———, living after 1749
  9. Thomas Poindexter (abt. 1670–1744) *m.* 1691 Sarah Crawford (1670–1752)
  10. GEORGE POINDEXTER (–aft. 1698) Sussanna
  George Poindexter, born in Isle of Wight, came to America 1657. He died after
  1698. His mother was Elizabeth Efford; her brother, Peter Efford, had previously
  come to America and living at York Town, Va.
  Complete history of Poindexter and Crawford families submitted with Mothers
  applications. Her National Number is S. & D. of Pilgrims 6624.

6263 BLOOM, Mrs. Frank   Recorded 1939
          100 S. Broadway, Irvington-on-Hudson, New York
  1. Etta Matha Lewis *m.* 1933 Frank Bloom
  2. Clement Lewis (1865–1935) *m.* 1890 Sarah Viola Fuller, *b.* 1868
  3. George Washington Fuller (1817–1881) *m.* 1856 Martha Barnhart (1837–1911)
  4. John Fuller (1780–1859) *m.* 1802 Peninah Langdon (1784–1873)
  5. Nathan Fuller (1739–1811) *m.* 1757 Phoebe Harris (1740–1822)
  6. Abial Fuller (1712–1783) *m.* 1738 Beulah Daggett (1719–1794)
  7. Capt. Mayhew Daggett (1686–1752) *m.* 1709 Joanna Biven, *b.* 1687
  8. John Daggett (1662–1724) *m. c.* 1685 Sarah Pease, *b.* 1668
  9. Thomas Daggett (1630–1691) *m.* 1657 Hannah Mayhew, *b.* 1635
  10. GOVERNOR THOMAS MAYHEW (1593–1682) *m.* Jane Bangs Paine
  Service: Governor Martha's Vineyard, Indian Teacher, Deputy General Court.
  Reference: Attleborough Vital Rec., New York in the Revolution, Daggett Genealogy,
          History Martha's Vineyard, by Col. Banks.

6514 BODEN, Mrs. Harry Clark
          Newark, Delaware
  1. Marguerite duPont *m.* Harry Clark Boden
  2. Julien Ortiz (1866–   ) *m.* 1906 (2nd) Alice Eugenie duPont (1876–1940)
  3. Dr. Alexis Iranee duPont (1843–1904) *m.* 1875 (2nd) Elizabeth Canby Bradford
          (1852–1925)
  4. Alexis Iranee duPont (1816–1857) *m.* 1836 Joanna Maria Smith (1815–1876)
  5. Francis Gurney Smith (1784–1873) *m.* 1807 Eliza Mackie (1787–1861)
  6. Daniel Smith (1755–1836) *m.* 1780 Elizabeth Shute (1760–1799)
  7. Richard Smith (1715–1760) *m.* 1740 Hannah Somers (1721–1762)
  8. James Somers (1695–1761) *m.* 1718 Abigail Adams
  9. JOHN SOMERS (1641–1723) *m.* 1684 (2nd) Hannah Hodgins (–1737)
  Service: Provincial Assembly of New Jersey, 1709; settled Somer's Point, New Jersey.

5975 BODINE, Mrs. Joseph R.   Recorded 1930, Pennsylvania
         36 Warwick Road, Haddonfield, New Jersey
      1. Eva Hallinger *m.* 1909 Joseph R. Bodine
      2. David B. Hallinger (1838–1924) *m.* 1858 Mary Godfrey (1838–1928)
      3. Andrew Godfrey (1791–1867) *m.* 1814 Sarah Stephenson (1795–1847)
      4. James Godfrey (1752–1835) *m.* 1781 Abigail Weaver (1767–1845)
      5. Andrew Godfrey (1699–1771) *m.* 1750 Ann Hathorn (1710–1769)
      6. Andrew Godfrey (1670–1736) *m.* 1698 Elizabeth
      7. BENJAMIN GODFREY (1632–1705) *m.* 1669 Mary Piggot (–1730)

      Service: Judge of the Court at Cape May, 1692.
      Reference: History of Cape May County, by Stevens; Mayflower Descendants.

6084 BOHN, Mrs. Jacob L.   Recorded 1935, Pennsylvania
         2444 W. 78th Street, Philadelphia, Pennsylvania
      1. Florence Cushman *m.* Jacob L. Bohn
      2. Ernest W. Cushman (1851–1922) *m.* 1879 Minnie Worthley (1858–)
      3. James Cushman (1818–1901) *m.* 1846 Jane Clough (1812–1901)
      4. Luther Cushman (1780–1849) *m.* 1807 Fannie Coleman (1785–1857)
      5. Ephraim Cushman (1741–1832) *m.* 1764 Sarah Colman (1745–1832)
      6. Allerton Cushman (1712–) *m.* 1734 Aletha Soule (1714–1747)
      7. Allerton Cushman (1683–1730) *m.* 1710 Mary Buck (–1725)
      8. Elkanah Cushman (1651–1727) *m.* 1682 Martha Cook (1659–1722)
      9. THOMAS CUSHMAN (1608–1692) *m.* 1635 Mary Allerton (1609–1699)

      Service:
      Reference: Cushman Genealogy, Vol. I.

6651 BOND, Mrs. O. F.   Recorded 1949
         5307 University Avenue, Chicago, Illinois
      1. Julia S. Hopkins *m.* 1912 Otto F. Bond
      2. Col. Owen J. Hopkins (1844–1902) *m.* 1865 Julia S. Allison (1846–1907)
      3. Col. Chas. W. B. Allison (1820–1876) *m.* 1844 Sophronia S. Lee (1825–1848)
      4. Dr. Elisha G. Lee (1785–1846) *m.* 1812 Elizabeth Israel (1791–1873)
      5. Moses Lee (1762–1802) *m.* 1783 Electa Guilford (1767–1832)
      6. Paul Guilford (1740–1811) *m.* 1761 Mary Burt (1742–)
      7. Thomas Burt (bap. 1697–1773) *m.* 1730 Mercy Phelps (1703–1779)
      8. William Phelps (1657–1745) *m.* 1678 Abigail Stebbins (1660–1748)
      9. JOHN STEBBINS (1626–1678) *m.* 1657 Abigail Bartlett

      Service: Served under Capt. Samuel Moseley, 1676 and 1675.
      Reference: Lin. Bk. Daus. of Col. Wars, No. 1776; Gen. Reg. of Henry and Ulalia
         Burt; Sheldon's History of Deerfield, Mass.; N. E. Hist. and Gen. Reg.
         Vol. 5.

6564 BOONE, Helen Garnsey   Recorded 1947
         Fairbury, Nebraska
      1. Helen Garnsey *m.* 1929 ——— Boone
      2. Oscar N. Garnsey (1869–1941) *m.* 1898 Winona Hanchett (1878–)
      3. Philemon H. Hanchett (1844–1918) *m.* 1866 Lucinda Givens (1842–1928)
      4. Silas H. Hanchett (1815–1852) *m.* 1841 Pamelia J. Smith (1821–1888)
      5. Ebenezer Hanchett (1785–1860) *m.* 1813 Mary Collins (1790–1883)
      6. Jonah Hanchett (1758–1860) *m.* 1782 Sarah Squares (1760–1860)
      7. Ebenezer Hanchett (1716–1785) *m.* Sarah
      8. John Hanchett (1679–1761) *m.* 1707 Lydia Hayward (1683–1777)
      9. John Hanchett (1649–1744) *m.* 1677 Esther Pritchett, *d.* 1711
      10. THOMAS HANCHETT (1610–) *m.* 1648 Oliverance Langton, *d.* 1718

      Service: Lt. Col. in French and Indian War, 1708–9.
      Reference: Salisbury Hist; Collections; Hist. of Pleasant Valley, N. Y.

5982 BOOZ, George V.   Recorded 1931
          301 N. Pennsylvania Avenue, Morrisville, Pennsylvania

   1. Calvin W. Booz (1852–1923) *m.* 1883 Catharine Van Horn (1854–1930)
   2. Moses H. Van Horn (1812–1885) *m.* 1843 Rebecca Scattergood (1820–1895)
   3. Henry Van Horn (1777–1849) *m.* 1798 Hanna Reeder
   4. Capt. Henry Van Horn (–1777) *m.* Elizabeth Vansant (–1807)
   5. Henry Van Horn (1707–1761) *m.* Susanna Van Vleeg (–1776)
   6. Christian Van Horn (1681–1751) *m.* Williamtji Van Dyck (1681–1760)
   7. Barendt Van Horn (1655–1726) *m.* Giertje Dircke
   8. CHRISTIAN BARENDI (–1658) *m.* Jarneta Jane ——— (–1694)

   Service: Assemblyman.
   Reference:

6529 BOREN, Mrs. Ella Chilton   Recorded 1946
          4117 Swiss Avenue, Dallas, Texas

   1. Ella Chilton *m.* Samuel H. Boren
   2. Horace Chilton (1853–1932) *m.* 1877 Mary Welch (1856–1924)
   3. George W. Chilton (1828–1884) *m.* 1853 Ella Goodman (1835–1916)
   4. Rev. Thomas Chilton (1798–1854) *m.* 1815 Frances Stoner (1797–1842)
   5. Rev. Thomas J. Chilton (1769–1840) *m.* 1786 Margaret Bledsoe (1770–1831)
   6. John Chilton (1739–1777) *m.* 1768 Letitia Blackwell (1750–1775)
   7. Thomas Chilton (1699–1775) *m.* 1722 Jemima Cook (*ca.* 1707–   )
   8. John Chilton (*ca.* 1726) *m.* Mary Watts
   9. JOHN CHILTON (1630–1706) *m.* Jane, *d.* 1706

   Service: Landed proprietor on Curryoman Bay in Westmoreland Co., Va.
   Reference: Baptist Ency., Cathcart; Hardy's "Colonial Families of the Southern
        States."

5930 BOWEN, Mrs. Albert   Recorded 1930, Colorado
          1694 Oneida Street, Denver, Colorado

   1. Amy Metcalf *m.* Albert Bowen
   2. John Conard Metcalf (1851–1898) *m.* 1879 Elizabeth May Love (1862–1908)
   3. John Wesley Love (1837–1927) *m.* 1860 Ellen Sophia Frost (1839–1898)
   4. Robert Frost (1809–1888) *m.* 1831 Elizabeth Wills (1812–1869)
   5. Noah Frost (1755–   ) *m.* 1787 Irene Edson (1767–   )
   6. Josiah Frost (1706–   ) *m.* 1739 Mary Polk
   7. Samuel Frost (1664–1739) *m.* 1691 Elizabeth Miller (1669–1731)
   8. Samuel Frost (1638–   ) *m.* 1663 Mary Cole (1639–1670)
   9. ELDER EDMUND FROST (1600–1660) *m.* Thomasine

   Service:
   Reference: The Frost Family; Savage Geneal. Dist. Nos. 7 and 8.

9353 BOWEN, Eugene Bucklin   Recorded 1941
          3 Main Street, Cheshire, Massachusetts

   1. Eugene Bucklin Bowen *m.* Lizzie Maria Percival
   2. Henry C. Bowen (1832–1916) *m.* 1855 Susan Eliza Bucklin (1832–1912)
   3. Major John Bucklin (1806–1880) *m.* 1828 Sabra Ann Smith (1811–1891)
   4. John Bucklin (1773–1859) *m.* 1795 Hepzibah Cooper (1778–1838)
   5. Jeremiah Bucklin (1745–1838) *m.* 1771 Rhoda Eaton (1751–1808)
   6. John Bucklin (1718–1803) *m.* 1740 Jerusha Eaton (1717–1823)
   7. Joseph Bucklin (1694–1751) *m.* Susannah
   8. Joseph Bucklin (1663–   ) *m.* 1691 Mehitabel Sabin
   9. JOSEPH BUCKLIN (Buckland) (*c.* 1638–1718) *m.* 1659 Deborah Allen, *d.* 1690

   Service: Died in R. I.
   Reference: V. R. Rehobeth, Mass.; Town Records of Cheshire and Adams, Mass.;
        "Bucklin Family;" Hist, of Cheshire, Mass.

5892 BOWEN, Mrs. Harold K. Recorded 1930, Iowa
    3113 Brooklyn Avenue, Kansas City, Missouri
1. Alta R. Brown *m.* 1930 Harold King Bowen
2. Luke E. Brown *m.* 1901 Ella Herbert (1880–)
3. Nathan B. Brown (1842–) *m.* Catherine E. Stevenson
4. Luke E. Brown (1808–) *m.* 1824 Ann Gleason (1805–)
5. Luke Brown (1766–) *m.* 1788 Mary Butler (1770–)
6. Abraham Brown (1738–) *m.* 1765 Zilpha Eddy
7. Jeremiah Brown (1716–1795) *m.* Abigail
8. Jeremiah Brown (1690–1757) *m.* 1715 Sarah Tucker
9. Daniel Brown (1645–1710) *m.* 1669 Alice Hearndon (1652–1719)
10. REV. CHAD Brown (1600–1665) *m.* 1626 Elizabeth Sharparowe
Service: Signer of Providence Plantations Compact; Original Proprietor of Providence Purchase; Successor to Roger Williams.
Reference: N. E. Gen. & Hist. Register, Vol. 80; Gen. Register of Nat'l. Society of Colonial Wars.

6764 BOWEN, Mrs. John B. Recorded 1952, Texas
    6940 Lakewood Boulevard, Dallas 14, Texas
1. Anna Rose Scott *m.* 1919 John B. Bowen
2. William Thomas Scott (1852–1901) *m.* 1890 Sarah Minna Chalk (1871–1948)
3. Robert Louis Chalk (1841–1914) *m.* 1870 Ann Margaret Butcher (1851–1891)
4. Edward Grady Butcher (1823–1892) *m.* 1844 Sarah Ann Wilson (1825–1878)
5. Ely Butcher (1779–1862) *m.* 1804 Elizabeth Hart (1788–1873)
6. Edward Hart (1755–1812) *m.* 1777 Nancy Stout (1756–1840)
7. St. Leger Codd Stout (1735–1767) *m.* 1753 Susannah (–1770)
8. James Stout (–1767) *m.* 1730 Mary Ann Codd (–1787)
9. Capt. St. Leger Codd (1680–1784) *m.* Mary Hand (1680–)
10. COL. ST. LEGER CODD (1635/6–1701) *m.* Anna Bennett (–1687)
Service: Born in England, Burgess of Va.
Reference: Families of Royal Descent, Part VI, 1950, Brookfield Publishing Co., Philadelphia; The Chalk Family of England and America, by Minna Chalk Scott Hyman. Naylor Press.

6569 BOWKER, Mrs. R. F. Recorded 1948, Ohio
    Plain City, Ohio
1. Jane Robinson *m.* 1937 Robert F. Bowker
2. Pearl O. Robinson (1869–1941) *m.* 1901 Elizabeth Lane (1876–)
3. Milton Lane, M.D. (1837–1889) *m.* 1874 Sophronia McCloud (1840–1904)
4. Dr. Charles McCloud (1808–1860) *m.* 1831 Mary J. Carpenter (1813–1911)
5. Benjamin Carpenter (1774–1855) *m.* 1793 Sarah Scovell, *d.* 1817
6. Gilbert Carpenter (1742–1838) *m.* 1772 Sarah (1744–1820)
7. Benjamin Carpenter (1691–1767) *m.* 1740 Mary Coons
8. Samuel Carpenter (1666/7–1745) *m.* Mary Becket
9. John Carpenter (1628–1695) *m.* Hannah Hope
10. WILLIAM CARPENTER (1605–1659) *m.* 1627/8 Abigail (1606–1687)
Service: Made town director of Rehoboth, Mass., 1647; made Captain 1642.
Reference: Abridged Compedium of American Genealogy.

6429 BRAMAN, Mrs. Sidney Royce Recorded 1943
    Windsor, Connecticut
1. Mattie Dunham *m.* Sidney Royce Braman
2. Isaac Watson Dunham (1827–1915) *m.* 1872 Martha A. Lindley (1847–1901)
3. Cyprian W. Dunham (1802–1860) *m.* 1826 Sarah Howes (1810–1885)
4. Samuel Fuller Dunham (1760–) *m.* 1707 Dorothy Watson (1776–1826)
5. Cornelius Dunham (1734–1782) *m.* 1756 Dorcas Woodruff (1739–1778)
6. Hezekiah Dunham (1698–1738) *m.* Jean Pease (1700–)
7. Jonathan Dunham (1658–1745) *m.* Mrs. Esther Huxford (–1724)
8. Jonathan Dunham (1632–1717) *m.* Mary DeLaNoye (Delano)
9. DEACON JOHN DUNHAM (1588–1669) *m.* 1619 Abigail Wood
Service: Deacon in church at Plymouth; Deputy, General Court, Plymouth.
Reference: Dunham Gen., First Fam. of America, Vol. 4.

6731   BRAND, SR., Mrs. Robert Lafayette   Recorded 1951, Georgia
            102 East Oxford Avenue, College Park, Georgia
       1. Lillian E. Kitchen *m.* 1916 R. L. Brand
       2. James Uriah Kitchen (1855–1924) *m.* 1875 Jennie Fielder (1858–1941)
       3. James Monroe Fielder (1816–1863) *m.* 1851 Roxanna Williamson (1831–1871)
       4. Obediah Martin B. Fielder (1789–1857) *m.* 1815 Elizabeth Thornbury Heard
            (1798–1847)
       5. Joseph Heard (1773–1848) *m.* 1795 Nancy Stuart (Stewart) (–1810
       6. Thomas Heard (1742–1808) *m.* 1765/66 Elizabeth Fitzpatrick (1745–1790)
       7. Joseph Fitzpatrick (1720/25–1777) *m.* bf. 1743 Mary Perrin Woodson *c.* (1727–
            1833 (106 years old)
       8. Benjamin Woodson (1684/92–1778) *m. c.* 1720 Frances Napier (1695–1727/8)
       9. John Woodson (1655–1700) *m. c.* 1677 Mary Tucker (*b. c.* 1660–1710)
      10. John Woodson 2nd (1632–1684) *m. c.* 1654 Judith (after 1684)
      11. Dr. John Woodson (1586–1644) *m.* bf. 1619 Sarah Winston (–after 1644)
      Service: Came with wife, 1619, as physician and surgeon to protect Colonists.
      Reference: Records of Morgan and Newton Co., by Herbert Fields; Southern Lineage,
            by A. E. Wynn, pgs. 142–3, 147; Thomas Heard's will, Green Co., Ga.,
            pgs. 44–46; will of Jos Fitzpatrick, Fluvania Co., Va.; Wm. & Mary Quar-
            terly, Vol. XI, pg. 53; Woodson Genealogy, pg. 43; 29 St. Peter's Par.
            Reg. 25.

5852   BRAY, Mrs. Patrick   Recorded 1929, Georgia
            658 Kennesaw Avenue N. E., Atlanta, Georgia
       1. Lillian Rogers *m.* 1923 Patrick Bray
       2. Jewett J. Rogers (1840–1906) *m.* 1864 Elizabeth Johnson (1837–1916)
       3. Dr. Mark M. Johnson (1804–1854) *m.* 1831 Caroline Alexander (1809–1874)
       4. Benjamin Johnson *m.* Elizabeth
       5. John Johnson (1752–)
       6. Benjamin Johnson (1734–1769) *m.* Mary Moorman (1731–)
       7. Benjamin Johnson (1705–) *m.* 1728 Agnes Clark (1712–)
       8. William Johnson *m.* 1698 Sarah Massie (–1711)
       9. Capt. Christopher Clark (1695–1754) *m.* Penelope Bolling
      Service: First Justice in Louisa County, Va.
      Reference: Wood's History of Albermarle Records.

5857   BREWER, Virginia Ann   Recorded 1929, Illinois
            403 Maple Avenue, Paris, Illinois
       1. Virginia Ann Brewer
       2. Rody Brewer (1820–1908) *m.* 1851 Martha M. Price (1835–1917)
       3. George Price (1784–1850) *m.* 1818 Annie Miller (1791–1877)
       4. Henry Price (1757–1845) *m.* 1782 Elizabeth Price (1759–1848)
       5. George Price (1695–1780) *m.* Mary
      Service: Landed Proprietor.
      Reference: Family Bible.

6661   BREWSTER, Kingman   Recorded 1949
            2500 Que Street N. W., Washington, D. C.
       1. Kingman Brewster *m.* Theo Urch 1930
       2. Charles K. Brewster (1843–1908) *m.* 1866 Celina S. Baldwin, *d.* 1917
       3. Elisha H. Brewster (1809–1878) *m.* 1832 Sophronia Kingman, *d.* 1879
       4. Elisha Brewster (1755–1833) *m.* 1788 Sarah Huntington, *d.* 1841
       5. Jonathan Brewster (1734–1800) *m.* 1754 Zipporah Smith, *d.* 1794
       6. Jonathan Brewster (1705–) *m.* 1725 Mary Parish
       7. Daniel Brewster *m.* 1686 Hannah Gager
       8. Benjamin Brewster *m.* Ann Dart
       9. Jonathan Brewster, *d.* 1661, *m.* Lucretia
      10. Elder William Brewster (1560–1643) *m.* Mary
      Service: Mayflower passenger.
      Reference: Brewster Gen., Mayflower Desc., History of Town of Worthington, Mass.

6746   BRIGGS, Mrs. Charles H.   Recorded 1952, Pennsylvania
            622 W. Elkins Avenue, Philadelphia, Pennsylvania
       1. Esther Marian Shallcross *m.* 1913 C. H. Briggs
       2. Frank Rorer Shallcross (1854–1929) *m.* 1886 Clara Matilda Rorer (1859–1914)

3. David Simmons Rorer (1826–1912) *m.* 1849 Mary Ann Woodington (1829–1901)
4. William Woodington (1809–1877) *m.* abt. 1827 Rebecca Dyer (1812–1880)
5. Samuel Dyer (1783–1855) *m.* 1808 Elizabeth Keen (1790–1832)
6. Joseph Dyer (1754–1815) *m.* abt 1780 Mary Ann (abt. 1756–1817)
7. James Dyer (1727–1803) *m.* 1751 Elizabeth
8. Charles Dyer (1697–   ) *m.* 1716 Elizabeth Shrief (1698–1778)
9. James Dyer (1669–   ) *m.* 1696
10. Charles Dyer (1650–1708) *m.* Mary
11. WILLIAM DYER (–1677) *m.* Mary (–1660)
Service: Sec. Portsmouth and Newport, R. I.; Attorney General, Commissioner.
Reference: Genealogical Directory of R. I., by Austin, pgs. 290–92; Statistics of R. I.;
Will B, 4, pg. 81; Will B, 6, pgs. 150–1; Elizabeth's Will B 3, pg. 364; Will of
Joseph Dyer, R. I. B 4, pg. 81.

6033 BROOKE, Miss Elmira   Recorded 1932
1509 Cayuga Street, Philadelphia, Pennsylvania
1. Josiah C. Brooke (1832–1916) *m.* 1856 Sarah Christman (1836–1877)
2. John Brooke (1798–1861) *m.* 1824 Maria Christman (1802–1877)
3. Capt. John Brooke (1740–1813) *m.* 1792 Mary Brant Kepner (1760–1837)
4. William Brooke (–1763) *m.* Rachel Kendall (–1780)
5. MATTHEW BROOKE (1680–1720) *m.* 1712 Ann Evans (1744)
Service:
Reference: Pennsylvania archives.

6034 BROOKE, Miss Mary   Recorded 1932
1509 Cayuga Street, Philadelphia, Pennsylvania
1. Josiah C. Brooke (1832–1916) *m.* 1856 Sarah Christman (1836–1877)
2. John Brooke (1798–1861) *m.* 1824 Maria Christman (1802–1877)
3. Capt. John Brooke (1740–1813) *m.* 1792 Mary Brant Kepner (1760–1837)
4. William Brooke (–1763) *m.* Rachel Kendall (–1780)
5. MATTHEW BROOKE (1680–1720) *m.* 1712 Ann Evans (–1744)
Service:
Referance: Penn. Archives, Vol. 3, page 678.

6600 BROOKS, Mrs. F. C.   Recorded 1948, Georgia
New Lyons Hotel, Lyons, Georgia
1. Ida Mae Bussey *m.* 1910 Felix C. Brooks
2. Wm. Thos. Bussey (1846–1897) *m.* 1879 Sarah J. Parkman (1859–1915)
3. Henry V. Parkman (1814–1892) *m.* 1842 Mary A. Glanton (1819–1903)
4. Serana Parkman (1778–1816) *m.* 1801 Lydia Huffman (1782–1862)
5. Henry Parkman, Jr. (*ca.* 1755–*aft.* 1817) *m.* 1775 Mercy Minter (1761–*aft* 1817)
6. Joseph Minter (*ca.* 1730 *aft* 1774) *m. ca.* 1754 Ann M. Goode (*ca.* 1735–1802)
7. Phillip Goode (*ca.* 1705–1791) *m. ca* 1730 Ann ——— (*ca.* 1709–*aft* 1791)
8. Samuel Goode (1655/8–*aft.* 1734) *m.* bef. 1700 Martha Jones
9. JOHN GOODE (*ca.* 1620–1709) *m.* aft. 1650 Frances Mackerness, *d.* 1661
Service: In Bacon's Indian Wars and assisted in settling the Colony of Virginia.
Reference: Virginia Cousins.

6156 BROOKS, Frances Elizabeth Furbee   Recorded 1937
69 Manchester Place, Newark, New Jersey
1. Frances Elizabeth Furbee Brooks (1896–   ) *m.* 1928 Harold Brooks
2. James S. Furbee (1864–   ) *m.* 1892 Louise Christine Mahon (1867–   )
3. Rev. Chas. LeDow Mahon, M.D. (1836–1872) *m.* 1866 Emily Frances Cloake
(1843–1878)
4. Capt. John Mahon (1812–1843) *m.* 1837 Harriet Scot Tomlinson (1818–1894)
5. William Tomlinson (1786–1826) *m.* 1808 Phebe Harris (1788–1841)
6. Samuel Tomlinson (1762–   ) *m.* Ann Garrison (1761–1824)
7. James Tomlinson (1735–1811) *m.* 1756 Barbara Brown (1736–1808)
8. Richard Tomlinson (1698–   ) *m.* Lydia Wells
9. Richard Tomlinson (W. P.   –1716) *m.* 1696 Sarah Buxby (W. P.   –1746)
Service: Will proved Jan. 4, 1716, in Oxford Township Co. of Philadelphia.
Reference: 8th Vol. of Wills, page 65 (84) Register of Wills, Philadelphia, Pa.; Abington Friends Rec. Minutes, Vol. 1, pg. 26; Monthly Meeting of 5 mo. 1696;
Morgan Edwards History of the Baptist, p. 61; Perm. Historical Society
Philadelphia, Pa.

6157   BROOKS, Harold Mahon   Recorded 1937
           (Junior)
           69 Manchester Place, Newark, New Jersey
    1. Harold Mahon Brooks (1930–)
    2. Harold Brooks (1898–) *m.* 1928 Frances Elizabeth Furbee (1896–)
    3. James S. Furbee (1864–) *m.* 1892 Louise Christine Mahon (1867–)
    4. Rev. Chas. Ledow Mahon M. D. (1836–1872) *m.* 1866 Emily Frances Cloake
        (1843–1878)
    5. Capt. James Mahon (1812–1843) *m.* 1837 Harriet Scot Tomlinson (1818–1894)
    6. William Tomlinson (1786–1826) *m.* 1808 Phebe Harris (1788–1841)
    7. Samuel Tomlinson (1762–) *m.* (I) Ann Garrison (1761–1824)
    8. James Tomlinson (1735–1811) *m.* 1756 Barbara Brown (1736–1808)
    9. Richard Tomlinson (1698–) *m.* Lydia Wells
   10. RICHARD TOMLINSON (W. P. 1716) *m.* 1696 Sarah Buxby (W. P. 1746)
    Service: Will proved Jan. 4, 1716, in Oxford Township, Philadelphia, Pa.
    Reference: 8th Vol. of Wills, page 65 (84) Register of Wills, Philadelphia, Pa.; Abington
         Friends Rec. Minutes, Vol. 1, pg. 26; Monthly Meeting of 5 mo., 1696;
         Morgan Edwards History of the Baptist, pg. 61; Perm. Historical Society,
         Philadelphia, Pa

6127   BROME, Mrs. W. S.   Recorded 1937, New York
           North Tarrytown, New York
    1. Sarah White *m.* 1921 W. S. Brome
    2. Selden S. White (1851–1932) *m.* 1887 Mary L. Wheeler (1857–)
    3. George H. Wheeler (1820–1900) *m.* 1842 Cornelia A. Fouguet (1823–1917)
    4. Douglas L. Fouguet (1802–1871) *m.* 1822 Rhoda O. Sperry (1801–1886)
    5. John Louis Fouguet (1772–1827) *m.* 1801 Abigail Douglas (1782–1855)
    6. Capt. John Douglas (1758–1808) *m.* 1779 Hannah Brown (1760–1853)
    7. Major Asa Douglas (1715–1792) *m.* 1737 Rebecca Wheeler (1718–1809)
    8. Dea. William Douglas (1672–1719) *m.* Sarah Proctor
    9. Dea. William Douglas (1645–1724) *m.* Abiah Hough (1648–1715)
   10. DEACON WILLIAM DOUGLAS (1610–1682) *m.* Anne Mattle
    Service: Commissary in King Philip's War in 1675; Deputy to General Court, 1672.
    Reference: The Wheeler Family in America; Douglas Genealogy.

5856   BROOM, Hubert Earl   Recorded 1929, Georgia
           658 Kennesaw Avenue N. E., Atlanta, Georgia

    1. Hubert Earl Broom
    2. CAPT. CHRISTOPHER CLARK (1695–1754) *m.* Penelope Bolling
    Lineage same as 5852.

5933   BROWNELL, Mrs. Francis E.   Recorded 1930, Georgia
           99 Roswell Road, Atlanta, Georgia

    1. Florence Haile Bowen *m.* Francis E. Brownell
    2. Charles W. Bowen (1836–1910) *m.* 1861 Mary T. Richardson (1837–1921)
    3. George Richardson (1812–) *m.* 1835 Lucina D. Warren (1812–1882)
    4. Moses Richardson (1774–1850) *m.* 1807 Eliza Andrews (1788–1844)
    5. Stephen Richardson, Jr. (1737–1808) *m.* 1765 Mary Fuller (1735–1804)
    6. Stephen Richardson, Sr. (1714–) *m.* 1736 Hannah Coy
    7. William Richardson (1678–) *m.* 1703 Rebecca Vinton (1683–1729)
    8. Stephen Richardson (1649–1718) *m.* 1674 Abigail Wyman (1659–1720)
    9. SAMUEL RICHARDSON (1610–1659) *m.* Joanna (–1666)
    Service: One of the Founders of Woburn, Mass., now Winchester, 1642.
    Reference: History of the Richardson Family, by Daggett; Vital Records of
         Providence, R. I.

6092 **BUCK, Mrs. Jessica Williams** Recorded 1935, Connecticut
Hubbard Street, Glastonbury, Connecticut
1. Jessica Williams *m.* 1922 ——— Buck
2. James S. Williams (1859–) *m.* 1887 Katherine P. Clarke (1857–)
3. James B. Williams (1818–1907) *m.* 1845 Jerusha Hubbard (1825–1866)
4. Solomon Williams (1783–1875) *m.* Martha Baker (1786–1869)
5. Dr. Joseph Baker (1748–1804) *m.* 1779 Lucy DeVotion (1754–1843)
6. Rev. Ebenezer Votion (1714–1771) *m.* Martha Lathrop (1715–1785)
7. Col. Simon Lathrop (1689–1774) *m.* 1714 Martha Lathrop (1696–1775)
8. Samuel Lathrop (1650–1732) *m.* 1675 Hannah Adgate (1653–1695)
9. Samuel Lathrop (–1700) *m.* 1644 Elizabeth Scudder
10. Rev. JOHN LATHROP (1584–1653) *m.* Hannah House
Service: First Pastor of Scituate in 1634.
Reference: Vital Records, Glastonbury, Ct.; Vital Records, Lebanon, Ct.; Robinson
Genealogy; Barnstable Church Register.

6086 **BUCKEY, Mrs. William G.** Recorded 1935, Maryland
1815 Park Avenue, Baltimore, Maryland
1. Ethel Close *m.* 1899 William G. Buckey
2. Albert Biggs Close (1850–1924) *m.* 1877 Mary E. Krise (1857–)
3. Elijah Close (1807–1883) *m.* 1839 Susan Wilson Biggs (1809–1884)
4. Frederick Biggs (1766–1840) *m.* 1795 Mary Wilson (1776–1842)
5. Joseph Wilson (1754–) *m.* Catherine Miller
6. Thomas Wilson (1720–1764) *m.* Mary
7. Capt. Thomas Wilson (–1744) *m.* Priscilla (Kent) Wilson
8. Absalom Kent (–1718) *m.* Mary Wadsworth
9. William Wadsworth (–1711) *m.* Elizabeth Clagett
10. CAPT. THOMAS CLAGETT, GENT. (1638–1703)
Service: Commissioner of Calvert Co., Md., 1680; Coroner, 1683; Capt. of Calvert
Co. Militia, 1683.
Reference: Scharf's History of Western Maryland, Vol. I, pp. 581–83; Baldwin's Wills,
Vols. 3 and 8.

6376 **BULL, Mary Ellen** Recorded 1942
50 West Gouveneur Avenue, Rutherford, New Jersey
(Junior)
1. Mary Ellen Bull
2. Jacob Edmund Bull (1908–) *m.* 1929 Henrietta Boyd, *b.* 1904
3. Charles A. Bull (1877–) *m.* 1903 Adelaide Mattoon, *b.* 1869
4. Ranson Dayton Mattoon (1839–1922) *m.* 1864 Harriet Carlin (1842–1910)
5. William Curtis Mattoon (1815–1897) *m.* 1836 Harriet Vanderhoof (1813–1884)
6. Bethel Mattoon (1784–1862) *m.* 1809 Hannah Williams, *d.* 1873
7. Amasa Mattoon (1758–1839) *m.* Elizabeth Dayton, *b.* 1759
8. David Mattoon (1715–1775) *m.* 1742 Jurusha Hall
9. John Mattoon (1682–1754) *m.* 1706 Phebe Curtis
10. PHILIP MATTOON, *d.* 1696, *m.* 1677 Sarah Hawks (1657–1751)
Service: Soldier in King Philip's War, under Capt. Turner, in Falls Fight, 1676.
Reference: Mattoon Genealogy; History of Deer Field, Mass., Sheldon.

5954 **BULLARD, Miss Irene B.** Recorded 1930, West Virginia
406 Professional Bldg., Charleston, West Virginia
1. Miss Irene B. Bullard
2. Daniel O. Bullard (1830–1886) *m.* 1869 Mariette Gernon (1834–1911)
3. Rev. Dexter Bullard (1799–1866) *m.* 1820 Juliana Sayles (1798–1871)
4. Daniel Sayles (1758–1844) *m.* 1778 Eunice Ballou (1760–1837)
5. Richard Sayles, Jr. (1723–) *m.* 1742 Abigail Hawkins
6. Richard Sayles, Sr. (1695–) *m.* 1720 Mercy Phillips (–1737)
7. John Sayles, Jr. (1654–1727) *m.* 1689 Elizabeth Olney (1666–1699)
8. John Sayles, Sr. (1633–1681) *m.* 1650 Mary Williams (1638–1681)
9. ROGER WILLIAMS (1603–1683) *m.* Mary Barnard
Service: Founder of Providence, R. I.

6766 BULLOCK, Mrs. Helena Mercy Smith   Recorded 1952, Massachusetts
      6 Channing Street, Cambridge 38, Massachusetts
1. Helen Mercy Smith *m.* 1895 ———— Bullock
2. Clinton George Smith (1846–1905) *m.* 1868 Alice Matilda White (1846–1918)
3. George Smith (1815–1876) *m.* 1844 Julia Wilmarth (1826–1904)
4. Jonathan Smith (1789–1865) *m.* 1815 Nancy Pierce (1791–1874)
5. Nathaniel Smith (1755–1839) *m.* 1783 Mary Barrett (1765–1851)
6. Nathaniel Smith (1721–1802) *m.* 1751 Priscilla Harris (1728/9–1814)
7. Nathaniel Smith (1697–1749) *m.* 1716 Esther ————
8. Nathaniel Smith (1644–1712) *m.* 1696 Esther Dickenson (–1674)
9. Joseph Smith (–1689) *m.* 1650 Lydia Huit (–1689)
Service: Contributed money in King Phillip's War.
Reference: History of Mason, New Hampshire, pg. 34; History of Watertown, Mass.,
      pgs. 77–8; Groton, Mass., Vital Records, p. 161; History of Windsor and
      Hartford, Conn.

6659 BUNCE, Mrs. Allen   Recorded 1949
      368 Ponce de Leon Avenue N. E., Atlanta, Georgia
1. Isabella Arnold *m.* 1900 Allen H. Bunce
2. Reuben Arnold, Sr. (1853–1914) *m.* 1897 Isabella R. Hope (1869–)
3. Samuel L. Hope (1830–1915) *m.* 1863 Orvilla Rogers (1833–1895)
4. Lemuel S. Rogers (1784–1858) *m.* 1820 Fanny Putnam (1796–1861)
5. Solomon Putnam (1755–1810) *m.* 1779 Miriam Elmer (1755–)
6. Stephen Putnam (1728–1803) *m.* 1754 Mary C. Gebbs (1737–)
7. Dea. Elisha Putnam (1685–1745) *m.* 1715 Susannah Fuller (1695–aft 1738)
8. Dea. Edward Putnam (bapt. 1654–1747) *m.* 1681 Mary Hale (1660–aft. 1731)
9. Lt. Thomas Putnam (bapt. 1614–1686) *m.* 1643 Ann Holyoke (1620–1665)
10. Edward Holyoke, *d.* 1660, *m.* 1612 Prudence Stockston
Service: Freeman, 5/14/1638, in Lynn, Mass.
Reference: Hist. of Putnam Family; Vital Records.

6508 BURNELL, Miss Polly Ann   Recorded 1945
      Charleston, West Virginia
1. Polly Ann Burnell (Miss)
2. John Phillips Burnell (1895–) *m.* 1921 Mary Ernestine Wagner (1899–)
3. Charles Newman Wagner (1870–1942) *m.* 1891 Lillie Leota Wolfe (1868–)
4. Alfred Wagner (1826–1903) *m.* 1853 Regina Sayre (1834–1897)
5. Daniel Sayre (1789–1836) *m.* 1807 Sinah Hayman (1789–1847)
6. Daniel Sayre (1760–1824) *m.* 1785 Sarah Hall (1762–)
7. David Sayre (1736–1826) *m.* 1758 Hannah Frazier (1741–1826)
8. Daniel Sayre (–1760) *m.* Rebecca Bond
9. Samuel Sayre (–1707) *m.* ———— Lyons
10. Daniel Sayre (–1708) *m.* 1659 Hannah Foster
11. Thomas Sayre (1597–1670) *m.* ————
Service: Selectman, Lynn, Mass., 1638, and given 60 acres of land; Founder of
      Southampton, N. Y.; 1651 chosen one of the Governors; served in French
      and Colonial Wars.

6507 BURNELL, Mrs. John Patrick   Recorded 1945
      Charleston, West Virginia
1. Mary Ernestine Wagner *m.* John Phillips Burnell
2. Charles Newman Wagner (1870–1942) *m.* 1891 Lillie Leota Wolfe (1868–)
3. Alfred Wagner (1826–1903) *m.* 1853 Regina Sayre (1834–1897)
4. Daniel Sayre (1789–1836) *m* 1807 Dinah Hayman (1789–1847)
5. Daniel Sayre (1760–1824) *m.* 1785 Sarah Hall (1762–)
6. David Sayre (1736–1826) *m.* 1758 Hannah Frazier (1741–1826)
7. Daniel Sayre (–1760) *m.* Rebecca Bond
8. Samuel Sayre (–1707) *m.* ———— Lyons
9. Daniel Sayre (–1708– *m.* 1659 Hannah Foster
10. Thomas Sayre (1597–1670) *m.* ————
Service: Selectman in Lynn, Mass., 1638, and given 60 acres of land; Founder at
      Southampton, N. Y.; 1651 chosen one of the Governors of Southampton;
      served in French and Colonial Wars.

6178 BURNEY, Minnie Melton   Recorded 1938
      1817 Senate Street, Columbia, South Carolina
   1. Minnie Malton Burney (1860–   ) m. William B. Burney
   2. Samuel W. Melton (1830–1889) m. 1857 Mary Helen Gore (1834–1901)
   3. Samuel Melton (1789–1861) m. Sarah Thompson Davis (1796–1851)
   4. George Davis (1762–1839) m. Anne Eakin (Aiken)
   5. David Davies (Davis) (–1778) m. Elizabeth James
   6. David Davies m. Sarah Dickinson
   7. Morgan A. Davies (1622–   ) m. Catherine
   Service: Captain in Indian Wars.
   Reference: Indenture, etc., Glamorgan, Caermarthen and Pembroke Counties,
        Wales; MS. Ashm 844fo. 6 Bodecian; Lib. Guild, p. 70; Harl MSS., 1422,
        fo78b, Visitation Wales, 1586; "History of Davis Family," by Maj.
        Harry Davis of Washington, D. C.; "Welsh Settlement of Pa;" "Sprague's
        Annals of the American Pulpit;" Early "History of Pa.;" Encyclopedia
        of the Southwest; Morgan Ap. David-Thomas Ap David, Witness a deed,
        22 Oct., 1647, in Wales.

6121 BURWELL, Miss Lena A.   Recorded 1936, Connecticut
      10 Forest Road W., Hartford, Connecticut
   1. Lena Almira Burwell
   2. John S. Burwell (1847–1924) m. 1874 Etta M. Baldwin (1843–1906)
   3. John Burwell (1816–1884) m. 1845 Annis E. Strong
   4. Elnathan Strong, Jr. (1775–1842) m. 1806 Annis Higley (1781–1842)
   5. Elnathan Strong (1736–1806) m. 1760 Rachel Warner (1744–1779)
   6. Capt. Joseph Strong (1701–1773) m. 1724 Elizabeth Strong (1704–1792)
   7. Justice Joseph Strong (1672–   ) m. 1694 Sarah Allen (1672–   )
   8. Thomas Strong (–1689) m. 1671 Rachel Holten
   9. ELDER JOHN STRONG (1605–1699) m. 1630 Abigail Ford (–1688)
   Service: Deputy of General Court, 1641–1644.
   Reference: Strong Family, Vol. I.

6299 BURT, Gertrude Leone   Recorded 1940
      46 Nichols Street, Rutland, Vermont
   1. Gertrude Leone Burt
   2. Alonzo Fremont Burt, d. 1939, m. 2nd 1899 Edith Zander (1877–   )
   3. James Burt (1810–1863) m. 2nd Pheby Crandall (1823–1908)
   4. Rix Burt (1772–1841) m. 1793 Miriam Wright (1776–1793)
   5. Rix Burt (1748–1777) m. 1772 Lucy Mun, b. 1744
   6. John Burt (1712–1794) m. 1733 Sarah Stebbins (1708–1761)
   7. Capt. John Burt (1687–1770) m. 1710 Abigail Rix (1689–1726)
   8. John Burt (1658–1712) m. 1684 Sarah Day (1664–1716)
   9. Deacon Jonathan Burt, d. 1715, m. 1651 Elizabeth Lobdel (1632–1684)
  10. HENRY BURT, d. 1662, m. 1619 Ulalia Marche (c. 1600–1690)
   Service: Helped lay out town of Springfield, Mass.
   Reference: "Life and Times of Henry Burt," pub. by Clark W. Bryan Co.; "The
        Emigrants who early settled at Springfield, Mass.," by Roderick H.
        Burnham.

5948 BURTS, Martha E.   Recorded 1930, Georgia
      24 N. Green Street, Gainesville, Georgia
   1. Martha E. Burts
   2. Ransom Burts (1906–   ) m. 1928 Kathleen Bailey (1909–   )
   3. Willard N. Bailey (1867–   ) m. 1894 Lucy Eavenson (1875–   )
   4. John W. Eavenson (1840–   ) m. 1865 (2) Josephine Oglesby (1846–1930)
   5. George Eavenson (1817–1898) m. 1839 Sarah Thornton (1824–1863)
   6. George Eavenson (1782–1842) m. Polly Hilly (1781–1855)
   7. Eli Eavenson (1760–1829) m. 1781 Rachel Seal (1769–1830)
   8. George Eavenson (1726–1816) m. 1755 Mary Williams (–1828)
   9. Joseph Eavenson (1689–1771) m. 1717 Catherine George
  10. Thomas Eavenson (1653–1726) m. 1677 Hannah Woodward
  11. RALPH EAVENSON (1625–1655) m. 1650 Cecily Orton
   Reference: See Nat'l. No. 5420.

5887   BUSSENIUS, Mrs. Frederick W.   Recorded 1929, Pennsylvania
       5365 Wyngohocking Terrace, Philadelphia, Pennsylvania
  1. Edith May Wharton *m.* 1896 Frederick W. Bussenius
  2. William F. Wharton (1846–1899) *m.* 1871 Eunice M. Pinneo (1851–   )
  3. William W. Pinneo (1822–1869) *m.* 1848 Eunice M. Eaton (1832–1896)
  4. Judah Eaton (1792–1849) *m.* 1817 Eunice Pineo (1798–1842)
  5. Erastus Pineo (1774–   ) *m.* 1795 Prudence Beckwith (1779–   )
  6. Major John Beckwith, Jr. (1738–1816) *m.* 1764 Catherine Chipman (1746–1812)
  7. Handley Chipman (1717–1799) *m.* 1740 Jane Allen
  8. Hon. John Chipman (1670–1756) *m.* Elizabeth Handley Pope
  9. John Chipman *m.* Hope Howland
 10. JOHN HOWLAND *m.* Elizabeth Tilley
Service: A passenger on the Mayflower.
Reference: History of King's County and N. E. Hist. & Gen. Register, Vol. 15,
       pp. 80–81, Vol. 48, p. 450.

6446   BUTTON, Mrs. Frank Rodman   Recorded 1944, Ohio
       McConnelsville, Ohio
  1. Evelyn True *m.* Frank Rodman Button
  2. Dr. Hiram L. True (1845–1912) *m.* 1874 Helen E. Moore (1846–1885)
  3. Austin True (1818–1906) *m.* 1844 Jane Fuller (1826–1853)
  4. Josiah True (1776–1855) *m.* 1804 Almira Tuttle (1788–1853)
  5. Capt. Solomon Tuttle (1757–1830) *m.* 1777 *ca.* Deborah Strong (1760–1814)
  6. Capt. Thomas Tuttle (1730–   ) *m.* 1753 Lydia Owen (*ca.* 1730–   )
  7. Thomas Tuttle (1705–   ) *m.* 1730 Silence Sperry (1701–   )
  8. Caleb Tuttle (1674–   ) *m.* 1699 Mary Hotchkiss (1680–1723)
  9. Samuel Hotchkiss (1645–1705) *m.* 1678 Sarah Talmadge (1652–1775)
 10. Robert Talmadge (–1662) *m.* 1648 *ca.* Sarah Nash (–1683 aft.
 11. THOMAS NASH (–1658) *m.* Margery Baker (–1655/57)
Service: Signed compact in New Haven, June, 1639; signed "Fundamental Agree-
       ment" soon after June 4, 1639; member General Court, 1640; a gunsmith
       by trade.
Reference: The Strong Fam., Benj. W. Dwight; Tuttle Fam., by Tuttle; Desc.
       Thomas Nash, Conn., by Nash; Desc. of John Owen of Windsor, Conn.

5952   BUTTRILL, Mrs. Thomas H.   Recorded 1930, Georgia
       2 Peachtree Street, Jackson, Georgia
  1. Ruby Durden *m.* 1910 Thomas H. Buttrill
  2. William M. Durden (1853–1918) *m.* 1883 Emma Kennedy (1863–1915)
  3. Albert Durden (1828–1904) *m.* 1851 Eliza L. Bruison (1833–1911)
  4. Benjamin E. Bruison (1800–1861) *m.* 1825 Mary Lewis (1804–1870)
  5. Adam Bruison II (1751–1825) *m.* 1786 Mary Sheppard (1760–1820)
  6. ADAM BRUISON I (1689–1769) *m.* 1715 Sarah Sterring (1693–1774)
Service: Soldier in Colonial Wars.
Reference: Colonial Records of North Carolina, Vol. 22, p. 343.

5985   BYERS, Mrs. Arthur M.   Recorded 1931
       631 Elkins Avenue, Philadelphia, Pennsylvania
  1. Katherine Edna Shallcross (1889–   ) *m.* 1913 Arthur M. Byers
  2. Frank R. Shallcross (1854–1929) *m.* 1886 Clara M. Rorer (1859–1914)
  3. David Simmons Rorer (1826–1912) *m.* 1849 Mary Ann Woodington (1829–1901)
  4. William Woodington (1809–1877) *m.* 1827 Rebecca Dyer (1812–1880)
  5. Samuel Dyer (1783–1855) *m.* 1808 Elizabeth Keen (1790–1832)
  6. Joseph Dyer (1754–1815) *m.* 1780 Mary Ann (1756–1817)
  7. James Dyer (1726–1803) *m.* 1751 Elizabeth ———
  8. Charles Dyer (1697–   ) *m.* 1716 Elizabeth Shrief (1698–1778)
  9. James Dyer (1669–   ) *m.* 1696 ———
 10. Charles Dyer (1650–1709) *m.* Mary ———
 11. WILLIAM DYER (–1677) *m.* Mary (–1660)
Service: Sec. Portsmouth and Newport, R. I.; Gen. Recorder; Atty. Gen.

6111   CAIRNS, Miss Anna W.   Recorded 1936, New Jersey
        221 Springs Avenue, Gettysburg, Pennsylvania
1. Miss Anna W. Cairns
2. James P. Cairns (1872–) *m.* 1894 Anna S. Ege (1872–)
3. Benjamin A. Ege (1833–1914) *m.* 1868 Hannah S. Henry (1841–1904)
4. Jonathan W. Ege (1799–1865) *m.* 1823 Emily Shaw (1802–1891)
5. Hanson Shaw (1770–1813) *m.* 1796 Rebecca Hendrickson (1776–1829)
6. Andrew Hendrickson (1748–1824) *m.* 1770 Judith Jones (1751–1792)
7. Peter Hendrickson (1718–1761) *m.* 1746 Catherine Locke (1729–1766)
8. Israel Locke (–1753) *m.* 1725 Rebecca Helm (1710–)
9. Hermanus Helm (1675–1740) *m.* Catherine
10. Israel Helm (1620–1701)
Service: A Magistrate under Capt. Carr in 1668.
Reference: "Delaware Finns," by E. H. Louke.

6110   CAIRNS, Mrs. James P.   Recorded 1936, New Jersey
        221 Springs Avenue, Gettysburg, Pennsylvania
1. Anna Ege *m.* 1894 James P. Cairns
2. Benjamin A. Ege (1833–1914) *m.* 1868 Hannah S. Henry (1841–1904)
3. Jonathan W. Ege (1799–1865) *m.* 1823 Emily Shaw (1802–1891)
4. Hanson Shaw (1770–1813) *m.* 1796 Rebecca Hendrickson (1776–1829)
5. Andrew Hendrickson (1748–1824) *m.* 1770 Judith Jones (1751–1792)
6. Peter Henrickson (1718–1761) *m.* 1746 Catherine Locke (1729–1766)
7. Israel Locke (–1753) *m.* 1725 Rebecca Helm (1710–)
8. Hermanus Helm (1675–1740) *m.* Catherine ——
9. Israel Helm (1620–1701)
Service: A Magistrate under Capt. Carr, 1668.
Reference: "Delaware Finns," by E. H. Louke.

6015   CALHOUN, Mrs. E. C.   Recorded 1932
        3429 Stuart Street, Denver, Colorado
1. Helen Waite (1894–) *m.* 1921 E. C. Calhoun
2. Daniel M. Waite (1863–1919) *m.* 1886 Anna R. Fairchild (1867–)
3. Nelson Fairchild (1823–1908) *m.* 1849 Hannah Eliz Alden (1829–1920)
4. Lyman Alden (1806–1886) *m.* 1837 Nancy Doran (–1887)
5. John Adams Alden (1762–1843) *m.* 1787 Hannah Daniels (1768–)
6. John Alden *m.* —— Adams
7. John Needham Alden (1731–) *m.* ——
8. John Alden (1663–1729) *m.* 1684 Eliz. Phelps (–1719)
9. John Alden (1622–1702) *m.* Elizabeth ——
10. John Alden (1589–1687) *m.* 1650 Pricilla Mullins
Service:
Reference:

6007   CALVERT, Carlyle C.   Recorded 1931
        Chelyan (Kanawha County), West Virginia
1. Carlyle C. Calvert (1894–) *m.* Erma D. Andrews
2. James William Calvert (1866–) *m.* Iva C. Little (1892–)
3. Cornelius Calvert (1838–1892) *m.* 1859 Drusilla Ann Oakes
4. Mills Witt Calvert *m.* Katherine Slack
5. Francis Calvert (1751–1823) *m.* 1791 Elizabeth Witt (1772–1806)
6. Jacob Calvert (1720–1772) *m.* 1750 Sarah Crupper (1730–1789)
7. John Calvert (1790–1835) *m.* 1810 Eliz. Harrison
8. George Calvert (1664–1740) *m.* 1688 Eliz Doyne
9. William Calvert (1642–1688) *m.* 1660 Eliz. Stone
10. Gov. Leonard Calvert (1606–1647) *m.* 1641 Anne Brent
11. Sir George Calvert (1579–1632) *m.* 1604 Anne Mynne (1579–1622)
Service: Colonizer and founder of the Province of Maryland.
Reference: Maryland His. Mag., Vol. 16, Vol. 25.

5032   CAMDEN, Mrs. Horace P.   Recorded 1932
            28 Roslyn Avenue, Glenside, Pennsylvania
   1. Mary Cunningham (1873–   ) *m.* 1897 Horace P. Camden
   2. Dav. Cunningham (1834–1925) *m.* 1860 Sarah C. Urwiler (1841–1908)
   3. John Urwiler (1803–1887) *m.* 1840 Oromina Stout (1810–1885)
   4. Reuben Stout (1766–1836) *m.* Abia La Boyteaux (1777–1850)
   5. Benijah Stout (1740–1836) *m.* 1760 Eliz. Hyde (1745–1827)
   6. Joseph Stout (1717–   ) *m.* Mary Hixon
   7. James Stout (1694–1731) *m.* 1712 Catherine Simpson
   8. David Stout (1669–   ) *m.* Rebecca Ashton
   9. RICHARD STOUT (1602–1705) *m.* 1644 Penelope Van Prencis
   Service: Member first Assembly; member of Constables Court.
   Reference: Stillwell's Misc., Vol. 4.

6639   CANNON, Mrs. Charles A.   Recorded 1949
            34 N. Union Street, Concord, North Carolina
   1. Ruth Coltrane *m.* 1912 Charles Albert Cannon
   2. Daniel Coltrane (1842–1937) *m.* 1884 Marian S. Winslow (1857–1915)
   3. William B. Winslow (1814–1883) *m.* 1847 Martha J. Woolfolk (1826–1905)
   4. William Winslow (1766–1838) *m.* 1791 Peggy Mills (1776–1816)
   5. Beverley Winslow (1734–1793) *m.* 1757 Katherine Robinson (1742–1789)
   6. William Robinson (1709–1792) *m.* 1737 Agatha Beverley (1716–bef. 1764)
   7. John Robinson (1683–1749) *m. ca.* 1701 Katherine Beverley
   8. CHRISTOPHER ROBINSON (1645–1693) *m.* Agatha Obert, *d.* 1685
   Service: Member Virginia Assembly, 1685, 86, 88; Clerk, Middlesex Co., 1675–88;
            Sec. of State of Va. Colony, 1692–3.
   Reference: Robinson Chart in Va. Mag., Vol. XV, pgs. 448–49; Colonial Va.
            Register, Vol. III, p. 3.

6531   CAPEN, Miss Ruth Mabee   Recorded 1946
            9 Ware Street, Cambridge, Massachusetts
   1. Ruth Mabee Capen
   2. Edgar L. Capen (1875–1946) *m.* 1899 Anna M. Cox
   3. Henry G. Capen (1829–   ) *m.* 1853 Mary J. Mabee, *d.* 1894
   4. Alexander Capen, Jr. (1800–1872) *m.* Elizabeth Cummings (1809–   )
   5. Alexander Capen, Sr. (1779–1873) *m.* 1799 Jane Kenwood (1774–1848)
   6. Benjamin Capen *m.* 1777 Elizabeth Greenwood (1760–   )
   7. Josiah Capen (1722–   ) *m.* 1744 Charity Dwelley (1725–   )
   8. Samuel Capen (1686–1751) *m.* Lydia Waterman (1700–1726)
   9. Samuel Capen (1648–1733) *m.* 1673 Susanna Payson (1655–1737)
  10. Capt. John Capen (1612–1692) *m.* 1647 Mary Bass (1632–1704)
  11. BARNARD CAPEN (1562–1638) *m.* 1596 Joan Purchase, *d.* 1653
   Service: Proprietor and one of the original Grantees of Dorchester, Mass.
   Reference: Capen Family and Cutter's Genealogical Memoirs of Massachusetts.

6616   CARLAN, Miss Florence E.   Recorded 1949
            76 Westmoreland Avenue, Arlington Heights, Massachusetts
   1. Florence Estelle Carlan
   2. James A. Carlan (1899–   ) *m.* 1922 Florence A. Whidden (1899–   )
   3. Ralph E. Whidden *m.* 1898 Florence E. Haskell (1878–1926)
   4. William Haskell (1844–1923) *m.* Jane M. Griffin (1849–1906)
   5. William Haskell (1809–   ) *m.* 1839 Lois Colby (1818–   )
   6. Edward Haskell (1780–   ) *m.* 1806 Nancy Marshall
   7. Josiah Haskell (1754–   ) *m.* 1772 Abigail Fellows
   8. John Haskell (1716–1769) *m.* 1743 Mary Bray
   9. Josiah Haskell (1687–1762) *m.* 1715 Mary Collins
  10. Dea. Benjamin Haskell (1648–1740) *m.* 1677 Mary Riggs (1659–1697/8)
  11. CAPT. DEA. WILLIAM HASKELL (1618–1693) *m.* 1643 Mary Tybbott (Tibbetts),
            d. 1693
   Service: Freeman Oct. 31, 1684; Soldier in King Phillip's War, 1675.
   Reference: Descendants of William Haskell.

6561 CARIAN, Mrs. James A. Recorded 1947
76 Westmoreland Avenue, Arlington Heights, Massachusetts
1. Florence A. Whidden *m.* 1922 James A. Carlin
2. Ralph E. Whidden *m.* 1898 Florence E. Haskell (1878–1926)
3. William Haskell (1844–1923) *m.* Jane M. Griffin (1849–1906)
4. William Haskell, Jr. (1809–) *m.* 1839 Lois Colby (1818–)
5. Edward Haskell (1780–) *m.* 1806 Nancy Marshall
6. Josiah Haskell (1754–) *m.* 1772 Abigail Fellows
7. John Haskell, Jr. (1716–1769) *m.* 1743 Mary Bray
8. Josiah Haskell (1687–1762) *m.* 1715 Mary Collins
9. Dea. Benjamin Haskell (1649–1740) *m.* 1677 Mary Riggs (1659–1697)
10. CAPT. DEA. WILLIAM HASKELL (1617–1693) *m.* 1643 Mary Tybbott, *d.* 1693
Service: Freeman 1684; soldier in King Philip's War, 1675; Lt. of Train Band; Selectman several times.
Reference: Descendants of William Haskell.

6410 CARLOCK, Mrs. Lyman Judy Recorded 1943
Champaign, Illinois
1. Lila Mabel Riddle *m.* Judge Lyman Judy Carlock
2. Dr. Hamilton Rush Riddle (1841–1926) *m.* 1868 Cordelia F. Constant (1849–1930)
3. Rezin Harlan Constant (1809–1887) *m.* 1847 Mary L. Halbert (1817–1863)
4. Dr. James Halbert (1785–1858) *m.* 1816 Nancy Rennolds (ab. 1798–1834)
5. James Halbert (bef. 1760–1819) *m.* 1783 Sarah Shaddock (–1811)
6. James Shaddock (–1795) *m.* 1759 Hannah Samuel
7. James Samuel (–1759) *m.* Sarah Boulware
8. James Boulware (–ab. 1717) *m.* Margery Gray
9. WILLIAM GRAY (–aft. 1673) *m.* Elizabeth ———
Service: Landed Proprietor Rappahannock Co., Va.
Reference: Early Set. Sagamon Co., Ill., Will Books Essex Co., Va.; Comp. A. Gen., Virkus, Vol. 7; D.A.C. 5971; Col. Wars 1570.

6491 CARLTON, Mrs. H. C. (2nd) Recorded 1945
Pomeroy, Ohio
1. Velma Wolf *m.* 1st Harry E. Feiger, 2nd H. C. Carlton
2. Thomas A. Wolf (1855–1936) *m.* 1882 Serena Pickens (1858–1924)
3. Philip E. Pickens (1832–1891) *m.* 1854 Mary E. Roush (1837–1923)
4. Thomas Pickens (1805–1882) *m.* 1829 Hannah Elliott (1809–1850)
5. Fuller Elliott (1772–1832) *m.* 1802 Serena Jones (1786–1826)
6. Aaron Elliott (1747–1829) *m.* 1767 Lydia Taylor (1745–1825)
7. James Taylor (1720–) *m.* 1741 Lydia Taylor (cousins) 1724–)
8. Caleb Taylor (1685–) *m.* 1707 Ann Roberts
9. THOMAS TAYLOR (–1691) *m.* 1671 Mary Hooper (–1697)
Service: Died North Reading, Mass.

6656 CARMAN, Bessie C. Recorded 1949
1529 E. Marquette Road, Chicago, Illinois
1. Bessie C. Carman
2. Marcus W. Carman (1854–1929) *m.* 1888 Roberta S. Duffy (1869–1917)
3. Lawrence E. Duffy (1842–1927) *m.* 1864 Catherine P. Herring (1846–1876)
4. Dr. Charles Duffy (1808–1892) *m.* 1835 Anne C. House (1820–1891)
5. Dr. Charles Duffy (ca. 1784–1840) *m.* 1806 Elizabeth Stringer (1790–1832)
6. Francis Stringer (ca. 1765–1804) *m.* 1789 Anne Mackilwean (ca. 1770–1800)
7. Francis Mackilwean (ca. 1720–1774) *m.* 1753 Mary Nixon (1737–)
8. Richard Nixon (1712–1746/7) *m. ca.* 1736 Mary Graves (1718–1781)
9. Richard Graves (ca. 1680–1730) *m.* 1714 Hannah Consolvoe (1675–aft. 1744)
10. Francis Graves (1630–1691) *m.* 1678 Jane Dougherty, *d.* 1694
11. CAPT. THOMAS GRAVES (ca. 1580–bef 1637) *m. ca.* 1605 Katherine Graves.
Service: 2nd Commander of the Plantations of Accomack; came to this country in the Mary and Margaret in 1608; was Burgess for Smythes Hundred in 1619.
Reference: Whitfield, Bryan, Smith and Related Families; Pearsall Family; Colonists of Carolina in lineage of Hon. W. D. Humphrey; N. C. Hist. and Gen. Reg., by Hathaway.

6167   CARMICHAEL, Caroline Willingham   Recorded 1937
              843 Piedmont Avenue, Atlanta, Georgia
   1. Caroline Willingham Carmichael (1888–) *m.* 1910 Ambrose Homer Carmichael.
   2. Benj. Lawton Willingham (1856–1919) *m.* 1887 Maggy Seely Wood (1860–1937)
   3. Thomas Henry Willingham III (1825–1891) *m.* Cecilia Matilda Baynard (1828–
      1914)
   4. Thomas Henry Willingham (1798–1873) *m.* 1823 Phoebe Sarah Lawton
      (1808–1862)
   5. Benj. T. d'I Lawton (1782–1846) *m.* 1803 Jane Mosse (1783–1857)
   6. Joseph Lawton (1754–1819) *m.* bf. 1782 Sarah Robert (1755–1839)
   7. Jacques (James) Robert (1711–1776) *m.* 1735 Sarah Jaodon (Jordon Jourdon)
      (1719–1779)
   8. Pierre Robert, Jr. (Bapt. 1675–1731) *m.* 2, Judith Videaul (born aft. 1697–1731)
   9. Dr. Pierre Robert (M.D.) (1656–1715) *m.* 1678 Jeanne Braye (Bayer) (Broye)
      (1660–1717)
  10. DANIEL ROBERT (1625–) *m.* Marie
  11. Jeane Bayer was dgt. of Susannah Bayer (Braye)
   Service: First Minister of the French Huguenot Church, St. James, at the French
              Settlement on the French Santee River a few miles from Charleston, S. C.
   Reference: "Our Family Tree," by Miller, pg. 381; D.A.R. Nat. No. 133630; S. C.
              Hist. & Gen. Mag. 23–47–2–7–99; Huguents of Col. S. C., by Hirsch,
              pgs. 17–61.

6185   CARMICHAEL, (Henry) Griffin   Recorded 1938, Georgia
              983 Crescent Avenue N. E., Atlanta, Georgia
              (Junior)
   1. Henry Griffin Carmichael (1921–)
   2. John Floyd Carmichael (1891–1938) *m.* 1918 Florrie Lewis Griffin (1895–1938)
   3. Henry Clay Griffin (1852–1933) *m.* (2) 1886 Frances Gray Lewis (1864–1896)
   4. Charles Thomas Lewis (1830–1909) *m.* 1857 Henrietta Montgomery Gray
      (1837–1910)
   5. Ninian Edwards Gray (1807–1859) *m.* 1834 Harriet Elizabeth Howell (1811–1892)
   6. Joseph Emlen Howell (1781–1827) *m.* 1808 Sallie (Sarah) Powel Montgomery
      (1782–1865)
   7. Capt. James Montgomery (–1810) *m.* (2) 1777 Hester Griffitts (1754–aft. 1782)
   8. William Griffitts (1724–1762) *m.* 1752 Abigail Powel (1735–1797)
   9. Samuel Powel (1704–1759) *m.* 1732 Mary Morris (1713–1759)
  10. Anthony Morris IV (1681–1763) *m.* 1704 Phoebe Guest
  11. ANTHONY MORRIS III (1654–1721)
   Service: Alderman 1691; J. P. & Courts 1692–93; J. C. of Common Pleas 1693–97;
              Member of Gov. Con., 1695–96; Justice of Supreme Court 1694–98; Mayor
              of Philadelphia 1703.
   Reference: Fulton Co., Ga., Rec.; D.A.R. Nat. No. 268440; Rec. at Philadelphia,
              Pa.; "Ancestral Recs. & Portraits," Vol. I, pg. 153; Pa. Archives, 2nd ser.,
              Vol. 9, pgs., 625–630–701–719–729–731; 1st Ser., Vol. I, pgs. 473–512–535–
              537–540.

6131   CARMICHAEL, Mrs. John F.   Recorded 1937, Georgia
              983 Crescent Avenue, Atlanta, Georgia
   1. Florrie L. Griffin *m.* 1918 John F. Carmichael
   2. Henry C. Griffin (1852–1933) *m.* 1886 Frances G. Lewis (1864–1896)
   3. Charles T. Lewis (1830–1909) *m.* 1857 Henrietta M. Gray (1837–1910)
   4. Isaac Lewis (1796–1856) *m.* 1824 Sarah B. Brent (1809–1889)
   5. George Lewis (1763–1810) *m.* 1794 Mary Forman (1772–1799)
   6. Thomas Forman (1740–1825) *m.* 1767 Jane Throckmorton (1750–)
   7. Ezekiel Forman (1706–1746) *m.* 1738 Elizabeth Seabrooke (–1747)
   8. Samuel Forman (1662–1742) *m.* 1684 Mary Wilbur (1666–1728)
   9. Aaron Forman (1637–1693) *m.* 1662 Dorothy
  10. ROBERT FORMAN (1605–1671) *m.* 1635 Johanna (–1670)
   Service: Magistrate of Hempstead, L. I., 1658.
   Reference: Forman Family, by Miss A. S. Dandridge; The Marshall Family, by W. M.
              Paxton.

6005 CARPENTER, Mrs. Eugene J. Recorded 1931
　　　300 Clifton Ave., Minneapolis, Minnesota
　　1. Merrette Lamb (1867–) *m.* 1894 Eugene Joseph Carpenter
　　2. Lafayette Lamb (1845–1917) *m.* 1866 Olivia A. Hufman (1849–1924)
　　3. Chancy Lamb (1816–1897) *m.* Jane Bevier (1820–1897)
　　4. David Bevier (1764–1829) *m.* Sally Ann Gear (1777–)
　　5. Amos Gear (1736–) *m.* Mary Wight (1737–)
　　6. Robert Gear, Jr. (1707–1801) *m.* 1733 Abigail Greenman (–1790)
　　7. Capt. Robert Gear (1675–1742) *m.* Martha Tyler (–1733)
　　8. GEORGE GEAR (1621–1726) *m.* 1658 Sarah Allyn
Service: General.
Reference: Geer Gen., by Walter Geer, N. Y. Bevier Gen.

5970 CARPENTER, Mrs. Williston C. Recorded 1930, Georgia
　　　259 Second Avenue S. E., Atlanta, Georgia
　　1. Estelle Burney *m.* 1907 Williston C. Carpenter
　　2. Julius A. Burney (1850–1914) *m.* 1873 Sarah M. Ware (1850–1896)
　　3. John F. Burney (1828–1887) *m.* 1849 Margaret E. Stanley (1828–1855)
　　4. Irce Stanley (1803–1858) *m.* 1828 Janet H. McCall (1807–1888)
　　5. Thomas McCall (1764–1840) *m.* 1798 Elizabeth M. Smith (1775–1831)
　　6. James L. Smith (1735–1792) *m.* 1763 Margaret M. Sanders (1738–)
　　7. Col. William Sanders (1705–1742) *m.* 1738 Margaret Moore (1707–1775)
　　8. James Moore, Jr. (1667–1723) *m.* 1706 Elizabeth Beresford (1675–)
　　9. Gov. JAMES MOORE, SR. (1640–1706) *m.* 1665 Margaret Berringer (1645–)
Service: Governor of South Carolina.
Reference: South Carolina History & Genealogical Magazine, Vol. 17, p. 92; Barbados
　　　Immigrants, 1665 to S. C.; Marriage Records found in Barbados by Jacob
　　　Mott; S. C. McCrady's South Carolina History.

5973 CASEY, Mrs. Joseph M. Recorded 1930, Iowa
　　　921 Avenue E., Fort Madison, Iowa
　　1. Sarah Johnson *m.* 1895 Joseph M. Casey
　　2. Nelson Johnson (1843–1917) *m.* 1870 Nancy Ann Porter (1841–1926)
　　3. Seth Johnson (1798–1888) *m.* 1821 Lavina Adams (1804–1894)
　　4. Daniel Johnson (1775–1869) *m.* 1794 Lucretia Prout (1774–1863)
　　5. Seth Johnson (1747–1794) *m.* 1769 Jemima Miller (1748–)
　　6. John Johnson (1722–1802) *m.* 1743 Grace Morris (1721–1766)
　　7. John Johnson (1698–) *m.* 1721 Mary Bow Davis (1687–)
　　8. Isaac Johnson (1670–1744) *m.* 1695 Margery Miller (1675–1764)
　　9. Isaac Johnson (1644–1720) *m.* 1669 Mary Harris (1657–1740)
　10. ISAAC JOHNSON (–1675) *m.* 1637 Elizabeth Porter (–1683)
Service: Captain in the Ancient & Honorable Artillery Company of Boston.
Reference: Drake's History of Roxbury; History of Ancient & Honorable Artillery
　　　Company of Boston.

6679 CASSIDY, Mrs. John Herbert, Jr. Recorded 1950
　　　1645 Ingleside Street, Baton Rouge, Louisiana
　　1. Catherine H. Williams *m.* 1935 John H. Cassidy
　　2. Louis Rendall Williams (–1939) *m.* Mary O. Hall (–1935)
　　3. Dr. Alfred Hall (1833–1880) *m.* 1858 Ophelia Brusle (1839–1906)
　　4. Dr. William Hall (1789–1867) *m.* 1815 Anne Poyas (1799–1863)
　　5. Dr. John E. Poyas (1765–1836) *m.* ——Catherine Smith
　　6. Hendry Smith (1727–1780) *m.* 1764 Elizabeth Hall
　　7. Thomas Smith (1663–1738) *m.* 1713 Mary Hyrne (1690–1766)
　　8. THOMAS SMITH (1648–1694) *m.* Barbara Atkins (–1687)
Service: First Lamdgrave.
Reference: "Our Family Circle," by Dr. Alfred Hall.

5893 CHAMBERLAIN, Mrs. Harry   Recorded 1930, Iowa
         486 W. First Street, Spencer, Iowa
    1. Inez E. Palmer *m.* 1918 Harry Chamberlain
    2. Daniel C. Palmer (1845–1920) *m.* 1875 Margaret E. Lahmon (1847–)
    3. Benjamin F. Palmer (1819–1894) *m.* 1842 Mary Hopkins (1822–1875)
    4. Daniel Palmer (1797–1861) *m.* 1818 Beulah Warner (1800–1867)
    5. Daniel Palmer (1763–1851) *m.* Joanna Deming (1763–1849)
    6. Samuel Palmer (1731–1773) *m.* Lucretia
    7. Daniel Palmer (1704–1773) *m.* 1731 Mary Palmer
    8. Daniel Palmer (1672–1762) *m.* 1700 Margaret Smith (–1727)
    9. Nehemiah Palmer (1637–1717) *m.* 1662 Hannah L. Stanton (1644–1727)
   10. WALTER PALMER (1585–1661) *m.* 1633 Rebecca Short
   Service: One of the Founders of Stonington, Conn., 1653; also of Charlestown, Mass.,
         1629.
   Reference: History of Stonington, pp. 504, 507, 508, 509, 512. Connecticut Vital
         Records.

5947 CHAMBERLAIN, Harry   Recorded 1930, Iowa
         486 First Street, Spencer, Iowa
    1. Harry Chamberlain *m.* 1875 Mary Ellis; *m.* 1918 Inez E. Palmer
    2. Alonzo Chamberlain (1818–1902) *m.* 1843 Betsy N. Phillips (1823–1852)
    3. Spencer Chamberlain (1786–1853) *m.* Millicent French (1786–1849)
    4. John Chamberlain (1720–1802) *m.* (2) Winona
    5. John Chamberlain (1692–1756) *m.* 1712 Abigail Woods
    6. Thomas Chamberlain (1667–1709) *m.* 1690 Elizabeth Hall (–1699)
    7. Thomas Chamberlain (–1727) *m.* 1666 Sarah Proctor (1646–)
    8. THOMAS CHAMBERLAIN (–1700) *m.* Mary (–1669)
   Service: One of the first settlers in Chelmsford, Mass.; Freeman of Woburn, Mass.,
         1644.
   Reference: Vital Records of Keene, N. H.; Vital Records of Groton, Mass., Vol. I,
         p. 49; Vol. II, p. 40; "One Branch of the Descendants of Woburn,"
         pp. 5, 6, 8, 9.

6512 CHANCE, Mrs. Jesse E.   Recorded 1946, Ohio
         London, Ohio
    1. Ada Beach *m.* Jesse E. Chance
    2. Dr. Timothy D. Beach (1848–1922) *m.* 1876 Talitha Bales (1855–1942)
    3. Uri Beach (1826–1906) *m.* 1845 Eleanor Downing (1825–1906)
    4. Uri Beach (1789–1832) *m.* 1816 Hannah Noble (1789–1854)
    5. Obil Beach (1758–1846) *m.* 1782 Elizabeth Kilbourne (1765–1826)
    6. Amos Beach (1724–1790) *m.* 1746 Sarah Rice (Royce) (1723–1820)
    7. Deacon John Beach (1690–1775) *m.* 1717 Mary Rays (1695–)
    8. John Beach (1655–1709) *m.* 1678 . . . . . .
    9. THOMAS BEACH (*ca.* 1622–1662) *m.* 1654 Sarah Platt (–1670)
   Service: Settled first in New Haven, Conn., 1648, had a house-lot in Milford, Conn.

6617 CHAPIN, Miss Lucy   Recorded 1949
         616 W. Church Street, Champaign, Illinois
    1. Lucy Chapin
    2. Edward B. Chapin (1856–1936) *m.* 1877 Lucy Pierce (1857–1924)
    3. Edward O. J. Chapin (1825–1902) *m.* 1850 Rosetta Smith (1827–1916)
    4. Daniel S. Chapin (1787–1840) *m.* 1810 Clarinda Hill (1786–1868)
    5. Abner Chapin (1749–1814) *m.* 1769 Rhoda Kibbe (1751–1824)
    6. Abner Chapin (1722–) *m.* 1742 Abigail Warner
    7. Henry Chapin (1679–1754) *m.* 1716 Esther Bliss (1688–1768)
    8. Henry Chapin (*ca.* 1630–1718) *m.* 1664 Bethia Cooley (1644–1711)
    9. DEA. SAMUEL CHAPIN (bapt. 1598–1675) *m.* 1623 Cicely Penny (bapt. 1601–1682)
   Service: One of the Founders of Springfield, Mass.
   Reference: Chapin Book.

6618 CHAPIN, Miss Mae   Recorded 1949
       616 West Church Street, Champaign, Illinois
1. Mae Chapin
2. Edward B. Chapin (1856–1936) *m.* 1877 Lucy M. Pierce (1857–1924)
3. Edward O. J. Chapin (1825–1902) *m.* 1850 Rosetta Smith (1827–1916)
4. Daniel S. Chapin (1787–1840) *m.* 1810 Clarinda Hill (1786–1868)
5. Abner Chapin (1749–1814) *m.* 1769 Rhoda Kibbe (1751–1824)
6. Abner Chapin (1722–   ) *m.* 1742 Abigail Warner
7. Henry Chapin (1679–1754) *m.* 1716 Esther Bliss (1688–1768)
8. Henry Chapin (*ca.* 1630–1718) *m.* 1664 Bethia Cooley (1644–1711)
9. DEA. SAMUEL CHAPIN (1598–1675) *m.* 1623 Cicely Penny (1601–1682/3)
Service: One of the Founders of Springfield, Mass.
Reference: Chapin Book.

6686 CHAPLAN, Mrs. Mildred Gorham   Recorded 1951
       28 Hayes Street, Meriden, Connecticut
1. Fred Jaynes Gorham (1878–1918) *m.* 1903 Ethelyn M. Keller (1878–)
2. George B. Gorham (1847–1873) *m.* Mary N. Farris (1852–1939)
3. Maj. John T. Farris (1830–1885) *m.* Malinda Overly (1828–1885)
4. Joseph B. Faris (1800–1833) *m.* 1821 Betsy Ann Finley (1805–1881)
5. John Faris (1766–1826) *m.* 1794 Eleanor Belt (1772–1794)
6. Marsham Belt (1735–1801) *m.* 1763 Elizabeth Gross
7. John Belt (1707–177–) *m.* 1727 Margaret Queen
8. Col. Joseph Belt (1680–1761) *m.* 1706 Hester Beall, *d.* 1726
9. COL. NINIAN BEALL (1625–1717) *m.* 1670 Ruth Moore
Service:
Reference:

6425 CHAPPEL, Richard Badger   Recorded 1943
       Silver Spring, Maryland
       (Junior)
1. Richard Badger Chappell
2. John George Chappell (1893–) *m.* 1916 Mollie Ozelah Badger (1893–)
3. Dr. Augustine P. Badger (1863–) *m.* 1886 Matilda Jones (1865–1951)
4. David Elliott Badger (1834–1886) *m.* 1855 Adelia Ann Lee (1834–1872)
5. James Badger (1793–) *m.* Mary Blaylock Bell
6. James Badger (1757–1817) *m.* 1786 Elizabeth Swint (1766–)
7. Joseph Badger (1736–) *m.* 1755 Rhoda Cox
8. Joseph Badger (1707–1765) *m.* 1730 Mrs. Catherine (Smith) Felch (1693–)
9. Stephen Badger (1671–1750) *m.* Mercy Kettell (1679–)
10. Sergt. John Badger (1643–1691) *m.* 1671 Hannah Swett (1651–)
11. GILES BADGER (–1647) *m.* 1642 *ca.* Elizabeth Greenleaf (ab. 1622–)
Service: Settled in Newbury, Mass., 1635.
Reference: V. R., Boston, Mass.; Rec., Newbury, Mass.; Nos. 5708, 5670, 5600, Pilgrim Index.

6576 CHARLTON, Mrs. Ernest Rogers   Recorded 1948
       1621 Parnell Avenue, Chicago, Illinois
1. Amy Broadway *m.* 1909 Ernest Rogers Charlton
2. John B. B. Broadway (1853–1921) *m.* 1876 Lillis Robinson (1859–1890)
3. Alvin Robinson (1830–1906) *m.* 1853 Mary M. Price (1831–1914)
4. Gideon Robinson (1800–1864) *m.* 1823 Mary Hammon (1802–1854)
5. Thomas Hammon (1773–1846) *m.* 1795 Susannah Place (1773/5–1849)
6. Benejah Place (1742–1815) *m.* 1761/2 Mary Perkins (1741–1829)
7. Enoch Place (1704–1787) *m.* 1730 Hannah Wilcox, *d.* aft. 1735
8. Thomas Place (1663–1725) *m.* 1687 Hannah Cole (1668–1727)
9. John Cole (bef. 1630–1707) *m.* 1651 Susannah Hutchinson (1633–1713)
10. WILLIAM HUTCHINSON (1586–1642) *m.* 1612 Anne Marbury (1591–1643)
Service: Second Gov. of R. I. Colony.
Reference: Cole Gen., Marbury Gen., R. I. Place Family.

6108   CHASON, Mrs. Gordon   Recorded 1936, Georgia
       Bainbridge, Georgia
   1. Stella Kornegay *m.* 1905 Gordon Chason
   2. Robert D. Kornegay (1852–1929) *m.* 1874 Eliza C. Kornegay (1857–)
   3. Col. Henry R. Kornegay (1823–1898) *m.* 1851 Jeanette Williams (1824–1868)
   4. George F. Kornegay (1793–1869) *m.* 1823 Sarah Glisson (1791–1859)
   5. Isaac Kornegay (1766–1838) *m.* 1792 Hester Hargett (1772–1817)
   6. William Kornegay (1735–1822) *m.* 1765 Elizabeth Outlaw (1743–1821)
   7. Edward Outlaw III (1715–1795) *m.* 1740 Patience Whitfield (1723–1789)
   8. William Whitfield II *m.* Rachel Bryan
   9. Col. Needham Bryan *m.* Annie Rambeau
   Service: Justice in 1690.
   Reference: First Families of Virginia, p. 128; Society of Colonial Dames in N. C.

6591   CHRYSLER, Jack Forker   Recorded 1948
       Chrysler Bldg., 405 Lexington Avenue, New York City
   1. Jack F. Chrysler *m.* 1941 Edith Helen Backus
   2. Walter P. Chrysler (1875–1940) *m.* 1901 Della V. Forker (1876–1938)
   3. George C. Forker (1844–1918) *m.* 1867 Sarah C. Weese (1847–1893)
   4. John C. Forker (1814–1875) *m.* Mancy McCullough (1815–1860)
   5. George Forker (1787–1846) *m.* 1814 Nancy Campbell (1795–1874)
   6. Adam Forker (1761–1835) *m.* Jane Green (1760–1836)
   7. Adam Forker *ca.* (1729–) *m.* 1749 Hannah Gaskill (1728–)
   8. Zerubbabel Gaskill *ca.* (1698–1752) *m.* 1729 Ann Lippincott
   9. Samuel Lippincott *ca.* (1675–1721) *m.* 1700 Ann Hulett
  10. Restore Lippincott (1653–1741) *m.* 1674 Hannah Shattuck (1654–1709)
  11. Richard Lippincott *d.* 1683, *m.* Abigail *d.* 1697
   Service: Member of first English Colony in N. J., in Gov.'s Council, 1669, deputy of
       Gen. Court, 1669, 70, 77.
   Reference: Lippincotts in England and America, N. J. Calendar of Wills.

5917   CLAPHAM, Lizzie Hartman   Recorded 1930, Pennsylvania
       227 E. Gowen Avenue, Philadelphia, Pennsylvania
       Married Hesser C. Clapham 1886
   1. John Markley Hartman (1840–1910) *m.* 1862 Ruth Anna LaRue (1843–1926)
   2. Nicholas LaRue (1807–1849) *m.* 1836 Catherine M. Bunting (1816–1882)
   3. Solomon Bunting (1786–1864) *m.* 1811 Ruth Mathias (1789–1868)
   4. Joseph Bunting, Jr. (–1830) *m.* 1783 Phoebe Moon
   5. John Bunting (1720–) *m.* 1745 Christina Headley (1723–)
   6. Samuel Bunting (1692–1759) *m.* 1716 Priscilla Burgess
   7. Job Bunting (–1703) *m.* 1689 Rachel Baker (1669–)
   Service: Job Bunting came to New Jersey 1678.
   Reference: History of Bucks County, Pa., Vol. III; Colonial and Revolutionary
       Families of Penna., Vol. II, John W. Jordan, LL.D.

6068   CLARK, Gaylord Lee   Recorded 1934, Connecticut
       Margaret Meadows, Stevenson, Maryland
   1. Gaylord L. Clark *m.* 1921 Juliana B. Keyser
   2. Gaylord B. Clark (1846–1893) *m.* 1881 Lettice Lee Smith (1855–1914)
   3. Francis B. Clark (1820–1910) *m.* 1845 Helen M. Shepherd (1822–1899)
   4. Wyllys F. Clark (1786–1858) *m.* 1812 Charity Barnard (1792–1861)
   5. Oliver Clark, Jr., (1748–1824) *m.* 1778 Elizabeth Fish (1756–1848)
   6. Oliver Clark, Sr., (1720–1777) *m.* 1744 Esther Eaton (–1757)
   7. Aaron Clark (1687–1744) *m.* 1711 Susannah Wade (1692–)
   8. Daniel Clark, Jr., (1654–) *m.* 1678 Hannah Pratt (–1751)
   9. Captain Daniel Clark (1622–1710) *m.* 1644 Mary Newberry (–1688)
   Service: A Magistrate in Windsor, Conn., 1650; Tax Assessor in 1654; Representative
       in the Colonial Assembly of Connecticut 1657–1661, and Secretary of
       State from 1658–1662.
   Reference: James Savage Genealogical Dictionary of the First Settlers of New Eng-
       land, Vol. I; History and Genealogy of Ancient Windsor, Conn., Vol. II.

6733 CLEMONS, Mrs. Heywood C.   Recorded 1951, Texas
     4810 Hopkins, Dallas, Texas

1. Harriett Atkinson *m.* 1947 Heywood Clemons
2. Hubert Leland Atkinson (1877–) *m.* 1898 Harriett Emily Williams (1878–1941) (1878–1941)
3. Herbert Williams (1844*–1890) *m.* 1875 Emily Massengale (1852–1898)
4. Alfred Madison Massengale (1814–1874) *m.* 1840 Emily McKinney McAdore (1814–1861)
5. Harria McKinney (1784–1864) *m.* 1810 Jency (Jane) Ivey (1797–1851)
6. Sampson Ivey (1765–1816) *m.* 1790 Milly *ca.* (1776–after 1816)
7. Adam Ivey, Jr., (1720–1789–1792) *m.* 1747 Mary Pebbles (Peoples) *ca* (1727–1792)
8. Adam Ivey, Sr., (1690–abt. 1762) *m.* Mary *ca.* (1695–after 1762)
9. George Ivey, Jr., *ca.* (1660 *bf.* 1718) *m.* 1685 Elizabeth Langley, *ca* (1665–1718)
10. William Langley, Jr., *ca.* (1640–1716) *m. ca.* 1660 Maraget Thelaball *ca.* (1645–after 1718)
11. JAMES THELABALL *b.* in France (–1692) *m.* 1637 Elizabeth Mason (–1692/3)

Service: Imported immigrants to Virginia 1659. Served as Church Warden of Lower Norfolk Co., Va.

Reference: James and Elizabeth Mason Thelaballs wills; Tarrance and Allied Families; The Wickersham Press, MCMXXXVIII, pg. 265.

6422 CLIFFORD, Merritt Willard   Recorded 1943
     New Haven, Connecticut

1. Merritt Willard Clifford *m.* Bessie Mae Kinsman
2. Elmanan Winchester Clifford (1844–1892) *m.* 1866 Ella Josephine Dunklee (1846–1901)
3. Simeon Willard Clifford (1800–1847) *m.* 1842 (2nd) Lois (Torrey) Cheney, wid. 1813–)
4. Simeon Clifford (1764–1838) *m.* 1794 Susan Martin (1772–1819)
5. Edward Clifford (1734–1824) *m.* 1760 Abigail Winslow (1742–1820)
6. Dr. Gilbert Winslow (1704–1777) *m.* Patience Seabury
7. Lieut. Gilbert Winslow (1673–1731) *m.* 1698 Mercy Snow (1675–)
8. Capt. Nathaniel Winslow (1639–1719) *m.* 1664 Faith Miller (–1729)
9. KENELM WINSLOW (1599–1672) *m.* 1634 Eleanor (Helen) Adams, wid. 1681 (prob. dau. of Ellen Newton, Plymouth Pilgrim)

Service: Prob. to Plymouth 1629; 1640 Surveyor at Plymouth; to Marshfield 1641; one of 26 original proprietors of Assonet (Freetown), Mass. Deputy to General Court, 1642–44, 1649–53.

References: Twn. Rec. Pittsford and Brandon, Vt.; V. R. Hardwick, Mass.; Hists., Marshfield, Situate, Bridgewater, Mass.

6424 CLIFFORD, Mrs. Merrit Willard   Recorded 1943
     New Haven, Connecticut

1. Bessie Mae Kinsman *m.* Merritt Willard Clifford
2. Henry Parker Kinsman (1836–1913) *m.* 1858 Mary Abigail Gibson (1842–1919)
3. Timothy Oakley Gibson (1810–1884) *m.* 1839 Abigail Perkins (1815–1885)
4. Timothy Gibson (1785–1857) *m.* 1808 Nancy Lawrence (1787–1868)
5. Abraham Gibson (1762–1832) *m.* 1782 Elizabeth Barker (1762–1835)
6. Deacon Steven Gibson (1719–1806) *m.* 1744 Sarah Goss (1719–1802)
7. Deacon Timothy Gibson (1679–1757) *m.* 1700 Rebecca Gates (1682–1754)
8. John Gibson (1641–1699) *m.* 1668 Rebecca Farrington (1713–1688)
9. JOHN GIBSON (1601–1694) *m.* Rebecca ——— (–1661)

Service: First appears at Cambridge, Mass., 1634; Removed to Hartford, Conn. *Reference:* Gibson Geneal. (Wilson), Hemenway's Gazateer of Vt., Vol. III; V. R. of Stow, Sudbury and Cambridge, Mass.

6559 CLOTHIER, Marjorie Elizabeth   Recorded 1947
        17085 Rancho Street, Encino, California
   1. Marjorie Elizabeth Clothier.
   2. Jos. V. Clothier, M.D. (1879–   ) *m.* 1908 Selma E. Sann (1880–1946)
   3. Samuel Clothier (1852–1922) *m.* 1874 Emma J. Elberson (1854–1935)
   4. Samuel Clothier (1813–1859) *m.* 1833 Margaret Vaughn (1812–1906)
   5. Samuel Clothier (1790–1832) *m.* 1811 Anna *d. aft.* 1832
   6. Samuel Clothier *c.* (1760–1804) *m.* 1780 Barbara
   7. James Clothier (1718–aft. 1770) *m.* 1755 Mary S. Allison (1727–aft. 1770)
   8. Henry Clothier *d.* 1732, *m.* 1717 Abigail Ridgway, *d.* 1724
   9. Richard Ridgway (1650–1723) *m.* 1693 Abigail Stockton, *d.* 1721
  10. RICHARD STOCKTON *d.* 1707, *m.* Abigail
   Service: Lt. of Horse Co., Lt. of Foot Co., Flushing, L. I.
   Reference: Stockton Genealogy.

6558 CLOTHIER, Ruth Schofield   Recorded 1947
        17085 Tancho Street, Encino, California
   1. Ruth Schofield Clothier
   2. Jos. V. Clothier, M.D. (1879–   ) *m.* 1908 Selma E. Sann (1880–1946)
   3. Samuel Clothier (1852–1921) *m.* 1874 Emma J. Elberson (1854–1935)
   4. Samuel Clothier (1813–1859) *m.* 1833 Margaret Vaughn (1812–1906)
   5. Samuel Clothier (1790–1832) *m. c.* 1811 Ann *d. aft.* 1832
   6. Samuel Clothier (1760–1804) *m.* 1780 Barbara
   7. James Clothier (1718–aft. 1770) *m.* 1756 Mary S. Allison (1727–aft. 1770)
   8. James Clothier *d.* 1732, *m.* 1717 Abigail Ridgway *d.* 1724
   9. Richard Ridgway (1650–1723) *m.* 1693 Abigail Stockton
  10. RICHARD STOCKTON *d.* 1707, *m.* Abigail *d. aft.* 1714
   Service: Lt. of Horse Co., Lt. of Foot Co., Flushing, L. I.
   Reference: Stockton Genealogy.

6557 CLOTHIER, Selma Vaughn   Recorded 1947
        17085 Rancho Street, Encino, California
   1. Selma V. Clothier
   2. Joseph V. Clothier, M.D. (1879–   ) *m.* 1908 Selma E. Sann (1880–1946)
   3. Samuel Clothier (1852–1922) *m.* 1874 Emma J. Elberson (1854–1935)
   4. Samuel Clothier (1813–1859) *m.* 1833 Margaret Vaughn (1812–1906)
   5. Samuel Clothier (1790–1832) *m.* 1811 Anne, *d. aft.* 1832
   6. Samuel Clothier *ca.* (1760–1804) *m.* 1780 Barbara ———
   7. James Clothier (1718–aft. 1770) *m.* 1755 Mary S. Allison (1727–aft. 1770)
   8. Henry Clothier *d.* 1732, *m.* 1717 Abigail Ridgway *d.* 1724
   9. Richard Ridgway (1650–1723) *m.* 1693 Abigail Stockton *d.* 1721
  10. RICHARD STOCKTON *d.* 1707, *m.* Abigail *d. aft.* 1714
   Service: Lt. of Horse Co., Lt. of Foot Co., Flushing, L. I.
   Reference: Stockton Genealogy, Gen. and Hist. of N. J.

6298 CLOTHIER, Dr. Joseph V.   Recorded 1949
        Kane Bldg., Pocatello, Idaho
   1. Dr. Joseph V. Clothier *m.* Selma Elaine Sann
   2. Samuel Clothier *b.* 1852, *m.* 1874 Emma Jane Elberson (1854–1935)
   3. Samuel Clothier (1813–1859) *m.* 1833 Margaret Vaughn (1812–1906)
   4. Samuel Clothier (1790–1832) *m.* 1811 Ann, *d. aft.* 1832
   5. Samuel Clothier (1760–1804) *m.* 1780 Barbara
   6. James Clothier (1718–*aft.* 1770) *m.* 1756 Mary Shinn Allison (widow), *b.* 1727
   7. Henry Clothier *d.* 1732, *m.* 1717 Abigail Ridgway *d.* 1724
   8. Richard Ridgway *d.* 1723, *m.* 1693 Abigail Stockton *d.* 1721
   9. RICHARD STOCKTON came 1656, *d.* 1707, *m.* Abigail
   Service: Lt. of Horse Co. 1665; Lt. of Foot. Co.
   Reference: "Shinn Family"; Stockton Genealogy, by Thomas Coates Stockton.

6252 COATES, Rev. Walter John
　　　　North Montpelier, Vermont
　　1. Walter John Coates (1880–　) *m.* 1902 Florence Webster; *m.* 1908 Nettie Allen, 2nd
　　2. Albert Spicer Coats (1845–1900) *m.* 1875 Frances Amanda Lee (1850–1894)
　　3. Benj. Franklin Coats (1804–1881) *m.* 1841 Lois Whitford (1810–1873)
　　4. Edward Whitford (1778–1862) *m.* 1799 Polly Maxson (1781–1862)
　　5. Asa Maxson (1750–1842) *m.* 1775 Lois Stillman (1756–1820)
　　6. David Maxson (1729–　) *m.* 1748 Abigail Greenman (1727–　)
　　7. John Maxson (1701–　) *m.* 1724 Thankful Randall
　　8. John Maxson, Jr. (1666–1747) *m.* 1687 Judith Clarke (1667–　)
　　9. John Maxson (1638–1720) *m.* 1664 Mary Mosher (1641–1718)
　10. RICHARD MAXSON
Services: Pastor.
Reference: Austin's Biog. Dict. of R. I.; Savage's Gen. Dict. of R. I.; Westerly and its
　　　　Witnesses, by Denison; Narragansett His.

6328 COBURN, Mrs. Carroll L.　　　　　　　　　　　　　　　　Recorded 1941
　　　　Twin Elms Farm, East Montpelier, Vermont
　　1. Edith Lillian Ellis *m.* 1932 Rep. Carroll Leander Coburn
　　2. Leon Glen Ellis (1879–　) *m.* 1902 Esther Isabel Keith (1881–　)
　　3. Ira Ellis, Jr. (1843–1917) *m.* 1865 Ortensa Goodall (1842–1925)
　　4. Ira Ellis (1808–　) *d. aft.* 1881, *m.* Sally Briggs Collier *d.* 1871
　　5. Benjamin Ellis (1779–　) *m.* Susanna Guernsey
　　6. Deacon Martin Ellis (1753–1832) *m.* 1777 Mary Kingsley
　　7. John Ellis (1735–1805) *m.* 2nd 1750 Mary Horton (widow)
　　8. John Ellis (1704–1792) *m.* Rose ——— (1709–1782)
　　9. John Ellis *d.* 1732, *m.* 1700 Mary Holmes
　10. LT. JOHN ELLIS *d.* 1677, *m.* 1645 Elizabeth Freeman
Service: Lt. Militia, Sandwich, Mass., 1653; engaged to train Company of Sandwich,
　　　　Plymouth Colony, 1660.
Reference: "Ancient Landmarks of Plymouth," Davis; Hist. of Richmond, N.H.,
　　　　Bassett; "Hist. of Vermont," Hemenway.

6246 COBURN, Mr. Carroll Leander
　　　　Twin Elms Farm, Montpelier, Vermont
　　1. Carroll Leander Coburn (1907–　) *m.* 1932 Edith Ellis (1909–　)
　　2. Lewis Dwight Coburn (1865–1936) *m.* 1891 Rosa Belle Hollister (1868–1937)
　　3. Joseph Leander Coburn (1830–1888) *m.* 1859 Caroline Alma Corliss (1834–1904)
　　4. Larned Coburn (1800–1872) *m.* 1823 Lovisa Livermore Allen (1804–1872)
　　5. Joseph Coburn (1774–1813) *m.* 1796 Mary Larned (1772–　)
　　6. John Coburn (1718–　) *m.* 1759 Sarah Dresser (1740–　)
　　7. Daniel Coburn (1678–1750) *m.* 1700 Elizabeth Conant (1682–　)
　　8. Robt. Coburn (1647–　) *m.* 1669 Mary Bishop
　　9. EDWARD COLBORNE (1618–　) *m.* Hannah ——— (　–1712)
Service:
Reference: Gen. Desc. of Edward Colburn; History of Ipswitch; His. of Charlton,
　　　　Mass.

5877 CODINGTON, Mrs. Joseph L.　　　　　　　　　　Recorded 1929, Nebraska
　　　　Hotel Hamilton, Omaha, Nebraska
　　1. Kate M. Smith *m.* 1902 Joseph L. Codington
　　2. Richard B. Smith (1830–1901) *m.* 1856 Margaret Chapman (1834–1903)
　　3. Benjamin Smith (1798–1873) *m.* 1818 Lydia Gardiner (1802–1832)
　　4. Diodate Smith (1772–1834) *m.* 1797 Rachel Alworth (1776–1848)
　　5. Thomas Smith, Jr. (1738–1821) *m.* 1760 Mary Greene (1736–1810)
　　6. Warren Greene (1712–1785) *m.* 1733 Mary Paine (　–1783)
　　7. William Greene (1684–1756) *m.* 1709 Desire Bacon (1688–1730)
　　8. John Bacon (1661–　) *m.* 1686 Mary Hawes (1664–1725)
　　9. Capt. John Hawes (　–1701) *m.* 1661 Desire Gorham (1644–1700)
　10. Capt. John Gorham (1621–1675) *m.* 1643 Desire Howland (1623–1683)
　11. JOHN HOWLAND (1592–1672) *m.* Elizabeth Tilley (1606–1687)
Service: One of the Founders of Plymouth Colony.
Reference: Mayflower Descendants, Vol. IV, p. 217.

6402   COLCORD, Elmer Danforth   Recorded 1943
              Provincetown, Massachusetts
       1. Dr. Elmer Danforth Colcord *m.* Evelyn Ruth Huntsinger
       2. Frederick Elmer Colcord (1875–) *m.* Sadie Holway Hill
       3. George Frederick Colcord (1850–) *m.* 1871 Mary Maria Clark (1857–1908)
       4. David B. Colcord (1802–1882) *m.* Louisa George (1810–1881)
       5. Joseph Colcord *m.* 1791 Sarah Bean
       6. Samuel Colcord (1722–1787) *m.* 1745 Mehitable Stevens
       7. Ebenezer Colcord (1695–1766) *m.* 1720 Hannah Fellows (1697–)
       8. Lieut. Samuel Colcord (1656–1736) *m.* 1681 Mary Ayer (1661–1739)
       9. EDWARD COLCORD (1616–1682) *m.* Ann Page
       Service: Deputy to General Court from Dover, N. H., to Boston 1642.
       Reference: State V. R. Sunapee, Springfield, N. H.; Histories: Sutton, Ceshire and
              New Fields, N. H.; Comp., Virkus.

5878   COLLINS, Mrs. Charles T.   Recorded 1929, New Jersey
              416 Doughty Road, Pleasantville, New Jersey
       1. Flora Stebbins *m.* 1892 Charles T. Collins
       2. Job Stebbins (1844–1926) *m.* 1866 Hester A. Adams (1847–)
       3. Martin Adams (1809–1848) *m.* 1831 Hester A. Risley (1814–1883)
       4. Richard N. Risley (1779–1831) *m.* 1801 Elizabeth D. Bevis (1784–1865)
       5. Nathaniel Risley (1754–) *m.* Sarah Steelman
       6. Jeremiah Risley (1734–1796) *m.* 1758 Margaret Doughty (1734–1796)
       7. Jeremiah Risley (1690–1767) *m.* Dinah Gale
       8. Richard Risley (1648–) *m.* Rebecca Adams
       9. RICHARD RISLEY (–1648)
       Service: One of the Original Proprietors of Hartford, Conn.
       Reference: Genealogy of the Lake Family, by Arthur Adams & Sarah R. Risley,
              pp. 205–6.

5956   COLLINS, Mrs. Francis A.   Recorded 1930, Texas
              915 Grigsby Avenue, Dallas, Texas
       1. Josephine Cunningham *m.* 1892 Francis A. Collins
       2. Louis A. Cunningham (1840–1889) *m.* 1861 Avaline Carson (1843–1880)
       3. Dr. John F. Cunningham (1819–1895) *m.* 1839 Mary H. Dolman (1820–1890)
       4. John Cunningham (1782–1838) *m.* 1810 Orpha Bingham (1787–1867)
       5. Chester Bingham (1761–1812) *m.* 1786 Deborah Rich (1769–)
       6. Jonathan Rich (1737–) *m.* 1760 Thankful Newcomb
       7. Capt. Ebenezer Newcomb (1712–1782) *m.* 1738 Thankful Freeman (1715–)
       8. Ebenezer Freeman (1688–1760) *m.* 1710 Abigail Young (1688–1781)
       9. Lt. Edmund Freeman (1657–) (1660–1717)
      10. Maj. John Freeman (1627–1719) *m.* 1649 Mercy Prence (1631–1711)
      11. Gov. Thomas Prence *m.* 1624 Patience Brewster
      12. ELDER WILLIAM BREWSTER (1566–1644)
       Service: Fourth signer of the Mayflower Compact.
       Reference: Mayflower Descendants, Vol. VI–VIII and X; Newcomb Genealogy;
              Freeman Genealogy.

6018   COLLINS, Miss Josephine Toy   Recorded 1932
              1057 Asylum Avenue, Hartford, Connecticut
       1. Fred. Starr Collins (1883–) *m.* 1907 Josephine Seymour Toy (1884–1909)
       2. Joseph Toy (1808–1887) *m.* 1882 Mary Florilla Seymour (1852–)
       3. Chester Seymour (1823–1895) *m.* 1849 Sabra Thankful Ensign (1826–1901)
       4. Chester Seymour (1793–1832) *m.* 1820 Florilla Mather (1796–1838)
       5. Asa Seymour (1760–1810) *m.* 1796 Eliz Denison (1766–1846)
       6. Capt. Daniel Seymour (–1815) *m.* 1750 Lydia King (1735–1829)
       7. Capt. Daniel Seymour (1698–1759) *m.* 1727 Mabel Bigelow (1703–1759)
       8. John Seymour (1666–1748) *m.* 1693 Eliz Webster (1690–1754)
       9. Lt. Robt. Webster (1627–1677) *m.* 1652 Susannah Treat (1629–1705)
      10. GOVERNOR JOHN WEBSTER (–1661) *m.* Agnes ———
       Service: Governor, Commissioner.
       Reference: Mather Gen.; Gen. Seymour Family; Hist. and Gen of Gov. John Webster.

6059 COLLINS, Miss Martha K.   Recorded 1933, New Jersey
      223 Retreat Avenue, Hartford, Connecticut
1. Martha Knowles Collins
2. Daniel E. Collins (1846–1923) *m.* 1867 Margaret T. Frambes (1850–1923)
3. Richard I. Frambes (1824–1903) *m.* 1845 Mary Tilton (1823–1906)
4. James Tilton (1796–1849) *m.* 1822 Margaret Lake (1804–1885)
5. John Lake (1773–1855) *m.* 1796 Abigail Adams (1775–1857)
6. Ens. John Adams (1738–1798) *m.* 1763 Margaret Garwood (1740–1826)
7. Thomas Garwood (1707–1796) *m.* 1733 Mary Ballenger (–1764)
8. Thomas Garwood (1669–1752) *m.* 1705 Margaret Hancock (1684–)
9. RICHARD HANCOCK (–1689) *m.* 1680 Elizabeth Denn
Service: Member of the Assembly of West New Jersey for Salem Co., 1682; Surveyor-
    General of Fenwick's Colony, 1676–1680; a Justice for Salem Co., 1682.
Reference: Genealogy of the Lake Family, Adams-Risley, 1915; Smith's History of
    New Jersey.

6024 COLVER, Clinton   Recorded 1932
      945 S. University Blvd., Denver, Colorado
1. Clarence Walker Collver (1858–) *m.* 1883 Amy Gillis (1861–1932)
2. Lyman Nelson Collver (1837–1891) *m.* 1856 Marg. Cecelia Bartlett (1838–1873)
3. Orrin Gabriel Collver *m.* Harriet Walker (–1882)
4. Gabriel Collver (1774–1841) *m.* Martha Culver (1776–1866)
5. Rev. Jabez Collver (1731–1818) *m.* Anna ——— (1739–1813)
6. Jabez Colver (1674–) ———
7. John Colver (1640–) *m.* 1672 Mary Winthrop
8. EDWARD COLVER (1600–1685) *m.* 1638 Ann Ellis
Service: Lieutenant.
Reference: Pioneers Sketches of Long Point Settlement, pages 84–89; Colver-Culver
    Gen.; Edward Colver-Colver-Culver Gen.

6147 CONDIT, Mrs. Ernest D.   Recorded 1937, Pennsylvania
      Morristown, Pennsylvania
1. Anna Thompson *m.* 1907 Ernest D. Condit
2. William W. Thompson (1856–1933) *m.* 1884 Martha A. McBride (1864–)
3. Samuel Thompson (1835–1869) *m.* 1854 Cecelia Ball (1837–1920)
4. William C. Ball (1804–1890) *m.* Margaret Ten Broeck (1805–1892)
5. Cyrus Ball (1783–1815) *m.* Sarah Cook (1785–1809)
6. Ellis Cook (1755–1832) *m.* 1777 Isabella Davis
7. Williams Cook
8. Ellis Cook (1703–1756) *m.* 1730 Mary Williams (1716–1754)
9. Abiel Cook (–1714) *m.* Sarah Moore
10. Joseph Moore (1661–1726) *m.* Sarah Halsey (1658–)
11. Rev. John Moore (1620–1659) *m.* Margaret Howell (1622–)
12. EDWARD HOWELL (1584–1655) *m.* Frances (–1630)
Service: Member of the Colonial Legislature, Hartford, Conn.
Reference: Colonial Families of the U. S., by Mackenzie; Howell's History of
    Southampton.

5915 CONDON, Richard Wathen   Recorded 1930, Maryland
      418 W. Oak St., Louisville, Ky.
1. Richard L. Condon (1855–1910) *m.* 1905 Emma Louise Wathen (1869–)
2. John Bernard Wathen (1844–1919) *m.* 1867 Margaret Adams (1844–)
3. James Adams (1802–1881) *m.* 1827 Ann Pamelia Hill (1807–1845)
4. Clement Hill (1776–1832) *m.* 1798 Mary Hamilton (1782–1833)
5. Thomas Hamilton (1723–1807) *m.* 1781 Ann Hodgkins (1757–1819)
6. James Hamilton (1715–1785) *m.* Mary Ann Coombs (1720–1785)
7. Thomas Coombs (–1753) *m.* Elizabeth Wharton (–1772)
8. DR. JESSE WHARTON (–1676) *m.* 1672 Elizabeth Sewall (–1710)
Service: Dr. Jesse Wharton was Deputy Governor of Maryland.
Reference: Maryland Archives, Vol. II; Side-lights on Maryland History, Vol. II.

5903   COOK, Charles Wenzel   Recorded 1930, New Jersey
           15 Southward Street, Trenton, New Jersey
       1. Charles Wenzel Cook (1896–   ) *m.* 1922
       2. Stephen C. Cook (1864–   ) *m.* 1886 Sara Etta Wenzel (1866–   )
       3. William Wenzel (1835–1916) *m.* 1850 Hannah H. Bowne (1830–1872)
       4. John Deats Bowne (1792–1860) *m.* 1819 Sarah Cronce
       5. William Bowne (1750–1842) *m.* 1788 Anna Deats
       6. James Bowne *m.* 1743 Elizabeth O. Hartshorne
       7. John Bowne (1670–   ) *m.* Elizabeth ———
       8. James Bowne (1636–1692) *m.* 1665 Mary Stout
       9. WILLIAM BOWNE (–1677) *m.* Ann
       Service: William Bowne, soldier in the Second Regiment, New Jersey Troops under
           Col. Ogden.
       Reference: Commissioner of Pensions, Washington, D. C.

6715   COOK, James Fielder   Recorded 1951, Georgia
           2 Gramercy Park, New York, New York
       1. James Fielder Cook *m.* 1950 Sarah E. Chamberlin
       2. George Lindsey Cook (1886–1949) *m.* Marion Fielder (1890–   )
       3. James Walton Fielder (1861–1923) *m.* 1888 Julia Martha Hodgkins (1866–   )
       4. Col. James Monroe Fielder (1816–1863) *m.* 1851 Roxanna Williamson (1831–1871)
       5. Obediah M. B. Fielder (1789–1857) *m.* 1815 Elizabeth Thornbury Heard (1798–
           1847)
       6. Joseph Heard (1773–1848) *m.* 1795–7 Nancy Stuart (–1810)
       7. Thomas Heard (1742–1808) *m.* 1765–66 Elizabeth Fitzpatrick (1745–1790)
       8. Joseph Fitzpatrick (1720–25–1777) *m.* Mary Perrin Woodson *circa* (1730–   )
       9. Benjamin Woodson *circa* (1684–1778) *m.* 1720 Francis Napier (1695–1727)
      10. John Woodson (1655–1700) *m.* Mary Tucker *circa* (1660–1710)
      11. John Woodson (1632–1684) *m.* Judith ———, died after 1684
      12. DR. JOHN WOODSON I (1586–after 1644) *m.* Sarah Winston (–after 1644)
       Service: Physician and surgeon for the early Colonists.
       Reference: Woodsons, Their Connection, by Henry M. Woods; pub. 1915; Southern
           Lineages, by A. E. Wynn, pg. 147; Jos. Fitzpatrick Will, Fluvania Co., Va.;
           Wm. and Mary Quarterly, Vol. XI, 53, Wills of John Woodson, 3rd and 2nd.
           Hotten's Emigrants to America.

5904   COOK, Sara Etta Wenzel   Recorded 1930, New Jersey
           15 Southard Street, Trenton, New Jersey
       1. Sara Etta Wenzel (1866–   ) *m.* 1886 Stephen C. Cook (1864–   )
       2. William Wenzel (1835–1916) *m.* 1850 Hannah H. Bowne (1830–1872)
       3. John Deats Bowne (1792–1860) *m.* 1819 Sarah Cronce
       4. William Bowne (1750–1842) *m.* 1788 Anna Dats
       5. James Bowne *m.* 1743 Elizabeth O. Hartshorne
       6. John Bowne (1670–   ) *m.* Elizabeth
       7. James Bowne (1636–1692) *m.* 1665 Mary Stout
       8. WILLIAM BOWNE (–1677) *m.* Ann
       Service: Served as a soldier in the Second Regiment, New Jersey Troops, under
           Col. Ogden.
       Reference: Commissioner of Pensions, Washington, D. C.

6742   COOPER, Mrs. Edward Richwood   Recorded 1952, Louisiana
           Natchitoches, Louisiana
       1. Olive Ray Long *m.* 1909 Edward Richwood Cooper
       2. Hughey Pierce Long (1852–1937) *m.* 1875 Caledonia Tison (1860–1913)
       3. John Murphy Long (1825–1901) *m.* 1845 Mary Elizabeth Wingate (1829–1901)
       4. James Long (1790–1850) *m.* 1823 Mary Kirtman (1793–1850)
       5. Hugh Long (1770–btw. 1794/1806) *m.* 1786 Margaret (–1794)
       6. James Long (1750–1807) *m.* 1763 Catherine, *d.* before 1790
       7. John Long (–1759) *m.* 1735 Ellenor Owens (1706–aft. 1759)
       8. Capt. Richard Owens (1668–aft. 1708) *m.* 1698 Rachael Beall (bef. 1678–aft.
           1708)
       9. COL. NINIAN BEALL (1625–1717) *m.* 1668 Ruth Moore (–1704)
       Service: Dept. Surveyor, Justice, Burgess of Md.
       Reference: Beal Genealogy, by F. M. Beall, pg. 49; Sons & Daughters National
           No. 6724.

5967 CORSON, Miss Mabel   Recorded 1930, Pennsylvania
      1559 Pratt Street, Philadelphia, Pennsylvania
1. Miss Mabel Corson
2. Robert T. Corson (1858–1921) *m.* 1878 Eliza O. Deal (1856–1918)
3. Rufus T. Corson (1826–1884) *m.* 1855 Caroline W. Thornton (1837–1862)
4. Amos Corson (1791–1836) *m.* 1820 Hannah W. Neff (1791–1878)
5. John Corson (1759–1826) *m.* 1787 Deborah Engle (1753–1840)
6. Cornelius Corson (1714–1774) *m.* 1755 Maragritta Van Enden
7. Benjamin Corson (1678–) *m.* 1713 Blandina Von Woglam
8. Cornelius Corssen (1645–1693) *m.* 1666 Maritje Jacobse (1649–1698)
9. Jacob L. Van der Grist *m.* 1648 Rebecca Lubbertsen
10. FREDERICK LUBBERTSEN (1603–1680) *m.* Styntje Jans
Service: Burgher of Brooklyn, 1641.
Reference: The Coursen Family, by P. G. Ullman; History of Brooklyn by Stiles.

6677 CORVEN, Mrs. Joseph E.   Recorded 1950, Ohio
      McConnelsville, Ohio
1. Anna Porter (1892–) *m.* 1922 Joseph E. Corven
2. Willard F. Porter, (1869–) *m.* 1891 Mary Gillespie (1866–)
3. Alfred Avery Porter (1845–1933) *m.* 1868 Mary Trainer (1849–1918)
4. Reuben Porter, Sr. (1773–1861) *m.* Lydia H. Stanley
5. Letti Stanley (1755–1827) *m.* 1781 Ann Hooker (1756–1808)
6. Samuel Hooker (1726–1807) *m.* 1756 Sarah Nortar (1731–1809)
7. Samuel Hooker (1688–1787) *m.* 1711 Mercy (Mary) Leete (1688–1751)
8. Samuel Hooker (1661–1730) *m.* 1687 Mehitable Hamlin (1664–1749)
9. Rev. Samuel Hooker (1633–1697) *m.* 1658 Mary Willet
10. REV. THOMAS HOOKER (1586–1647) *m.* 2nd Susanna. Descendant of Rev.
     Thomas Hooker, Edward Hooker
Service:
Reference:

6450 COULSON, Mrs. Fred D.   Recorded 1944, Ohio
      Malta, Ohio
1. Beryl Goodwin *m.* Fred D. Coulson
2. Albert D. Goodwin (1862–1899) *m.* 1885 Nellie M. Boutelle (1867–1895)
3. Augustus Copp Goodwin (1834–1907) *m.* 1855 Susannah A. Lewis (1839–1901)
4. William L. Lewis (1806–1889) *m.* 1825 Sarah Chadwick (1807–1888)
5. Col. Elihu Chadwick (1759–1837) *m.* 1789 (2nd) Rebekah Jeffrey (1764–1841)
6. John Chadwick (1713–1783) *m.* 1735 Ann Martha Jackson (1713–1795)
7. Hugh Jackson (1683–1760) *m.* 1716 bef. Mercy Potter (1690–)
8. Ephraim Potter (–1717) *m.* Sarah Brown (1669–1715)
9. Abraham Brown (1665–1714) *m.* Mary Potter
10. NICHOLAS BROWN (–1694) *m.* Frances (wid. Parker) (–1669 aft.)
Service: Resident of Portsmouth, R. I., 1638; 1639 one of 29 who joined to create them-
     selves a "Civill body politicke."
Reference: Hist. McKean, Elk, Cameron, Potter Counties, Pa.; Chadwick Fam.,
     Allegheny Valley, Pa., by Jordan.

6540 COVINGTON, Frank H.   Recorded 1947
      311 Fayetteville Avenue, Bennettsville, South Carolina
1. Frances Harllee Covington
2. Benjamin H. Covington (1858–1940) *m.* 1883 Annie M. Coxe (1860–1938)
3. Benjamin H. Covington (1812–1866) *m.* 1847 Mary A. Harllee (1829–1876)
4. Col. David S. Harllee (1800–1864) *m.* 1823 Harriett P. Barnes (1807–1855)
5. Thomas Harllee (1767–1827) *m.* 1789 Elizabeth Stewart (1767–1817)
6. Peter Harllee (1699–1784) *m.* 1759 Jane Leake (1714–1810)
7. Richard Leake *ca.* (1691–1784) *m.* 1712 Elizabeth, *d.* 1784
8. WILLIAM LEAKE (*ca.* 1664–*ca.* 1714) *m.* Mary Bostic, *d.* 1717
Service:
Reference: Kinfolks, by Col. Wm. C. Harllee.

5861 COX, Mrs. William   Recorded 1929, New Jersey
            29 Prospect St., Trenton, New Jersey
   1. Frances Field *m.* William Cox
   2. William R. Field (1821–1892) *m.* 1856 Sarah E. Kline (1832–1891)
   3. Richard W. Field (1783–1876) *m.* 1804 Sarah VanderVoort (1783–1868)
   4. Hendrick Field (1751–1844) *m.* 1774 Hannah Lane (1752–1855)
   5. Richard Field (1726–1800) *m.* 1749 Elizabeth Smock (1728–1805)
   6. Jeremiah Field (1689–1746) *m.* 1712 Mary Seneicke (1687–1742)
   7. John Field (1659–1729) *m.* Margaret (1657–1728)
   8. Anthony Field (1632–1691 *m.* Susannah
   9. ROBERT FIELD (1605–1673) *m.* 1630 ( ) Elizabeth Taylor
   Service: First reported at Newport and Portsmouth in 1638 with Roger Williams.
   Reference: History of Westchester County, N. J. Family Bibles.

5978 CRAGG, Mrs. Richard P.   Recorded 1931
            4341 Paul Street, Frankford, Philadelphia, Pennsylvania
   1. Florence Eva Woodington (1882   ) *m.* 1912 Richard P. Cragg
   2. Fred Woodington (1856–1916) *m.* 1879 Elizabeth Evans Miller (1859–1928)
   3. James Woodington (–1915) *m.* 1853 Julia Gardner (1834–1909))
   4. William Woodington (1809–1877) *m.* 1827 Rebecca Dyer (1812–1880)
   5. Samuel Dyer (1783–1855) *m.* 1808 Elizabeth Keen (1790–1832)
   6. Joseph Dyer (1754–1815) *m.* Mary Ann ———
   7. James Dyer (1727–1803) *m.* 1751 Elizabeth ———
   8. Charles Dyer (1697–) *m.* 1716 Elizabeth Shrief (1698–1778)
   9. James Dyer (1669–) *m.* 1696 ———
   10. Charles Dyer (1650–1709) *m.* Mary ———
   11. WILLIAM DYER (1677–) *m.* Mary ——— (–1660)
   Services: Sec. Portsmouth and Newport, R. I., 1640–1647; 1648, Gen Recorder; 1650, Atty. Gen.
   Reference: William Dyer Gen.; Directory of R. I. by Austin.

5880 CRAIG, Mrs. A. J.   Recorded 1929, Illinois
            1003 South Seventh Street, Charleston, Illinois
   1. Lulu Foreman *m.* 1925 A. J. Craig
   2. Isaac P. Foreman (1852–1923) *m.* 1886 Laura O'Hair (1859–)
   3. John Foreman (1823–1900) *m.* 1842 Harriet Richardson (1820–1881)
   4. William H. Richardson (1790–) *m.* 1811 Susanna Bowman
   5. Samuel M. Richardson (1760–1831) *m.* 1782 Catherine B. Hall (1760–1837)
   6. William Richardson (1720–) *m.* 1745 Isabel de la Calmes
   7. Joseph Richardson (1678–1740) *m.* 1705 Sarah Thomas
   8. WILLIAM RICHARDSON (1614–1698) *m.* 1667 Elizabeth Talbot (nee Ewan)
   Service: Member of the House of Burgesses from 1676 to 1683.
   Reference: Cartmell, "Shenandoah Valley Pioneers & Descendants," pages 74 to 261.
   Founders of Anna Arundal & Howard Counties, Maryland, page 175.

6615 CRANKSHAW, Mrs. Charles W.   Recorded 1949
            Pleasant Valley Road, South Windsor, Connecticut
   1. Mildred G. Rowley *m.* Dr. Charles W. Crankshaw
   2. Chester J. Rowley (1868–1921) *m.* 1891 Grace W. Hathaway (1873–1946)
   3. Hiram E. Rowley (1837–1911) *m.* 1864 Anna M. Watts (1845–1916)
   4. Roger E. Rowley (1802–1870) *m.* 1828 Hannah S. Osgood (1810–1853)
   5. Roger Rowley *d.* 1841, *m.* 1801 Rebecca Latimer (1782–1828)
   6. Hezekiah Latimer (1761–1841) *m.* 1782 Rebecca Thrall (1766–1852)
   7. Hezekiah Latimer (1736–1818) *m.* 1758 Tryphena Gillet (1746–1791)
   8. Jonah Gillet (1708–1782) *m.* Elizabeth Hoskins, *d.* 1753
   9. Thomas Gillett (1676–) *m.* 1704 Hannah Clarke (1688–1708)
   10. John Clarke (1656–1717) *m.* 1685 Mary Crow
   11. DANIEL CLARKE *d.* 1710, *m.* 1644 Mary Newberry *d.* 1688
   Service: Founder, Magistrate, Captain, Patentee to Royal Charter, 1662.
   Reference: Stiles' Windsor, Barbaer Coll., Windsor; Vital records, Brockton, Mass., Rochester, Mass., Raynham Center, Mass., Pawtucket, R. I.

6442 CRAWFORD, Mrs. William Milton   Recorded 1944, Georgia
      Route 4, Box 285, Atlanta, Georgia
   1. Emily Page Drake *m.* Wm. Milton Crawford
   2. Benjamin M. Drake (1868-   ) *m.* 1895 Mary I. Hunnicutt (1874-   )
   3. James B. Hunnicutt (1836-1904) *m.* 1862 Emily Jane Page (1843-1886)
   4. Dr. James E. P. Hunnicutt (1805-1884) *m.* 1830 Martha Lundie Atkinson
      1809-1851
   5. John Pepper Atkinson (1768-1840) *m.* 1801 Eliz. Bland Lundie (1782-1854)
   6. Rev. Thomas Lundie (1740-1798) *m.* 1770 Lucy Yates (1750-1823)
   7. Rev. William Yates (1720-1764) *m.* 1740-45 Elizabeth Randolph (1720-1784)
   8. Edward Randolph (1690-1756) *m.* 1720 bef. Miss Grosvenor (-1720-25)
   9. COL. WILLIAM RANDOLPH (1651-1711) *m.* 1680 abt. Mary Isham
   Service: Member House of Burgesses 1685-1710); Speaker House of Burgesses 1698;
      Clerk House of Burgesses 1702; Atty. General. 1696; Clerk of Henrico Co.,
      Va., 1673-1680; Col. commanding Militia Forces of Henrico Co., Va., etc.
   Reference: Coweta County Chronicles; Jones & Reynolds; Haydens' Va. Genealogies;
      Virg. Mag. of H&B, Vol. 7; William & Mary Quart., Vol. 7.

6027 CROOK, Mrs. John Anthony   Recorded 1932, Colorado
      70 South Birch Street, Denver 7, Colorado
   1. Minnie C. Dalbey *m.* 1899 John Anthony Crook
   2. George W. Dalbey (1857-1930) *m.* 1878 Samantha L. Jones (1857-1940)
   3. Fletcher Jones (1827-1918) *m.* 1852 Mary Ann Ring (1830-1900)
   4. Ira Ring (178?-1869) *m.* 1816 Sarah Moore (1794-1862)
   5. Joseph Ring (1751-1806) *m.* 1780 Penelopy Patch (1754-1837)
   6. Jonathan Ring (1702-1767) *m.* 1747 Sarah Mitchell (1719-1777)
   7. Eleazer Ring (1654-1749) *m.* 1687 Mary Shaw (1665-1730)
   8. ANDREW RING (1617-1692) *m.* 1646 Deborah Hopkins (1625-1666)
   Service: Born in Scotland, died in Massachusetts where he served in King Phillip's
      War.
   Reference: Pioneers of Mass., 2, p. 386; New England Historical & Genegoloical
      Register, Vol. IV, p. 34; Ancient Land Mark of Plymouth, Mass., 2,
      pp. 216-17, No. 3, pp. 234-36, 239; Mass. Soldiers & Sailors, Vol. XIII,
      p. 341.

5955 CUMMINGS, Mrs. Peter S.   Recorded 1930, Georgia
      Brinson, Georgia
   1. Lela Youmans *m.* Peter Sidney Cummings
   2. Augustus M. Youmans (1846-1894) *m.* 1867 Margaret Johnston (1848-1874)
   3. William C. Johnston (1823-1894) *m.* 1840 Rebecca Hamilton (1826-1882)
   4. Thomas Hamilton (1787-1844) *m.* Cherry Anderson (1803-1883)
   5. Thomas Hamilton (1744-1791) *m.* 1770 Rebecca Dixon (1752-1795)
   6. Thomas Dixon (1720-1769) *m.* 1755 Elizabeth H. Smith (1722-1756)
   7. Thomas Smith II (1669-1738) *m.* Mary Hyrne (1677-1777)
   8. THOMAS SMITH I (1648-1694) *m.* 1668 Barbara Atkins
   Service: Colonial Governor of North and South Carolina, 1690.
   Reference: National No. 5934.

6240 CURRIN, Mrs. J. B.   Recorded 1939, Texas
      2727 N. Washington, Dallas, Texas
   1. Elizabeth Heafer (1904-   ) *m.* 1924 Joe Bailey Currin
   2. Henry Wallace Heafer (1876-   ) *m.* 1899 Mittie Purl (1876-   )
   3. James Henry Heafer (1848-1931) *m.* 1870 Nancy Maria Waring (1853-1925)
   4. Frances Waring (1826-1908) *m.* 1851 Harriet Ward Williams (1827-1866)
   5. Wm. Williams (1787-1875) *m.* 1826 Maria Denny (1797-1883)
   6. Isaac Denny (1765-1813) *m.* 1793 Grace Tibb (-1859)
   7. Samuel Denny (1731-1817) *m.* 1757 Elizabeth Henshaw (1737-1787)
   8. Daniel Henshaw (1701-1781) *m.* 1724 Elizabeth Bass (1703-1774)
   9. Joseph Bass *m.* Mary Belcher
  10. John Bass (-1716) *m.* 1657 Ruth Alden
  11. JOHN ALDEN (-1687) *m.* Priscilla Mullins
   Service: Signer of Mayflower Compact.
   Reference: Denny Gen. in Eng. and Am., by C. C. Denny; Garr. Gen.; Bowie Book
      page 471; N. Eng. & His. & Gen. Reg.

6451   CURRIN, Nancy Eleanor (Miss)   Recorded 1944, Texas
           5404 Miller Avenue, Dallas 6, Texas
                        JUNIOR MEMBERSHIP
   1. Nancy Eleanora Currin
   2. Joseph Bailey Currin (1904–) *m.* 1924 Eleanora Eliz. Heafer (1904–)
   3. Henry Wallace Heafer (1875–) *m.* 1899 Mittie Belle Purl (1876–)
   4. James Henry Heafer (1848–1931) *m.* 1870 Nancy Marie Waring (1853–1925)
   5. Francis Waring (1826–1908) *m.* 1851 Harriet Ward Williams (1827–1866)
   6. William Williams (1787–1875) *m.* 1826 Maria Denny (1797–1883)
   7. Isaac Denny (1765–1813) *m.* 1793 Grace Tibb (–1859)
   8. Samuel Denny (1731–1817) *m.* 1757 Elizabeth Henshaw (1737–1787)
   9. Daniel Henshaw (1701–1781) *m.* 1724 Elizabeth Bass (1703–1774)
  10. Joseph Bass *m.* Mary Belcher
  11. John Bass (–1716) *m.* 1657 Ruth Alden
  12. JOHN ALDEN (–1687) *m.* Priscilla Mullins
  Service: Signer Mayflower Compact.
  Reference: No. 5464 S. & D. P ; N. E. H. & G. Rec.; Rec. Mason County, Ky.; Bowie
           Book, 471–476.

6452   CURRIN, Jo Anna Belle   Recorded 1944, Texas
           5404 Miller Avenue, Dallas 6, Texas
   1. Jo Anna Belle Currin
   2. Joseph Bailey Currin (1904–) *m.* 1924 Eleanor Eliz. Heafer (1904–)
   3. Henry Wallace Heafer (1875–) *m.* 1899 Mittie Belle Purl (1876–)
   4. James Henry Heafer (1848–1931) *m.* 1870 Nancy Marie Waring (1853–1925)
   5. Francis Waring (1826–1908) *m.* 1851 Harriet Ward Williams (1827–1866)
   6. William Williams (1787–1875) *m.* 1826 Maria Denny (1797–1883)
   7. Isaac Denny (1765–1813) *m.* 1793 Grace Tibb (–1859)
   8. Samuel Denny (1731–1817) *m.* 1757 Elizabeth Henshaw (1737–1787)
   9. Daniel Henshaw (1701–1781) *m.* 1724 Elizabeth Bass (1703–1774)
  10. Joseph Bass *m.* Mary Belcher
  11. John Bass (–1716) *m.* 1657 Ruth Alden
  12. JOHN ALDEN (–1687) *m.* Priscilla Mullins
  Service: Signer Mayflower Compact.
  Reference: No. 5464 S. & D. of P.; N. E. H. & G. Reg.; Mason County, Ky., Rec.;
           Bowie Book, 471–476.

6052   CUSHMAN, Miss Frances   Recorded 1933, Texas
           3411 Swiss Avenue, Dallas, Texas
   1. Frances Cushman
   2. Alonzo R. Cushman (1851–1904) *m.* 1879 Nancy Spain (1858–1885)
   3. Horatio B. Cushman (1822–1904) *m.* 1843 Elizabeth Edwards (1829–1876)
   4. Calvin Cushman (1784–1841) *m.* 1809 Laura Bardwell (1782–1862)
   5. Caleb Cushman (1749–1809) *m.* 1774 Bathsheba Spaulding (1756–1805)
   6. Allerton Cushman (1712–) *m.* 1748 Deborah Cushman (2) (–1751)
   7. Elkanah Cushman (1678–1714) *m.* 1702 Hester Barnes
   8. Thomas Cushman (1608–1691) *m.* 1635 Mary Allerton (1609–1699)
   9. ROBERT CUSHMAN (1580–1625)
  Reference: Cushman Genealogy, by Henry W. Cushman, Pub. 1855.

6288   CULLER, Mrs. John M.   Recorded 1940, Maryland
           12 West Third Street, Frederick, Maryland
   1. Mary Ada Biggs *m.* 1909 John M. Culler
   2. Milton E. Biggs (1835–1901) *m.* 1871 Fannie E. Copeland (1850–1912)
   3. William Biggs (1796–1876) *m.* 2nd 1835 Elizabeth Chaney (1812–1849)
   4. Frederick Biggs (1766–1840) *m.* 1795 Mary Wilson (1776–1842)
   5. Joseph Wilson *c.* 1754– *d. aft.* 1799 *m.* Catherine Miller
   6. Thomas Wilson (1720–*aft.* 1764) *m.* Mary
   7. Capt. Thomas Wilson *d.* 1744, *m.* Priscilla Kent
   8. Absalom Kent *d.* 1718, *m.* Mary Wadsworth
   9. William Wadsworth *d.* 1711, *m.* Elizabeth Clagett *d. aft.* 1734
  10. CAPT. THOMAS CLAGETT, Gent. (1644–1703) *m.* Mary Hooper
  Service: Captain.
  Reference: Scharp Hist. W. Maryland, vol. I; Maryland History Queen Ann; "Bowie
           Kindred."

6712 D'AGOSTIN, MRS. HENRY   Recorded 1951 (New Jersey (Md.))
            243 Fulton Terrace, Cliffside Park, New Jersey
    1. Alice Muriel Lemart *m*. 1926 Dr. Henry D'Agostin
    2. Nicholas D LaHert (1862–1915) *m*. 1887 Mary Mattoon (1867–Living)
    3. Randsom Dayton Mattoon (1839–1922) *m*. 1864 Harriet E. Carlin (1842–1910)
    4. William Curtis Mattoon (1815–1897) *m*. 1836 Harriet Vanderhoof (1814–1884)
    5. Bethel Mattoon (1784–1862) *m*. 1809 Hannah Williams (–1873)
    6. Amasa Mattoon (1758–1829) *m*. 1780 Elizabeth Dayton (1759–   )
    7. David Mattoon (1715–1775) *m*. 1742 Phebe Curtis (1719–1776)
    8. John Mattoon (1682–1754) *m*. 1706 Jerusha Hall (1687–1760)
    9. Philip Mattoon (–1696) *m*. 1677 Sarah Hawkes (1657–1751)
    Service: Soldier in King Phillip's Wars.
    Reference: Connecticut Men of the Revolution, pg. 500; History of Deerfield, Vol. I,
            pg. 300; Sheldon's History of Deerfield, Vol. I, pg. 180.

6341 DALE, HON. TIMOTHY CHRISTOPHER   Recorded 1941
            Elm Street, Island Pond, Vermont
    1. Timothy Christopher Dale *m*. 1920 Emma Everheart Hemmig
    2. Porter Hinman Dale (1867–1933) *m*. 1891 Amy Katherine Bartlett, *d*. 1910
    3. George Needham Dale (1834–1903) *m*. 1863 Helen Maria Hinman (1842–1917)
    4. Porter Hinman (1812–1880) *m*. 1836 Mary Porter Wilder
    5. Timothy Hinman (1762–1850) *m*. 1786 Phoebe Stoddard (1769–1858)
    6. Lt. Adam Hinman (1718–1796) *m*. 1754 Sarah Porter
    7. Judge Noah Hinman (1689–1766) *m*. 1711 Anna Knowles, *b*. 1689
    8. Benjamin Hinman (1662–1727) *m*. 1684 Elizabeth Lamb
    9. Sergt. Edward Hinman *d*. 1681, *m*. Hannah Stiles
    Service: With Capt. John Underhill, under Stuyvesant, fought against the Indians.
    Reference: Congressional Directory; "Vermont, the Green Mountain State,"
            Crockett; Legislative Directories of Vermont; "Hon. Timothy Hinman,"
            Brigham; "Hist. of Ancient Woodbury."

5931 DANIEL, Mrs. Erdis Gray   Recorded 1930 (Georgia)
            Graysville, Georgia
    1. Erdis Gray *m*. ——— Daniels
    2. Charles A. Gray (1860–   ) *m*. 1890 Cora Linthicum (1864–   )
    3. George W. Linthicum (1837–1912) *m*. 1860 Catherine Linthicum (–1911)
    4. Philip Linthicum (1805–   ) *m*. Eleanor McElfresh (1805–   )
    5. Frederick Linthicum (1774–   )
    6. Zacharia Linthicum (1735–   ) *m*. Sarah Prather
    7. John Linthicum (1700–   )
    8. Thomas Linthicum, Jr. (1660–   ) *m*. 1698 Jane
    9. Thomas Linthicum, Sr. (1630–1701) *m*. Deborah Wayman
    Reference: All Hallows, Records, Md.

6206 DANIEL, Mrs. Will H.   Recorded 1938
            Huntington, West Virginia
    1. Miss Iven Smith (1888–   ) *m*. 1913 Will Horton Daniel
    2. Hugh Cox Smith (1854–   ) *m*. 1882 Virginia Henry Ivey (1860–   )
    3. John Cato Ivey (1830–1862) *m*. 1859 Delia Maria Beekman (1836–1906)
    4. Dr. Peter Quick Beekman (1812–1852) *m*. 1835 Virginia Everett (1815–1840)
    5. George Beekman (1768–1840) *m*. 1794 Margaret Quick (1776–1816)
    6. Christopher Beekman (1730–1829) *m*. 1765 Martha Veght (1741–1817)
    7. Gerardus Christopher (1707–1778) *m*. Catherine Van Dyke (1708–   )
    8. Christopher Beekman (1681–1724) *m*. 1704 Maria Delancy
    9. Abraham De Lancy (1642–1702) *m*. Juliana Cornelia Jacobsa
    10. Abraham De Lancy (1620–   ) *m*. Marie Lubberts
    11. Henry Martin DeLancy *m*. Agnes Batteel
    Service:
    Reference: First Families in America, Delanc.; F. D. Roosevelt's Colonial Anc., by
            Alvin Page Johnson; Dist. Fam. in America Descended from Wil. and Jan.
            Thomas Van Dyke, by Aitken.

6602 DANIELS, Mrs. Fay L.   Recorded 1948
          4930 N. Talman Avenue, Chicago 25, Illinois
      1. Fay Lowenthal *m.* —— Daniels
      2. Julius L. Lowenthal (1878–1947) *m.* 1904 Emma J. Cross (1884–)
      3. Eugene C. Cross (1863–) *m.* 1883 Alvina D. Green (1865–1943)
      4. William A Cross (1831–1908) *m.* 1858 Jane E. Elliott (1841–1907)
      5. Charles E. Elliott (1813–1892) *m.* 1837 Lucy M. Barber (1818–1891)
      6. Asa Elliott (1785–1852) *m.* 1807 Betsy Williams (1788–1855)
      7. Laban Elliott (1757–1830) *m.* Mehitable Harrington
      8. David Elliott (1716–1798) *m.* 1739 Mehetabel Aldrich (1716–1794)
      9. Peter Aldrich (1686–1748) *m.* Hannah Hayward (1680–1746)
      10. Jacob Aldrich (1652–1695) *m.* 1674/5 Huldah Thayer (1657–)
      11. FERDINANDO THAYER (*bap.* 1625–1713) *m.* 1652 Huldah Hayward, *d.* 1690
      Service: In Mendon, Mass., before King Phillip's War.
      Reference: Gen. Dict. of New England, New England Families, First Families of
          America.

6741 DANIEL, Mrs. Horace Milton   Recorded 1952 (Georgia)
          2424 Collier Road, N. W., Atlanta, Georgia
      1. Lucy King *m.* 1928 Horace Milton Daniel
      2. John Henry King (1853–1935) *m.* 1872 Hannah Jane Dickson (1855–1942)
      3. Willis Dickson (1823–1874) *m.* 1851 Nancy Cleveland (1833–1909)
      4. Jeremiah Cleveland (1809–1892) *m.* 1832 Clara Isbell (1810–1892)
      5. Benjamin Cleveland (1778–1830) *m.* 1808 Peggy (Margaret) Holland (1784–1857)
      6. Rev. John Cleveland (1730–1821) *m.* 1760 Molly (Mary) McCann (1740–1809)
      7. John Cleveland (1695–1765) *m.* 1728 Martha Coffee (1710–1805)
      8. Alexander Cleveland (1659–1707) *m.* 1694 Milly Presley (1667–1707)
      9. ALEXANDER CLEVELAND, SR., (1617–) *m.* 1650 Margaret
      Service: Landed proprietor of Virginia.
      Reference: Cleveland Genealogy, Vol. 3, pp. 2105–2158, 207 Court House; Carnesville,
          Franklin Co., Ga., will Bk. Court House, S. C. Roll. 274; Deed C. 476,
          Cleveland, vol. 3, 2056, 2058, –070; Compendium of American
          Genealogy, Vol. I, pg. 972, Vol. 7, page 554.

6506 DARBY, Mrs. Van Buren, Jr.   Recorded 1945
          Charleston, West Virginia
      1. Beulah Wagner *m.* Van Buren Darby, Jr.
      2. Charles Newman Wagner (1870–1942) *m.* 1891 Lillie Leota Wolfe (1868–)
      3. Alfred Wagner (1826–1903) *m.* 1853 Regenia Sayre (1834–1897)
      4. Daniel Sayre (1789–1836) *m.* 1807 Sinah Hayman (1789–1847)
      5. Daniel Sayre (1760–1824) *m.* 1785 Sarah Hall (1762–)
      6. David Sayre (1736–1826) *m.* 1758 Hannah Frazier (1741–1826)
      7. Daniel Sayre (–1760) *m.* Rebecca Bond
      8. Samuel Sayre (–1707) bef. *m.* —— Lyons
      9. Daniel Sayre (–1708) *m.* 1659 Hannah Foster
      10. THOMAS SAYRE (1597–1670) *m.* ——
      Service: Settled in Lynn, Mass., 1638 and was given 60 acres of land; Founder of
          Southampton, N. Y.; 1651 chosen one of the Governors of Southampton;
          Served in French and Colonial Wars.

6364 DARLING, Hon. Charles Hial, LL.D.   Recorded 1942
          447 Main St., Burlington, Vermont
      1. Charles Hial Darling *m.* 1889 Agnes Chritmas Norton
      2. Jason Darling (1829–1897) *m.* 1854 Ellen Paul (1835–1888)
      3. Jason Darling (1796–1864) *m.* 1813 Nancy Marcy
      4. Seth Darling (1764–1825) *m.* 1786 Chloe Marsh (1768–1838)
      5. Thomas Darling, *b.* 1730 *m.* 1749 Rachel White
      6. Benjamin Darling (1687–1772) *m.* 1708 Mehitable White (1689–1760)
      7. DENNIS DARLING (1641–1717) *m.* 1662 Hannah Francis
      Service: He went from Braintree, Mass., to Mandon, Mass., about 1681.
      Reference: Crockett's "Hist. of Vermont;" Reces. of Town of Woodstock; V. R.
          Montpelier, Vt.; Town Records of Mendon, Mass.; V. R. of Braintree,
          Mass.

6332 DARLING, Hon. Henry George   Recorded 1941
East Burke, Lyndonville, Vermont
1. Henry George Darling
2. Lucius Albro Darling (1850–1937) *m.* 1892 Margaret McDonald (1873–)
3. Henry George Darling (1816–1902) *m.* 1845 Mehitabel Whitcomb
4. Major Ebenezer Darling (1787–) *m.* Abigail Fisher
5. Peter Darling, *b.* 1752, *m.* Rebecca Burbank
6. Lt. John Darling, *b.* 1714, *m.* 1739 Hannah Morse
7. Jon Darling, *b.* 1683, *m.* 1708 Mary Page
8. Capt. J. Darling
Service: Came to America after 1640; settled in Kingston, N. H.
Reference: "Gen. & Family History of Vermont," Carleton; Salisbury, Mass., V. R.;
"Old Families of Salisbury & Amesbury," Hoyt.

6023 DARTE, Mrs. George   Recorded 1932
175 W. 76th Street, New York, New York
1. Mary Eggleston Cushman (1876–) *m.* George Dockhart Darte
2. John Thompson Cushman (1853–1880) *m.* 1873 Sallie R. Fourgureau (1857–1918)
3. Robert Smith Cushman (1813–1871) *m.* 1848 Mary Jane Thompson (1822–1860)
4. Paul Cushman (1767–1833) *m.* 1802 Marg. McDonald (1779–1868)
5. Seth Cushman
6. James Cushman
7. Eleazar Cushman (1656–) *m.* 1687 Eliz. Combes (1609–1722)
8. Elder Thomas Cushman (1608–) *m.* 1635 Mary Allerton
9. Robert Cushman (1589–1625) *m.* Marg. Clunzelton
Service: Preached first sermon in New England; Elder.
Reference: Cushman Gen., by Henry Wyles Cushman.

5981 DAVIDSON, Mrs. Charles E.   Recorded 1931
405 W. Washington Street, Greenville, Illinois
1. Martha S. C. McNeil (1872–) *m.* 1896 Charles E. Davidson
2. Abraham McNeil (1832–1909) *m.* 1853 Elizabeth Etzler (1831–1905)
3. Neilly McNeill (1800–1883) *m.* 1829 Minerva Mills (1810–1884)
4. Andrew G. Mills (1773–1858) *m.* 1797 Mary Trotter (1780–1848)
5. Benjamin Mills (1750–1822) *m.* 1770 Elizabeth Collier (1751–1822)
6. Doughty Collier (–1755) *m.* 1737 Priscilla Nicholson (1716–1775)
7. Robert Collier (1681–1757) *m.* 1703 Ann Cannon (1677–1762)
Service:
Reference: Bond Co., Illinois, Records; Dashiell Family Records, Vol. I, pgs. 34–35.

6737 DAVIS, Mrs. Robert W.   Recorded 1952 (Louisiana)
609 North Vienna Street, Ruston, Louisiana
1. Charlotte Long *m.* 1908 Robert W. Davis
2. Hugh Pierce Long (1852–1937) *m.* 1875 Caledonia Tison (1860–1913)
3. John Murphy Long (1825–1901) *m.* 1845 Mary Elizabeth Wingate (1829–1901)
4. James Long (1790–1850) *m.* 1823 Mary Kirtman (1793–1850)
5. Hugh Long (1770–1800) *m.* 1789 Margaret ———— (–1794)
6. James Long (1750–1806) *m.* 1767–9 Catherine, *before* 1790
7. John Long (*abt.* 1692–1759) *m.* 1735 Ellenir Owens (1706–)
8. Capt. Richard Owens *m.* 1698 Rachael Beall (1678–)
9. Col. Ninian Beall (1625–1717) *m.* 1668 Ruth Moore (–1704)
Service: Burgess and High Sherriff of Calvert Co., Md.
Reference: Md. Archives, B. 8 F, 170; Bk. 3, F 170, Maltimore wills; Beall Genealogy
by F. F. M. Beall, p. 40.

5908   DEAN, Agnes Louise   Recorded 1930 (Minnesota)
              106 E. Twenty-fourth Street, Minneapolis, Minnesota
       1. Alfred J. Dean (1853–) *m.* 1880 Carrie Louise Chamberlain (1858–)
       2. James T. Chamberlain (1827–1861) *m.* 1854 Caroline Eliz. Emery (1831–1919)
       3. Jonathan Emery (1786–1863) *m.* 1810 Hannah Chaney (1786–1848)
       4. David Emery (1754–1838) *m.* 1782 Abigail Goodwin (1763–1830)
       5. Jonathan Emery (1722–1807) *m.* 1753 Jerusha Barron (1735–1781)
       6. James Emery (1698–1762) *m.* 1719 Ruth Watson
       7. Jonathan Emery (1651–1723) *m.* 1676 Mary Woodman
       8. John Emery (1598–1683) *m.* 1650 Mary Webster (–1694)
       9. JOHN EMERY (1578–) *m.* Agnes
       Service: Landed in Boston, 1635.
       Reference: Descendants of John and Anthony Emery, pub. Salem, 1890.

5909   DEAN, Carolyn Elizabeth   Recorded 1930 (Minnesota)
              106 E. Twenty-fourth Street, Minneapolis, Minnesota
       1. Alfred Joseph Dean (1853–) *m.* 1880 Carrie Louise Chamberlain (1858–)
       2. James Thwing Chamberlain (1827–1861) *m.* 1854 Caroline Eliz. Emery (1831–1919)
       3. Jonathan Emery (1786–1863) *m.* 1810 Hannah Cheney (1786–1848)
       4. David Emery (1754–1838) *m.* 1782 Abigail Goodwin (1763–1830)
       5. Jonathan Emery (1722–1807) *m.* 1753 Jerusha Barron (1735–1781)
       6. James Emery (1698–1762) *m.* 1719 Ruth Watson
       7. Jonathan Emery (1651–1723) *m.* 1676 Mary Woodman
       8. John Emery (1598–1683) *m.* 1650 Mary Webster (–1694)
       9. JOHN EMERY (1578–) *m.* Agnes
       Service: Landed in Boston 1635.
       Reference: Descendants of John and Anthony Emery, published Salem, 1890.

6039   DEER, Mrs. Rufus L.   Recorded 1933
              Oreland, Pennsylvania
       1. Carrie E. Reid (1868–) *m.* 1890 Rufus L. Deer
       2. Lawson P. Reid (1832–1908) *m.* 1866 Susan C. Wherritt Tishwick (1835–1908)
       3. George Wherritt (1808–1895) *m.* 1829 Marg. Fisher (1806–1880)
       4. John Fisher (1776–1820) *m.* 1810 Ann Eliz. Judd (–1823)
       5. Peter Fisher (1745–1782) *m.* 1767 Eliz. Heylmun
       6. Thomas Fisher (1717–1767) *m.* 1743 Abigail Cooper
       7. William Fisher (1696–1739) *m.* Tabitha
       8. John Fisher (1671–) *m.* Elizabeth Light
       9. JOHN FISHER *m.* Margaret Hindle
       Service:
       Reference: Gen. of the Fisher Fam.

6652   DEJONG, Mrs. John A.   Recorded 1949
              Route 1, Box 100-A, Baker, Louisiana
       1. Louka Adele Garrett *m.* (2) John A. DeJong 1929
       2. John W. Garrett, M.D., (1851–1895) *m.* 1878 Mattie B. Gaines (1862–1883)
       3. James R. Gaines (1828–1896) *m.* 1861 Sarah E. B. Jackson (1835–1903)
       4. James H. Gaines (1796–1848) *m.* 1822 Anne B. Henderson (*ca.* 1805–1851)
       5. Heirome Gaines, Jr., (*ca.* 1758–1815) *m.* 1792 Ann T. Adams (1776–1815)
       6. Heirome Gaines, *d. ca.* 1786, *m. ca.* 1748 Margaret Taliaferro, *d. bef.* 1784
       7. Col. John Taliaferro (1687–1744) *m.* 1708 Mary Catlett
       8. Col. John Catlett, Jr., (1658–1724) *m.* Elizabeth Gaines
       9. COL. JOHN CATLETT, *d.* 1670, *m.* 1657 Elizabeth (Underwood) Slaughter.
       Service: Came to Rappahannock Co., Va., 1650; Member of Colonial Militia.
       Reference: Gen. of Lewis Family, History of two Virginia Families, by Stubbs.

6187   DEMPSEY, Georgia Page Hunnicutt   Recorded 1938
              218 Pond Street, Toccoa, Georgia
       1. Georgia Page Hunnicutt Dempsey (1883–) *m.* 1906 Rev. Elam Franklin Dempsey
       2. James Benjamin Hunnicutt (1836–1904) *m.* 1852 Emily Jane Page (1843–1856)

3. Dr. James Edward P. Hunnicutt (1805–1884) *m.* 1830 Martha Lundie Atkinson 1809–1862) *ca.*
4. John Pepper Atkinson, Sr., (1768–1840) *m.* 1801 Elizabeth Bland Lundie (1782–1854)
5. Rev. Thomas Lundie, Scotland (*ca.* (1740–1798) *m. ca.* 1770 Lucy Yates *ca.* (1750–1823)
6. Rev. William Yates (1720–1764) *m. ca.* 1740/1745 Elizabeth Randolph (–1784)
7. Edward Randolph *ca.* (1695/1700–died in Eng. aft. 1756) *m.* in Eng. *ca.* 1720/5 Miss Grosvenar, of Bristol, England.
8. Col. WILLIAM RANDOLPH, Eng. (1651–1711) *m.* 1680 Mary Isham

Service: Clerk of Henrico, 1673–1683; Justice, Henrico, 1683–1711; Member of House of Burgesses, 1685–1699, 1703–04–05–1710; Att. Gen., 1696; Speaker of H. of B., 1698; Clerk of H. B., 1702.
Reference: Recs. Fulton and Coweta Cos., Ga.; Brunswick Co., Va.; Will bk. No. 6, pa. 133, No. 9, pg. 290; Va. Mag. H. & B., 7, pgs. 91–436 et al.; Hayden's Gen., pgs. 121–122; Wm. & Mary Quart., 24, pgs. 206–209; Ibid., I, pgs. 158–9; Ibid., 7, pgs. 122–124; Meade's "Old Churches," Vol. I, pgs. 138–139, 333; Va. Mag. H. & B. XV, pgs. 437–442; Tyler's Cyclo. Va. Biog. 4, pg. 517, I, pg. 311.

6583 DENEEN, Florence   Recorded 1948
500 Englewood Ave., Chicago 21, Illinois
1. Florence Deneen
2. Samuel H. Deneen (1835–1895) *m.* 1859 Mary F. Ashley (1836–1914)
3. Rev. Wm. L. Deneen (1798–1879) *m.* 1831 Verlinda Moore (1802–1855)
4. Risdon Moore (1760–1828) *m.* 1790 Anna Dent (1767–1845)
5. Col. Wm. Dent (1730–1805) *m. ca.* 1756/8 Verlinda Beall (1736–1815)
6. Peter Dent (1693–1757) *m.* 1729 Mary Brooke (1709–)
7. Maj. Wm. Dent (1652–1704) *m.* 1684 Elizabeth Fowke (1653–)
8. JUDGE THOMAS DENT (1630/1–1676) *m. bef.* 1652 Rebecca Wilkinson

Service: High Sheriff of St. Mary's Co., Md.; delegate for St. Mary's Co., Md., 1669.
Reference: Desc. Shields Moore, Mackenzie–Col. Family.

6095 DENNIS, Mrs. Frank A.   Recorded 1936 (Georgia)
Eatonton, Georgia
1. Katie F. Jordan *m.* 1919 Frank A. Dennis
2. Lee Newman Jordan (1879–) *m.* 1898 Alice F. Oquinn (1880–)
3. Elisha W. Jordan (1815–1881) *m.* 1875 Penelope Ann Watkins (1836–1918)
4. Thomas Jordan (1758–1840) *m.* 1790 Catherine Daniel (1760–1845)
5. Josiah Jordan (1735–1789) *m.* 1755 Elizabeth Newby (1737–1758)
6. Matthias Jordan (1710–1762) *m.* 1730 Miriam Copeland (1712–1789)
7. Matthew Jordan (1676–1747) *m.* 1702 Susanna (Jones) Bressey (1675–1710)
8. Thomas Jordan, J. (1634–1699) *m.* 1658 Margaret Brashieur (1642–1708)
9. Thomas Jordan, Sr., (1600–1685) *m.* 1630 Lucy Corker (1610–1688)
10. SAMUEL JORDAN (1570–1624) *m.* Cecilly (–1626)

Service: Member of the House of Burgesses, Virginia, 1619.
Reference: Records of Charles City, Va.; Stanard's Colonial Virginia Register.

6209 DENISON, Miss Evelyn Mattocks   Recorded 1938
Yonkers, New York
1. Adelbort S. Dennison (1846–1932) *m.* 1869 Estelle Mattocks (1851–1935)
2. Oscar Alanson Dennison (1817–1901) *m.* 1844 Adaline Stoddard (–1850)
3. Isaac Dennison (1778–1867) *m.* 1798 Electa Newall (1780–)
4. Elisha Dennison (1734–1809) *m.* 1758 Keturah Minor (–1813)
5. °Avery Dennison (1712–1775) *m.* 1734 Thankful Williams (–1767)
6. Williams Dennison (1677–1730) *m.* 1698 Mary Avery (1680–1762)
7. Capt. John Dennison (1646–1698) *m.* 1667 Phebe Lay (–1699)
8. Capt. Geo. Dennison (1618–1694) *m.* 1645 Ann Borodell (1615–1712)
9. WILLIAM DENNISON (1586–1653) *m.* Margaret

Service:
Reference: Desc. of Capt. Geo. Dennison.

5994   DICK, Mrs. Frank M.   Recorded 1931
          Glenburn Avenue, Cambridge, Maryland
       1. Minette G. Mills *m.* Frank M. Dick
       2. Stephen Dow Mills (1828–1885) *m.* 1855 Angelina Barkley White (1826–1890)
       3. Stephen Mills (1786–1840) *m.* Lavina Morris (1783–1842)
       4. William Mills (1743–1823) *m.* Elizabeth Cottingham (1768–)
       5. David Cottingham (1743–1785) *m.* 1767 Mary Gunby (1753–1803)
       6. Thomas Cottingham (1718–1791) *m.* 1741 Mary Long
       7. John Cottingham (1678–1723) *m.* 1703 Mary Conner
       8. THOMAS COTTINGHAM (–1688) *m.* 1666 Mary Dixon
       Service: Indian Fighter in expedition against the Nanticoke Indians.
       Reference: Maryland Archives for Col. Service; Col. Wars of Mass.

5995   DICK, Miss Minnie F.   Recorded 1931
          Glenburn Avenue, Cambridge, Massachusetts
       1. Stephen Morris Mills (1853–1894) *m.* 1877 Alexine Anne Bradley (1851–1929)
       2. Lemuel Morris Mills (1811–1870) *m.* 1844 Mary M. Bradley (1819–1875)
       3. Stephen Mills (1786–1840) *m.* Lavina Morris (1783–1842)
       4. William Mills (1743–1823) *m.* Elizabeth Cottingham (1768–)
       5. David Cottingham (1743–1785) *m.* 1767 Mary Gunby (1753–1803)
       6. Thomas Cottingham (1718–1791) *m.* 1741 Mary Long
       7. John Cottingham (1678–1723) *m.* 1702 Mary Conner
       8. THOMAS COTTINGHAM (–1688) *m.* 1666 Maxy Dixon
       Service: Indian Fighter, expedition against Nanticoke Indians.
       Reference: Daughters of Founders and Patriots of America, Nat. 2841.

6315   DIECKMANN, Mrs. Christian W.   Recorded 1941
          135 Erie Avenue, Decatur, Georgia
       1. Emma Pope Moss *m.* 1915 Dr. Christian W. Dieckmann
       2. H. B. Moss (1860–1939) *m.* 1892 Adelle Pope (1868–1934)
       3. John Pope (1826–1890) *m.* 1844 Martha Allen (1826–1895)
       4. David Pope (1807–) *m.* ———— Bruce
       5. John Pope (1778–1849) *m.* Susannah ———— (1780–1844)
       6. Henry Pope *b.* 1748, *m.* Charity *b.* 1747
       7. William Pope, *b. c* (1725–) *m.* Mary ————, *b. ca* 1727
       8. John Pope, *c* (1697–1735) *m.* 1723 Elizabeth Pope *b. ca.* 1699
       9. Nathaniel Pope, *d.* 1719, *m.* Jane Brown, *d.* 1752
      10. NATHANIEL POPE, *c.* (1610–1660) *m.* Lucy ————
       Service: Lt. Col. of Westmoreland Co., Va. Militia, 1655.
       Reference: "Nathaniel Pope and His Descendants," Beale; "Georgia Descendants of
             Nathaniel Pope of Virginia," Humphries.

6475   DIEFENBACH, Mrs. Howard B.   Recorded 1945
          Akron, Ohio
       1. Josephine Conrad Zartman *m.* Howard B. Diefenbach, D.D.
       2. Allan King Zartman (1849–1937) *m.* 1877 Elizabeth Ann Conrad (1855–1929)
       3. Benjamin Conrad (1823–1910) *m.* 1852 Mary Ann Heldenbrand (1825–1897)
       4. Adam Heldenbrand (1798–1882) *m.* 1818 Ann King (1800–1881)
       5. Michael Heldenbrand (1766–1850) *m.* 1791 Elizabeth Schlenger (1774–1846)
       6. Jn. Geo. Nicholas Heldenbrand (1733–1804) *m.* 1757 Anna Maria Hill
       7. Jacob Hill (–1775) *m.* 1739 Maria Appolonia Merkle (–1776 aft.)
       8. JOHN CHRISTIAN MERKLE (1678–1766) *m.* 1698 Jemima Weurta (–bef. 1766)
       Service: Settled in Bucks Co., Pa., 1703; purchased 1500 acres of land from the
             Penns; was a coach maker, operated a wagon shop, smith and grist-mill and
             owned Moselem mines. The well-known "Crystal Cave" is on his land.

6275   DIMON, Mrs. Raymond C.   Recorded 1939
          129 Elizabeth Street, Hartford, Connecticut
       1. Eleather Mowry *m.* 1920 Raymond Clark Dimon
       2. David Lyman Mowry, *b.* 1873, *m.* 1892 Stella Harris, *b.* 1872

3. William Windsor Mowry (1842–1911) *m.* 1865 Hannah Swan (1841–1935)
4. David Ballou Mowry (1818–1891) *m.* 1841 Elizabeth (1824–1888)
5. Welcome Mowry (1786–1862) *m.* 1810 Joanna Ballou (1790–1846)
6. Richard Mowry (1749–1825) *m.* Hannah (Eddy) Arnold (1755–1790)
7. Ananias Mowry (1705–1789) *m.* 1745 Zerniah Angell (1718–1806)
8. John Mowry II *m.* 1701 Marjory Whipple
9. John Mowry, *c.* (1645–1690) *m.* Mary (?), *d.* 1690
10. ROGER MOWRY, *d.* 1666, *m.* Mary Johnson, *d.* 1679

Service: Became a freeman in Boston, 1631. Later with his kinsman, Roger Williams, he became citizen of Plymouth, Salem, and Providence; Commissioned from Providence to Court at Warwick.
Reference: Descendants of John Mowry of Rhode Island, by William A. Mowry; Rhode Island Colonial Records.

5914 DISBROW, William Cooke   Recorded 1930 (New York)
     220 Hyde Park Avenue, Tampa, Florida
     Married Elizabeth Bulger, 1875

1. William Cook Disbrow (1816–1893) *m.* 1848 Margaret Dill (1828–1912)
2. Samuel Warne Disbrow (1778–1783) *m.* 1811 Sarah Cook (1792–1875)
3. Benjamin Disbrow (1754–1794) *m.* 1775 Deborah Robinson (1754–)
4. Griffin Disbrow (1712–1754) *m.* Hannah
5. Benjamin Disbrow (1672–1733) *m.* Mary Griffin (–1737)
6. HENRY DISBROW (–1699) *m.* Margaret

Service: Henry Disbrow was a magistrate, 1673, in New York; erected "Disbrow House," 1677.
Reference: New York Gen. & Biog. Register, Vol. V; Hist. & Gen. Miscellany, Stillwell, Vol. IV.

5922 DISBROW, William Cook   Recorded 1930 (New York)
     Tampa, Florida

1. William Cook Disbrow IV
2. William Cook Disbrow (1885–) *m.* 1909 Anna Dykstra (1882–)
3. William Cook Disbrow (1851–) *m.* 1875 Elizabeth Bulger (1856–1919)
4. William Cook Disbrow (1816–1893) *m.* 1848 Margaret Wessels Dill (1828–1912)
5. Samuel Warne Disbrow (1778–1873) *m.* 1811 Sarah Cook (1792–1875)
6. Benjamin Disbrow (1754–1794) *m.* 1775 Deborah Robinson (1754–)
7. Griffin Disbrow (1712–1754) *m.* Hannah
8. Benjamin Disbrow (1672–1733) *m.* Mary Griffin (–1737)
9. Henry Disbrow (–1699) *m.* Margaret

Service: Henry Disbrow, of West Chester, New York; a Magistrate, 1673.
Reference: N. Y. Gen. & Biog. Rec., Vols. 51 and 59; Hist. & Geneal. Miscellany— Stillwell, Vols. 2 and 4.

6281 DOBBS, Mrs. Herbert Clifton   Recorded 1939
     10 Sheridan Drive N. E., Atlanta, Georgia

1. Annie Von Schélé Hahr *m.* 1890 Herbert Clifton Dobbs
2. Franz Joseph Hahr, C.S.A. (1825–1877) *m.* 1859 Alice Mulvinal Hartman (1841–1873)
3. William Murchson Hartman (1813–1853) *m.* 1831 Martha Cade (1810–aft. 1841)
4. James Waddell Cade (*c.* 1770–*c.*) *m.* 1797 Margaret Daniel, *d.* bef. 1864
5. William Cade, *b.* 1735, *m.* Elizabeth Smith, *d. aft.* 1821
6. Stephen Cade, *b.* 1715, *m.* 1734 Mary ———, *d. aft. 1735*
7. Robert Cade, Jr., *c.* 1680, *d.* 1769, *m.* 1713 Susannah Crump (1682–after 1720)
8. Stephen Crump (*c.* 1655–1700) *m.* Susannah ———, *d.* aft. 1727
9. William Crump, *d.* bef. 1680, *m.* Eliza, *d.* 1726.
10. Lt. Thomas Crump, *d.* bef. 1680, *m.* Eliza, *d.* 1726.
11. REV. RICHARD BUCK, *b.* Eng., *d.* 1623, *m.* in Eng.

Service: Came to Virginia, 1610; Minister at Jamestown, 1610–1623; Chaplain of 1st General Assembly in America, 1619.
Reference: "Kinfolks," by Harlee; St. Peter's Parish Reg., New Kent Co., Va.

6676   DODEZ, Edward Cramer   Recorded 1950
         1425 W. Main Street, Fort Wayne, Indiana
1. Edward C. Dodez *m.* 1941 June V. Merriman
2. Dr. Edward Wright Dodez (1875–1939) *m.* 1900 Lilla May
3. Jared Morse Cramer (1834–1917) *m.* 1860 (Cramer 1874 ——) Josephine M. Harlow (1837–1912)
4. Daniel H. Harlow (1800–1877) *m.* 1823 Mercy Austin (1801–1875)
5. Elijah Harlow, Jr. (1768–1833) *m.* 1792 Molly ——
6. Elijah Harlow, Sr. (1743–1778) *m.* 1766 Patience Drew (1746–)
7. Thomas Harlow, Jr. (1712–1753) *m.* 1736 Patience Telson (1718–1753)
8. Thomas Harlow, Sr. (1686–1746) *m.* 1709 Judiah Churchill (1689–1729)
9. Sgt. William Harlow, Jr. (1656–1711) *m.* 1686 Lydia Cushman (1658–1718)
10. LIEUT. WILLIAM HARLOW, SR. (1624–1691) *m.* 1649 Rebecca Bartlett, *d.* 1664
Service: Dept. Gen. Ct. King Philip; built Harlow house, still standing.
Reference:

6490   DONALDSON, Miss Clara Rosella (dec'd)   Recorded 1945
         Greenwich, Ohio
1. Miss Clara Rosella Donaldson
2. John H. Donaldson (1834–1919) *m.* 1860 Lura Permelia Barker (1836–1897)
3. Daniel Gilbert Barker (1803–1887) *m.* 1829 Eliza Baker (1800–1865)
4. Marshall Baker (1774–1848) *m.* 1796 Elizabeth Ward (1778–1849)
5. Sylvanus Ward (1753–1834) *m.* 1775 Hannah Goddard (1753–1812)
6. Robert Goddard (1728–1807) *m.* 1752 Hannah Stone (1726–1757)
7. Edward Goddard (1697–1777) *m.* 1722 Hepzibah Hapgood (1704–1763)
8. Thomas Hapgood (1669–1763) *m.* 1690/3 Judith Barker (1671–1759)
9. John Barker (1646–1718) *m.* 1668 Judith Simonds (1646–17)
10. WILLIAM SIMONDS (1611–1672) *m.* 1644 Judith Phippen Hayward (1619–1689/90)
Service: Early settler of Concord, Mass., and was a landed proprietor of Woburn, Mass., as early as 1645. He held various town offices, and was a man of prominence there. During the Indian Wars his home was barricaded and used as a garrison house.

6478   DORN, Mrs. Charles   Recorded 1945
         London, Ohio
1. Jessie Field *m.* Charles Dorn
2. Dr. Orestes G. Field (1832–1895) *m.* 1868 Josephine (Dille) Latham (1846–1928)
3. Dr. Abel Wakelee Field (1802–1851) *m.* 1826 Zilpha Witter (1802–1894)
4. Francis Field (1757–1812) *m.* 1780 Naomi Wakelee (1756–1812)
5. Nathaniel Field (1727–1803) *m.* 1748 Mary Goodrich
6. Joshua Field (1695–1783) *m.* 1719 Elizabeth Cooley (1696–1781)
7. Sergt. Samuel Field (1651–1697) *m.* 1676 Sarah Gilbert (1655–1712)
8. ZECHARIAL FIELD (1596–1666) *m.* 1641 Mary —— (–1670)
Service: Died 1666, Hatfield, Mass. Colonist, planter, soldier and landed proprietor, Hartford, Conn.

6449   DOUGAN, Mrs. C. Earl   Recorded 1944
         McConnelsville, Ohio
1. Nettie T. Henery *m.* C. Earl Dougan
2. George N. Henery (1857–1893) *m.* 1877 Nettie Tavenner (1856–1896)
3. Joseph J. Henery (1829–1897) *m.* 1852 Lovina Noyes (1835–1901)
4. Josephus Noyes (1812–1890) *m.* 1834 Sybil Blake (1811–1875)
5. Joseph Noyes (1770–1856) *m.* Ann Cherry
6. Col. Peter Noyes (1731–1803) *m.* 1752 Hannah Merrill (1728–1805)
7. Joseph Noyes (1686–1755) *m.* 1711 Jane Dole (1672–)
8. Cutting Noyes (1649–1734) *m.* 1673 Elizabeth Knight
9. NICHOLAS NOYES (1615–1701) *m.* 1640 *ca.* Mary Cutting
Service: Deputy General Court, Boston, from Newbury, Mass., 1660, 1679, 1680–81.
Reference: Noyes Genealogy, Vol. 1.

6533 DOW, Mrs. Ernest F. Recorded 1946
Plymouth, Massachusetts
1. Euphemia Coffrin Pevear *m.* Ernest Fairman Dow
2. Frank W. Pevear (1854–1921) *m.* 1876 Maria E. Parfitt (1849–1881)
3. George F. Pevear (1832–1900) *m.* 1853 Sarah Lye (1827–1853)
4. John Lye (1801–1860) *m.* 1824 Mary Lindsay (1803–1874)
5. Joseph Lye, Jr. (1759–1807) *m.* 1787 Anna Hart (1767–1848)
6. Joseph Hart (1739–1806) *m.* 1766 Eunice Burrill (1747–1816)
7. Samuel Burrill (1717–1797) *m.* 1740 Anna Alden (1722–1795)
8. Capt. John Alden (1690–1727) *m.* 1718 Anna Braeme (1694–1764)
9. Capt. John Alden (1662/3–1729/30) *m.* 1684 Elizabeth Phelps (1669–1719)
10. Capt. John Alden (abt. 1626–1701/2) *m.* 1660 Elizabeth (Phillips) Everell (1640–1695)
11. Hon. John Alden (1599–1687) *m.* abt. 1621 Priscilla Mullins, *d. c.* 1687
Service: Mayflower passenger, Compact signer, Deputy to General Court, Treas. of Colony, Dep. Governor.
Reference: Lynn, Mass., Vital Records, Records of the Alden Kindred of America.

6768 DOWLING, Miss Etta Genevieve Recorded 1952 (Colorado)
2289 South Williams Street, Denver, Colorado
1. Miss Genevieve Etta Dowling
2. Nicholas Dowling (1842–1910) *m.* 1882 Etta Guthrie Pugeley (1860–1933)
3. Horatio Nelson Pugeley (1817–1893) *m.* 1847 Margaret Davis Silvey (1821–1904)
4. Peter Van Allen Pugeley (1789–1843) *m.* 1813 Samantha Per Lee (1790–1857)
5. Edmund Per Lee (1750–1822) *m.* 1779 Zayde Winans (1752–1827)
6. James Winans (1715–1795) *m.* 1736 Sarah Reynolds (1714–1802)
7. Conrad Winans (1680–1727/8) *m.* Sarah Palmer
8. John Winans (1640–1694) *m.* 1664 Susannah Melyn (1643–1692)
9. Cornelius Melyn (1602–aft. 1662) *m.* abt. 1627 Jenetie
Service: Came to America from Holland, 1639; Patroon of Staten Island 1639–1657.
Reference: New Amsterdam and its People, by J. H. Innes, Chap XI and Appendix II; Records filed with applicants; two Sisters Application Papers in S. & D. Pilgrims, 1939 Vol., and No. 6243.

6243 DOWLING, Miss Marguerite Silvey
901 East Alameda Ve., Denver, Colorado
1. Nicholas Dowling (1842–1910) *m.* 1882 Etta Guthrie Pugsley (1860–1933)
2. Horatio Nelson Pugsley (1817–1893) *m.* 1847 Margaret Davis Silvey (1821–1904)
3. Peter Van Allan Pugsley (1789–1843) *m.* 1813 Samantha Per Lee (1790–1857)
4. Edmund Per Lee (1750–1822) *m.* 1779 Zayde Winans (1752–1827)
5. James Winans (1716–1795) *m.* 1735 Sarah Reynolds (1714–1802)
6. Conrad Winans (1680–1727) *m.* Sarah Palmer
7. John Winans (1640–1694) *m.* 1664 Susannah Melyn (1643–1688)
8. Cornelius Melyn (1602–1662) *m.* 1627 Janetie ———
Service: Patroon of Staten Isle.
Reference: Gen. 4—Bockee Gen., page 110; New Amsterdam and its People, by Innes; Early Residents of Amenia.

6244 DOWLING, Per Lee Recorded 1939
901 East Alameda Ave., Denver, Colorado
1. Nicholas Dowling (1842–1910) *m.* 1882 Etta Guthrie Pugsley (1860–1933)
2. Horatio Nelson Pugsley (1817–1893) *m.* 1847 Margaret Davis Silvey (1821–1904)
3. Peter Van Allen Pugsley (1789–1843) *m.* 1813 Samantha Per Lee (1790–1857)
4. Edward Pugsley (1760–1836) *m.* 1786 Mary Lapham (1764–1848)
4. Benjamin Lapham (1727–) *m.* 1749 Margaret Page
5. John Lapham (1703–) *m.* 1726 Desire Howland (1696–)
6. Benjamin Howland (1659–1727) *m.* 1684 Judith Sampson
7. Zoeth Howland (1636–1676) *m.* 1656 Abigail ———
8. Henry Howland (1600–1671) *m.* 1649 Mary Newland
Service: Constable; Grantee of Bridgewater.
Reference: Bockee Gen.; Abr. Comp. of Am. Gen., Vol. 6; Gen. Dic. of N. E., by Savage; Pioneers of Mass., by Pope.

5962   DOWNEY, Mrs. James H.   Recorded 1930 (Georgia)
        29 Academy Street, Gainesville, Georgia
   1. Lillie Farrara *m.* 1903 James H. Downey
   2. Capt. L. L. Farrara (1839–   ) *m.* 1866 Lucinda F. Pruner (1847–1927)
   3. William W. Pruner (–1869) *m.* 1844 Elizabeth McGhee (1826–1870)
   4. Henry Pruner III (1795–1877) *m.* 1816 Sarah A. Boggess (1785–1876)
   5. Henry Boggess (1736–1785) *m.* 1764 Mary Ann Lindsay (1747–1822)
   6. Robert Lindsay II (1704–1784) *m.* 1745 Susanna
   7. Opie Lindsay (1659–1727)
   8. Robert Lindsay I (1640–1665)
   9. DAVID LINDSAY (1603–1667) *m.* 1638 Susanna (–1665)
   Service: Clergyman of the Episcopal Church in Wicomico Parish for 20 years.
   Reference: Lyndsay Family in America.

5854   DOZIER, Mrs. Walter S.   Recorded 1929 (Georgia)
        321 Crawford Street, Dawson, Georgia
   1. Susie Bright Geise *m.* 1878 Walter S. Dozier
   2. Reuben Geise (1821–1880) *m.* 1848 Jerusha Halsey Wood (1837–1885)
   3. Lewis Wood (1797–1836) *m.* 1822 Mary Ann (1800–1857)
   4. Joseph Wood (1760–1815) *m.* 1780 Joanna Tuttle (1762–1843)
   5. Jonathan Wood (1723–1804) *m.* 1753 Jerushia Halsey (1728–1803)
   6. Samuel Halsey
   7. Isaac Halsey (1628–1725) *m.* Mary
   8. THOMAS HALSEY (1592–1678) *m.* 1625 Phoebe (–1649)
   Service: Member of General Court at Hartford, Conn., 1664–1669.
   Reference: Halsey Genealogy.

4609   DRAKE, Rev. James Hunnicutt   Recorded 1943
        Atlanta, Georgia
   1. James Hunnicutt Drake *m.* Hazel Bennett Runyan (2nd wife)
   2. Benjamin Magruder Drake (1868–   ) *m.* 1895 Mary Iula Hunnicutt (1874–   )
   3. James Benjamin Hunnicutt (1836–1904) *m.* 1862 Emily Jane Page (1843–1886)
   4. Dr. James E. P. Hunnicutt (1805–1884) *m.* 1830 Martha Lundie Atkinson
        (1809–1851)
   5. John Pepper Atkinson (1768–1840) *m.* 1801 Elizabeth Bland Lundie (1782–1854)
   6. Rev. Thomas Lundie (1740–1798) *m.* 1770 Lucy Yates (ab. 1750–1823)
   7. Rev. William Yates (1720–1764) *m.* 1740/45 Elizabeth Randolph (ab. 1720–1784)
   8. Edward Randolph (ab. 1690–1756) *m.* 1720 bef. Miss Grosvenor
   9. COL. WILLIAM RANDOLPH (1651–1711) *m.* 1680 Mary Isham (ab. 1660–   )
   Service: Member of House of Burgesses, 1685–1710; Speaker of the House, 1698;
        Clerk of the House, 1702; Attorney General, 1696; Clerk of Henrico Co.,
        Va., 1673–1680; Justice, 1683–1711; Colonel Commanding Militia Forces of
        Henrico; one of the Founders and Trustees of William and Mary College.
   Reference: Coweta Co. Chronicals; Rec. Brunswick Co., Ga.; Va./Mag. H&B, Vol. 7;
        Wm. & Mary Quart., Vol. 7.

5989   DRUMMOND, Mrs. Edward H.   Recorded 1931
        5618 Marrimac Street, Dallas, Texas
   1. Zou White *m.* 1927 Edward H. Drummond
   2. John White (1837–1906) *m.* 1859 Julia Elenore (1839–1919)
   3. Albert Elmore (1812–1883) *m.* 1838 Thirga Whitney (1814–1844)
   4. Moses Whitney (1772–1816) *m.* 1794 Lydia Allen (1777–1860)
   5. Joseph Whitney (1748–1813) *m.* 1771 Abagail Barnard (1751–1813)
   6. Joseph Whitney (1716–1796) *m.* 1744 Hannah Chandler (1727–1788)
   7. Thomas Whitney (1681–   ) *m.* 1704 Mary Baker (1682–   )
   8. Thomas Whitney (1656–1742) *m.* 1679 Elizabeth Lawrence (1659–1741)
   9. Thomas Whitney (1629–1719) *m.* 1654 Mary Kettle
  10. John Whitney (1589–1673) *m.* Elinor ——— (1584–1659)
  11. THOMAS WHITNEY (–1637) *m.* 1583 Mary Bray (–1629)
   Service: Town Clerk, Constable.
   Reference: Whitney Gen., Frederick; D. A. R. Lineage.

6216 DUCH, Mrs. Andrew J. Recorded 1938
   120 Stacy Avenue, Trenton, New Jersey
   1. Bessie G. Cramer *m.* Andrew J. Duch
   2. Watson D. Cramer (1855–1921) *m.* 1877 Lucy Ann Weeks (1856–1926)
   3. Capt. Wm. Theo Wake (1824–1908) *m.* 1854 Lucy Ann Sooy (1824–1880)
   4. James Weeks (1798–1856) *m.* 1820 Phebe Watson (1796–1875)
   5. Curtis Wilson (1769–1855) *m.* 1790 Sarah Sooy (1778–1853)
   6. John Sooy (1742–1792) *m.* 1770 Abigail Osborn (1747–1792)
   7. Joost Sooy, Jr. (1710–1742) *m.* 1737 Eliz Smith (1720–1742)
   8. Joost Sooy, Sr. (1684–1737) *m.* 1707 Sarah Van Lienhoven Balk (1681–1794)
   9. Dr. Luijkas Van Lienhoven (1649–1714) *m.* 1680 Tryntje Boarding (1657–1714)
   10. CORNELIS VAN LIENHOVEN (–1656) *m.* 1649 Rachel Vinjee (–1663)
   Service: Attorney General, Magistrate.
   Reference: History New York, Putnam; Abridged Comp. of Am. Gen.

6754 DUCOURNAU, Mrs. Jackson P. Recorded 1952 (Louisiana)
   496 Walnut Street, New Orleans, Louisiana
   1. Caledonia V. Cooper *m.* 1931 Jackson P. Ducournau
   2. Edward Richmond Cooper (1882–1913) *m.* 1909 Olive Long Cooper (1885, living)
   3. Hugey Pierce Long (1852–1937) *m.* 1875 Caledonia Tison (1860–1913)
   4. John Murphy Long (1825–1901) *m.* 1845 Mary Elizabeth Wingate (1829–1901)
   5. James Long (1790–1850) *m.* 1823 Mary Kirtman (1793–1850)
   6. Hugh Long (1770–bet. 1794 and 1800) *m.* 1789 Margaret (–1794)
   7. James Long (1750–1807) *m.* 1768 Catherine (–bef. 1790)
   8. John Long (abt. 1692–1759) *m.* 1735 Ellenor Owens (1706–aft. 1795)
   9. Capt. Richard Owens (1668–aft. 1708) *m.* 1698 Racheal Beall (bf. 1678–aft. 1708)
   10. COL. NINIAN BEALL (1625–1717) *m.* 1668 Ruth Moore (–1704)
   Service: Dep. Surveyor; Justice and Burgess of Md.
   Reference: Beall Genealogy, by F. M. Beall, p. 49; Baltimore Wills B 8 F–170–180;
   Archives of Md., Vol. 22, pgs. 421–2; Sons and Daughters of Pilgrims
   Nat. No. 6724.

6120 DUNBAR, Mrs. F. W. Recorded 1936 (New York)
   Manchester, Vermont
   1. Edith Flanders *m.* 1900 Francis W. Dunbar
   2. Rev. Alonzo B. Flanders (1828–1898) *m.* 1853 Sarah Anne Ide (1827–1920)
   3. James Flanders (1805–1878) *m.* 1826 Cynthia Clifford (1805–1839)
   4. Jacob Flanders (1759–1840) *m.* Ann Kenerson (1762–1829)
   5. Zebulon Flanders (1737–1799) *m.* Miriam (–1807)
   6. Josiah Flanders (1700–1781) *m.* 1724 Mehitable Osgood (1706–1782)
   7. John Flanders (1659–1716) *m.* 1687 Elizabeth Sargent (1668–1713)
   8. STEVEN FLANDERS (–1684) *m.* Jane (–1683)
   Service: Early Settler.
   Reference: The Flanders Family, by Edith Flanders Dunbar.

6150 DUNBAR, Mrs. Helen Flanders Recorded 1937 (New York)
   730 Park Avenue, New York City
   1. Helen F. Dunbar *m.* 1932 Dr. Theodore Wolfe
   2. Francis W. Dunbar (1868–) *m.* 1900 Edith V. Flanders (1871–)
   3. Rev. Alonzo B. Flanders (1828–1898) *m.* 1853 Sarah Ann Ide (1827–1920)
   4. James Flanders (1805–1878) *m.* 1826 Cynthia Clifford (1805–1839)
   5. Jacob Flanders (1759–1840) *m.* Ann Kenerson (1762–1829)
   6. Zebulon Flanders (1737–1798) *m.* Miriam ——— (–1807)
   7. Josiah Flanders (1700–1781) *m.* 1724 Mehitabel Osgood (1706–1782)
   8. Corp. John Flanders (1659–1716) *m.* 1687 Elizabeth Sargent (1668–1713)
   9. STEVEN FLANDERS (–1684) *m.* Jane ——— (–1683)
   Service: Early Settler.
   Reference: The Flanders Family from Europe to America, by Edith Flanders Dunbar.

64 SOCIETY OF THE SONS AND

6750 DUNBAR, Miss Katherine Elise Recorded 1952 (Louisiana)
561 Lakeland Drive, Baton Rouge, Louisiana
1. Miss Katherine Elise Dunbar, *b.* 1901
2. Winder Crough Dunbar (1862–1927) *m.* 1894 Eliz. Posey Prescott (1869–living 1952)
3. Capt. Lewis D. Prescott (1836–1900) *m.* 1856 Lucy Glenn Offutt (1847–1929)
4. William Marshall Prescott (1808–1854) *m.* 1830 Evelina S. Moore (1812–1875)
5. Judge John Moore (abt. 1788–1867) *m.* 1810 S. Adelaide Demarest (abt. 1791–)
6. Major Lewis Moore (abt. 1768–) *m.* Rebecca Henshaw (1770–)
7. Capt. Wm. Henshaw (1736–1799) *m.* Agnes Anderson (1735–)
8. Nicholas Henshaw (1704–) *m.* Rebecca Smith
9. John Henshaw (1683–) *m.* Mary Stubman
10. Joshua Henshaw (1661–1719) *m.* 1682 Elizabeth Sumner (–1728)
11. William Sumner, Jr. (abt. 1636–) *m.* 1660 Elizabeth Clement
12. WILLIAM SUMNER, SR., *b.* Eng., *d.* 1688, *m.* 1635 Mary West (–1676)
Service: Came to Massachusetts 1635.
Reference: Genealogy of Sumner Family, by W. B. Trask; Sons and Daughters of Pilgrim Nat. No. 6678.

6747 DUNBAR, Mrs. Otto C. Recorded 1952 (Illinois)
515 East Washington Street, Macomb, Illinois
1. Meta Pillsbury *m.* 1909 Otto Carl Dunbar
2. Francis Ithamer Pillsbury (1851–1893) *m.* 1884 Minnie I. Blackwelder (1857–1887)
3. Ithamer Pillsbury (1794–1862) *m.* 1837 Caroline Miller (1818–1896)
4. Joshua Pillsbury (1743–1825) *m.* 1770 Elizabeth Sawyer (1750–1816)
5. Caleb Pillsbury (1717–1778) *m.* 1742 Sarah Kimball (1722–1761)
6. Caleb Pillsbury (1681–1751) *m.* 1703 Sarah Morss
7. Moses Pillsbury (1645–1701) *m.* 1668 Sussannah Worth
8. WILLIAM PILLSBURY (1615–1686) *m.* Dorothy Crosby
Service: Born in England, died Newberyport, Mass. His home, built by him, is still standing and is marked.
Reference: Pillsbury Family, by Pillsbury & Getchell, pgs. 1–9, 14–16, 25–26, 81, 158. Caleb 4 and Joshua 5 were in American Revolution; 5 died in service. Bible and abstracts from family history filed with applications.

6745 DUNBAR, Mrs. William R. Recorded 1952 (Pennsylvania)
Kellers Church, Bucks County, Pennsylvania
1. Helen Holland *m.* 1940 W. Reed Dunbar
2. William Fowler Holland (1884–Living 1952) *m.* 1911 Edna M. Nightlinger (1889–Living 1952)
3. Clarence P. Holland (1856–1937) *m.* 1882 Addie V. Fowler (1856–1922)
4. Thomas Holland (1819–1881) *m.* 1851 Susan Eccleston (1835–1882)
5. Nathaniel G. Eccleston (1798–) *m.* 1827 Susan Pattison (1801–1869)
6. Richard Pattison (1759–1823) *m.* 1788 Mary MacKeele (1769–1825)
7. Capt. John Mac Keele (*c.* 1743–) *m.* Wife
8. Capt. Thomas Mac Keele (*c.* 1720–1762) *m.* Mary Stevens (*c.* 1721–aft. 1762)
9. Thomas Mac Keele (–1685) will *m.* Claire Gary
10. JOHN MAC KEELE (–1696) will *m.* a dau. of John Custis, (*c.* 1642–)
Service: Came to America, 1640; served in campaign against the Nanticoke Indians; a Justice of Dorchester Co., Va., 1685; appointed a Commissioner to lay out towns in Virginia; his grandson served in the American Revolution.
Reference: History of Mac Keel Family; History of Dorchester Co., Va., pgs. 41, 45 51, 56, 224; MacKeele wills.

6751 DUNBAR, Mrs. Windor Crouch Recorded 1951 (Louisiana)
561 Lakeland Drive, Baton Rouge, Louisiana
1. Eliza Posey Prescott *m.* 1894 W. C. Dunbar
2. Capt. Lewis D. Prescott (1836–1900) *m.* 1856 Lucy Glenn Offutt (1847–1929)
3. William Marshall Prescott (1808–1854) *m.* 1830 Evelina S. Moore (1812–1875)
4. Judge John Moore (abt. 1788–1867) *m.* 1810 S. Adelaide Demarest (abt. 1791–)
5. Major Lewis Moore (abt. 1768–) *m.* Rebecca Henshaw (1770–)
6. Capt. Wm. Henshaw (1736–1799) *m.* Agnes Anderson (1735–)
7. Nicholas Henshaw (1704–) *m.* Rebecca Smith
8. John Henshaw (1683–) *m.* Mary Stubman

9. Joshua Henshaw (1661–1719) *m.* 1682 Elizabeth Sumner (–1728)
10. William Sumner, Jr. (abt. 1636–) *m.* 1660 Elizabeth Clement
11. WILLIAM SUMNER, SR. (–1688) *m.* 1635 Mary West (–1676)
Service: Wm. Sumner, Sr., came to Massachusetts, 1635.
Reference: Genealogy of Sumber Family, by Wm. B. Trask; Nat. No. of Sons and Daughters of Pilgrims 6678.

5920 DUNCAN, Mary Fields   Recorded 1930 (Texas)
      723 N. Beacon Street, Dallas, Texas
1. Mary Fields *m.* Chester A. Duncan
2. Theo F. Fields (1844–1883) *m.* 1873 Clara Oram (1846–1908)
3. Daniel Fields (1810–1871) *m.* 1835 Eliza Smedley (1808–1886)
4. John Smedley (1755–1815) *m.* 1804 Mary Baker (1781–1855)
5. George Smedley (–1783) *m.* 1750 Patience Mercer (1731–1812)
6. Thomas Smedley (1688–1758) *m.* 1710 Sarah Baker (1682–1765)
7. GEORGE SMEDLEY (–1723) *m.* 1687 Sarah Goodwin (–1709)
Service: George Smedley purchased 250 acres of land from William Penn in 1682.
Reference: Smedley Genealogy.

5986 DUNLAP, Walter Eugene Briggs   Recorded 1931
      203 Eureka Avenue, Montevideo, Minnesota
1. Walter E. B. Dunlap (1886–) *m.* 1913 Amey Pearson
2. Walter Clarence Dunlap (1857–1918) *m.* 1885 Minnie Emma Briggs (1862–)
3. Allen Erasmus Briggs (1835–1898) *m.* 1856 Frances Augusta Peabody (1835–1903)
4. Thomas Millen Briggs (1813–) *m.* Phoebe Spaulding
5. Ephriam Allen Briggs (1783–1861) *m.* 1806 Sally Townsend (1785–1869)
6. Rev. Samuel Briggs (1744–1800) *m.* 1770 Ruth Paul (–1830)
7. John Briggs (1719–1796) *m.* 1742 Tabatha Allen (1724–1753)
8. Ephriam Allen (1689–) *m.* Zipporah Crane
9. Samuel Allen (1660–1736) *m.* 1685 Rebecca Carey (1665–1697)
10. Samuel Allen (1632–1703) *m.* 1658 Sarah Partridge
11. SAMUEL ALLEN (1588–1648) *m.* Ann
Service:
Reference: Asa W. Allen's Gen.; Allen & Witter Fam.; Reg. Published 1926 by Or. Founders & Patriots.

6492 DYER, Mrs. Wilbur C.   Recorded 195?
      87 Tibet Road, Columbus 2, Ohio
1. Marion Woolson Corey *m.* Wilbur Clyde Dyer
2. Harry Hibbard Corey (1861–1929) *m.* 1888 Claribel Quimby (1865–1934)
3. Kimball H. Quimby (1833–1909) *m.* 1858 Mary Rebecca Woolson (1838–1906)
4. Amos Woolson (1803–1888) *m.* 1830 Hannah Dodge Temple (1804–1891)
5. Elijah Woolson (1769–) *m.* 1797 Rebecca Batchellor (1776–1814)
6. Nehemiah Batchellor (1741–1822) *m.* 1766 Lucy Hayward (1747–1822)
7. Nehemiah Batchellor (1716–) *m.* 1738 Experience Perham
8. David Batchellor (–1747) *m.* Susannah Whipple (–1764)
9. John Batchellor (–1698) *m.* 1665 (2nd) Sarah Goodale (–1729)
10. JOSEPH BATCHELLOR (–1647) *m.* Elizabeth ———
Service: One of the original members of church in Wenham, Mass. First representative of Wenham in General Court in 1644.

6457 EASTELL, Mrs. Eldred W. (dec'd)   Recorded 1945
      1824 Lawrence Avenue, Toledo 6, Ohio
1. Jessie Cosgrave Seagrave *m.* Eldred W. Eastell
2. Francis Eugene Seagrave (1843–1916) *m.* 1869 Charlotte Caroline Lee (1843–1912)
3. Lyman W. Lee (1817–1901) *m.* 1837 Mary Louise Miner (1818–1863)
4. Charles Lee (1776–1823) *m.* 1799 Esther Tennant (1780–1848)
5. Solomon Lee (1747–1811) *m.* 1775 bef. Ann Brewster (1755–1824)
6. Nathan Brewster (1724–1808) *m.* 1751 Rachel Partridge (1726–1757)
7. Joshua Brewster (1698–1776) *m.* 1721 Deborah Chandler (1703–1769)
8. Dea. William Brewster (1645–1723) *m.* 1672 Lydia Partridge (–1742/3)
9. Love Brewster (–1650) *m.* 1634 Sarah Collier
10. ELDER WILLIAM BREWSTER (1566–1644) *m.* Mary ——— (–1627)
Service: Elder, Church, Plymouth. Mayflower passenger.
Reference: Gen. Seagrave Family; Brewster Genealogy.

6011 EATON, Miss Grace Caroline   Recorded 1932
          2581 Dexter Street, Denver, Colorado
1. Allen Smith Eaton (1829–1914) *m.* 1857 Martha Adelia Smith (1836–1914)
2. William Eaton (1792–1866) *m.* 1819 Rebecca Sherman (1799–1848)
3. Luther Eaton (1758–1829) *m.* 1780 Sally Rice (–1842)
4. Nathaniel Eaton (1728–1804) *m.* 1755 Sarah Johnson
5. Nathaniel Eaton (1704–1785) *m.* 1727 Esther Parry (1710–1769)
6. Thomas Eaton (1675–1848) *m.* 1697 Kydia Starr Gay (1679–1748)
7. John Eaton (1636–1694) *m.* Alice ——— (–1694)
8. JOHN EATON (–1658) *m.* Abigail Damat
Service: Surveyor.
Reference: His. & Gen. Biog. of Eaton Families; Nathaniel Eaton, by Nellie Z. R. Molyneaux; John Eaton, by Nellie Z. R. Molyneaux.

6418 EATON, Robert Clark   Recorded 1943
          Woodstock, Vermont
1. Robert Clark Eaton
2. Herbert Clark Eaton (1856–1917) *m.* 1882 Emma Elnora Fuller (1864–1917)
3. Clark Eaton *m.* Mary Green (1821–1904)
4. Asa Eaton (1778–1858) *m.* Matilda (Melinda) ——— (1785–1841)
5. Rev. Asa Eaton (1746–) *m.* 1772 Abigail Goodell (1750–)
6. David Eaton (1706–1777) *m.* 1741 (2nd) Bethia Tiffany
7. Thomas Eaton (1675–1748) *m.* 1697 Lydia Gay (1679–1748)
8. John Eaton (1636–1694) *m.* Alice ——— (–1694)
9. JOHN EATON (1611–1658) *m.* 1630 Abigail Damon (widow)
Service: Surveyor of Highways, Dedham, Mass. Other town offices. (Early (1630) at Watertown, Mass.)
Reference: Twn. Rec., Vt. Rochester, Pittsfield, Westminster, Woodstock; Hists: Woodstock, Bowen; Windham Co., Conn.; Watertown, Mass.; Eaton Fam., Molyneaux.

6752 EATON, Mrs. William W.   Recorded 1952, Pennsylvania
          22 East Vassar Road, Audubon, Camden County, New Jersey
1. Frances Maria Sweet *m.* 1889 W. W. Eaton
2. Simon Elon Sweet (1836–1922) *m.* 1857 Sallie Maria Noxon (1836–1930)
3. James Pascho Moxon (1798–1876) *m.* 1833 Anna Wilkinson (1809–1892)
4. Jeremiah Wilkinson (1771–1812) *m.* 1808 Phoebe Eldridge (abt. 1788–1814)
5. Jeremiah Wilkinson 2nd (1741–1831) *m.* Hope Mosher (1751–1774)
6. Jonathan Mosher, Jr. (1726–) *m.* 1749 Ann Mott (–1810)
7. Jonathan Mosher, Sr., (1699–) *m.* 1720 Isabel Potter (1703–)
8. Joseph Mosher (1670–1754) *m.* 1695 Lydia Taber (1673–1743)
9. Phillip Taber (–1692) *m.* abt 1668 Mary Cooke (–1714)
10. John Cooke (–before 1708) *m.* Sarah Warren
11. RICHARD WARREN (will 1628) *m.* Elizabeth Jarratt
Service: Signer of Mayflower Compact, 1620.
Reference: Wilkinson Genealogy, pgs. 132–3, 171–3; '38, 409–413; Mosher Genealogy, 15 Dartmouth V. R., I, 167–188; The Mayflower Descendant, Vol. 10, pgs. 44–6—16: 22. Vol. 16, pgs. 228–30–31. Colonial Families of America, 2: 29 (1928).

5829 EAVENSON, John William   Recorded 1929
          Bowman, Georgia
1. John William Eavenson (1840–) *m.* 1865 Jane Josephine Oglesby
2. George Eavenson (1817–1898) *m.* 1839 Sarah Thornton (1824–1863)
3. George Eavenson, Sr. (1782–) *m.* Polly Hilly (1781–1803)
4. Eli Eavenson (1760–) *m.* 1781 Rachael Seals (1760–)
5. George Eavenson (1726–1816) *m.* Mary Williams (–1828)
6. Joseph Eavenson (1689–1771) *m.* 1717 Catherine George
7. Thomas Eavenson (1653–) *m.* Hannah Woodward (1677–)
8. RALPH EAVENSON (1625–1655) *m.* 1650 Cicely Orton
Service: Same as 5829.
Reference:

6070 ECKEL, Mrs. John Leonard (dec'd)   Recorded 1934, New York
        589 Delaware Avenue, Buffalo, New York
  1. Berenice Long *m.* 1914 John Leonard Eckel
  2. Clement R. Long (1851–) *m.* 1875 Nellie Devol (1852–)
  3. Charles Mc. Devol (1827–1895) *m.* 1849 Phebe Ann Williams (1828–1857)
  4. Alpha Devol (1789–1871) *m.* 1814 Nancy Champlin (1780–1830)
  5. Joseph Champlin *m.* Anna Prentice (1759–1837)
  6. Stephen Prentice (1728–1799) *m.* 1750 Anna Starr (1731–1798)
  7. Samuel Starr (1699–1786) *m.* 1726 Anna Bushnell (1705–1796)
  8. Jonathan Starr (1673–1747) *m.* 1698 Elizabeth Morgan (1678–1763)
  9. Samuel Starr (–1688) *m.* 1664 Hannah Brewster (1641–1691)
  10. Jonathan Brewster (–1659) *m.* 1624 Lucretia Oldham (–1678)
  11. WILLIAM BREWSTER *m.* Mary Peame
  Service: Religious Leader of the Pilgrims.
  Reference: Mayflower Descendants; Starr Family; Morgan Genealogy; Norwich
        Vital Records; Prentice Genealogy; N. E. Historical & Genealogical
        Register.

6077 EDLER, Miss Emma K.   Recorded 1934, Pennsylvania
        3518 Powelton Avenue, Philadelphia, Pennsylvania
  1. Emma K. Edler
  2. William C. Edler (1868–) *m.* 1892 Sarah G. Graham (1870–)
  3. William H. Edler (1841–1904) *m.* 1866 Emma R. Custer (1845–1893)
  4. David L. Custer (1796–1871) *m.* 1829 Catherine Cline (1806–1880)
  5. Jonathan Custer, Jr. (1768–1823) *m.* 1790 Rosanna Ludwig (1770–1832)
  6. Jonathan Custer (1734–1823) *m.* 1760 Hannah Peters (1735–1805)
  7. Paul Custer (1710–1783) *m.* Sarah Ball (1722–1779)
  8. Arnold Custer (1674–1734) *m.* Elizabeth
  9. PAUL KUSTER (1640–1708) *m.* Gertrude Streypers (–1708)
  Service: Helped form the first colony of 13 families who settled in Germantown,
        Pa., in 1684.
  Reference: Custer Family; Berks County Wills.

6071 EDGERLY, Mrs. Webster   Recorded 1934, New Jersey
        349 West State Street, Trenton, New Jersey
  1. Edna Reid Boyts *m.* 1892 Webster Edgerly
  2. Franklin Boyts (1840–1911) *m.* 1870 Cecelia M. Reid (1849–1923)
  3. James D. Reid (1813–1856) *m.* 1834 Mary Henry (1817–1901)
  4. Edward Henry (1782–1859) *m.* 1805 Mary McCauley (1785–1859)
  5. Edward Henry (1750–1855) *m.* 1776 Christena Trout (–1786)
  6. Robert Henry, Jr. (1707–1786) *m.* 1740 Sarah Davison (–1761)
  7. WILLIAM DAVISON *m.* 1700 Elizabeth
  Service: Early settler in West Caln Twp., Pa., in 1684.
  Reference: Boyts Genealogy; Penna. Archives; Egles Notes and Queries; Harvey's
        Miscellany, Vol. III, p. 19.

6586 EDWARDS, Mrs. J. L.   Recorded 1948
        1041 Wooster Road West, Barberton, Ohio
  1. Ruth K. Ridgway *m.* 1920 Joseph L. Edwards
  2. Samuel E. Ridgway (1858–1938) *m.* 1885 Julia A. Bellen (1862–1934)
  3. Samuel Ridgway (1824–1901) *m.* 1848 Eliza Hyde (1824–1907)
  4. Elijah Hyde (1791–1863) *m.* Diadama Comstock
  5. Elijah C. Hyde (1758–1837) *m.* Sarah Taylor (1761–1801)
  6. Maj. Elijah Hyde (1735–1800) *m.* 1757 Mary Clark (1738–1813)
  7. Elijah Hyde (1705–1783) *m.* 1730 Ruth Tracy (1711–1773)
  8. John Tracy II *d.* 1726, *m.* 1697 Elizabeth Leffingwell (1676–)
  9. Capt. John Tracy (1642–1702) *m.* 1670 Mary Winslow (1646–1721)
  10. LT. THOMAS TRACY *m.* 1641 Widow of Edward Mason
  Service: Active in founding of Wethersfield and Saybrook, Conn. An original pro-
        prietor of Norwich, Conn.
  Reference: Hyde Genealogy.

5976   EDWARDS, Mrs. James P.   Recorded 1931
            Prospect, Jefferson County, Kentucky
    1. Margaret Wathen, *m.* 1911 James P. Edwards
    2. John Bernard Wathen (1844–1919) *m.* 1867 Margaret Adams (1844–1930)
    3. James Adams (1802–1881) *m.* 1827 Ann Pamelia Hill (1807–1846)
    4. Clement Hill (1776–1832) *m.* 1798 Mary Hamilton (1782–1833)
    5. Thomas Hamilton (1745–1819) *m.* 1781 Ann Hodgkins (1757–1819)
    6. Capt. James Hamilton (1715–1785) *m.* Mary Ann Coombs (1720–aft. 1785)
    7. Thomas Coombs (–1753) *m.* Elizabeth Wharton (–1772)
    8. Dr. Jesse Wharton (–1676) *m.* Elizabeth Sewall (–aft. 1676)
    9. Hon. Henry Sewall (–1665) *m.* Lady Jane Low (–1701)
    Service: Sec. to Lord Baltimore; Justice and Keeper of the Acts.
    Reference: Founders of Anne Arundel County, Maryland; Colonial Families of
        America; Side-lights on Maryland History.

6312   ELLIS, Mrs. Francis D.   Recorded 1941
            High Street, Farmington, Connecticut
    1. Carolyn Welles *m.* Francis D. Ellis
    2. Martin Welles (1859–   ) *m.* 1888 Mary Amelia Paeton, *b.* 1864
    3. Roger Welles (1829–1904) *m.* 1858 Mercy Delano Aikin (1832–1922)
    4. Samuel Smith Aikin (1790–1866) *m.* 1821 Sarah Coffin (1804–1883)
    5. Bartholomew Aikin (1750–1835) *m.* 1782 Mercy Delano (1755–1812)
    6. Benjamin Aikin (1715–1802) *m.* 1739 Eunice Taber (1711–1762)
    7. Saueb Taber (1683–1773) *m.* Sarah West (1686–1775)
    8. Stephen West, *d.* 1748, *m.* Mercy Cooke (c. 1654–1733)
    9. John Cooke, *d.* 1696, *m.* 1634 Sarah Warren
    10. Francis Cooke, *d.* 1663, *m.* Hester
    Service: Mayflower Passenger.
    Reference: The Mayflower Descendants; Delano Genealogy; Taber Genealogy,
        Randall; Stiles Hist. of Ancient Wethersfield, Conn.

6444   ELLIS, Mrs. Harry Hay   Recorded 1944
            741 Piedmont Avenue N. E., Atlanta, Georgia
    1. Grace Gregorie *m.* Harry Hay Ellis
    2. Henry Hutson Gregorie (1836–1900) *m.* 1780 Matilda Kemp (1854–   )
    3. Charles Colcock Gregorie (1799–1843) *m.* 1835 Emily Gregorie (cousins)
        (1817–1897)
    4. James Gregorie (1777–1834) *m.* 1801 Ann Gibbes Landson (1784–1824)
    5. James Landson (1753–1812) *m.* 1778 Judith Smith (1761–1820)
    6. Benjamin Smith (1717–1770) *m.* 1760 Mary Wragg (1720–1777)
    7. Thomas Smith (1691–1723) *m.* 1714 Sabina Smith (cousins) (1699–1734)
    8. Thomas Smith (1664–1738) *m.* 1686/9 Ann C. Van Myddagh (1672–1712)
    9. Thomas Smith (1630–1694) *m.* 1664 Barbara Atkins (1650–   )
    Service: Cassique; Governor of the Province; Member of the Grand Council; Deputy
        for Thomas Amy, one of the Lords Proprietors; High Sheriff of Berkeley
        Co., Carolina.
    Reference: S. C. Hist. & Gen. Mag., Vol. 4—(Thomas Smith), Vols. 2, 12, 13, 20, 22.

6682   ERVING, Mrs. Morris M.   Recorded 1950
            2895 Peachtree Road N. C., Atlanta, Georgia
    1. Dorothy Fielder (1893–   ) *m.* Morris M. Erving
    2. James W. Fielder (1861–1923) *m.* 1888 Julia M. Hodgkins (1866–   )
    3. James M. Fielder (1816–1863) *m.* 1851 Roxanna Williamson (1831–1871)
    4. Lt. Col. James M. Fielder (1789–1857) *m.* 1815 Elizabeth T. Heard (1798–1847)
    5. Joseph Heard (1773–1848) *m.* 1795/7 Nancy Stuart (Stewart), *d.* 1810 *c.*
    6. Thomas Heard (1742–1808) *m.* 1765/6 Elizabeth Fitzpatrick (1745–1790)
    7. Joseph Fitzpatrick (1720–1777) *m.* 1743 Mary P. Woodson (1727–1833)
    8. Benjamin Woodson (1684/92–1778) *m.* 1720 Frances Napier (1660–1710)
    9. John Woodson (1655–1700) *m.* 1677 Mary Tuckes (1660–1710)
    10. John Woodson (1632–1684) *m.* 1654 ———— ————, *d.* 1654
    11. Dr. John Woodson (1586 Eng.–1644) va. *m.* 1619 Sarah Weston, *d.* 1644
    Service:
    Reference:

6226 ESTLACK, Mr. Walter Forrest   Recorded 1938
      4111 Baltimore Avenue, Philadelphia, Pennsylvania
  1. Horace Datson Estlack (1848–1913) *m.* 1872 Cordelia Matilda Gregg (1845–1917)
  2. Thos. Estlack, Jr. (1823–1902) *m.* Sallie Watson
  3. Thomas Estlack, Sr. (1792–1865) *m.* Eliza Shim (1790–1868)
  4. Hezekiah Estlack (1762–1836) *m.* Anne Marshall (1759–1802)
  5. Restore Estlack (1734–1773) *m.* Sarah
  6. Francis Estlack (1707–1733) *m.* Phebe Driver (1711–1779)
  7. Joseph Estlack (1674–) *m.* 1698 Anne Powell
  8. FRANCIS ESTLACK
Service:
Reference: "First Settlers of Newton Township, N. J."

6395 ETHELL Mrs.   Recorded 1942
      1441 Logan Street, Denver, Colorado
  1. Charity I. Borton *m.* ——— Ethell
  2. James William Borton (1849–1911) *m.* 1873 Columbia Ann Carnal (1853–)
  3. William Borton (1825–) *m.* 1846 Charity Dillon (1821–)
  4. James Borton (1801–) *m.* 1822 Mariah Wilson (1801–1851)
  5. Benjamin Borton (1761–) *m.* 1780 Charity Rogers (–1821)
  6. Obidiah Borton (1708–1761) *m.* 1749 Mary Driver
  7. John Borton (1669–) *m.* 1707 ———
  8. JOHN BORTON (–1687) *m.* 1668 Ann ———
Service: Constable of London Tenth, 1682. Died Hillsdown, New Jersey.
Reference: Borton & Mason Families, F. C. Mason, pages 10, 12, 80, 95.

6431 EVEREST, Russell Elmer   Recorded 1943
      17 Wheeler Street, Boston, Massachusetts
  1. Russell Elmer Everest *m.* Florence Bessie Clifford
  2. Geo. Champlin Everest (1866–) *m.* 1897 Jane Butler Elmer (1870–)
  3. Seymour J. Everest (1837–1879) *m.* Phoebe L. Thorpe (1843–1918)
  4. John H. Everest (1812–1871) *m.* Caroline Champlin (1817–1894)
  5. Dr. Ira W. Everest (1785–1876) *m.* 1844 Pheney Booth (1785–1873)
  6. Lieut. Benj. Everest (1752–1843) *m.* Martha Fuller (1762–1843)
  7. Benjamin Everest (1718–1768) *m.* 1741/2 Hester Dudley
  8. Benjamin Everest *m.* 1708 Hannah Jones (1687–)
  9. Isaac Everest (–1697) *m.* Joanna ——— (–1706)
 10. ANDREW EVEREST (–1682 aft.) *m.* Barbara ———
Service: Died probably in York, Me., his son moved to Conn.; Constable York, Me.,
      in 1672.
Reference: V. R. Sec. St. office, Mont., Vt.; Hemenwat's Vt. Gazeteer, Vol. I; Am.
      Gen., Vol. I; Hist York, Me., Banks.

6430 EVEREST, Mrs. Russell Elmer   Recorded 1943
      85 Shawrunt Avenue, Boston, Massachusetts
  1. Florence Bessie Clifford *m.* Russell Elmer Everest
  2. Merritt Willard Clifford (1875–) *m.* 1896 Bessie Mae Kinsman (1877–)
  3. Henry Parker Kinsman (1836–1913) *m.* 1858 Mary Abigail Gibson (1842–1919)
  4. Timothy Oakley Gibson (1810–1884) *m.* 1835 Abigail Perkins (1815–1885)
  5. Capt. Moses Perkins (1786–1858) *m.* 1807 Hulda Williams (1790–1864)
  6. Arthur O. Williams (1761–) *m.* Dorcas Field (1766–1840)
  7. Jeremiah Williams (1736–1767) *m.* 1756 Bethiah Williams
  8. Jeremiah Williams (1700–1789) *m.* 1735 Abigail Mathewson (–1775)
  9. Joseph Williams (1673–1752) *m.* Lydia Hearnden (–1763)
 10. Joseph Williams (1643–1724) *m.* 1669 Lydia Olney (1646–1724)
 11. ROGER WILLIAMS (–1683) *m.* 1629 Mary Bernard (–1676)
Service: Religious leader; defender of liberty of conscience.
Reference: Pilgrim Index, No. 6422, 6424; Hist. of Rufus Perkins Fam., V. T.; Roger
      Williams' Desc., Calif; Gen. Dict. R. I., Austin.

6152 EYERS, Clara Victoria Preston (Mrs. Walter)   Recorded 1937
        Farmington, Connecticut
    1. Clara Victoria Preston Eyers (1891–   )
    2. Miles Barber Preston (1850–1911) *m.* (2d) 1890 Nellie Fenetta Dole (1866–1931)
    3. Truman Welles Preston (1825–1896) *m.* 1846 Mary Etta Brong
    4. Argabus Drake Preston (1795–1859) *m.* 1821 Laura Barber (1796–1869)
    5. Truman Barber (1769–1827) *m.* 1793 Alice Beebe (1768–1825)
    6. Bildad Barber (1745–1816) *m.* 1768 Lois Humphrey (1746–1810)
    7. Jonathan Barber (1717–1745) *m.* (1st) 1740 Jemima Cornish (1718–1791)
    8. Samuel Barber (1613–1725) *m.* Sarah Holcomb (1691–1787)
    9. Lt. Thomas Barber (1644–1713) *m.* 1660 Mary Phelps (1663–   )
   10. Thomas Barber (abt. 1614–1662) *m.* 1640 Jane ———
    Service: Soldier in the Pequot War.
    Reference: Hartford Records, pgs. 10, 11, 15, 78, 246, 493; N. H. Records, Vol. 2,
        pg. 615; Barber Gen., pgs. 18, 21, 22, 37, 54, 90; Phelps Family, Vol. I,
        pg. 86, No. 25.

6386 FARR, Mrs. George Cassius   Recorded 1942
        Monkton, Vermont
    1. Marjorie Zoe Palmer *m.* George C. Farr
    2. George Wallace Palmer (1853–1924) *m.* 1880 Lettie Alice Kennedy (1858–1928)
    3. Simeon Dana Palmer (1827–1898) *m.* Rosemond Besse (1832–1902)
    4. Otis Besse (Bessy, Bessee) (1798–1876) *m.* 1816 Susannah Goodwin
    5. Abraham Besse (1768–   ) *m.* 1796 Mary Bliss
    6. Nehemiah Bessee *m.* Sarah ———
    7. Nehemiah Bessee (1682–   ) *m.*
    8. Nehemiah Bessee (164?–   ) *m.* Mary ———
    9. Anthony Besse (ab. 1611–1657) *m.* Jane ———
    Service: Came in 'James' 1635 from London; one of those able to bear arms in
        Plymouth, 1643; many years "active in holy service to the Indians."
    Reference: V. R., Richmond, Duxbury, Huntington, V. T.; N. G. Gen. Reg., V. 15;
        Savage Vol. 1; Hist. Bridgewater, Mitchell, Woodstock, Vt., Henry Dana.

6333 FARR, Shirley   Recorded 1941
        53 Park Street, Brandon, Vermont
    1. Shirley Farr
    2. Albert George Farr (1851–1913) *m.* 1873 Alice Parkhurst (1852–1888)
    3. Daniel B. Parkhurst (1823–1890) *m.* 1851 Cynthia Cole Capron (1825–1918)
    4. Otis Capron (1793–1872) *m.* 1814 Julia Amanda Alden (1795–1856)
    5. Joseph Capron III (1760–1827) *m.* 2nd Cynthia Cole (1761–1841)
    6. Joseph Capron, Jr. (1722–1784) *m.* 1745 Sarah Robeson, *d.* 1761
    7. Joseph Capron (1691–1776) *m.* 1714 Judith Peck (1690–1734)
    8. Banfield Capron (1660–1752) *m.* Callender, *d.* 1735.
    Service: Settled in Massachusetts.
    Reference: "Gen. of Descendants of Banfield Capron," Holden; "Vermont of Today,"
        Stone.

5898 FARNAM, G. Oscar   Recorded 1930
        718 Riverside Drive, Trenton, New Jersey
    1. G. Oscar Farnam (1882–   ) unm.
    2. George Farnam (1846–1925) *m.* 1873 Elizabeth J. Lippincott (1852–   )
    3. Daniel H. Farnam (1810–1887) *m.* 1838 Lucy M. Knapp (1806–1879)
    4. Joseph Farnam (1779–1843) *m.* 1803 Miriam Hickcox (1781–1820)
    5. Seth Farnam (1733–1820) *m.* 1766 Dinah Gibbs (1741–1816)
    6. John Farnam (1702–   ) *m.* 1725 Hannah Crittenden
    7. Peter Farnam (–1703) *m.* 1686 Hannah Wilcoxon
    8. Henry Farnam (1636–1700) *m.* Johanna Ruttke (–1689)
    Service: Deacon and joiner in Windsor and Killingworth.
    Reference: American Ancestry, Vol. VII.

6612 FARRAR, Harry Allen   Recorded 1949
      Andover, R. F. D., Chester, Vermont

1. Rev. Harry Allen Farrar *m.* 1916 Agnes B. Field
2. George P. Farrar (1853–1933) *m.* 1884 Myrta D. Fuller (1866–   )
3. Olivar Farrar (1808–1884) *m.* 1841 Sarah A. Burt (1814–1884)
4. Oliver Farrar (1774–1855) *m.* 1807 Elizabeth Taylor, *d.* 1829
5. Nathaniel Farrar (1708/9–   ) *m.* 1773 Rachel Fletcher
6. Cornet Jacob Farrar (1669–1722) *m.* 1692 Susanna Rediate, *d.* 1737/8
7. Jacob Farrar (bapt. 1641–1675) *m.* 1668 Hannah Hayward (1647–   )
8. JACOB FARRAR (bapt. 1614–1677) *m.* 1640 Grace Deane

Service: In Dedham, Mass., 1653; in Lancaster, Mass., 1652.
Reference: Farrar Memoir, History of Lancaster, Mass.

5919 FARRELL, Laura Frances   Recorded 1930
      828 W. Main Street, Norristown, Pennsylvania

1. John Barry Farrell II (1820–1884) *m.* 1866 Carolyn Barton Davis (1832–1887)
2. William Barton (1794–1855) *m.* 1817 Rachel Supplee (1794–1879)
3. Jacob Supplee (1759–1825) *m.* 1782 Rebecca Ramsey (1760–1823)
4. Josiah Supplee (–1823) *m.*
5. Jacob Supplee (1727–   ) *m.* 1746 Margaret Yocum (1726–   )
6. Jacob Supplee (1690–1749) *m.* 1720 Elizabeth Enoch (1698–1748)
7. ANDREAS SUPPLEE (1634–1726) *m.* Gertrude

Service: Andreas Supplee was the First Sheriff, Germantown, Pa.
Reference: History of Germantown; Watson's Annals; Stapleton's "Memorials of the Huguenots."

5900 FARNAM, Lucy A.   Recorded 1930
      718 Riverside Avenue, Trenton, New Jersey

1. Lucy A. Farnam (1878–   ) unm.
2. George Farnam (1846–1925) *m.* 1873 Elizabeth Jane Lippincott (1852–   )
3. Daniel H. Farnam (1810–1887) *m.* 1838 Lucy M. Knapp (1806–1879)
4. Joseph Farnam (1779–1843) *m.* 1803 Miriam Hickcox (1781–1820)
5. Seth Farnam (1733–1820) *m.* 1766 Dinah Gibbs (1741–1816)
6. John Farnam (1702–   ) *m.* 1725 Hannah Crittenden
7. Peter Farnam (–1703) *m.* 1686 Hannah Wilcoxon
8. HENRY FARNAM (1636–1700) *m.* Johanna Ruttke (–1689)

Service: Deacon and joiner in Windsor and Killingworth.
Reference: American Ancestry, Vol. VII.

6541 FARWELL, Mrs. Frank Squire   Recorded 1947
      131 Killington Avenue, Rutland, Vermont

1. Alberta Olive Ford *m.* Frank Squire Farwell
2. Benjamin W. Ford (1847–1918) *m.* 1871 Lydia A. Merrill (1852–   )
3. Heman Ford (1815–1884) *m.* Phebe Farwell (1815–1886)
4. Gladden Farwell (1778–1865) *m.* 1802 Mehitable Parker (1783–1847)
5. Rev. Wm. Farwell, Jr. (1748–1823) *m.* 1771 Phebe Crosby (1749–1835)
6. William Farwell (1712–1801) *m.* 1744 Bethiah Eldredge (1726–1812)
7. Isaac Farwell (1678–1753) *m.* 1704/5 Elizabeth Hyde (1680–   )
8. Ensign Joseph Farwell (1640–1722) *m.* 1666 Hannah Learned (1649–   )
9. HENRY FARWELL *ca.* (1605–1670) *m.* 1629 Olive Welby (bapt. 1604–1691/2)

Service: One of the first settlers of Concord, Mass., later in Chelmsford, Mass. Took oath of Freeman 1638/9.
Reference: Genealogy of Farwell Family.

5837   FAXON, Mrs. Walter Collyer   Recorded 1929
          926 Asylum Avenue, Hartford, Connecticut
       1. Nellie A. White (1857–) *m.* 1877 Walter Collyer Faxon (–1920)
       2. Josiah White, Jr. (1831–1907) *m.* 1854 Hannah C. Pease (1830–1896)
       3. Josiah White (1800–1882) *m.* 1819 Hanna J. Cushing (1798–1863)
       4. Elija White (1778–1856) *m.* 1799 Lucy Pierce (1778–1855)
       5. Ebenezer White (1733–1817) *m.* Sarah Church (1736–1802)
       6. Ebenezer White (1702–1733) *m.* 1730 Ruth Atherton (1700–1785)
       7. Deacon Nathaniel White (1652–1742) *m.* 1678 Elizabeth Savage (1655–1742)
       8. Capt. Nathaniel White (1629–1711) *m.* Elizabeth ——— (1625–1690)
       9. ELDER JOHN WHITE (1595–1605)
       Service:
       Reference: Commemorative Record Biographies Hartford County, Conn., pages 128
              and 1010; Memorial of Elder John White, by Allyn S. Kellog, page 286;
              Encyclopedia of Biography Representative Citizens Conn., page 287.

6530   FENWICK, Carroll Robert, Jr.   Recorded 1946
          Barre, Vermont
       1. Carroll Robert Fenwick, Jr.
       2. Carroll Robert Fenwick, Sr. (1891–) *m.* 1918 Rena C. White (1894–)
       3. Robert Fenwick (1855–) *m.* 1876 Effie M. Boutwell (1868–)
       4. Ira C. Boutwell (1842/3–1925) *m.* 1863 Lavinia M. Bates (1842–1887)
       5. Asa Bates (1795–1876) *m.* 1830 Phebe Ainsworth
       6. Carver Bates (1760–1832) *m.* bef. 1795 Eunice
       7. John Bates (1731–) *m.* 1753 Elizabeth Taylor
       8. Comfort Bates (1691–) *m.* Desire
       9. Caleb Bates (1666–1747) *m.* 1691 Mary Lane (1671–1715)
      10. JOSEPH BATES *c.* (1630–1706) *m.* 1657/8 Esther Hilliard, *d.* 1709
       Service: Bricklayer, constable and sexton of parish.
       Reference: Vital Records of Vt., Abington, Mass., and History of Hingham, Mass.

6048   FIELD, Mrs. Chas. P.   Recorded 1933
          109 Jackson Street, Trenton, New York
       1. Jessie Bronson Howell (1879–) *m.* 1904 Chas. P. Field
       2. Lewis Ammor Howell (1838–1922) *m.* 1878 Jennie Angie Standiford Hill
          (1845–1929)
       3. Jos. Brittain Howell (1808–1893) *m.* Sarah P. Garrison (1815–1848)
       4. Ezekiel Howell *m.* Charity Brittain (1757–1847)
       5. Isaac Howell (1735–1814) *m.* Hannah Carter (1736–1804)
       6. Christopher Howell (1689–1779) *m.* Hannah ——— (1698–1789)
       7. Richard Howell, Jr. *m.* Sarah Schott
       8. Richard Howell, Sr (1629–) *m.* Eliz. Halsey
       9. EDWARD HOWELL (1584–1656) *m.* Frances ———
       Service: Member Col. Legislature; Gov. Council.
       Reference: Early Settlers of Ewing.

6382   FIELD, Hon. Benj. Reuben   Recorded 1942
          Cornwall, Vermont, R. F. D. Middlebury, Vermont
       1. Hon. Benjamin Reuben Field *m.* Mary E. James
       2. Arthur Jesse Field (1855–1926) *m.* 1877 Minnie Amanda Sampson (1857–)
       3. Benjamin Stearns Field (1820–1886) *m.* 1841 Emily Ellsworth (1818–1869)
       4. Major Orin Field (1792–1882) *m.* 1815 Maria Atwood (1797–1826)
       5. Elisha Field, Jr. (1763–1852) *m.* 1790 Ruth Kirkham (1770–1835)
       6. Ensign Elisha Field, Sr. (1717–1791) *m.* 1753 Betty Pratt (1726–1809)
       7. Deacon Joseph Field (1689–1754) *m.* 1716 Mary Smith (1697–1767)
       8. Captain Joseph Field (1658–1736) *m.* 1683 Joanna Wyatt (1663–1722)
       9. ZECHRIAH FIELD (1596–1666) *m.* 1641 Mary ——— (–1670)
       Service: French and Indian War; arr. Boston, 1629; in Dorchester; Hartford, Conn.,
              1636; Northampton, Mass., 1659; and Hatfield, Mass., 1663. One of those
              to go with Rev. Thomas Hooker to Connecticut.
       Reference: Field Gen., 2 vol., pg. 908 ("History of Cornwall, Vt.")

5925 FIELDS, Mrs. J. J. Recorded 1930
    Forest Hills, Long Island, New York
1. Victoria Wykes Kilsby *m.* J. J. Fields
2. John Wykes Kilsby (1804–1893) *m.* 1864 Mary Dingman (1826–1907)
3. Andrew Dingman (1803–1889) *m.* 1825 Caroline Eliza Sayre (1804–1885)
4. Daniel W. Dingman (1775–1862) *m.* 1795 Mary Westbrook (1774–1857)
5. Andrew Dingman (1752–1839) *m.* 1774 Jane Westbrook (1755–1838)
6. Andrew Dingman (1711–1801) *m.* 1741 Cornelia Kermer (1720–1765)
7. Jacob Dingman *m.* 1698 Eva Swartwout
8. ADAM DINGMAN (–1720) *m.* 1676 Aeltie Jacobs Flodder (–1720)
Service: Early settler of Greenbuch, 1663.
Reference: Munsell's Hist. of Albany, N. Y., vol. 4, pages 117 and 125.

5996 FIELD, Colonel James Thomas, Jr. Recorded 1931
    Bath Avenue, Boyd Co., Ashland, Kentucky
1. James Thomas Field (1890–) *m.* Townsella Jones (1893–)
2. Ben. Dickinson Jones (1849–1928) *m.* Townsella Randolph (1853–1921)
3. Chandler Jones *m.* Isabella Ann Wilson
4. Wyley Jones (–1822) *m.* 1816 Mary Dickinson (1787–)
5. Daniel Dickinson (1763–) *m.* 1780 Rebecca Grubb (–1851)
6. Samuel Grubb (1722–1762) *m.* 1746 Rebecca Hewes (1727–1766)
7. William Hewes *m.* 1713 Mary Withers
8. JOSEPH HEWES *m.* Rebecca ———
Service:
Reference: The Grubb Fam. of Penna.; Dickinson Family, Amherst, Mass.

6186 FINCH, George Griffin, Jr. Recorded 1938
    983 Crescent Avenue N. E., Atlanta, Georgia
1. George Griffin Finch, Jr. (1922–)
2. George Griffin Finch, Sr. (1902–) *m.* 1921 Martha Burt Miller (1903–1927)
3. Royall James Miller (1861–) *m.* 1889 Belle McLendon (1864–)
4. John Thomas Miller (1829–1891) *m.* 1855 Rebecca E. Royall (1836–1896)
5. Andrew Jackson Miller (1806–1856) *m.* 1828 Martha Burt Olive (1809–1880)
6. Thomas Harvey Miller (1779–1844) *m.* 1801 Mary Scott Jackson (1783–1855)
7. Andrew Miller (1734–1784) *m.* 1763 Elizabeth Warth Blount (1747–aft. 1782)
8. Charles Worth Blount (1721–1784) *m. ca.* 1742 Mary Clayton *ca.* (1723/25–)
9. John Blount (1669–1726) *m.* 1695 Elizabeth Davis (1679–1732/3)
10. JAMES BLOUNT *ca.* (1635–1686) *m.* 1664/5 Anne (Willis) Roscoe, Ipswich, Mass.—
    in Va.
Service: Member of the Assembly and Court; member of the Gov.'s Council; of the
    "Great Council;" Capt. of the Militia.
Reference: Recs. in Fulton and Thomas Cos., Ga.; D.A.R. Nat. No. 173327; Will of
    John Blount; Chowan Co., N. C.; "Grimes," N. C.; Wills and Inv., pgs.
    56–60, 34–35; "Ancestral Rec'ds & Portraits," from Arch of C. D. of A.,
    Vol. 2, pgs. 581–582; Col. Recs. of N. C. I, pgs. 259–273, 281–282, 299.

6047 FISCHELIS, Mrs. Robert P. Recorded 1933
    640 West State Street, Trenton, New Jersey
1. Juniata C. Deer (1896–) *m.* 1919 Robert P. Fischelis
2. Rufus L. Deer (1866–1931) *m.* 1890 Carrie E. Reid (1868–1931)
3. John Martin Deer (1837–1916) *m.* 1858 Ann Elya McLellan (1832–1886)
4. Wm. McLellan (1797–1878) *m.* 1826 Marg. Rebekah Wright (1809–1883)
5. Jos. McLellan, Jr. (1762–1844) *m.* 1788 Rebecca Stone (1766–1825)
6. Benj. Stone (1728–1806) *m.* 1758 Rebecca Littlefield (1733–1802)
7. James Littlefield *m.* 1723 Lydia ———
8. Lt. Josiah Littlefield (1670–1712) *m.* Lydia Masteis (1670–1707)
9. Capt. John Littlefield (1624–) *m.* 1650 Patience ———
10. Edmonds Littlefield (1592–1661) *m.* Annis Austin (1596–1678)
11. FRANCIS LITTLEFIELD (1565–1618) *m.* Mary ———
Service: Lieut., Commissioner, Capt.
Reference: His. Brunswick; Old Fam. of Salisbury and Amesbury.

6104 FISHER, Mrs. Margaret C.   Recorded 1936 (New York)
        Tarrytown, New York
    1. Margaret Cassell *m.* 1935 ——— Fisher
    2. Edward L. Cassell (1885–) *m.* 1903 Harriet Benedict (1881–)
    3. Charles H. Benedict (1858–) *m.* 1880 Margaret Hagerty (1856–1914)
    4. Enoch Benedict (1816–1861) *m.* 1849 Hester Van Lent (1830–1877)
    5. Hercules Van Lent (1795–1871) *m.* Hetty Morntross (1797–1835)
    6. John H. Van Lent (1767–1841) *m.* Letitia Morntross (1769–1835)
    7. Hercules Van Lent (1737–1816) *m.* 1760 Lavinia Van Tasse (1733–1826)
    8. Hendrick Van Lent (1712–1782) *m.* 1734 Elizabeth Storms
    9. Harck Van Lent (1681–1766) *m.* 1700 Cornelia Van Wart
    Service: Early settler.

6416 FISH, Galen Burch   Recorded 1943
        Reading, Vermont
    1. Galen Burch Fish *m.* Lina Maude Chamberlin
    2. Arnold Burch Fish (1833–1918) *m.* 1858 Amelia Maria Pearson (1836–1924)
    3. John Pearson (1813–1883) *m.* 1836 Olive Lucinda Walbridge (1814–1883)
    4. Capt. Elezer Walbridge (1779–1849) *m.* 1808 Olive Billings (1752–1832)
    5. Corp. Elezer Walbridge (1748–1815) *m.* 1768 Abigail Washburne (1779–)
    6. Eleazer Walbridge (1725–1748) *m.* 1747 Margaret Jewett
    7. Henry Walbridge (1696–1727) *m.* 1722 Mary Jewett (1700–)
    8. Henry Walbridge (–1729) *m.* 1688 Anna Amos (1666–1760)
    Service: Inhabitant of Dedham, Mass., Preston, Conn., and Norwich, Conn., in 1702.
    Reference: Twn. Rec. V. T., Randolph; Childs' Gazeteer, Orange Co.; Twn. Rec .
        Stamford, Conn.; Walbridge Gen.; Desc. of Henry Walbridge; Twn.
        Rec., Preston and Norwich, Conn.

6415 FISH, Verdi Mack Martin   Recorded 1943
        Flechville (Reading) Vermont, Windsor Co.
    1. Rev. Verdi Mack (Martin) Fish *m.* 1st G. H. Martin; 2nd, Burch Fish
    2. Alonzo Shaw Mack (1827–1900) *m.* 1850 Maria Sarah Felton (1827–1892)
    3. Benjamin Mack (1781–1862) *m.* 1813 Abijah Shaw (1789–1884)
    4. Benjamin Mack (1756–1831) *m.* 178? Nabby Lord
    5. Nehemiah Mack (1724–) *m.* 1749 Mrs. Eunice (Beckwith)
    6. John Mack (1682–1734) *m.* 1704 Love Bennett (1685–1732)
    7. John Mack (1653–1721) *m.* 1681 Sarah Bagley (1663–)
    Service: Land owner, Conn. (prob. Lyme).
    Reference: Town Rec. V. T., Woodstock; Hist. Woodstock, Dana; Mack Gen.—
        John Mack of Lynn, Vol. 2 (Conn.).

6357 FISHER, Mrs. John R.   Recorded 1941 (Vermont 27)
    1. Dorothy Canfield *m.* 1907 Dr. John Redwood Fisher
    2. James Hulme Canfield, Litt.D. (1847–) *m.* 1877 Flavia Camp, *d.* 1930
    3. Rev. Eli H. Canfield (1817–1898) *m.* 1846 Martha Crafts Hulme
    4. Nathaniel Canfield (1785–1853) *m.* Almira Hawley (1787–1874)
    5. Israel Canfield (1733–1827) *m.* 1758 Mary Sackett, *d.* 1817
    6. Azariah Canfield, *b.* 1695, *m.* 1719/20 Mary Baldwin
    7. Jeremiah Canfield (1662–*c.* 1739) *m.* Alice Hine
    8. Sergt. and Rep. Thomas Canfield, *d.* 1689, *m.* Phebe Crane
    Service: Freeman, 1669; M. Sergeant, Train Band, 1669; Rep. from Milford in Gen.
        Court of Conn., 1674, 1676.
    Reference: "General & Family Hist. of Vt.," Carleton; "New Bridgewater, Conn.,
        Orcutt; "History of Thomas Canfield and Geneology of N. J. Descend-
        ants;" "American Genealogy," Vol. 9; Conn. V. R., Milford.

6254 FLANDERS, Ralph Edward
Cherry Hill Street, Springfield, Vermont
1. Ralph Edward Flanders (1880–) *m.* 1911 Helen E. Hartness
2. Albert Wellington Flanders (1852–) *m.* 1879 Mary L. Gilfillan (1860–1938)
3. Hiram Flanders (1821–1879) *m.* 1845 Mary Alexander (1825–1919)
4. Philip Flanders (1781–1855) *m.* 1809 Lydia Hall (1784–1844)
5. Christopher Flanders (1749–1825) *m.* 1770 Joanna Smith (–1817)
6. Phillip Flanders (1712–1754) *m.* 1735 Hannah Morrill (1713–1793)
7. Phillip Flanders (1681–) *m.* 1710 Joanna Smith (1686–)
8. Steven Flanders (1646–1689) *m.* 1670 Abigail Carter (1652–1747)
9. STEVEN FLANDERS (–1684) *m.* Jane ——— (–1683)
Service:
Reference: The Flanders Fam. from Europe to America, by Edith Flanders Dunbar.

6513 FLING, Mrs. Maud Hammond   Recorded 1946
Lincoln, Nebraska
1. Maud Hammond *m.* ——— Fling
2. Charles Hammond (1859–1916) *m.* 1866 Ann Rosaltha Kirby (1845–1933)
3. Williard Hammond (1813–1864) *m.* Susan Norton Gower (1819–1887)
4. James Gower *m.* 1800 Susannah Norton (1771–)
5. Cornelius Norton (1746–) *m.* 1765 Lydia Claghorn (1744–)
6. Peter Norton (1718–1792) *m.* 1740 *ca.* Sarah Bassett, *ca.* (1720–1804)
7. Samuel Bassett (1693–1770) *m.* Martha Pease (1695–1774)
8. Nathan Bassett (1667–) *m.* 1690 *ca.* Mary Huckins (1673–1743)
9. John Huckins (–1678) *m.* 1670 Hope Chipman (1652–1678)
10. John Chipman (1614–1708) *m.* 1646 Hope Howland (1629–1684)
11. JOHN HOWLAND, *ca* (1592–1673) *m.* Elizabeth Tilley (–1687)
Service: Signed Mayflower Compact.

5968 FOOTE, Miss Rachel M.   Recorded 1930
5523 Tremont Road, Dallas, Texas
1. Miss Rachel Mulliner Foote
2. Willis O. Foote (1856–1929) *m.* 1887 Myra Mulliner (1859–1926)
3. David S. Foote (1821–1864) *m.* 1850 Hulda Merritt (1826–1904)
4. Russell Foote (1786–1842) *m.* 1809 Belinda Mead (–1832)
5. David Foote (1753–1851) *m.* 1777 Mary Scovel (–1838)
6. Samuel Foote (1723–1776) *m.* 1750 Mary Lyon (–1782)
7. Dr. Thomas Foote (1699–1776) *m.* Elizabeth Sutliffe (–1789)
8. John Foote (1670–1713) *m.* 1696 Mary
9. Robert Foote (1627–) *m.* 1659 Sarah Potter
10. NATHANIEL FOOTE (1593–1644) *m.* 1615 Elizabeth Deming (1595–1683)
Service: One of the first settlers of Wethersfield, Conn., 1636; Delegate to the General
Court, 1644.
Reference: Foote History & Genealogy, Vol. I, published by Marble City Press,
Rutland, Vt.

6683 FORD, Mrs. Victor   Recorded
3105 Washington Avenue, Baton Rouge Louisiana
1. Iria Jagers *m.* 1900 Victor Ford
2. James E. Jagers (1860–1889) *m.* 1879 Elizabeth Lewis (1860–1921)
3. James E. Jagers (1822–1881) *m.* 1857 Margaret R. Butter (1838–1897)
4. Decater Butter (–1898) *m.* 1836 Martha Wilkinson (1820–1907)
5. Roland Wilkinson (1797–) *m.* 1819 Margaret Cain (–1867)
6. Micajah Wilkinson (1776–) *m.* 1791 Mary Kennedy (1774–1836)
7. John Wilkinson III (1744–1786) *m.* 1765 Ann Douglas
8. William Wilkinson (1723–1796) *m.* 1743 Hulda Godwin, *b.* 1727
9. John Wilkinson Fr. (1690–1756) *m.* 1716 Rebecca Scott
10. John Wilkinson (1654–) *m.* 1689 Deborah Whipple (1670–1748)
11. LAWRENCE WILKINSON (–1692–RI) *m.* Susanna Smith
William Wilkinson, Esq., England, 1659.
Service: Commissioner, Deputy, 1667–73.
Reference: Wilkinson Family Memoirs, by Rev. Israel Wilkinson.

6445 FOSTER, Miss Belle   Recorded 1944
        979 Middle Turnpike West, Manchester, Connecticut
   1. Miss Belle Foster
   2. Truman Ransom Foster (1847–1930) *m.* 1876 Emma Annette Cushman
      (1852–1939)
   3. Monroe F. Cushman (1818–1909) *m.* 1850 Adeline Lull (1820–1898)
   4. Salmon Cushman (1778–   ) *m.* 1802 Cynthia Church (1781–1865)
   5. Isaac Cushman (1734–1813) *m.* 1758 Thankful Raymond (1736–1806)
   6. Capt. Nathaniel Cushman (1712–1793) *m.* 1733 Sarah Coomer (1713–1753)
   7. Isaac Cushman (1676–1727) *m.* 1700 Sarah (Warner) Gibbs (1682–1716)
   8. Isaac Cushman (1647–1739) *m.* 1675 *ca.* Rebeckah Rickard (1654–1727)
   9. Rev. Thomas Cushman (1608–1691) *m.* 1635/6 Mary Allerton (1609–1699)
   10. ROBERT CUSHMAN
   Service: Intermediary between the Plymouth Colony and English Government.
        Ruling Elder of Church, Plymouth (Rev. Thomas Cushman).
   Reference: Cushman Genealogy, Henry Cushman; Plympton V. R., Mass.

6266 FOX, Alice Virginia   Recorded 1939
        6936 Walnut Avenue, Merchantville, New Jersey
   1. Alice Virginia Fox
   2. William Albert Fox, *b.* 1900, *m.* 1921 Lelia Stout, *b.* 1896
   3. Llewellyn Stout (1808–1927) *m.* 1896 Lelia Gill Mather (1862–1931)
   4. John Atkinson Mather (1837–1921) *m.* 1861 Louisa Wallace Dawson (1842–1923)
   5. James Carr Dawson (1815–1872) *m.* 1838 Elizabeth Barber Cade (1818–1895)
   6. Isaac Cade (1780–1823) *m.* 1804 Judith Hendrickson (1784–1867).
   7. Andrew Henricsson (1748–1793) *m.* 1770 Judy Jones (1751–1793)
   8. Peter Henricsson (1718–1761) *m.* Catherine Lock (1729–1766)
   9. ANDRES HENRICSSON *m.* Beata
   Service: Swedish settler of Western New Jersey by 1698—"Original Settlers on the
        Delaware," by Benjamin Forrest.
   Reference: Same as Number 6265.

6267 FOX, John Mather   Recorded 1939
        6939 Walnut Avenue, Merchantville, New Jersey
   1. John Mather Fox
   2. William Albert Fox, *b.* 1900, *m.* 1921 Lelia Stout, *b.* 1896
   3. Llewellyn Stout (1808–1927) *m.* Lelia Gill Mather (1862–1931)
   4. John Atkinson Mather (1837–1921) *m.* 1861 Louisa Wallace Dawson (1842–1923)
   5. James Carr Dawson (1815–1872) *m.* 1838 Elizabeth Barber Cade (1818–1895)
   6. Isaac Cade (1780–1823) *m.* 1804 Judith Hendrickson (1784–1867)
   7. Andrew Henricsson (1748–1793) *m.* 1770 Judy Jones (1751–1793)
   8. Peter Hendricsson (1718–1761) *m.* Catherine Lock (1729–1766)
   9. ANDRES HENRICSSON *m.* Beata
   Service: Swedish settler of Western New Jersey by 1698—"Original Settlers on the
        Delaware," by Benjamin Forrest.
   Reference: Same as Number 6265.

6198 FOX, Lelia Mather Stout   Recorded 1938
        6936 Walnut Avenue, Merchantville, New Jersey
   1. Lelia Mather Stout Fox (1896–   ) *m.* William Albert Fox
   2. Llewellyn Stout (1858–1929) *m.* (2) 1896 Lelia Gill Mather (1862–1931)
   3. John Atkinson Mather (1837–1921) *m.* 1861 Louisa W. Dawson (1842–1923)
   4. James Carr Dawson (1815–1872) *m.* 1838 Elizabeth B. Cade (1818–1895)
   5. Isaac Cade (1780–1823) *m.* 1804 Judith A. Hendrickson (1784–1867)
   6. Andrew Hendrickson (1748–   ) *m.* 1770 Judy Jones (1751–1793)
   7. Peter Henricsson (1718–   ) *m.* bef. 1748 Catherine Lock(2) (1725– or 1729–   )
   8. ANDRES HENRICSSON *m.* bef. 1713 Beata
   Service: A Swedish settler of West New Jersey before 1700.
   Reference: Church Records, Ch. of Ascension, Phila.; St. Peter's, Clarksboro, N. J.;
        Trinity P. E., Swedesboro, N. J., pgs. 11, 203–204, 310, 343, 376. Spelling
        of the name Hendrickson, Henrickson, Henricsson, ?Henrixon all occur
        in the Swedish records of Trinity Ch. of Swedesboro; that is the same
        family is shown by dates and Christian names. Translated copy in the
        Penna. Hist. Soc.

6051 FREEMAN, Mrs. Gaylord A.   Recorded 1933 (Illinois)
       10502 S. Seeley Avenue, Chicago, Illinois
1. Frances L. Tollerton *m.* Gaylord A. Freeman
2. William J. Tollerton (1870–1926) *m.* 1906 Clara Horsely (1876–)
3. Louis L. Horsley (1846–1883) *m.* 1866 Florentine Gunn (1850–1926)
4. William C. Gunn (1814–1855) *m.* 1849 Elizabeth Moreland (1831–1917)
5. Andrew Moreland (1782–1859) *m.* 1811 Elizabeth Rucker (1796–1868)
6. John Rucker (1766–1812) *m.* 1788 Fancy Shelton (1767–1860)
7. Isaac Rucker (1740–1799) *m.* 1761 Mildred Plunkett (1754–1813)
8. Capt. John Rucker (–1742) *m.* Susanna (–1742)
9. PETER RUCKER (1670–1743) *m.* Elizabeth (1670–1752)
Service: A Captain in the Colonial Militia in Virginia, 1640.
Reference: Va. 1790 Census; Boddie & Allied Genealogies, by John T. Boddie & John
       B. Boddie, 1918; Scott's History of Orange Co., Va.; Hennings Statute,
       Vol. 11.

6542 FRENCH, Rev. Edward Goodhue   Recorded 1947
       Johnson, Vermont
1. Rev. Edward G. French *m.* Nellie Maria Osgood
2. Levi W. French (1834–1923) *m.* 1859 Julia A. Goodhue (1837–1924)
3. Hiram French (1808–1892) *m.* 1832 Sarah P. Williams (1811–1883)
4. Levi French (1777–1859) *m.* 1805 Matilda Osgood (1789–1863)
5. Jonas Osgood (1765–1812) *m.* Francena Pond
6. Benjamin Osgood (1726–1812) *m.* 1753 Mary Carter
7. Benjamin Osgood (1700–1789) *m.* Hannah Divoll
8. Hooker Osgood (1668–1748) *m.* Dorothy Woodman (1669–)
9. Stephen Osgood (1638–1690) *m.* 1663 Mary Hooker
10. JOHN OSGOOD (1595–1651) *m. ca.* 1627 Sarah Booth, *d.* 1667
Service: Representative to Gen. Court, admitted Freeman in Mass., 1639, one of first
       ten members of Church in Andover, Mass.
Reference: Osgood Genealogy.

6009 FRUEAUFF, Miss Margaret Hall   Recorded 1931
       510 Park Avenue, New York, New York
1. Frank Wheatcroft Frueauff *m.* Antoinnette Hall Perry
2. Will. Russel Perry *m.* 1887 Minnie B. Hall (1873–)
3. Chas. Levias Hall (1836–1907) *m.* 1862 Mary Mellissa Hill Nye (1838–1890)
4. Asahel Hill (1797–1877) *m.* 1816 Betsey Wood Ripley (1799–1856)
5. Hesikiah Ripley (1771–1846) *m.* 1795 Priscilla Wood (1776–1843)
6. Ephrain Wood 3rd (1744–1831) *m.* 1773 Sarah French
7. Ephrain Wood 2nd (1715–1781) *m.* 1742 Mary Lazell
8. Ephrain Wood, Sr. (1679–1744) *m.* Susanna Howland
9. Isaac Howland (1659–1723) *m.* 1677 Elizabeth Vaughan (1653–1727)
10. JOHN HOWLAND (1593–) *m.* Elizabeth Tilley
Service:
Reference: John Howland Family, Plymouth Rec.; Isaac Howland, Hist. of Middle-
       borough, Mass.

6496 FRYE, Mrs. Harley E.   Recorded 1945
       Lowell, Ohio
1. Maude Chapman *m.* Harley E. Frye
2. Hiram A. Chapman (1841–1889) *m.* 1868 Harriett L. Morris (1849–1919)
3. Wheeler Chapman (1808–1881) *m.* 1836 Louisa True (1812–1876)
4. John True (1781–1841) *m.* 1811 Jerusha Tollman (–1861)
5. Ephraim True (1756–1835) *m.* 1776 Mercy Martha Eaton (1749–)
6. John True (1703–) *m.* 1730 Mary Brown (1714–)
7. Deacon John True (1678–) *m.* 1702 Martha Merrill (1683–)
8. Capt. Henry True (1645–1735) *m.* 1668 Jane Bradbury (1645–1729)
9. CAPT. HENRY TRUE *m.* 1644 *ca.* Isreal Pike (–1699)
Service: Early Settler of Salem, Mass., 1644, and of Salisbury, Mass., 1657.

6649 FRANKLIN, Reginald M.   Recorded 1949
           4305 N. Pershing Drive, Arlington, Virginia
    1. Reginald M. Franklin, Jr., *m.* 1943 Lillie A. Henderson
    2. Reginald M. Franklin (1892–1942) *m.* 1920 Edith M. Christian (1899–)
    3. Leslie E. Franklin (1867–1932) *m.* 1891 Lyda C. Anderson (1866–)
    4. William L. Franklin (1830–1913) *m.* 1860 Caroline E. Morton (1843–1922)
    5. Alexander Morton, Jr. (1796–1876) *m.* 1820 Martha Anderson (1798–1881)
    6. Alexander Morton, Sr. (1759–1822) *m.* 1784 Ruth Strong (1762–1850)
    7. Elijah Strong (1733–1774/5) *m.* 1756 Ruth Loomis (1729–)
    8. Lt. Jebediah Strong (1700–1737) *m.* 1722 Elizabeth Webster (1701–)
    9. Capt. John Webster (1672–1735) *m.* bef. 1701 Elizabeth ———, *d.* bef. 1709
   10. Thomas Webster, *d.* 1686, *m.* 1663 or 66 Abigail Alexander, *d.* bef. 1690
   11. Gov. JOHN WEBSTER, *ca.* (1585/90–) *m.* 1609 Agnes Smith, *d.* 1667
Service: Orig. Prop., Hartford, Conn., 1636; Dep. Gen. Conn., 1637; Gov. Asst. and
           Magis., 1639–55; Commr. Unit. Colonies, 1654; Royal Gov. Conn., 1656–57.
Reference: Desc. Jno. Webster, Lin. Book. Daus. Col. War.

5993 FRETWELL, Charles Burlington   Recorded 1931
           235 Pine Street, Spartanburg, South Carolina
    1. Charles B. Fretwell (1887–) *m.* 1917 Julia Alexander
    2. James B. Fretwell (1853–1918) *m.* 1880 Katie Linthicum Pearson (1856–1893)
    3. Rev. Chas. Garland Linthicum (1822–1903) *m.* 1850 Ann Louise Pearre
           (1830–1901)
    4. Amasa Linthicum (1765–1823) *m.* 1799 Rachel Johnson (1782–)
    5. Hezekiah Linthicum (1723–1767) *m.* Sarah Bateman (1713–1778)
    6. Thomas Linthicum, Jr. (1674–1741) *m.* 1698 Deborah Wayman
    7. THOMAS LINTHICUM, Sr. (1640–1701) *m.* Jane ———
Service:
Reference: Maryland His. Magazine, Vol. XXV; Natl. No. of Soc. of Sons &
           Daughters of Pilgrims 5844.

6391 FULLER, Alexander Lemuel   Recorded 1942
           Rock Island, Quebec, Canada
    1. Alexander Lemuel Fuller *m.* Nelle Leon Ives
    2. Damon Fuller (1818–1875) *m.* 1886 Eliza Chalmers (1829–1906)
    3. Lemuel Fuller (1794–1848) *m.* 1817 Betsy Sherman (1794–)
    4. Lemuel Fuller (1754–1840) *m.* Eleanor Gibbs (–1803)
    5. Judah Fuller (1715–) *m.* 2-11-17— Abigail Wentworth (1723–)
    6. Serg. Samuel Fuller (1676–1716) *m.* 1700 Elizabeth Thacher (1672–)
    7. Lieut. Samuel Fuller (–1676) *m.* Mary ———
    8. CAPT. MATTHEW FULLER (1603–1678) *m.* Frances ———
Service: Juryman, Plymouth, 1642; Serg. Military Co.; Rep. from Barnstable in
           Colony Court; Lieut. of Militia at Barnstable; 1654 Lieut. under Miles
           Standish; King Philip's War Capt. of Plymouth forces.
Reference: Rec. of Bradfort V. T.; Granby, Quebeck; Rec. of Bradford V. T.; Gen. of
           descendants of Mathew Fuller, numbers 1, 4, 13.

6484 FULLER, Mrs. Edwin M.   Recorded 1945
           Kent, Ohio
    1. Gertrude Townsend Melcher *m.* Edwin M. Fuller
    2. Wm. Davis Melcher (1866–1938) *m.* 1893 Charlotte Townsend (1867–1945)
    3. Sylvester C. Melcher (1838–1908) *m.* 1853 Abby Ann Townsend (1842–1911)
    4. Charles Jarvis Townsend (1808–1849) *m.* 1829 Mary Cochran (1808–1891)
    5. Samuel Cochran (1774–1840) *m.* 1807 Mary Bailey (1787–1843)
    6. Daniel Bailey (1759–1826) *m.* 1783 Molly Standley (1762–1817)
    7. Jonathan Bailey (1719–) *m.* 1745 Susannah Trull (1720–)
    8. David Bailey (1687–1721) *m.* 1713 Experience Putnam (1698–1782)
    9. Isaac Bailey (1654–1740) *m.* 1683 Sarah Emery (–1694)
   10. JOHN EMERY (1598–1685) *m.* 1650 (2nd) Mary (Shatswell) Webster, widow.
Service: Selectman, Grand Juror, Member of Jury of Trials.

6137 GAERTNER, Mrs. Herman J.   Recorded 1937 (Georgia)
      De Kalb County, Georgia
1. Nell Hornbeck *m.* 1894 Herman J. Gaertner
2. Lorenzo D. Hornbeck (1845–1911) *m.* 1874 Quiteria Wood (1851–1929)
3. Solomon Hornbeck (1820–1899) *m.* 1841 Katherine Currence (–1852)
4. Joseph Hornbeck (1791–1865) *m.* 1819 Nancy (1797–1865)
5. Benjamin Hornbeck (1754–1829) *m.* 1782 Lydia Currence (–1840)
6. Jonathan Hornbeck (1730–) *m.* 1751 Sara Vernooy (1732–)
7. JOHANNES VERNOOY (1681–) *m.* 1724 Janneken Louw (1701–)
Service:
Reference:

6211 GAERTNER, Herman Julius, Jr.   Recorded 1938
      Atlanta, Georgia
1. Herman Julius Gaertner, Jr. (1903–) *m.* 1936 Anne Retsch
2. Herman Gaertner (1866–) *m.* 1894 Nellie Hornbeck (1875–)
3. Lorenzo Dow Hornbeck (1745–1911) *m.* 1874 Quinteria Wood (1851–1929)
4. Solomon Hornbeck (1820–1899) *m.* 1841 Katherine Aurreva (–1852)
5. Joseph Hornbeck (1791–1865) *m.* 1819 Nancy Light (1797–1865)
6. Benjamin Hornbeck (1754–1827) *m.* 1782 Lydia Aurreva (1763–1840)
7. Jonathan Hornbeck (1730–) *m.* 1751 Sara Vernooy (1732–)
8. Johannes Hornbeck (1685–) *m.* 1716 Ursulla Westbrook (1697–)
9. Warnaar Hornbeck (1645–) *m.* 1670 Anna De Hooges (1650–1688)
10. Anthony De Hooges (–1658) *m.* 1647 Eva Albertse Bradt
11. ALBERT ANDRIESE (–1672) *m.* Annetie Barentse Van Rotvers (–1662)
Service: Lieutenant Colonel.
Reference: Ye Olde Ulster, Vol. 6; History of Randolph Co., W. Va., Bosworth; Coll.
      of N. Y. Gen. Society, Vol. 7, by Vosburgh.

6322 GAERTNER, Nellie Jane   Recorded 1941
      1447 Peachtree Street N. E., Atlanta, Georgia
1. Nellie Jane Gaertner
2. Herman J. Gaertner (1866–) *m.* 1894 Nellie Hornbeck (1875–)
3. Lorenzo Dow Hornbeck (1845–1911) *m.* 1874 Quiteria Wood (1851–1929)
4. Solomon Hornbeck (1820–1899) *m.* 1841 Katherine Currence, *d.* 1852
5. Joseph Hornbeck (1791–1865) *m.* 1818 Nancy Light
6. Benjamin Hornbeck (1754–1827) *m.* 2nd 1782 Lydia Currence (1763–1845)
7. Lt. Col. Jonathan Hoornbeck (1730–1768) *m.* 1751 Sara Vernooy, bpt. 1732
8. Lt. Col. Johannes Hoornbeeck 1685–) *m.* 1716 Corseltjen Westbrook (1697–)
9. Warnaar van Hoornbeeck (1645–) *m.* 1670 Annetie de Hooges, *d.* 1688
10. ANTHONY DE HOOGES, *d.* 1658, *m.* 1647 Eva Albertse Bradt.
Service: Secretary of Colony of Rennsylaerwyck, N. Y.; Cecommiteerde; Voorlesser in
      the Church.
Reference: Hist. Randolph Co., W. Va.; N. Y. Gen. & Biog. Rec.; M. & B. Records Old
      Dutch Reformed Ch., Rochester, N. Y.; Hoes' Compilations; New Nether-
      land Register, V; Ecclesiastical Hist. State of N. Y.

6274 GALE, Lydia Hammond   Recorded 1939
      7 Dana Avenue, Albany, New York
1. Lydia Hammond Gale
2. William Bradford Gale (1851–1922) *m.* 1873 Georgeanna Cutler, *b.* 1850
3. Jacob Gale (1803–1868) *m.* 1837 Mary Lucinda Maben (1809–1887)
4. John Maben (1787–1843) *m.* 1807 Pamelia Bradford (1791–1865)
5. David Bradford (1748–1794) *m.* 1770 Rhoda Palmer
6. William Bradford (1718–1780) *m.* 3rd 1743 Mary Cleveland (1720–1765)
7. James Bradford (1689–1762) *m. c.* 1712 Edith
8. Thomas Bradford *c.* (1657–1731) *m. c.* Ann Raymond (1664, *d.* before 1705)
9. William Bradford (1624–1703/4 *m.* 1654 Alice Richards *c.* (1627–1671)
10. WILLIAM BRADFORD (1588–1657) *m.* 2nd 1623 Alice Carpenter (1590–1670)
Service: Governor Plymouth Colony; President Council of War; Commissioner of
      United Colonies.
Reference: Mayflower Descendants; Parkins "Old Homes of Norwich;" Cleveland
      Genealogy American Ancestry; Albany V. R.; New England Register.

6392 GALE, Royce Larebee   Recorded 1942
            Waterville, Quebec, Canada
      1. Royce Larebee Gale *m.* Doris Colquhoun
      2. Frank Gilbert Gale (1855–1927) *m.* 1885 Olivia Iola Larebee (1862–1938)
      3. George Gale (1824–1892) *m.* 1846 Dorothy Davis (1815–1892)
      4. Amos Curtis Gale (1793–1885) *m.* 1818 Rhoda Royce (1797–1877)
      5. Lieut. Elisha Gale (1743–1827) *m.* 1767 Mary Singletary (1747–1835)
      6. Capt. Isaac Gale (1708–1793) *m.* 1731 ab. Judith Sawyer
      7. Abraham Gale (1674–   ) *m.* 1699 Rachel Parkhurst
      8. Abraham Gale (1643–1718) *m.* 1673 Sarah Fiske (1656–1728)
      9. Richard Gale (1614–1678) *m.* 1640 Mary Castle (–1681)
      Service: Settled in Watertown, Mass., 1640; town officer; Selectman.
      Reference: Waterville, Que., Col. Wood (Vol. 5); Richard Gale Yoeman of Water-
            ville, Quebeck, Gale; Gale Fam. Rec. in Eng. and U. S., by Gale.

6200 GARMAN, Helen Sonnenschein   Recorded 1938
            1724 F Lincoln, Nebraska
      1. Helen Sonnenschein Garman (1905–   ) *m.* LeRoy C. Garman
      2. Louis Carl Sonnenschein (1882–   ) *m.* 1904 Nellie Blanche Mitchell (1879–   )
      3. James Milton Mitchell (1842–1929) *m.* 1869 Rosetta Blanchard (1850–1932)
      4. Mason Marshall Blanchard (1825–1894) *m.* 1845 Amanda Bliss (1826–1908)
      5. Zenas Gooding Bliss (1793–1868) *m.* 1815 Mabel Gillet (1798–1882)
      6. Zenas Bliss (1767–1853) *m.* Sarah Anton, *d.* bef. 1816
      7. Daniel Bliss (1723–   ) *m.* 1745 Eunice Newcomb
      8. Rev. John Bliss (1690–1741) *m.* 1709 Anna
      9. Samuel Bliss (1657–1729) *m.* 1681 Anna Elderkin
     10. Thomas Bliss (1615/18–1688) *m.* 1644 Elizabeth
      Service: Early settler of Saybrook.
      Reference: Bliss Family in America, 1881, pgs. 610–611–613–614–610–47–40–34–35,
            by John Homer Bliss Savage; Vol. 1, pgs. 201–202.

6563 GARNSEY, Winora Hanchett   Recorded 1947
            Fairbury, Nebraska
      1. Winora Hanchett *m.* 1898 Oscar N. Garnsey
      2. Philemon H. Hanchett (1844–1918) *m.* 1866 Lucinda E. Givens (1842–1928)
      3. Silas H. Hanchett (1815–1852) *m.* 1841 Jennie P. Smith (1821–1888)
      4. Ebenezer Hanchett (1785–1860) *m.* 1813 Mary Collins (1790–1883)
      5. Jonah Hanchett (1758–1860) *m.* 1782 Sarah Squares (1760–1860)
      6. Ebenezer Hanchett (1716–1785) *m.* Sarah
      7. John Hanchett (1679–1761) *m.* 1707 Lydia Hayward (1683–1777)
      8. John Hanchett (1649–1744) *m.* 1677 Ester Pritchett
      9. Thomas Hanchett *ca.* 1610–   *m.* 1648 Oliverance Langton, *d.* 1718
      Service: Lt. Col. in French and Indian War, 1708–9
      Reference: Salisbury Hist. Collections, Hist. of Pleasant Valley, N. Y.

6432 GALLUP, Walter Palmer, Jr.   Recorded 1943
            Woodstock, Vermont
      1. Walter Palmer Gallup
      2. Walter Palmer Gallup (1892–   ) *m.* 1918 Ruth Elna Robinson (1895–   )
      3. Joseph Adam Gallup (1849–1921) *m.* 1878 Sarah A. Shaw (1856–1933)
      4. Elisha Swan Gallup (1805–   ) *m.* Harriet Darling
      5. William Gallup (1767–1828) *m.* 1794 Lucy Avery
      6. William Gallup (1735–1803) *m.* 1761 Lucy Denison
      7. Capt. Joseph Gallup (1695–1760) *m.* 1720 Eunice Williams (1701–1772)
      8. Benadam Gallup (1655–1727) *m.* Esther Prentice (1660–1751)
      9. Capt. John Gallup *m.* 1643 Hannah Lake
     10. John Gallup (1590–1650) *m.* Christobel ———
      Service: Of Dorchester and Boston, Mass.; Capt. in Swamp Fight, 1675; Ind.
            interpreter; Commissioner.
      Reference: Hists. of Woodstock, Hartland, Windsor, Vt.; Gallup Gen.; Rec., Stoning-
            ton, Conn.

5853   GENTRY, Mrs. James Clay   Recorded 1929 (Georgia)
       3051 Piedmont Road, Atlanta, Georgia
       1. Leila Thornton *m.* 1882 Capt. James C. Gentry
       2. Capt. Jackson L. Thornton (1824–1894) *m.* 1861 Mary Lindsay Maﬁsﬁeld
          1840–)
       3. Capt. Anthony Thornton (1790–1855) *m.* 1816 Nancy Twyman (1793–1867)
       4. Samuel Twyman (1759–1823) *m.* 1790 Frances Rogers (1765–1824)
       5. Giles Rogers (1719–1789) *m.* 1757 Ann Iverson Lewis (1720–1789)
       6. John Rogers (1680–1768) *m.* 1716 Mary Byrd (1682–1763)
       7. GILES ROGERS (1643–1730) *m.* 1672 Rachel Eastham
       Service: Came in his own ship bringing laborers and material for building, 1670.
       Reference: Underwood's History, "Virginia Descendants of John Rogers the
          Martyr."

6000   GERTH, Mrs. R. E.   Recorded 1931
       New Britain Avenue, West Hartford, Connecticut
       1. Maude Chatﬁeld (1885–) *m.* R. E. Gerth
       2. Edwin Hubert Chatﬁeld (1863–1890) *m.* 1885 Annette McCartney (1861–)
       3. Edwin Chatﬁeld (1840–1917) *m.* 1862 Catherine Thompson (–1878)
       4. Joel Ray Chatﬁeld (1804–1894) *m.* Mary Tomlison (1810–)
       5. Joel Chatﬁeld (1757–1836) *m.* 1785 Ruth Stoddard (1760–1831)
       6. Elnathan Chatﬁeld (–1733) *m.* Hannah Northrop (1704–)
       7. Ebenezer Chatﬁeld (1703–) *m.* 1728 Abegail Prindle (1704–)
       8. John Chatﬁeld (1661–) *m.* 1684 Amah Hargar (1668–)
       9. GEORGE CHATFIELD (–1671) *m.* 1659 Isabella Nettleton
       Service: Colonel, Constable.
       Reference: Settlers of Conn., by Hinman; Early Puritan; Chatﬁeld Gen.; Past and
          Present, by Rev. Hollis A. Campbell.

6707   GILLIAM, Mrs. R. L.   Recorded 1951 (Arkansas)
       239 Oak Street, Hot Springs, Arkansas
       1. Mamie Bell *m.* 1898 Reuben Lynch Gilliam
       2. John Jeptha Bell (1851–1895) *m.* 1869 Mary Ashworth (1850–1903)
       3. Joseph Bell (1813–1879) *m.* 1849 Martha Binns Jones (1826–1878)
       4. Rev. John Cargill Jones (1795–1864) *m.* 1826 Mary Ann Walker (1805–1878)
       5. Capt. John Jones (1764–1840) *m.* 1787 Lucy Binns Cargill (1768–abt. 1810)
       6. Col. John Jones (1735–1793) *m.* 1758 Elizabeth Binns (1740–1803)
       7. Charles Binns (abt 1698–1749 Will) *m.* Judith Eldridge (–1760 Will)
       8. Thomas Eldridge, *circa* (1700–1748 Will) *m.* Judith Kennon (–1759 Will)
       9. RICHARD KENNON (–1696 Will) *m.* Elizabeth Worsham (–after 1696)
       Service: London Merchant and Burgess Henrica Co., Va.
       Reference: Cemetery stones and wills in Camden, Wilcox Co., Ala., and wills in
          Brunswick. Surry, Sussex and Henrico Co., Va.
       She and husband, Thomas Eldridge mentioned in her mother's will.—Elizabeth
          Worship Epes, 1678.

6126   GILMORE, Mrs. Albert D.   Recorded 1937 (New York)
       Yonkers, New York
       1. Maud M. Edmonds *m.* Albert D. Gilmore
       2. William Edmonds (1841–1881) *m.* 1866 Jeanette Estey (1847–1924)
       3. Warren D. Estey (1819–1898) *m.* 1846 Maryette Bliss (1829–1908)
       4. Calvin Bliss, Jr. (1794–1866) *m.* 1822 Mary A. Braisted (1792–1868)
       5. Calvin Bliss (1754–1849) *m.* 1777 Ruth Janes (1756–)
       6. Henry Bliss (1726–1761) *m.* 1749 Rubie Brewster (1733–1761)
       7. Oliver Brewster (1708–) *m.* 1732 Martha Wadsworth
       8. William Brewster (1683–) *m.* 1707 Abigail Wadsworth
       9. Dea. William Brewster *m.* 1672 Lydia Partridge (–1742)
      10. Love Brewster (–1650) *m.* 1634 Sarah Collier
      11. ELDER WILLIAM BREWSTER (1566–) *m.* Mary (1569–)
       Service: Mayﬂower Passenger; one of the founders of Plymouth Colony.
       Reference: Bliss Family Genealogy; Brewster Family Genealogy.

6305 GILMORE, Mrs. Thomas Warthen   Recorded 1940
1. Winifred Rawlings *m.* 1924 Thomas W. Gilmore
2. Benj. Tarbutton Rawlings (1855–1921) *m.* 1883 Mattie Belle Bangs (1859–1910)
3. Major Joseph Bangs (1813–1883) *m.* 1851 Martha Brown (1829–1898)
4. Joseph Bangs (1783–1839) *m.* 1809 Mary Warner (1786–1819)
5. Deacon Joseph Bangs (1757–1809) *m.* 1778 Desire Sears (1760–aft. 1804)
6. Allen Bangs (1733/4–1793) *m.* 1753/4 Rebecca Howes (1732–1793)
7. Joseph Howes, *d.* aft 1732, *m.* Elizabeth Paddock
8. Samuel Howes, *d.* aft. 1700, *m.* ———
9. Jeremiah Howes (1627–1706) *m.* 1650 Sarah Prence
10. Gov. Thomas Prence (1600–1673) *m.* 1624 Patience Brewster, *d.* 1634
11. ELDER WILLIAM BREWSTER (1563–1643) *m.* Mary
Service: Fourth Signer of Mayflower Compact; Ruling Elder; Chaplain of 1st Military
    Co. at Plymouth.
Reference: "Hist. and Genealogy of Bangs Family," by Dean Dudley; "Morton's
    Memorials," by Davis; Hunter's "First Colonists of New Eng."

6413 GILMORE, Thomas Warthen, Jr.   Recorded 1943
        Sandersville, Georgia
                (JUNIOR MEMBERSHIP)
1. Thomas Warthen Gilmore, Jr.
2. Thomas Warthen Gilmore (1892–) *m.* 1924 Sarah Winifred Rawlings (1900–)
3. Benj. Tarbutton Rawlings (1855–1921) *m.* 1883 Mattie Belle Bangs (1859–1910)
4. Maj. Joseph Bangs (1813–1883) *m.* 1851 Martha Brown (1829–1898)
5. Joseph Bangs (1783–1839) *m.* 1809 Mary Warner (1786–1819)
6. Deacon Joseph Bangs (1757–1809) *m.* 1778 Desire Sears (1760–1804)
7. Allen Bangs (Rev. Sold.) (1733–1793) *m.* 1754 Rebecca Howes (1732–1793)
8. Joseph Howes (ab. 1700–1733) *m.* 1725/30 Elizabeth Paddock
9. Samuel Howes (1650/55–1700) *m.* ———
10. Jeremiah Howes (1627–1706) *m.* 1650 Sarah Prence
11. Gov. Thomas Prence (1600–1673) *m.* 1624 Patience Brewster (–1634)
12. ELDER WILLIAM BREWSTER (1563–1643) *m.* Mary ———
Service: Fourth Signer Mayflower Compact.
Reference: Hist. Washington Co., Ga., Mitchell; Hist. Gen. Bangs Fam., Dean Dudley;
    Gen. Dict., Savage, Vol. 3; Gen. Reg. IV, Vol. ?

6207 GLADSTONE, Mrs. Robert Taylor   Recorded 1938
        1211 Tenth Street, Huntington, West Virginia
1. Elizabeth Boone (1883–) *m.* 1900 Robert Taylor Gladstone
2. John Wm. Boone (1840–1901) *m.* 1874 Rachel Price (1855–1923)
3. Abram R. Boone (1812–1888) *m.* 1839 Eliz. Ban Nort (1819–1895)
4. Jacob Van Nort (1777–1861) *m.* 1806 Edia Le Hew (1780–1857)
5. Spencer Le Hew (1735–1802) *m.* 1762 Ann Foley (1740–1815)
6. Peter Le Hew (1702–1780) *m.* 1733 Frances Allen (1706–1736)
7. PETER LE HEW (1677–1733) *m.* ———
Service:
Reference:

6765 GLOVER, Mrs. Hugh Wallace   Recorded 1952 (Michigan)
        124 Ashman Street, Midland, Michigan
1. Frances Reed *m.* 1918 Hugh W. Clover
2. Austin Breckway Reed (1857–1931) *m.* 1879 Pheebe Linnie Tainter (1859–1936)
3. William Asa Reed (1829–1888) *m.* 1856 Weltha Sholes (1839–1924)
4. Austin Brown Reed (1804–1852) *m.* 1824 Mary Richardson (1803–1891)
5. Ebenezer Reed (1774–1831) *m.* 1799 Eunice Brockway (1778–1859)
6. Rev. Thomas Brockway (1754/5–1807) *m.* 1772 Eunice Lathrop (1753–1823)
7. Elijah Lathrop (1720–1814) *m.* 1745/6 Susanna Lord (1724–1808)
8. Judge Richard Lord (1690–1776) *m.* 1720 Elizabeth Lynde (1694–1778)
9. Judge Nathaniel Lynde (1659–1729) *m.* 1688 Susanna Willoughby (1664–)
10. DEP. GOV. FRANCIS WILLOUGHBY (1613–1671) *m.* 1659 Margaret Locke (–1683)
Service: Asst. Gov., 1640.
Reference: Generation 1 to 9 accepted 1951 in Barons of Runnemede; Ellington Book
    of Marriages, 1820, pg. 13; Descendants of Thomas Lord, 1946, pgs. 199, 194;
    Ibid., pg. 194, Vol. 30; New England Genealogy, pg 77; Brockway Family,
    by Frances Brockway, pg. 47.

6566 GOODWIN-PERKINS, Charles Almon Recorded 1947
Piankeshaw Place, Hoopeston, Illinois
1. Charles A. Goodwin-Perkins
2. Emmett H. Goodwin-Perkins (1866–1946) *m.* 1889 Elizabeth Hunt (1865–1939)
3. Stephen Badger Goodwin (1821–1886) *m.* 1845 Mary P. Wyman (1825–1902)
4. John Goodwin (1794–1867) *m.* 1816 Elvira Gould (1794–1879)
5. Nathan Gould (1767–1844) *m.* 1792 Elizabeth Goodwin (1766–1848)
6. Gideon Gould (1741–1821) *m.* 1766 Hannah Heath (1746–1843)
7. Joseph Gould (1700–1752) *m.* 1726 Abigail Hoyt (1705–)
8. Samuel Gould (1668–1725/6) *m.* 1693 Sarah Rowell (1673/4–)
9. NATHAN GOULD (1614–1693) *m.* Elizabeth
Service: One of the Incorporators of Amesbury, 1690; Oath of Allegiance under
Maj. Robert Pike.
Reference: Morrill Kindred in America; Hist. of Newport, New Hampshire.

6133 GORDON, Miss Lenorah F. Recorded 1937, Georgia
Rome, Georgia
1. Miss Lenorah Frances Gordon
2. James B. Gordon (1873–) *m.* 1904 Jessie Jennings (1873–)
3. William T. Gordon (1825–1891) *m.* 1870 Ella Frances Nix (1853–1894)
4. William Gordon (1787–1852) *m.* Patsy (1791–1840)
5. Capt. Thomas Gordon (1758–1826) *m.* 1777 May Buffington (1760–1837)
6. Joseph Buffington (1737–1798) *m.* 1759 May Few (1741–1808)
7. Joseph Few (1708–1761) *m.* 1733 Mary Astor
8. Isaac Few (1664–1734) *m.* 1699 Hannah Stanfield (1683–)
9. FRANCIS STANFIELD (–1692) *m.* Grace (–1691)
Service: Member of the Pennsylvania Assembly, Chester Co., 1685.
Reference: Colonial Dames of the 17th Century.

6173 GOWDY, Nellie Peters Recorded 1938
1038 Farmington Avenue, West Hartford Connecticut
1. Nellie Peters Gowdy (1863–) *m.* 1884 Willis Gowdy
2. Samuel A. Peters (1827–) *m.* 1859 Sarah Hurlbut (1826–1876)
3. John T. Peters (1799–1867) *m.* 1824 Sophie Chester (1803–1884)
4. David Chester (1768–) *m.* 1797 Prudence Fox
5. Joseph Chester (1730–1803) *m.* 1757 Elizabeth Otis (1798–)
6. John Chester (abt. 1690–1771) *m.* 1716 Marcy Starr (1696–1774)
7. Thomas Starr (1668–1711/12) *m.* 1694 Mary Morgan (1670–1765)
8. Samuel Starr (–1687) *m.* 1664 Hannah Brewster (1643–)
9. Jonathan Brewster *m.* Lucretia
10. WILLIAM BREWSTER
Service: A member of the Plymouth Colony.
Reference: Peters of N. W., pgs. 173–175; Montville Rec., Barbour; History of Montville, Conn., pg. 240; Starr Gen., pgs. 14–16.

6728 GRAFF, Mrs. J. A. Recorded 1951, North Carolina
203 East Street, Waynesville, North Carolina
1. Lillian Pearl Campbell *m.* 1905 John A. Graf
2. John W. Campbell (1855–1879) *m.* 1876 Jennie Irene Coffin (1857–1920)
3. Wm. Carey Coffin, Sr. (1821–1893) *m.* 1854 Jane McCormick Osborne (1827–1892)
4. Nathan Emery Coffin (1778–1850) *m.* 1803 Eunice Coffin (2nd cou.) (1782–1854)
5. Eliphalet Coffin (1737–1812) *m.* 1760 Lydia Emery (4th cou.) (1741–1823)
6. John Coffin (1694–1764) *m.* 1726 (2nd wife) Hannah Cheney (Gr. Dau. of noted
Hannah Dustin
7. Stephen Coffin (1664–1725) *m.* 1685 Sarah Atkinson
8. Tristram Coffin, Jr. (1632–1706) *m.* 1652 Judith Somerby (1625–1705)
9. TRISTRAM COFFIN, SR. (1605–1681) *m.* 1630 Dionis Stevens, Dau. of Robert of
Brixton
Service:
Reference: Coffin Gatherings, pgs. 11, 140, 25; Coffin History of Newbury (67 and 7),
published by Appleton; Old Families of Salsbury and Amesbury, pg. 342,
and many wills.

6489   GRAHAM, Mrs. John Lincoln   Recorded 1945
            Lancaster, Ohio
   1. Fannie P. Musser *m.* John Lincoln Graham
   2. Andrew J. Musser (1838–1911) *m.* 1875 Elizabeth Courtright (1849–1914)
   3. Zephaniah Courtright (1819–1897) *m.* 1845 Sarah Williamson (1827–1893)
   4. Abraham Van Courtright (1787–1862) *m.* 1809 Elizabeth McFarland (1787–1870)
   5. Abraham Van Courtright (1748–1825) *m.* 1776/78 Effie Drake (1752–1825)
   6. Maj. Johannes Courtright (1714–1783) *m.* 1735 Margaret Demmerken
   7. Cornelius Hendrickson Courtright (1680–   ) *m.* 1701 Christina Rosecrans
   8. Hendrick J. Van Courtright *m.* 1672 Catherine Hansen
   9. JAN BASTIAENSEN KORTRIGHT (1618–   ) *m.* ———
   Service: Came to New Amsterdam in 1663 from Leesdam, Holland.

*4820   GRANT, Mrs. R. J.
            622 Humboldt Street, Denver, Colorado
   1. Leslie Hayden *m.* 1894 Robert J. Grant
   2. Julius Hayden (1838–1894) *m.* 1866 Estelle Matilda Whitaker (1841–1901)
   3. Sidney Hayden (1813–1892) *m.* 1836 Flora Miller (1814–1868)
   4. Luke Hayden (1773–1854) *m.* 1804 Ruth Humphrey
   5. Augustin Hayden (1740–1823) *m.* 1796 Cynthia Filer (–1835)
   6. Serg. Samuel Hayden (1707–   ) *m.* 1737 Abigail Heil
   7. Lt. Samuel Hayden (1677–1742) *m.* 1703 Ann Holcolm (1675–1756)
   8. Lt. Daniel Hay (1640–1714) *m.* Hannah Wilcoxon (1641–1712)
   9. WILLIAM HAYDEN (1600–1669) *m.* Margaret Wilcoxson
   Service: A founder of Windsor, Conn.
   Reference: First three generations—"Sketch and Gen. of Conn., Haydens."
   * Omitted from Vol. I

6102   GRAY, Harry L.   Recorded 1936, Georgia
            3219 Alta Vista, Chattanooga, Tennessee
   1. Harry L. Gray *m.* 1923 Nell Clemens
   2. Charles A. Gray (1861–   ) *m.* 1880 Cora Linthicum (1863–   )
   3. George W. Linthicum (1840–1912) *m.* 1860 Catherine T. Webb (1840–1911)
   4. Philip Linithicum (1802–1856) *m.* 1823 Eleanor McElfresh
   5. Frederick Linithicum (1774–1836) *m.* 1801 Rachel McElfresh
   6. Zachariah Linithicum (1735–1808) *m.* Sarah Prather (1738–1797)
   7. Thomas Linithicum (1701–   ) *m.* 1724 Sarah Burton
   8. Thomas Linithicum (1660–   ) *m.* 1698 Deborah Wayman
   9. THOMAS LINITHICUM, SR. (1638–1701) *m.* Jane
   Service: Early settler.
   Reference: Maryland Historical Society

6134   GRAY, Mrs. J. E.   Recorded 1937, West Virginia
            3218 Seminary Avenue, Richmond, Virginia
   1. Ada Gordon *m.* 1918 J. E. Gray
   2. Walter W. Gordon (1854–1924) *m.* 1884 Sarah Payne (1863–1934)
   3. John F. Gordon (1812–1905) *m.* 1841 Roberta Ward (1824–1907)
   4. John J. Gordon (1782–1856) *m.* 1799 Frances Fousher (1783–1856)
   5. Thomas Gordon (1749–1834) *m.* 1781 Mary Gordon (1756–1787)
   6. Rev. Alexander Gordon (1727–1782) *m.* 1748 Ann Rush (1729–1791)
   7. James Rush (1679–1727) *m.* 1710 Rachel Peart (1682–   )
   8. William Rush (1652–1685) *m.* 1675 Aurelia Rush (1656–1683)
   9. JOHN RUSH (1620–1699) *m.* 1648 Susannah Lucas (1627–1694)
   Service: Early settler and commanded Troop of Horse in Cromwell's Army.
   Reference: Rush Genealogy.

6040   GREEN, Mrs. Harry C.   Recorded 1933
            228 Cumberland Street, Brooklyn, New York
   1. Hortense Wagner (1870–   ) *m.* 1908 Dr. Harry Clifford Green
   2. Arnold H. Wagner (1831–1901) *m.* 1858 Cecilia A. Gerard (1839–1909)

3. Geo. Wash. Gerard (1813–1882) *m.* 1836 Amanda Lent Forbes (1817–1908)
4. Colin Van Gelder Forbes (1776–1865) *m.* 1798 Eliza Bullock
5. Wm. Gilbert Forbes (1751–1840) *m.* 1771 Catherine Van Gelder (1748–1834)
6. Gelyn Van Gelder (1720–1775) *m.* 1745 Maria Heyer (1723–   )
7. Johannes Van Gelder (1689–1776) *m.* 1713 Neeltje Oncklebog (1691–   )
8. Gerrit Oncklebog (1670–1733) *m.* 1690 Eliz Van Schaick (1671–   )
9. ADRIAN VAN SCHAICK (1642–1694) *m.* 1662 Rebecca Idens
Service: Asst. Alderman, Councilman, Capt.
Reference: N. Y. Gene. & Biog.; Valentines Common Council No. 1853.

6736 GREEN, Mrs. Lucius Felton   Recorded 1951, Louisiana
          609 N. Vienna Street, Ruston, Louisiana
1. Mary Olive Davis *m.* 1934
2. Robert W. Davis (1865–1934) *m.* Charlotte Long (1875–   )
3. Hughey Pierce Long, Sr. (1852–1937) *m.* 1875 Calendonia Tison (1860–1913)
4. John Murphy Long (1825–1901) *m.* 1845 Mary Elizabeth Wingate (1829–1901)
5. James Long (1790–1850) *m.* 1823 Mary Kirtman (1793–1850)
6. Hugh Long (1770–betw. 1794 and 1800) *m.* 1789 Margaret (–1794)
7. James Long (1750–1806) *m. c.* 1767/9 Catherine (–bef. 1790)
8. John Long (abt. 1692–1795) *m.* 1735 Ellenor Owens (1706–aft. 1750)
9. Capt. Richard Owens *m.* 1698 Racheal Beall (1678–   )
10. COL. NINIAN BEALL (1625–1717) *m.* 1668 Ruth Moore (–1704)
Service: High Sheriff of Calvert Co., Md., 1692, also Burgess.
Reference: Md. Archives B. & F; 170 Baltimore Wills, 1807; Beall Genealogy, by
          F. F. M. Beall, p. 49.

6718 GRIGGS, Wilkinson Garrett   Recorded 1951, Louisiana
          1923 Hardman Avenue, Apt. D, Macon, Georgia
1. Wilkinson Garrett Griggs *m.* 1941 Margaret Elizabeth Thompson
2. John E. Griggs (1879–   ) *m.* 1908 Sallie Lee Garrett (1886–   )
3. John Wilkinson Garrett (1851–1898) *m.* 1883 Annie Lee Gaines (1865–1925)
4. James Ralph Gaines (1828–1896) *m.* 1861 Sarah E. B. Jackson (1835–1903)
5. James Henry Gaines (1796–1848) *m.* 1822 Anne Banks Henderson (–1851)
6. Heirome Gaines, Jr. (abt. 1758–Will 1815) *m.* 1792 Anne T. Adams (–1815)
7. Heirome Gaines, Sr. (abt. 1730–aft. 1786) *m.* 1750 Margaret Taliaferro (–aft.
          1896)
8. Col. John Taliaferro, Jr. (1687–   ) *m.* 1708 Mary Catlett (abt. 1688–   )
9. Col. John Catlett *m.* Elizabeth Gaines (–1705)
10. Capt. Daniel Gaines (1632–1684) *m.* 1657 Margaret Bernard (–bef. 1670)
11. COL. WILLIAM BENARD died in Isle of Wight Co., Va. He was born in Wales.
Service: Col. in Colonial Militia of Va.
Reference: History of Albemarle Co., Va., by Edgar Wood; Hening's Statues, p. 432,
          shows Margaret Bernard dau. of Col. Wm. Bernard of Isle of Wight mar.
          Capt. Daniel Gaines.

6493 GRIMSLEY, Mrs. G. Reed   Recorded 1945
          East Fultonham, Ohio
1. Hazel Meloy *m.* G. Reed Grimsley
2. John Morton Meloy (1862–1944) *m.* 1889 Ella O. Nickels (1869–1937)
3. William H. Meloy (1836–1923) *m.* 1858 Emily Candace Tuttle (1836–1880)
4. Solomon Tuttle (1794–1848) *m.* 1820 Nancy Holdridge (1797–1881)
5. Enos Tuttle (1762–1843) *m.* 1783 Candace Hotchkiss (–1863)
6. Enos Tuttle *ca.* (1718–1802) *m.* 1741 2nd Martha Breckett (1721–1807)
7. Nathaniel Tuttle (1675–1728) *m.* Esther Blakesle (1680–1756)
8. Jonathan Tuttle (1637–   ) *m.* Rebecca Bell
9. WILLIAM TUTTLE (1609–1673) *m.* Elizabeth Waterman (1612–   )
Service: William Tuttle, born in England, 1609, came to America 1635 in the
          "planter." Settled in New Haven, Conn.

5875   GRISWOLD, Mrs. Julius E.   Recorded 1929, Connecticut
            17 S. Marshall Street, Hartford, Connecticut
   1. Alma L. Griswold *m.* 1878 Julius E. Griswold
   2. Albert C. Griswold (1827–1892) *m.* 1853 Caroline L. Goodrich (1831–1908)
   3. James Griswold (1784–1863) *m.* 1812 Lucy Robbins (1783–1855)
   4. Ozias Griswold (1735–1815) *m.* 1766 Anner Stanley (1742–1825)
   5. Major Josiah Griswold (1700–1769) *m.* 1727 Mabel Belden (1707–1789)
   6. Jacob Griswold (1660–1737) *m.* 1685 Mary Wright (1665–1735)
   7. Michael Griswold (–1684) *m.* Anna
   Service: A Freeman, 1659. Also an Assessor.
   Reference: Stile's History of Ancient Wethersfield, Vol. 11, pp. 395, 398, 404; Vol. I,
            p. 274.

6670   GROOM, Mrs. Avery Burr   Recorded 1950
            511 Holly Avenue, Winston-Salem, North Carolina
   1. Elizabeth Fearington *m.* 1916 Avery Burr Groom (1875–1947)
   2. Joseph Peyton Fearington (1862–1928) *m.* 1889 Mary Franklin Pass (1862–1940)
   3. James Cornelius Pass (1830–1882) *m.* 1861 Mary Eleanor Ireland (1838–1915)
   4. Samuel Ross Ireland (1802–1888) *m.* 1835 Elizabeth Newton (1810–1896)
   5. James Newton (1750–1809) *m.* 1805 Eleanor Bourdeaux (1781–1862)
   6. Daniel Bourdeaux (1745–1815) *m.* Elizabeth Miller (1756–1787)
   7. Anthony de Bourdeaux (1739–1767) *m.* Priscilla; all in will
   8. Antoine de Bourdeaux Grenoble France. D.–S.C. *m.* Marianna (1693–1770)
   9. Jacques de Bourdeaux (1699–) *m.* Madeleine Garilion (1685–)
   Service: One of first councilmen, Charlestown, S. C.
   Reference: Rec. in office of Sec., Columbia, S. C.; Back to 1682.

6607   GUMBART, Mrs. George C.   Recorded 1948
            622 Beverly Drive, Compton Park, Macomb, Illinois
   1. Aimee Christy *m.* 1919 George C. Gumbart
   2. William E. Christy (1879–1933) *m.* 1898 Viola Abbott (1878–)
   3. James L. Christy (1846–1923) *m.* 1872 Celinda J. Watson (1850–1927)
   4. Elisha W. Watson (1823–1874) *m.* 1849 Roxy (Fry(e) (1829–1856)
   5. Olney Fry(e) (1802–1894) *m.* 1824 Celinda J. Bennett (1802–1859)
   6. Jeffrey A. Frye *m.* 1789 Polly (Mary) Lyons
   7. Thomas Frye (1723–1805) *m. ca.* 1745 Penelope Rhodes
   8. Joseph Rhodes (1693–1738) *m.* Mary Arnold (1696–1745)
   9. John Rhodes *m.* 1685 Waite Waterman
   10. Resolved Waterman *m.* 1659 Mercy Williams (1640–1705)
   11. Roger Williams (1599–1683) *m.* Mary Barnard
   Service: Founded Colony of Rhode Island; Gov. of R. I. 1654–1656.
   Reference: Gen. Dict. of R. I.; Frye Gen.

5951   GUNN, Mrs. Edgar R.   Recorded 1930, Georgia
            504 Washington Street S. W., Atlanta, Georgia
   1. Willie Ross *m.* 1911 Edgar Ross Gunn
   2. Leonard G. Ross, Jr. (1857–1920) *m.* 1881 Loula K. Martin (1859–)
   3. Leonard G. Ross, Sr. (1813–1866) *m.* 1846 Martha G. Fain (1824–1863)
   4. Col. Theodorus Ross (1780–1844) *m.* 1806 Elizabeth Ganserrott (1784–1850)
   5. Leonard Ganserrott (1754–1834) *m.* 1777 Marie VanRensselaer (1760–1843)
   6. Col. Killian VanRensselaer (1717–1781) *m.* 1742 Ariantia Schuyler (1720–1763)
   7. Nicholas Schuyler (1691–1748) *m.* 1714 Elsie Wenchel (1689–)
   8. Philip Schuyler (1666–1724) *m.* 1687 Elizabeth De Meyer (–1712)
   9. Nicholas De Meyer *m.* 1664 Lydia Van Dych
   Service: First Mayor of New York City, 1676.
   Reference: History of New York, by Van Renssalaer, Vol. I, p. 214; Vol. II, pp. 209,
            445; History of Long Island.

5840 GUNTHER, Jack Disbrow Recorded 1929
Grand View-on-Hudson, Nyack, New York
1. Jack Disbrow Gunther, 1908–)
2. Charles O. Gunther (1879–) *m.* 1901 Beatrice Disbrow (1881–)
3. William Cook Disbrow (1851–) *m.* 1876 Elizabeth Bulger (1860–1919)
4. William Cook Disbrow (1816–1893) *m.* 1848 Margaret Wessello Dill (1828–1912)
5. Samuel Warne Disbrow (1778–1873) *m.* 1811 Sarah Cook (1792–1875)
6. Benjamin Disbrow (1754–1794) *m.* 1775 Deborah Robinson (1755–1785)
7. Griffin Disbrow (1712–1754) *m.* Hannah ———
8. Benjamin Disbrow (1672–1733) *m.* Mary Griffin (–1737)
9. HENRY DISBROW (–1699) *m.* Margaret
Service: Magistrate, Mamaroneck, 1673.
(Same as 5838.)
Reference: N. J. Archives, First Series Abstract of Wills, Vol. 3, p. 94; Register of
N. Netherland, 1626–1674, O'Callaghan, p. 99; History of Westchester
Co., N. Y., by Shonnard & Spooner, p. 176; Historical and Gen. Misc.
Stillwell, Vol. 4, p. 75.

5838 GUNTHER, Mrs. Charles Recorded 1929
Grandview-on-Hudson, Nyack, New York
1. Beatrice Disbrow (1881–) *m.* 1901 ——— Gunther
2. William Cook Disbrow (1851–) *m.* 1876 Elizabeth Bulger (1860–1919)
3. William Cook Disbrow (1816–1893) *m.* 1848 Margaret Wessello Dill (1828–1912)
4. Samuel Warne Disbrow (1778–1873) *m.* 1811 Sarah Cook (1792–1876)
5. Benjamin Disbrow (1754–1794) *m.* 1775 Deborah Robinson (1755–1785)
6. Griffith Disbrow (1712–1754) *m.* Hannah ———
7. Benjamin Disbrow (1672–1733) *m.* Mary Griffin (–1737)
8. HENRY DISBROW (–1699) *m.* Margaret ———
Service: Magistrate, Mamaroneck, 1673; erected "Disbrow House" in 1677.
Reference: History of St. Peter's Church in Perth Amboy, N. J., p. 246; Oyster Bay
Town Records, Vol. 1, p. 2; History of Westchester County, N. Y., Shonnard & Spooner, p. 176; Historical & Gen. Misc., Stillwell, Vol. 4, p. 75.

6487 HADDOX, Miss Rosalie Recorded 1945
Columbus, Ohio
1. Miss Rosalie Haddox
2. Louis Cass Haddox (1849–1912) *m.* 1876 Caroline B. Ireland (1852–1935)
3. Alexander Ireland (1824–1918) *m.* 1851 Mary Maxwell (1828–1907)
4. Thomas Ireland (1798–1869) *m.* 1820 Catherine Lowther (1798–1855)
5. Alexander Ireland (1772–1843) *m.* 1795 Elizabeth Ragan (1771–1855)
6. William Ireland *m.* 1770 ———
7. Col. William Ireland (–1775) *m.* Mary Hickman
8. Thomas Ireland *m.* Elizabeth (Wilson) Kent
9. Joseph Wilson (–1731 bef.) *m.* Frances Hillary (–1736)
10. Thomas Hillary (–1697) *m.* Eleanor Sprigg
11. THOMAS SPRIGG (1630–1704) *m.* 1668 bef. Eleanor Nuthall (1648–1694)
Service: One of the Justices of Calvert Co., Md., and of the Quorum in 1658, 1661,
1667, 1669, 1670, 1674. In 1661 was Presiding Justice and was commissioned
High Sheriff.

6231 HAGEN, Mrs. J. W. Recorded 1938
1101 Sixth Avenue, Huntington, West Virginia.
1. Emma Rece (1860–) *m.* 1879 James W. Hagen
2. Rev. John Calvin Rece (1818–1879) *m.* 1855 Margaret Ann George (1824–1906)
3. Rev. Wm. George (1790–1871) *m.* 1820 Nancy Byrd Eastham (1794–1879)
4. George Eastham (1755–1818) *m.* Susan Woodside
5. Col. Robert Eastham (1706–1790) *m.* Ann Lawson
6. GEORGE EASTHAM *m.* 1682 Ann Taylor
Service: First Fam of Am., Vol. 5, p. 588, by Virkus; Battle of Point Pleasant, by
Poffenbarger; Hist. of Kanawha Valley; P. C. Eastham Gen.; Hardesty's
Hist of Mason Co.

5828 HAINES, Mrs. Oscar M.   Recorded 1929, Georgia
        1401 Fairmont Street N. W., Washington, D. C.
    1. Winifred Strickland *m.* 1927 Oscar M. Haines
    2. A. H. Strickland (1855–1926) *m.* 1889 Sexta Eavenson (1868–   )
    3. Capt. J. W. Eavenson (1840–   ) *m.* 1865 Jane J. Oglesby (1846–   )
    4. George Eavenson (1817–1898) *m.* 1839 Sarah Thornton (1824–1863)
    5. George Eavenson, Sr. (1782–   ) *m.* Polly Hilly (1781–1803)
    6. Eli Eavenson (1764–   ) *m.* 1781 Rachel Seal (1760–   )
    7. George Eavenson (1726–1816) *m.* Mary Williams (–1828)
    8. Joseph Eavenson (1689–1771) *m.* 1717 Catherine George
    9. Thomas Eavenson (1653–   ) *m.* Hannah Woodward (1677–   )
   10. RALPH EAVENSON (1625–1655) *m.* 1650 Cicely Orton
    Service: Early settler.
    Reference: "Eavenson-Thornton" Genealogy, by Sexta E. Strickland.

5944 HALL, Mrs. Arthur   Recorded 1930, Colorado
        975 Vine Street, Denver, Colorado
    1. Lorena Eliz. Nash *m.* Arthur Hall
    2. Eugene Nash (1841–1894) *m.* 1871 Sarah C. Hurlbut (1849–   )
    3. David Nash, Jr. (1814–1846) *m.* 1839 Philena Nash (1817–1883)
    4. David Nash, Sr. (1784–1856) *m.* 1813 Ruth Colson
    5. Daniel Nash (1742–1823) *m.* 1773 Susannah Richards (–1820)
    6. Peter Nash (1710–1773) *m.* 1735 Mary Noyes (1718–1795)
    7. Ens. James Nash (1678–1725) *m.* Hannah
    8. Lt. Jacob Nash (1640–1718) *m.* 1666 Abigail Dyer (1647–   )
    9. LT. JAMES NASH *m.* Alice Burgess
    Service: A Freeman of Mass. Bay Colony, 1645.
    Reference: Vital Records, Abington, Mass.; History of Weymouth, Mass.

6641 HALL, Mrs. Howard B.   Recorded 1949
        469 East Main Street, Meriden, Connecticut
    1. Gertrude Wetmore *m.* 1905 Howard Baldwin Hall
    2. Seth A. Wetmore (1849–1928) *m.* 1871 Frances E. Wilcox (1849–1924)
    3. Asa Wilcox (1829–1896) *m.* 1845 Nancy Allen (1829–1910
    4. Hazard Wilcox (1787–1874) *m.* 1825 Polly Wright (1797–1887)
    5. Robert Wilcox *ca.* (1753–1808) *m.* 1777 Sarah Wilbur (1762–1854)
    6. Joseph Wilbur (1736–   ) *m.* 1758 Sarah Hall
    7. Benjamin Wilbur (1699–   ) *m.* 1724 Deborah Gifford
    8. Christopher Gifford (1658–1748) *m.* Deborah Perry (1665–1724)
    9. Edward Perry *m.* Mary Freeman
   10. Gov. EDMUND FREEMAN (1590–1682) *m.* Elizabeth ———, *d.* 1675
    Service: One of the first men to establish a town on the Cape, in the County of
        Barnstable and named Sandwich. Grant was from the King and was dated
        1637.
    Reference: Austin's Genealogy, Arnold's Genealogy, Wilbur's Genealogy.

6407 HAM, Mrs. Albert Henry   Recorded 1943
        North Hatley, Quebec, Canada
    1. Bertha Edith Bean *m.* Albert Henry Ham
    2. Edwin Bean (1840–1913) *m.* 1871 Elizabeth Jane Colt (1851–1917)
    3. Mark Bean (1805–1897) *m.* Praxina Gordon
    4. Moses Bean (1774–1826) *m.* 1802 Betsey Kezar (1776–1830)
    5. Simon Kezar (1753–1817) *m.* 1769 Mehitable Foster (1747–1801)
    6. Ebenezer Kezar (1730–1793) *m.* Hannah Moulton (1725–   )
    7. John Kezar (1678–   ) *m.* 1730 Judith Heath (–1756)
    8. John Kezar (1651–   ) *m.* 1677 Hannah Davis
    9. GEORGE KEZAR (ab. 1612–1690) *m.* Elsha ——— (–1659)
    Service: Grandjuryman in Salem, Mass., 1668, 1670, 1677, 1679, 1680, 1684, 1685;
        Surveyor, 1666–67; Constable, 1669.
    Reference: V. R. kept in Church (Universalist), Huntingville, Que., Canada; Forest
        & Clearings or Hist. of Stanstead Co., Que.; V. R., Haverfield, Mass.,
        Vol. 2; Hist. Haverhill, Mass., Salem, Mass., Perley.

5907 HAMILTON, Mary Burnham   Recorded 1930, Connecticut
139 Sigourney Street, Hartford, Connecticut

1. Mary A. Burnham (1864–) *m.* 1897 Morrison Clark Hamilton
2. Col. George S. Burnham (1828–1893) *m.* 1862 Mary Archer (1832–1893)
3. Thomas Archer III (1793–1880) *m.* 1820 Lucy Remington (1797–1867)
4. Thomas Archer II (1758–1797) *m.* 1778 Roxelanna Hancock
5. Thomas Archer I *m.* 1749 Azuba Olds (1727–)
6. Nathaniel Olds (1702–) *m.* 1722 Mercy S——? (1701–)
7. Robert Olds (1670–1728) *m.* 1689 Dorothy Granger (1665–)
8. LANCELOT GRANGER (1642–1689) *m.* 1664 Joanna Adams (1634–)

Service: Early settler in Connecticut.

6664 HAMMOND, Miss Marian   Recorded 1950
6018 Drexel Road, Philadelphia 31, Pennsylvania

1. Marian Hammond
2. Irving W. Hammond (1854–1924) *m.* 1888 Mary E. Rawson (1855–1896)
3. Dennis C. Rawson (1822–1922) *m.* 1846 Eliza Copeland (1823–1857)
4. Rev. Nath'l Rawson (1780–1845) *m.* 1811 Betsey Fitch (1786–1824)
5. Rev. Elijah Fitch (1746–1788) *m.* 1766 Hannah Fuller (1743–1824)
6. Capt. John Fitch (1705–1760) *m.* 1731 Alice Fitch (1713–)
7. Ebenezer Fitch (1689–1724) *m.* 1712 Bridget Brown
8. Maj. James Fitch (1649–1727) *m.* 1687 Mrs. Alice Bradford (1661–)
9. Maj. William Bradford (1624–) *m.* Alice Richards (1627–1671)
10. Gov. WILLIAM BRADFORD (1589–1657) *m.* (2) Mrs. Alice Carpenter Southworth (1590–1670)

Reference: Hammond, Rawson, Fitch Genealogies; Shepards' Gov. Bradford & Son Maj. William.

6116 HANCE, James Harold   Recorded 1936
College, Alaska
MEMBER-AT-LARGE

1. James Harold Hance
2. Henry Hance (1837–1927) *m.* 1870 Mary E. Emery (1848–1908)
3. James Moore Hance (1807–1894) *m.* 1835 Francis Stewart (1812–1838)
4. Samuel Stewart (1769–1847) *m.* Sarah Drake (1773–1855)
5. William Stewart (1738–1810) *m.* 1769 Frances Sherred (1737–1803)
6. Jacob Sherred *m.* 1731 Catherine Anderson (–1756)
7. Joshua Anderson (1667–1731) *m.* 1695 Engeltie Opdyck
8. Johannes Opdyck (1634–1729) *m.* Catherine
9. LAURIS JANSEN OPDYCK (1600–1659) *m.* Christian Stencila (–1660)

Service: Member of Committee of Safety, Gravesend, L. I., 1659.
Reference: Early Germans of New Jersey, Chambers.

6404 HANCOCK, Mrs. Howard B.   Recorded 1943
Bridgeton, New Jersey

1. Sarah Sheppard *m.* Howard B. Hancock
2. Daniel Maskell Sheppard (1821–1892) *m.* 1866 Frances A. Cook (1840–1917)
3. David Cook (1805–1891) *m.* 1831 Harriet Parvin (1807–1877)
4. David Cook *m.* 1795 Mary Bacon
5. Eldad Cook (–1786) *m.* Deborah Bowen (bef. 1729–)
6. Dan Bowen (1690–1729) *m.* Mary Walling
7. Rev. Samuel Bowen (1659–1729) *m.* 1684 Elizabeth (Wood) Wheaton
8. Obediah Bowen (1627–1710) *m.* 1649 Mary Clifton
9. RICHARD BOWEN (1600–1676) *m.* Anna —— (–1648)

Service: Emigrated to America 1640.
Reference: Local references and Bible records.

6761   HANSON, Miss Maybelle Marie   Recorded 1952, Illinois
           5601 N. Pulaski Road, Chicago, Illinois
       1. Miss Maybelle Marie Hanson
       2. Ellick Hanson (1865–1900) *m.* 1893 Sarah Broughton (1869–1939)
       3. Eli Broughton (1829–1896) *m.* 1855 Maria Barnes (1839–1890)
       4. Elisha Barnes (1791–1848) *m.* 1819 Eunice Tanner (1802–1863)
       5. William Tanner (1761–1835) *m.* 1785 Lois Johnson (1765–1831)
       6. James Tanner (1733–1775) *m.* 1753 Mary Wilcox
       7. Benjamin Tanner (1692–1767 *m.* Joanna Lewis, *d.* aft. 1733
       8. William Tanner (1660–   ) *m.* Mary Babcock (1668–   )
       9. Job Babcock (1646–1718) *m.* Jane Crandall (–1715)
      10. James Babcock (1612–1679) will *m.* Sarah (–1665)
      Service: One of Founders of Westerly, R. I.; made a Freeman 1648.
      Reference: Barnes Genealogy, by Rev. N. Barnes, pgs. 182–3; Wm. Tanner, Sr., His
           Descendants of South Kingston, R. I., p. 32, by Rev. George Clinton
           Tanner, pgs. 18, 6, 23, 32; Babcock Genealogy, by Stephen Babcock,
           pgs. 1–12.

6722   HARBAUGH, Mrs. L. C.   Recorded 1951, West Virginia
           607 Sixth Street, Ironton, Ohio
       1. Elizabeth Davidson *m.* 1902 L. O. Harbaugh
       2. Jonathan C. Davidson (1829–1888) *m.* 1851 Cynthia Anne Thomas (1836–1904)
       3. Joseph Wm. Davidson (1806–1872) *m.* 1826 Jane Bryson (1809–1889)
       4. William Davidson (1747–1811) *m.* 1784 Barbara McDowell (1768–1831)
       5. Lewis Davidson (1712–1793) *m.* 1746 Comfort Warrington (1716–1749)
       6. William Warrington (1690–1755) *m.* 1710 Comfort Tilney (1687–1721)
       7. William Tilney (1661–1695) *m. c.* 1686 Elizabeth Bagwell (1666–1720)
       8. Thomas Bagwell (1642–1690) *m.* 1665 Ann Stockley (1645–1695)
       9. Henry Bagwell (1590–1650) *m.* 1636 Alice (Hawkins) Stratton (1600–1664)
      Service: Clerk of Accomack Co. Court until 1640.
      Reference: Davidson Genealogy, by Elizabeth Davidson Marbaugh, pgs. 7, 11, 117,
           145, 129, 134; Court Orders, pgs. 118, 119, 112, 113, 112 to 115,
           Henry Bagwell, 99 to 105.

6403   HARDING, Mrs. George M.   Recorded 1943
           Philadelphia, Pennsylvania
       1. Elizabeth Fisher *m.* George H. Harding
       2. Wm. Lafayette Fisher (1829–1895) *m.* 1857 Elizabeth Carback (1833–1891)
       3. Elisha Carback (1806–1893) *m.* 1827 Sarah Gawthrope (1803–1893)
       4. William Carback (1763–1807) *m.* 1785 Jane Wright (1770–1835)
       5. Nathaniel Wright (1750–1783) *m.* 1769 Sophia Rutledge
       6. John Rutledge (–1773) *m.* 1742 Elizabeth Milhughes
       7. Thomas Rutledge (1702–   ) *m.* 1725 Mary Jenney
       8. Thomas Jenney (1667–1696) *m.* Rachel Pownall
      Service: Member of Provincial Council, 1684, 85, 86, 91; Judge of Quarter Sessions
           Common Pleas and Orphans Courts, Pa., 1685.
      Reference: (See lineage-book, DAC, V. 2, p. 28.) Penna. Magazine, Vol. 27, pgs.
           232–235.

6313   HARPER, John Lampkin   Recorded 1941, Georgia
           126 Twelfth Street N. E., Atlanta, Georgia
       1. John Lampkin Harper *m.* 1905 Leila Adella Bartlett
       2. Roderick C. B. Harper (1860–1921) *m.* 1881 Leila Ocea Doyal (1860–1931)
       3. John Lampkin Doyal (1836–1899) *m.* 1859 Mary Elizabeth Alexander (1841–1913)
       4. James Ludlow Alexander (1815–1863) *m.* 1837 Mary Ann Lake (1820–1879)
       5. Abraham Lake (1784–1866) *m.* 1810 Elizabeth Acree (1793–1861)
       6. Richard Lake, *d.* 1800, *m.* 1783 Elizabeth Lanning *d.* bef. 1834
       7. Abraham Lake, *d.* 1796, *m.* Elizabeth ———, *d.* aft. 1796
       8. Thomas Lake, Jr. *d.* 1787, *m.* Eleanor ———, *d.* 1777
       9. Thomas Lake, *d.* 1765, *m. c.* 1712 Jane ———, *d.* aft. 1755
      10. John Lake, Jr., *d.* 1729, *m.* Neeltje Claessen, *d.* aft. 1696
      11. John Lake, *d.* bef. 1696, *m.* Anne Spicer, *d.* aft. 1709
      Service: A Founder of Colony of Gravesend, L. I.; Owned extensive lands on Long
           Island.
      Reference: "The Lake Family in America," by Devereux Lake.

6314 HARPER, Mrs. John Lampkin   Recorded 1941, Georgia
          126 Twelfth Street N. E., Atlanta, Georgia
    1. Leila Adelle Bartlett *m.* 1905 John L. Harper
    2. William L. Bartlett (1858–1906) *m.* 1884 Julia Nancy M. Butler (1864–1925)
    3. William M. Butler (1835–1873) *m.* Martha Ann Fariss (1834–1910)
    4. John Fariss (1803–1898) *m.* Julia Ann Fitzpatrick, *d.* 1907
    5. Joseph Fitzpatrick (1788–1830) *m.* 1810 Nancy Hunter, *b.* 1796
    6. Benjamin Fitzpatrick (1746–1821) *m.* 2nd 1784 Sarah Jones (1761–1830)
    7. Joseph Fitzpatrick, *d.* 1777, *m.* Mary Perrin Woodson (1727–1833)
    8. Benjamin Woodson, *b.* 1692, *m.* Frances Napier (1695–1778)
    9. Robert Napier, *d.* 1724, *m.* 1689 Mary Perrin, *d.* aft. 1705
   10. Dr. Patrick Napier (1610–1669) *m.* 1655/6 Elizabeth Booth, *d.* aft. 1672
   11. Robert Booth, *d.* 1657, *m.* Frances, *b.* 1609
   Service: Burgess for York Co., Va., 1653–1654; Clerk of York Co., *c.* 1640–1652.
   Reference: "Southern Lineages," by A. Evans Wynn; Wm. & M. Quart., Vol. II, 13;
          "Hist. and Gen. of the Woodson Family;" "Annals of Henrice Parish
          & St. John's Ch.," by Burton.

5949 HARRIS, Mrs. Norris   Recorded 1930, Maryland
          2906 Almeda Blvd., Baltimore, Maryland
    1. Winifred Mitchell *m.* 1917 Norris Harris
    2. H. C. Welch Mitchell (1871–   ) *m.* 1894 E. Elizabeth Devilbiss (1870–1921)
    3. Hendrick G. Mitchell (1840–1872) *m.* 1869 Susan A. Owens (1846–1897)
    4. Gassaway Owens (1807–1887) *m.* 1833 Artridge E. Foggett (1810–1848)
    5. Nicholas Owens (1775–1830) *m.* 1801 Susan Shepherd (1775–1850)
    6. James Owens, Sr. (1748–1797) *m.* 1771 Elizabeth Owens (1757–   )
    7. James Owens (1718–1786) *m.* Elizabeth
    8. Joseph Owens *m.* (2) Jane
    9. Joseph Owens
   Service: A settler in Maryland, 1658.
   Reference: Land Records in Annapolis, Maryland Historical Society.

6581 HARRIS, Mrs. Robert Austin   Recorded 1948
          803 Belleforte Avenue, Oak Park, Illinois
    1. Margaret Louise Carlock *m.* 1930 Robert Austin Harris
    2. Judge L. J. Carlock (1868–1903) *m.* 1893 Lila M. Riddle (1872–   )
    3. Dr. Hamilton R. Riddle (1841–1926) *m.* 1868 Cordelia F. Constant (1849–1930)
    4. Rezin H. Constant (1809–1887) *m.* 1847 Mary L. Halbert (1817–1863)
    5. Dr. James Halbert, Jr. (1785–1858) *m.* 1816 Nancy Rennolds *ca.* (1794–1834)
    6. James Halbert, Sr. (bef. 1760–1819) *m.* 1783 Sarah Shaddock, *d.* aft. 1823
    7. James Shaddock, *d.* 1795, *m.* bef. 1739 Hannah Samuel
    8. James Samuel, *d.* 1759, *m.* Sarah Boulware
    9. James Boulware, *d.* bef. 1718, *m.* Margery Gray
   10. William Gray, *d.* aft. 1673, *m.* Elizabeth
   Service: Landed proprietor in Old Rappahannock Co., Va.
   Reference: Comp. Amer. Genealogy.

5881 HARRIS, Mrs. William T.   Recorded 1929, Texas
          Rockledge, Route 5, Dallas, Texas
    1. Susanna Wilcox *m.* 1900 William T. Harris
    2. Ephraim Wilcox (1843–1903) *m.* 1869 Mary L. Hopkins (1850–1926)
    3. William L. Hopkins (1804–1852) *m.* 1836 Susanna R. Warfield (1807–1888)
    4. Major David Hopkins (1753–1824) *m.* 1801 Isabella Ford (1781–   )
    5. Rev. Samuel Hopkins (1721–1803) *m.* 1748 Joanna Ingersol (1725–1793)
    6. Timothy Hopkins (1691–1748) *m.* 1719 Mary Judd (1701–1744)
    7. Lt. John Hopkins (1653–1732) *m.* 1683 Hannah Strong (1661–1730)
    8. Sliphur Hopkins (1634–   ) *m.* Dorcas Brown (–1697)
    9. John Hopkins (–1697) *m.* Jane Strong
   Service: Made a Freeman, 1635.
   Reference: First Settlers of New England, by Savage.

6549 HARRISON, Mrs. M. M.   Recorded 1947, Ohio
            Route 1, Peninsula, Ohio
      1. Kernon Bedford *m.* 1916 Marion M. Harrison
      2. Samuel W. Bedford (1861–1916) *m.* 1889 Winifred M. Bowden (1870–1941)
      3. Thompson W. Bedford, M.D. (1836–1909) *m.* 1860 Susan M. Houtchens
            (1842–1915)
      4. Asa K. L. Bedford (1811–1846) *m.* 1834 Davidella Ware (1812–1875)
      5. Archibald Bedford (aft. 1769–1826) *m.* 1796 Letty Clay (1782–)
      6. Henry Clay, M.D. (1736–1820) *m.* 1753 Rachel Povall (1739–1820)
      7. Henry Clay *ca.* (1712–1764) *m.* 1735 Lucy Green (1717–)
      8. Henry Clay (1672–1760) *m.* 1708/9 Mary Mitchell (1693–1777)
      9. Charles Clay (1638–1686) *m.* bef. 1672 Hannah Wilson
     10. CAPT. JOHN CLAYE *m.* Anne
      Service: Immigrated to Virginia in 1613. Received Patent Grants for 1200 acres
            near Chesterfield County, Va.
      Reference: Clay Family, Hotten's List of Emigrants to America, 1600–1700.

6230 HART, Mrs. John Freeman   Recorded 1938, Georgia
            Macon, Georgia
      1. Elsie Gibson (1885–) *m.* 1904 John Freeman Hart
      2. John Carter Gibson (1861–) *m.* 1884 Josephine Winkles (1863–1900)
      3. Levi Winkles (–1780) *m.* 1862 Lavinia Harrison Sawyer (1840–1874)
      4. John Swift Sawyer (1814–1895) *m.* 1836 Elmira Harrison (1810–1846)
      5. Asahel Harrison (1778–1823) *m.* 1808 Miriam Harris (1786–1868)
      6. Ebenezer Harris (1738–1823) *m.* 1779 Abigail Burnham (1756–1834)
      7. Gibson Harris (1694–1761) *m.* 1720 Phebe Denison (1696–)
      8. Samuel Harris (1666–1725) *m.* 1687 Elizabeth Gibson
      9. Gabriel Harris (–1684) *m.* 1653 Elizabeth Abbot (–1702)
     10. WALTER HARRIS (–1654) *m.* Mary (–1655)
      Service: Ensign.
      Reference: Walter Harris Gen.; Ebenezer Harris, pg. 17; Samuel Harris, pg. 12.

6293 HARTLEY, Mrs. James R.   Recorded 1940
      1. Miriam Elizabeth Barbash *m.* 1937 James R. Hartley
      2. Samuel Barbash, M.D. (*b.* 1884–) *m.* 1908 Anna May Tomlinson (1881–1931)
      3. George Tomlinson (1844–1921) *m.* 1874 Mary Augusta Bowen (1849–1928)
      4. James Tomlinson (1783–1831) *m.* 1805 Prudence Bowen (–1849)
      5. Moses Bowen (bef. 1727–aft. 1778) *m.* Eve Sheppard, *d.* 1765
      6. Samuel Bowen (1687–1727) *m.* Martha Dickson
      7. Samuel Bowen (1650–1729) *m.* Elizabeth Wood (Wheaton)
      8. Obidiah Bowen (1627–1710) *m.* Mary Clifton (1628–1697)
      9. RICHARD BOWEN (1580–1674) *m.* Ann
      Service: Came to America 1630; was Deputy to Court of Plymouth.
      Reference: Town Bk. of Rehoboth; Barbers Col. of Mass.; Plymouth Records, 1633–
            1689; Pope's Pioneers of Mass.; Genealogical Dic. of R. I.

6427 HARTLEY, Mernan Ruth   Recorded 1943
            Mattawan, New Jersey
                        (JUNIOR MEMBERSHIP)
      1. Mernan Ruth Hartley
      2. James Roy Hartley (1915–) *m.* 1937 Miriam Barbash (1914–)
      3. Dr. Samuel Barbash (1884–) *m.* 1908 Anna May Tomlinson (1881–1931)
      4. George Tomlinson (1844–1921) *m.* 1874 Mary Augusta Bowen (1849–1928)
      5. James T. Tomlinson (1813–1859) *m.* 1841 Margaret Adams (1814–1855)
      6. James Tomlinson (1783–1831) *m.* 1805 Prudence Bowen (1787–1849)
      7. Moses Bowen (1727–1778) *m.* Eva Sheppard (–1765)
      8. Samuel Bowen (1687–1727) *m.* Martha Dickson
      9. Samuel Bowen (1650–1729) *m.* 1684 Elizabeth Wood Wheaton
     10. OBEDIAH BOWEN (1580–1674) *m.* Ann ——— (–1647)
      Service: Deputy to the Court of Plymouth.
      Reference: Town Book Rehoboth; Tilton's Hist Rehoboth; Plymouth Colony Rec.
            1633/89; Gen. Dicy. of R. I.; Pope's Pioneers.

6067 HARVEY, Miss Althea   Recorded 1934, Connecticut
          4 Park Avenue, Windsor, Connecticut
     1. Althea Harvey
     2. Charles G. Harvey (1877–   ) *m.* 1902 Cora Alford (1876–   )
     3. Samuel Alford (1847–1915) *m.* 1875 Nellie Brockett (1824–1884)
     4. James E. Brockett (1824–1884) *m.* 1845 Sarah C. Case (1822–1898)
     5. George Brockett (1799–1835) *m.* 1823 Lydia Mose (1803–1858)
     6. Michael Mose (1766–1816) *m.* 1797 Anna Crane (1781–1858)
     7. Samuel Crane (1752–1818) *m.* 1776 Charity Higley (1756–1842)
     8. Josiah Higley (1725–   ) *m.* 1755 Hepzibah Cotton
     9. Josiah Higley (1701–1751) *m.* 1724 Dinah Gilette
    10. Captain John Higley (1649–1718) *m.* 1696 Sarah Strong (Bissell) (1664–   )
    11. Return Strong (1641–1726) *m.* 1663 Sarah Wareham (1642–1678)
    12. JOHN WAREHAM (REV.) (–1670) *m.* Jane Newberry
     Service: First minister at Windsor, Conn., and Dorchester, Mass.
     Reference: John Mose of Plymouth, p. 65; Crane Family, Vol. II; The Higleys and
          Their Ancestry, p. 660; Stiles History of Windsor.

5859 HARVEY, Mrs. Harold C.   Recorded 1929, New Jersey
          Bel Air River Road, Trenton, New Jersey
     1. Sarah Rice *m.* 1914 Harold C. Harvey
     2. James Kearney Rice (1849–1920) *m.* 1876 Julia Grant Neilson (1852–   )
     3. Theodore G. Neilson (1827–1920) *m.* 1847 Catherine B. Rutgers
     4. Anthony Rutgers (1799–1836) *m.* 1825 Sarah A. Johnson (1806–   )
     5. Robert C. Johnson (1766–1806) *m.* 1795 Catherine Bayard (1774–1806)
     6. Nicholas Bayard (1736–1798) *m.* 1762 Catherine Livingston (1743–   )
     7. Nicholas Bayard (1698–   ) *m.* 1729 Elizabeth Rynders (1704–1763)
     8. Samuel Bayard (1667–1745) *m.* 1696 Margaret Van Cortlandt
     9. NICHOLAS BAYARD (–1709) *m.* 1666 Judith Varlet
     Service: Member of Governor's Council, 1685, New York.
     Reference: Valentine's Manual, pp. 454–472.

6470 HARVEY, Mrs. James Rice   Recorded 1945
          69 West State Street, Athens, Ohio
     1. Elma Paul *m.* James Rice Harvey
     2. George B. Paul (1845–1931) *m.* 1868 Sophia McKee (1847–1893)
     3. Eldridge McKee (1810–1862) *m.* 1835 Rebecca Morris (1812–1870)
     4. Jabish McKee (1782–1857) *m.* Asenath Hollister (–1866)
     5. Nehemiah Hollister (1748–1820) *m.* 1776 Abigail House (–1787)
     6. Thomas Hollister (1707–1784) *m.* 1734 Abigail Talcott (1717–1812)
     7. Thomas Hollister (1672–1741) *m.* 1695 *ca.* Dorothy Hills (1677–1741)
     8. John Hollister (1644–1711) *m.* 1667 Sarah Goodrich (–1700)
     9. JOHN HOLLISTER (1612–1665) *m.* Joanna Treat (–1694)
     Service: He died in Weathersfield, Conn.
     Reference: Hollister Genealogy, pgs. 25, 26, 32, 41, 64–65; Gen. Ancient Weathers-
          field, 429.

6135 HATTER, Mrs. Leroy R.   Recorded 1937, Maryland
          Linthicum Heights, Maryland
     1. Edith A. Junkins *m.* LeRoy R. Hatter
     2. Joseph W. Junkins (1850–1913) *m.* 1877 Alice V. Davis (1850–1905)
     3. Oliver Junkins (1817–1878) *m.* 1842 Elizabeth Arnold (1820–1878)
     4. Daniel Junkins (1773–1848) *m.* 1800 Hannah Shaw (1778–1849)
     5. Daniel Junkins (1735–1800) *m.* 1756 Alice Chase
     6. Daniel Junkins (1705–1746) *m.* Eleanor
     7. Alexander Junkins (1685–1760) *m.* Hannah McIntire
     8. Alexander Junkins (1660–1740) *m.* Catherine
     9. ROBERT JUNKINS (1620–1696) *m.* Sara
     Service: Captured at the Battle of Dunbar, 1650.
     Reference: Vol. II, "York," by Col. Bangs; Sprague's History of Maine.

6578 HAWKINS, Mrs. Rex W.   Recorded 1948
         4211 N. Kedvale Avenue, Chicago, Illinois
    1. Ednah Doty *m.* 1921 Rex Willard Hawkins
    2. Russell B. Doty (1847–1919) *m.* 1876 Edna A. Webster (1859–1946)
    3. Charles P. Webster (1817–1877) *m.* 1844 Hannah C. Austin (1827–1899)
    4. Isaac Webster (1771–1858) *m. ca.* 1791 Lucy Whitcomb (1772–1848)
    5. Samuel Webster (1744/5–1817) *m.* 1770 Jerusha Smith
    6. Benajah Webster (1713–1751) *m.* 1739 Eunice Strong (1711–1750)
    7. George Webster (1670–1721) *m.* 1695 Sarah Bliss (1677–)
    8. Thomas Webster, *d.* 1686, *m.* 1663 Abigail Alexander, *d.* bef. 1690
    9. JOHN WEBSTER, *c.* (1585–1661) *m.* 1609 Agnes Smith, *d.* 1667
    Service: Gov. of Connecticut, an original proprietor of Hartford, Conn., a founder
         of Hadley, Mass.
    Reference: Webster Genealogy.

6233 HAY, Mrs. Parks Lee   Recorded 1938, Georgia
         Macon, Georgia
    1. Maude Saxon (1877–) *m.* D. D. Murphy 1st, Parks Lee Hay, 2nd
    2. Robt. B. Saxon (1845–1912) *m.* 1876 Tyree Martin (1855–1932)
    3. Rev. John Martin (1821–1917) *m.* 1838 Martha Truitt (1821–1908)
    4. Riley Truitt 2nd (1788–1821) *m.* 1813 Bonetta Smith (1788–1821)
    5. Purnall Truitt (1757–1841) *m.* 1783 Polly Godley (1758–1810)
    6. Riley Truitt 1st (–1770) *m.* 1754 Margaret
    7. James Truitt (–1775) *m.* ———
    8. James Truitt *m.* Mary Riley
    9. GEORGE TRUITT (–1670) *m.* 1652 Alice Watson
    Service:
    Reference: Va. Immigrants, old vol. 5; Pioneers and Cavaliers, page 405, by Nugunt.

6136 HAYS, Mrs. James E.   Recorded 1937, Georgia
         Montezuma, Georgia
    1. Louise Frederick *m.* 1902 James E. Hays
    2. Maj. James D. Frederick (1827–1899) *m.* 1877 Medora Ann Keene (1842–1916)
    3. Dr. Benjamin F. Keene (1809–1856) *m.* 1841 Ann Eliza Reese (1824–1843)
    4. Josiah Keene (1781–1847) *m.* 1803 Avis Swift (1781–1867)
    5. Silas Swift (1746–1837) *m.* 1772 Elizabeth Bumpus (1753–1828)
    6. Benjamin Swift *m.* 1741 Waitstill Bowerman (–1801)
    7. Benjamin Swift (1682–) *m.* 1703 Hannah Wing
    8. William Swift (1654–1701) *m.* Elizabeth Thompson (1654–)
    9. John Thompson (1616–1696) *m.* Mary Cooke (1625–1714)
   10. FRANCES COOKE (1583–1663) *m.* 1603 Hester Mahieu
    Service: One of the signers of the Mayflower Compact.
    Reference: Colonial Dames of America; Mayflower Society.

6648 HEADLEY, Mrs. H. C.   Recorded 1949
         909 Hillwood Avenue, Falls Church, Virginia
    1. Hazel Jane Clow *m.* 1919 Holland C. Headley
    2. David H. Clow (1862–1938) *m.* 1882 Louisianna Deary (1866–)
    3. William L. Clow (1819–1899) *m.* 1857 Sarah J. Conant (1834–1908)
    4. Lot Conant (1785–1864) *m.* 1814 Mary McClellan (1792–1879)
    5. James Conant (1755–1801) *m.* 1778 Dorothy Bullard
    6. Timothy Conant (1732–1777) *m.* 1754 Hannah Blackman (1782–)
    7. Lot Conant (1689–1774) *m.* 1710/11 Deborah Lovell, *d.* 1773
    8. Nathaniel Conant (1650–1732) *m.* Hannah Mansfield
    9. Lot Conant (1624–1674) *m.* 1649 Elizabeth Walton (1629–)
   10. ROGER CONANT (1593–1679) *m.* 1618 Sarah Horton
    Service: Came to Plymouth, Mass., 1623. Was first Governor of Massachusetts Bay
         Colony.
    Reference: Conant Family.

6647 HEADLEY, Holland Columbus   Recorded 1949
       909 Hillwood Avenue, Falls Church, Virginia
  1. Holland C. Headley *m.* 1919 Hazel Jane Clow
  2. Heister K. Headley (1851–1917) *m.* 1882 Evaline B. Hadsell (1851–1934)
  3. Thomas D. Headley (1816–1897) *m.* 1847 Laura Keeler (1820–1853)
  4. Asa Keeler (1780–1867) *m.* 1807 Betsey Newman (1785–1849)
  5. Paul Keeler, Jr. (1756–1812) *m.* 1775 Sarah B. Cornwell (1756–1826)
  6. Paul Keeler, *d.* 1787, *m.* ―――― Smith
  7. Joseph Keeler (1683–1757) *m.* Elizabeth Whitney (1684–1763)
  8. Samuel Keeler (1656–1713) *m.* 1682 Sarah Sention (Saint John) (1659–1714)
  9. RALPH KEELER (1613–1672) *m.* 1652 Sarah Whelpley
  Service: Came to Hartford, Conn., in 1637.
  Reference: Rockwell and Keeler Genealogy

5964 HEAFER, Buford   Recorded 1930, Texas
       1038 King's Highway, Dallas, Texas
  1. Buford Heafer
  2. James H. Heafer (1848–   ) *m.* 1870 Nancy M. Waring (1853–1925)
  3. Francis Waring (1826–1908) *m.* 1851 Harriet W. Williams (1827–1866)
  4. Thomas T. G. Waring (1782–1864) *m.* 1799 Nancy Mefford (1784–1862)
  5. Thomas T. G. Waring (1752–1818) *m.* 1780 Lydia Walton (1755–   )
  6. Frances Waring (1715–1776) *m.* 1740 Mary Holliday (1719–   )
  7. Basil Waring (1683–1733) *m.* 1709 Martha Greenfield (1687–1758)
  8. Basil Waring (1650–1688) *m.* 1682 Katherine Marsham (1653–   )
  9. CAPT. SAMSON WARING (1617–1668) *m.* 1648 Sarah Leigh
  Service: Member of the Assembly; one of the Parliamentary Commissioners to the
       Governor of Maryland, 1654.
  Reference: Garr Genealogy (1894); McKenzie's Colonial Families of U. S., Vol. I,
       pp. 553, 571; Records of Mason County, Ky.; Jones Genealogy; Old King
       William County, Virginia, Families.

6296 HEAFER, Henry Wallace   Recorded 1940
  1. Henry Wallace Heafer *m.* 1899 Mittie Purl
  2. James Henry Heafer, *b.* 1848, *m.* 1870 Nancy Maria Waring (1853–1925)
  3. Frances Waring (1826–1908) *m.* 1851 Harriet Ward Williams (1827–1866)
  4. William Williams (1787–1875) *m.* 1826 Maria Denny (1797–1883)
  5. Isaac Denny (1765–1813) *m.* 1793 Grace Tibb, *d.* 1859
  6. Samuel Denny (1731–1817) *m.* 1757 Elizabeth Henshaw (1737–1787)
  7. Daniel Henshaw (1701–1781) *m.* 1724 Elizabeth Bass (1703–1774)
  8. Joseph Bass *m.* Mary Belcher
  9. John Bass, *c.* (1632–1716) *m.* 1657 Ruth Alden, *d.* 1674
 10. JOHN ALDEN (1599–1687) *m.* Priscilla Mullins
  Service: Youngest signer of Mayflower Compact and last signer to die; a founder of
       Duxbury, Mass.; Acting Governor of Plymouth, 1664.
  Reference: Denny Genealogy, by C. C. Denny; Garr Genealogy, 1894; Records of
       Mason Co., Ky.; V. R., Mass.; Mayflower Descendants.

6500 HEATH, Mrs. Homer H.   Recorded 1945, Ohio
       Toledo, Ohio
  1. Pamelia Pray *m.* Homer Harvey Heath, M.D.
  2. John Lansing Pray (1839–1911) *m.* 1866 Pamelia C. Hall (1841–1881)
  3. John L. Pray (1812–1838) *m.* 1832 Lucina Cross (1814–1892)
  4. John Pray (1783–1872) *m.* 1809 Lucy Dunham (1789–1874)
  5. Rev. John Pray (1749–1830) *m.* 1775 Deborah Wade (1755–1832)
  6. Samuel Wade (1715–1788) *m.* 1741 Martha (Upham) Newell (1714–   )
  7. James Upham (1687–   ) *m.* 1709 Dorothy Wigglesworth (1687–   )
  8. REV. MICHAEL WIGGLESWORTH (1661–1705) *m.* Martha Mudge (1662–1690)
  Service: Preached selection sermon Ancient and Honorable Artillery Co. of Mass.,
       1686, and the Artillery sermon in 1696.

6482 HEAUME, Mrs. John S.   Recorded 1945, Ohio
        Springfield, Ohio
    1. Julia Douglas Moler *m.* John Salladay Heaume
    2. James Douglas Moler (1836–1891) *m.* 1881 (2nd) Millie Amelia Oakes (1854–1944)
    3. Alexander Oakes (1815–1863) *m.* 1838 Jane Amelia Beardsley (1820–1857)
    4. Eliphalet Beardsley (1787–1880) *m.* 1814 Hamutal Rolfe (1793–1844)
    5. Benjamin Beardsley (1754–1837) *m.* 1783 Amelia Stevens (1759–)
    6. Ens. Benjamin Beardsley (1727–1802) *m.* 1751 Thankful Beardsley (1729–1787)
    7. Josiah Beardsley *ca.* (1690–) *m.* 1712 Mary Whittemore (1694–)
    8. Joseph Beardsley (1634–1712) *m.* 1665 Abigail Phoebe Dayton
    9. WILLIAM BEARDSLEY (1605–1661) *m.* 1630 ca. Marie ———
    Service: Deputy to the General Court for 8 sessions and in 1639 was one of the
Founders of Stratford, Conn. Name on Memorial to the Founders in Stratford.

5965 HEDLEY, Mrs. Thomas Wilson   Recorded 1930, Pennsylvania
        1015 S. 47th Street, Philadelphia, Pennsylvania
    1. Evalena G. Fryer *m.* 1904 Thomas W. Hedley
    2. John P. Fryer (1835–1920) *m.* 1857 Mary E. Goheen (1838–1893)
    3. Stephen S. Goheen (–1897) *m.* 1828 Margaret Goheen (cousin) (1811–1896)
    4. James Goheen (1783–1831) *m.* Sarah Stackhouse (1785–)
    5. Steven Stackhouse (–1834) *m.* 1784 Amy Van Dyke (–1804)
    6. John Stackhouse *m.* Elizabeth Buckingham
    7. Thomas Stackhouse (1706–1781) *m.* Rachel
    8. JOHN STACKHOUSE (–1757) *m.* 1702 Elizabeth Pearson (1682–1743)
    Service: Early Settler; came with William Penn in the "Welcome," 1682, to Bucks
        County.
    Reference: Stackhouse Genealogy by Powel Stackhouse.

5935 HENDERSON, Lindsay P., Sr.   Recorded 1930, Georgia
        104 E. Hull Street, Savannah, Georgia
    1. Lindsay P. Henderson *m.* Stella I. Ihly
    2. Thomas H. Henderson (1869–) *m.* 1890 Annie I. Patterson (1870–)
    3. Charles B. Patterson (1845–1920) *m.* 1869 Annie M. Lester (1851–1896)
    4. Charles B. Patterson (1809–1858) *m.* 1838 Susannah B. Ash (1824–1907)
    5. George Adam Ash (1793–1861) *m.* 1814 Eliza Gorham (1794–1839)
    6. Joseph Gorham (1758–1805) *m.* 1784 Elizabeth Alley (1761–1849)
    7. Timothy Gorham (1723–) *m.* 1749 Sara Rowe Brown (1725–1778)
    8. Isaac Gorham (1689–1739) *m.* 1717 Hannah E. Miles (1697–)
    9. Jabez Gorham (1656–) *m.* Hannah Sturges (Gray) (widow)
    10. Capt. John Gorham (1621–1676) *m.* 1643 Desire Howland (–1683)
    11. JOHN HOWLAND (1592–1672) *m.* Elizabeth Tilley
    Service: Founder of Plymouth, Mass., 1620.
    Reference: New England Hist. & Geneal. Register, Vol. 2, p. 67; Vol. 50, p. 34; Vol. 52,
        p. 358.

5934 HENDERSON, Mrs. Lindsay P.   Recorded 1930, Georgia
        104 E. Hull Street, Savannah, Georgia.
    1. Stella Ihly *m.* Lindsay Patterson Henderson
    2. Montreville D. Ihly (1878–1905) *m.* 1899 Ella L. Garvin (1883–)
    3. James B. Garvin (1836–1908) *m.* 1863 Rosa R. Johnston (1848–)
    4. William C. Johnston (1823–1894) *m.* 1840 Rebecca Hamilton (1826–1882)
    5. Thomas Hamilton (1787–1844) *m.* Cherry Anderson (1803–1883)
    6. Thomas Hamilton (1744–1791) *m.* 1770 Rebecca Dixon (1752–1795)
    7. Thomas Dixon (1720–1769) *m.* 1745 Elizabeth H. Smith (1722–1756)
    8. Thomas Smith II (1669–1738) *m.* 1713 Mary Hyrne (1677–1777)
    9. THOMAS SMITH I (1648–1694) *m.* 1668 Barbara Atkins
    Service: Colonial Governor of the Province of North and South Carolina, 1690.
    Reference: South Carolina Genealogical Magazine, Vol. 28, pgs. 169–175; Vol. 30,
        pgs. 255–256.

5936 HENDERSON, Lindsay P., Jr. Recorded 1930, Georgia
      104 E. Hull Street, Savannah, Georgia
1. Lindsay P. Henderson, Jr.
2. Thomas H. Henderson (1869–) *m.* 1890 Annie I. Patterson (1870–)
3. Charles B. Patterson (1845–1920) *m.* 1869 Annie M. Lester (1851–1896)
4. Charles B. Patterson (1809–1858) *m.* 1838 Susannah B. Ash (1824–1907)
5. George Adam Ash (1793–1861) *m.* 1814 Eliza Gorham (1794–1839)
6. Joseph Gorham (1758–1805) *m.* 1784 Elizabeth Alley (1761–1849)
7. Timothy Gorham (1723–) *m.* 1749 Sara Rowe Brown (1725–1778)
8. Isaac Gorham (1689–1739) *m.* 1717 Hannah E. Miles (1697–)
9. Jabez Gorham (1656–) *m.* Hannah Sturges (Gray) (widow)
10. Capt. John Gorham (1621–1676) *m.* 1643 Desire Howland (–1683)
11. JOHN HOWLAND (1592–1672) *m.* Elizabeth Tilley
Service: Founder of Plymouth, Mass., 1620.
Reference: New England Hist. & Geneal. Register, Vol. 2, p. 67; Vol. 50, p. 34; Vol. 52,
      p. 358.

5937 HENDERSON, Robert Thomas Recorded 1930, Georgia
      104 E. Hull Street, Savannah, Georgia
1. Robert Thomas Henderson
2. Thomas H. Henderson (1869–) *m.* 1890 Annie I. Patterson (1870–)
3. Charles B. Patterson (1845–1920) *m.* 1869 Annie M. Lester (1851–1896)
4. Charles B. Patterson (1809–1858) *m.* 1838 Susannah B. Ash (1824–1907)
5. George Adam Ash (1793–1861) *m.* 1814 Eliza Gorham (1794–1839)
6. Joseph Gorham (1758–1805) *m.* 1784 Elizabeth Alley (1761–1849)
7. Timothy Gorham (1723–) *m.* 1749 Sara Rowe Brown (1725–1778)
8. Isaac Gorham (1689–1739) *m.* 1717 Hannah E. Miles (1697–)
9. Jabez Gorham (1656–) *m.* Hannah Sturges (Gray) (widow)
10. Capt. John Gorham (1621–1676) *m.* 1643 Desire Howland (–1683)
11. JOHN HOWLAND (1592–1672) *m.* Elizabeth Tilley
Service: Founder of Plymouth, Mass., 1620.
Reference: New England Hist. & Geneal. Register, Vol. 2, p. 67; Vol. 50, p. 34; Vol. 52,
      p. 358.

5938 HENDERSON, Mrs. Thomas H. Recorded 1930, Georgia
      104 E. Hull Street, Savannah, Georgia
1. Ivie Patterson *m.* Thomas Hunter Henderson
2. Thomas H. Henderson (1869–) *m.* 1890 Annie I. Patterson (1870–)
3. Charles B. Patterson (1845–1920) *m.* 1869 Annie M. Lester (1851–1896)
4. Charles B. Patterson (1809–1858) *m.* 1838 Susannah B. Ash (1824–1907)
5. George Adam Ash (1793–1861) *m.* 1814 Eliza Gorham (1794–1839)
6. Joseph Gorham (1758–1805) *m.* 1784 Elizabeth Alley (1761–1849)
7. Timothy Gorham (1723–) *m.* 1749 Sara Rowe Brown (1725–1778)
8. Isaac Gorham (1689–1739) *m.* 1717 Hannah E. Miles (1697–)
9. Jabez Gorham (1656–) *m.* Hannah Sturges (Gray) (widow)
10. Capt. John Gorham (1621–1676) *m.* 1643 Desire Howland (–1683)
11. JOHN HOWLAND (1592–1672) *m.* Elizabeth Tilley
Service: Founder of Plymouth, Mass., 1620.
Reference: New England Hist. & Geneal. Register, Vol. 2, p. 67; Vol. 50, p. 34; Vol. 52,
      p. 358.

5939 ADAMS, Inez Gray Recorded 1930, Georgia
      123 Ridgeside Road, Chattanooga, Tennessee
1. Inez Gray *m.* Walter S. Adams
2. Erdis Gray *m.* ——— Daniels
3. Charles A. Gray (1860–) *m.* 1890 Cora Linthicum (1864–)
4. George W. Linthicum (1837–1912) *m.* 1860 Catherine Linthicum (–1911)
5. Philip Linthicum (1805–) *m.* Eleanor McElfresh (1805–)
6. Frederick Linthicum (1774–)
7. Zacharia Linthicum (1735–) *m.* Sarah Prather
8. John Linthicum (1700–)
9. Thomas Linthicum, Jr. (1660–) *m.* 1698 Jane
10. THOMAS LINTHICUM, SR. (1630–1701) *m.* Deborah Wayman
Reference: All Hallows, Records, Md.

5998 HENDERSON, Mrs. W. L. Recorded 1931, Georgia
    504 Washington Street S. W., Atlanta, Georgia
    1. Virginia Woodson (1850–   ) *m.* 1871 W. L. Henderson
    2. John Prosser Woodson (1815–1885) *m.* 1848 Sarah Ann Hill (1830–1886)
    3. William Woodson (1784–1861) *m.* 1814 Mary Richardson (1796–1872)
    4. Capt. Chas. Woodson (1759–1830) *m.* 1780 Judith Leake (1762–1851)
    5. Drury Woodson (1722–1788) *m.* 1756 Lucy Christian (1735–   )
    6. William Woodson (1690–1785) *m.* 1712 Sarah Allen (1695–   )
    7. Benj. Woodson (1666–1723) *m.* 1688 Sarah Porter (1668–1722)
    8. Robert Woodson (1634–   ) *m.* 1656 Elizabeth Ferris (1636–   )
    9. Dr. John Woodson (1586–1644) *m.* Sarah Winston
    Service: Doctor.
    Reference: Footes "Sketches of Virginia;" Meads "Old Churches and Families;"
        Hist. Gen. of the "Woodsons and their Connections."

6354 HENSON, Mrs. Arthur Nellow Recorded 1941, West Virginia
    Hamlin, West Virginia
    1. Inez Varnum *m.* 1932 Dr. Arthur Nellow Henson
    2. George Griffith Varnum, *b.* 1880, *m.* 1902 Norma Burcham, *b.* 1880
    3. Leander Varnum, Jr. (1849–1922) *m.* 1879 Anna M. Griffith, *d.* 1929
    4. Leander Varnum (1821–1911) *m.* 1846 Angelina Cole Mason (1823–1898)
    5. Moses Varnum (1784–1865) *m.* 1812 Sophia Stacy (1792–1854)
    6. Moses Varnum (1759–1833) *m.* 1773 Sarah Dean (1762–1833)
    7. John Varnum (1721–1786) *m.* 1741 Ann Staul
    8. Col. Joseph Varnum (1672–1749) *m.* 1697 Ruth Jewett (or Jouett) (1681–1728)
    9. Samuel Varnum (1619–aft. 1702) *m.* 1645 Sara Langton, *d.* aft. 1698
    10. George Varnum *c.* (1580–1649) *m.* Hannah
    Service: Landed in Ipswich *c.* 1635.
    Reference: "The Varnums of Dracutt, Mass.," by J. M. Varnum.

6090 HERBERT, Mrs. Henry A. Recorded 1935, New York
    444 W. 20th Street, New York City
    1. Mary G. Waterman *m.* 1897 Henry A. Herbert
    2. William H. Waterman (1846–1917) *m.* 1869 Mary Waring (1844–1919)
    3. James D. Waring (1812–1897) *m.* 1841 Maria Dederick (1823–1900)
    4. James Waring (1781–1847) *m.* 1810 Betsey Whitney (1785–1855)
    5. Daniel Whitney (1754–1826) *m.* 1776 Hannah Selleck (1761–1849)
    6. Daniel Whitney (1723–   ) *m.* 1745 Hester Clason
    7. Richard Whitney (1687–   ) *m.* 1709 Hannah Darling (1689–1744)
    8. John Whitney (1644–1720) *m.* 1674 Elizabeth Smith
    9. Henry Whitney (1620–1673)
    Service: With four other townsmen he was selected to carry on the affairs of
        Huntington, L. I.
    Reference: Whitney Family, 3 volumes, by S. Whitley, Phoenix, 1876.

6041 HESS, Mrs. Frank F. Recorded 1933
    159 Fairview Avenue, Rutherford, New Jersey
    1. Julia Roberty (1876–   ) *m.* 1901 Frank F. Hess
    2. Jas. H. Roberts (1844–1919) *m.* 1869 Julia F. Waring (1849–   )
    3. Jas. Darling Waring (1812–1897) *m.* 1841 Maria Dederick (1823–1900)
    4. James Waring (1781–1847) *m.* 1810 Betsey Whitney (1785–1855)
    5. Daniel Whitney (1754–1826) *m.* 1776 Hannah Selleck (1761–1849)
    6. Daniel Whitney (1723–   ) *m.* 1745 Hester Clason
    7. Richard Whitney (1687–   ) *m.* 1709 Hannah Darling (1689–1744)
    8. John Whitney (1644–1720) *m.* 1674 Eliz. Smith
    9. Henry Whitney (1620–1673) *m.*
    10. Thomas Whitney (–1657) *m.* Mary Roach
    Service:
    Reference: Daniel Whitney, Vol. 1; James Darling Waring, Vol. 2; Whitney Family.

6744 HESS, Miss Jamie   Recorded 1952, Texas
5825½ Victor Street, Dallas, Texas
1. Miss Jamie Hess
2. Edward Daniel Hess (1862–1949) *m.* 1892 Theodocia Miller (1873–1941)
3. George Phillip Hess (1836–1897) *m.* 1861 Martha Emeline Lemon (1842–1918)
4. John Lemon (1804–1881) *m.* 1826 Elizabeth Johnson (1808–1857)
5. Henson Johnson (1763–1858) *m.* 1798 Jane Johnson (1772–1846)
6. John Johnson (1738–1827) *m.* Lydia Watkins (1759–)
7. Benjamin Watkins (–will 1753) *m.* Jane Watkins (–will 1778)
8. Thomas Watkins (1691–1760). Wife unknown
9. Henry Watkins *c.* (1660–1714) *m.* 1680 Mary ——
10. Henry Watkins (1637–will 1691)
11. HENRY WATKINS (1) born in Wales, 1600; was Burgess of Henrico Co., Va., 1623; listed as dead same year, 1923.
Service: Burgess of Henrico Co., Va., 1623; listed as dead same year.
Reference: Copies with applications of family records, wills and deeds filed with application. Virginia House of Burgesses, 1619–1658.

6551 HETT, Mrs. C. H.   Recorded 1947
Hotel Gettysburg, Gettysburg, Pennsylvania
1. Naomi Reifsnider *m.* Clarence Henry Hett
2. Samuel Reifsnider (1855–1921) *m.* 1880 Sarah A. Hollinger (1854–1926)
3. David Reifsnider, Jr. (1808–1858) *m.* 1840 Sarah Shoemaker (1820–1870)
4. David Reifsnider, Sr. (1775–1841) *m.* 1802 Elizabeth Maus (1783–1844)
5. George Maus (1748–1825) *m.* 1775 Anna M. von Kitzmiller (1757–1832)
6. Lt. John J. von Kitzmiller, *d.* 1731, *m.* Elizabeth Sell (1738–1811)
7. Peter Sell (1715–1776) *m.* 1735 Anna M., *d.* 1769
8. John Sell (1690–1764) *m.* ——
9. HENRY SELL, SR. (1663–1738) *m.* Margaret
Service: Came to America in 1683 and helped to settle Germantown, Penna.
Reference: General Studies of Some Provident Families.

6227 HEWITT, Mrs. Edmund   Recorded 1938
115 Martine Avenue North, Fanwood, New Jersey
1. Mary Frances Broome (1857–) *m.* 1908 Rev. Edmund Hewitt, D.D.
2. David Lawrence Broome (1825–1885) *m.* 1847 Elizabeth Gray (1830–1902)
3. Abel Broome (1780–1852) *m.* 1818 Rachel Clifford (1790–1874)
4. John Broome *m.* 1775 Sarah Isdall
5. Thomas Broome (1714–) *m.* 1740 Grace Stackhouse
6. Thomas Broome (1686–1739) *m.* 1712 Elizabeth Coley
7. John Broome (1656–1730) *m.* 1678 Winifred Margaret Jones
8. John Broome *m.* Margaret ——
9. SIR JOHN BROOME *m.* Maude ——
Service: Founder of Calverton, Calvert Co., Md.
Reference: N. J. Archives, Vol. 22, p. 34; Col. Families of U. S., Mackenzie, Vol. 1.

5888 HICKMAN, Mrs. W. H.   Recorded 1929, Illinois
426 W. Madison Street, Paris, Illinois
1. Elma Dick *m.* 1913 William Henry Hickman
2. Jesse N. Dick (1857–1917) *m.* 1879 Hariette E. Luse (1857–)
3. Jacob Luse (1818–1893) *m.* 1845 Charlotte Martin (1821–1891)
4. Ephraim Martin (1792–1868) *m.* 1814 Rhoda Sayers (1798–1881)
5. Josiah Sayers (1763–1857) *m.* Rhoda Drake (1764–1827)
6. William Sayers (1729–1796) *m.* 1762 Mary Fithian (1731–1809)
7. David Sayers (–1742) *m.* Ruth
8. David Sayers
9. Daniel Sayers (–1708)
10. THOMAS SAYERS (–1645)
Service: One of the founders of Southampton, L. I., in 1640.
Reference: McKenzie "Colonial Families of the U. S. of America" (1907).

6053 HILL, Annie Laura   Recorded 1933, Georgia
          1161 Peachtree Street N. E., Atlanta, Georgia
    1. Annie Laura Hill
    2. Ludowick J. Hill (1846–1930) *m.* 1871 Mary Henderson (1849–1918)
    3. Gen. Robert Henderson (1822–1891) *m.* 1846 Laura E. Wood (1829–1899)
    4. Cary Wood (1794–1857) *m.* 1823 Mary R. Billups (1803–1874)
    5. William Billups (1763–1817) *m.* 1787 Mary Richardson (1763–1803)
    6. Col. Richard Richardson (1741–1818) *m.* 1761 Dorcas Nelson (1741–1834)
    7. Gen. Richard Richardson (1704–1781) *m.* 1737 Mary Cantey (1715–1767)
    8. William Cantey (1680–1729) *m.* 1703 Arabella Oldys (1685–1722)
    9. GEORGE CANTEY (1650–1714) *m.* 1670 Martha
    Service: A member of the Commons for Berkely; Assessor and member of the Jury.
    Reference: The Hills of Wilkes Co., Ga., and Allied Families, by L. J. Hill; South
          Carolina Historical and Genealogical Magazine, Vol. XI, p. 203.

6080 HILL, Mrs. DeLos L.   Recorded 1935, Georgia
          91 Eleventh Street, Atlanta, Georgia
    1. Gussie Parkhurst *m.* 1899 DeLos Lemuel Hill
    2. William F. Parkhurst (1839–1901) *m.* 1868 Anna A. McDonald (1847–1918)
    3. Lebbeus G. Parkhurst (1816–) *m.* 1838 Adaline Knight (1817–1850)
    4. Alexander Parkhurst (1779–1819) *m.* 1806 Mary Thayer (1785–1822)
    5. Ichabod Thayer, Jr. (1745–1820) *m.* 1765 Mary Marsh (1745–)
    6. Ichabod Thayer (1721–1796) *m.* Hannah (Bigelow) (Cheney)
    7. Isaac Thayer (1695–) *m.* 1716 Meriam Thayer (cousin) (1699–)
    8. Josiah Thayer (–1728) *m.* 1690 Sarah Bass
    9. John Bass (1632–1716) *m.* 1657 Ruth Alden (1631–1674)
   10. SAMUEL BASS (1600–1694) *m.* Anne (1600–1693)
    Service: First Deacon of the Church at Braintree, Mass. In 1641 and for 12 years
          after, he represented the town in General Court.
    Reference: Vital Records, Mendon, Mass.; Braintree Records.

5876 HINCKLEY, Mrs. Arthur G.   Recorded 1929, Connecticut
          243 Laurel Street, Hartford, Connecticut
    1. Alice M. Hills *m.* 1899 Arthur Guy Hinckley
    2. Augustus C. Hills (1845–1893) *m.* 1868 Julia G. Litchfield (1847–1912)
    3. Elizur Hills (1815–1875) *m.* Mary D. Mumford (1816–1880)
    4. Joel Hills (1778–1851) *m.* 1802 Milly Keeney (1781–1824)
    5. Ebenezer Hills (1756–1826) *m.* 1775 Ruth Deming (1754–1802)
    6. Ebenezer Hills (1733–1773) *m.* Hepzibah Keeney (1733–1826)
    7. Ebenezer Hills (1708–1772) *m.* Hannah Arnold
    8. Ebenezer Hills (1676–1750) *m.* Abigail Benjamin
    9. William Hills (1646–1693) *m.* Sarah
   10. WILLIAM HILLS (1608–1683) *m.* 1632 Phillis Lyman (1611–1648)
    Service: Freeman, 1634, in Roxbury, Mass.
    Reference: Hills Genealogy, pp. 5, 7, 13, 26, 53, 102, 168, 222.

6188 HINES, Cecilia Lopez   Recorded 1938, Georgia
          1420 Peachtree Street N. E., Atlanta, Georgia
    1. Cecilia Lopez Hines (1882–) *m.* 1905 Dr. Joseph Howard Hines (1878–)
    2. Moses E. Lopez (1836–1907) *m.* 1862 Cecilia Cohen (1843–1909)
    3. David Lopez (1809–1884) *m.* (I) 1832 Catherine Dobbs Hinton (1814–1843)
    4. John Hinton (1787–1863) *m.* 1809 Sarah Rebecca Hammond (1791–1848)
    5. Joshua Hammond (1757–1853) *m. ca.* 1780/85 Sarah Hammond (cousins)
          (1755–1816)
    6. Charles Hammond (1716–1794) *m.* 1745 Elizabeth Steele (cousins) (1721–1798)
    7. John Hammond (1685–1764) *m. ca.* 1712 Katharine Dobyns (1688–1764)
    8. John Hammond (Eng. *ca.* 1640–) *m.* bef. 1685 name unknown, (–aft. 1685)
    Service: Came to America prior to 1685 and settled in what was later (1692) Richmond
          Co., Va.
    Reference: Fulton Co., Ga., and Charleston, S. C., D.A.R. Nat. No. 52486; Rec. of
          Richmond Co., Va., and Farnham Parish, Va.; Old Hammond Bible
          printed 1608, owned by Samuel Hammond, of Edgefield Dist., S. C.

6175 HINE, Ruth Eldridge Pember   Recorded 1938
      24 Pelham Road, West Hartford, Connecticut
1. Ruth Eldridge Pember Hine (1891–   ) *m.* 1917 Harold M. Hine
2. Edward E. Pember (1863–   ) *m.* 1889 Minna Kearny Cohn (1865–   )
3. Milo Warner Pember (1832–1905) *m.* 1857 Julia Laura Ripley (1833–1914)
4. David S. Pember (1795–1854) *m.* 1820 Martha Warner (1797–1891)
5. Capt. Nathaniel Warner (1769–1828) *m.* 1796 Martha Gifford (1774–1814)
6. Ziba Gifford (1735–   ) *m.* 1761 Edith Gifford (1742–   )
7. John Gifford, Jr. (1710–1742) *m.* 1739 Martha Arnold
8. John Gifford (1673–1747) *m.* 1708 Martha Gallop (bap. 1683–1775)
9. John Gallop (1646–   ) *m.* 1675 Elizabeth Harris (1654–   )
10. Capt. John Gallop, Jr. (–1675) *m.* 1643 Hannah Lake (–1655)
11. JOHN GALLOP, SR., *b.* in Eng. (1590–1650) *m.* in Eng. Christobel, *d.* 1655
Service: Came to Dorchester in the "Mary & John" in 1630. Admitted to church,
      Boston, Jan. 5, 1634. Made Freeman same year.
Reference: History of New London, Caulkins, pgs. 291, 154; Gifford Gen., pg. 88,
      No. 6, pg. 89, No. 10; Gallop Gen.

6129 HOBART, Leonora   Recorded 1937, New York
      156 Robert Lane, Yonkers, New York
1. Leonora Hobart
2. Heustin H. Hobart (1845–   ) *m.* 1872 Ellen J. Manchester (1849–1934)
3. George W. Manchester (1809–1877) *m.* Jane McClusky (1818–1900)
4. George Manchester (1778–1856) *m.* Jael Kent (1787–1864)
5. John Manchester II (1752–1794) *m.* Mary Whitman
6. Matthew Manchester (1720–1801) *m.* Freelove Gorton (1725–1796)
7. Stephen Manchester (1689–1733)
8. Job Manchester
9. THOMAS MANCHESTER (–1691) *m.* Margaret Wood
Service: Early settler in Conn., in 1639.
Reference: Family Records.

6459 HOBART, Mrs. Lowell Fletcher   Recorded 1945, Ohio
      2912 Vernon Place, Cincinnati 19, Ohio
1. Edith Irwin *m.* Lowell Fletcher Hobart
2. James Taylor Irwin (1833–1905) *m.* 1860 Anna Underwood Reed (1837–1885)
3. Capt. Edwin Reed (1814–1854) *m.* 1835 Jane Gibson
4. Daniel Reed (1791–1856) *m.* 1813 Rachel Cutter Loring (1794–1865)
5. John Mason Loring (1768–1839) *m.* 1793 Mehitable Mitchell (1772–1834)
6. Bezaleel Loring (1739–1822) *m.* Elizabeth Mason (1741–1810)
7. Judge Jonas Mason (1708–1801) *m.* Mary Chandler (1704–1787)
8. John Mason (1677–   ) *m.* 1699 *ca.* Elizabeth Spring (1675–   )
9. John Mason (1645–1730) *m.* Elizabeth Hammond (1656–1715)
10. Capt. Hugh Mason (1605–1698) *m.* 1632 Hester Wells (1611–1692)
Service: Early settler Watertown, Mass.; Representative General Court, 1644–45,
      1671–74–77; Selectman for 29 years, 1639–78; Lieut. in 1649; Capt., May 5,
      1652.
Reference: Hist. Newton, Mass.; Hist. Lexington, Mass., by Huston; N. E. H. & G.
      Reg., Vol. 154, p. 189; Vol. 78, p. 256.

6344 HOCKENHULL, Mrs. Alman Guynn   Recorded 1941, Georgia
      Roswell, Georgia
1. Lucille Eliza Wing *m.* 1938 Almann Guynn Hockenhull
2. George Washington Wing (1854–1918) *m.* 1874 Eliza Jane Weldon (1853–   )
3. Jehu Lowery Wing (1823–1877) *m.* 1848 Mary Rebecca Johnson (1829–1882)
4. John Wing (1780–1848) *m.* 2nd 1821 Mary Tullis (1807–1877)
5. Edward Wing (1745–1804) *m.* 1775 Mary Lowery *c.* (1755–1826)
6. John Wing (1701–aft. 1745) *m.* 1727 Mary Tucker (1708–aft. 1774)
7. John Wing (1661–1728) *m.* 1685 Mary Perry, *d.* 1714
8. Edward Perry (1630–1695) *m.* 1653 Mary Freeman, *d.* aft. 1704
9. EDMUND FREEMAN (1590–1682) *m.* Elizabeth
Service: Came to America, 1635; Freeman, 1637; Lt. Governor serving with Governor
      William Bradford, 1640–1646; Member, Council of War, 1642.
Reference: Same as Number 6343.

6177   HODGSON, Beatrice-Alice (Tomlinson)   Recorded 1938, Georgia
             40 Standish Avenue N. W., Atlanta, Georgia
       1. Beatrice-Alice Tomlinson Hodgson (1905-) *m.* 1926 Thomas Salkald Hodgson
          (1903-)
       2. Alfred Clark Tomlinson (1872-) *m.* 1895 Beatrice Alice Laning (1875-)
       3. William Laning (1864-1910) *m.* 1874 Alice Patterson Inskeep (1861-1929)
       4. Joseph Stockton Inskeep *ca.* (1806-1885) *m.* 1838 Rebecca Allen (-1885)
       5. Thomas Inskeep (1771-1813) *m.* 1796 Mary Stockton *ca.* (1776/77-)
       6. William Stockton (1750-1838) *m.* 1775 Mary Naglie
       7. William Stockton (1712-1781) *m.* 1736 Mary Bryan (1720-1806)
       8. Job Stockton (1676-1732) *m.* Ann Petty (-1746)
       9. Richard Stockton *ca.* (1630-1707) *m.* 1652 Abigail, *d.* aft. 1714
       Service: Lieutenant of Horse, Flushing, L. I., Troop; April 22, 1665, commissioned by
          Col. Richard Nicols.
       Reference: "The Stockton Family," by T. C. Stockton, San Diego, Cal., pgs. 33-57;
          Lineage Book of Nat. Soc. S.D.P., pg. 94; Penn. "Mag. of Hist. & Biog.,"
          April, 1914.

6667   HOFFMAN, Mrs. A. W.   Recorded 1950
             128 N. Dawson Avenue, Raleigh, North Carolina
       1. Francis Williams *m.* 1916 A. W. Hoffman
       2. Franklin Pearce Williams (1856-1921) *m.* 1882 Julia York (1859-1908)
       3. Richard W. York (1839-1893) *m.* 1857 Louisa F. Foushee (1838-1881)
       4. Amrose Foushee (1812-) *m.* 1834 Rebecca Farrar (1816-1841)
       5. Thomas Farrar (1781-1858) *m.* 1814 Polly Robards (-1851)
       6. Peter Farrar (1743-1802) *m.* 1766 Trephenah LaForce
       7. John Farrar (1691-1769) *m.* Temperance Batte
       8. Thomas Farrar (1665-1742) *m.* 1686 Katherine Perriu
       9. Thomas F. Farrar (1620-1678)
      10. WILLIAM FARRAR (1593-1637) *m.* Cicely Jordan
       Service: Member Council of Virginia, 1623-1633.
       Reference: Virginia Magazine, VIII: 427; Farrar Family, Va. Mag. of History, Vol. VII.

6479   HOLLOWAY, Mrs. W. S. M.   Recorded 1945, Ohio
             Columbus, Ohio
       1. Esther Cadwalader *m.* Warren Scott McLane Holloway
       2. Dallas Isaac Cadwalader (1872-1932) *m.* 1900 Emma Jane Clark
       3. Isaac Cadwalader (1831-1872) *m.* 1853 Esther Allmon (1834-1878)
       4. Mifflin Cadwalader (1803-1886) *m.* 1829 Ellen Sharpless (1806-1836)
       5. John Cadwalader (1774-1815) *m.* 1798 Ann Cattell (1778-1811)
       6. Jonas Cattell (1740-1828) *m.* 1775 Elizabeth Roberts (1747-1837)
       7. Enoch Roberts (1717-1748) *m.* 1744 Rachel Coles (1716-)
       8. John Roberts (-1747) *m.* 1712 Mary Elhinton (-1759)
       9. JOHN ROBERTS (-1695) *m.* Sarah ―――――
       Service: Signer of the "Concessions and Agreements of the Proprietors, Freeholders
          and Inhabitants of West Jersey." He died in Burlington, N. J.

6538   HOLMES, Homer Benjamin Durwood   Recorded 1946
             641 Pine Street, Abilene, Texas
       1. Homer Benjamin Durwood Holmes
       2. Benjamin G. Holmes (1888-) *m.* 1912 Lucille B. Edwards (1893-)
       3. James W. Holmes (1841-1905) *m.* 1866 Sarah R. Ogilvie (1846-1930)
       4. John Holmes (1820-1863) *m.* 1840 Eliza T. Ogilvie (1825-1863)
       5. Robert Holmes, Jr. (1775-1820) *m.* 1806 Sarah Pope (1787-1851)
       6. Burwell Pope (1751-1800) *m.* 1772 Priscilla Wootten (1756-1806)
       7. Henry Pope *ca.* (1723-1764) *m. ca.* 1748 Tabitha, *d.* 1808
       8. John Pope (1698-1745) *m.* 1721/2 Mourning McKinnie *ca.* (1704-*ca.* 1750)
       9. Col. Barnaby McKinnie *ca.* (1673-1740) *m.* 1703 Mary E. Ricks *ca.* (1679-aft.
          1719
      10. MICHAEL MACKQUINNEY *ca.* (1635-1686) *m.* 1660/65 Elizabeth *ca.* (1640-1704)
       Service: "Was possessed of a Patent of Land." Emigrated to Virginia from Scotland.
       Reference: Hills of Wilkes Co., Ga., and Allied Families; Record of Isle of Wight
          Co., Va.

6518 HOLSTEN, Mrs. Walter H.   Recorded 1946
     7 W. Palmer Avenue, Collingswood, N. J.
1. Elizabeth E. Mather *m.* 1942 Walter Holsten
2. John S. Mather (1891–) *m.* 1916 Harriet E. Hanger (1889–1917)
3. John A. Mather (1865–1917) *m.* 1889 Lizzie B. Weatherby (1866–1898)
4. John A. Mather (1837–1921) *m.* 1861 Louisa W. Dawson (1842–1923)
5. James C. Dawson (1815–1872) *m.* 1838 Elizabeth B. Cade (1818–1895)
6. Isaac Cade (1780–1823) *m.* 1804 Judith Hendrickson (1784–1867)
7. Andrew Henricsson (1748–1823) *m.* 1770 Judy Jones (1751–1793)
8. Peter Hendricsson (1718–1761) *m.* bef. 1748 Catherine Lock (1729–1766)
9. ANDERS HENRICSSON (bef. 1700–aft. 1724) *m.* bef. 1713 Beata ———
Service: A Swedish pioneer and settler on N. J. near Swedesboro before 1699.
Reference: Hist. and Gen. of Fenwick's Colony, by Thomas Shourd.

6369 HOLSWADE, Mrs. James F.   Recorded 1942, West Virginia
1. Daisy Staats *m.* 1909 James Frederick Holswade
2. Coleman Alkin Staats (1851–1899) *m.* 1871 Emma Watkins Keeney (1854–1933)
3. Joshua Hamilton Staats (1828–1860) *m.* 1851 Rebecca M. Alkire (1828–1866)
4. Alexander White Alkire (1802–1886) *m.* 1825 Margaret Coleman (1801–1834)
5. Adam Alkire (1776–aft. 1833) *m.* 1800 Margaret White (1780–1833)
6. Alexander White, Jr. (1752–c. 1814) *m.* 1769 Mary Clifford, *d.* 1826
7. Alexander White (1709–1776) *m.* 1735 Mary McMurtrie, *b.* 1711
8. Jonathan White (1658–1736) *m.* 1682 Esther Nickerson, *d.* 1703
9. PEREGRINE WHITE (1620–1704) *m.* 1646 Sarah Bassett, *d.* 1711
Service: Born on Mayflower, 1620; Lt. and Capt. of Colonial Forces; Deputy to
    General Court.
Reference: "White Family Records."

6609 HOLTON, Ethel Elaine   Recorded 1948
     3261 Wrightwood Avenue, Chicago 47, Illinois
1. Ethel Elaine Holton
2. Charles A. Holton (1848–1922) *m.* 1874 Elizabeth A. Dyche (1850–1903)
3. Wm. A. W. Holton (1808–1896) *m.* 1846 Bernetta Vosburg (1828–1900)
4. Alexander Holton (1779–1823) *m.* 1806 Harriet Warner (1783–1879)
5. Joel Holton (1738–1821) *m.* 1768 Bethia Farwell (1747–1813)
6. John Holton (1707–1793) *m.* 1731 Hehitable Alexander (1713–1792)
7. William Holton (1675–1755) *m.* 1706 Abigail Edwards (1680–)
8. John Holton, *d.* 1712, *m.* 1667 Abigail Fisher (1649–)
9. DEACON WILLIAM HOLTON (1611–1691) *m.* Mary ———, *d.* 1691
Service: One of the founders of Hartford Conn., Northampton, Mass., and Northfield,
    Mass.
Reference: Hist of Northfield, Mass., John Holton—Judd Manuscript, Hist. of
    Hadley, Vermont Gazeteer.

6553 HORTON, Gail Nora   Recorded 1947, Georgia
     1240 W. Wesley Road N. W., Atlanta, Georgia
         (JUNIOR)
1. Gail Nora Horton
2. William C. Horton (1908–) (adopted by aunt, Nora Eavenson Horton) *m.* 1941
    Eva. H. Mitchell, *d.* 1942
3. O. C. Eavenson (1884–1938) *m.* Annie N. Whittemore
4. Capt. John W. Eavenson (1840–1935) *m.* 1865 Josephine Oglesby (1846–1930)
5. George Eavenson, Jr. (1817–1898) *m.* 1839 Sarah Thornton (1824–1863)
6. John Thornton (1805–1854) *m.* Frances Adams (1807–)
7. Benjamin Thornton (1781–1854) *m.* 1800 Sarah Upshaw, *d.* 1805
8. Dozier Thornton (1755–1843) *m.* 1773 Lucy Hill (1760–1836)
9. Mark Thornton (1725–) *m.* Susannah Dozier (1739–1782)
10. William Thornton *ca* (1705–) *m.* Elizabeth Fitzhugh
11. Col. Francis Thornton (1682–) *m.* Mary Taliaferro
12. Francis Thornton (1651–1726) *m.* Alice Savage
13. WILLIAM THORNTON, *d.* 1708
Service: His Arms are on his tombstone.
Reference: Eavenson-Strickland and Allied Families.

6595   HORTON, Gloria Lucille   Recorded 1948, Georgia
              1240 West Wesley Road, N. W., Atlanta, Georgia
       1. Gloria Lucille Horton
       2. Wm. C. Horton (1908–) (adopted by aunt, Nora Eavenson Horton) *m.* 1945
              Hyldred G. Harris (1920–)
       3. O. C. Eavenson (1884–1938) *m.* Annie N. Whittemore
       4. Capt. John W. Eavenson (1840–1935) *m.* 1865 Josephine Oglesby (1846–1930)
       5. George Eavenson, Jr. (1817–1898) *m.* 1839 Sarah Thornton (1824–1863)
       6. John Thornton (1805–1854) *m.* Frances Adams (1807–)
       7. Benjamin Thornton (1781–1854) *m.* 1800 Sarah Upshaw, *d.* 1805
       8. Dozier Thornton (1755–1843) *m.* 1773 Lucy Hill (1760–1836)
       9. Mark Thornton (1725–) *m.* Susannah Dozier (1739–1782)
      10. William Thornton *ca.* (1705–) *m.* Elizabeth Fitzhugh
      11. Col. Francis Thornton (1682–) *m.* Mary Taliaferro
      12. Francis Thornton (1651–1726) *m.* Alice Savage
      13. WILLIAM THORNTON, *d.* 1708
       Reference: Eavenson-Strickland and Allied Families.

6552   HORTON, William C.   Recorded 1947, Georgia
              1240 W. Wesley Road N. W., Atlanta, Georgia
       1. William C. Horton (adopted by aunt, Nora Eavenson Horton) *m.* 1941 Mrs.
              Eva Hilley Mitchell
       2. Ora C. Eavenson (1884–1938) *m.* Annie N. Whittemore
       3. Capt. John W. Eavenson (1840–1935) *m.* 1865 Josephine Oglesby (1846–1930)
       4. George Eavenson, Jr. (1817–1898) *m.* 1839 Sarah Thornton (1824–1863)
       5. George Eavenson, Sr. (1782–1842) *m.* 1803 Polly Hilly (1781–1855)
       6. Eli Eavenson (1760–1829) *m.* 1781 Rachel Seals (1760–1830)
       7. George Eavenson (1726–1816) *m.* 1755 Mary Williamson *ca.* (1728–1828)
       8. Joseph Eavenson (1689–1771) *m.* 1717 Catherine George
       9. Thomas Eavenson (1653–1726) *m.* 1669 Hannah Woodward
      10. RALPH EAVENSON *ca.* (1625–1665) *m.* 1650 Cicely Orton (1630–)
       Service: Died in Chester County, Penna., 1665.
       Reference: Eavenson-Strickland and Allied Families.

5851   HORTON, Mrs. William C.   Recorded 1929, Georgia
              Winder, Georgia
       1. Nora Eavenson *m.* 1903 William C. Horton
       2. Capt. John W. Eavenson (1840–) *m.* 1865 Jane J. Oglesby (1846–)
       3. George Eavenson, Jr. (1817–1898) *m.* 1839 Sarah Thornton (1824–1863)
       4. George Eavenson, Sr. (1782–1842) *m.* Polly Hilly (1781–1855)
       5. Eli Eavenson (1764–1829) *m.* 1781 Rachel Seal (1760–1830)
       6. George Eavenson (1726–1816) *m.* 1755 Mary Williams (–1828)
       7. Joseph Eavenson (1689–1771) *m.* 1717 Catherine George
       8. Thomas Eavenson (1653–1726) *m.* 1677 Hannah Woodward
       9. RALPH EAVENSON (1625–1665) *m.* 1650 Cicely Orton
       Reference: Palmer & Trimble Genealogy.

6324   HOSCH, Millicent   Recorded 1941, Georgia
                                     (JUNIOR)
       1. Millicent Coleman Hosch
       2. William Henry Hosch, *d.* 1935, *m.* 1915 Leta Coleman
       3. Edward T. Coleman (1863–1929) *m.* 1890 Margaret Durden (1872–)
       4. Jeremiah T. Coleman (1833–1909) *m.* 1861 Zilphia Roundtree (1839–1915)
       5. Elisha Coleman (1789–1860) *m.* 1829 Mary Lucretia Scott (1797–1878)
       6. Gen. John Baytop Scott (1773–1839) *m.* 1795 Eliza Coleman (1779–1839)
       7. Capt. James Scott (1732–1799) *m.* 1750 Frances Collier, *b.* 1735
       8. Capt. John Collier (1695–1765) *m.* Anne Eppes, *b.* 1690
       9. Col. Francis Eppes (1659–1765) *m.* 1680 Ann Isham
      10. Col. Francis Eppes, *c.* (1628–1678) *m.* ———
      11. COL. FRANCIS EPPES in Va. before 1625
       Service: Member Va. Convention, 1625; Col. Va. Militia; Justice Gen Court, 1626;
              House of Burgesses, 1727, '28, '31, '32, '39, '45. Councillor 1652.
       Reference: Same as 6323.
       Reference: Journ. House of Burgesses, Henrico Co., Va.; Va. House of Burgesses,
              Vol. III; Nicholson's Rent Rolls; Amben Papers, Lib. of Congress.

6323 HOSCH, Mrs. William Henry   Recorded 1941, Georgia
    414 E. Washington Street, Gainesville, Georgia
1. Leta Coleman *m.* 1915 William Henry Hosch
2. Edward T. Coleman, M.D. (1863–1929) *m.* 1890 Margaret Durden (1872–)
3. Jeremiah T. Colman (1833–1909) *m.* 1861 Zilphia Roundtree (1839–1915)
4. Elisha Coleman (1789–1860) *m.* 1829 Mary Lucretia Scott (1797–1878)
5. Gen. John Baytop Scott (1773–1839) *m.* 1795 Eliza Coleman (1779–1839)
6. Capt. James Scott (1732–1799) *m.* 1750 Frances Collier, *b.* 1735
7. Capt. John Collier (1695–1765) *m.* Anne Eppes, *b.* 1690
8. Col. Francis Eppes (1659–1765) *m.* 1680 Ann Isham
9. Col. Francis Eppes *c.* (1628–1678) *m.* ———
10. Col. Francis Eppes in Va. before 1625
Service: Member Va. Convention, 1625; Col. Va. Militia; Justice Gen. Court, 1626; House of Burgesses, 1727, '28, '31, '32, '39, '45; Councillor, 1652; Receiver of Land Grants.
Reference: Journ. House of Burgesses, Henrico Co., Va.; Va. House of Burgesses, Vol. III; Nicholson's Rent Rolls; Amben Papers. Lib. of Congress.

6297 HOUCK, Mrs. Oliver F.   Recorded 1940
    27 Westland Avenue, West Hartford, Connecticut
1. Helene Otis *m.* 1919 Oliver Frederick Houck
2. Amos Thatcher Otis (1865–1930) *m.* 1889 Josie Peters (1862–)
3. Samuel Andrew Peters, *b.* 1827, *m.* 1859 Sarah Hurlbut (1826–1876)
4. John T. Peters (1799–1867) *m.* 1824 Sophia Chester (1803–1884)
5. David Chester, *b.* 1768, *m.* 1797 Prudence Fox
6. Joseph Chester (1730–1803) *m.* 2nd 1757 Elizabeth Otis, *d.* 1757
7. John Chester *c.* (1690–1771) *m.* 1716 Marcy Starr (1696–1774)
8. Thomas Starr (1668–1711) *m.* 2nd 1694 Mary Morgan (1670–1765)
9. Samuel Starr, *d.* 1687, *m.* 1664 Hannah Brewster (1643–aft. 1671)
10. Jonathan Brewster (1593–1659) *m.* 1624 Lucretia Oldham, *d.* 1679
11. William Brewster (1560–1644) *m.* Mary, *d.* 1627
Service: Fourth Signer of Mayflower Compact.
Reference: "Signers of Mayflower Compact," by Annie Arnous Haxton; Starr Genealogy; History of Montville, Conn.

6030 HOUGHTON, Mrs. Harold George   Recorded 1932
    720 West State Street, Trenton, New Jersey
1. Mae Van Lieu (1891–) *m.* Harold G. Houghton
2. Oliver Durham Van Lieu (1870–) *m.* 1887 Katharine Holtzman (1869–)
3. William Van Lieu (1838–1920) *m.* 1861 Sarah Rebecca Durham (1841–1920)
4. Richard Van Lieu (1815–1880) *m.* 1836 Permelia Quick (1805–1887)
5. Abraham Quick (1770–1822) *m.* 1803 Rachel Stout (1770–1865)
6. Moses Stout (1750–1833) *m.* 1773 Abigail Hart (1754–1801)
7. John Stout *m.* 1734 Rachel Merrill
8. James Stout (1694–1731) *m.* 1712 Catharine Simpson (1692–1749)
9. David Stout (1667–) *m.* 1688 Rebecca Ashton (1669–)
10. James Ashton (–1705) *m.* 1667 Deliverance Throckmorton
11. John Throckmorton (–1684) *m.* Rebecca ———
Service: Throckmorton Family, Sitherwood; Hist. Gen., Stillwell.

6464 HOWARD, Hon. Charles Benjamin   Recorded 1945
    Howardene, Sherbrooke, Quebec, Canada
1. Charles Benjamin Howard *m.* 1st Alberta Campbell
2. Benjamin Cate Howard (1865–1923) *m.* 1885 Helen Eloisa Salls (1863–)
3. James Howard (1825–1892) *m.* 1863 Clarinda Hunt (1841–1932)
4. Orin Hunt (1806–1871) *m.* 1838 Mehitable White (1807–1874)
5. Caleb White (1776–1868) *m.* 1797
6. Caleb White (1747–1830) *m.* 1767 Rebecca Marsh (1751–1785)
7. Josiah White *m.* 1737 Mary Taylor
8. Josiah White (1654–) *m.* Remember Reid (1657–)
9. Paul Resolved White (1614/15–1695/96) *m.* 1640 Judith Vassal (ab. 1619–1670)
10. William White (–1621) *m.* 1612 Susanna Fuller (–1682)
Service: Eleventh signer of Mayflower Compact.
Reference: Forest & Clearings, Hubbard; Hist. Sutton, Mass., Benedict & Tracy; Mayflower Desc., I, 10, etc.

6043 HOWITZ, Mrs. A. A.   Recorded 1933
           201 Parkway Avenue, Chester, Pennsylvania
    1. Janie Howison (1877–) m. Alfred A. Howitz
    2. John Howison (1812–1879) m. 1876 Lucy Mary Rawlings (1842–1929)
    3. Jas. Boswell Rawlings (1809–1882) m. Ann Eliz. Cason (1816–1883)
    4. Richard Rawlings (1781–1862) m. 1807 Lucy Scott Herndon (1789–1870)
    5. James Rawlings (1752–1804) m. ———
    6. Jas. Rawlings (1715–1784) m. Sarah Holladay (–1788)
    7. Capt. John Holladay (–1742) m. Eliz. Brocas
    8. CAPT. THOMAS HOLLADAY
    Reference: Abridged Comp. of Am. Gen., Vol. 2; Immigrant Anc.

6675 HUCKABAY, Mrs. Sybil S.   Recorded 1950
           6588 Goodwood Avenue, Baton Rouge 12, Louisiana
    1. Sybil Slocum m. J. E. Huckabay
    2. Chas. F. Slocum (1853–1906) m. 1883 Lula Aline Van Norman (1869–1916)
    3. Philemon B. Van Norman (1844–1880) m. 1858 Susan E. McAdams (1846–1933)
    4. William McAdams (1812–1889) m. 1838 Abigail Doughty (1821–1895)
    5. R. Doughty (1784–1830) m. 1813 Mary Reese (1795–)
    6. Levi Doughty (1763–1864) m. 1782 Abigail Morgan (1766–1825)
    7. Benjamin Doughty (1721–) m. 1748 Lydia Mundine
    8. James Doty (1686–1739) m. 1712 Phoebe Slater (1693–1745)
    9. Samuel Doty (1643–1715) m. 1678 Mary Jean Harmon (1651–1717)
   10. EDWARD DOTY (Mayflower) (1600–1655) m. 1635 Faith Clark (1619–)
    Reference: Mayflower Descendants.

6481 HUFF, Mrs. George H.   Recorded 1945, Ohio
           Columbus, Ohio
    1. Mary Evelyn Blue (resigned) m. George Harry Huff
    2. Joel Gilbert Blue (1840–1889) m. 1866 Ann Eliza Johnston (1846–1902)
    3. David Byron Blue (1814–1889) m. 1839 Wealthy Bartlett (1822–1899)
    4. John Bartlett (1787–1836) m. 1809 Obedience Mix (Meeks) (1785–1858)
    5. Amos Mix (1754–1847) m. 1779 Amelia Pennoyer (1762–1832)
    6. Capt. John Mix (1720–1796) m. Sarah ———
    7. John Mix (1676–1721) m. 1702 Sarah Thompson (1671–1711)
    8. John Mix (1649–1711) m. Elizabeth Heaton (1650–1711)
    9. THOMAS MIX (1623–1691) m. Rebecca Turner
    Service: Lived in New Haven, Conn.

6550 HUGHES, Mrs. John V.   Recorded 1947, Texas
           401 South Chilton Avenue, Tyler, Texas
    1. Vannie Henderson m. 1911 John V. Hughes
    2. E. M. Henderson (1851–1934) m. 1876 Mary A. Trommell (1854–1938)
    3. Eli Henderson (1803–1858) m. 1828 Mary Darby (1810–1865)
    4. Nathaniel Henderson, Jr. (1756–1821) m. 1784 Rebecca J. Branson (1766–1818)
    5. Nathaniel Henderson (1736–1803) m. Rebecca N. Holliday
    6. Samuel Henderson (1700–1783) m. 1732 Elizabeth Williams (1714–)
    7. Richard Henderson m. Mary Washer
    8. ENSIGN WASHER
    Service: Member House of Burgesses, 1619, the first legislative assembly in America.
    Reference: Family History, by Horton; Colonial Families of the United States of
        America.

6149 HYMPHRIES, Miss Annis J.   Recorded 1937, Georgia
           914 E. Rock Springs Road N. E., Atlanta, Georgia
    1. Miss Annis Jones Humphries
    2. John David Humphries (1873–) m. 1900 Lillie Jones (1878–)
    3. Amos D. Humphries (1848–1910) m. 1870 Annis E. Pope (1852–1884)
    4. John Hewell Pope (1818–1902) m. 1840 Emily E. Crow (1821–1870)
    5. John Pope (1778–1849) m. Susannah ——— (1780–1844)

6. Henry Pope (1748–) *m.* Charity ———— (1747–)
7. William Pope (1725–) *m.* Mary ————
8. John Pope *m.* Elizabeth Pope
9. Nathaniel Pope (–1719) *m.* 1690 Jane Brown (–1752)
10. Nathaniel Pope (1638–) *m.* Mary Sisson
11. NATHANIEL POPE (–1660) *m.* Luce ————

Service: Commissioned Lt. Col. of Westmoreland County, Virginia Troops, 1655.
Reference: Descendants of Nathaniel Pope, by John D. Humphries.

6593 HUMPHRIES, Damaris G. Recorded 1948, Georgia
914 E. Rock Springs Road N. E., Atlanta, Georgia
(JUNIOR)
1. Damaris Guest Humphries
2. John D. Humphries, Jr. (1910–) *m.* 1941 Demaris Keene (1917–)
3. John D. Humphries (1873–1942) *m.* 1900 Lillie M. Jones (1877–1943)
4. Amos D. Humphries (1848–1910) *m.* 1870 Annis E. Pope (1852–1884)
5. John H. Pope (1813–1902) *m. ca.* 1840 Emily Crow (1821–1870)
6. John Pope (1778–1849) *m. ca.* 1802 Susannah ———— (1780–1844)
7. Henry Pope (1748–) *m.* Charity ———— (1747–)
8. William Pope *ca* (1725–) *m. ca.* 1746 Mary ———— *ca* (1727–)
9. John Pope *ca.* (1697–) *m.* Elizabeth Pope *ca.* (1699–)
10. Nathaniel Pope, *d.* 1719, *m. ca.* 1690 Jane Brown
11. Nathaniel Pope *m.* Mary Sisson
12. COL. NATHANIEL POPE *ca.* (1610–1660) *m. ca.* 1630 Lucy ————

Service: Lt. Col. of Westmoreland County, Va., Militia, 1655.
Reference: Desc. Nathaniel Pope.

6342 HUMPHRIES, John David, Jr. Recorded 1941, Georgia
914 E. Rock Springs Road N. E., Atlanta, Georgia
1. John David Humphries, Jr. *m.* 1941 Demaris Keene
2. John David Humphries (1883–) *m.* 1900 Lillie Marvin Jones (1877–)
3. Amos Daniel Humphries (1849–) *m.* Annis Elizabeth Pope (1852–1884)
4. John Howell Pope (1818–1902) *m.* Emily E. Crow (1821–1870)
5. John Pope (1778–1849) *m.* Susannah ———— (1780–1844)
6. Henry Pope (1748–) *m.* Charity ———— (1747–)
7. William Pope *c.* (1725–) *m. c.* 1746 Mary *c.* (1727–)
8. John Pope *c.* (1697–1735) *m. c.* 1723 Elizabeth Pope *b. c.* 1699
9. Nathaniel Pope, *d.* 1719, *m.* Jane Brown, *d.* 1752
10. Nathaniel Pope *m.* Mary Sisson
11. NATHANIEL POPE *c.* (1610–1660) *m. c.* 1636 Luce ————

Service: Commissioned Lt. Col., Westmoreland Co., Va., 1655.
Reference: "Georgia Descendants of Nathaniel Pope of Va.," by J. D. Humphries;
"Col. Nathaniel Pope and His Descendants," G. W. Beale.

6594 HUMPHRIES, John David 3rd Recorded 1948, Georgia
914 E. Rock Springs Road N. E., Atlanta, Georgia
1. John David Humphries, 3rd
2. John D. Humphries, Jr. (1910–) *m.* 1941 Damaris Keene (1917–)
3. John D. Humphries (1873–1942) *m.* 1900 Lillie Jones (1877–1943)
4. Amos D. Humphries (1848–1910) *m.* 1870 Annis E. Pope (1852–1884)
5. John H. Pope (1818–1902) *m.* 1840 Emily Crow (1821–1870)
6. John Pope (1778–1849) *m. ca.* 1802 Susannah ———— (1780–1844)
7. Henry Pope (1748–) *m.* Charity ———— (1747–)
8. William Pope (1725–) *m. ca.* 1746 Mary ———— (1727–)
9. John Pope *ca.* (1697–1735) *m. ca.* 1723 Elizabeth Pope (1699–)
10. Nathaniel Pope, *d.* 1719, *m. ca.* 1690 Jane Brown
11. Nathaniel Pope *m.* Mary Sisson
12. COL. NATHANIEL POPE *ca.* (1610–1660) *m. ca.* 1630 Lucy ————

Service: Lt. Col. of Westmoreland County, Va., Militia, 1655.
Reference: Desc. Nathaniel Pope.

6148 HUMPHRIES, John D.   Recorded 1937, Georgia
            914 E. Rock Springs Road, Atlanta, Georgia
      1. John David Humphries *m.* 1900 Lillie Jones
      2. Amos D. Humphries (1848–1910) *m.* 1870 Annis E. Pope (1852–1884)
      3. John H. Pope (1818–1902) *m.* 1840 Emily E. Crow (1821–1870)
      4. John Pope (1778–1849) *m.* Susannah ——— (1780–1844)
      5. Henry Pope (1748–) *m.* Charity ——— (1747–)
      6. William Pope (1725–) *m.* Mary ———
      7. John Pope *m.* Elizabeth Pope
      8. Nathaniel Pope (–1719) *m.* 1690 Jane Brown (–1752)
      9. Nathaniel Pope (1638–) *m.* Mary Sisson
     10. NATHANIEL POPE (–1660) *m.* Luce ———
      Service: Commissioned Lt. Col. of Westmoreland County, Va., Troops, 1655.
      Reference: Descendants of Nathaniel Pope, by John D. Humphries.

6397 HUMPHRIES, Lillie Jones   Recorded 1942, Georgia
            Atlanta, Georgia
                              (JUNIOR MEMBERSHIP)
      1. Lillie Jones Humphries
      2. John David Humphries (1910–) *m.* 1941 Demaris Keene
      3. John David Humphries (1873–) *m.* 1900 Lillie Jones (1877–)
      4. Amos Daniel Humphries (1848–1910) *m.* 1870 Annis E. Pope (1852–1884)
      5. John Hewell Pope (1818–1902) *m.* 1840 Emily Crow (1821–1870)
      6. John Pope (1778–1848) *m.* 1802 Susannah ——— (1780–1844)
      7. Henry Pope (1748–) *m.* Charity ——— (1747–)
      8. William Pope (1725–) *m.* 1746 Mary ——— (1727–)
      9. John Pope (1697–1735) *m.* 1723 Elizabeth Pope (1699–)
     10. Nathaniel Pope (–1719) *m.* 1690 Jane Brown
     11. Nathaniel Pope *m.* Mary Sisson
     12. COL. NATHANIEL POPE (1610–1660) *m.* 1636 Lucy ———
      Service: Lieut. Col. of Westmoreland County, Va., Militia, 1655.
      Reference: Col. Nathaniel Pope & Ancestors, W. G. Beale; W. & M. Quart., Vol. XII;
            Georgia Desct. of Nathaniel Pope, by J. D. Humphries.

6366 HUNT, Mrs. Elvid   Recorded 1942, New York
            508 Monroe Avenue, Philipse Manor, New York
      1. Ruth Brockway *m.* 1905 Lt. Elvid Hunt, U. S. Army
      2. Mortimer E. Brockway (1839–1903) *m.* 1859 Emma R. Sowle (1840–1914)
      3. Gideon Sowle (1806–1870) *m.* 1830 Sally Brower (1812–1878)
      4. Robert Sowle (1767–1848) *m.* 1793 Merebah Durfee (1768–1817)
      5. Joseph Sowle (1733–1820) *m.* 1763 Charity Tripp, *b.* 1747
      6. William Soule *m.* 1733 Junema Baker, *d.* bef. 1747
      7. Sylvanus Soule *c.* (1675–) *m.* bef. 1715 Sarah
      8. Nathaniel Soule, *d.* 1699, *m.* Rose Thorn, *d.* aft. 1699
      9. GEORGE SOULE, *d.* 1680, *m.* 1622 Mary Beckett, *d.* 1677
      Service: In Duxbury, Mass., 1680; Collaborator in Revision of Colonial Laws with
            Gov. Prince and others; Original Proprietor of Bridgewater, Duxbury, Middle-
            boro and Dartmouth; Representative Gen. Court in Plymouth, 1642, '45,
            '46, '50, '51, '53, '54; Volunteer in Pequote War and in move against
            Miantomah.
      Reference: Soule Generalogy, by G. T. Redlon; Tripp Genealogy, Durfee Genealogy.

5891 HUNT, John O.   Recorded 1929, New Jersey
            833 Berkeley Avenue, Trenton, New Jersey
      1. John Osborne Hunt *m.* Nellie Edwards
      2. John R. Hunt *m.* 1872 Amy Van Cleaf
      3. Edward C. Hunt (1790–1868) *m.* 1844 Jemima Vliet (1819–1878)
      4. John Hunt (1750–1824) *m.* 1784 Rhoda Read
      5. Edward Hunt (–1792) *m.* 1746 Charity Cornell (–1793)
      6. Ralph Hunt (1656–1727) *m.* Elizabeth
      7. RALPH HUNT (1613–1678) *m.* 1649 Elizabeth Jessups
      Service: Was Lieut. of Newtown Company, Province of New York, 1665; Member of
            Provincial Assembly, 1673.
      Reference: Annals of Newtown, by Ricker, 0. 85; Colonial War Register, 1640–1677;
            Hale's History of Hopewell Church.

6724 HUNT, Mrs. Stewart S. Recorded 1951, Louisiana
    Ruston, Louisiana
1. Lucille Long *m.* 1919 Stewart Hunt
2. Hughty Pierce Long, Sr. (1852–1937) *m.* 1875 Caledonia Tison (1860–1913)
3. John Murphy Long (1825–1901) *m.* 1845 Mary Elizabeth Wingate (1829–1901)
4. James Long (1790–1850) *m.* 1823 Mary Kirtman (1793–abt. 1850)
5. Hugh Long (1770–abt. 1794) *m. c.* 1789 Margaret (buried in Md., 1794)
6. James Long (1750–1806) *m. c.* 1768/9 Catherine, *d.* bef. 1790
7. John Long *b.* Balt., Md., *m.* Ellenor Owens (1706–)
8. Capt. Richard Owens, *b.* Ann. Ar. Co., Md., *m.* 1690 Racheal Beall, *b.* bef. 1678
9. Col. Ninian Beall (1625–1717) *m.* 1668 Ruth Moore (–1704)
Service: Peace Officer Calvert Co., Md.; Major of Calvert Co., 1690, Burgess Pr.
    Geo. Co., Md.
Reference: Records of Winn Parish, La.; Md. Archives B. 8 F., 170 Baltimore Co.
    Wills Book and Settlement of Baltimore Estates; Beall Genealogy, by
    F. F. M. Beall, p. 49.

6325 HUNTER, Priscilla Jane. Recorded 1941
    (Junior)
1. Priscilla Jane Hunter
2. Edgar Leslie *m.* 1924 Catherine Thompson
3. T. G. Pratt Thompson (1876–1934) *m.* 1900 Charlotte Jepson, *b.* 1876
4. George Edwin Jepson (1842–1915) *m.* 1871 Emma Almira Fitch (1843–1916)
5. Austin Green Fitch (1813–1891) *m.* 1840 Mary Charlotte March (1816–1911)
6. Jacob March (1786–1823) *m.* 1814 Mary LeBaton Monro (1791–1869)
7. Stephen Monro (1758–1826) *m.* 1790 Susannah LeBaron (1767–1811)
8. Lazarus LeBaron (1744–1827) *m.* 1767 Susannah Johonnet (1738–1774)
9. Lazarus LeBaron (1721–1784) *m.* 1743 Margaret Newsome
10. Lazarus LeBaron (1698–1773) *m.* 1720 Lydia Bartlett (1697–1742)
11. Joseph Bartlett *c.* (1665–1703) *m.* 1692 Lydia Griswold (1672–1752)
12. Joseph Bartlett, *c* (1639–1711) *m.* Hannah Pope, *d.* 1710
13. Robert Bartlett, *d.* 1676, *m.* 1628 Mary Warren
14. Richard Warren *m.* ——
Service: Mayflower Pilgrim.
Reference: Mayflower Descendants; LeBaron Genealogy; Sutton's V. R.

6543 HUNTING, Clifford Herbert Recorded 1947
    Huntingville, Quebec, Canada
1. Clifford H. Hunting *m.* 1901 Nettie Louise Simons
2. William H. Hunting (1852–1937) *m.* 1891 Emily E. Ford (1871–)
3. William Hunting (1815–1892) *m.* 1847 Mariah Whitcomb (1826–1903)
4. William Hunting, Jr. (1783–1832) *m.* 1809 Mary Stone (1782–1853)
5. Capt. Leonard Stone (1746–1818) *m.* 1781 Catherine Kendall (1753–1810)
6. Benjamin Stone (1706–1758) *m.* 1736 Emma Parker (1713–1782)
7. Dea. Simon Stone (1656–1741) *m. ca.* 1685 Sarah Farnsworth (1663–)
8. Dea. Simon Stone *ca.* (1630–1707/8) *m. ca.* 1655 Mary Whipple *ca.* (1634–1720)
9. Dea. Simon Stone (1586–1665) *m.* 1616 Joane Clark, *d.* 1654
Service: Came to America on ship "Increase," 1635; admitted Freeman 1636; select-
    man on Watertown, Mass.
Reference: Deacon Simon Stone Genealogy.

6501 HUNTINGTON, Kenneth William Recorded 1945
    Lennoxville, Vermont
1. Kenneth William Hunting *m.* Alice Maude Call
2. William H. Hunting (1852–1937) *m.* 1891 Emily Ella Ford (1871–1945)
3. William Hunting (1815–1892) *m.* 1847 Mariah Whitcomb (1826–1903)
4. William Hunting (1783–1832) *m.* 1809 Mary Stone (1782–1853)
5. William Hunting (1753–1844) *m.* 1779 Lydia Wheelock (1763–1804)
6. Stephen Hunting (1719–1815) *m.* M. E. Tyler
7. Stephen Hunting (1687–) *m.* 1709 Rebecca Woodward (1683–)
8. John Hunting (1628–1718) *m.* Elizabeth Paine (1648–)
9. Elder John Hunting (1597–1689) *m.* 1617 Hester Seaborne
Service: First Ruling Elder of First Church at Dedham, Mass.

6544   HUNTING, Mrs. Clifford Herbert   Recorded 1947
           Huntingville, Quebec, Canada
   1. Nettie Louise Simons *m*. 1925 Clifford H. Hunting
   2. Charles A. Simons (1870–   ) *m*. 1896 Emma L. Haines (1873–   )
   3. Simon C. Haines *ca*. (1827–1908) *m*. Louise Richardson, *d*. 1873
   4. Daniel G. Richardson, *d*. 1845, *m*. Olive Huntington (1801–   )
   5. Thomas Huntington (1767–1811) *m*. 1795 Submit Huntington *ca*. (1769–   )
   6. James Huntington (1728–1812) *m*. Hannah Marsh, *d*. 1795
   7. Caleb Huntington (1693/4–   ) *m*. 1720 Lydia Griswold (1696–   )
   8. Samuel Huntington (1665–1717) *m*. 1686 Mary Clark, *d*. 1743
   9. Dea. Simon Huntington (1629–1706) *m*. 1653 Sarah Clarke, *d*. 1721
  10. SIMON HUNTINGTON (1583–1631/33) *m*. 1627 Margaret Baret
   Service: One of first settlers at Norwich, Conn.
   Reference: Huntington Genealogy Memoir.

6224   HUNTTING, Mrs. C. H.   Recorded 1938
           15 Vanderbilt Road, West Hartford, Connecticut
   1. Mary Alexander Newton *m*. Charles Hand Huntting
   2. Duane E. Newton (1833–1906) *m*. 1857 Clarissa Ludington (1837–1891)
   3. Norman Bemis Newton *m*. Mary Alexander
   4. Ivah Newton (1784–1840) *m*. Sarah Rugg (1785–1882)
   5. Winslow Newton (1756–1790) *m*. 1777 Anna Bemis
   6. Lemuel Newton (1718–1793) *m*. Abigail ———
   7. Samuel Newton (1695–1771) *m*. 1716 Mary Tozer (1693–   )
   8. Daniel Newton (1655–1739) *m*. 1679 Susanna Morse (1662–1729)
   9. RICHARD NEWTON (1600–1701) *m*. Anne Loker (–1697)
   Service: Proprietor.
   Reference: Newton Gen., by Leonard, p. 648.

6066   HUSTON, Mrs. H. K.   Recorded 1934, Pennsylvania
           1 Bartol Avenue, Ridley Park, Pennsylvania
   1. Elizabeth Rogers *m*. 1896 Howard K. Huston
   2. Charles W. Rogers (1843–1889) *m*. 1865 Evelyn Woodward (1848–1921)
   3. Reuben S. Woodward (1823–1857) *m*. 1847 Susanna G. Leishman (1824–1907)
   4. Henry Leishman (–1868) *m*. 1822 Theodosia Lippincott (1800–1876)
   5. Jacob Lippincott (1778–1826) *m*. 1799 Elizabeth Stockton (1778–1841)
   6. William Stockton, Jr. (1750–1836) *m*. 1775 Mary Naglee (1755–1795)
   7. William Stockton, Sr. (1712–1781) *m*. 1736 Mary Brian
   8. Job Stockton (–1732) *m*. Ann Petty (–1746)
   9. RICHARD STOCKTON
   Service: Patentee, Freeholder, Lieut. of Horse in Flushing, L. I., 1665–1690.
   Reference: New Jersey Genealogies, by F. B. Lee., Vol. IV; The Stockman Family
           of New Jersey, by Lee.

6289   HUTCHINSON, Emma Fuller   Recorded 1940, Connecticut
           1 Main Street, Manchester, Connecticut
   1. Emma Fuller Hutchinson
   2. Myron H. Hutchinson (1828–1908) *m*. Wealthy White (1830–1915)
   3. Horace White (1801–1893) *m*. 1827 Asenath Fuller (1802–1866)
   4. Irad Fuller (1766–1849) *m*. 1788 Thankful Smith (1768–1803)
   5. Capt. Jehiel Fuller (1735–1796) *m*. 1759 Sarah Day (1742–1815)
   6. Thomas Fuller (1717–1802) *m*. 1734 Martha Rowley (1710/11–1760)
   7. Thomas Fuller *c*. (1679–   ) *m*. Elizabeth ———, *d*. 1784
   8. John Fuller (1656–1726) *m*. 1678 Mehitable Rowley (1660/1–*c*. 1732)
   9. Samuel Fuller (1612–1683) *m*. 1635 Jane Lathrop
  10. EDWARD FULLER, *d*. 1621, *m*. Ann
   Service: Settler of Plymouth, Mass.
   Reference: Fuller Genealogy, Vol. I.

6213 IRONSIDE, Mrs. Stanley   Recorded 1938
         416 Broadway, Camden, New Jersey
    1. Edith Woodward (1889–   ) m. 1910 Stanley Ironside
    2. Geo. D. Woodward (1863–1904) m. 1883 Laura Catherine Powell (1865–   )
    3. James S. Woodward (1836–1915) m. 1857 Rachel Shaw Davenhower (1837–1915)
    4. Geo. M. Woodward (1787–1850) m. 1811 Margaret Wyskoop (1793–1870)
    5. Geo. Woodward (1744–1817) m. 1780 Margaret Mount (1756–1830)
    6. Anthony Woodward (–1784) m. 1718 Constant Williams
    7. Anthony Woodward (1657–1729) m. 1686 Hannah Foulkes (–1760)
    8. THOMAS FOULKES
    Service: Commissioner, Administrator.
    Reference: Gen. Miscellany, by Stillwell; Smith's Hist. of New Jersey, p. 93; Borden-
         ton & Environs, by Woodward.

6318 IRVIN, Anne Hill   Recorded 1941, Georgia
         323 Robert Toombs Avenue, Washington, Georgia
    1. Anne Hill Irvin
    2. Isaiah Tucker Irvin (1876–1925) m. 1913 Ida Lee Hill, b. 1886
    3. Lodowick M. Hill (1856–1902) m. 1884 Annie Lee Hudson, b. 1865
    4. Dr. Abraham Chandler Hill (1831–1867) m. 1855 Rachel E. Hampton (1835–1863)
    5. Col. Lodowick M. Hill (1804–1883) m. 1824 Nancy Hill Johnson (1808–1846)
    6. Wylie Hill (1775–1844) m. 1799 Martha (Patsey) Pope (1782–1853)
    7. Burwell Pope (1751–1800) m. 1772 Priscilla Wooten (1756–1806)
    8. Henry Pope, d. 1764, m. c. 1748 Tabitha ———, d. 1808
    9. John Pope (1698/9–1745) m. Mourning McKinnie, d. c. 1750
   10. Col. Barnaby McKinnie, d. 1740, m. 1703 Mary Exum Ricks (widow), d. aft. 1719
   11. MICHAEL MACKQUINNEY, d. 1686, m. Elizabeth ———, d. aft. 1704
    Service: Landed Proprietor in Isle of Wight Co., Va., before 1673.
    Reference: "Wilkes of Co. Ga., and Allied Families."

6598 ISBELL, Sarah Rachel   Recorded 1948
         1205 Ogden, Denver, Colorado
    1. Sarah Rachel Isbell
    2. Harvey G. Isbell (1859–1943) m. 1891 Mary E. White (1862–   )
    3. Horace S. Isbell (1825–1884) m. 1848 Olive J. Fisher (1825–1922)
    4. Nathan Isbell, Jr. (1801–1856) m. 1823 Sophia Jarvis (1801–1872)
    5. Nathan Isbell (1765–1839) m. 1789 Abigail Smith (1764–1834)
    6. Noah Isbell (1727–1801) m. 1748 Jerusha Ward (1728–bef. 1775)
    7. Robert Isbell, b. 1700, m. Miriam Carter, d. 1728
    8. Eleazer Isbell (1675–   ) m. 1698 Elizabeth French
    9. ROBERT ISBELL, d. 1655, m. Ann Kingman
    Service: Received grant of land in Salem, Mass., 1637.
    Reference: Descendants of Robert Isbell.

6763 ISBELL, Mrs. Luther   Recorded 1952, Georgia
         107 W. Paces Ferry Road N. W., Atlanta, Georgia
    1. Sarah Lillie Wells m. 1908 Luther Isbell
    2. Thomas Scales Wells (1839–1922) m. 1873 Sarah Frances Moss (1854–1920)
    3. Wm. Calton Moss (1829–1915) m. 1851 Elizabeth Arendall (Arundell) (1828–1887)
    4. Hudson Moss (1786–1863) m. 1808 Nancy Greenwood (1790–bf. 1863)
    5. Alexander Moss (1730/40–1800) m. 1760 Anne Thurman (1735/45–abt. 1786)
    6. John Moss (abt. 1700–1785) (Will) m. Elizabeth Massie (bap. 1708–aft. 1785)
    7. Charles Massie (abt. 1685–   ) m. Ann Macon
    8. PETER MASSIE (1639/40–1719)
    Service: One of the signers of Blissland Grievance; Surveyor of Highways, 1684–86;
         his son charles Massie appointed to help with clearing.
    Reference: Wm. & Mary, Vol. 13; St. Peter's Parish Vestry Bk. 1734 and 1739;
         Wills in Goochland Co., Va.; Data filed with application.

6118   IVES, Mrs. Robert F.   Recorded 1936, New York
         962 Ocean Avenue, Brooklyn, New York
   1. Mildred Card *m.* 1897 Robert F. Ives
   2. Benjamin F. Card (1837–1921) *m.* 1862 Abigail M. Bliss (1836–1917)
   3. Albert Card (1805–1868) *m.* 1835 Catherine Storrs (1809–1898)
   4. Benjamin Storrs (1782–1860) *m.* 1807 Mindwell Crosby (1778–1858)
   5. Jonathan Crosby (1744–1788) *m.* 1762 Martha Hayward (1743–   )
   6. Jonathan Crosby (1722–1775) *m.* 1743 Rebecca Coburn (1719–   )
   7. Edward Coburn (1691–1771) *m.* 1713 Elizabeth Richardson (1696–1743)
   8. Daniel Coburn (1654–1712) *m.* 1685 Sara Blood (1658–1741)
   9. Robert Blood *m.* 1653 Elizabeth Willard
  10. Major Simon Willard (1605–1676) *m.* Mary Dunston (1630–1715)
   Service: Founder of Concord, Mass.; Magistrate, Assistant Judge of General Court,
         1654, 1666, 1675.
   Reference: Willard Genealogy, Storrs Genealogy, Coburn Genealogy.

5862   IVINS, Mrs. Nathan R.   Recorded 1929, New Jersey
         115 W. State Street, Trenton, New Jersey
   1. Madeline Woodcock *m.* 1916 Nathan R. Ivins
   2. Leonard M. Woodcock (1838–1910) *m.* 1862 Martha J. Gillette (1839–1874)
   3. William R. Gillett (1809–1846) *m.* 1837 Diana Coe (1814–1890)
   4. Jesse Coe (1780–   ) *m.* 1803 Mary Brainard (1776–   )
   5. Morris Coe (1752–1799) *m.* 1775 Lucy Rossiter (1754–1797)
   6. Ensign Simeon Coe (1720–1782) *m.* 1745 Anna Morris (1728–1813)
   7. John Coe (1693–1751) *m.* 1717 Hannah Parsons (1698–1760)
   8. Capt. John Coe (1658–1741) *m.* 1682 Mary Hawley (1663–1731)
   9. Robert Coe (1626–1659) *m.* 1650 Hannah Mitchell (1631–1702)
  10. Robert Coe (1596–   ) *m.* 1623 Mary (–1628)
   Service: Settled in New England, 1634.
   Reference: Coe Genealogy; Vital Records of Conn.

6205   JACKSON, Miss Harriett DeLance   Recorded 1938
         Tarrytown, New York
   1. Miss Harriett DeLance Jackson
   2. David L. Jackson (1831–1911) *m.* 1871 Julia Jane DeLance (1851–1905)
   3. Delevan DeLance (1818–1898) *m.* 1839 Sarah Palmer (1822–1874)
   4. John DeLance (1775–1840) *m.* 1810 Betsy Chandler (1793–1857)
   5. Jonathan Chandler (1762–1830) *m.* 1784 Pilly Marvin (1766–1830)
   6. John Marvin (1726–   ) *m.* 1747 Sarah Brooker (1726–   )
   7. John Brooker (1695–1742) *m.* 1717 Sarah Grinnell
   8. Daniel Grinnell (1668–1740) *m.* 1683 Lydia Pabodie (1667–1748)
   9. Wm. Pabodie (1620–1707) *m.* 1644 Elizabeth Alden (1634–1717)
  10. John Alden *m.* Priscilla Mullens
  11. Wm. Mullens
   Service:
   Reference:

6406   JACKSON, Harold Charles LeBaron   Recorded 1943
         Detroit, Michigan
   1. Harold Charles LeBaron Jackson *m.* Gretchen Dold
   2. Prof. Archibald C. Jackson (1872–   ) *m.* 1892 Mary Ellen LeBaron (1874–   )
   3. Benjamin LeBaron (1832–1915) *m.* 1857 Almira Achsa Huntington (1838–1910)
   4. Chauncey LeBaron (1803–1879) *m.* Cordelia Hitchcock (1810–1883)
   5. Japhet LeBaron (1767–1845) *m.* 1792 Betsy Prouty (1777–1811)
   6. Joshua LeBaron (1729–1806) *m.* 1761 Grace Bush (1744–1819)
   7. James LeBaron (1696–1744) *m.* 1720 Martha Benson
   8. Dr. Francis LeBaron (1668–1704) *m.* 169? Mary Wilder (1668–1737)
   Service: Useful citizen of Plymouth, Mass.
   Reference: LeBaron Gen., Huntington Fam. Hist.; Hist of Stanstead Co., Quebec.
         Desc. Francis LeBaron of Plymouth, Mass., Stockwell.

6622 JACKSON, Mrs. M. O. Recorded 1949
23 Mt. Vernon Circle, Asheville, North Carolina
1. Alma S. Hough *m.* 1899 Marshall Oscar Jackson
2. Alverson S. Hough (1817–1890) *m.* 1874 Mary F. Brown (1838–1907)
3. Ephraim Hough III (1789–1876) *m.* 1816 Jerusha Sanford (1793–1870)
4. Dea. Ephraim Hough II (1745/6–1815) *m.* 1785 Lydia Alling (1754–)
5. Samuel Alling (1725/6–) *m.* 1752 Mary Leek (1721–)
6. Nathan Alling (1695/6–1774) *m.* Hannah Todd (1702/3–1771)
7. Michael Todd (1653–1713) *m.* Elizabeth Brown (bapt. 1642–1714)
8. Eleazer Brown (bapt. 1642–1714) *m.* Sarah Bulkeley (1640–1723)
9. Thomas Bulkeley *ca.* (1617–1658) *m.* Sarah Jones *ca.* (1620–1682)
10. Rev. Peter Bulkeley (1582/3–1658/9) *m.* 1613 Jane Allen (–1626)
Service: Founder and Minister of Concord, Mass.
Reference: Bulkeley Genealogy, Todd Genealogy.

6123 JAMES, Howard K. Recorded 1936
Almeda, California
(Member-at-Large)
1. Howard K. James
2. Henry L. James (1842–1920) *m.* 1865 Ann F. Leavitt (1844–1890)
3. Caleb Leavitt III (1808–1897) *m.* 1834 Velina Robertson (1807–1888)
4. Caleb Leavitt II (1780–) *m.* Nancy Sewall (1783–1872)
5. Caleb Leavitt I *m.* Sarah Beal
6. Elijah Beal *m.* Sarah Jones
7. Thomas Jones *m.* Catherine Caswell
8. Joseph Jones *m.* Patience Little
9. Thomas Little *m.* Ann Warren
10. Richard Warren
Service: Early settler.
Reference: Colonial Families of America, by Rhoades.

6154 JELKS, Lila Napier Recorded 1937, Georgia
315 Merritt Street, Hawkinsville, Georgia
1. Lila Napier (1878–) *m.* 1900 Nathaniel Augustus Jelke (1873–)
2. Robert Freeman Napier (1847–1886) *m.* 1871 Mattie C. Wimberly (1851–1911)
3. Skelton Napier (1800–1866) *m.* 1820 Jane Gage (1804–1890)
4. Thomas Napier (1768–1838) *m.* 1790 Tabitha Easter (1771–1800)
5. Rene Napier, Jr. (1734–) *m.* 1765 Rebeka Hurt (1740–1803)
6. Rene Napier, Sr. (1714–1751) *m.* bef. 1734 Wene ——— (1716–aft. 1751)
7. Booth Napier (1692–1755) *m.* 1712 Sarah LaForce (1694–)
8. Robert Napier (1658–1698) *m.* 1689 Mary Perrin (1675–1708)
9. Dr. Patriarch Napier (1610–1672) *m.* 1649/50 Elizabeth Booth (1628/30–1678)
10. Robert Booth (Bouth) (1590/1600–1657) *m.* bef. 1628 Frances (1609–aft. 1657)
Service: Member of Virginia House of Burgesses, 1653 and 1654; Clerk of York Co.
Court, 1639 et seq.
Reference: Rec. of Houston, Bibbs, Pulaski Counties, Ga.; Goochland Co., Va.;
Douglas Register, pgs. 259, 36, 70; Wm. & M. Quar. 15, pp. 28, 116, 117,
118; II, p. 53; 13, p. 269; Va. Mag. 22, p. 316; Goochland Co. Will Book,
p. 180; New Kent Co., Va.; St. Peter's Parish Reg., p. 25; Henrico Par.
Reg., p. 225; Stanard's Colonial Reg., pp. 70–71.

6223 JENNE, Mrs. S. A. Recorded 1938
24 Meadowbrook Road, West Hartford, Connecticut
1. Elva Hawkes *m.* 1913 Sherman Austin Jenne
2. Geo. Herbert Hawkes (1859–1936) *m.* 1881 Hester Ann Bulis (1852–1929)
3. Lynman Hawkes (1830–1900) *m.* 1855 Mary Tritton (1831–1906)
4. Abner Hawkes (1796–) *m.* 1822 Ruth Van Duzen (1805–1890)
5. Ira Hawkes (1766–) *m.* 1785 Cynthia Mitchell (1768–)
6. Gershom Hawkes (1715–1799) *m.* 1744 Thankful Corse (1722–1800)
7. James Corse (1694–1783) *m.* 1721 Thankful Munn (1703–)
8. Benj. Munn (1683–) *m.* 1702 Thankful Nims (1684–1746)
9. Godfrey Nims (–1704) *m.* 1677 Mary Miller (–1688)
Services: Cordwainer.
Reference: His. of Deerfield, Mass., p. 243; 6th Gen.

6681 JOHNSON, Frances   Recorded 1950
       204 Broad Street, Plainville, Connecticut
       1. Frances Sullivan (1901–) *m.* 1946
       2. Daniel F. Sullivan (1874–1944) *m.* 1890 Eva Noyes (1875–)
       3. Charles Noyes (1854–1920) *m.* 1873 Hannah Long (1853–1898)
       4. Chaney Noyes (1824–1874) *m.* Sarah V. Carver (1827–1915)
       5. Reuben Carver (1797–1890) *m.* 1820 Hannah C. Wood (1798–1856)
       6. Thaddeus Carver (1751–1832) *m.* 1776 Hannah Hall (1759–)
       7. Reuben Carver (1718–1800) *m.* Mary Phillips
       8. William Carver (1685–1763) *m.* 1712 Abigail Branch (1693–)
       9. William Carver (1659–1760) *m.* 1682 Elizabeth Foster (1664–1715)
      10. John Carver (1637–1679) *m.* 1658 Willicent Ford
      11. ROBERT CARVER (1594–1680) *m.* Christian ——, *d.* 1658
      Reference: Carver Family of N. Eng., 1935, Clifford M. Carver.

6590 JOHNSON, Margaret E. W.   Recorded 1948, Maryland
       921 Highland Drive, Silver Spring, Maryland
       1. Margaret Estelle Walker *m.* 1912 —— Johnson
       2. George A. Walker (1862–1933) *m.* 1887 Margaret A. Giesler (1867–1947)
       3. John P. Walker (1813–1882) *m.* 1845 Lucinda Parker (1828–1921)
       4. Henry S. Walker (1767–1854) *m.* 1800 Sophia Badger (1771–1838)
       5. John Walker, Jr. (1740–1796) *m.* 1761 Elizabeth Stuart, *d.* 1837
       6. Benjamin Stuart, *d.* 1766, *m.* Matilda Scarburgh (1728–)
       7. Andrew Stuart, *d.* 1745, *m.* Sarah ——
       8. Andrew Stuart, *d.* 1697, *m.* Judeth Harmanson
       9. THOMAS HARMANSON
      Service: Member of House of Burgesses and Patentee of 500 acres of land in Eastern
             Virginia.
      Reference: The Harmanson Family; Va. Mag. Hist. and Biol.

6627 JOHNSON, Mrs. Nathan M.   Recorded 1949
       Dunn, North Carolina
       1. Elizabeth H. Denning *m.* Nathan M. Johnson
       2. Dr. Ollin L. Denning (1862–1927) *m.* Meda L. McDaniel (1865–1938)
       3. Randall McDaniel (1816–1887) *m.* Elizabeth Hodges (1824–1896)
       4. Dr. Samuel Hodges *ca.* (1789–1841) *m.* Elizabeth Johnson (1798–1832)
       5. Robert Hodges (1758–1816) *m.* 1779 Mary Lloyd (Lide) (1763–1816)
       6. Maj. Robert Lloyd (Lide) (1734–1802) *m.* 1760 Sarah Kolb (1736–1789)
       7. Davis Lloyd (1707–1773) *m. ca.* 1729 Ann Crawford (1710–*ca.* 1740)
       8. Robert Lloyd (1669–1714) *m.* 1698 Lowry Jones (1680–1762)
       9. THOMAS LLOYD (1640–1694) *m.* Mary Jones
      Service: Deputy Governor of Pennsylvania.
      Reference: Americans of Royal Descent, Brownings.

5957 JOHNSTON, Mrs. Robert J.   Recorded 1930, Connecticut
       Humbolt, Iowa
       1. Mary H. Stoddard *m.* 1888 Robert J. Johnston
       2. James G. Stoddard (1826–1871) *m.* 1863 Margaret Barr (1844–1922)
       3. Jonathan Stoddard (1783–1859) *m.* 1812 Hannah Morgan (1787–1867)
       4. Israel Morgan (1757–1816) *m.* 1777 Elizabeth Brewster (1757–1826)
       5. William Morgan (1723–1777) *m.* 1744 Temperance Avery (1725–1801)
       6. William Morgan (1693–1729) *m.* 1716 Mary Avery (1696–1780)
       7. John Morgan (1645–1712) *m.* Elizabeth J. Williams (1664–)
       8. Dep. Gov. William Jones (1624–1706) *m.* 1659 Hannah Eaton (1633–1707)
       9. Theophilus Eaton (1590–1657) *m.* (2) Ann Lloyd Yale (–1659)
      10. REV. GEORGE LLOYD *m.* Anna Wilkinson
      Service: Governor, Connecticut.
      Reference: N. E. Hist. & Gen. Register, Jan., 1910; Atwater's Hist. of New Haven
             Colony; Genealogy, James Morgan and his Descendants; Avery Genealogy;
             Records, N. Y. Historical Collection, Vol. II.

6193 JONES, Carolyn Annette   Recorded 1938, Georgia
       805 Woodrow, Dublin, Georgia
1. Carolyn Annette Jones (1934–)
2. Mrs. Josephine Humphries (1909–) *m.* 1932 Wilbur Sparks Jones
3. John D. Humphries (1873–) *m.* 1900 Lillie Jones (1877–)
4. Annis Elizabeth Pope (1852–1884) *m.* 1870 Amos D. Humphries (1848–1910)
5. John H. Pope (1818–1902) *m.* 1840 Emily Crow (1821–1870)
6. John H. Pope (1778–1849) *m.* abt. 1803 Susannah (1780–1844)
7. Henry Pope (1748–) *m.* Charity (1747–)
8. William Pope, *b.* abt. 1725, *m.* abt. 1746 Mary, *b.* abt. 1727
9. John Pope (abt. 1697–1735) *m.* abt. 1723 Elizabeth Pope, *b.* abt. 1699
10. Nathaniel Pope *m.* abt. 1690 Jane Brown
11. Nathaniel Pope *m.* Mary Sisson
12. NATHANIEL POPE, *d.* 1660, *m.* Lucy ⸻
Service: Lieutenant Colonel of Westmoreland Co., Va., Troops.
Reference: Ga. Desc. of Nathaniel Pope, by John D. Humphries, pgs. 5, 6, 7, 8, 9, 10, 12, 15, 17, 18.

6262 JONES, Dean Crawford   Recorded 1939, New Jersey
       110 N. Wyoming Avenue, Ventnor City, New Jersey
                      (JUNIOR)
1. Dean Crawford Jones
2. Armand F. Jones, *b.* 1907, *m.* 1933 Margaret T. Crawford, *b.* 1908
3. Dean B. Crawford, *b.* 1881, *m.* 1907 Agnes A. Thompson, *b.* 1887
4. George Carllin Thompson (1861–1898) *m.* 1884 Margaret Rachel Thomas (1866–1926)
5. Jesse Thomas (1839–1919) *m.* 1865 Eunice Smith Lee (1847–1922)
6. Abel Lee (1811–1895) *m.* 1839 Margaret Smith (1820–1900)
7. Constant Smith (1781–1861) *m.* 1814 Eunice Somers (1783–1860)
8. Thomas Somers (1750–1826) *m.* 1780 Alice Higby (1755–1835)
9. John Somers (1723–1783) *m.* 1744 Esther Risley, *d.* 1786
10. James Somers (1695–1761) *m.* Abigail Adams (1695–1772)
11. JOHN SOMERS (1640–1723) *m.* Hannah Hodgkins (1667–1738)
Service: Road Supervisor, Constable, Great Egg Harbor, 1693; Member Fourth Assembly, 1708.
Reference: Journals House of Representatives, N. J.; Hall's History of Atlantic Co.; Wills, Deeds and Records.

6192 JONES, Gwendolyn Joanne   Recorded 1938, Georgia
       Dublin, Georgia
1. Gwendolyn Joanne Jones (1934–)
2. Mrs. Josephine Humphries (1909–) *m.* 1932 Wilbur Sparks Jones
3. John D. Humphries (1873–) *m.* 1900 Lillie Jones (1877–)
4. Annis Elizabeth Pope (1852–1884) *m.* 1870 Amos D. Humphries (1848–1910)
5. John H. Pope (1818–1902) *m.* 1840 Emily Crow (1821–1870)
6. John H. Pope (1778–1849) *m.* 1803 Susannah ⸻ (1780–1844)
7. Henry Pope (1748–) *m.* Charity ⸻ (1747–)
8. William Pope, *b.* abt. 1725, *m.* abt. 1746 Mary, *b.* abt. 1727
9. John Pope (abt. 1697–1735) *m.* 1723 Elizabeth Pope, *b.* abt. 1699
10. Nathaniel Pope *m.* abt. 1690 Jane Brown
11. Nathaniel Pope *m.* Mary Sisson
12. NATHANIEL POPE, *d.* 1660, *m.* Lucy
Service: Lieutenant Colonel of Westmoreland Co., Va., Troops.
Reference: Ga. Desc. of Nathaniel Pope, by John D. Humphries, pgs. 5, 6, 7, 8, 9, 10, 12, 15, 17, 18; S.D.P. No. 6148.

6138 JONES, Mrs. James J.   Recorded 1937, Georgia
       Graceville, Florida
1. Katherine Brinson *m.* 1931 James J. Jones
2. Homer H. Brinson (1878–) *m.* 1898 Caroline E. Jones (1878–)
3. Simeon Brinson (1847–1918) *m.* 1875 Hattie Russell (1857–1883)
4. Adam Brinson (1812–1859) *m.* 1842 Catherine Hodges (1806–)
5. John Brinson (1767–1840) *m.* 1807 Martha (1787–)
6. ADAM BRINSON I (1689–1769) *m.* Sarah Sterring (1693–1774)
Service: Fought in the Colonial Wars in North Carolina.

6162 JONES, Josephine Humphries   Recorded 1937, Georgia
          805 Woodrow Street, Dublin, Georgia
      1. Josephine Humphries Jones (1909–) *m.* 1932 Wilbur Sparks Jones
      2. John D. Humphries (1873–) *m.* 1900 Lillie Marvin Jones (1877–)
      3. Amos D. Humphries (1848–) *m.* 1870 Annis Elizabeth Pope (1852–1884)
      4. John H. Pope (1818–1902) *m.* abt. 1840 Emily Crow (1821–1870)
      5. John Pope (1778–1849) *m.* abt. 1803 Susanna (1780–1844)
      6. Henry Pope (1748–) *m.* Charity ———— (1747–)
      7. William Pope *b.* abt. 1725, *m.* abt. 1746 Mary ————, *b.* abt. 1727
      8. John Pope (abt. 1697–1735) *m.* abt. 1723 Elizabeth Pope (abt. 1699–)
      9. Nathaniel Pope *m.* 1690 Jane Brown
      10. Nathaniel Pope *m.* Mary Sisson
      11. NATHANIEL POPE, *d.* 1660, *m.* Lucy
      Service: Lieutenant-Colonel of Westmoreland County, Va., Troops.
      Reference: S.D.P. Nat. No. 6148 and 6149; Ga. Desc. of Nathaniel Pope, by John D.
          Humphries, pgs. 5, 6, 7, 8, 9, 10, 12, 15, 17, 18.

6290 JONES, Mariluise Crawford   Recorded 1920, New Jersey
          110 N. Wyoming Avenue, Ventor City, New Jersey
                          (JUNIOR)
      1. Mariluise Crawford Jones
      2. Armand F. Jones (1907–) *m.* 1933 Margaret Thompson Crawford, *b.* 1908
      3. Dean B. Crawford *m.* 1907 Agnes A. Thompson, *b.* 1887
      4. George Carlin Thompson (1861–1898) *m.* 1884 Margaret Rachel Thomas
          (1866–1926)
      5. Jesse Thomas (1839–1919) *m.* 1865 Eunice Smith Lee (1842–1865)
      6. Abel Lee (1811–1895) *m.* 1839 Margaret Smith (1820–1900)
      7. Constant Smith (1781–1861) *m.* 1814 Eunice Somers (1783–1860)
      8. Thomas Somers (1750–1826) *m.* 1780 Alice Higby (1755–1835)
      9. Edward Higby (1714–1793) *m.* 1738 Jemima Risley
      10. Richard Risley (1693–1740) *m.* Hester Conover (1698–aft. 1737)
      11. Peter Conover (bapt. 1669–1704) *m.* 2nd Mary, *d.* 1731
      12. Pieter Wolfertse, *c.* (1614–1675) *m.* 2nd 1668 Aeltje Sibrants, *d.* 1670
      13. WOLFERT GERRETSEN VAN COUVENHOVEN (1588–aft. 1660) *m.* 1605 Neeltje
          Janse
      Service: Supt. of Farms for Patron Van Rennslaer; a Founder of Flatlands, L. I.
          (New Amersfoort).
      Reference: N. J. Cal. of Wills Lib. 1, 2, 3; Gloucester Co. Wills; Somerset Co. Hist.
          Quart. (1916), Vol. V.

6301 JONES, Miriam Jeannette   Recorded 1940, New Jersey
      1. John W. W. Jones (1894–) *m.* 1922 Rosa May Rickenbach (1894–)
      2. Hon. Samuel Jones (1859–1914) *m.* 1884 Sarah Jeannette Wriggins (1858–)
      3. Charles Wriggins (1821–1896) *m.* 1847 Sarah Ann Howey (1825–1885)
      4. Thomas Wriggins (1790–1866) *m.* 1810 Sarah Barber (1788–1864)
      5. James Barber (1752–1832) *m.* 1780 Pennuia Barker (*c* 1760–bef. 1832)
      6. Aquila Barber (1710–1759) *m.* 1736 Hannah Hucking (1708–1762)
      7. Aquila Barber (1678–1762) *m.* Mary Patterson
      8. JOHN BARBER, *d.* 1682, *m.* Elizabeth
      Service: Name follows that of William Penn on Passenger List.
      Reference: Craig Genealogy; Records Salem and Trenton, N. J.; Records Trinity
          Church, Swedesboro.

6056 JONES, Mrs. Ralph   Recorded 1933, New Jersey
          928 Gaunt Street, Gloucester City, New Jersey
      1. Cerillie Zara Ogden *m.* Ralph Jones
      2. Edward C. Ogden (1861–) *m.* 1886 Elizabeth Holdcraft (1869–)
      3. Elmer Ogden (1832–1886) *m.* 1858 Mary Ann Duffy (–1886)
      4. Jason Ogden (1777–1845) *m.* 1822 Elizabeth Taylor (1801–1876)
      5. Jason Ogden (–1801) *m.* Joanna Davis (1744–)
      6. David Ogden *m.* Mary Elmer
      7. John Ogden (1671–1746) *m.* Mary Dimon
      8. RICHARD OGDEN, SR. (1610–1687) *m.* 1639 Mary Hall
      Reference: South Jersey Ogdens; New Jersey Archives, First Series, Vol. XXXII.

6498 JONES, Miss Sarah C. Recorded 1945
Beachwood, New Jersey
(JUNIOR MEMBERSHIP)
1. Miss Sarah Crawford Jones
2. Armand Jones (1907–) *m.* 1933 Margaret T. Crawford (1908–)
3. Dean B. Crawford (1881–) *m.* 1907 Agnes A. Thompson (1887–)
4. George C. Thompson (1861–1898) *m.* 1884 Margaret R. Thomas (1866–1926)
5. Jesse Thomas (1839–1919) *m.* 1865 Eunice Smith Lee (1847–1922)
6. Abel Lee (1811–1895) *m.* 1839 Margaret Smith (1820–1900)
7. Constant Smith (1781–1861) *m.* 1814 Eunice Somers (1783–1860)
8. Thomas Somers (1750–1826) *m.* 1780 Alice Higby (1755–1835)
9. John Somers (1723–1783) *m.* 1744 Esther Risley (–1786)
10. James Somers (1695–1761) *m.* Abigail Adams (1695–1772)
11. JOHN SOMERS (1640–1738) *m.* 1684 (2nd) Hannah Hodgkins (1667–1738)
Service: Road Supervisor; Constable Great Egg Harbor, N. J., 1693; Member 4th
Assembly, 1708.

6347 JONES, Mrs. Vincent Weaver Recorded 1941, Connecticut
47 Westwood Road, West Hartford, Connecticut
1. Elizabeth Boardman Post *m.* Vincent W. Jones
2. David J. Post (1861–1933) *m.* 1887 Grace Elizabeth Boardman (1864–1936)
3. Major Chauncey B. Boardman (1839–1905) *m.* 1863 Sarah Lamb (1836–1905)
4. Major Allen C. Boardman (1806–1850) *m.* Elizabeth Barnard (1802–1856)
5. Capt. Benjamin J. Boardman (1782–1829) *m.* 1803 Sally Clark (1786–1846)
6. Elizur Boardman (1738–1790) *m.* Rebecca Sage (1739–1810)
7. Edward Boardman (1702–1772) *m.* 1726/7 Dorothy Smith (1703–1777)
8. Isaac Boardman, Jr. (1666–1719) *m.* 1699 Rebecca Benton
9. Isaac Boreman (1642–1719) *m.* Abiah Kimberly (1641–1722/3
10. SAMUEL BOREMAN (1615–1673) *m.* Mary Betts, *d.* 1684
Service: Entered grant on Town Book of Ipswich, Mass., 1693.
Reference: Boardman Genealogy.

6505 JULIAN, Mrs. William L Recorded 1945
Evanston, Illinois
1. Elizabeth Virginia Stoolman *m.* William Lincoln Julian
2. Almon Winfield Stoolman (1876–) *m.* 1909 Lois Gertrude Franklin (1881–)
3. William Lyman Franklin (1830–1913) *m.* 1860 Caroline E. Morton (1843–1922)
4. Alexander Morton (1796–1876) *m.* 1820 Martha Anderson (1798–1881)
5. Alexander Morton (1759–1822) *m.* 1784 Ruth Strong (1762–1850)
6. Elijah Strong (1733–) *m.* 1756 Ruth Loomis (1729–)
7. Jedediah Strong (1700–) *m.* 1722 Elizabeth Webster
8. Capt. John Webster (1672–1735) *m.* 1709 Grace Loomis
9. Thomas Webster (–1686) *m.* 1663 Abigail Alexander
10. Gov. JOHN WEBSTER (–1661) *m.* 1609 Agnes Smith (–1667)
Service: Founder of Hartford, Conn.; Gov. of Colony of Conn., 1656–57; Died 1661 at
Hadley, Mass.

6463 KAISER, Mrs. Oliver B. Recorded 1945, Ohio
Drake Road, Indian Hill, Cincinnati 27, Ohio
1. Grace Edwards *m.* Oliver B. Kaiser
2. Thomas H. H. Edwards (1850–1933) *m.* 1874 Eva Williams (1854–1933)
3. Alexander H. Edwards (1807–) *m.* 1832 Charlotte Atlee (1815–)
4. Abraham Edwards (1781–1860) *m.* 1805 Ruth Hunt (1788–)
5. Col. Thomas Hunt (1754–1808) *m.* 178? Eunice Wellington (1768–)
6. John Hunt (1716–1777) *m.* 173? Ruth Fessenden (1717–1800)
7. Samuel Hunt (1689–1774) *m.* 171? (2nd) Katharine Thayer (–1737)
8. Thomas Hunt (1648–1721) *m.* 167? Judith Torrey (–1693)
9. Ephraim Hunt (1610–1686) *m.* 164? Anna Richards
10. ENOCH HUNT *m.* (2nd) Sarah Barker
Service: Freeman, Newport, R. I., 1638; Town Offices, Weymouth, Mass., 1651.
Reference: Hunt Gen., by W. L. G. Hunt; Atlee Gen.; Gen. Early Sett. Watertown,
Mass.; Pioneers of Mass., Pope.

6462   KAISER, Ramona (Miss)   Recorded 1945, Ohio
       Drake Road, Indian Hill, Cincinnati 27, Ohio

1. Miss Ramona Kaiser
2. Oliver B. Kaiser (1877–) *m.* 1902 Grace Edwards (1881–)
3. Thomas H. H. Edwards (1850–1933) *m.* 1874 Eva Williams (1854–1933)
4. Alexander H. Edwards (1807–) *m.* 1832 Charlotte Atlee (1815–)
5. Abraham Edwards (1781–1860) *m.* 1805 Ruth Hunt (1788–)
6. Thomas Hunt (1754–1808) *m.* 178? Eunice Wellington (1768–)
7. John Hunt (1716–1777) *m.* 173? Ruth Fessenden (1717–1800)
8. Samuel Hunt (1689–1774) *m.* 171? (2nd) Katherine Thayer (–1737)
9. Thomas Hunt (1648–1721) *m.* 167? Judith Torrey (–1693)
12. Ephraim Hunt (1610–1686) *m.* 164? Anna Richards
11. ENOCH HUNT *m.* (2nd) Sarah Barker

Service: Freeman at Newport, R. I., 1638; Town Officer, Weymouth, Mass., 1651.
Reference: Hunt Gen., by W. L. G. Hunt; Atlee Gen.; Gen. Early Sett. Watertown,
       Mass.; Pioneers of Mass., Pope.

6532   KALISH, Mrs. David Francis   Recorded 1946, Ohio
       Commodore Perry Hotel, Toledo 3, Ohio

1. Harriet Nichols *m.* 1915 David Francis Kalish
2. Addison Nichols (1852–1907) *m.* 1881 Alida Madden (1857–1886)
3. Isaac B. Nichols (1823–1917) *m.* 1843 Harriet Phillips (1824–1908)
4. John Phillips (1783–1868) *m.* 1811 Abigail Raymond (1794–1833)
5. David Raymond (1767–1852) *m.* 1788 Abigail Sherwood (1770–1832)
6. David Sherwood (1745–1817) *m.* 1769 Abigail Ogden (1756–1813)
7. Joseph Sherwood (1702–1790) *m.* 1731 Sarah Osborn (1711–1793)
8. Serg. David Osborn (1686–1727) *m.* Dorothy Bulkley (1687–1734)
9. Dr. Peter Bulkley (1643–1691) *m.* Margaret Foxcroft *d.* 1690
10. REV. PETER BULKLEY, M.A. (1582–1659) *m.* Grace Chetwood (1602–1669)

Service: One of the Founders of Concord, Mass.
Reference: Families of Old Fairfield; Sherwood Gen.; Bulkley Genealogy.

6203   KAUFFMAN, Alice Lianne   Recorded 1938
       207 Ridgewood Avenue, Charlotte, North Carolina

(JUNIOR MEMBERSHIP)

1. Alice Lianne Kauffman
2. Charles Crouch Kauffman, Sr. (1902–) *m.* 1927 Dorothy Dorough (1904–)
3. Ovrin F. Kauffman (1876–1930) *m.* 1900 Gertrude Evangeline Curtis (1879–)
4. Ezra Sager Curtis (1848–) *m.* 1873 Mary Josephine Winder (1855–1927)
5. Thomas Orchard Sager (–1885) *m.* 1836 Mary R. Curtis (1820–1876)
6. Ezra S. Curtis (1790–1864) *m.* 1819 Irene Sprague (1794–1869)
7. Ezra St. John Curtis (1758–) *m.* ———— Ryan
8. Caleb Curtis, Jr. (1727–1774) *m.* 1754 Phebe St. John (1736–)
9. Caleb Curtis (1703–1777) *m.* 1726 Jemima Calkins (1708–1789)
10. Samuel Curtice (1681–1740) *m.* 1702 Mary ———— (–1724)
11. Caleb Curtis (1646–1730) *m.* 1670 Elizabeth Ryder (–1711)
12. RICHARD CURTIS (–1671) *m.* Sarah ————

Reference: Hist. of Salem, by Sidney Perly, Vol. 2, 1926; Records of Southold, L. I.;
       Hebron, Conn.; Savage's Gen. Dict. of New Eng., Vol. 1.

5895   KAUFFMAN, Benjamin Curtis   Recorded 1930, Georgia
       477 W. Ontario Avenue S. W., Atlanta, Georgia

1. Benjamin Curtis Kauffman
2. Orrin Frederick Kauffman (1876–) *m.* 1900 Gertrude Evangeline Curtis
       (1879–)
3. Ezra Sager Curtis (1848–) *m.* 1873 Mary Josephine Winder (1855–1927)
4. Thomas Orchard Sager (–1885) *m.* 1836 Mary R. Curtis (1820–1876)
5. Ezra S. Curtis (1790–1864) *m.* 1819 Irene Sprague (1794–1869)

6. Ezra St. John Curtis (1758–) *m.* —— Ryan
7. Caleb Curtis, Jr. (1727–1774) *m.* 1754 Phoebe St. John (1736–)
8. Ezra St. John (1707–1740) *m.* 1733 Anne St. John (1717–)
9. CAPTAIN MATTHEW ST. JOHN (1686–1755) *m.* 1709 Anne Whitney (1690–1732)

Service: Ensign, Lieut. and Captain; Original Settler, Wilton Parish, Norwalk.
Reference: Colonial Records, 126, 297.

6202 KAUFFMAN, Charles Crouch, Jr.
207 Ridgewood Avenue, Charlotte, North Carolina

(JUNIOR MEMBERSHIP)

1. Charles Crouch Kauffman (1902–) *m.* 1927 Dorothy Dorough (1904–)
2. Orrin Frederick Kauffman (1876–1930) *m.* 1900 Gertrude E. Curtis (1879–)
3. Ezra Sager Curtis (1848–1927) *m.* 1873 Mary Josephine Winder (1855–)
4. Thomas Orchard Sager (–1885) *m.* 1836 Mary R. Curtis (1820–1876)
5. Ezra S. Curtis (1790–1864) *m.* 1819 Irene Sprague (1794–1869)
6. Vine Sprague (1772–1813) *m.* 1793 Mary Sherwin (1768–1813)
7. Capt. Elkanah Sprague (1732–) *m.* 1754 Mehitable Moulton
8. Benjamin Sprague (1686–1754) *m.* Abigail Hodges (wid. Elkanck Tisdale) 11th Child of
9. Henry Hodges (1652–1717) *m.* 1674 Esther Gallup (1653–)
10. John Gallup (in Eng. –1675) *m.* Hannah Lake
11. CAPT JOHN GALLUP (in Eng. 1590–1650)

Service: Capt. Conn. Co., King Philip War.
Reference: Sprague Fam. America, Sprague; Gen. Hodges Fam., Hodges; Gen. Gallup Fam., Gallup.

6204 KAUFFMAN, Dorothy Dee   Recorded 1938
207 Ridgewood Avenue, Charlotte, North Carolina

1. Dorothy Dee Kauffman
2. Chas. C. Kauffman, Sr. (1902–) *m.* 1927 Dorothy Dorough (1904–)
3. Orrin Fred. Kauffman (1876–1930) *m.* 1900 Gertrude E. Curtis (1879–)
4. Ezra Sager Curtis (1848–) *m.* 1873 Mary J. Winder (1855–1927)
5. Thomas Orchard Sager (–1885) *m.* 1836 Mary R. Curtis (1820–1876)
6. Ezra S. Curtis (1790–1864) *m.* 1819 Irene Sprague (1794–1869)
7. Ezra St. John Curtis (1758–) *m.* —— Ryan
8. Caleb Curtis, Jr. (1727–1774) *m.* 1754 Phebe St. John (1736–)
9. Ezra St. John (1707–1740) *m.* 1733 Anne St. John (1717–)
10. Ebenezer St. John (1660–1723) *m.* Elizabeth Comstock (1674–)
11. Christopher Comstock (–1702) *m.* 1663 Hannah Platt (1642–1684)
12. DEACON RICHARD PLATT (1603–1684) *m.* Mary —— (–1676)

Reference: Comstock Gen., by Cyrus B. Comstock; St. John Gen., by Orline St. John Alexander.

6158 KEATES, Anna Mary   Recorded 1937
1713 Atlantic Avenue, Atlantic City, New Jersey

1. Anna Mary Keates (1866–) *m.* 1886 George H. Keates
2. Evan Jeffries (1831–1904) *m.* 1854 Hannah Rette D. Adams (1837–1915)
3. Richard Adams (1800–1877) *m.* Sarah Ela (1802–1852)
4. Joshua Adams (1771–1809) *m.* Sarah Boice (1767–1861)
5. John Adams (1737–W.P. 1798) *m.* 1763 Margaret Garwood (1740–1825)
6. John Adams (abt. 1700–1770) *m.* prob. Mary Cowenhoven
7. Jonathan Adams (1668–W.P. 1727) *m.* Barbara
8. John Adams (abt. 1637–1670) *m.* Abigail Smith
9. Jeremy Adams, *d.* 1683, *m.* abt. 1637 Rebecca (widow of Samuel Greenhill)

Service: Came to Cambridge in 1632; Original Proprietor of Hartford, 1636, where he kept the famous Inn. Served in Indian Wars.
Reference: Genealogy of the Lake Family, Adams & Risley, pages 165–166.

6377   KEATS, George H.   Recorded 1942, New Jersey
          16 S. Martindale Avenue, Ventnor City, New Jersey
                                    (JUNIOR)
    1. George H. Keats
    2. Howard Paxson Keats (1894–   ) *m*. 1926 Marion Knerr
    3. George H. Keats (1860–1934) *m*. 1886 Anna Jeffries, *b*. 1866
    4. Evan Jeffries (1831–1904) *m*. 1854 Hannah Rette Adams (1837–1915)
    5. Richard Adams (1800–1877) *m*. Sarah Ela (1802–1852)
    6. Joshua Adams (1771–1807) *m*. Sarah Boice (1767–1861)
    7. John Adams (1737–1798) *m*. 1763 Margaret Garwood (1740–1825)
    8. John Adams *d*. aft. 1770, *m*. Mary Von Cowenhoven
    9. Jonathan Adams (1668–1727) *m*. Barbara White, *d*. 1727
   10. John Adams (1637–1670) *m*. 1657 Abigail Smith, *d*. 1690
   11. JEREMY ADAMS (1604–1683) *m*. 1636 Rebecca Greenhill, *d*. 1678

    Service: Fought in Indian Wars; was Collector of Customs and Indian Agent; one of
       the Founders of Hartford, Conn.
    Reference: Genealogy of the Lake Family.

6378   KEATS, H. Paxson   Recorded 1942, New Jersey
          16 S. Martindale Avenue, Ventnor, New Jersey
                                    (JUNIOR)
    1. H. Paxson Keats
    2. Howard Paxson Keats (1894–   ) *m*. 1926 Marion Knerr
    3. George H. Keats (1860–1934) *m*. 1886 Anna Jeffries (1866–   )
    4. Evan Jeffries (1831–1904) *m*. 1854 Hannah Rette Adams (1837–1915)
    5. Richard Adams (1800–1877) *m*. Sarah Ela (1802–1852)
    6. Joshua Adams (1771–1807) *m*. Sarah Boice (1767–1861)
    7. John Adams (1737–1798) *m*. 1763 Margaret Garwood
    8. John Adams, *d*. aft. 1770, *m*. Mary Von Cowenhoven
    9. Jonathan Adams (1668–1729) *m*. Barbara White, *d*. 1727
   10. John Adams (1637–1670) *m*. 1657 Abigail Smith, *d*. 1690
   11. JEREMY ADAMS (1604–1683) *m*. 1636 Rebecca Greenhill, *d*. 1678

    Service: Fought in Indian Wars; Collector of Customs and Indian Agent; a Founder
       of Hartford, Conn.
    Reference: Genealogy of the Lake Family.

6502   KELLEY, Miss Konstance W.   Recorded 1945
          Greenwich, Connecticut

    1. Miss Konstance Walker Kelley
    2. George Fergus Kelley (1888–   ) *m*. 1912 Pearl Ann Walker (1885–   )
    3. Charles Andrew Walker (1854–1917) *m*. 1880 Ann Howard Hartsook (1856–1934)
    4. David Hillary Hartsook (1824–1912) *m*. 1846 Nancy Emaline Sherman
       (1827–1919)
    5. Elisha Sherman (1780–1845) *m*. 1811 (2nd) Nancy Cook (1782–   )
    6. Seth Sherman (1754–1804) *m*. 1772 Mary Harkness
    7. Nehemiah Sherman (1722–1802) *m*. 1745 Experience Wing
    8. David Sherman (1680–1755) *m*. 1710 Abigail Hathaway
    9. Edmund Sherman (1641–1719) *m*. Dorcas ———
   10. PHILIP SHERMAN (1610–1687) *m*. 1633 Sarah Odding

    Service: Original proprietor of Portsmouth, R. I.; Secretary of Portsmouth Colony,
       1639; General Recorder, 1648–1651; Commissioner to General Court, 1656.

6631   KELLENBERGER, Mrs. John A.   Recorded 1949
          McConnell Road, Greensboro, North Carolina

    1. May Gordon Latham *m*. 1920 John A. Kellenberger
    2. James E. Latham (1866–1946) *m*. 1892 Maude Moore (1871–   )
    3. James W. Moore (1848–1913) *m*. 1869 Sarah J. Gorton (1851–1932)
    4. John S. Gorton (1830–1898) *m*. 1850 Catherine Flinn (1833–1862)

5. Ethan Gorton (1807–1861) *m.* 1828 Mary Sague, *d.* 1861
6. Joseph Gorton (1773–1851) *m.* 1796 Charlot Schriver (1774–abt. 1851)
7. William Gorton, Jr. (1748–abt. 1834) *m.* 1770 Phebe Daniels, *d.* bef. 1805
8. William Gorton, Sr. (1706–1761) *m.* 1736 Lydia Collins (1714–1809)
9. John Gorton, Jr. (abt. 1675–aft. 1750) *m.* 1700 Patience Hopkins (abt. 1678–bef. 1717)
10. John Gorton, Sr. (abt. 1639–1714) *m.* 1665 Margaret Weeden (abt. 1642–)
11. Samuel Gorton, Sr. (bapt. 1592–1677) *m.* bef. 1630 Mary Maplet, *d.* aft. 1677
Service: Founded town of Warwick, R. I.; Asst. to Gov. Roger Williams; Pres. of Colony of R. I.
Reference: Life and Times of Samuel Gorton.

6720 KENDALL, Mrs. John W.   Recorded 1951, Indiana
       632 W. First Street, Marion, Indiana
1. Agnes Lownsdale *m.* 1908 J. W. Kendall
2. Thomas N. Lownsdale (1841–1914) *m.* 1877 Alice Delilah Bothwell (1852–1935)
3. John T. Bothwell (1816–1911) *m.* 1848 Indiana Seawell Mabry (1827–1872)
4. Benjamin Seawell Mabry (1794–1871) *m.* 1813 Delilah Zora Murphy (1792–1858)
5. Seth Mabry (1752–aft. 1803) *m.* 1771 Elizabeth Seawell (1747–1803)
6. Henshaw Mabry, Jr. (1720–1755) *m.* Celia Evans (1722–bef. 1755)
7. Henshaw Mabry, Sr. (1697–aft. 1726) *m.* Frances Parham (abt. 1700–aft. 1726)
8. Francis Mabry (abt. 1665–1712) *m.* Elizabeth Gilliam (–1715)
9. John Gilliam, Jr. (abt. 1614–1672) *m.* Margery Henshaw (–1714)
10. John Gilliam, Sr. (abt. 1580–will 1651)
Service: Landed Proprietor.
Reference: History of Clay Co., Ill., pg. 178; History of Benjamin Seawell and Sarah Hicks; Wills of William Seawell, Col. Benjamin Seawell, of William Evans and Ephream Parram, in Surry Co., Va.; Wills of Henshaw Mabry, Frances Mabry, Elizabeth Gilliam Mabry, all recorded in Surry Co., Va.; Will of John Gilliam, Sr., recorded in Norfolk Co., Va., 1651.

5843 KENT, Mrs. Kate Stratton   Recorded 1929
       622 State Street, St. Joseph, Michigan
1. Kate Stratton (1863–) *m.* 1883 ——— Kent
2. Robt. Folger Stratton (1831–1918) *m.* 1859 Cornelia J. Chapman (1842–)
3. William Stratton (1781–1849) *m.* 1809 Abbey May Clarke (1788–1878)
4. Hezekiah Stratton (1746–1834) *m.* 1778 Eunice Haywood (1760–1836)
5. Hezekiah Stratton (1714–) *m.* 1737 Dorothy Hubbard (1719–1768)
6. Sam. Stratton (1684–) *m.* 1709 Sarah Allen
7. Samuel Stratton (1660–1717) *m.* 1683 Elizabeth Fletcher (1663–1762)
8. Samuel Stratton (–1707) *m.* 1651 Mary Frye (–1674)
9. Samuel Stratton (1592–1672) *m.* Alice ———
Reference: Stratton Genealogy.

6356 KEYSER, Mrs. Frank Ray   Recorded 1941, Vermont
       Chelsea, Vermont
1. Frank Ray Keyser *m.* 1921 Ellen Larkin
2. Winfield Scott Keyser (1872–1938) *m.* 1893 Harriet B. Bailey (1872–1930)
3. Scott Winfield Keyser *m.* Mary E. Stocker, *d.* 1922
4. Franklin Kezar *m.* Hannah Gale
5. Stephen Gale *d. c.* 1836, *m.* Margaret Sanborn (1779–1855)
6. Major Theopholus Sanborn (1753–1839) *m.* 1779 Mary Sleeper (1758–)
7. Daniel Sanborn (1728–1812) *m.* 1748 Anna Tilton, *d.* 1759
8. Abraham Sanborn (1696–1757) *m.* 1718 Dorothy Smith, *d.* 1788
9. Joseph Sanborn *m.* 1682 Mary Gove
10. Lt. John Sanborne (1620–1792) *m.* Mary Tuck, *d.* 1668
Service: Lieutenant.
Reference: Hist. of Woodsville, N. H.; Hist. of Haverhill, N. H.; "Hist. of N. H.," by R. W. Musgrave.

6497   KEZAR, Mrs. Guy Foster   Recorded 1945
          North Hatley, Quebec, Canada
   1. Lois Gladys Colt *m.* Guy Foster Kezar
   2. Stephen Samuel Colt (1858–1930) *m.* 1887 Alice Gertrude Hovey (1864–1918)
   3. Wright Hovey (1832–1884) *m.* 1860 Lois Hitchcock (1841–1922)
   4. Edward Hitchcock (1806–1874) *m.* Mehitable Kezar (1809–1843)
   5. Amos Kezar (1783–1837) *m.* Dorcas Lowell (1787–1875)
   6. Simon Kezar (1753–1817) *m.* Mehitable Foster (1747–1801)
   7. Ebenezer Kezar (1720–1793) *m.* 1745/6 Hannah Moulton (1725–   )
   8. John Kezar (1678–   ) *m.* Judith Heath (–1758)
   9. John Kezar *m.* 1677 Hannah Davis
  10. George Kezar (Keaser) *ca.* (1612–1690) *m.* Elsha ———— (–1659)
   Service: Grand Juryman in Salem, Mass., 1668, 1670, 1677, 1679, 1680, 1684, 1685;
          Surveyor, 1666–67; Constable, 1669.

6380   KIDDER, Hon. Harley Walter   Recorded 1942, Vermont
          61 Summer Street, Barre, Vermont
   1. Harley Walter Kidder *m.* 1927 Ruth Esther Lander
   2. Walter Daniel Kidder (1862–1910) *m.* 1887 Nellie Louise Johnson (1850–   )
   3. Charles Childs Johnson (1820–1901) *m.* 1842 Jemima Whipple Whitney
          (1820–1905)
   4. Moses Whitney (1786–1876) *m.* 1812 Susannah Hall (1792–1866)
   5. Ephraim Whitney, Jr., (1756–1827) *m.* 1778 Jemima Whipple (1753–1795)
   6. Ephraim Whitney (1722–1797) *m.* 1749 Thankful Harrington (1730–1795)
   7. Nathaniel Whitney III (1696–1776) *m.* 1721 Mary Childs (1699–1776)
   8. Nathaniel Whitney, Jr. (1675–1730) *m.* 1695 Mercy Robinson (1676–1740)
   9. Nathaniel Whitney (1646–1732) *m.* 1672 Sarah Hager (1651–1746)
  10. John Whitney, Jr. (1624–1692) *m.* 1642 Ruth Reynolds
  11. John Whitney, Sr. *c.* (1589–1673) *m.* Elinor, *b.* 1599
   Service: Selectman, Watertown, Mass., 1638–1655; Constable, 1641; Town Clerk,
          1655.
   Reference: "Memorials of Vermonters" (1917); "Hist. of Town of Milford, Mass.," by
          A. Ballou; "John Whitney of Watertown," W. L. Whitney; "Whitney
          Family," Henry Melville; Magna Charta Barons and Descendants, C. H.
          Browning.

6729   KILLIAN, Mrs. James W.   Recorded 1951, North Carolina
          805 Boyd Avenue, Wanesville, North Carolina
   1. Eva Truby *m.* 1910 J. W. Killian
   2. Jacob Truby (1847–1933) *m.* 1873 Mary Ellen Weller (1855–   )
   3. Jacob Truby (1816–1884) *m.* 1832 Lucy Hotchkiss (1807–1884)
   4. Jesse Hotchkiss (1780–   ) *m.* 1799 Abigail Thrasher
   5. Ladwick Hotchkiss (1752–1823) Rev. Soldier, *m.* 1773 Martha Lee (1754–1813)
   6. Capt. Ladwick Hotchkiss (1728–1803) Rev. Soldier, *m.* 1743 Molly North
          (1716–1775)
   7. Josiah Hotchkiss (1680–1732) *m.* 1715 Abigail Parker (–1732)
   8. John Hotchkiss (1643–1689) *m.* 1672 Elizabeth Peck
   9. Samuel Hotchkiss (–1663) *m.* 1642 Elizabeth Cleverly
   Service: Assisted in establishing town of New Haven, Conn.
   Reference: The marriage of Samuel Hotchkiss to Elizabeth Cleverly is recorded in
          Court of Hew Haven, Conn., family has been published from County
          records; family history in Library of State of Conn., New Haven, Conn.,
          Mag., 8 pg. 1549–50–51; Vol. 2, pg. 1552; Vol. 3, pg. 1551; Hartford, Conn.,
          Court, 1657; Memorial History of Hartford, Conn., by J. Hammond
          Trumbull, Vol. I, pg. 266; Family History with all references submitted
          with application.

6471   KING, Mrs. Orion   Recorded 1945, Ohio
          148 West High Street, Circleville, Ohio
   1. Laura Millar *m.* Orion King
   2. Michael See Millar (1847–1924) *m.* 1874 (2nd) Sarah Jane Hickman (1849–1920)

3. Adam Millar (1815–1891) *m.* 1841 Nancy Robinson Howell (1819–1906)
4. William Millar (1778–1863) *m.* 1808 Mary Sudduth (1783–1860)
5. Isaac Millar (1751–1815) *m.* 1777 Elizabeth See (1756–1794)
6. William Millar (1706–1778) *m.* 1743 Catherine Du Bois (1715–1778)
7. Isaac Du Bois (1691–1729) *m.* 1714 Rachel Du Bois
8. Solomon Du Bois (1670–1759) *m.* 1690 Teyntje Gerretson Cornelius (1671–)
9. Louis Du Bois (1626–1695) *m.* 1655 Catherine Blanchan (–1706)

Service: Settler Kingston, N. Y.; Patentee of New Paltz.
Reference: Nillar-DuBois Genealogy; Lefevers' Hist. of New Paltz; Hist. Hampshire Co., Va., Hist. Dunmore Co., Va.

6237   KINNE, Donna Kay   Recorded 1939, Georgia
            121 De Soto Place, Macon, Georgia
1. Erwin Newton Kinne (1905–) *m.* 1933 Mary Waring Lewis-Mayben (1908–)
2. Dr. John Waring Lewis (1879–1931) *m.* 1906 Effie Baldock (1880–1931)
3. Philip Winston Lewis (1846–1924) *m.* 1878 Mary Latane Lewis (1851–1922)
4. Dr. John Lewis (1820–) *m.* 1844 Barbara Joanna Winston (1823–1879)
5. Warner Lewis (1786–1873) *m.* 1810 Ann Susanna Latane (1799–1822)
6. Dr. John Taliferro Lewis *m.* 1782 Susanna Waring
7. Capt. Chas. Lewis (1729–) *m.* 1750 Lucy Taliaferro
8. John Lewis 3rd (1694–1752) *m.* 1718 Frances Fielding (–1731)
9. John Lewis 2nd (1669–1725) *m.* 1690 Elizabeth Warner (1673–)
10. Col. John Lewis (1645–) *m.* 1666 Isabelle Warner (1644–)
11. Robt. Lewis (1579–1645) *m.* Elizabeth ⸺
12. Sir Edmund Lewis *m.* Anne Sackville

Reference: Wm. & Mary Col. Quarterly, Vol. 10.

6165   KINNE, Mary Waring Lewis Mayben   Recorded 1938, Georgia
            Macon, Georgia
1. Mary Waring Lewis-Mayben (1908–) *m.* 1933 Erwin Newton Kinne (1905–)
2. Dr. John Waring Lewis (1879–) *m.* 1906 Effie Baldock (1880–)
3. Philip Winston Lewis (1846–1924) *m.* 1878 Mary Latane Lewis (1851–1922)
4. Dr. John Lewis (1820–) *m.* (?) 1844 Barbara Joanna Winston (1823–1879)
5. Warner Lewis (1786–1873) *m.* 1810 Ann Susanna Latane (1799–1822)
6. Dr. John Taliaferro Lewis *m.* 1782 Susanna Waring
7. Capt. Charles Lewis (1729–) *m.* 1750 Lucy Taliaferro
8. John Lewis III (1694–1752) *m.* 1718/19 Frances Fielding
9. John Lewis II (1669–1725) *m.* 1690 Elizabeth Warner (1673–)
10. Col. John Lewis (1645–) *m.* 1666 Isabella Warner (1644–)
11. Robert Lewis, Breacon Wales (1579–1645) *m.* Elizabeth ⸺
12. Sir Edmund Lewis, Willy Co., Eng. *m.* Anne Sackville, dtr. Earl of Dorset

Service: Founder of the family in 1?35 and a distinguished soldier.
Reference: See Nat. No. 146427 D.A.R.; William & Mary College Quart, Vol. 19, 1900–01, pg. 261; Vol. 10, No. 1, July, 1901, pgs. 48–54; Hotten's List of Immigrants.

6480   KINNEY, Mrs. James E.   Recorded 1945, Ohio
            Columbus, Ohio
1. Bertha Rankin *m.* James Edgar Kinney
2. Lewis Lincoln Rankin (1860–1918) *m.* 1882 Harriet Rathmell (1861–1944)
3. Swan Innis Rankin (1832–1913) *m.* 1855 Sarah Melissa Denune (1836–1909)
4. Alexander Burrell Denune (1807–1886) *m.* 1831 Mary Ann Agler (1814–1882)
5. John Duvall Denune (1767–1838) *m.* 1798 Sarah Burrell
6. Alexander Burrell *m.* 1757/9 Eleanor Dent
7. Peter Dent (1693–1757) *m.* 1726 Mary Brooke (1709–1781)
8. Major William Dent *ca.* (1652–1705) *m.* 1684 Elizabeth Fowke (1664–)
9. Col. Gerard Fowke *ca.* (1606–1669) *m.* 1661 Ann Thoroughgood *ca.* (1632–)
10. Adam Thoroughgood (1602–1640) *m.* 1627 Sarah Offley (–1657)

Service: Landed Proprietor, Virginia; Captain; built the first or one of the first homes in Virginia. He died 1640, Lynn Haven, Princess Ann County, Va.

6368   KIRK, Mrs. Cary Benedict   Recorded 1942, Illinois
           Mansfield, Illinois
    1. Clara Hughes *m.* 1908 Cary Benedict Kirk
    2. Solomon Hughes (1839–1908) *m.* 1868 Mary Susan DeHass (1849–1911)
    3. Charles DeHass (1822–1899) *m.* 1848 Elizabeth Florence (1829–1914)
    4. Thomas Florence (1801–1886) *m.* 1827 Mary Springer, *d.* 1827
    5. John Springer *c.* (1780–1843) *m.* 1807 Rebecca Stockwell (1786–1860)
    6. Nathan Springer (1752–1831) *m.* Hannah McDaniel
    7. Dennis Springer (1712–1760) *m.* 1736 Anne Prickett
    8. JACOB SPRINGER (1668–1731) *m.* 1704 Phoebe
    Service: Came to America 1692, sailing from Rotterdam. Born in Stockholm.
           With his brother Carl, founded Wilmington, Delaware.
    Reference: Records in Court House, Hillsboro, Ohio; Recs., Uniontown, Penna.;
           Certified copies of wills, deeds, etc.

6755   KIRKLAND, Rev. Henry Burnham   Recorded 1952, New Jersey
           401 Maywood Avenue, Maywood, New Jersey
    1. Rev. Henry Burnham Kirkland *m.* 1912 Helen J. Mays
    2. Henry Sterling Kirkland (1856–1935) *m.* 1881 Josephine Hooker (1860–1912)
    3. Nathaniel Wood Hooker (1819–1895) *m.* 1856 Honoria Elizabeth Cashman
           (1825–1889)
    4. Timothy Judson Hooker (1782–   ) *m.* Charlotte Wood
    5. William Hooker (1729–1815) *m.* (2nd) 1764 Mary Moseley (1743–1833)
    6. Hezekiah Hooker (1688–1756) *m.* 1716 Abigail Curtis (1695–   )
    7. John Hooker (1664–1745) *m.* 1687 Abigail Standley (1669–1742)
    8. Rev. Samuel Hooker (1633–1697) *m.* 1658 Mary Willet (1637–1712)
    9. REV. THOMAS HOOKER (1586–1647) *m.* 1621 Susanna Garland Hooker (1593–1676)
    Service: Came to America 1633. Pastor at Newtown, Mass.; moved with family
           and congregation to Hartford, 1636.
    Reference: The Descendants of Rev. Thomas Hooker, by Edward Hooker, pgs.
           3, 10, 19, 35, 55, 116, 211, 344; Affidavit of dates, wills, and family sketch.

6326   KIRKLAND, Mrs. Spencer A.   Recorded 1941, Georgia
           106 Peachtree Battle Avenue N. W., Atlanta, Georgia
    1. Nell May Fielder *m.* 1922 Dr. Spencer Atkinson Kirkland
    2. William Kendall Fielder (1855–1937) *m.* 1884 May Jordan (1856–1933)
    3. James Monroe Fielder (1816–1863) *m.* 1851 Roxanna Williamson (1831–1871)
    4. Obidiah Martin B. Fielder (1789–1857) *m.* 1815 Elizabeth T. Heard (1798–1847)
    5. Joseph Heard (1773–1848) *m.* Nancy Stuart (Stewart), *d.* aft. 1810
    6. Thomas Heard (1742–1808) *m.* 1765/6 Elizabeth Fitzpatrick, *d.* 1790
    7. Joseph Fitzpatrick, *d.* 1777, *m.* Mary Perrin Woodson, *d.* 1833
    8. Benjamin Woodson, *d.* 1778, *m.* 1720 Frances Napier (1695–aft. 1727)
    9. John Woodson (1655–1700) *m.* Mary Tucker, *d.* 1710
   10. John Woodson (1632–1684) *m.* ————, *d.* aft. 1684
   11. DR. JOHN WOODSON (1586–1644) *m.* Sarah Winston
    Service: Physician and Surgeon; came to Virginia in 1619, as Surgeon for Company
           of soldiers sent over for protection of the Colonists.
    Reference: "Woodsons and their Connections," H. M. Woodson; "Southern Lineages."

6355   KNIGHT, Mabel Emma   Recorded 1941, Vermont
           Shrewsbury Center, R. F. D., Cuttingsville, Vermont
    1. Mabel Emma Knight
    2. Orrin George Knight (1863–1937) *m.* 1886 Phoebe Ann Ray (1866–   )
    3. Albert Knight (1836–1898) *m.* Ellen L. Phalen (1843–1918)
    4. Orrin Knight, *d.* 1866, *m.* Diantha Richardson
    5. Luther Knight (1775–1859) *m.* Sarah Saunders (1781–1822)
    6. Amos Knight, *b.* 1747, *m.* 1771 Susanna Maynard, *b.* 1748
    7. Ensign Joseph Maynard (1725–1769) *m.* 1746 Abigail Jennings, *b.* 1724
    8. Johnanthan Maynard (1685–1763) *m.* 1714 Mehitable Needham, *d.* 1767
    9. Zachary (Zechariah) Maynard (1647–1724) *m.* 1678 Hannah Goodrich or
           Coolidge
   10. JOHN MAYNARD, *d.* 1672, *m.* (2nd) 1646 Mary Exdell
    Service: Petr. for Marlboro, Mass., 1656.

Reference: "Hist of Framington, Mass.," J. H. Temple; Lancaster, Mass., Vital Records, by Nourse; "Hist of Fitzwilliam, N. H., J. F. Norton; V. R. in office of Sec. of State, Montpelier, Vt.

6083 KNIGHT, Mrs. H. S. Recorded 1935, Pennsylvania
103 Chestnut Street, Sunbury, Pennsylvania
1. Mary Martin Knight *m.* 1896 Harry S. Knight
2. Albert Martin (1841–1919) *m.* 1864 Martha J. Brown (1842–1912)
3. Lewis Martin (1803–1886) *m.* 1830 Sarah Berryhill (1819–1890)
4. Thomas Martin (1759–1829) *m.* 1791 Mary Montgomery (1776–1846)
5. Robert Martin (1720–1800) *m.* 1758 Mary Bloomfield (1739–   )
6. Peter Martin (1693–1756) *m.* Sarah
7. Benjamin Martin (1656–1732) *m.* 1688 Margaret Ellstone
8. John Martin (–1687) *m.* Esther Roberts (1631–1687)
9. THOMAS ROBERTS (1600–1674)
Service: President of Court of Dover, 1639, and Governor of New Hampshire, 1640–43.
Reference: History of Lycoming County, Pa., by Meginnis (John F.); New Jersey Archives, 1st Series, Vol. 32; Landmarks in Ancient Dover, Thompson; New England Hist. & Gen. Register, Vol. 7.

5868 KNIGHT, Mrs. Reuben E. Recorded 1929, Nebraska
907 Cheyenne Avenue, Alliance, Nebraska
1. Florence McKean *m.* 1910 Reuben Edward Knight
2. William T. McKean (1844–1924) *m.* 1875 Edith E. Partridge (1854–1924)
3. Chester Partridge (1811–1868) *m.* 1843 Rachel Mattison (1820–1888)
4. James Mattison (–1850) *m.* 1811 Catharine Dickinson (1791–1860)
5. James Dickinson (1767–1840) *m.* 1790 Samantha Case (1772–1816)
6. Philip Case (1731–1815) *m.* 1760 Lydia Soverill
7. Timothy Case (1708–   ) *m.* 1730 Sarah Holcomb (1713–   )
8. Capt. Richard Case (1669–1746) *m.* 1701 Amy Reed (1678–   )
9. JOHN CASE (1616–1703) *m.* 1656 Sarah Spencer (1636–1691)
Service: Elected first constable of Simsbury, Conn., 1669.
Reference: See Case Line in "New England Families," by William R. Cutter; Directory of Ancestral Heads of New England Families.

6743 KNOTT, Mrs. William M. Recorded 1952
Mississippi Avenue, Many, Louisiana
1. Clara Long, *m.* 1914 William M. Knott
2. Huey Pierce Long (1852–1937) *m.* 1875 Caledonia Tison (1860–1913)
3. John Murphy Long (1825–1901) *m.* 1845 Mary Elizabeth Wingate (1829–1901)
4. James Long (1790–1850) *m.* 1823 Mary Kirtman (1793–1850)
5. Hugh Long (1770–btw. 1794 & 1806) *m.* 1789 Margaret (–1794)
6. James Long (1750–1807) *m.* 1768 Catherine, *d.* bef. 1790
7. John Long, *d.* 1759, *m.* 1735 Ellenor Owens (1706–aft. 1759)
8. Capt. Richard Owens (1668–aft. 1708) *m.* 1698 Racheal Beall (bef. 1678–aft. 1708)
9. COL. NINIAN BEALL (1625–1717) *m.* 1668 Ruth Moore (–1704)
Service: Dep. Surveyor; Justice and Burgess of Md.
Reference: National Number in Sons & Daughters of Pilgrims 6724.

6311 KNOX, Mrs. James Whitney Recorded 1941, Connecticut
561 Wethersfield Avenue, Hartford, Connecticut
1. Myrtle Havens *m.* 1913 James Whitney Knox
2. Herman Edgar Havens (1854–1935) *m.* 1882 Jessie Fremont Beebe (1860–   )
3. Capt. Samuel A. Beebe (1820–1878) *m.* 1840 Louise Frances Beckwith (1820–1910)
4. David B. Beebe (1781–1855) *m.* 1808 Mary Lamb (1781–1858)
5. Samuel Lamb (1748–1834) *m.* 1774 Tabitha Wightman (1756–1834)
6. Rev. Timothy Wightman (1719–1796) *m.* 1747 Mary Stoddard (1725–1817)
7. Rev. Valentine Wightman (1681–1749) *m.* 1703 Susannah Holmes
8. John Holmes (1649–1712) *m.* (2nd) Mary Sayles Green (widow) (1652–1717)
9. John Sayles (1631–1681) *m.* 1650 Mary Williams (1633–1681)
10. ROGER WILLIAMS *c.* (1599–1683) *m.* 1629 Mary Barnard, *d.* 1676
Service: Founded Providence, first colony in R. I.
Reference: Austin's Genealogical Dict. of R. I.; New Eng. Regist., Vol. V.

5905 KNUDSON, Frank M. L.   Recorded 1930, Colorado
          2357 Clayton Street, Denver, Colorado
      1. Frank M. L. Kirk (1898–   ) *m.* 1926 Clarence Milton Knudson
      2. Charles M. Kirk (1865–   ) *m.* 1897 Jennie M. L. Moore (1876–   )
      3. James Elliott Kirk (1832–1921) *m.* 1861 Mary Ellen Hull (1840–1894)
      4. John W. Kirk *m.* 1831 Elizabeth A. Whitcomb (1812–1889)
      5. Perez Whitcomb (1774–1853) *m.* 1798 Priscilla Litchfield (1780–1843)
      6. James Litchfield (1738–1786) *m.* 1770 Elizabeth Litchfield (1744–1835)
      7. Nicholas Litchfield (1708–   ) *m.* 1737 Sarah Studley
      8. Nicholas Litchfield (1680–1750) *m.* 1704 Bathsheba Clark
      9. Josiah Litchfield (1647–   ) *m.* 1671 Sarah Baker
     10. LAWRENCE LITCHFIELD (–1657) *m.* Judith Dennis
      Service: Member of Ancient and Honorable Artillery Company, 1640.

4995 *KRAFT, Mrs. Charles   Recorded 1928
          810 East Colfax Avenue, Denver, Colorado
      1. Mary Phelps *m.* Charles Kraft
      2. Hulbut L. Phelps (–1903) *m.* 1898 Katherine Frisbee
      3. Frederick Phelps (1797–   ) *m.* Lucy Whitman Hulbut (–1812)
      4. Capt. Daniel Phelps (1766–1850) *m.* 1790 Hulda Whiting (1769–   )
      5. Benj. Phelps (1736–1781) *m.* Isabelle Loomis
      6. Capt. Benj. Phelps *m.* Rachel Barber Brown
      7. William Phelps (1684–   ) *m.* 1706 Thankful Edwards
      8. William Phelps (1651–   ) *m.* 1672 Abigail Stebbins
      9. NATHANIEL PHELPS, *b.* England, to New England 1630/31, *m.* Elizabeth Coplen,
          1630/31

6029 KUHN, Miss Florence Calvert   Recorded 1932
          Marmet, Kanawha Co., Kanawha, West Virginia
      1. Florence Calvert Kuhn
      2. Joseph J. Kuhn (1830–1897) *m.* 1854 Sally Calvert (1837–1909)
      3. John Lewis Calvert (1803–1863) *m.* 1825 Elizabeth Slack (1807–1882)
      4. Francis Calvert (1751–1823) *m.* 1791 Elizabeth Witt (1755–1806)
      5. Jacob Calvert (1720–1772) *m.* 1750 Sarah Krupper (1730–1789)
      6. John Calvert (1690–1735) *m.* 1710 Elizabeth Harrison
      7. Geo Calvert (1664–1740) *m.* 1688 Eliz. Doyne
      8. William Calvert (1642–1682) *m.* 1660 Elizabeth Stone
      9. Gov. Leonard Calvert (1606–1647) *m.* 1641 Anne Brent
     10. SIR GEORGE CALVERT (Lord Baltimore) (1579–1632) *m.* 1604 Anne Mynne
          (1579–1622)
      Reference: Maryland Hist. Mag., Vol. 16.

6650 KUNSE, Lois Jean   Recorded 1949
          5630 Rawles Avenue, Indianapolis, Indiana
      1. Lois Jean Kunse
      2. Robert Kunse (1889–   ) *m.* 1913 Lois B. Franklin (1895–   )
      3. Leslie E. Franklin (1867–1932) *m.* 1891 Lyda C. Anderson (1866–   )
      4. William L. Franklin (1830–1913) *m.* 1860 Caroline E. Morton (1843–1922)
      5. Alexander Morton, Jr. (1796–1876) *m.* 1820 Martha Anderson (1798–1881)
      6. Alexander Morton, Sr. (1759–1822) *m.* 1784 Ruth Strong (1762–1850)
      7. Elijah Strong (1733–1774/5) *m.* 1756 Ruth Loomis (1729–   )
      8. Lt. Jebediah Strong (1700–1737) *m.* 1722 Elizabeth Webster (1701–   )
      9. Capt. John Webster (1672–1735) *m.* bef. 1701 Elizabeth, *d.* bef. 1709
     10. Thomas Webster, *d.* 1685, *m.* 1663 or 66 Abigail Alexander, *d.* bef. 1690
     11. Gov. JOHN WEBSTER *ca.* (1585/90–1661) *m.* 1609 Agnes Smith, *d.* 1667
      Service: Orig. Proprietor Hartford, Conn., 1636; Dep. Gen. Conn., 1637; Gov. Asst.
          and Magis., 1639–55; Commr. Unit. Colonies, 1654; Dept. Gov. Conn., 1654;
          Royal Gov. Conn., 1656–57.
      Reference: Desc. Jno Webster, Lin. Bk. Daus. Col. Wars.

6711   LA HART, Miss Ethel Louise   Recorded 1951, Maryland
           Troy Hills, N. J., R. F. D. 1, Box, 368
           Parsippany, New Jersey

   1. Miss Ethel Louise La Hart
   2. Nicholas D. La Hart (1862–1915) *m.* 1887 Mary Mattoon (1867–)
   3. Randsom Dayton Mattoon (1839–1922) *m.* 1864 Harriet Carlin (1842–1910)
   4. William Curtis Mattoon (1815–1897) *m.* 1836 Harriet Vanderhoof (1814–1884)
   5. Bethel Mattoon (1784–1862) *m.* 1809 Hannah Williams (–1873)
   6. Amasa Mattoon (1755–1829) *m.* 1780 Elizabeth Dayton (1759–)
   7. David Mattoon (1715–1775) *m.* 1742 Phebe Curtis (1719–1776)
   8. John Mattoon (1682–1754) *m.* 1706 Jerusha Hall (1687–1760)
   9. PHILLIP MATTOON (–1696) *m.* 1677 Sarah Hawks (1657–1751)
   Service: Soldier in King Phillip's Wars.
   Reference: Connecticut Men of Revolutionary War, pg. 500; History of Deerfield,
           Vol. I, pg. 300; Sheldon's History of Deerfield, Vol. I, pg. 180.

6713   LA HART, Miss Helen May   Recorded 1951, Maryland
           Troy Hills, N. J., R. F. D. 1, Box 368
           Parsippany, New Jersey

   1. La Hart, Miss Helen May
   2. Nicholas D La Hart (1862–1915) *m.* 1887 Mary Mattoon (1867–)
   3. Randsom Dayton Mattoon (1839–1922) *m.* 1864 Harriet E. Carlin (1842–1910)
   4. William Curtis Mattoon (1815–1897) *m.* 1836 Harriet Vanderhoof (1814–1884)
   5. Bethel Mattoon (1784–1862) *m.* 1809 Hannah Williams (–1873)
   6. Amasa Mattoon (1755–1829) *m.* 1780 Elizabeth Dayton (1759–)
   7. David Mattoon (1715–1775) *m.* 1742 Phebe Curtis (1719–1776)
   8. John Mattoon (1682–1754) *m.* 1706 Jerusha Hall (1687–1760)
   9. PHILIP MATTOON (–1698) *m.* 1667 Sarah Hawks (1657–1751)
   Service: Soldier in King Philip's War.
   Reference: Connecticut Men of the Revolution, pg. 500; History of Deerfield, Vol. I,
           pg. 300; Sheldon's History of Deerfield, Vol. I, pg. 180.

6210   LA HART, Mrs. Nicholas D.   Recorded 1938
           R. F. 1, Troy Hills, Whippany, New Jersey

   1. Mary Mattoon (1867–) *m.* 1887 Nicholas D. La Hart
   2. Randson D. Mattoon (1839–1922) *m.* 1864 Harriet Carlin (1842–1910)
   3. William Curtis Mattoon (1815–1897) *m.* 1836 Harriet Vanderhoof (1814–1884)
   4. Bethel Mattoon (1734–1862) *m.* 1809 Hannah Williams (–1873)
   5. Amasa Mattoon (1758–1829) *m.* 1780 Elizabeth Dayton (1759–)
   6. David Mattoon (1715–1775) *m.* 1742 Phebe Curtis (1719–1776)
   7. John Mattoon (1682–1754) *m.* 1706 Jerusha Hall (1687–1760)
   8. PHILIP MATTOON (–1696) *m.* 1677 Sarah Hawks (1657–1751)
   Service: Soldier in King Philip's War.
   Reference: Sheldon's Hist. of Deerfield, Vol. 1.

6721   LA LANCE, Mrs. Charles V.   Recorded 1951, West Virginia
           326 Seventh Avenue, Huntington, West Virginia

   1. Eugenia Pollard *m.* 1902 Charles La Lance
   2. John C. Pollard (1839–1902) *m.* 1868 Frances Johnston (1844–1926)
   3. Henry Brown Pollard (1810–1851) *m.* 1833 Sophia Timberlake Poage (1814–1860)
   4. George Poage (1787–1847) *m.* 1811 Judith Blair Kemper (1788–1848)
   5. Rev. James Kemper (1753–1834) *m.* 1772 Judith Hathaway (1756–1846)
   6. Capt. John Hathaway (1732–1786) *m.* 1754 Sarah Timberlake (1739–1795)
   7. William Hathaway III (1695–) *m.* 1732 Sarah Lawson (1705–)
   8. William Hathaway II (1666–1725)
   9. WILLIAM HATHAWAY I (1636–1692) *m.* Lettie Lawson
   Reference: Kemper Genealogy; Wills, pg. 201; pgs. 55–90; Hathaway & Lawson
           Families, by McComb, Va, pgs. 18–98.

6352   LAMB, Leonard Illman   Recorded 1941, Massachusetts
          191 S. Main Street, Attleboro, Massachusetts
       1. Leonard Illman Lamb *m*. 1912 Gertrude Emerson Knapp
       2. Louis Jacob Lamb (1852–1906) *m*. 1898 Elizabeth Becket (1850–1920)
       3. Norval Bacon Lamb (1827–1918) *m*. Caroline Frances Manchester (1838–1904)
       4. Gerson Lamb (1800–1885) *m*. 1826 Lois Bacon
       5. Nahum Lamb (1759–1842) *m*. 1781 Lydia Daggett, *d*. 1836
       6. Samuel Lamb (1734–aft. 1778) *m*. 1753 Sarah Dana
       7. Ebenezer Lamb (1706–   ) *m*. 1730 Anna Green
       8. Abial Lamb (1679–bef. 1771) *m*. 1699 Hannah Taylor, *d*. 1771
       9. Abial Lamb (1646–bef. 1710) *m*. Elizabeth
      10. THOMAS LAMB, *d*. 1646, *m*. (2nd) Dorothy Harbittle
       Service: Came with Winthrop to Boston, 1630.
       Reference: Records of Attleboro, Mass.; V. R. of Charlton, Mass.; Hist. of Oxford,
          Mass., by Daniels.

6017   LAMPHIER, Mrs. George A.   Recorded 1932
          Watertown, Connecticut
       1. Mary Perry (1869–   ) *m*. 1898 George Arthur Pamphier
       2. Herman Perry (1835–1914) *m*. 1864 Josephine Mitchell (1839–1922)
       3. Chas. Perry (1802–1876) *m*. 1833 Maria L. Curtiss (1808–1882)
       4. Japhel Curtiss (1779–1864) *m*. 1805 Lucy Strong (1783–1857)
       5. Benjamin Curtiss (1757–1798) *m*. 1778 Esther Benham (1759–1847)
       6. Israel Curtiss (1716–1796) *m*. 1738 Martha Towner
       7. Stephen Curtiss (1673–1723) *m*. 1699 Sarah Minor (1678–1731)
       8. Capt. John Minor (1634–1719) *m*. 1658 Eliz. Booth (1634–1732)
       9. Thomas Minor (1608–1690) *m*. 1634 Grace Palmer (–1690)
      10. Clement Minor (–1640)
      11. William Minor (–1585) *m*. Isabella H. de Frilbay
      12. William Minor
      13. THOMAS MINOR (1436–1480) *m*. Bridget De St. Martins
       Service: Capt., Surveyor, Deacon, Signer of Fundamental Articles
       Reference: Sharp's South Britain; Gen. Curtis Family.

5911   LANDRUM, Lillie Noell   Recorded 1930, West Virginia
          Buena Vista, Virginia
       1. Lillie Noell *m*. 1900 Ernest Lynwood Landrum
       2. Matthias B. Noell (1844–1921) *m*. 1866 Octavia S. Robinson (1846–1916)
       3. Robert Noell *m*. Barbara Ann Seay
       4. Robert Noell *m*. Polly A. Ryan
       5. Richard Noell *m*. 1787 Mary Crutchfield (–1800)
       6. Rice Noell
       7. Richard Noell
       8. INCREASE NOELL (–1655) *m*. Parnell Gray
       Increase Noell came over in the Arabella, 1630.
       Service: A prominent member of the Bay Colony, and assistant treasurer until 1655.
       Reference: Mass. Bay Colony.

6074   LANE, Mrs. John E.   Recorded 1934, Georgia
          South Oak Street, Jackson, Georgia
       1. Rosa Thornton *m*. 1911 John Edward Lane
       2. George W. Thornton (1822–1893) *m*. 1856 Mary E. Moore (1836–1905)
       3. Zachariah Thornton (1763–1830) *m*. 1795 Mary Oakes (1776–1864)
       4. Presley Thornton (1730–1812) *m*. 1762 Mary (–1829)
       5. Rowland Thornton (1685–1748) *m*. Elizabeth Catlett (1689–1751)
       6. Francis Thornton (1651–   ) *m*. Alice Savage (1660–1705)
       7. WILLIAM THORNTON (–1710) *m*. 1648 Elizabeth Rowland
       Service: Vestryman of Pettsworth Parish, 1677.
       Reference: The Thornton Family, by W. G. Stanard, Vol. II, p. 230; Vol. IV, pp.
          92–93; William & Mary Quarterly, Vols. V and VI.

6217   LANING, Miss Mary Wolfe   Recorded 1938
          291 E. Commerce Street, Bridgeton, New Jersey
       1. Chester Laning (1883–1927) *m*. 1908 Blanche Hitchner (1888–1923)

2. Chas. Ewing Laning (1845–1924) *m.* Mary Wolfe (1850–1931)
3. David Laning (1809–1883) *m.* Catherine Ewing (1816–1880)
4. Thomas Ewing (1780–1867) *m.* 1803 Mahetabel Shaw (1778–1853)
5. Samuel Ewing (1739–1783) *m.* Mary Miller
6. Thomas Ewing (1695–1747) *m.* 1720 Marcy Maskell (1700–1784)
7. Thomas Maskell, Jr. (1665–1732) *m.* 1700 Marcy Stathem
8. THOMAS MASKELL (–1671) *m.* 1662 Bathia Parsons

Reference: "Ewing," by Roberty Patterson; "Thomas Maskell at Simsbury, Conn.";
Records of Windsor, Conn., by Savage.

6375 LARSEN, Lyle Franklin   Recorded 1942, New Jersey
      170 Myrtle Avenue, Millburn, New Jersey
      (JUNIOR)
1. Lyle Franklin Larsen
2. Oscar Christian Larsen (1893–   ) *m.* 1923 Rose Marian Lyle (1886–   )
3. Albert Franklin Lyle, LL.D. (1839–1910) *m.* 1872 Louisa Thomas (1841–1932)
4. John Jacobs Thomas (1810–1895) *m.* 1838 Mary Slocum Howland (1815–1900)
5. Humphrey Howland (1780–1862) *m.* 1810 Sarah T. Field (1794–1842)
6. Benjamin Howland (1754–1831) *m.* 1777 Mary Slocum
7. Benjamin Howland (1716–1755) *m.* Mary Chase
8. Nicholas Howland (–Will 1722) *m.* 1697 Hannah Woodman (–Will 1734)
9. Zoeth Howland, *d.* 1676, *m.* 1656 Abigail Howland
10. HENRY HOWLAND, *d.* 1671, *m.* Mary Newland, *d.* 1674

Service: Constable of Duxbury, Mass., 1635; on Grand Jury 1636–1656; Surveyor of
Highways; Proprietor, Dartmouth, Mass., 1652.
Reference: "A Brief Gen. & Bio. Hist. of Arthur, Henry and John Howland," by
Franklyn Howland; Colonial Families of U. S. A., Vol. IV, by Gen. N.
MacKenzie.

6374 LARSEN, Marian Howland   Recorded 1942, New Jersey
      170 Myrtle Avenue, Millburn, New Jersey
      (JUNIOR)
1. Marian Howland Larsen
2. Oscar Christian Larsen (1893–   ) *m.* 1923 Rose Marian Lyle (1886–   )
3. Rev. Albert F. Lyle, LL.D. (1839–1910) *m.* 1872 Louisa Thomas (1841–1932)
4. John Jacobs Thomas (1810–1895) *m.* 1838 Mary Slocum Howland (1815–1900)
5. Humphrey Howland (1780–1862) *m.* 1810 Sarah T. Field (1794–1842)
6. Benjamin Howland (1754–1831) *m.* Mary Slocum (1755–1840)
7. Benjamin Howland (1716–1755) *m.* Mary Chase
8. Nicholas Howland *d. c.* 1722, *m.* 1697 Hannah Woodman
9. Zoeth Howland, *d.* 1676 *m.* 1656 Abigail Howland
10. HENRY HOWLAND, *d.* 1671, *m.* Mary Newland, *d.* 1674

Service: Constable of Duxbury, Mass., 1635; on Grand Jury 1636–1656; Surveyor of
Highways; Proprietor, Dartmouth, Mass., 1652.
Reference: "A Brief Gen. & Bio. Hist. of Arthur, Henry and John Howland," by
by Franklyn Howland; Colonial Families of U. S. A., Vol. IV, by Geo. N.
MacKenzie.

6346 LARSEN, Mrs. Oscar C.   Recorded 1941, New Jersey
1. Rosa Marian Lyle *m.* 1923 Oscar Christian Larsen
2. Albert Franklin Lyle, LL.D. (1839–1910) *m.* 1872 Louisa Thomas (1841–1932)
3. John Jacobs Thomas (1810–1895) *m.* 1838 Mary Slocum Howland (1815–1900)
4. Humphrey Howland (1780–1862) *m.* 1810 Sarah T. Field (1794–1842)
5. Benjamin Howland (1754–1831) *m.* 1777 Mary Slocum (1755–1840)
6. Benjamin Howland (1716–1755) *m.* Mary Chase
7. Nicholas Howland *d. c.* 1722, *m.* 1697 Hannah Woodman, *d. c.* 1734
8. Zoeth Howland, *d.* 1676, *m.* 1656 Abigail Howland
9. HENRY HOWLAND *c.* (1600–1671) *m.* Mary Newland, *d.* 1674

Service: Constable of Duxbury, Mass., 1635; on Grand Jury, 1636–1656; Surveyor of
Highways; Proprietor at Dartmouth, Mass., 1652.
Reference: "A Brief Genealogical & Biographical Hist. of Arthur, Henry, and John
Howland," by Franklyn Howland; Henry Howland, Colonial Families of
U. S. A., by George N. MacKenzie, Vol. IV.

6629 LATHAM, Mrs. James E.   Recorded 1949
          306 Parkway, Greensboro, North Carolina
    1. Maude Moore, *m.* 1892 James E. Latham
    2. James W. Moore (1848–1913) *m.* 1869 Sarah J. Gorton (1851–1932)
    3. John S. Gorton (1830–1898) *m.* 1850 Catherine Flinn (1833–1862)
    4. Ethan Gorton (1807–1861) *m.* 1828 Mary Sague, *d.* 1861
    5. Joseph Gorton (1773–1851) *m.* 1796 Charlot Schriver (1774–abt. 1851)
    6. William Gorton, Jr. (1748–1834) *m.* 1770 Phebe Daniels, *d.* bef. 1805
    7. William Gorton, Sr. (1706–1761) *m.* 1735 Lydia Collins (1714–1809)
    8. John Gorton, Jr. (abt. 1675–aft. 1750) *m.* 1700 Patience Hopkins (abt. 1678–bef.
          1717)
    9. John Gorton, Sr. (abt. 1639–1714) *m.* 1665 Margaret Weeden (abt. 1642–)
   10. SAMUEL GORTON, SR. (bapt. 1592–1677) *m.* 1630 Mary Maplet, *d.* aft. 1677
    Service: Founded town of Warwick, R. I.; Asst. to Gov. Roger Williams; Pres. of
          Colony of R. I.
    Reference: Life and Times of Samuel Gorton

6196 LAWRENCE, Emily Frances   Recorded 1938
          303 Sixth Street S. W., Canton, Ohio
                              (JUNIOR)
    1. Emily Frances Lawrence (1937–)
    2. Arthur E. Lawrence (1894–) *m.* 1930 Sarah Louise Furbee (1904–)
    3. James S. Furbee (1864–) *m.* 1892 Louise Christine Mahon (1867–)
    4. Rev. Chas. LeDow Mahon, M.D. (1836–1872) *m.* 1866 Emily Frances Cloake
          (1843–1878)
    5. Cap. John Mahon (1812–1843) *m.* 1837 Harriet Scot Tomlinson (1818–1894)
    6. William Tomlinson (1786–1815) *m.* 1808 Phebe Harris (1788–1841)
    7. Samuel Tomlinson (1762–1842) *m.* Ann Garrison (1761–1808)
    8. James Tomlinson (1724–1811) *m.* (1) 1756 Barbara Brown (1736–1808)
    9. Richard Tomlinson (1698–) *m.* Lydia Wells
   10. RICHARD TOMLINSON *d.* W. P. 1716, *m.* 1696 Sarah Buzby, *d.* W. P. 1746
    Reference: 8th Vol. D. of Wills, pg. 65 (No. 84) Reg. of Wills, Phila., Pa.; Abington
          Friends Monthly Meeting Rec., Minutes, Vol. 1, pg. 26; Mo. M. held 27th
          of 5 mo. 1696; Rec. of Trinity Oxford Ch., Phila., Pa.; Chettenham Twp.,
          Book 8 of deeds, pg. 102; Bridgeton C. H., N. J., Baptist Cem., 5th St.
          below Market, Phila., Pa.; Penn. Hist. Soc., Phila., Pa.

6270 LAWRENCE, Mrs. Arthur Lee   Recorded 1939
          R. D. No. 1, Canton, Ohio
    1. Sarah Louise Furbee *m.* Arthur E. Lawrence
    2. James S. Furbee, *b.* 1864, *m.* 1892 Louise Christine Mahon, *b.* 1867
    3. Rev. Charles LeDow Mahon, M.D. (1836–1872) *m.* 1866 Emily Frances Cloake
          (1843–1878)
    4. Capt. John Mahon (1812–1843) *m.* 1837 Harriet S. Tomlinson (1818–1894)
    5. William Tomlinson (1786–1822) *m.* 1808 Phoebe Harris (1788–1841)
    6. Samuel Tomlinson (1762–1842) *m.* Ann Garrison (1761–1824)
    7. James Tomlinson (1724–1811) *m.* 1756 Barbara Brown (1736–1808)
    8. Richard Tomlinson, *b.* 1698, *m.* Lydia Wells
    9. RICHARD TOMLINSON, *d.* 1716, *m.* 1696 Sarah Buzby, *d.* 1746
    Reference: Register of Wills, Phila., Pa.; Abington Friends Monthly Meetings;
          Morgan Edward History of the Baptist Records, Trinity Oxford Church,
          Phila., Pa.; Bk. 8 of Deeds, Bridgeton, N. J.; Historical Sketch Seventh
          Day Baptist, by Julius F. Sachse; Penn. Historical Soc., Phila., Pa.;
          Abington Presbyterian Ch. Rec., Abington, Pa.

6271 LAWRENCE, Florence Louise   Recorded 1939
          R. D. No. 1, Canton, Ohio
                              (JUNIOR)
    1. Florence Louise Lawrence
    2. Arthur Lawrence (1894–) *m.* 1930 Sarah Louise Furbee, *b.* 1904

3. James S. Furbee, *b.* 1864, *m.* 1892 Louise Christine Mahon, *b.* 1867
4. Rev. Charles LeDow Mahon, M.D. (1836–1872) *m.* 1866 Emily Frances Cloake (1843–1878)
5. Capt. John Mahon (1812–1843) *m.* 1837 Harriet S. Tomlinson (1818–1894)
6. William Tomlinson (1786–1822) *m.* 1808 Phoebe Harris (1788–1841)
7. Samuel Tomlinson (1762–1842) *m.* Ann Garrison (1761–1824)
8. James Tomlinson (1724–1811) *m.* 1756 Barbara Brown (1736–1808)
9. Richard Tomlinson, *b.* 1698, *m.* Lydia Wells
10. RICHARD TOMLINSON, *d.* 1716, *m.* 1696 Sarah Buzby, *d.* 1746

Reference: Register of Wills, Phila, Pa.; Abington Friends Monthly Meetings; Morgan Edward History of the Baptist Records, Trinity Oxford Church, Phila., Pa., Bk. 8 of Deeds, Bridgeton, N. J.; Historical Sketch Seventh Day Baptist, by Julius F. Sachse; Penn. Historical Soc., Phila., Pa.; Abington Presbyterian Ch. Rec., Abington, Pa.

6285 LEARY, Mary Gertrude   Recorded 1940
       138 Hazel Street, Providence, Rhode Island
1. Mary Gertrude Leary
2. Serg't James Leary (1844–1918) *m.* 1869 Mary Jane Foster (1848–1902)
3. George Washington Foster (1823–1862) *m.* 1847 Margaret Fay (1827–1871)
4. Capt. Elisha Foster (1775–1852) *m.* 1803/4 Sarah Turner
5. Lt. Elisha Foster (1745–1827) *m.* 1769 Grace Barstow
6. Deacon Elisha Foster (1708–1771) *m.* 1738 Temperance Freeman, *b.* 1715
7. Benjamin Freeman, *b.* 1685, *m.* 1709 Temperance Dimmick
8. John Freeman, Jr., *b.* 1651, *m.* 1672 Sarah Merrick
9. Major John Freeman *c.* (1627–1719) *m.* 1649/50 Mercy Prence (1630/1–*d.* age 80
10. Governor Thomas Prence (1600–1673) *m.* 1624 Patience Brewster (1600–1634)
11. ELDER WILLIAM BREWSTER (1566/7–1644) *m.* Mary Wentworth, *c.* (1569–1627)

Service: Postmaster, Teacher, One of Founders of Plymouth Colony, Ruling Elder.
Reference: Freeman Genealogy; Mayflower Index; Freeman's Annals of Cape Cod; Compendium of Amer. Genealogy, Vol. V.

5827 LEATHERBEE, Mrs. Albert Thompson   Recorded 1929
       176 Park Street, Boston, Mass.
                   (AT LARGE)
1. Ethel Brigham (1878–   ) *m.* 1901 Albert Thompson Leatherbee
2. Edwin Howard Brigham (1840–1926) *m.* 1871 Jane Spring Pierce (1845–1923)
3. Elijah S. Brigham (1813–1863) *m.* 1840 Sarah Jane Rogers (1822–1912)
4. Elijah Brigham (1776–1861) *m.* 1803 Sophia Houghton (1775–1816)
5. Lt. Elijah Brigham (1742–1804) *m.* 1768 Ruth Taylor (1747–1811)
6. Lt. Nathan Brigham (1693–1784) *m.* 1729 Elizabeth Ward
7. Capt. Nathan Brigham (1671–1746) *m.* Elizabeth (How) (1665–1733)
8. Thomas Brigham (1640/1–1717) *m.* 1665 Mary Rice (1646–1695)
9. THOMAS BRIGHAM (1603–1653) *m.* 1637 Mercie Hurd (–1693)
Service: Constable and Board of Townsmen, Cambridge, Mass.
Reference: Gen. Reg. of Several Ancient Puritans, Vol. 2, Rev. Abner Morse; Hist. Brigham Fam. N. E., 1907, E. E. & W. E. Brigham.

6001 LEE, Mrs. Homer   Recorded 1931
       410 Riverside Drive, New York City, New York
1. Charlotte Buffington Riddle (1865–   ) *m.* Homer Lee
2. Samuel Riddle (1799–1888) *m.* 1860 Lydia Carter Doyle (1837–1915)
3. Rev. Wm. W. Doyle (–1842) *m.* 1834 Charlotte Temple Buffington
4. Jesse Buffington (1786–1846) *m.* 1809 Martha Taylor (1785–1864)
5. Richard Buffington 4th (1751–1803) *m.* Rachael Baker (1752–1841)
6. Richard Buffington 3rd (1715–1781) *m.* Anna Pyle Woodward
7. Richard Buffington 2nd (1679–1741) *m.* Phoebe Grubb (–1769)
8. RICHARD BUFFINGTON, 1st (1653–1748) *m.* Frances Grubb (–1712)
Service: Constable.
Reference: History of Chester Co., Penna., by Fiethey & Cope; Jesse Buffington, p. 489.

6062 LEIRER, Mrs. W. E.   Recorded 1934, Pennsylvania
          Kelvin Avenue, Somerset, Philadelphia, Pennsylvania
      1. Marion Holland *m.* 1917 W. E. Leirer
      2. Clarence P. Holland (1856–) *m.* 1882 Addie Fowler (1856–1922)
      3. Thomas Holland (1819–1881) *m.* 1851 Susan Eccleston (1835–1882)
      4. Nathaniel G. Eccleston (1798–) *m.* 1827 Susan Pattison (1801–1869)
      5. Richard Pattison (1759–1823) *m.* 1788 Mary McKeel (1769–1825)
      6. John McKeel
      7. Thomas McKeel (–1762) *m.* 1748 Mary Stevens
      8. Thomas McKeel *m.* Clare Gary
      9. John McKeel (1640–1696) *m.* ——— Custis
      Service: Court Justice, 1692–1694.
      Reference: Dorchester County, Md., History.

6163 LEITCH, Eleanor Woodhull   Recorded 1937
          178 North Whitney Street, Hartford, Connecticut.
      1. Eleanor Woodhull (1873–) *m.* Charles Andrew Leitch
      2. Charles Smith Woodhull (1844–1875) *m.* 1867 Mattie Jeannette Leete (1848–1923)
      3. Anson Lewis Leete (1823–1893) *m.* 1846 Jeannette Betsy Norton (1824–1895)
      4. Absalom Leete (1782–1857) *m.* Sally Pease (1793–1852)
      5. Absalom Leete (1747–1800) *m.* Jane Dudley (1745–1800)
      6. Jordon Leete (1720–1773) *m.* 1746 Rebecca Watrous (1722–1788)
      7. William Leete (1671–1736) *m.* 1699 Hannah Stone (1678–)
      8. Andrew Leete (1643–1702) *m.* 1669 Elizabeth Jordon (1645–1701)
      9. Gov. William Leete (1613–1683) *m.* 1638 Anne Payne (1615–1668)
     10. John Leete
      Service: Governor of the New Haven Colony, 1661, 1662, 1663, 1664; Comm. to Mass.
          Colony, 1653, 1654; Com. to United Colonies, 1665, 1656, 1657, 1658, 1659,
          1660, 1661, 1662, 1663, 1664.
      Reference: The Family of William Leete, by S. L. Leete, pg. 9, No. 1; pg. 10, No. 3;
          pg. 14, No. 19; pg. 23, No. 53; pg. 31, No. 116; pg. 62, No. 261; pg. 111,
          No. 534; pg. 144, No. 721.

6189 LEWIS, Ada R. Root   Recorded 1938
          18 Westland Avenue, West Hartford, Connecticut
      1. Ada R. Root (1868–) *m.* 1890 George A. Lewis
      2. Joseph S. Root (1831–1874) *m.* 1865 Julia E. Felt (1842–1903)
      3. Matthew D. Root (1800–1883) *m.* abt. 1825 Roxanna Potter (1805–1893)
      4. Rev. Samuel Potter (1778–1833) *m.* 2nd) Chloe Brockett (1781–1861)
      5. Zenas Brockett (1752–1838) *m.* 1780 Abigail Johnson (1753–1813)
      6. Samuel Brockett (1714–1796) *m.* Ruth Bradley (1716–1780)
      7. Samuel Brockett (1683–) *m.* 1699 Rachel Brown (1677–1718)
      8. Samuel Brockett (1652–1742) *m.* 1682 Sarah Bradley (1665–)
      9. John Brockett (1609–1690) *m.* in Eng. Puritan Wife, born in Eng.
     10. Sir John Brockett, of Brockett Hall, of Hertfordshire, Eng.
      Service: Surgeon in King Phillip's War from June, 1675 to June, 1676; Deputy to the
          General Court, 1671–1685.
      Reference: Brockett Gen., pgs. 14, 15, 17, 24, 25, 30, 33, 36, 50, 108, 109; History of
          Southington, Ct., pg. 74; June 4, 1639, the name of John Brockett appears
          as a signer of the Covenant for Civil Government; Year Book of Colonial
          Wars, 1899, 1902.

6212 LEWIS, Anna Newton (Miss)   Recorded 1938
          Laramie, Wyoming
      1. Anne Newton Lewis
      2. Geo. Henry Lewis (1842–1913) *m.* 1869 Elmina Buell (1847–1896)
      3. Geo. Lewis (1814–1845) *m.* 1838 Lucy Peck Gages (1816–1852)
      4. Erastus Lewis (1774–1826) *m.* 1801 Salome Booth (1785–1866)
      5. Adonijah Lewis (1722–1799) *m.* 1760 Mary Bronson (1742–1790)
      6. Capt. Jonathan Lewis (1697–1769) *m.* 1719 Elizabeth Newell (1689–)
      7. Wm. Lewis 3rd (1656–1737) *m.* 1679 Sarah Moore (1661–1725)
      8. Capt. Wm. Lewis, Jr. (1620–1690) *m.* 1644 Mary Hopkins (–1670)
      9. Wm. Lewis (1594–1683) *m.* 1618 Felix Collins (–1671)
     10. William Lewis (1561–) *m.* 1592 Sarah Cathcart

Services: Capt. Engager; Deputy, Lieut.
Reference: History of New Britain, Conn., by David N. Camp; Gen. & Ecc. Hist. of
    New Britain; Am. Gen. & New Haven Gen. Magazine; His. of City &
    Town of Waterbury; His. of Connecticut Valley in Mass.; His. of Hadley,
    Mass., Judd; Gen. Dictionary, Savage.

5984   LEWIS, Miss Harriet Teese   Recorded 1931
          4615 Penn Street, Frankford, Philadelphia, Pennsylvania
    1. Harriet Teese Lewis
    2. George Lewis (1837–1906) *m.* 1865 Harriet J. Teese (1829–1914)
    3. Charles Lewis (1801–1873) *m.* 1830 Mary Smith (1803–1881)
    4. Robt. Lewis (1773–1850) *m.* 1795 Sarah Fish (1778–1860)
    5. Ellis Lewis (1734–1776) *m.* 1763 Mary Deshler (1740–)
    6. Robert Lewis (1714–1790) *m.* 1733 Mary Pyle (1714–1782)
    7. Ellis Lewis (1680–1750) *m.* 1713 Elizabeth Newlin (1687–)
    8. Nathaniel Newlin (–1729) *m.* 1685 Mary Mendenhall
    9. Nicholas Newlin (–1699) *m.* Elizabeth Paggot (–1717)
    Service: Member Governor's Counsel, Penna.; Justice Peace, Chester Co., Pa.
    Reference: Penna. Archives, 2 Series, Vol. 9; Gen. Rec. by Lewis, pg. 236; Merion
        in the Welsh Tract.

6106   LEWIS, Mrs. Frank E.   Recorded 1936
          Centerdale, Rhode Island
    1. Charlotte L. Houston *m.* Frank E. Lewis
    2. John Houston (1819–1865) *m.* 1844 Amanda Greene (1827–1881)
    3. Ransom J. Greene (1792–) *m.* 1823 Susan B. Gorton (1799–1865)
    4. David Gorton (1768–1830) *m.* 1789 Alice Whitford (1770–1855)
    5. Joseph Gorton (1741–1821) *m.* 1762 Mary Barton (1750–1772)
    6. Samuel Gorton III (1690–1784) *m.* 1715 Freelove Mason
    7. Samuel Gorton II (1630–1724) *m.* 1684 Susannah Burton (1665–1737)
    8. Samuel Gorton (1592–1677) *m.* Mary Mayplet
    Service: Founder of the settlement of Old Warwick, R. I.
    Reference: The Gorton Genealogy; Rhode Island Historical Society.

6128   LEWIS, Mrs. Ed.   Recorded 1937, New York
          80 Eighth Avenue, New York City
    1. Myrtle Mosher *m.* 1904 Ed. Lewis
    2. Eugene H. Mosher (1853–1928) *m.* 1875 Alice E. Dean (1855–1889)
    3. Charles Dean (–1912) *m.* 1854 Rachel Bunker (1836–1889)
    4. Hussey Bunker (1805–1873) *m.* 1826 Matilda Wood (1808–)
    5. Jonathan Wood (1760–1838) *m.* 1783 Rachel White
    6. Daniel Wood (1729–1773) *m.* 1752 Susannah Chase
    7. Jonathan Wood (1697–1757) *m.* 1724 Peace Davis (1702–)
    8. Timothy Davis *m.* 1690 Sarah Perry
    9. Edward Perry (–1694) *m.* Mary Freeman
    10. Edmund Freeman (1590–1692) *m.* Elizabeth (–1675)
    Service: Assistant to Gov. Bradford, 1640–46.
    Reference: The Descendants of John Wood, by E. D. Preston; The Perrys of Rhode
        Island; Freeman Genealogy.

6258   LIDE, Mrs. David M.   Recorded 1939, Texas
          6864 Turtle Creek Lane, Dallas, Texas
    1. Nita De Loach *m.* 1917 David M. Lide
    2. Lawrence E. De Loach (1872–1920) *m.* 1895 Margaret Watts (1878–)
    3. Alfred Burton De Loach *m.* Fannie E. Young (1849–1933)
    4. Benjamin F. Young (1810–1863) *m.* 1840 Ann E. Peters (1819–1912)
    5. James Peters, *b.* 1791, *m.* 1817 Rebecca Boddie, *b.* 1792
    6. George Boddie (1769–1842) *m.* 1790 Susanna P. Hill (1767–1798)
    7. Nathan Boddie (1732–1797) *m.* 1762 Chloe Curdup (1745–1781)
    8. John Curdup (1720–1753) *m.* 1743 Monning Dixon (1722–1781)
    9. Thomas Dixon, Jr. (1698–1747) *m.* 1720 Penelope ————, *b.* 1700
    10. Thomas Dixon, *d.* 1670, *m.* Marie
    Reference: "Boddie Families."

6261 **LINTHICUM, Lillian M.** Recorded 1939, Maryland
159 Conduit Street, Annapolis, Maryland
1. Lillian M. Linthicum
2. Thomas Jefferson Linthicum (1835–1907) *m.* 1858 Mary Delilah Smith (1837–1905)
3. Mathias Linthicum (1806–1879) *m. c.* 1830 Ann Jacobs
4. Amasa Linthicum (1765–1823) *m.* 1799 Rachel Johnson
5. Hezekiah Linthicum (1723–1767) *m.* 1750 Sarah Bateman (1713–1778)
6. Thomas Linthicum, Jr. (1674–1740) *m.* 1698 Deborah Wayman
7. THOMAS LINTHICUM, SR., *b. c.* 1640, *d.* 1701
Service: Secured grant of land 1677, when he patented Linthicum Stopp.
Reference: Anne Arundal Co. Gentry, by Harry Wright Newman.

6241 **LINTHICUM, Miss Mabel I.** Recorded 1939, Maryland
159 Conduit Street, Annapolis, Maryland
1. Mabel I. Linthicum
2. Thos. Jefferson Linthicum (1835–1907) *m.* 1858 Mary Delilah Smith (1837–1905)
3. Mathias Linthicum (1806–1879) *m.* 1830 Ann Jacobs
4. Amasa Linthicum (1765–1823) *m.* 1799 Rachel Johnson
5. Hezekiah Linthicum (1723–1767) *m.* 1750 Sarah Bateman (1713–1778)
6. Thos. Linthicum, Jr. (1674–1740) *m.* 1698 Deborah Wagman
7. THOS. LINTHICUM (1640–1701) *m.* 1668 Jane ———
Service: Secured grant of land, 1677.
Reference: Anne Arundel Co. Gentry, Newman.

6257 **LINTHICUM, Sarah Louise** Recorded 1939, Maryland
Linthicum Heights, Maryland
1. Sarah Louise Linthicum
2. Sweetser Linthicum, Jr. (1862–1935) *m.* 1888 Sarah Crisp (1868–1927)
3. Sweetser Linthicum (1824–1905) *m.* 1847 Laura Ellen Smith (1829–1910)
4. William Linthicum (1798–1866) *m.* 1823 Elizabeth Sweetser (1800–1875)
5. Abner Linthicum (1763–1848) *m.* 1791 Rachel Jacob, *d.* 1825
6. Hezekiah Linthicum (1723–1767) *m.* 1750 Sarah Bateman (1713–1778)
7. Thomas Linthicum, Jr. *m.* 1698 Deborah Wayman
8. THOMAS LINTHICUM SR. *d.* 1701, *m.* Jane
Service: Captain 22nd Regiment, Anne Arundel Co., Md., 1809. Member State Legislature for some years after War of 1812.
Reference: Linthicum Book, by Matilda J. Badger.

5839 **LLEWELLYN, Mrs. Frederick B.** Recorded 1929
47 N. Fullerton Avenue, Montclair, New Jersey
1. Beatrice Gunther (1904–) *m.* 1924 Frederick B. Llewellyn
2. Charles O. Gunther (1879–) *m.* 1901 Beatrice Disbrow (1881–)
3. William Cook Disbrow (1851–) *m.* 1876 Elizabeth Bulger (1860–1919)
4. William Cook Disbrow (1816–1893) *m.* 1848 Margaret Wessello Dill (1828–1912)
5. Samuel Warne Disbrow (1778–1873) *m.* 1811 Sarah Cook (1792–1875)
6. Benjamin Disbrow (1754–1794) *m.* 1775 Deborah Robinson (1755–1785)
7. Griffin Disbrow (1712–1754) *m.* Hannah ———
8. Benjamin Disbrow (1672–1733) *m.* Mary Griffin (–1737)
9. HENRY DISBROW (–1699) *m.* Margaret ———
Service: Magistrate Mamaroneck, 1673.
Reference: Register of New Netherland, 1626–1674, by O'Callaghan, page 99; Oyster Bay Town Records, Vol. 1, page 3; N. Y. Gen. & Biog. Rec., Vol. 51, page 41.

6197 **LODER, Carolyn Maude** Recorded 1938
67 Washington Street, Bridgeton, New Jersey
1. Carolyn Maude Loder (1921–)
2. LeRou Ward Loder (1883–) *m.* 1913 Maude Woodruff (1887–)
3. Adrian Bateman Woodruff (1854–1910) *m.* 1878 Kate N. Tomlin (1859–)

4. David Tomlin (1821–1881) *m.* 1846 Martha Steelman (1826–1892)
5. Jonas Steelman (1798–1876) *m.* 1820 Rachel Champion (1800–1874)
6. Joseph Champion (1768–1828) *m.* 1795 Sarah Smith (1778–1854)
7. William Smith (1754–1832) *m.* 1776 Martha Scull (1757–1843)
8. Jeremiah Smith (1723–   ) *m.* 1747 Abigail Somers (1725–   )
9. James Somers (1695–1761) *m.* Abigail Adams (1695–1772)
10. John Somers (1640–1723) *m.* (2nd) 1684 Hannah Hodgens (1667–1738)
  The said Abigail Adams (referred to in art. 9) was the dau. of
11. Jeremiah Adams (1664–1735) *m.* 1688 Rebecca (–1752)
12. John Adams (1637–1670) *m.* 1657 Abigail, dau. of Richard Smith, Sr., of
  Weatherfield
13. JEREMY ADAMS (1604–1683) *m.* abt. 1637 Rebecca Greenhill, *d.* abt. 1678
Service: An Original Proprietor of Hartford, Conn.
Reference: Gen. of Lake Family, pg. 165; Early Rec. Penn. Hist. Soc.; Hinman's
  Early Puritans, 13th & Locust Sts., Phila., Pa.

6168 LODER, Maude Woodruff   Recorded 1937
         67 Washington Street, Bridgeton, New Jersey
1. Maude Woodruff Loder (1887–   ) *m.* 1913 LeRoy Ward Loder
2. Adrian Bateman Woodruff (1854–1910) *m.* 1878 Kate N. Tomlin (1859–   )
3. David Tomlin (1821–1881) *m.* 1846 Martha Steelman (1826–1892)
4. Jonas Steelman (1798–1876) *m.* 1820 Rachel Champion (1800–1874)
5. Joseph Champion (1768–1828) *m.* 1795 Sarah Smith (1778–1854)
6. William Smith (1754–1832) *m.* 1776 Martha Scull (1757–1854)
7. Jeremiah Smith (1723–   ) *m.* 1747 Abigail Somers (1725–   )
8. James Somers (1695–1761) *m.* Abigail Adams (1695–1772)
9. Jeremiah Adams (1664–1735) *m.* 1688 Rebecca (–1752)
10. John Adams (1637–1670) *m.* 1657 Abigail Smith (–1670)
11. JEREMY ADAMS (1604–1683) *m.* abt. 1637 Rebecca Greenhill (widow) *d.* abt. 1678
Service: An Original Proprietor of Hartford, Conn.
Reference: Gen. Lake Family, pg. 165; Gen. Tomlin Family, Part I, pg. 5; Penn.
  Hist. Soc., 13th & Locust Sts., Phila., Pa.; Hinman's Early Puritans,
  Vol. I, starting pg. 26.

5980 LOHMULLER, Miss Delmah Loretta   Recorded 1931, Maryland
         3901 Greenway, Baltimore, Maryland
1. Delmah Loretta Lohmuller (1908–   )
2. John Lohmuller *m.* 1907 Eureth Linthicum (1882–   )
3. John Telison Brown *m.* 1874 Eureth Linthicum
4. Hezelsiah Linthicum (1801–1890) *m.* 1825 Matilda Philips (1809–1881)
5. Abner Linthicum (1763–1848) *m.* 1791 Rachael Jacobs (–1825)
6. Hezelsiah Linthicum (1723–1767) *m.* 1750 Sarah Bateman
7. Thomas Linthicum, Jr., *m.* Deborah Wayman
8. THOMAS LINTHICUM, SR. (1640–1701) *m.* Jane ———
Service: Capt. in 22nd Regiment.
Reference: Early Settlers, List Md. 1633 Historical Society, page 398.

6035 LONG, Mrs. Alford Thomas   Recorded 1932
         25 Middlemay Circle, Forest Hills, Long Island, New York
1. Anne Victoria Fields (1896–   ) *m.* 1917 Alford Thomas Long
2. J. J. Fields (1863–1923) *m.* 1887 Victoria Wykes Kilsby (1868–   )
3. John Wykes Kilsby (1804–1893) *m.* 1864 Mary Dingman (1826–1907)
4. Andrew Dingman (1803–1889) *m.* 1826 Caroline Eliza Sayre (1804–1886)
5. Dariel Westbrook Dingman (1775–1862) *m.* 1795 Mary Westbrook (1774–1851)
6. Andries Dingman (1752–1839) *m.* 1774 Jane Westbrook (1755–1838)
7. Andries Dingman (1711–1801) *m.* 1741 Cornelia Kermer (1720–1765)
8. Jacob Dingman *m.* 1698 Eva Swartuvat
9. ADAM DINGMAN *m.* Aeltil Jacobs Flodder
Reference: Gen. Dayre Family; Jerseymen in the Rev. War, page 574.

6396 LONG, Mrs. Lewis E.   Recorded 1942
          3279 Grove Street, Denver, Colorado
      1. Martha E. Montgomery *m.* Lewis E. Long
      2. George B. Montgomery (1851–1902) *m.* 1873 Georgia V. Wallace (1857–1925)
      3. William S. Montgomery (1821–1895) *m.* 1845 M. Elizabeth Pike (1823–1854)
      4. Thomas Montgomery (1782–1854) *m.* 1811 Martha Woodbury (1786–1868)
      5. William Woodbury (1758–) *m.* 1784 Hannah Kelley
      6. Zachariah Woodbury (1731–1815) *m.* Hannah Corning (1733–1802)
      7. William Woodbury *m.* 1720 Martha
      8. WILLIAM WOODBURY (1580–) *m.* Agnes ——
      Service: Deputy to General Court from Salem, Mass., 1635, 1638; 1637, Selectman.
      Reference: Hist. Acworth, N. H., 4, 5, 6, 7th Gen.; Hist. Francestown, N. H.

6448 LOONEY, Mrs. Charles   Recorded 1939, Texas
          4328 Lorraine Avenue, Dallas 5, Texas
      1. Ida Mitchell *m.* Charles Looney
      2. James Reid Mitchell (1850–1920) *m.* 1879 Ida Monroe (1856–1932)
      3. Jn. Tompkins Monroe (1822–1871) *m.* 1845 Rebecca K. Shepard (1826–1889)
      4. William Shepard (1779–1845) *m.* 1813 Ann Moore (1793–1864)
      5. John Shepard (–1794) *ca. m.* 1771 Miriam Wallace (–1815) *ca.*
      6. John Wallace (–1777) *m.* Elizabeth Caskill (–1789)
      7. Robt. Wallace of Cartoret (1700–1737) *m.* 1727 *ca.* Esther West (–1743)
      8. ROBT. WALLIS of Pasquotank (1646–1712) *m.* Prudence ——
      Service: Assistant Deputy, North Carolina; Member of the House of Commons;
          Magistrate.
      Reference: Cartaret Co., N. Carolina Court Rec. Deeds, Wills and Marriages.

6398 LOTHROP, Rev. Donald G.   Recorded 1942
          Brookline, Massachusetts
      1. Rev. Donald G. Lothrop *m.* Helena Lukomska
      2. Chester H. Lothrop (1879–) *m.* 1904 Mary Hilts (1882–)
      3. Henry Allen Lothrop (1851–1927) *m.* Agnes Harper (1855–)
      4. Henry Allen Lothrop (1831–) *m.* Elizabeth Matthews (–1912)
      5. Capt. John Lothrop (1794–1866) *m.* 1817 Maria Baxter (–1862)
      6. David Lothrop (1770–1850) *m.* Sarah ——
      7. Jonathan Lothrop (1719–1784) *m.* 1762 (2nd) Eunice Cobb
      8. Barnabas Lothrop (1686–1756) *m.* 1718 (2nd) Hannah Chipman (–1763)
      9. Captain John Lothrop (1644–1727) *m.* 1671 Mary (Colgrain) Cobb (1653–1694)
     10. REV. JOHN LOTHROP (1584–1653) *m.* 1635 (2nd) Anna (Hammond), wid. (–1687)
      Service: Clergyman, Scituate and Barnstable, Mass.
      Reference: Gen. Mem. Lo-Lathrop Family, Rev. Huntington; V. R., Chelsea, Mass.;
          Freman's Cape Cod, Vol. II; Trayson's Hist. Barnstable, 220, 411.

6605 LOWENTHAL, Mrs. Julius L.   Recorded 1938
          4930 N. Talman Avenue, Chicago 25, Illinois
      1. Emma Jane Cross *m.* 1904 Julius L. Lowenthal
      2. Eugene C. Cross (1863–) *m.* 1883 Alvina D. Green (1865–1943)
      3. Wm. A. Cross (1831–1908) *m.* 1858 Jane E. Elliott (1841–1907)
      4. Charles E. Elliott (1813–1892) *m.* 1837 Lucy M. Barber (1818–1891)
      5. Asa Elliott (1785–1852) *m.* 1807 Betsey Williams (1788–1855)
      6. Laban Elliott (1757–1830) *m.* Mehitable Harrington
      7. David Elliott (1716–1798) *m.* 1739 Mehetabel Aldrich (1716–1794)
      8. Peter Aldrich (1686–1748) *m.* Hannah Hayward (1680–1746)
      9. Jacob Aldrich (1652–1695) *m.* 1674/5 Huldah Thayer (1657–)
     10. FERDINANDO Thayer (bap. 1625–1713) *m.* 1652 Huldah Hayward, *d.* 1690
      Service: In Mendon, Mass., before King Phillip's War.
      Reference: Gen. Dict. of New England, New England Families, First Families of
          America.

5863 LUPTON, Mrs. Alfred H. Recorded 1929, New Jersey
  286 Atlantic Street, Bridgeton, New Jersey
 1. Mary A. Smith *m.* 1884 Alfred Holmes Lupton
 2. David P. Smith (1821–1868) *m.* 1852 Esther Townsend (1821–1899)
 3. Samuel Townsend (1783–1852) *m.* 1802 Hannah Humphries (1782–1829)
 4. Richard Humphries (1748–1824) *m.* 1780 Esther Aldrich (1757–1825)
 5. Abraham Humphries *m.* 1747 Hannah Smart (1718–)
 6. Nathan Smart (1690–1756) *m.* 1713 Deborah (1691–1762)
 7. Isaac Smart (1658–1700) *m.* 1683 Elizabeth Thompson (1666–)
 8. ANDREW THOMPSON (1637–1696) *m.* 1664 Isabella Marshall
 Service: Magistrate of the Colony, 1682; Commissioner of Highways, 1685.
 Reference: Shourd's History of the Thompson Family, pp. 283, 284, 285, 286.

6440 LUPTON, Mrs. B. Frank Recorded 1944
  286 Atlantic Street, Bridgeton, New Jersey
 1. Edna Townsend Smith *m.* B. Frank Lupton
 2. David P. Smith (1822–1868) *m.* 1852 (2nd) Esther Townsend (1821–1899)
 3. Samuel Townsend (1783–1852) *m.* 1802 Hannah Humphries (1782–1829)
 4. Richard Humphries (1748–1824) *m.* 1780 Esther Aldrich (1757–1835)
 5. Abraham Humphries *m.* 1747 Hannah Swarts (1718–)
 6. Nathan Swarts (1690–1756) *m.* 1713 Deborah ——— (1691–1762)
 7. Isaac Swarts (1658–1735) *m.* 1683 Elizabeth Thompson (1666–)
 8. ANDREW THOMPSON (1637–1696) *m.* 1664 Isabell Marshall
 Service: Came from England 1677 to Fenwick Colony; Magistrate of Colony; Member
  of Assembly 1682–83; Commissioner of Highways 1685.
 Reference: Shroud's Hist. Thompson Fam.; Salem Meeting, Vol. I.

6339 LYONS, Edwin James Recorded 1941
  125 Hickory Grove Drive, Larchmont, New York
 1. Edwin James Lyons, Jr.
 2. Edwin James Lyons *m.* 1928 Marjorie Thomas
 3. John Godhou Thomas, *b.* 1875, *m.* 1898 Maria Taylor Collins (1876–)
 4. Richard S. Collins (1841–1919) *m.* 1867 Adeline S. Green (1841–1927)
 5. John Collins (1806–1900) *m.* 1831 Elizabeth Clark (1809–1855)
 6. Levi Collins (1772–1813) *m.* 1801 Asenath Lake (1783–1860)
 7. Daniel Lake *c.* (1740–1799) *m.* 1764 Sarah Lucas
 8. Daniel Lake *c.* (1697–1774) *m.* 1730 Gartara Steelman
 9. William Lake *d.* 1717, *m.* Sarah
 10. John Lake, *d.* bef. 1696, *m.* Anne Spicer, *d.* aft. 1709
 11. THOMAS SPICER, *d.* 1658, *m.* Ann
 Service: Signed Compact at Newport, 1638; Treas. Portsmouth, 1642; Original
  Proprietor of Gravesend (Brooklyn) 1645; Magistrate of Gravesend, 1658.
 Reference: "Genealogy of Lake Family," by Adams and Risley.

6472 McARTHUR, Mrs. Vernon E. Recorded 1945
  Hutchinson, Kansas
 1. Virginia S. Bostick *m.* Vernon E. McArthur
 2. Lewis Thornton Bostick (1858–1933) *m.* 1888 Mattie L. Shackleford (1860–1931)
 3. George Shackleford (1798–1864) *m.* 1854 (2nd) Mrs. Ann Pitt Hall (Bassett)
  (1821–1902)
 4. Lyne Shackleford (1762–1806) *m.* 1790 *ca.* Elizabeth Price Dabney (1764–1806)
 5. Lyne Shackleford (1731–1776) *ca.* *m.* 1758 *ca.* Elizabeth Taliaferro (1738/40)
 6. William Taliaferro (1710–1778) *m.* Lucy Baytop
 7. Lawrence Taliaferro (1683–1726) *m.* Sarah Thornton (1680–)
 8. John Taliaferro (1656–1720) *m.* 1683 bef. Sarah Smith
 9. MAJOR LAWRENCE SMITH (bef. 1660–1700) *m.* Mary ——— (said to be dau. of
  Col. Augustine Warner, Sr.)
 Service: Officer in the Colonial Army of Va. Militia against Bacon, 1676; Lawyer;
  Burgess.

6045 McLEAN, Mrs. Allan   Recorded 1933
         1465 East Nineteenth Street, Brooklyn, New York

1. Grace Chalmers Patton (1867–   ) *m.* 1914 Allan McLean
2. John Vevirs Patton (1844–1920) *m.* 1867 Kate Combs (1843–1923)
3. Wm. Harrison Combs (1820–1895) *m.* 1841 Grace Chalmers (1816–1898)
4. Wm. Combs, Jr. (1791–1849) *m.* 1808 Jane A. Nutt (1792–1849)
5. Wm. Combs (1758–1840) *m.* 1787 Thankful Fletcher (1766–1800)
6. Oliver Fletcher (1743–1775) *m.* 1766 Tabitha Richardson (1746–1775)
7. John Richardson, Jr. (1711–1765) *m.* 1733 Esther Pirver (1711–1803)
8. John Richardson (1669–1746) *m.* 1693 Eliz. Farwill (1672–1728)
9. Josiah Richardson (1635–1695) *m.* 1689 Remembrance Underwood (1641–1718)
10. ESEKIEL RICHARDSON (1602–1647) *m.* Susanna ――――

Service: Constable.
Reference: Richardson Me., page 27; Manchester, N. H., His.

6636 McCLAMROCH, Grace West   Recorded 1949
         122 West Smith Street, Greensboro, North Carolina

1. Grace West *m.* 1901 ―――― McClamroch
2. Samuel E. West (1838–1879) *m.* 1859 Oceana W. Gwaltney (1840–1877)
3. William M. West (1806–1866) *m.* 1836 Lucy C. Warren (1817/8–1893)
4. Jesse P. Warren, *d.* 1829 (?), *m.* 1814 Sarah C. Bell, *d.* 1836 (?)
5. Lt. Jesse Warren, *d.* 1794 (?), *m.* Martha
6. Allen Warren III, will probated 1780, *m.* ――――
7. Allen Warren, Jr., will probated 1733, *m.* Anne Hart
8. Allen Warren (1663–1738) *m.* Elizabeth Clements
9. THOMAS WARREN (1624–1670) *m.* (3) Jane King (w. John)

Service: Member Va. House of Burgesses from Surry Co., Va., 1644, 45, 58, 59, 62, 63, 66.
Reference: Surry County Records, D.A.C. No. 8490.

5855 McCLELLAN, Miss Marianne   Recorded 1929, Georgia
         201 Clermont Avenue, East Point, Georgia

1. Marianne McClellan
2. John Marcus McClellan (1854–1908) *m.* 1879 Mamie Bradford Taul (1856–1929)
3. William Blount McClellan (1798–1881) *m.* 1825 Martha Roby (1808–1858)
4. John McClellan (1768–1842) *m.* 1794 Mary Wallace (1774–1856)
5. William Wallace (1737–1799) *m.* 1758 Mary Wallis
6. James Wallace (1690–   )
7. WILLIAM WALLACE

Service: Settled in Bucks County, Pa., 1690.
Reference: Bucks County Historical Society.

6654 McCLENDON, Mrs. J. H.   Recorded 1949
         Amite, Louisiana

1. Elizabeth Treiley *m.* 1912 Dr. Jesse H. McClendon
2. George J. Reiley (1854–1936) *m.* 1877 Mary A. S. Dunn (1856–1906)
3. Valeria H. Dunn (1809–1903) *m.* 1833 Mary Ann Bostwick (1815–1899)
4. John Bostwick (1789–1885) *m.* 1812 Catherine Fraser (1789–1817)
5. John W. Bostwick (1761–1835) *m.* 1783 Anna Collins (1758–1826)
6. Arthur Bostwick (1729–1802) *m.* 1752 Eunice Warriner (1729–1801)
7. Nathaniel Bostwick (1699–1756) *m.* 1727 Esther Hitchcock (1705–1747)
8. John Bostwick (1667–1747) *m. ca.* 1687 Abigail Walker (1672/3–   )
9. John Bostwick (bapt. 1638–bef. 1688) *m. ca.* 1665 Mary Brinsmead (1640–bef. 1704)
10. ARTHUR BOSTWICK (bapt. 1603–aft. 1680) *m.* 1627/8 Jane Whittel.

Service: Baptized in Tarpoley, Chesshire C., England; died after 1680 in Stratford, Conn.
Reference: Gen. of the Bostwick Family in America.

6183   McCORD, Clinton Duncan, Jr.   Recorded 1938
             183 Nacoochee Dr., Atlanta, Georgia
                              (JUNIOR)
   1. Clinton Duncan McCord (1935–)
   2. Clinton D. McCord (1906–) *m.* (I) 1933 Nancy Orme (1913–)
   3. Frank Orme (1870–1921) *m.* (I) 1909 Mary Phillips (1883–)
   4. Francis Hodgson Orme (1834–1913) *m.* (I) 1867 Ellen Vail Woodward (1843–1921)
   5. Archibald Orme (1795–1840) *m.* (I) 1818 Lucy Priestly (1800–1883)
   6. John Orme (1763–1824) *m.* (I) 1785 Sarah McAllister (1765–1806)
   7. Col. Archibald Orme (1730–1812) *m.* bf. (I) 1763 Elizabeth Johns (1734/5–abt.
             1808)
   8. Rev. John Orme, V.D.M. (1691/2–1758) *m.* (I) 1720 Ruth Edmondston
             (1705–1775)
   9. Col. Archibald Edmondston, *d.* 1734, *m.* (I) bef. 1705 Jane Beall, *b.* 1667/8
   10. COL. NINIAN BEALL (1624/5–1717) *m.* (I) Ruth Moore.
   Service: Was commissioned first as Lieutenant, then as Captain, then as Major and
             finally as Colonel.
   Reference: Vol. 2, McKenzie "Colonial Family," pgs. 66–563; "Descendants of
             Archibald McAllister of Cumberland Co., Md., by Miss Mary McAllister;
             Hist. W. Md., Vol. I, pgs. 126–128; also archives of Md. Journal of the
             Com. of the Council of Safety, Jan. 1 to Mar. 10, 1777; Records Annapolis
             in N. W. No. 6, Folio 509, dated 1–17–1717, proven 2–28–1717.

6061   McCLESKY, Mrs. Waymon B.   Recorded 1934, Georgia
             23 Riverview Park Drive, Columbus, Ohio
   1. Flossie Jones *m.* 1916 Waymon B. McCleskey
   2. Claudius C. Jones (1844–1915) *m.* 1872 Mildred McCurry (1856–)
   3. James W. Jones (1809–1877) *m.* 1842 Mildred E. White (1819–1865)
   4. Eppy White (1791–1854) *m.* 1815 Catherine Herndon (1797–1885)
   5. Edward Herndon (1768–1827) *m.* 1791 Nancy Rucker (1770–1840)
   6. Edward Herndon (1738–1831) *m.* 1762 Mary Gaines (1744–1820)
   7. William Herndon (1706–) *m.* 1730 Sarah Ann Drysdale (widow of Thomas
             Leftwich)
   8. Edward Herndon (1678–1742) *m.* 1698 Mary Waller (1674–)
   9. William Herndon *m.* 1677 Catherine Digges (1654–1727)
   10. GOVERNOR EDWARD DIGGES (1620–1675) *m.* Elizabeth Page (–1691)
   Service: Member of Virginia Council, 1654–75; Governor of Virginia, 1656–58.
   Reference: Manuscript on Herndon, Digges, Henderson, Street and Allied Families, by
             Mrs. Frances McCauley Johnson; Genealogy, of the Fitzhugh, Edmonds,
             Digges, Page, Taylor and Allied Families, by Fitzhugh Knox, Atlanta,
             Ga., 1932.

6181   McCORD, Clinton Duncan, Sr.   Recorded 1938
             183 Macoochee Drive, Atlanta, Georgia
   1. Clinton Duncan McCord, Sr. (1906–) *m.* 1933 Nancy Orme
   2. John Lawrence McCord (1879–) *m.* 1905 Laura Katherine Pate (1884–)
   3. Dr. Redding Hamilton Pate (1834–1896) *m.* 1863 Zeph Eugenia Laidler
             (1847–1896)
   4. Redding Hamilton Pate (1796–1836) *m.* 1829 Elizabeth Miller (1809–1888)
   5. John Pate (1760–1829) *m.* 1794 Nancy Cowart (2nd wife) 1779–1823)
   6. Jacob Pate (1710–) *m.* (I) Zillah Broach
   7. Matthew Pate (bpt. 1686–) *m.* (I) 1708 Anne Reade
   8. Frances Reade, *d.* 1694, *m.* (2) Anne (Rec. only mentions wife Anne)
   9. Col. George Reade (1608–1674) *m.* (I) Elizabeth Martiau (Martin) (1605–1676)
   10. NICHOLAS MARTIN (MARTIAU) (1591–1657) *m.* (2) Jane Berkeley
   Service: First Representative in Va. Assembly from Chiskiach and Kent Island;
             Justice of York; Burgess of Kent Island and York, 1632–57.
   Reference: Hotten's List of Emigrants, pgs. 99, 176, 249; Va. Mag., IV, pgs. 248,
             249, 204; Vol. XIX, pgs. 255, 256, 257; Hening's, Vol., pgs. 129, 154, 179,
             203; Vol., pgs. 358, 414, 421, 429, 432, 499, 505; Vol. V, pgs. 483–85; Vol. 8,
             pg. 483.

6191   McCORD, Laura Katherine Pate   Recorded ——
       517 Ridgecrest Road, Atlanta, Georgia
   1. Laura Katherine Pate McCord (1884–) *m.* 1905 John Lawrence McCord
      (1878–)
   2. Dr. Reddington Hamilton Pate (1834–1896) *m.* 1863 Zep Eugenia Laidler
      (1874–1896)
   3. Reddington Hamilton Pate (1796–1836) *m.* 1829 Elizabeth Miller (1809–1888)
   4. John Pate (1760–1829) *m.* (2) 1794 Nancy Cowart (1779–1823)
   5. Jacob Pate (1710–) *m.* Zillah Broach
   6. Matthew Pate, bpt. 1686, *m.* 1708 Annie Reade
   7. Frances Reade (1637–1694) *m.* 1676 Annie (2nd wife)
   8. George Reade (1609–1674) *m.* Elizabeth Martian (Martiou) (1605–1676)
   9. ROBERT READE, *b.* Yorkshire, Eng., *m.* Mildred Winebank (Windebank) dau. of
      Sir. Thomas Windebank, "Clerk of the Signet" to Queen Elizabeth

   Service: Sec. (*pro tem*) of Va., 1640, Council of Va. Burgesses; House of Burgesses,
       1649–56–57–71.
   Reference: Recs. of Dooly, Pulaski and Washington Cos., Georgia; Reg. of Land
       Grant, Book XXX, pg. 345, Sec'y of State Office, State Cap., Atlanta,
       Ga.; Wm. & Mary Quar., Vol. V, pg. 279; Vol. VII, pgs. 119–120; Vol. XIX,
       pg. 117; Vol. XII, Qua. III, pg. 39; Henning's Statutes, Vol. 1, pgs. 358,
       414, 421, 429, 432, 499, 505; Vol. VII, pg. 483.

6182   McCORD, Nancy (Orme)   Recorded 1938
       183 Nacoochee Dr., Atlanta, Georgia

   1. Nancy Orme (1913–) *m.* 1933 Clinton Duncan McCord, Sr.
   2. Frank Orme (1870–1921) *m.* (I) 1909 Mary Phillips (1883–)
   3. Francis Hodgson Orme (1834–1913) *m.* (I) 1867 Ellen Vail Woodward (1843–1921)
   4. Archibald Orme (1795–1840) *m.* (I) 1818 Lucy Priestly (1800–1883)
   5. John Orme (1763–1824) *m.* (I) 1785 Sarah McAllister (1765–1806)
   6. Col. Archibald Orme (1730–1812) *m.* (I) bef. 1763 Elizabeth Johns (1734/5–abt.
      1808)
   7. Rev. John Orme, V.D.M. (1691/2–1758) *m.* (I) 1720 Ruth Edmondston
      (1705–1775)
   8. Col. Archibald Edmondston, *d.* 1734, *m.* (I) bef. 1705 Jane Beall, *b.* 1667/8
   9. COL. NINIAN BEALL (1624/5–1717) *m.* (I) Ruth Moore

   Service: Was commissioned first as Lieutenant, then as Captain, then as Major, and
       finally as Colonel.
   Reference: Descds. of Archibald McAllister of Cumberland Co., Md., by Mary
       McAllister; History of Western Md., Vol. I, pgs. 126–128, also archives
       of Md., Journal of Com., Council of Safety, Jan. 1 to Mar. 10, 1777;
       Beall & Edmondston Wills, Liber TD, folio 159, Annapolis, dated Mar.
       13, 1734, proven June 28, 1734; also Col. Ninian Beall will, Annapolis,
       in N. W. No. 6, Folio 509, dated Jan. 17, 1717, proven 2–28–1717.

6160   McDOUGALL, Irene Gantt   Recorded 1937
       30 Fifth Avenue, New York, New York

   1. Irene Gantt (1888–) *m.* 1908 John Franklin McDougall
   2. Pleasant Jordan Gantt (1853–1916) *m.* 1877 Florence Minerva Reed
   3. Dr. Charles Alfred Gantt (1826–1901) *m.* 1852 Margaret Jane Mask
   4. Pleasant Marshall Mask (1787–1847) *m.* 1820 Winifred T. Pemberton (1794–1859)
   5. William Stith Pemberton (1763–1819) *m.* 1783 Martha Jennings (1765–1823)
   6. Col. John Jennings (abt. 1734–) *m.* Lydia Batte (1740–)
   7. Charles Jennings (bef. 1680–1747) *m.* Jane Lattimore (Latimer)
   8. CHARLES JENNINGS (1651–abt. 1700) *m.* as early as 1680 Mary (1652–1710)

   Service: Clerk of the Court of Elizabeth City County, Virginia.
   Reference: Tyler's Quarterly Magazine, Vol. 4, pgs. 425, 426, 431; William & Mary
       Quarterly, Vol. 9, pg. 124; Vol. 26, pg. 107; Va. VI 4, pages 216, 321, 308;
       Va. Mag. & Biography, Vol. 30, pg. 342.

6130 McDOUGALL, Mrs. William L. Recorded 1937
Atlanta, Georgia
1. Mary A. Thomas *m.* 1922 Dr. William L. McDougall
2. Dr. Joseph M. Thomas (1865–1925) *m.* 1896 Addavale Kincaid (1875–)
3. William J. Kincaid (1841–1923) *m.* 1872 Mary A. Phelps (1852–1915)
4. Augustus B. Phelps (1813–1887) *m.* 1840 Mary (Burnley) Seals (1815–1857)
5. Richmond Burnley (1789–1817) *m.* 1810 Sarah Veazey (1790–)
6. John Veazey (1767–1847) *m.* 1790 Jane Rabun (1766–1855)
7. James Veazey, Jr. (1725–1790) *m.* 1750 Mrs. Elizabeth H. Johnston (1727–1812)
8. James Veazey, Sr. (1685–1758) *m.* 1716 Mary Mercer (1695–1766)
9. JOHN VEAZEY (1645–1698) *m.* 1670 Martha Brocas (–1697)
Service: Landed Proprietor, Church Warden, 1698.
Reference: McKenzie's Colonial Families; Hubert's Barksdale Family History.

6709 McGUIRE, Mrs. Victor Virgil Recorded 1951, North Carolina
75 St. Dunston Circle, Asheville, North Carolina
1. Blanche Emerson Duke *m.* 1923 V. V. McGuire
2. Robert Duke (1862–1903) *m.* 1888 Laura Emerson (1867–1946)
3. Robert Jehu Emerson (1835–1902) *m.* 1857 Cornelia Lewis Hudson (1835–1873)
4. John Emerson (1792–1886) *m.* 1834 Aseneath Stuart (1813–1907)
5. Robert Stuart (1766–abt. 1820) *m.* 1793 Martha Beeson (abt. 1775–1819)
6. Isaac Grubb Beason (1722–) *m.* Phoebe Stroud (1733–)
7. Richard Beason (1684–1777) *m.* 1706 Charity Grubb (1687–1761)
8. EDWARD BEASON (–1714) *m.* Rachel Pennington
Service: Born in England, came to America 1684; a landed proprietor and founder
of West Nottingham, Pa.
Reference: Stuart and Allied Families, pgs. 26, 20; Henshaw's "Encyclopedia of
American Quakers," pgs. 5, 17, 571, 573; The Grubb Family of Del.,
Vol. I; Smith's History of New Jersey, pg. 539; Meetings of Penn's Commissioners of Philadelphia, 1701; Beeson Genealogy, by J. L. Beason
of Alabama.

5923 McHALE, Mrs. John Recorded 1930, Rhode Island
Providence, Rhode Island
1. Julia Brown Knowles *m.* John McHale
2. Martin Van Buren Knowles (1836–1886) *m.* 1866 Mary Jane Brown (1848–1883)
3. John Knowles Brown (1821–1898) *m.* 1841 Mercy Congdon (1820–1895)
4. Thomas Brown (1779–1854) *m.* 1817 Margaret Knowles (1791–1850)
5. Perleg Brown (1757–1831) *m.* 1778 Mary Coggeshall (1761–1837)
6. Joshua Coggeshall (1722–) *m.* 1752 (2) Anne Dennis (1731–)
7. Thomas Coggeshall (1688–1771) *m.* 1708 Mary Freeborn (1692–1776)
8. Joshua Coggeshall (1656–1723) *m.* 1681 Sarah (–1697)
9. Joshua Coggeshall (1623–1688) *m.* 1652 Joan West (1631–1676)
10. JOHN COGGESHALL (1591–1647) *m.* Mary (1604–1684)
Service: President of the Colony, 1647.
Reference: Vital Records of Rhode Island; Austin's Dictionary of Rhode Island
Families, page 49.

6093 McLUCAS, Mrs. Benjamin W. Recorded 1935
1103 G Street, Fairbury, Nebraska
1. Cora Cropsey *m.* Benjamin W. McLucas
2. Daniel B. Cropsey (1848–1930) *m.* 1873 Myra Caldwell (1854–1928)
3. William E. Caldwell (1817–1890) *m.* 1840 Amy J. Banning (1821–1909)
4. Benjamin Banning (1780–1827) *m.* 1807 Mary Munger (1791–1868)
5. Abner Banning (1755–1829) *m.* 1775 Annah Sparrow (1751–1820)
6. John Sparrow (1719–1764) *m.* 1740 Anna Atwood (–1806)
7. Stephen Sparrow (1694–1785) *m.* 1717 Anna Mulford (1691–1772)
8. John Sparrow (1656–1734) *m.* 1683 Apphia Tracey (–1739)
9. John Tracy (1633–1718) *m.* Mary Prence (1639–1696)
10. Gov. THOMAS PRENCE (1600–1673) *m.* Mary Collier (–1662)
Service: Governor of Massachusetts.
Reference: Mayflower Descendants; Historical Sketch of Gov. Prence; Plymouth
Colony Records.

6476 McMILLEN, Mrs. Frank O.   Recorded 1945
            518 W. Market, Akron 3, Ohio
    1. Frances Burnett *m*. Frank Orlando McMillen
    2. Ralph P. Burnett (1858–1929) *m*. 1884 F. Lillian Ayres (1861–1936)
    3. Hiram Jefferson Ayers (1823–1907) *m*. 1852 Frances Freelove Smith (1834–1864)
    4. Hiram J. Smith (1800–1845) *m*. Elsie Adams
    5. Joshua Smith (1766–1835) *m*. 1796 Rhoda Kittridge (1775–1835)
    6. Joshua Smith (1744–1793) *m*. Freelove Kibbe (1749–1840)
    7. Joshua Smith (1720–1774) *m*. 1742 Mercy Snow (1722–1774)
    8. James Smith (1685–   ) *m*. 1713 Hannah Rogers (1689–   )
    9. John Rogers (1642–   ) *m*. 1669 Elizabeth Twining (–1725)
   10. Joseph Rogers (1607–1678) *m*. Hannah ———
   11. THOMAS ROGERS (–1621) *m*. Grace ———
    Service: Signer Mayflower Compact.

6020 McMURRY, Mrs. E. R.   Recorded 1932
            210 Hartwell Road, Lavonia, Georgia
    1. Anetta Higginbotham (1875–   ) *m*. Edward R. McMurry
    2. Thos. Benj. Higginbotham (1855–   ) *m*. 1874 Susan Jane Ledbitler (1854–   )
    3. Benj. Thos. Higginbotham (1830–1864) *m*. 1849 Frances Eliz. Cook (1831–1915)
    4. W. Tos. Oliver Cook (1809–1902) *m*. 1828 Nancy Tennyson Ridgway (1803–1885)
    5. Wm. Thos. Cook (1777–1814) *m*. Frances Oliver
    6. Dionysius Oliver (1735–1808) *m*. 1758 Mary Ann Winfrey (1740–1802)
    7. Peter Oliver *m*. Anne McCartie (1706–   )
    8. JOHN OLIVER
    Service:
    Reference: Early Settler of Ala., by Col. James Edmonds Saunders, N. Orleans,
            1899; McCarty Family.

6381 McNUTT, Mrs. James C.   Recorded 1942, Illinois
            803 Hester Avenue, Normal, Illinois
    1. Margaret Newkirk *m*. 1902 James Carson McNutt
    2. Enoch Jas. Newkirk (1844–1902) *m*. 1869 Mary E. Williams (1851–1936)
    3. Adam Clark Williams (1820–1911) *m*. 1843 Margaret Conchman Reed (1826–1880)
    4. Abel Lewis Williams (1786–1881) *m*. 1811 Tabitha Keener (1794–1876)
    5. Isaac Williams (1742–aft. 1789) *m*. 1765 Rachel Pike (1746–1789)
    6. John Pike (1702–1774) *m*. 1731 Abigail Overman (1709–1781)
    7. Ephraim Overman, *d*. 1732, *m*. 1708 Sarah Belman, *b*. 1688
    8. John Belman, *d. c.* 1706, *m*. 1687 Sarah Wilson
    9. ROBERT WILSON (1629–1696) *m*. Ann Blount
    Service: Came to America age 6, 1635; had Land Grant, Surrey Co., Va., 1648.
    Reference: "The Williams Family," by E. H. Joseph; Hinshaw's Quaker Records;
            Hist. of Perq. Co., Va., by Winslow.

5966 MacPHAIL, Mrs. D. R.   Recorded 1930, Pennsylvania
            322 E. 21st Street, Chester, Pennsylvania
    1. Jessie Bowker *m*. 1906 D. R. MacPhail
    2. John J. Bowker (1856–   ) *m*. 1882 Lavinia Davis (1856–   )
    3. Joseph Davis (–1864) *m*. 1836 Leah Ireland (1815–1889)
    4. Elijah Ireland (1780–1823) *m*. 1805 Rachel Somers (1785–1840)
    5. Japhet Ireland (1744–1810) *m*. 1767 Mary Townsend (1746–1801)
    6. Thomas Ireland (1721–1773) *m*. 1741 Mary Creasey
    7. Daniel Ireland (1680–1762) *m*. Ruth Williams (1699–1757)
    8. Thomas Ireland (1647–1710) *m*. Mary (–1723)
    9. THOMAS IRELAND (–1668) *m*. Joan
    Service: One of the 50 Founders of Hempstead, Long Island.
    Reference: Essex County, N. J., Records; Camden County, N. J., Records; Hemp-
            stead Town Records; New York Geneal & Bio. Records, Vol. 10, p. 11;
            American Ancestry, Vol. 3, p. 91.

5864 MacPHERSON, Mrs. Ronald   Recorded 1929, New Jersey
        Morrisville, Bucks Co., Pennsylvania
    1. Mary B. Hendrickson *m.* 1905 Ronald MacPherson
    2. Mahlon K. Hendrickson (1843–) *m.* 1869 Rachel H. Scattergood (–1909)
    3. John Hendrickson *m.* 1834 Margaretta Yardley (1808–1871)
    4. Joseph Yardley (1771–1831) *m.* 1798 Sarah Field
    5. William Yardley (1716–1774) *m.* 1756 Sarah Kirkbride
    6. Thomas Yardley (1680–) *m.* 1706 Ann Biles
    7. WILLIAM BILES *m.* Johanna (–1687)
    Service: Arrived in Penna 1679 and was Justice of the Peace in 1681, 1685, 1689;
        member of the Assembly in 1686, 1689, 1694; Judge of the Supreme Court
        in 1699, 1701.
    Reference: History of Bucks County, by Davis; Yardley Genealogy; Friends' Records
        of Bucks County, Pa.

5961 MAHON, Miss Harriette W.   Recorded 1930, New Jersey
        101 East Avenue, Bridgeton, New Jersey
    1. Harriette Warrick Mahon
    2. Rev. Charles L. Mahon (1836–1872) *m.* 1866 Emily F. Cloak (1843–1878)
    3. Capt. John Mahon (1812–1843) *m.* 1835 Harriet S. Tomlinson (1818–1894)
    4. William Tomlinson (1786–1826) *m.* 1808 Phebe Harris (1788–1841)
    5. Samuel Tomlinson (1762–1842) *m.* Ann Garrison (1761–1824)
    6. James Tomlinson (1735–1811) *m.* 1756 Barbara Brown (1736–1808)
    7. Richard Tomlinson (1698–) *m.* Lydia Wells
    8. RICHARD TOMLINSON (–1716) *m.* 1696 Sarah Buzby (–1746)
    Reference: Abington Friends' Monthly Meeting Records, Vol. I, p. 26; Records of
        Trinity Oxford Church, Phila., Pa.; Historical Sketch of Seventh Day
        Baptist, by Julius F. Sachse.

6176 MALONE, Chaste Alberta   Recorded 1938
        747 Juniper Street N. E., Atlanta, Georgia
    1. Chaste Alberta Malone (1883–)
    2. Frank Nettles Malone (1853–1897) *m.* 1876 Alberta Elizabeth Scruggs (1856–1915)
    3. Gross Scruggs (1829–1863) *m.* 1854 Chaste Helen Noble (1839–1902)
    4. Gross Scruggs (1790–1835) *m.* 1821 Mary Earle Lundy (–aft. 1833)
    5. Gross Scruggs (1758–1822) *m.* (2) 1788/9 Margaret Earle (–1799)
    6. Jesse Scruggs (1736–aft. 1774) *m.* 1756 ———
    7. Richard Scruggs *ca.* (1689/90–aft. 1736) *m.* 1716/17 Martha, *d.* aft. 1738
    8. Henry ("Henery") Scruggs, *ca.* (1660–aft. 1723) *m.* 1685/6 Anne Grose (Gross)
        ca. (1665–)
    9. RICHARD SCRUGGS, Gentleman, *ca.* (1630–aft. 1669) min. Va. *ca.* 1660
    Service: Came to America and settled in Va. in 1655; Landed Proprietor—owner of
        several thousand A. in James City and New Kent Cos., Va.; Rec'd as Crown
        Grant.
    Reference: Recs. of Fulton Co., Ga., and Clark Co., Ala., Vol. 2–1834–65, pg. 209,
        Book I, pg. 131; "Ga. Landmarks, Memorials and Legends," L. L. Knight,
        pgs. 701–703; "St. Peter's Par. Recs." (New Kent Co., Va.), pgs. 50,
        103, 123, et al.; Land Patents in Va. Land Office, Richmond, Va.; Scruggs
        Gen., by Ethel H. S. Dunklin.

6626 MALONE, Mrs. E. P.   Recorded 1949
        617 Fox Street, Aurora, Illinois
    1. Vivian D. Haggard *m.* 1929 E. P. Malone
    2. R. J. Haggard (1867–1946) *m.* 1895 Lily M. Givler (1865–1940)
    3. David Givler (1829–1919) *m.* 1848 Mary J. Eckman (1829–1902)
    4. Henry Givler (1765–1835) *m.* 1826 Rebecca Line (1795–1872)
    5. William Line (1749–1842) *m.* 1773 Maria Bear (1746–1826)
    6. George Line (1714–1786) *m.* 1746 Salome Carpenter (1727–1807)
    7. Gabriel Carpenter (1704–1767) *m. ca.* 1726 Appolina Hermann (1710–1793)
    8. DR. HENRY CARPENTER (1673–1747) *m.* 1701 Salome Rufener (1675–1742)
    Service:
    Reference: Gen. History of Carpenter Family; D.A.R., D.C.W., 1812 records; Hist.
        Lancaster Co., by Rupp.

6100   MANLEY, Mrs. John W.   Recorded 1936, Texas
                602 South Peak Street, Dallas, Texas
       1. Frederick Moseley *m.* John Walter Manley
       2. Rev. Hillery Moseley (1830–1883) *m.* 1858 Judith Ayers (1835–1922)
       3. John F. Moseley (1790–1862) *m.* 1814 Frances E. Cooper (1795–1854)
       4. John Moseley (1757–1816) *m.* 1784 Anna Finney Willson (1760–)
       5. William Moseley (1732–1763) *m.* 1755 Mary Watkins (1737–1792)
       6. Arthur Moseley, Jr. (–1736) *m.* Martha Cock
       7. John Cock (–1759) *m.* 1696 Obedience Branch (–1746)
       8. John Branch (–1688) *m.* Martha Goode (–1699)
       9. William Branch (1625–1676) *m.* Jane Hatcher (1640–)
      10. CHRISTOPHER BRANCH (1602–1682) *m.* 1619 Mary Addie
       Service: One of the Representatives of Henrico County, Va., in the House of Burgesses;
                Justice of the Peace in 1656.
       Reference: Branch Family; Wm. & Mary Quarterly, Vol. 25; Va. Hist. Mag., Vol. 5;
                Henrico Records, Vol. 1734–46.

6008   MANN, Mrs. H. C.   Recorded 1931
                Lyons, Georgia
       1. Lucille E. Mann (1905–) *m.* 1929 Herman C. Mann
       2. Ora Carl Eavenson (1884–) *m.* 1904 Annie Nora Whittemore (1889–)
       3. John Wm. Eavenson (1840–) *m.* 1865 Josephine Oglesby (1846–1930)
       4. Geo. Eavenson (1817–1898) *m.* 1839 Sarah Thornton (1824–1863)
       5. Geo. Eavenson (1782–1842) *m.* 1803 Polly Hilly (1781–1855)
       6. Eli Eavenson (1760–1829) *m.* Rachael Seal (1760–1830)
       7. Geo. Eavenson (1726–1816) *m.* 1753 Mary Williamson (–1828)
       8. Joseph Eavenson (1689–1771) *m.* 1717 Catherine George
       9. Thomas Eavenson (1653–1726) *m.* Hannah Woodward
      10. RALPH EAVENSON (1625–1665) *m.* Cecil Orton
       Service:
       Reference:

5924   MANN, Mrs. Washington L.   Recorded 1930, New York
                444 W. Twentieth Street, New York, New York
       1. Viola Waring *m.* Washington L. Mann
       2. James Darling Waring (1812–1897) *m.* 1841 Maria Dederick (1823–1900)
       3. James Waring (1781–1847) *m.* 1810 Betsy Whitney (1785–1855)
       4. Daniel Whitney (1754–1826) *m.* 1776 Hannah Sellead (1761–1849)
       5. Daniel Whitney (1723–) *m.* 1745 Hester Claton
       6. Richard Whitney (1687–) *m.* 1709 Hannah Darling (–1774)
       7. John Whitney (1644–1720) *m.* 1674 Elizabeth Smith
       8. Henry Whitney (1620–1673) *m.* ——————
       9. THOMAS WHITNEY (–1657) *m.* Mary Roach
       Service: Selected with other townsmen to carry on the affairs of Huntington, L. I.,
                1664.
       Reference: Whitney Family, 3 Volumes, by S. Whitney, Phoenix, 1878.

6638   MARKHAM, Mrs. Charles B.   Recorded 1949
                204 N. Dillard Street, Durham, North Carolina
       1. Sadie Hackney *m.* 1909 Charles B. Markham
       2. Edward C. Hackney (1856–1903) *m.* 1884 Lina Mallory (1863–1909)
       3. Joshua W. Hackney (1820–1892) *m.* 1841 Harriet Stone (1823–1876)
       4. John L. Stone *m.* 1812 Sylvia Booth (1780–)
       5. Daniel Booth (1723–1801) *m.* Priscilla Moore
       6. Zachariah Booth (1694–1762) *m.* Anna Curtis
       7. Joseph Booth (1656–1703) *m.* Hannah Wilcox
       8. RICHARD BOOTH (1607–1702) *m.* Elizabeth Hawley
       Service: Came to America in 1639 and settled in Stratford, Conn. Came to Virginia
                to help set the boundary line between Virginia and North Carolina in
                1661–1667.
       Reference: Durham County, N. C., records; Chatham County, N. C., records; Orange
                County records.

6097 MARSH, Mrs. Charles T. Recorded 1936, Illinois
1010 Grant Avenue, Rockford, Illinois

1. Cora E. Marsh *m.* 1901 Charles T. Marsh
2. Jacob E. Vande Mark (1833–1893) *m.* 1859 Jane Henderson (1838–1920)
3. Evert Vande Mark (1797–1893) *m.* 1819 Fanny Wentworth (1800–1860)
4. Henry Wentworth (1740–1810) *m.* 1791 Annatie Romer (1772–1852)
5. Ezekiel Wentworth (1723–1772) *m.* Mary Gibbons
6. Shubael Wentworth (1690–1759) *n.* 1717 Damaris Hawes (1696–1739)
7. James Hawes (1664–1718) *m.* 1692 Damaris Bird (1675–1715)
8. John Bird (1641–1732) *m.* 1673 Elizabeth Williams (1647–1724)
9. RICHARD WILLIAMS (1606–1692) *m.* 1632 Frances Dighton (1611–1724)

Service: Founder, Freeman, Member of the General Court. Militiaman in 1643.
Reference: Wentworth Genealogy, Vol. I; N. E. Genealogical Society.

5972 MARTIN, Mrs. Robert S. Recorded 1930, Illinois
503 N. Main Street, Paris, Illinois

1. Mabel Puffer *m.* 1908 Robert Stanwood Martin
2. Morgan Puffer (1846–1923) *m.* 1875 Susan E. Whalen (1852–   )
3. Reuben Puffer, Jr. (1825–1909) *m.* 1846 Harriet Depuy (1827–1897)
4. Reuben Puffer, Sr. (–1825) *m.* 1821 Diadema Mack (1801–1891)
5. Elisha Mack, Jr. (1775–   ) *m.* 1793 Hannah Graves
6. Elisha Mack, Sr. (1745–1830) *m.* 1769 Diadema Rathburne
7. Ebenezer Mack (1697–1777) *m.* 1728 Hannah Huntley
8. Jack Mack (1653–1721) *m.* 1681 Sarah Bagley (1663–   )
9. Orlando Bagley *m.* 1653 Sarah Colby (1637–1700)
10. ANTHONY COLBY (–1661) *m.* Susannah (–1682)

Service: Came with Gov. Winthrop, 1630, to America.
Reference: Mack History, Vols. I and II.

6534 MASSENGALE, Alice May Recorded 1946
198 Ponce de Leon Avenue, Atlanta, Georgia

1. Alice May Massengale
2. Andrew M. Massengale (1840–1899) *m.* 1874 Hattie E. Brinn (1846–1935)
3. Dr. T. E. Massengale (1809–1859) *m.* 1835 E. Angelina Pettit (1816–1874)
4. John Pettit (1757–1821) *m.* 1787 Betsy Kennon (1772–1846)
5. John Pettit *m.* Anne Fauntleroy
6. Lt. Col. Wm. Fauntleroy (1684–1757) *m.* Apphia Bushrod
7. William Fauntleroy *m.* 1680 Katherine Griffin
8. COL. MOORE FAUNTLEROY (1610–1663) *m. ca.* 1650 Mary Hill

Service: Commissions by Va. Assembly; Captain, Major, Lt. Colonel, and Colonel of Virginia Militia.
Reference: Wm. and Mary Quarterly; Va. Hist. Mag.; Browning's Col. Dames of Royal Descent.

6428 MAST, Mrs. Guy L. Recorded 1943
La Porte City, Iowa

1. Margaret Eleanor Hagen *m.* Guy L. Mast
2. James William Hagen (1880–   ) *m.* 1905 Mary Eleanor Ogdin (1881–   )
3. James William Hagen (1852–1928) *m.* 1879 Emma Rece (1860–   )
4. John Calvin Rece (1818–1879) *m.* 1855 Margaret Ann George (1824–1906)
5. Rev. William George (1790–1875) *m.* 1817 Nancy Byrd Eastham (1794–1879)
6. George Eastham (1755–1818) *m.* Susan Woodside
7. Col. Robert Eastham (1706–1790) *m.* Ann Lawson
8. GEORGE EASTHAM *m.* 1682 Ann Taylor

Service: Married in Va. in 1682; lived in Fauquier Co., Va.
Reference: Hist. Papers of Virginia; First Families of America, Vol. 5, p. 588, Virkus; Hist. Kanawah Valley, Poffenbarger; Eastham Gen.

6268   MATHER, John Augustus II   Recorded 1939, New Jersey
           26½ Tanner Street, Haddonfield, New Jersey
                                (JUNIOR)
       1. John Augustus Mather II
       2. John Sidney Mather, *b*. 1891, *m*. 1920 Edith Barton Dale
       3. General John Augustus Mather (1865–1917) *m*. 1890 Lizzie Weatherby (1866–1899)
       4. John Atkinson Mather (1837–1921) *m*. 1861 Louisa Wallace Dawson (1842–1923)
       5. James Carr Dawson (1815–1872) *m*. 1838 Elizabeth Barber Cade (1818–1895)
       6. Isaac Cade (1780–1823) *m*. 1804 Judith Hendrickson (1784–1867)
       7. Andrew Henricsson (1748–1793) *m*. 1770 Judy Jones (1751–1793)
       8. Peter Henricsson (1718–1761) *m*. Catherine Lock (1729–1766)
       9. ANDERS HENRICSSON *m*. Beata
       Service: Swedish settler of Western New Jersey by 1698; "Original Settlers on the
           Delaware," by Benjamin Forrest.
       Reference: Same as Number 6265

6340   MATHER, John Sidney   Recorded 1941, New Jersey
       1. John Sidney Mather *m*. 1916 Evangeline Hanger; *m*. 1920 Edith Barton Dale
       2. Capt. John A. Mather (1865–1917) *m*. Lizzie Weatherby (1866–1899)
       3. John Atkinson Mather (1837–1921) *m*. 1861 Louisa W. Dawson (1842–1923)
       4. James Carr Dawson (1815–1872) *m*. 1838 Elizabeth B. Cade (1818–1925)
       5. Isaac Cade (1781–1823) *m*. 1804 Judith Hendrickson (1784–1867)
       6. Andrew Hendrickson (1748–1821) *m*. 1770 Judy Jones (1751–1793)
       7. Peter Henricsson (1718–1761) *m*. Catherine Lock (1729–1766)
       8. ANDRES HENRICSSON, *b*. bef. 1700, *m*. Beata, *d. c.* 1722
       Service: Settler in Swedesboro, N. J.; helped build Old Swedes Church at Christiana,
           Del., 1699.
       Reference: Records Trinity Church, Swedesboro; Records St. Paul's P. E. Church,
           Camden, N. J.; Records St. Peter's Church, Clarksboro, N. J.

6719   MAYE, Miss Lily Adele   Recorded 1951
           114 S. Second Street, Warrington, Florida
       1. Miss Lily Adele Maye
       2. James McKenzie Maye (1892–1940) *m*. 1914 Lillie Corinne Garrett (1891–   )
       3. John Wilkinson Garrett (1851–1895) *m*. 1883 Annie Lee Gaines (1864–1925)
       4. James Ralph Gaines (1828–1896) *m*. 1851 Sarah E. B. Jackson (1835–1903)
       5. James Henry Gaines (1796–1848) *m*. 1822 Anne Banks Henderson (abt.1805–1851)
       6. Heirome Gaines, Jr. (1758–1815) *m*. 1792 Anne Thompson Adams (1775–1815)
       7. Heirome Gaines, Sr. (–abt. 1786) *m*. 1748 Margaret Taliaferro (–bef. 1784)
       8. Col. John Taliaferro (1687–1744) *m*. 1708 Mary Catlett
       9. Col. John Catlett (1658–   ) *m*. abt. 1676 Elizabeth Gaines (abt. 1660–   )
      10. Capt. Daniel Gaines (aft. 1632–1684) *m*. 1652 Margaret Bernard (–bef. 1690)
      11. THOMAS GAINES (abt. 1605–abt. 1667) *m*. Margaret
       Service:
       Reference: Genealogy of Lewis Family, by Wm. Trevell Lewis, pgs. 15, 213; Lineage
           Book No. 1, Sons and Daughters of Pilgrims, pg. 508; Pat. of 1,000 A. to
           Thomas Gains and wife Margaret, 1665, Deed Book 3, pg. 296, Rap-
           pahannock Co., Va.; Vol. I, pg. 77, Notable Southern Families, by Zella
           Armstrong.

6575   MAYFIELD, Mrs. John B.   Recorded 1948
           1311 West Oakwood, Tyler, Texas
       1. Hattie Belle Patterson *m*. 1899 John B. Mayfield
       2. John P. Patterson (1847–1911) *m*. 1873 Lelia Davenport (1856–1921)
       3. Dr. Jos. Davenport (1826–1909) *m*. 1848 Isabella Dial (1827–1891)
       4. Isaac M. Dial (1772–1835) *m*. 1801 Anna A. Coker (1784–1826)
       5. William Coker, *d. ca*. 1830, *m*. 1780 Elizabeth H. Garlington (1760–   )
       6. Christopher Garlington (1729–*ca*. 1805) *m. ca*. 1765 Hannah (?) Yonge
       7. Christopher Garlington, *d. ca*. 1753, *m*. 1724 Elizabeth Conway

8. Christopher Garlington (*ca.* 1660–*ca.* 1704) *m.* Margaret Jones
9. Christopher Garlington (*ca.* (1630–1709/14) *m.* Sara ——
10. Christopher Garlington *m.* Elisabet Wyatt
11. SIR DUDLEY WYATT, *d. ca.* 1652

Service: One of the original proprietors of Northern Neck, Va.
Reference: Va. Mag. Hist. & Biog.; Va. Historical Collection.

6303 MEADOR, Mrs. Thomas Dent   Recorded 1940, Georgia
       245 Peachtree Circle N. E., Atlanta, Georgia
1. Josephine Blankenship *m.* 1909 Thomas Dent Meador, Jr.
2. William H. H. Blankenship (1840–1929) *m.* 1863 Martha A. J. Hallenbeck (1846–1913)
3. Garret Hallenbeck (1796–1868) *m.* (2nd) 1838 Martha Trotter (1824–1874)
4. Isaac Hallenbeck (1767–1855) *m.* Magdalena Slingerland (1769–1838)
5. Garrit T. Slingerland (1723/4–1816) *m.* 1757 Egie Van Der Zee (1737–1814)
6. Teunis Arentse Slingerland (1694–1746) *m.* 1719 Elizabeth Van Der Zee (1698–1724)
7. Arent Slingerland (*c.* 1665–1712/3) *m.* (2nd) Gertruy Cobuse Van Vorst
8. Teunise Corneliese Slingerland (1617–aft. 1684) *m.* Engeltie Albertse Bratt (*c.* 1638–)
9. ALBERT ANDRIESE BRATT (BRADT) *d.* 1686, *m.* Annetje Barentrese Van Rotmers

Service: New Amsterdam, 1637; Original Landed Proprietor; established a trading post at New Amsterdam; Pearson's "First Settlers of Albany;" "The Kip Family in America," by Frederick Kip; "Washington Ancestry and Records of the McClain, Johnson and 40 Other Colonial Families."

9394 MEARS, Dorothy Warren   Recorded 1942
       3102 Hilton Street, Baltimore, Maryland
            (JUNIOR MEMBERSHIP)
1. Dorothy Warren Mears
2. Christian Emmerich Mears (1894–) *m.* 1919 Dorothy M. Packham (1895–)
3. Adelbert W. Mears (1870–) *m.* 1893 Ellen Emmerich (1873–)
4. George Emmerich (1846–1916) *m.* 1872 Mary E. Shepherd (1851–1882)
5. Joseph Shepherd (1819–1895) *m.* 1851 Priscilla Drury (1827–1912)
6. Henry Childs Drury (1797–1873) *m.* 1823 Mary Ann Owens (1802–1870)
7. Samuel Drury (1759–1843) *m.* 1779 Ann Ijams
8. Plummer Ijams (1718–1793) *m.* Ruth Childs (–1793)
9. William Ijams (–1738) *m.* 1696 Elizabeth Plummer (–1762)
10. Thomas Plummer (–1728) *m.* Elizabeth Yates (–1699)
11. George Yates (–1691) *m.* Mary Wells (–1698)
12. RICHARD WELLS (–1667) *m.* Frances ——

Service: Member General Assembly Md., 1654; appointed Prov. Commissioner Md., 1654.
Reference: Archives of Maryland, Vol. 1, 3; Warfield's Founders (Wells); No. 5784 Pilgrims.

6515 MENKE, Mrs. J. D.   Recorded 1946
       520 Grove Avenue, Crete, Nebraska
1. Edna May Worden *m.* 1907 John D. Menke
2. Ferris B. Worden (1849–1910) *m.* 1870 Mary E. Muchmore (1851–1910)
3. Dr. Benj. P. Muchmore (1827–1881) *m.* 1845 Eliz. J. Hardisty (1828–1869)
4. Robert B. Hardisty (1806–1881) *m.* 1827 Mary A. Rideout (1813–1845)
5. John G. Rideout (1769–) *m.* 1793 Elizabeth Getchell (1769–)
6. Benj. Rideout, Sr. (1731–1793) *m.* 1752 Mary Getchell (–1732)
7. Nicholas Rideout *m.* 1730 Mary Ingersoll (1713–1733)
8. Benjamin Ingersoll (1687–) *m.* 1711 Mary Hunt (1691/2–1733)
9. Joseph Ingersoll (1646–) *m.* Sarah Coe
10. George Ingersoll (1618–aft. 1652) *m.* 1642 Elizabeth ——
11. RICHARD INGERSOLL, *d.* 1644, *m.* 1616 Ann Langley, *d.* 1677

Service: Original householder in Salem, 1638.
Reference: Ipswich V. R. and N. E. Hist. and Gen. Register.

6486 MERKLE, Mrs. Edward J.   Recorded 1945
           Granville, Ohio
    1. Daisy Brooke *m.* Edward Joseph Merkle
    2. Banner Mark Brooke (1849–1933) *m.* 1871 Amelia Lucinda Jones (1850–1897)
    3. Calvin Kingsley Jones (1824–1915) *m.* 1845 Elisa Richardson (1831–1875)
    4. Samuel Jones (1773–1839) *m.* 1812 (2nd) Lucinda Kingsley (1790–1882)
    5. Calvin Kingsley (1745–1839) *m.* 1773 Susanna Lathrop (1754–1790/1805)
    6. Nathan Kingsley (1715–1796) *m.* 1744 Betty Dunbar (1722–   )
    7. Samuel Kingsley (1690–   ) *m.* 1714 Mary Packard (1689–   )
    8. Samuel Kingsley (1662–1713) *m.* bef. 1689 Mary Washburn (1661–1740)
    9. Samuel Kingsley (1630–1662) *m.* 1655 Hannah Brackett *ca.* (1634–1706)
   10. STEPHEN KINGSLEY (–1673) *m.* Elisabeth ———— (–1668)
    Service: Deputy to the General Court; Original Proprietor Braintree, Mass.; Representative to Congress; Original Inhabitant of Dorchester; Ruling Elder of Braintree, Mass.

5845 MERRIN, Miss Cynthia   Recorded 1929
           Flemington, Georgia
    1. Cynthia Merrin (1928–   )
    2. James F. Merrin (1897–19–) *m.* Hazel Cubberly (1904–   )
    3. Fred Cubberly (1869–   ) *m.* Etta Hancock (1870–   )
    4. Geo. Cubberly (1821–1896) *m.* 1865 Sarah Frazier (1848–   )
    5. Amariah Cubberly (1797–1838) *m.* 1816 Sarah Barber (1800–1889)
    6. Wm. Cubberly (1757–1838) *m.* 1784 Mary Sinclair (1764–1804)
    7. John Cubberly (1724–1795) *m.* Mary ———— (–1809)
    8. James Cubberly (–1754) *m.* Mary Pearson (1690–1772)
    9. ROBERT PEARSON
    Service:
    Reference:

6026 MEYER, Mr. Chandler O.   Recorded 1932
           2026 S. Fillmore Street, Denver, Colorado
    1. Chandler O. Meyer (1890–   ) *m.* 1918 Adda M. Burnett
    2. C. H. Oho Meyer (1856–1926) *m.* 1880 Emma Belle Fargher (1856–   )
    3. Wm. Fargher (1831–1904) *m.* 1855 Sarah Angeline Chandler (1829–1863)
    4. John Chandler (1799–1841) *m.* 1828 Rhoda Barber (–1837)
    5. Capt. David Chandler, Jr. (1754–   ) *m.* Hannah Peabody (1754–   )
    6. David Chandler (1724–1776) *m.* 1750 Mary Ballard (1732–   )
    7. Josiah Chandler (1683–1752) *m.* 1707 Sarah Ingalls (–1754)
    8. Serg. Wm. Chandler (1661–1727) *m.* Sarah Buckminister (–1735)
    9. Wm. Chandler *m.* Mary Dane (1638–1679)
   10. WILLIAM CHANDLER (–1641) *m.* Annis Allcock (–1683)
    Service:
    Reference: William and Annis Chandler; Dav. Chandler Fam., Library of Congress.

6055 MEYER, Mrs. C. Otto   Recorded 1933, Colorado
           310 W. Church Street, Newark, Ohio
    1. Emma B. Fargher *m.* 1880 C. H. Otto Meyer
    2. William Fargher (1831–1904) *m.* 1855 Sarah A. Chandler (1829–1863)
    3. John Chandler (1799–1841) *m.* 1828 Rhoda Barber (–1837)
    4. Capt. David Chandler (1754–   ) *m.* Hannah Peabody (1754–   )
    5. David Chandler (1724–1776) *m.* 1750 Mary Ballard (1732–   )
    6. Sgt. William Chandler (1661–1727) *m.* Sarah Buckminister (–1735)
    7. Josiah Chandler (1637–1752) *m.* 1707 Sarah Ingalls (–1754)
    8. William Chandler (–1698) *m.* Mary Dane (–1679)
    9. WILLIAM CHANDLER (–1641) *m.* Annis Allcock (–1683)
    Service: Early settler in Roxbury, Mass., 1637.
    Reference: David Chandler Family, Library of Congress.

6634 MICHIE, Mrs. O. E.   Recorded 1949
           121 S. Columbia Street, Chapel Hill, North Carolina
    1. Sallie Markham *m.* 1931 O. E. Michie

2. John W. Markham (1856–1917) *m.* 1891 Luna Cheek (1872–)
3. William A. Markham (1819–1895) *m.* 1842 Nancy Mason (1823–1913)
4. Edmund Markham (1798–1829) *m.* 1820 Nancy Mason (1802–1862)
5. Thomas Markham (Marcum), *d.* 1838, *m.* 1773 Frances Herndon (1754–1839)
6. Edmund Herndon *ca.* (1708–1769) *m.* 1730 Elizabeth Williams (–1750)
7. Edward Herndon (1678–1745) *m.* 1698 Mary Waller (1669–1720)
8. William Herndon (1649–1722) *m.* 1677 Catherine Digges (1654–1727)
9. EDWARD DIGGES (1620–1675) *m.* Elizabeth Page (–1691 *ca.*)

Service: Col. of Horse and Foot, member of Council, 1654–56, 1670–75; Governor of Virginia, 1655–58; Envoy to England, 1659; Auditor General of Virginia, 1670–75.
Reference: Herndon Family of Virginia, Vol. I; Herendon-Hurst and Allied Families.

6320 MIDDLETON, Mary Ann   Recorded 1941, Pennsylvania
   642 Twickenham Road, Glenside, Pennsylvania
       (JUNIOR)

1. Mary Ann Middleton
2. Edwin B. Middleton (1902–) *m.* 1936 Marian T. McCormick (1906–)
3. Edwin G. Middleton (1873–1940) *m.* 1901 Elizabeth H. Braddock (1871–)
4. Lemuel Middleton (1834–1889) *m.* 1866 Martha Shinn (1834–1892)
5. Urias Shinn (1812–1878) *m.* 1832 Elizabeth Bisham (1813–1867)
6. Benjamin Bisham (1790–1844) *m.* 1812 Ann Ivins (Ivens) (1794–1887)
7. Benjamin Bisham *m.* 1783 Hope Fortune (Fortiner)
8. Thomas Bisham (1732–1770) *m.* 1754 Sarah Hinchman
9. John Hinchman III (1690–1754) *m.* Sara (?)
10. John Hinchman, Jr. (1665–1721) *m.* 1689 Sara Hunt Harrison
11. John Hinchman, *d.* 1699, *m.* 1660 Elizabeth Emmons
12. EDMOND HINCHMAN (1598–1668) *m.* Elizabeth (?)

Service: Came to Mass., 1637. Founder of Hinchman Family in America.
Reference: Genealogy of Bisham Family; Hist. of Shinn Fam.; New Eng. Register, Vol. I, 19; Records of Flushing, L. I., N. Y.; Early Settlers of Newton Twp., N. J.

6571 MILLER, Arthur Barrett   Recorded 1948
   47 South Fullerton Avenue, Montclair, New Jersey

1. Arthur B. Miller *m.* Edith A. Canning
2. William Miller (1849–1915) *m.* 1872 Adelaide G. Barrett (1850–1935)
3. Samuel Barrett (1801–1877) *m.* 1829 Anne J. Eddy (1806–1888)
4. Zachariah Eddy (1780–1860) *m.* 1803 Sarah Edson (1781–1850)
5. Capt. Joshua Eddy (1748–1833) *m.* 1778 Lydia Paddock (1756–1838)
6. Zachariah Eddy (1712–1777) *m.* 1757 Mercy Morton (1721–1802)
7. Ebenezer Morton (1696–1750) *m.* 1720 Mercy Foster (1698–1782)
8. John Morton (1650–1718) *m.* 1687 Mary Ring (1657–1731)
9. Andrew Ring *m.* Deborah Hopkins
10. STEPHEN HOPKINS

Service: Mayflower passenger.
Reference: Eddy Family in America; Mayflower Index.

6584 MILLER, Edith A. C.   Recorded 1948
   47 South Fullerton Avenue, Montclair, New Jersey

1. Edith Almena Canning *m.* 1902 Arthur B. Miller
2. Wm. P. Canning (1844–1903) *m.* 1871 Ella F. Churchill (1848–1916)
3. Charles Churchill (1814–1866) *m.* 1837 Hyrena F. Purington (1816–)
4. Joseph Churchill (1768–1824) *m.* 1794 Sally Tash
5. Thomas Churchill (1730–) *m.* 1757 Mary S. Ewer (1737–)
6. Barnabas Churchill (1686–) *m.* 1714 Lydia Harlow (1688–)
7. William Harlow, Jr. (1657–1711/2) *m.* Lydia Cushman
8. William Harlow *ca.* (1624–1691) *m.* 1649 Rebecca Bartlett, *d.* bef. 1658
9. Robert Bartlett *m.* Mary Warren
10. RICHARD WARREN

Service: Mayflower passenger.
Reference: Churchill Family in America.

6292 MILLER, Mrs. Philip H.   Recorded 1940, New York
        300 S. Broadway, Tarrytown, New York
    1. Dorma Peet *m*. 1931 Philip H. Miller
    2. Fred Norton Peet (1859–1936) *m*. 1882 Matilda A. Ellis (1861–1937)
    3. Fred Plum Peet (1812–1878) *m*. 1845 Mary Ann Norton (1821–1895)
    4. Dr. Abiram Lewis Peet (1772–1812) *m*. Lois Bidwell (1772–1835)
    5. Dr. Abiram Peet (1737–1786) *m*. 1767 Anna Lewis (1739–1807)
    6. Lt. Richard Peet (1696–1760) *m*. 1724 Sarah Curtis, *b*. 1705
    7. Benjamin Peet (1665–1704) *m*. 1688 Priscilla Fairchild, *b*. 1669
    8. Benjamin Peet (1640–1704) *m*. 1662 Phoebe Butler, *b*. 1642
    9. JOHN PEET (1597/8–1684) *m*. Anne
    Reference: Peet Family Chart, by Robert A. Peet; "The Peet Family," Janett
        Raymond Dorr.

6180 MILNER, Caroline (Howell)   Recorded 1938
        945 Garden St. S. W., Atlanta, Georgia
    1. Caroline Howell Milner (1879–   ) *m*. 1907 McWhorter Milner (1875–   )
    2. George Arthur Howell (1849–1905) *m*. 1876 Mary Adair (1855–1927)
    3. George Washington Adair (1823–1899) *m*. 1854 Mary Jane Perry (1832–1910)
    4. John Fisher Adair (1785–1856) *m*. (2) 1814 Mary Radcliff Slaven (1790–1825)
    5. Noecut Slaven (born in France (–aft. 1788) *m. ca*. 1785 Ann (Nancy) Holliday
        ca. (1770/72–aft. 1795)
    6. Capt. John Holliday, Jr., Rev., *ca*. (1745–1781) (died in Rev. War) *m. ca*. 1770
        Mildred Thomas (–*ca*. 1796)
    7. John Holliday, Sr. *ca*. (1725–1781) *m. ca*. 1740/5 Elizabeth Rawlings (I) wife
        (*ca*. 1775/76)
    8. Capt. John Holliday *ca*. (1690/92–1742) *m*. ca. 1715/1720 Elizabeth, *d*. bet.
        1735 and 1742
    9. Joseph Holliday (1669–1712/13) *m*. ca. 1690/1692 Charity ———, *d*. aft. 1692
    10. Anthony Holliday, *b*. in Eng., *d*. 1718, *m*. in Va., *ca*. 1669 his 1st wife, name
        unknown; she died before 1674; *m*. (2nd) wid. Col. John Brewer
    11. THOMAS HOLLIDAY *b*. in Eng. *ca*. (1625–aft. 1680) *m*. in Eng. (I) wife; name
        unknown
    Service: Came to Va. *ca*. 1655/56 and received Patent for large tracts of land, 1657
        and later.
    Reference: Spotsylvania Co., Va., Vol. I, pgs. 6–36–37–75–274–335–406–425–482, et al.

6179 MILNER, Mr. McWhorter   Recorded 1938
        945 Garden Street, Atlanta, Georgia
    1. McWhorter Milner (1875–   ) *m*. 1907 Caroline Howell
    2. Pleasant P. Milner (1840–1878) *m*. 1865 Mary McWhorter (1845–1930)
    3. James Hamilton McWhorter (1811–1885) *m*. 1832 Eliza Jane Penn (–1867)
    4. Hugh McWhorter (1788–1825) *m*. 1810 Helena Ligon (1792–1853)
    5. Joseph Ligon (1759–1822) *m*. 1778 Mary Church (1758/9–1827)
    6. Joseph Ligon (1725/30–1780) *m. ca*. 1754 Judith, *d*. aft. 1787
    7. Joseph Ligon *ca*. (1704–1752) *m*. bef. 1740 Judith Stewart (2nd wife), *d*. 1784
    8. William Ligon, Jr. (1682–1764) *m. ca*. 1702 Elizabeth Batte, *d*. aft. 1764
    9. William Ligon, Sr., *ca*. (1651–1689) *m*. 1678/9 Mary Tanner, *d*. aft. 1696
    10. LT. COL. THOMAS LIGON (1620/25–1675) *m. ca*. 1650
    Service: Burgess for Henrico, 1655; Justice and Commissioner, Henrico Co., 1669;
        Surveyor.

6585 MINNERLY, Arthur Greenleaf   Recorded 1948
        95 Beekman Avenue, North Tarrytown, New York
    1. Arthur G. Minnerly *m*. Virginia M. Church
    2. Percy C. Minnerly (1878–   ) *m*. 1901 Phermetta E. Miller (1881–   )
    3. Constantine E. Minnerly (1845–1929) *m*. 1877 Lucy I. Nossiter (1851–1927)
    4. Andrew J. Minnerly (1815–1894) *m*. 1833 Harriet Wicks (1811–1883)
    5. William Minnerly (1781–1844) *m*. 1803 Elizabeth Lambert (1785–1845)

6. Jacobus Minnerly (1742–1825) *m.* 1762 Catherine Martling (1745–1826)
7. Abraham Martling (bapt. 1719–1786) *m.* 1739 Jeannetie Ackerman (1720–1782)
8. ABRAHAM MARTLING (1693–1761) *m.* 1715 Rachel DeVeaux (1695–   )
Service: One of the Founders of the Manor of Phillipsburg.
Reference: Quarterly Bulletin of West. Co. Hist. Soc., N. Y.; The Huguenot, Staten
   Island Hist. Pub.

6644 MINNERLY, Roger Charles   Recorded 1949
      95 Beekman Avenue, No. Tarrytown, New York
                          (JUNIOR)
 1. Roger Charles Minnerly
 2. Arthur G. Minnerly (1904–   ) *m.* 1937 Virginia M. Church (1913–   )
 3. Percy C. Minnerly (1878–   ) *m.* 1901 Phermetta E. Miller (1881–   )
 4. Constantine E. Minnerly (1845–1929) *m.* 1877 Lucy I. Nossitter (1851–1927)
 5. Andrew J. Minnerly (1815–1894) *m.* 1835 Harriet Wicks (1811–1883)
 6. William Minnerly (1781–1844) *m.* 1803 Elizabeth Lambert (1785–1845)
 7. Jacobus Minnerly (1744–1823) *m.* 1762 Catherine Martling (1745–1826)
 8. Albert Minne or Mennely (1703–   ) *m. ca.* 1734 Helena Smallens or Dinse
 9. Albert Minne (1655–   ) *m.* 1684 Meenske Jans
10. MINNE JOHANNIS *m.* Rensie Feddes
Service: Constable at Flatbush, N. Y., 1673, 74, 77; one of the first settlers at Haver-
   straw, N. Y.
Reference: History of Rockland Co., N. Y., by Rev. D. Cole; Holland Society Year
   Book, 1902, p. 27.

6643 MINNERLY, Robert Church   Recorded 1949
      95 Beekman Avenue, No. Tarrytown, New York
                          (JUNIOR)
 1. Robert Church Minnerly
 2. Arthur G. Minnerly (1904–   ) *m.* 1937 Virginia M. Church (1913–   )
 3. Percy C. Minnerly (1878–   ) *m.* 1901 Phermetta E. Miller (1881–   )
 4. Constantine E. Minnerly (1845–1929) *m.* 1877 Lucy I. Nossitter (1851–1927)
 5. Andrew J. Minnerly (1815–1894) *m.* 1835 Harriet Wicks (1811–1883)
 6. William Minnerly (1781–1844) *m.* 1803 Elizabeth Lambert (1785–1845)
 7. Jacobus Minnerly (1744–1823) *m.* 1762 Catherine Martling (1745–1826)
 8. Albert Minne or Mennely (1703–   ) *m. ca.* 1734 Helena Smallens or Dinse
 9. Albert Minne (1655–   ) *m.* 1684 Meenske Jans
10. MINNE JOHANNIS *m.* Rensie Feddes
Service: Constable at Flatbush, N. Y., 1673, 74, 77; one of the first settlers at Haver-
   straw, N. Y.
Reference: History of Rockland Co., N. Y., by Rev. D. Cole; Holland Society Year
   Book, 1902, p. 27.

6260 MITCHELL, Mrs. Alexander (M.-at-Large)   Recorded 1939
      50 Curtis Street, W. Somerville, Massachusetts
 1. Emily Ida Egee *m.* 1903 Alexander Mitchell
 2. Benjamin Allan Egee (1833–1914) *m.* 1868 Hannah Spiers Henry (1841–1904)
 3. Jonathan Egee (1799–1865) *m.* 1823 Emily Shaw (1802–1891)
 4. Hanson Shaw (1770–1813) *m.* 1796 Rebecca Hendrickson (1776–1829)
 5. Andrew Hendrickson (1748–1824) *m.* 1770 Judith Jones (1751–1792)
 6. Peter Hendrickson (1718–1761) *m.* 1746 Catherine Locke (1729–1766)
 7. Israel Locke, Jr. (1675–1753) *m.* 1725 Rebecca Helm (1705–*c.* 1740)
 8. Hermanus Helm (1675–1740) *m.* Catherine ————
 9. ISRAEL HELM came to Amer. 1641, *d.* 1701, *m.* Magdalene ————
Service: Captain.
Reference: Records Episcopal Church, Swedesboro, N. J.; Archives Penna. and N. J.;
   Israel Amline, History of Chester Co., Pa.; Samuel Wiley, History of
   Delaware Co., Pa.; George Smith, History of Pennsylvania; Penna.
   Courts, by Ed. Armstrong; Watson's Annals.

5889 MITCHELL, Miss Anna A.   Recorded 1929, New Jersey
        653 Adams Avenue, Elizabeth New Jersey
    1. Miss Anna A. Mitchell
    2. William J. Mitchell (1838–) *m.* 1860 Emma Bragg (1841–)
    3. Horatio Bragg *m.* 1835 Elizabeth Reed (1815–1883)
    4. Jacob Reed *m.* 1814 Effie Hoffman (1796–)
    5. Frederick Hoffman (–1824) *m.* 1783 M. Delana Schuyler (–1796)
    6. Philip Schuyler (1717–1784) *m.* 1754 Ann Anderson (1725–1796)
    7. Philip Schuyler (1687–1764) *m.* 1712 Hester Kingslant (–1736)
    8. Arent Schuyler (1662–1730) *m.* 1684 Jenneke Tiller (–1700)
    9. PHILIP PIETERSE SCHUYLER (1628–1683) *m.* 1650 Margarita Van Slechtenhorst
        (–1711)
    Service: Captain on Provincial Forges, 1667.

6280 MITCHELL, Eugene Muse II   Recorded 1939, Georgia
        1401 Peachtree Street N. E., Atlanta, Georgia
                            (JUNIOR)
    1. Eugene Muse Mitchell II
    2. Stephens Mitchell *b.* 1896, *m.* 1927 Carolyn Reynolds
    3. Joseph Shewmake Reynolds (1869–1935) *m.* 1901 Frances Hansberger, *b.* 1866
    4. John William Reynolds (1841–1913) *m.* 1865 Mary Lou Shewmake (1854–1927)
    5. James Madison Reynolds (1809–1878) *m.* 1832 Mary Ann Jones (1814–1884)
    6. Thomas Jones *c.* 1766, *d.* aft. 1822, *m. c.* 1800 Hannah Hadley
    7. Abraham Jones (1720–1771) *m. c.* 1743 Martha Jones (not related), *d.* 1788
    8. Abraham Jones (1690–1758) *m.* Sarah Batte
    9. Lt. Peter Jones, *d.* 1726, *m.* 1688 Mary Batte, *d.* 1741
   10. MAJOR PETER JONES, *d.* aft. 1674, *m.* Margaret Wood, *d.* 1719
    Service: Major in Virginia Militia; Commander of Fort at Petersburg, Va.
    Reference: Peter Jones and Richard Jones Genealogies, Augusta B. Fothergill; A Lost
        Arcadia, Walter A. Clark.

6279 MITCHELL, Joseph Reynolds   Recorded 1939, Georgia
        1401 Peachtree Street N. E., Atlanta, Georgia
                            (JUNIOR)
    1. Joseph Reynolds Mitchell
    2. Stephens Mitchell, *b.* 1896, *m.* 1927 Carolyn Reynolds
    3. Joseph Shewmake Reynolds (1869–1935) *m.* 1901 Frances Hansberger, *b.* 1866.
    4. John William Reynolds (1841–1913) *m.* 1865 Mary Lou Shewmake (1854–1927)
    5. James Madison Reynolds (1809–1878) *m.* 1832 Mary Ann Jones (1814–1884)
    6. Thomas Jones, *b. c.* 1766, *d.* aft. 1822, *m. c.* 1800 Hannah Hadley
    7. Abraham Jones (1720–1771) *m. c.* 1743 Martha Jones (not related), *d.* 1788
    8. Abraham Jones (1690–1758) *m.* Sarah Batte
    9. Lt. Peter Jones, *d.* 1726, *m.* 1688 Mary Batte, *d.* 1741
   10. MAJOR PETER JONES, *d.* aft. 1674, *m.* Margaret Wood, *d.* 1719
    Service: Major in Virginia Militia, Commander of Fort at Petersburg, Va.
    Reference: Peter Jones and Richard Jones Genealogies, Augusta B. Fothergill; A Lost
        Arcadia, Walter A. Clark.

6278 MITCHELL, Mrs. Stephens   Recorded 1939, Georgia
        1401 Peachtree Street N. E., Atlanta, Georgia
    1. Carolyn Louise Reynolds *m.* 1927 Stephens Mitchell
    2. Joseph Shewmake Reynolds (1869–1935) *m.* 1901 Frances Hansberger (1866–)
    3. John William Reynolds (1841–1913) *m.* 1865 Mary Lou Shewmake (1854–1927)
    4. James Madison Reynolds (1809–1878) *m.* 1832 Mary Ann Jones (1814–1884)
    5. Thomas Jones, *b. c.* 1766, *d.* aft. 1822, *m. c.* 1800 Hannah Hadley
    6. Abraham Jones (1720–1771) *m. c.* 1743 Martha Jones (not related), *d.* 1788
    7. Abraham Jones (1690–1758) *m.* Sarah Batte
    8. Lt. Peter Jones, *d.* 1726, *m.* 1688 Mary Batte, *d.* 1741
    9. MAJOR PETER JONES, *d.* aft. 1674, *m.* Margaret Wood, *d.* 1719
    Service: Major in Virginia Militia, Commander of Fort at Petersburg, Va.
    Reference: Peter Jones and Richard Jones Genealogies, Augusta B. Fothergill; A Lost
        Arcadia, Walter A. Clark.

6006 MOHLER, Mrs. Thomas H.   Recorded 1931
          320 B. Street, St. Albans, West Virginia
    1. Lavinia Campbell (1864–   ) *m.* 1884 Thomas Howard Mohler
    2. John Wesley Campbell (1841–1876) *m.* 1863 Adaline Calvert (1843–   )
    3. John Lewis Calvert (1803–1853) *m.* 1825 Elizabeth Ann Slack (1807–1882)
    4. Francis Calvert (1751–1823) *m.* 1791 Elizabeth Witt (1772–1806)
    5. Jacob Calvert (1720–1772) *m.* 1750 Sarah Crupper (1730–1789)
    6. John Calvert (1690–1735) *m.* 1710 Elizabeth Harrison
    7. George Calvert (1664–1740) *m.* 1688 Elizabeth Doyne
    8. William Calvert (1642–1682) *m.* 1660 Elizabeth Stone
    9. Gov. Leonard Calvert (1606–1647) *m.* 1641 Anne Brent
   10. Sir George Calvert (1579–1632) *m.* 1604 Anne Mynne (1579–1622)
    Services: Colonizer and Founder of the Province of Maryland.
    Reference: Maryland Hist. Magazine, Vol. 16, pg. 196; Vol. 25.

6087 MOHR, Mrs. F. A.   Recorded 1935, Texas
          3313 St. Johns Drive, Dallas, Texas
    1. Grace E. Cassell *m.* 1898 Frederick A. Mohr
    2. Harrison O. Cassell (1839–1893) *m.* 1866 Maria E. Edgerton (1842–1910)
    3. Urban C. Edgerton (1816–1863) *m.* 1841 Harriet Damon (1818–1918)
    4. Ebenezer Edgerton (1794–   ) *m.* 1816 Edna A. Harris (1795–1830)
    5. Jedediah Edgerton (1759–1848) *m.* 1780 Lucy Curtis (1760–1819)
    6. Simeon Edgerton (1732–1809) *m.* 1758 Abiah Hough (1737–1821)
    7. Joseph Edgerton (1696–   ) *m.* 1722 Elizabeth Haskins
    8. Richard Edgerton, Jr. (1665–1729) *m.* 1692 Elizabeth Scudder (1667–1762)
    9. Richard Edgerton (–1692) *m.* 1653 Mary Sylvester
    Service: Original Proprietor of Norwich, Conn.; a Freeman, 1669; a Constable, 1680.
    Reference: History of Pawlet, Vt., pp. 185–86; Vital Records of Norwich, Conn.;
          History of Norwich, Conn.

6025 MONETTE, Mr. Orra Eugene   Recorded 1932
          350 S. Oxford Avenue, Los Angeles, California
    1. Orra Eugene Monette (1873–   ) *m.* Ella Eliz. Crim
       Carrie Lucille Janeway
       Helen Marie Kull
    2. Mervin Jeremiah Monnette (1847–1931) *m.* 1869 Olive Adelaide Hull (1849–1912)
    3. Abraham Monnett (1811–1881) *m.* 1836 Catherine Braucher (1815–1875)
    4. Jeremiah Crabb Monnett (1784–1864) *m.* 1805 Alice Slagle (1788–1868)
    5. Abraham Monnett (1748–1810) *m.* 1772 Ann Hilleary (1748–1833)
    6. Isaac Monnett (1726–1798) *m.* 1745 Eliz. Osborne (1726–1798)
    7. Wm. Monett (1702–   ) *m.* Eliz. Kent
    8. Isaac Monnet (1670–1756) *m.* 1700 Eliz. Williams (1672–1751)
    9. Pierre Monnet, Sr. *m.* Catherine Pillot
    Service:
    Reference: Monnet Fam. Gen., 1911; Colonial Families of U. S. A., Vol. 3; Abridged
          Compendium of Am. Gen.; Armorial Fam. of Am.

6458 MONKS, Mrs. Paul McKee   Recorded 1945
          Logan, Ohio
    1. Flossie Goodwin *m.* Paul McKee Monks
    2. Carlos Goodwin (1853–1931) *m.* 1877 Laura Souders (1857–1906)
    3. John Goodwin (1826–1900) *m.* 1849 Sarah Chidester (1829–1903)
    4. John Goodwin (1794–1867) *m.* 1816 Alvira Gould (1794–1879)
    5. Nathan Gould (1767–1844) *m.* 1792 Elizabeth Goodwin (1766–1848)
    6. Gideon Gould (1741–1821) *m.* 1766 Hannah Heath (1746–1843)
    7. Joseph Gould (1700–1752) *m.* 1726 Abigail Hoyt (1705–   )
    8. Samuel Gould (1667–1726) *m.* 1693 Sarah Rowell (1673–   )
    9. Nathan Gould (1614–1693) *m.* Elizabeth Putnam
    Service: Grant of land, 1657, Salisbury, Mass.; Oath of Allegiance in 1677.
    Reference: Hist. Newport, N. H., Wheerel; Gen. and Fam. Hist. of N. H., Stearns;
          Hoyt Gen., by Hoyt; Gould Gen., by Gould.

6562   MOOK, Mrs. Leonard C.   Recorded 1947
      160 Hamilton Road, Lancaster, Pennsylvania
1. Hazel Dean *m.* 1911 Dr. Leonard C. Mook
2. Kit C. Dean (1862–1943) *m.* 1885 Jessie M. Dilley (1866–1886)
3. Wilson Dean (1838–1911) *m.* 1858 Mary Muse (1838–1910)
4. James Muse (1801–1865) *m.* 1835 Hannah Condit (1809–1888)
5. Rev. Ira Condit (1772–1836) *m.* 1800 Mary Miller (1781–1836)
6. Jabez Condit (1739–1804) *m.* Phoebe Smith (1736–1813)
7. Philip Condit (1709–1801) *m.* Mary Day (1713–1785)
8. Peter Condit, *d.* 1714, *m.* 1695 Mary Harrison, *d.* 1738
9. Samuel Harrison *ca.* (1653–1724) *m.* Mary Ward (1654–1738)
10. Richard Harrison, *d.* 1691, *m.* ———
11. RICHARD HARRISON, *d.* 1653, *m.* ———
Service: Ensign of Newark, N. J., 1673.
Reference: N. J. Archives.

6389   MOON, Mrs. Owen M.   Recorded 1942
      South Woodstock, Vermont
1. Margaret Scott *m.* Owen Moon
2. E. Irving Scott (1846–   ) *m.* 1872 Sarah Frances Hoyt (1847–1916)
3. Alexander Hamilton Scott (1804–1879) *m.* 1838 Sophronia Wood Seymour (1816–1897)
4. Thomas Seymour (1788–1882) *m.* Rebecca Maria Wood (1790–1854)
5. Nathaniel Seymour (1757–1846) *m.* 1784 Mercy Carter (1761–1806)
6. Capt. Thomas Seymour (1702–1796) *m.* Elizabeth ——— (1724–1794)
7. Capt. Matthew Seymour (1669–1735) *m.* Sarah Hayes (1673–   )
8. Thomas Seymour (1632–1722) *m.* 1654 Hannah Marvin (1634–   )
9. RICHARD SEYMOUR (1604–1655) *m.* 1631 Mercy Ruscoe (ab. 1610–   )
Service: Elected Townsman and Selectman of Norwalk, Conn.
Reference: Seymore Gen., No. 1, 2, 6, 16, $5; Colonial Dames of America; N. J. Register.

6170   MOORE, Mabel Roberts   Recorded 1937
      The Oaks, Wakesfield Blvd., Winsted, Connecticut
1. Mabel Roberts Moore (1873–   ) *m.* 1897 Burton Elizur Moore
2. Samuel Judah Roberts (1835–1901) *m.* 1855 Eunice Loomis (1837–1893)
3. Miles Loomis (1799–1854) *m.* 1828 Esther Alford (1803–1884)
4. Elias Loomis (1776–1831) *m.* in Torrington Mary Rood (1776–1837)
5. Ephraim Loomis (1731–1812) *m.* 1764 Jane Campbell
6. Aaron Loomis (1686–1773) *m.* 1719 Deborah Eggleston (–1783)
7. David Loomis (1668–1751/2) *m.* 1692 Lydia Marsh Lyman (1667–   )
8. Nathaniel Loomis (1626–1688) *m.* 1653 Elizabeth Moore (1638–1723)
9. Joseph Loomis (abt. 1590–1658) *m.* 1614 Mary White (bapt. 1590–1652)
Service: Joseph Loomis sailed from London Apr. 11, 1638, in the ship "Susan and Ellen," and arrived at Boston July 17, 1638. Land granted him in Windsor, 1640.
Reference: The Loomis Family in America, Revised, by Elisha Loomis, pgs. 121, 131, 138, 152, 175, 235, 352.

6434   MOORE, Mrs. W. T.   Recorded 1943
      173 E. State Road, Chesapeake, Ohio
1. Frances Flesher *m.* W. T. Moore
2. Benjamin T. Flesher (1855–1928) *m.* 1877 Mary A. Francis (1860–1920)
3. Andrew Jackson Flesher (1827–1898) *m.* 1847 Sarah M. Weaver (1827–1857)
4. Daniel Weaver (1800–1851) *m.* 1824 Hannah Sayre (1808–1865)
5. Thomas Sayre (1776–1845) *m.* 1798 Martha Sams (1775–1866)
6. David Sayre (Rev. War) (1736–1826) *m.* 1758 Hannah Frazier (1741–1826)
7. Daniel Sayre (–1760) *m.* Rebecca Bond
8. Samuel Sayre (–1707 bef.) *m.* ———
9. Daniel Sayre (–1708) *m.* Hannah Foster
10. THOMAS SAYRE (1597–1670) *m.* ———

Service: One of the "Lynn Undertakers." Oct. 10, 1649, at a general court he was chosen "to govern town affairs on Long Island," etc.; 1650 ordered to train with the company of town soldiers.
Reference: Sayre Book, by Banta; also Nellie Alexander Armstrong, No. 5817.

6547 MORISON, Henrietta Forster Shissler   Recorded 1947
      1250 N. 53rd Street, Philadelphia, Pennsylvania
1. Henrietta Foster Shissler *m.* 1906 Charles S. Morison
2. Alberto E. Shissler (1848–1929) *m.* 1873 Martha C. Klase (1851–1898)
3. Edward Shissler (1824–1901) *m.* 1847 Louise J. Foster (1829–1869)
4. Jesse Foster (1792–1885) *m.* 1818 Eliza A. Toppan (1797–1888)
5. Enoch C. Toppan (1765–1845) *m.* 1793 Mary Clark Nichols (1760–1846)
6. Enoch Clark (1735–1774) *m.* 1759 Mary March (1732–1816)
7. Enoch Clark (1709–1759) *m.* bef. 1730 Hannah ——— (1711–1746)
8. Henry Clarke (1673–1749) *m.* 1695 Elizabeth Greenleaf (1678–1723)
9. Capt. Stephen Greenleaf, Jr. (1652–1743) *m.* 1676 Elizabeth Gerrish (1654–1712)
10. Capt. Stephen Greenleaf (bapt. 1628–1690) *m.* 1651 Elizabeth Coffin, *d.* 1678.

Service: Made Freeman at Newbury, 1671; Dep. to Gen Court, 1676, 1689, 1690.
Reference: Clarke Genealogy; Newbury Vital Records (Mass.).

6526 MORRIS, Mrs. Esther Smith   Recorded 1946
      Salem, New Jersey
1. Esther Smith *m.* 1915 ——— Morris
2. Elmer H. Smith (1863–1920) *m.* 1888 Elizabeth M. A. Davis (1865–)
3. David E. Davis (1841–1875) *m.* 1862 Esther C. Miller (1840–1923)
4. Franklin Miller (1815–1841) *m.* 1838 Elizabeth W. Acton (1818–1843)
5. William F. Miller (1778–1847) *m.* 1806 Esther Cooper (1777–1828)
6. Mark Miller (1740–1800) *m.* Phebe Foster (1749–1828)
7. Ebenezer Miller (1702–1744) *m.* 1724 Sarah Collier
8. Joseph Miller, *m.* ———

Service: Deputy Surveyor of Fenwick's Tenth.
Reference: Shourd's History.

6125 MORRIS, Mrs. John F.   Recorded 1937, Connecticut
      West Hartford, Conn.
1. Caroline T. Huntington *m.* 1909 John F. Morris
2. William Huntington (1839–1918) *m.* 1871 Caroline Saxton (1842–1923)
3. Eleazer Huntington (1808–1870) *m.* 1835 Betsey F. Throop (1808–1883)
4. William Huntington (1765–1834) *m.* 1788 Mary Gray (1767–1856)
5. William Huntington (1732–1816) *m.* 1757 Bethia Throop (1738–1799)
6. Samuel Huntington (1691–1785) *m.* 1722 Hannah Metcalf (1702–1791)
7. Samuel Huntington (1665–1717) *m.* 1686 Mary Clark (–1743)
8. Simon Huntington (1629–1706) *m.* 1653 Sarah Clark (1633–1721)
9. Simon Huntington (1583–1633) *m.* 1627 Margaret Baret

Service: Early settler in Norwich, Conn., 1660.
Reference: Huntington Genealogical Memoirs, 1633 to 1915.

6042 MORTON, Mrs. F. N.   Recorded 1933
      36th and Powelton Ave., Powelton Apt. No. 8, Philadelphia, Pa.
1. Ellen Harwood Rich (1865–) *m.* 1892 ——— Morton
2. Chas. Wright Rich (1817–1889) *m.* 1863 Lorinda C. Harwood Hayden (1830–1896)
3. Benj. Ruggles Harwood (1794–1858) *m.* 1828 Louisa Ball Williams (1793–1869)
4. Benj. Harwood (1766–1852) *m.* 1782 Eliz. Cutler (1766–1849)
5. Abel Harwood (1742–1770) *m.* 1765 Sarah Ruggles (1743–1823)
6. Capt. Benj. Ruggles (1713–1790) *m.* 1736 Alice Merrick (1725–1756)
7. Nathaniel Merrick (1673–1743) *m.* Alice Freeman (1725–1756)
8. Ensign William Merrick (1643–1732) *m.* 1667 Abigail Hopkins (1644–)
9. Giles Hopkins (1607–1690) *m.* 1639 Catherine Wheldon (–1689)
10. Stephen Hopkins (1583–1644)

Service: Signer of Mayflower Compact; member first council of Gov. Assts.
Reference:

6046   MOSS, Mrs. John L.   Recorded 1933
          6017 Enright Avenue, St. Louis, Mississippi
   1. Arline B. Nichols (1876–   ) *m.* 1901 John Trigg Moss
   2. Edwin Phillips Nichols (1852–1928) *m.* 1872 Belle Arline Matlack (1854–1906)
   3. Earl Matlack (1834–1864) *m.* 1853 Sabrina Ann Macbeth (1834–1919)
   4. George Matlack (1809–1884) *m.* 1838 Eliz. Norris (1806–1878)
   5. George Matlack (1782–   ) *m.* 1805 Anna Bispham (1784–   )
   6. Jos. Bispham (1759–1832) *m.* 1783 Susanna Pearson (–1831)
   7. Joshua Bispham (1706–   ) *m.* 1743 Ruth Atkinson (1718–   )
   8. Sam. Atkinson (1685–1775) *m.* 1714 Ruth Stacy Beakes (1680–1755)
   9. MAHLON STACY (1638–1704) *m.* 1668 Rebecca Ely (–1711)
   Service: Member Assembly; Council of Royal Gov.; Proprietor.
   Reference: Great Britain and U. S., by Bispham; States of Am., by Norbury; Hist.
        of Burlington and Mercer Counties, N. J.

6255   MOUNCE, Leroy L.
          South Woodstock, Vermont
   1. Grace Turner Strong (1884–   ) *m.* 1915 Leroy L. Mounce
   2. Wm. Jackson Strong (1832–1915) *m.* 1869 Lucy Spaulding (1842–1926)
   3. Hiram Spaulding (1806–1898) *m.* 1831 Eliza Totman (1808–1888)
   4. Thomas Totman (1777–1863) *m.* Abigail Eaton (1783–1855)
   5. Ebenezer Totman (1731–1781) *m.* 1752 Grace Turner (1740–1832)
   6. Hawkins Turner (1704–1771) *m.* Lucy Starr (1708–1809)
   7. Jonathan Starr (1674–1747) *m.* 1699 Elizabeth Morgan (1678–1747)
   8. Samuel Starr (1640–1687) *m.* 1664 Hannah Brewster (1643–1691)
   9. Jonathan Brewster (1593–   ) *m.* Lucretia
  10. WILLIAM BREWSTER (1566–1644) *m.* Mary ——— (1569–1627)
   Service: Elder.
   Reference:

6435   MULFORD, Mrs. William Cornwell   Recorded 1943
          138 Atlantic Street, Bridgton, New Jersey
   1. Alice Probasco *m.* Wm. Cornwell Mulford
   2. Franklin Clement Probasco (1829–1905) *m.* 1865 Hannah Miller Minch
        (1841–1920)
   3. John Smalley Probasco (1804–1891) *m.* 1833 (2nd) Mary Hand Bacon (1808–1849)
   4. William Bacon (1775–1838) *m.* 1806 Mary Hand Bowen
   5. Smith Bowen (1763–1840) *m.* Mary Hand (1763–1791)
   6. Jonathan Bowen (1737–1804) *m.* 1762 (2nd) Sarah Smith (1736–1821)
   7. Jonathan Bowen (1714–1782) *m.* 1760 (2nd) Mrs. Rachel Remington (1723–   )
   8. Dan Bowen (1690–1729) *m.* Mary Walling (–1757)
   9. Samuel Bowen (1659–1728) *m.* Mrs. Elizabeth Wheaton
  10. Obadiah Bowen (1627–1710) *m.* Mary Clifton
  11. RICHARD BOWEN (–1674/6) *m.* Anna ———
   Service: Deputy General Court, Plymouth, Mass. (Buried at Rehoboth, Mass.)
   Reference: Shepherd's History Glouster and Salem County; Minutes Prov. Congress
        and Council of Safety. (Qualified Col. Dames of America, N. J.)

6117   MULFORD, Mrs. Vera Wandling   Recorded 1936
          Berkeley, California
   1. Vera Wandling *m.* ——— Mulford
   2. Adam R. Wandling (1843–1928) *m.* 1872 Lucy Stewart (1855–   )
   3. Jacob M. Stewart (1836–1918) *m.* Elizabeth Stephen (1837–1917)
   4. William I. Stewart (1810–1878) *m.* Amanda Sharp
   5. Samuel Stewart (1769–1847) *m.* Sarah Drake (1773–1855)
   6. William Stewart (1738–1810) *m.* 1769 Frances Sherred (1737–1803)
   7. Jacob Sherred *m.* 1731 Catherine Anderson (–1756)
   8. Joshua Anderson (1667–1731) *m.* 1695 Engeltie Opdyck
   9. Johannes Opdyck (1604–1729) *m.* Catherine
  10. LAURIS JANSEN OPDYCK (1600–1659) *m.* Christian Stenelia
   Service: Member of Committee of Safety, Gravesend, L. I., 1659.
   Reference: Early Germans of New Jersey, Chambers.

6310 MURPHY, Mrs. Thomas Edward   Recorded 1941, New Jersey
        45 Short Hills Avenue, Short Hills, New Jersey

1. Frances Irene Banta *m.* 1919 Thomas Edward Murphy
2. Charles Franklin Banta (1856–1920) *m.* 1889 Anna McClure (1864–)
3. Jacob Banta (1826–1901) *m.* 1853 Elizabeth Phillips (1825–1914)
4. David Banta (1801–1874) *m.* 1824 Sarah DeMott (1805–1882)
5. Jacob Banta (1771–1861) *m.* 1795 Mary Banta (1778–1806)
6. Albert Banta (1728–1810) *m.* 1756 Magdalena Van Voorhees (1739–1810)
7. Hendrick Banta, *b.* 1696, *m.* 1717 Gurtruy Terhune, *b.* 1694
8. Henrick Epke Banta (1665–) *m.* Angenita Hendricks
9. EPKE JACOBS BANTA, *b.* 1686, *m.* Sitska, *b.* 1624

Service: 1679, Judge of Special Court.
Reference: Banta Genealogy.

6734 NELSON, Miss Christine Louise   Recorded 1951, Connecticut
        84 Forest Street, Hartford 5, Connecticut

1. Miss Christine Louise Nelson
2. Clinton H. Nelson (1835–1922) *m.* 1873 Mary Hinman Dewey (1846–1944)
3. William Dewey (1809–1898) *m.* 1837 Eunice Cooley (1812–1890)
4. Aaron Dewey (1781–1826) *m.* 1810 Louisa Gillett (1787–1860)
5. Aaron Dewey, Sr. (1747–1825) *m.* Bedee Gillett (1747–1840)
6. Isaac Dewey (1708–) *m.* 1734 Abigail Bagg (1707–1773)
7. David Dewey (1676–1712) *m.* Sarah ——— (1682–1756)
8. Israel Dewey (1645–1678) *m.* 1668 Abigail Drake (1648–1696)
9. THOMAS DEWEY (–1648) *m.* 1639 Frances Clark (–1690)

Reference: Dewey Family History, by Louis Marimus, pub. by Westfield Mass.,
        pgs. 216, 225, 228, 781, 750, 737, 731, 724, 726.

5987 NELSON, Lloyd Leonard   Recorded 1931
        714 Boissavain Avenue, Norfolk, Virginia

1. Henry Elmer Nelson (1830–) *m.* 1903 Agnes Alma Leonard (1880–)
2. Jas. Montgomery Leonard (1833–1904) *m.* 1877 Mary Agnes Berry (1848–)
3. Thomas H. Leonard (1805–1876) *m.* Susan Leonard Collins (1800–1878)
4. Jonathan Leonard (1761–1830) *m.* Sarah Haddaway Kirby (1767–1848)
5. Thomas Leonard (1725–1777) *m.* Elizabeth Robson (1725–1786)
6. JOHN ROBSON (1680–1745) *m.* Elizabeth (1688–1745)

Service:
Reference:

6259 NEWBURY, Mrs. Alice Lane   Recorded 1939
        1822 Bennett Avenue, Dallas, Texas

1. Alice Lane Newbury *m.* 1911 John Orrin Newbury
2. Alvin V. Lane (1860–1938) *m.* 1886 Lulie Hughey (1865–)
3. Joseph Hughey (1827–1904) *m.* 1859 Mary Ann Peters (1834–1902)
4. Norman Peters –1788–1874) *m.* 1827 Mary Eliza Hill (1799–1874)
5. Eber Peters (1768–1841) *m.* 1787 Catherine McCullough *c.* (1764–1836)
6. William Peters (1746–1805) *m.* 1766 Deborah Strong, *b.* 1745, *d.* aft. 1805
7. Eleazer Strong (1725–1815) *m. c.* 1743 Abigail Chapwell (1724–1805)
8. Eleazer Strong (1695–1779) *m.* 1720 Gemima Stiles (1700–1780)
9. Jedediah Strong (1667–1709) *m.* 1688 Abijah Ingersoll (1663–1732)
10. Jedediah Strong (1639–1733) *m.* 1662 Freedom Woodward (1642–1681)
11. ELDER JOHN STRONG, *c.* (1605–1699) *m. c.* 1630 Abigail Ford *c.* (1608–1688)

Service: Deputy, Plymouth General Court from Taunton, Mass., 1641–1643; Ruling
        Elder, Northampton Church, 1663–1669.
Reference: Peters of New England, by Peters; Hebron, Conn., Vital Records; Boxford,
        Mass., V. R.; Strong Family, by Dwight; Emery's History of Taunton,
        Mass.; Trumbull's History of North Hampton, Mass.

6019 NEWTON, Mrs. Charles W.   Recorded 1932
          461 Farmington Avenue, Hartford, Connecticut
    1. Nellie M. Berry (1862–) *m.* 1884 Capt. Chas. Watson Newton
    2. Capt. Wm. Berry (1841–1889) *m.* 1861 Frances Elizabeth Russell (1842–1921)
    3. Stephen Russell (1818–1900) *m.* 1840 Julia Ann F. Ackley (1819–1882)
    4. Nathan Ackley (1780–1854) *m.* 1766 Eliz. Fuller (1747–)
    5. Amasa Ackley (1747–1808) *m.* 1766 Sarah Fuller (1747–)
    6. Elijah Ackley (1719–1804) *m.* 1761 Abigail Blakesley (1723–1784)
    7. Samuel Blakesley (1697–1761) *m.* 1737 Eliz. Doolittle (1700–)
    8. Daniel Doolittle (1675–1755) *m.* 1698 Hannah Cornwall (1677–1736)
    9. John Cornwall (1640–1707) *m.* 1665 Martha Peck (1641–1708)
   10. DEACON PAUL PECK (1608–1695) *m.* Martha Hale
    Service: Founder of Hartford; Proprietor.
    Reference: East Haddam Gen., by Patterson; History of Hartford County; Families of
          Ancient N. Haven, by Jacobus.

6680 NICHOLS, Miss Anita
    1. Miss Anita Nichols
    2. Foster Nichols (1848–1912) *m.* 1883 Clara Brinck (1860–1921)
    3. Gen. Geo. S. Nichols (1820–1916) *m.* Ann N. Foster (1814–1895)
    4. Sylvester Nichols (1795–1868) *m.* 1817 Lucy Hamilton (1798–1888)
    5. John Nichols (1748–1815) *m.* 1775 Sarah Hoston (1754–1838)
    6. Capt. George Nichols (1714–1788) *m.* 1741 Susanna Hichox (1714–1788)
    7. Joseph Nichols (1680–1733) *m.* Elizabeth Wood
    8. Isaac Nichols, Jr. (1654–1690) *m.* Mary (Bald?)
    9. Isaac Nichols (–1694/95) *m.* Margaret ———
   10. FRANCIS NICHOLS (1600–) *m.* Ann Wines
       Francis Nichols of Ampthill, Eng., *m.* Margaret Bruce, *d.* 1622.
    Service: Original Proprietor of Stratford, Conn.
    Reference: Serg. Francis Nicholls, by Walter Nicholls.

6295 NICHOLS, Mrs. Walter C.   Recorded 1940, Rhode Island
          813 Eddy Street, Providence, Rhode Island
    1. Mary Chace Herrick *m.* 1893 Walter C. Nichols
    2. George L. Herrick (1844–1900) *m.* 1866 Martha M. Tucker (1855–1922)
    3. Asahel Herrick (1811–1871) *m.* 1833 Eliza Chace (1813–1877)
    4. John Chace (1753–1833) *m.* Mary ———
    5. Caleb Chace, *b.* 1722, *m.* 1740 Ruth Payne
    6. Benjamin Chace, Jr. *b.* 1682, *m.* 1703 Mercy Simmons
    7. Benjamin Chace *m.* Phileppa Sherman
    8. WILLIAM CHACE. *c.* (1595–*c.* 1659) *m.* Mary ———
    Service: Freeman, 1634. Constable at Yarmouth, 1639.
    Reference: Certified Family Bibles and Tombstone records.

6063 NICHOLSON, Ralph M.   Recorded 1934, Iowa
          2527 Thirty-fourth Avenue, South, Seattle, Washington
    1. Ralph M. Nicholson *m.* 1913 Edna Preston
    2. John P. Nicholson (1855–) *m.* 1880 Leviette J. Luther (1857–1925)
    3. George H. Luther (1823–1907) *m.* 1845 Esther Silverthorne (1825–1908)
    4. Jabez Luther (1801–1888) *m.* 1820 Catherine Adams (1801–1864)
    5. Jabez Luther (1759–1818) *m.* 1782 Lydia Brown (1760–)
    6. Jabez Luther (1725–) *m.* 1749 Alice Pearce
    7. Caleb Luther (1696–) *m.* 1714 Mary Cole
    8. Samuel Luther, Jr. (1663–1714) *m.* Sarah
    9. Samuel Luther (1636–1716) *m.* 1661 Mary Abell
   10. CAPT. JOHN LUTHER (–1644)
    Service: One of the first proprietors of Taunton, Mass.
    Reference: Luther Genealogy; Descendants of Rev. Chad Browne, by William B.
          Browne; History of Erie Co., Pa., Part VI, Warner, Beers & Co., 1884.

6028 NICKERSON, Mrs. Alvin A.   Recorded 1932
     914 Carterett Avenue, Trenton, New York
1. Florence Platt *m.* Alvin A. Nickerson
2. Louis Henry Platt (1858–1892) *m.* 1882 Mary Louise Marsh (1860–1932)
3. Gilbert M. Platt *m.* Caroline Hoffman
4. Gilbert Platt (–1835) *m.* Charity Purdy
5. Bartholomew Purdy (1777–1833) *m.* ———
6. Elijah Purdy (1756–1826) *m.* Lavina Haght (–1811)
7. Jonathan Purdy (1693–1772) *m.* 1721 Mary Hart (1697–1734)
8. Joseph Purdy (1661–1709) *m.* Elizabeth Ogden (–1742)
9. FRANCIS PURDY (1595–1658) *m.* 1642 Mary Brundage (1616–)
Service:
Reference:

6433 NOBLE, Mrs. Kenneth B.   Recorded 1943
     71 Searborough Road, Hartford, Connecticut
1. Lydia Bryan *m.* Kenneth B. Noble
2. William Alden Bryan (1853–1932) *m.* Anna S. Williams (1865–1937)
3. William B. Bryan *m.* 1848 Lydia A. Palmer
4. Timothy Wells Palmer (1783–) *m.* 1818 Desire Smith
5. Stephen Palmer (1735–1809) *m.* 1759 Rachel Harrison (1740–1817)
6. Joseph Harrison (1700–1748) *m.* 1729 Sarah Foote (1706–1743)
7. Stephen Foote (1672–1762) *m.* 1702 Elizabeth Nash (–1739)
8. Robert Foote (1627–1681) *m.* 1659 Sarah Potter
9. Gov. NATHANIEL FOOTE *m.* 1615 Elizabeth Deming (–1683)
Service: Governor of Connecticut.
Reference: V. R. Brauford, Conn.; Foote Fam. History, Vol. I.

6161 NOBLE, Martha Rogers   Recorded 1937
     169 Avery Drive N. E., Atlanta, Georgia
1. Martha Rogers (1892–) *m.* 1917 George Henry Noble, Jr. (1890–)
2. Luther Woodman Rogers (1856–1914) *m.* 1890 Annie Drummond (1866–1936)
3. James Drummond (1825–1888) *m.* 1852 Martha Farrington (1831–1911)
4. J. Leonard Farrington (1804–1851) *m.* 1829 Betsy Reynolds (1801–1891)
5. Capt. Ichabod Reynolds (1773–1855) *m.* 1796 Polly Brett (1777–1866)
6. Isaac Brett (1738–1828) *m.* 1765 Priscilla Jackson (1740–1777)
7. Samuel Brett (1714–1807) *m.* 1737 Hannah Packard (1715–1802)
8. Seth Brett (1688–1722) *m.* 1712 Sarah Alden (1688–aft. 1714)
9. Isaac Alden (1660–1727) *m.* 1685 Mehitable Allen (1665–1688)
10. Joseph Alden (1624/27–1697) *m.* 1659 Mary Simonons (1625/30–aft. 1674)
11. JOHN ALDEN (1599–1687) *m.* 1623 Priscilla Mullins
Service: Seventh Signer of the Mayflower Compact; Member of Capt. Miles Standish's
    Company at Duxbury.
Reference: The Brett Gen., pgs. 65, 130, 174; Savage's Gen. Dict. of New England,
    Vol. 1, pgs. 23, 24; Vol. 3, pg. 253; Vol. 4, pg. 100; N. Eng. Hist. & Gen.,
    Vol. 3, pg. 338.

6525 NOBLE, Dr. Ralph Edward   Recorded 1946
     Montpelier, Vermont
1. Ralph E. Noble *m.* Bertha Damaris Eddy
2. Henry J. Noble (1866–) *m.* 1895 Bertha A. Dearing (1872–1938)
3. William T. Dearing, *d.* 1896, *m.* 1852 Melissa A. Grow (1827–1896)
4. Isaac Grow (Groo) (1777–1871) *m.* Rebecca Grow (1787–1849)
5. Edward Groo (Grow) (1746/7–1831) *m.* Joanna Nichols (1742–1812)
6. John Grow (1720–1775) *m.* 1742 Mary Farrington (1712–)
7. Edward Farrington (1662–) *m.* 1690 Martha Browne
8. Joseph Farrington, *d.* 1666, *m.* Elizabeth
9. EDMUND FARRINGTON (1588–1670) *m.* Elizabeth, *b.* 1586
Service: Came to America on "Hopewell." Built corn mill and water course on
    Water Hill, called "Farrington's Canal."
Reference: Grow Family History and Savage's Geneal. History.

5870   NORMAN, Mrs. Praber   Recorded 1929, Colorado
        135 N. 26th Street, Corvallis, Oregon
1. Nettie A. Hall *m.* 1892 Praber Norman
2. Henry G. Hall (1832–1893) *m.* 1868 Jane Morrison (1846–)
3. Asahel Hall (1799–1877) *m.* 1816 Betsy Wood Ripley (1799–1856)
4. Hezekiah Ripley (1771–1846) *m.* 1795 Priscilla Wood (1776–1843)
5. Ephraim Wood III (1744–1831) *m.* 1733 Sarah French (1753–)
6. Ephraim Wood, Jr. (1715–1781) *m.* 1742 Mary Lazell (–1752)
7. Ephraim Wood, Sr. (1679–1744) *m.* 1710 Susanna Howland (1690–1743)
8. Samuel Wood (1647–1718) *m.* 1679 Rebecca Tupper (1651–1718)
9. Henry Wood *m.* Abigail Janney
Service: None given.
Reference: Landmarks of Plymouth; Mayflower Descendants.

6171   NORRIS, Miss Olivia Jones   Recorded 1938
        214 Grosvenor Street, Douglaston, Long Island
1. Olivia Jones Norris
2. John Norris (1856–1914) *m.* 1881 Emma Virginia Jones (1857–)
3. Robert Jones (1829–1910) *m.* 1853 Olivia Jackson (1832–1918)
4. Enoch Jackson (Eng.) (1808–1875) *m.* 1831 Sophia Hughes Bennett (1816–1865)
5. John Bennett (1780–1834) *m.* 1800 Mary Hughes (1780–1862)
6. Jacob Hughes (1746–1796) *m.* 1773 Ann Lawrence (1753–1817)
7. Jacob Hughes (1711–1772) *m.* 1743 Priscilla Leaming (1710–1758)
8. Thomas Leaming (1674–1723) *m.* 1701 Hannah Whilldin (1683–1728)
9. Joseph Whilldin *m.* (Plymouth Col.) 1683 Hannah Gorman (1663–aft. 12–17–1708)
10. Papo John Gorman *m.* Desire Howland
    Desire Howland was the dau. of John Howland.
Service: Signer of Mayflower Compact.
Reference: The Mayflower Descendants, Vol. 4, pg. 220; Vol. 5, pgs. 176–177; Howe's Mayflower Desc., Pg. 148; Stillwell's "Leamings of Cape May, Vol. 4, pgs. 429, 433; Hughes "Divine Covenant," pg. 20; Penn.; Book A, Cape May Marriages, Divine Covenant," pg. 20.

6762   NORTON, Miss Ethel May   Recorded 1952, Illinois
        526 East Carroll Street, Macomb, Illinois
1. Miss Ethel May Norton
2. Edward J. Norton (1858–1939) *m.* 1884 Ethel J. Walker (1862–1888)
3. Edward I. Walker (1833–1906) *m.* 1856 Sarah Ann Gibbs (1835–1897)
4. Roswell Walker (1805–1855) *m.* 1830 Huldah S. Harkness (1803–1889)
5. Isaac Walker (1767–1839) *m.* 1794 Polly Porter (1769–1847)
6. Samuel Walker (1721–1817) *m.* 1750 Mary Stratton (1723–1794)
7. Seth Walker (1691–1772) *m.* 1716 Eleanor Chandler (1695–1769)
8. Joseph Walker (1645–1729) *m.* 1669 Sarah Wyman (1650–1728)
9. Samuel Walker (1615–1685) *m.* 1650 (Wife listed but name not given in Reading Church)
10. Captain Richard Walker (1592–1687) *m.* Jane Talmage
Service: 1638 was chosen to lay our farms.
Reference: Chandler's History of Town of Shirley, Mass., pgs. 627-8-9-26, 30–36–653–58, by Chandler, Pub. at Fitchburg, Mass., 1883, copy in Newbury Library, Chicago, Ill.

6674   O'DONNELL, Mrs. James Edward   Recorded 1950
        2769 Larkspur Avenue, Baton Rouge 7, Louisiana
1. Lenore Babers *m.* 1917 Edward J. O'Donnell
2. Darling Babers (1840–1904) *m.* 1876 Sarah E. Rowe (1855–1927)
3. Benjamin Rowe (1829–1894) *m.* Elizabeth E. McNulty (1835–1855)
4. John McNulty (1786–1837) *m.* 1827 Evaline L. Orr (1810–1875)
5. Dr. James Orr (1755–1817) *m.* 1800 Elizabeth DeLoach
6. Ruffin DeLoach (1764–1835) *m.* 1783 Abba Mercer (1768–1860)
7. William DeLoach (1745–1800) *m.* 1763 Purity Ruffin
8. William Ruffin (1719–1781)
9. William Ruffin (1683–1739) *m.* 1704 Faith Gray (1686–1719)

10. Robert Ruffin (1646–1693) *m.* Elizabeth Prime (1648–1714)
11. WILLIAM RUFFIN I, Immigrant (1603–1674)
Service:
Reference:

6139 O'NEAL, Mrs. David L.   Recorded 1937, Georgia
       Decatur, Georgia
1. Leila Thornley *m.* 1908 David L. O'Neal
2. Ernest S. Thornley (1856–1904) *m.* 1877 Elizabeth Thornley (1861–1893)
3. John L. Thornley, Jr. (1828–1900) *m.* 1855 Elizabeth T. McFall (1829–1863)
4. John L. Thornley, Sr. (1800–1833) *m.* 1826 Louisa (Chollet) Hutchinson (1800–1871)
5. Alexander P. Chollet –1799) *m.* 1787 Elizabeth Ripault (1765–1800)
6. John Ripault (1729–1805) *m.* 1755 ──────
7. Dr. James Ripault (1690–1743) *m.* 1720 Elizabeth Colleton (1695–1750)
8. MAJOR JAMES COLLETON (1665–1727) *m.* 1690 Anne (Mrs. Henry Russell) (–1735)
Service: Major in the Provincial Forces.
Reference: History of South Carolina under Proprietary Government.

6474 OEHLKE, Mrs. Theodore R.   Recorded 1945
       Lorain, Ohio
      (Mrs. Oehlke was a member in 1922. Her Application Blanks were lost. Not recorded. Given new number and recorded as above.)
1. Mary Emily Kingsbury *m.* Theodore R. Oehlke
2. Edward Kingsbury (1829–1917) *m.* 1863 Caroline F. Tallack (1838–1925)
3. Eliphalet Kingsbury (1804–1882) *m.* 1825 Mary Ann Briggs (1802–1887)
4. Solomon Briggs (1771–1875) *m.* 1798 Chloe Tucker (1777–1850)
5. Joseph Tucker (1736–1790) *m.* 1763 Abigail Nason (1743–)
6. Presward Tucker (1707–) *m.* 1729 Rebecca Esty (1708–)
7. Deacon Joseph Tucker (1679–1745) *m.* 1701 Judith Clapp (1680–1738/9)
8. Joseph Tucker (1643–) *m.* ──────
9. ROBERT TUCKER (1604–1682) *m.* Elizabeth ────── (–aft. 1682)
Service: Held office in Weymouth, Mass.; first recorder, town of Gloucester, Mass.; first recorder, town of Milton, Mass.; Selectman for several years; represented town at General Court, 1680–1681.

6606 OKESON, Miss Margaret A.   Recorded 1948
       1232 Greenwood Avenue, Wilmette, Illinois
1. Margaret Albertson Okeson
2. Wm. B. Okeson (1828–1910) *m.* 1860 Margaret J. Hardy (1835–1913)
3. William Okeson (1795–1873) *m.* 1818 Jane Black (1798–1881)
4. Nicholas A. Okeson (1757–1852) *m.* 1779 Susan Silverthorn (1762–1841)
5. Daniel Okeson (1724–1801) *m.* 1748 Angelshe Van de Water (1732–1807)
6. Nicholas Albertson (1700–1760) *m.* Angelshe Van de Water (1709–1760)
7. Cornelius Van de Water (1673–) *m.* 1698 Dorothea Loysee
8. JACOBUS VAN DE WATER (1642–1730) *m.* 1665 Engeltie Julians
Service: Major of New Amsterdam.
Reference: Pioneers of New Jersey; Early Settlers of Kings County, N. Y.

6096 OLSEN, Miss Sophia B.   Recorded 1936, Pennsylvania
       235 Gowen Avenue, Philadelphia, Pennsylvania
1. Sophia B. Olsen
2. Thorston Y. Olsen (1879–) *m.* 1905 Margarita McKinley (1881–)
3. A. A. McKinley (1853–1927) *m.* 1878 Annie R. Winchester (1855–1915)
4. Benjamin B. McKinley (1810–1883) *m.* 1839 Mary Sarah Elfreth (1815–1883)
5. John McKinley (1770–1852) *m.* 1807 Abigail Brannan (1780–1828)
6. Benjamin Brannan (1739–1825) *m.* 1767 Eunice Este (1744–1820)
7. Moses Este *m.* 1736 Eunice Pengilly (1719–)
8. Isaac Este, Jr. (1656–1714) *m.* 1689 Abigail Kymbal
9. Isaac Este (–1712) *m.* 1655 Mary Towne (1634–1692)
10. WILLIAM TOWNE *m.* 1620 Joanna Blessing (–1635)
Service: Early settler in Mass.
Reference: Ashmeade's History of Delaware County; Salem Register of Deeds.

6469 OSELAND, Mrs. Zimri Christian   Recorded 1945
            695 Merriman Road, Akron 3, Ohio

1. Erma Holden *m.* Zimri Christian Oseland
2. Melvin Elsworth Holden (1866–1935) *m.* 1890 Cynthia Stafford (1870–   )
3. James Delap Holden (1819–1892) *m.* 1864 (3rd) Hannah Ray (1840–1901)
4. Samuel Holden (1772–1858) *m.* 1797 Jane Farnsworth (1776–1813)
5. Jabez Holden (1735–1787) *m.* 1761 Rachel Farnsworth (1738–1829)
6. Nathaniel Holden (1691–1740) *m.* 1718 Abigail Stone (1691–1757)
7. Stephen Holden (1658–1715) *m.* 1685 Hannah Lawrence (1664–1735)
8. RICHARD HOLDEN (1609–1695) *m.* 1640 Martha Fosdick (1620–1681)

Service: Died in Groton, Mass., 1696.
Reference: Holden Genealogy, by Puiman.

6420 OSGOOD, Marian Curtis Stone   Recorded 1943
            Minneapolis, Minnesota.   (New number)

1. Marian Curtis (Stone) Osgood
2. David T. Stone (1835–   ) *m.* 1860 Sarah Jewett Cobb (1840–1912)
3. Curtis Stone (1808–1891) *m.* abt. 1834 Mary N. Stanley (1798–1867)
4. Thomas Stone (1762–aft. 1808) *m.* Margery Force (1762–   )
5. Lieut. Samuel Stone (1736–1775) *m.* Dorothy Fletcher (1745–1840)
6. Samuel Stone (1708–abt. 1776) *m.* Mindwell Stevens (1713/14–   )
7. Capt. Samuel Stone (1684–1769) *m.* Abigail Reed (1686–1767)
8. Deacon Samuel Stone (1631–1715) *m.* Sarah Stearns (1635–1700)
9. GREGORY STONE (1592–1672) *m.* Lydia Cooper (–1674)

Service: Deputy to the Mass. General Court; Signer of "Cambridge Petition," 1684.
Reference: Lost.

6419 OSGOOD, Dr. Phillips E.   Recorded 1943
            Minneapolis, Minnesota.   (New number)

1. Dr. Phillips Endecott Osgood *m.* ———
2. Geo. Endecott Osgood (1854–   ) *m.* 1879 Helen Frances Reed (1853–1918)
3. Moses E. Osgood (1824–1895) *m.* 1853 Sarah C. Gleason (–1903)
4. Dr. George Osgood (1784–1813) *m.* Nancy Endecott (1788–1869)
5. Moses Endecott (1767–1807) *m.* Anna Towne
6. John Endecott (1741–1816) *m.* Martha Putnam
7. John Endecott (1717–1783) *m.* Elizabeth Jacobs
8. Samuel Endecott (–1766) *m.* Anna Endecott (his cousin) (–1723)
9. Samuel Endecott (1666–1694) *m.* Hannah Felton
10. Zerrubbabel Endecott (–1684) *m.* Mary ———
11. Gov. JOHN ENDECOTT (1588–1665) *m.* Elizabeth Gibson

Service: Governor Mass. Bay Colony.
Reference: Lost.

5882 PAINE, Mrs. William M.   Recorded 1929, Texas
            303 Argyle Avenue, Dallas, Texas

1. Florence Thomas *m.* William Miller Paine
2. Melville Thomas (1842–1888) *m.* Louise W. Burr (1843–1924)
3. William E. Burr (1793–1872) *m.* 1826 Amanda F. Jones (1808–1889)
4. Ezekiel Burr (1755–   ) *m.* 1785 Hulda Merchant
5. Jabez Burr (1739–1770) *m.* Elizabeth
6. Daniel Burr *m.* 1678 Abigail Glover
7. JEHU BURR (1600–1672)

Service: Was a Freeman, 1632.
Reference: "Burr Family," by Charles Burr Todd.

6384 PARKER, Mrs. James R.   Recorded 1942
            Hartford, Connecticut

1. Dorothy Ely Williams *m.* James R. Parker
2. Wm. David Williams (1860–1922) *m.* 1895 Lilla Ely (1855–1941)
3. Frederick Everest Ely (1827–1892) *m.* 1849 Elizabeth Thompson Martin
      (1831–1887)
4. Rev. James Ely (1798–1890) *m.* 1822 Louisa Everest (1792–1848)

5. Richard Hayes Ely (1769–1844) *m.* Lucretia Ray
6. James Ely (1744–1809) *m.* 1768 Catherine Hayes (1744–1809)
7. James Ely (1719–1766) *m.* 1741 Dorcas Andrews
8. William Ely (1690–1760) *m.* 171– Hannah Thompson (1690–1733)
9. CAPT. AND JUDGE WILLIAM ELY (1647–1717) *m.* 1681 Elizabeth Smith (1645–1750)

Service: Deputy from Lyme to the General Court in Hartford, Conn., 1689–98, and Judge of the County Court of New London, Conn.
Reference: National Number 5790; Ely Ancestry—Lin. Richard Ely; Calmut Press, 1902, pgs. 32, 33, 38, 40, 55, 87, 145, 267, 487; Lynn V. R., Vol. I, 122.

6351 PARKHURST, Rev. John Queen   Recorded 1941, Massachusetts
      97 Mason Terrace, Brookline, Massachusetts

1. John Queen Parkhurst *m.* 1937 Mary Isabel Robinson
2. Rev. Henry Adams Parkhurst (1874–1929) *m.* Anna Belle Archibald (1879–)
3. John Adams Parkhurst (1834–) *m.* (2nd) 1871 Abbie Almira Queen
4. Henry Parkhurst, *b.* 1792, *m.* 1817 Abigail Taylor, *d.* 1868
5. Leonard Parkhurst (1763–1821) *m.* 1790 Hannah Hills (1769–1862)
6. Lt. Joel Parkhurst (1741–1808) *m.* 1762 Betty Cummings (1744–1837)
7. Ensign Ebenezer Parkhurst (1699–1757) *m.* Sarah
8. EBENEZER PARKHURST *m.* Mary

Service: In America before 1699.
Reference: Records of Universalist Gen. Con. Year Books; "Hist. of Dunstable, Mass.," Fox; "Hist. of Chelmsford, Mass."

6390 PARKHURST, Dr. Lewis   Recorded 1942
      Winchester, Massachusetts

1. Dr. Lewis Parkhurst *m.* Emma J. Wilder
2. Thomas Henry Parkhurst (1825–1907) *m.* 1848 Sarah Wright (1829–1896)
3. Henry Parkhurst (1792–1865) *m.* 1817 Abigail Taylor (1798–1868)
4. Leonard Parkhurst (1763–1821) *m.* 1790 Hannah Hills (1769–1862)
5. Lieut. Joel Parkhurst (1741–1808) *m.* 1762 Elizabeth Cummings (1744–1837)
6. Ensign Ebenezer Parkhurst (1699–1757) *m.* 1721 Sarah Blogget
7. EBENEZER PARKHURST *m.* 169– Mary ——— (–1732)

Service: War; town official; church official.
Reference: Hist. Winchester, Mass., Chapman; Hist. Dunstable, Chelmsford, Fox.

6401* PARKHURST, Wallace Archibald   Recorded 1943
      Situate, Massachusetts

1. Wallace Archibald Parkhurst *m.* Louisa M. Howard
2. Rev. Henry Adams Parkhurst (1874–1929) *m.* Anna Belle Archibald (1879–)
3. John Adams Parkhurst (1834–) *m.* (2nd) 1871 Abbie Almira Queen
4. Henry Parkhurst (1793–) *m.* 1817 Abigail Taylor (–1868)
5. Leonard Parkhurst (1763–1821) *m.* 1790 Hannah Hills (1769–1862)
6. Lieut. Joel Parkhurst (1741–1808) *m.* 1762 Betty Cummings (1744–1837)
7. ENS. EBENEZER PARKHURST (1699–1757) *m.* Sarah ———

Service: War; town officer; church official.
Reference: Mass. Town Rec. Histories; Dunstable, Mass., by Fox. Chelmsford.

6735 PARROTT, Mrs. Robert U.   Recorded 1951, Louisiana
      2821 Georges Lane, Alexandria, Louisiana

1. Charlotte E. Davis *m.* 1931 Robert Parrott
2. Robert W. Davis (1865–1934) *m.* 1908 Charlotte Long (1876–)
3. Huey Pierce Long (1852–1937) *m.* 1875 Caledonia Tison (1860–1915)
4. John Murphy Long (1825–1901) *m.* 1845 Mary Elizabeth Wingate (1829–1901)
5. James Long (1790–1850) *m.* 1823 Mary Kirtman (1793–1850)
6. Hugh Long (1770–1794 & 1800) *m.* 1789 Margaret ——— (–1794)
7. James Long (1750–1806) *m.* 1768 Catherine (–bef. 1790)
8. John Long (abt. 1692–1759) *m.* 1735 Eleanor Owens (1706–aft. 1759)
9. Capt. Richard Owens (1668–aft. 1708) *m.* 1698 Rachael Beall (bf. 1678–aft. 1708)
10. COL. NINIAN BEALL (1625–1717) *m.* 1668 Ruth Moore (–1704)

Service: Dept. Surveyor; Justice, and Burgess of Md.
Reference: National Number 6724 in Sons & Daughters of the Pilgrims.

6194   PASCHALL, C. Augusta Wille   Recorded 1938
          6531 Irving Avenue, Merchantville, New Jersey
   1. C. Augusta Wille (1896–   ) *m.* 1924 Henry Curtis Paschall
   2. George A. Wille (1865–1937) *m.* 1891 Louisa Dawson Mather (1867–   )
   3. John Atkinson Mather (1837–1921) *m.* 1861 Louisa W. Dawson (1842–1923)
   4. James Carr Dawson (1815–1872) *m.* 1838 Elizabeth B. Cade (1818–1895)
   5. Isaac Cade (1780–1823) *m.* 1804 Judith A. Hendrickson (1784–1867)
   6. Andrew Henricsson (1748–   ) *m.* 1770 Judy Jones (1751–1793)
   7. Peter Henricsson (1718–   ) *m.* bef. 1748 Catherine Lock(e) (–1725 or 1729)
   8. ANDERS HENRICSSON *m.* bef. 1713 Beata
   Service: A Swedish settler of West N. J. before 1700.
   Reference: Recs. of Church of Ascension, Phila.; St. Paul's P. E., Camden, N. J.;
          St. Peter's P. E., Clarksboro, N. J.; Trinity P. E., Swedesboro, N. J.,
          pgs. 206, 300, 343, 376, 203–11.
   Spelling of the name Henrickson, Hendrickson, Henrixon, all occur in the records of
          Trinity P. E. Ch. At that time it is all one family is shown by dates and Christian
          names. Translation of rec. in Penna. Hist. Soc., Phila., 18th and Locust Sts.

6265   PASCHALL, Louise Mather   Recorded 1939, New Jersey
          6531 Irving Avenue, Merchantville, New Jersey
   1. Louise Mather Paschall
   2. H. Curtis Paschall *b.* 1895, *m.* 1924 Caroline Augusta Wille, *b.* 1896
   3. George August Wille (1865–1937) *m.* 1891 Louisa Dawson Mather, *b.* 1867
   4. John Atkinson Mather (1837–1921) *m.* 1861 Louisa Wallace Dawson (1842–1923)
   5. James Carr Dawson (1815–1872) *m.* 1838 Elizabeth Barber Cade (1818–1895)
   6. Isaac Cade (1780–1823) *m.* 1804 Judith Hendrickson (1784–1867)
   7. Andrew Henricsson (1748–1793) *m.* 1770 Judy Jones (1751–1793)
   8. Peter Henricsson (1718–1761) *m.* Catherine Lock (1729–1766)
   9. ANDRES HENRICSSON *m.* Beata
   Service: Swedish settler in New Jersey near Swedesboro before 1699.
   Reference: Original Settlers on the Delaware, by Benjamin Forrest; Genealogy of
          the Fenwick Colony, by Shourds; Records St. Paul's Ch., Camden, N. J.;
          Rec. St. Peter's Ch., Clarksboro, N. J.; Rec. Trinity P. E. Ch., Swedes-
          boro, N. J.; Rec. Old Swede's Ch., Wilmington, Del.

6725   PATTERSON, Alice Carol   Recorded 1951, Georgia
          238 Garland Avenue, Decatur, Georgia
                              (JUNIOR)
   1. Alice Carol Patterson, Jr., *b.* 1938
   2. Turner Whitfield Patterson (1909–   ) *m.* 1937 Mary Edna Smith (1915–   )
   3. Turner Whitfield Patterson (1873–1917) *m.* 1901 Alto Lee Harrell (1882–   )
   4. Turner Whitfield (1832–1908) *m.* Ellen Frances Allen
   5. Turner Dennis Patterson (1810–1875) *m.* 1829 Belerma E. Rowlett (Rullett)
          (1810–1856)
   6. Lt. Thomas Rowlett (1787–1841) *m.* 1809 Lucy Bruce (2nd Acree) (1791–1850)
   7. Wm. Rowlett (Rullett) (aft. 1760–   ) *m.* 1785 Elizabeth Gill (1767–   )
   8. William Rowlett (1730–1785) *m.* 1752 Sarah ———
   9. Peter (Pierre) Rowlett (Rulett) (–1749) *m.* (2nd) ——— Cooke (–1777)
  10. PIERRE RULLETT (Rowlett) (1637–will 1702)
   Reference: Huguenot 1698 publication 13, Manakintown Huguenot Society, 1945–1947;
          Rullett Coat of Arms, pg. 147–8; Henrico Co., Va., will b. no. 1, p. 263;
          Chesterfield Co., Va., will b. no. 1, pg. 45, bk, 3, pg. 517.

6727   PATTERSON, Donna Lee   Recorded 1951, Georgia
          238 Garland Avenue, Decatur, Georgia
                              (JUNIOR)
   1. Donna Lee Patterson *b.* 1944
   2. Turner Whitfield Patterson (1909–   ) *m.* 1937 Mary E. Smith (1915–   )
   3. Turner Whitfield 2nd (1873–1917) *m.* 1901 Alto Lee Harrell (1882–   )

4. Turner Whitfield Patterson (1832–1908) *m.* Ellen Frances Allen, *b.* N.C.D. Va.
5. Turner Dennis Patterson (1810–1875) *m.* 1829 Belerma E. Rowlett (Rulett) (1810–1856)
6. Lt. Thomas Rowlett (1787–1841) *m.* 1809 Lucy Bruce (2nd) Acree (1790–1850)
7. William Rowlett (abt. 1760–) *m.* 1785 Elizabeth Gill (1767–)
8. William Rowlett (1730–1785) *m.* 1752 Sarah ———
9. Peter (Pierre) Rullett (–1749) *m.* (2nd) ——— Cook (–1777)
10. PIERRE RULLETT (1637–will 1702)

Reference: Huguenot, 1689, publication of Manakintown Huguenot Society of Va., 1945–1947; Rullett Coat of Arms, pgs. 147–8; Henrico Co., Va., will bk. no. 1, pg. 263; Chesterfield Co., Va. will b. no 3, pg. 517.

6726 PATTERSON, Mary Patricia   Recorded 1951
        238 Garland Avenue, Decatur, Georgia
                              (JUNIOR)
1. Mary Patricia Patterson
2. Turner W. Patterson (1909–) *m.* 1937 Mary Smith (1915–)
3. Turner W. Patterson (1873–1917) *m.* 1901 Alto Lee Harrell (1882–)
4. Turner Whitfield Patterson (1832–1908) *m.* Ellen Frances Allen
5. Turner Dennis Patterson (1810–1875) *m.* 1829 Belerma E. Rowlett (Rulette) (1810–1856)
6. Lt. Thomas Rowlett (1787–1841) *m.* 1809 Lucy Bruce (1790–1850)
7. William Rowlett (abt. 1760–) *m.* 1785 Elizabeth Gill (1767–)
8. William Rowlett (1730–1785) *m.* 1752 Sarah ———
9. Peter (Pierre) Rowlett (–1749) *m.* ——— Cook (–1777)
10. PIERRE ROWLETT (–1702-will)

Reference: Huguenot 1689 publication of Manakintown, Huguenot Society of Va., 1945–1947; Henrico Co., Va., will; Chesterfield Co., Va. will b. 3, pg. 517.

6460 PATTON, Mrs. James B.   Recorded 1945
        1676 Franklin Avenue, Columbus 5, Ohio
1. Marguerite Courtright *m.* James B. Patton
2. Samuel W. Courtright (1842–1913) *m.* 1865 Jennie R. Martin (1843–1914)
3. Jesse D. Courtright (1811–1873) *m.* 1831 Sarah Stout (1808–1881)
4. John Courtright (1779–1863) *m.* Elizabeth Grubb (1780–1852)
5. Abram Van Cortright (1748–1825) *m.* Effie Drake (1752–1824)
6. John Van Cortright (1714–1783) *m.* 1735 Margaret Denneonecken (1712–)
7. C. H. Van Cortright (1680–) *m.* 1701 Christina Roesenkrans (1671–)
8. H. J. Van Cortright (1648–1741) *m.* 1672 Catherine Hansen Weber
9. J. B. VAN KORTRYK (1618–) *m.* in Holland ———

Service: Left Holland April 16, 1663, and settled in Ulster Co., N. Y.
Reference: Rikers' Hist. Harlem; Hist. Ulster Co., by Clearwater; Gen. Western N. Y., by Cutler.

6101 PAUL, Miss Alice   Recorded 1936, New Jersey
        Moorestown, New Jersey
1. Miss Alice Paul
2. William M. Paul (1850–1902) *m.* 1881 Tacie Parry (1859–1930)
3. William M. Paul (1806–1850) *m.* 1829 Mary Ann Thorne (1810–1850)
4. Cooper Paul (1781–1813) *m.* 1803 Sybil Mickle (1785–1856)
5. Joshua Paul (1745–1785) *m.* 1779 Mary Lippincott (–1780)
6. Nathan Paul (1710–1754) *m.* 1740 Deborah Van Iman
7. Samuel Paul (1679–1730) *m.* 1703
8. PHILIP PAUL (1657–)

Service: Early settler.
Reference: Records of Friends Meetings, Newton, New Jersey; Friends Meetings of Woodbury, Haddonfield, and Moorestown, New Jersey.

6360 PAWLEY, Mrs. William Douglas   Recorded 1941, Georgia
      3190 Pine Tree Drive, Miami Beach, Florida
      1. Annie Hahr Dobbs *m*. 1919 William Douglas Pawley
      2. Herbert Clifton Dobbs (1867–1939) *m*. 1890 Annie von Schele Hahr, *b*. 1870
      3. Major Franz Joseph Hahr (1825–1877) *m*. 1858 Alice Mulvinal Hartman
         (1841–1873)
      4. William Murchison Hartman (1813–1853) *m*. 1831 Martha Cade (1810–aft. 1841)
      5. James Waddell Cade, *d*. 1865/6, *m*. 1797 Margaret McDaniel, *d*. bef. 1864
      6. William Cade (Rev. War) (1735–   ) *m*. Elizabeth Smith, *d*. aft. 1821
      7. Stephen Cade (1715–   ) *m*. 1734 Mary ———, *d*. aft. 1735
      8. Robert Cade (1690–1769) *m*. 1713 Susannah Crump (1682–aft. 1720)
      9. Stephen Crump *c*. (1655–1700) *m*. Susannah, *d*. aft. 1727
     10. WILLIAM Crump, *d*. bef. 1680, *m*. Eliza, *d*. 1653/4
     12. Lt. Thomas Crump, *d*. bef. 1655, *m*. Elizabeth Buck, *d*. aft. 1655
     13. REV. RICHARD BUCK, *d*. 1623, *m*. bef. 1609
      Service: Came to Jamestown, Va., 1610; 2nd Minister of Church at Jamestown,
         1610–1623; Chaplain of first Legislative Assembly in America, July 30, 1819.
      Reference: "Kinfolks," by Wm. C. Harlee; Hotten's "Immigrants, 1600–1700";
         Stanard's "Colonial Virginia Register"; "Cradle of the Republic," Tyler;
         "Genesis of U. S."; St. Peter's Parish Register of New Kent Co., Va.
         (Pub. Ed.)

5846 PEABODY, Miss Agnes L.   Recorded 1929
      464 W. 20th St., New York City, New York
      1. Miss Agnes L. Peabody
      2. Joseph Norton Peabody (1844–1903) *m*. 1867 Anna Brady (1847–1915)
      3. Linn Van Ness Peabody (1816–1858) *m*. 1843 Mary Eleanor Norton (1817–1881)
      4. Asa Peabody (1784–1828) *m*. Mary Van Ness
      5. John Tyng Peabody (1756–1822) *m*. 1778 Elizabeth Strange (–1787)
      6. Asa Peabody (1717–1788) *m*. 1742 Mary Prentice
      7. Richard Peabody (1691–1769) *m*. Ruth Kimball (1693–   )
      8. William Peabody (1646–1699) *m*. 1684 Hannah Hale
      9. Francis Peabody (1612–1697) *m*. Mary Foster
     10. JOHN PEABODY *m*. Lydia Isabel
      Service:
      Reference: Peabody Gen., N. Y. Public Library.

6016 PECKHAM, Dr. Herbert   Recorded 1932
      1328 Franklin Street, Denver, Colorado
      1. Stephen Farnum Peckham (1839–1918) *m*. 1865 Mary Chase Peck (1839–1892)
      2. Chas. Peckham (1816–1901) *m*. 1838 Hannah Lapham Farnum (1813–1906)
      3. Thomas Peckham (1783–1843) *m*. 1809 Sarah Wardwell (1785–1868)
      4. Samuel Wardwell (1755–1819) *m*. 1777 Lydia Wardwell (1757–1817)
      5. John Wardwell (1720–1770) *m*. 1741 Phoebe Howland (1720–1794)
      6. Samuel Howland (1686–   ) *m*. 1708 Abigail Carey (1684–1737)
      7. Jabiz Howland *m*. Bethia Thatcher
      8. JOHN HOWLAND (1593–1673) *m*. Elizabeth Tilley (1607–1687)
      Service:
      Reference: Peckham Gen.; Howland Gen.; Mayflower Desc., Vol. 7; Howland Gen.,
         page 333.

5841 PEDRONCELLI, Miss M. D.   Recorded 1929
      18 Summit Street, East Orange, New Jersey
      1. Margaret Disbrow Pedroncelli (1911–   )
      2. William John Pedroncelli (1879–   ) *m*. 1900 Eterline Disbrow (1879–   )
      3. William Cook Disbrow (1851–   ) *m*. 1876 Elizabeth Bulger (1860–1919)
      4. William Cook Disbrow (1816–1893) *m*. 1848 Margaret Wessells Dill (1828–1912)
      5. Samuel Warne Disbrow (1778–1873) *m*. 1811 Sarah Cook (1792–1875)
      6. Benjamin Disbrow (1754–1794) *m*. 1775 Deborah Robinson (1755–1785)
      7. Griffin Disbrow (1712–1754) *m*. Hannah ———
      8. Benjamin Disbrow (1672–1733) *m*. Mary Griffin (–1737)
      9. HENRY DISBROW (–1699) *m*. Margaret
      Service: Magistrate of Mamaroneck, 1673.
      Reference: Reg. of New Netherland, 1626–1674, by O'Callaghan; N. Y. Gen. & Biog.
         Rec., Vol. 51, page 41.

5834 PEENE, Mrs. John G.   Recorded 1929
          1 Leighton Avenue, Yonkers, New York

1. Ava Lenora Holder (1853–   ) *m.* 1883 John Garrison Peene
2. Francis T. Holder (1833–1912) *m.* 1852 Arabella P. Davis (1834–1898)
3. David Holder (1788–1864) *m.* Ruth Bassett
4. Thomas Holder (1764–1830) *m.* Sarah Gaskill (–1836)
5. Daniel Holder (1721–   ) *m.* 1748 Hannah ——
6. Christopher Holder, Jr. (1666–1720) *m.* 1691 Elizabeth Daniell
7. CHRISTOPHER HOLDER (1631–1688) *m.* 1666 Hope Clifton

Services: Founder of the Quaker faith in America.
Reference:

6673 PELAYO, Mrs. Sidney F. M.   Recorded 1950
          1204 North Street, Baton Rouge, Louisiana

1. Myrtle Kershaw *m.* 1889 Sidney Frederick Pelayo
2. Henry de Solas Kershaw (1860–1893) *m.* 1881 Fannie Wiskell (1858–1929)
3. Richard H. Wiskell (1811–1869) *m.* 1834 Martha S. Cary (1816–1883)
4. Augustin Wiskell (1772–   ) *m.* 1793 Mary Blackwell
5. John Blackwell (1735–   ) *m.* Judith Churchill Jones (1743–   )
6. Col. Armistead Churchill (1697–1767) *m.* Hannah Harrison
7. Nathaniel Harrison (1677–1727) *m.* Mary (Cary Young) (1678–1732)
8. Benjamin Harrison (1654–1713) *m.* Hannah ——
9. BENJAMIN HARRISON, Eng. (–1649) *m.* Mary

Service: Emigrant.
Reference: La. Geo. Reg., Vol. 1, 104; Va. History Magazine, Vol. 31, 278.

6414 PENNOYER, Dr. Charles H.
          159 Grove Street, Rutland, Vermont
          Recorded Member during time of the Founder, Hon. Thomas W. Bicknell;
      original papers lost. Copy, April 15, 1943.

1. Dr. Charles H. Pennoyer (Ass't Gov. General) *m.* Emma Hindley
2. Hon. Henry Jesse Pennoyer (1835–1911) *m.* 1862 Mary Emma Huntington
      (1842–1896)
3. Jesse Peabody Pennoyer (1803–1889) *m.* Pamelia Blossom (1816–1885)
4. Nathan Blossom (abt. 1795–1847) *m.* 1815 Susan Beardsley (1787–1885)
5. Capt. David Blossom (1755–1835) *m.* Seana Miner
6. Seth Blossom (1721–   ) *m.* 1754 (2nd) Abigail Crocker
7. Peter Blossom (1698–   ) *m.* 1720 Hannah Isum
8. Thomas Blossom (1667–   ) *m.* 1695 Fear Robinson (1676–   )
9. Peter Blossom (1627–1700) *m.* 1663 Sarah Bodfish
10. DEACON THOMAS BLOSSOM (ab. 1580–1632) *m.* Anna (1590–   )

Service: First Deacon of the Leyden-Plymouth Churches.
Reference: Hists. Richmont, V. T. Barnstable, Trayser; Cape Cod, Freeman; Amer.
      Ancestry, Vol. 7; Hist. Reg., Vol. 2.

6399 PENNOYER, Lucius Huntington   Recorded 1942
          Beaumont, California

1. Lucius Huntington Pennoyer *m.* Maud Elizabeth Fuller
2. Henry Jesse Pennoyer (1835–1911) *m.* 1862 Mary Emma Huntington (1842–1896)
3. Jesse Peabody Pennoyer (1803–1889) *m.* Pamelia Blossom (1816–1885)
4. Maj. Jesse Pennoyer (1760–1825) *m.* Martha Ferguson
5. Rev. Joseph Pennoyer (1734–1815) *m.* Lucy —— (1737–1819)
6. John Pennoyer (1698–1785) *m.* ——
7. Thomas Pennoyer (1658–   ) *m.* 1685 Lydia Knapp
8. ROBERT PENNOYER (1614–1680) *m.* Widow Schofield

Service: Agent for his brother, William Pennoyer (Merchant and Philanthropist of
      London).
Reference: N. E. H. G. Rec. II, xlv, xlvi, xlvii; Histories: Sharon, Conn., Sedgwick,
      Stamford, Conn., Huntington.

6588   PEOPLES, Mrs. Hillery L.   Recorded 1948
            5440 Vanderbilt, Dallas, Texas
   1. Mrs. H. L. Peoples *m.* 1897
   2. Oliver H. Allen (1846–1926) *m.* 1872 Martha A. Granade (1856–1903)
   3. Leland Allen (1799–1890) *m.* 1823 Elizabeth B. White (1808–1851)
   4. Micajah White (1788–1825) *m.* 1807 Judith David (1784–1828)
   5. Pierre David III (1748–1798) *m.* 1780 ——— White (1760/1–1792)
   6. Pierre David II (1703–   ) *m.* 1737 Elizabet
   7. PIERRE DAVID *ca.* (1680–1729) *m. ca.* 1700 Ann, *d.* 1750
   Service: Among French refugees who settled Manakin; received grant of land from
            English Crown for 88 acres of land.
   Reference: Virginia Magazine of History; Our Kin.

6756   PERRY, Mrs. Helen Holton Evans   Recorded 1952, Illinois
            215 N. Union, Lincoln, Illinois
   1. Mrs. Helen Holton Evans *m.* 1920 ———
   2. David Grant Evans (1868–1911) *m.* 1890 Pauline Holton (1868–1944)
   3. Thomas Tilgham O. Holton (1839–1925) *m.* 1862 Ellen Margaret Campbell
            (1833–1921)
   4. William B. Holton (1799–1881) *m.* 1825 Sarah Price Tilgham (1804–1890)
   5. Jacob Morris Tilgman *c.* (1770–1821) *m.* 1798 Sarah Price Lewis (–pr. to 1859)
   6. Thomas Tilman (1740–   ) *m. c.* 1760 Susan Moon
   7. Thomas Tilman, Sr. (1720–1813) *m.* Lucy Hix (–1763)
   8. Robert Tilman (1675–1738) *m.* 1718 Hannah Morris
   9. Roger Tilgman (1650–   ) *m.* 1674 Winifred Austin
  10. CHRISTOPHER TILGHAM *c.* (1600–   ) *m.* Ruth Devonshire
   Service: Landed Proprietor of James City Co., Va.
   Reference: Tilgham Family Register, by Col. Stephen F. Tilgham; Holton Family
            History by Thomas T. Holton; Affidavit of dates and family history filed
            with Application.

6556   PEW, Mrs. Frederick C.   Recorded 1947
            3139 North Mount Curve, Altadena, California
   1. Lydia G. Smith, *m.* 1897 Frederick C. Pew
   2. William Smith (1839–1917) *m.* 1869 Caroline Butler (1841–1938)
   3. Charles Butler (1804–1886) *m.* 1829 Dorcas P. Patt (1807–1891)
   4. Aaron Pratt (1765–1835) *m.* 1788 Rosanna Pratt (1760–1816)
   5. Gerard Pratt (1739–1825) *m.* 1763 Dorcas Ashley (1736–1813)
   6. David Ashley (1692–1757) *m.* 1722 Mary Dewey (1701–1774)
   7. Adijah Dewey (1666–1742) *m.* 1688 Sarah Root (1670–   )
   8. Thomas Dewey, Jr. (1640–1690) *m.* 1663 Constance Hawes (1642–1702/3)
   9. THOMAS DEWEY, SR. *d.* 1648, *m.* Frances Clark
   Service: Came to Mass. Bay Colony, 1633, and settled in Dorchester, Mass.
            Removed to Windsor, Conn.
   Reference: Ashley Genealogy, Dewey Genealogy, Hist. of Northampton.

5847   PHILLIPS, Mrs. Frank Forest   Recorded 1929
            510 Adams Street, Ironton, Ohio
   1. Beulah Wyatt (1884–   ) *m.* 1912 Frank Forest Phillips
   2. Joseph Wadkins Wyatt (1847–1926) *m.* 1873 Mary Augusta Wilson (1852–   )
   3. Wm. Wilson (1820–1880) *m.* 1843 Hannah Shepardson Bailor (1821–1873)
   4. John Barton (1784–1859) *m.* 1820 Laodicea Eddy (1793–1868)
   5. Nathaniel Eddy (1768–1803) *m.* 1793 Hannah Shepardson (1765–1813)
   6. Nathan Eddy (1733–1804) *m.* 1757 Eunice Sampson (1737–   )
   7. Samuel Eddy (1696–1746) *m.* 1732 Lydia Alden (1710–1802)
   8. John Alden (1671–1730) *m.* 1701 Hannah White (1681–   )
   9. Joseph Alden (1627–1696) *m.* 1659 Mary Sunmons
  10. JOHN ALDEN (1599–1687) *m.* 1622 Priscilla Mullins (1602–165–)
   Service: Treasurer of Colony; member of Council; member of Council of War for
            Plymouth
   Reference: Eddy Bulletin No. 14; Eddy book of 1884, page 262; The Alden Kindred of
            America.

6085 PITCHER, Mrs. Charles W.   Recorded 1935, New Jersey
     New Jersey State Hospital, Trenton, New Jersey
1. Helen E. Martin *m.* 1918 Charles W. Pitcher
2. Thomas C. Martin (1852–) *m.* 1882 Carrie E. Doane (1861–1927)
3. George W. Doane (1827–1899) *m.* 1846 Mary E. Shattuck (1828–1905)
4. Leonard Doane (1798–1868) *m.* 1819 Harriet White (1801–1890)
5. Samuel D. Doane (1774–1809) *m.* 1797 Sally Lombard (1778–1867)
6. Nehemiah Doane (1737–1785) *m.* 1766 Lydia (Higgins) Dill (1741–)
7. Solomon Doane (1705–1789) *m.* 1727 Alice Higgins
8. Samuel Doane (1673–1756) *m.* 1696 Martha Hamblen (1672–)
9. John Doane (1635–1708) *m.* 1662 Hannah Bangs (1644–)
10. JOHN DOANE (1590–1685) *m.* Lydia
Service: Member of Gov. Bradford's Council, 1632; one of the founders of Eastham, Mass.
Reference: The Doane Family, by Alfred A. Doane; Mayflower Descendants.

6075 PITTMAN, Mrs. C. E.   Recorded 1934, Georgia
     95 North Broad Street, Commerce, Georgia
1. Frances Brooke *m.* 1902 Clarence E. Pittman
2. George W. Brooks (1816–1890) *m.* 1873 Elizabeth McCarter (1847–1900)
3. James Brooks, Jr. (1782–1832) *m.* 1800 Judith Seward (1785–1830)
4. James Brooks, Sr. (–1812) *m.* 1777 Sarah Woolford (1757–1831)
5. Roger Woolford (1730–1800) *m.* 1750 Elizabeth Jones
6. Thomas Woolford (1700–1751) *m.* Sarah Stevens
7. John Stevens, Jr. (1670–) *m.* 1695 Ann Brooke Cooke
8. JOHN STEVENS, SR. (1645–1692) *m.* Dorothy Preston (–1710)
Service: Member of House of Burgesses, 1678–1681, Dorchester County, Md.
Reference: Jones History of Dorchester County, Maryland, p. 148; Maryland Historical Society.

6021 PLUMB, Miss Margaret Grant   Recorded 1932
     195 Claremont Avenue, New York, N. Y.
1. Miss Margaret Grant Plumb
2. Henry Grant Plumb (1847–1930) *m.* 1886 Mary Eliz. Bogart Leverich Witte (1856–1901)
3. Melchior Conrad Gerhard Witte (1813–1883) *m.* 1851 Mary Eliz. Bogard Leverich (1831–1904)
4. John Leverich (1789–1858) *m.* 1814 Aletta Berrien (1788–1873)
5. Jesse Leverich (1756–1829) *m.* 1780 Ghashe (Grace) Berrien (1759–1831)
6. William Leverich (1723–1787) *m.* 1751 Dorothy Morse (1728–1814)
7. John Leverich (1696–1790) *m.* 1720 Amy Moore
8. John Leverich *m.* Hannan ———
9. Caleb Leverich (–1717) *m.* Martha ———
10. REV. WILLIAM LEVERICH (1605–1677) *m.* ———
Service: First Minister of Dover, N. H.; Minister of Pres. Church.
Reference: Annals of Newtown, by Abraham Riker; Gen. of Leverich Family; His. of Pres. Church.

6250 PLUMLEY, Hon. Chas. A., LL.D.   Recorded 1939, Vermont
     12 Prospect St., Northfield, Vermont
     County of Washington
1. Chas. Albert Plumley (1875–) *m.* Emile Adele Stevens
2. Frank Plumley (1844–1924) *m.* 1871 Lavina L. Fletcher (1848–1906)
3. Hiram Fletcher (1811–1868) *m.* Mary Smith (1819–1880)
4. Ebenezer Fletcher (1782–1834) *m.* Biby Spaulding
5. Ebenezer Fletcher (1761–1831) *m.* Mary Cummings (1758–1812)
6. Samuel Cummings (1718–1796) *m.* 1741 Sarah Spaulding (1723–1801)
7. John Cummings (1682–1759) *m.* 1705 Elizabeth Adams (1680–1759)
8. Peletiah Adams (1646–) *m.* Ruth ———
9. Thomas Adams
10. HENRY ADAMS (–1646) *m.* ———
Service:
Reference: Desc. of Robt. Fletcher of Concord, Mass., by E. H. Fletcher; Gen. Dict. of First Settlers of N. E.; Col. Fam. of the U. S.; Emigrants, etc., by Hotten; Hist. of New Ipswich; Gen. Hist. of Henry Adams.

5865 POTTS, Miss Florence H.   Recorded 1929, New Jersey
          361 Garfield Avenue, Trenton, New Jersey
      1. Florence Henrietta Potts
      2. Morris L. Potts (1884–1922) *m.* 1915 Florence Edwards (1890–1918)
      3. Joseph G. Edwards (1851–1923) *m.* 1877 Achsah Ewan Cox (1851–1915)
      4. John E. Cox (1815–1892) *m.* 1846 Elizabeth L. Curlis (1823–1891)
      5. William Curlis (1797–1858) *m.* Mary S. Lippincott (1803–1880)
      6. Jacob Lippincott (1778–) *m.* Elizabeth Stockton
      7. William Stockton (1750–) *m.* 1775 Mary Naigle
      8. William Stockton (1712–1781) *m.* 1736 Mary Bryan (1720–1806)
      9. Job Stockton (1676–1732) *m.* Anna Pitty (–1746)
     10. Richard Stockton (–1707) *m.* Abigail
     Service: Commissioned Lieut. in 1665.
     Reference: Stockton Genealogy in N. J. State Library.

6105 POUCH, Mrs. William H.   Recorded 1936, New York
          135 Central Park West, New York, N. Y.
      1. Helena R. Hellwig *m.* William H. Pouch
      2. Maurice Hellwig (1851–) *m.* 1873 Helen E. Abbott (1851–1927)
      3. James E. Abbott (1828–1881) *m.* 1850 Rebecca Wilson (1827–1916)
      4. Isaac Abbott (1805–1888) *m.* 1827 Elizabeth Fisher (1807–1871)
      5. William Abbott (1783–1862) *m.* 1804 Mary Patterson (1784–1855)
      6. John Abbott (1759–1840) *m.* 1779 Alice Akers (1755–1845)
      7. William Abbott (1735–1793) *m.* Catherine Prall (1739–1823)
      8. James Abbott (–1765) *m.* Catherine Brown
      9. James Abbott (1660–) *m.* 1690 Martha
     Service: Early Settler.
     Reference: Hempstead Town Records; Col. Dames of the 17th Century.

6509 POWELL, Mrs. Herbert B.   Recorded 1945
          Letart Falls, Ohio
      1. Genevieve Wagner *m.* Herbert B. Powell
      2. Charles Newman Wagner (1870–1924) *m.* 1891 Lillie Leota Wolfe (1868–)
      3. Alfred Wagner (1826–1903) *m.* 1853 Regina Sayre (1834–1897)
      4. Daniel Sayre (1789–1836) *m.* 1807 Sinah Hayman (1789–1847)
      5. Daniel Sayre (1760–1824) *m.* 1785 Sarah Hall (1762–)
      6. David Sayre (1736–1826) *m.* 1758 Hannah Frazier (1741–1826)
      7. Daniel Sayre (–1760) *m.* Rebecca Bond
      8. Samuel Sayre (–bef. 1707) *m.* ——— Lyons
      9. Daniel Sayre (–1708) *m.* 1659 Hannah Foster
     10. Thomas Sayre (1597–1670) *m.* ———
     Service: Selectman in Lynn, Mass., 1638, and given 60 acres of land; Founder of
          Southampton, N. Y.; 1651 chosen one of the Governors of Southampton,
          N. Y.; served in French and Colonial Wars.

6308 PRITCHARD, Mary   Recorded 1940, Georgia
          187 Fourteenth Street N. E., Atlanta, Georgia
      1. Mary Pritchard
      2. William Latham Pritchard (1877–) *m.* 1902 Ruby Cornelia Jones (1877–)
      3. James Dunwody Jones (1842–1904) *m.* 1870 Mary Cornelia Ashley (1848–1924)
      4. John Jones, D.D. (1815–1893) *m.* 1841 Jane Adaline Dunwody (1820–1884)
      5. Col. James Dunwody (1789–1833) *m.* Elizabeth West Smith (1794–1879)
      6. James Smith (1766–1854) *m.* 1793 Seymour Munro (1775–1828)
      7. James Lawrence Smith (1736–1792) *m.* 1763 Margaret Moore Sanders (1738–1775)
      8. James Smith (1715–1768) *m.* Margaret Lawrence *c.* (1718–aft. 1736)
      9. Thomas Smith II (1663–1738) *m.* (2nd) Mary Hyrne (1690–1776)
     10. Thomas Smith, d. 1694, *m.* Schenckingh, d. bef. 1688
     Service: Gov. Province of Carolina; member of Grand Council; Landgrave; a Lord
          Proprietor.
     Reference: "Hist. and Gen. of Bayard, Houston and Bolton Fams.," by J. G. B.
          Bulloch; "Hist. and Gen. Habersham Fam.," Bulloch; Records of St.
          George's Parish, Dorchester, S. C.; South Car. Hist. and Gen. Mag.

6421 PROCTOR, Hon. Mortimer Robinson   Recorded 1943
      Proctor, Vermont
1. Mortimer Robinson Proctor *m.* Lillian W. Bryan
2. Hon. Fletcher D. Proctor (1860–1911) *m.* 1886 Minnie E. Robinson
3. Col. Redfield Proctor (1831–1908) *m.* 1858 Emily J. Dutton (1835–)
4. Jabez Proctor (1780–1839) *m.* 1817 Betsy Parker (1792–1881)
5. Capt. Leonard Proctor (1734–1827) *m.* Mary Keep (1743–1827)
6. Thomas Proctor (1698–1750) *m.* 1722 Hannah Barron (1703–1774)
7. Samuel Proctor (1665–1740) *m.* Sarah ——— (–1757)
8. Robert Proctor (–1697) *m.* 1645 Jane Hildreth (–1688)
Service: Concord, Mass., 1643; Chelmsford, Mass., 1654, and one of the organizers
      there.
Reference: Vt. of Today, Stone; Enc. Vt. Biography, Dodge; Twn. Rec., Proctorsville;
      V. R., Montpelier, Vt.; Twn. Rec. Westford, Chelmsford, Mass.

6685 PROCTOR, Mrs. Creasy K.   Recorded 1950
      2008 Hillsboro St., Raleigh, North Carolina
1. Matilda Culpeper (1889–) *m.* Creasy K. Proctor
2. Cicero Culpeper (1861–1943) *m.* 1885 Margaret Lancaster (1860–1947)
3. Henry H. Culpeper (1820–1889) *m.* 1852 Catherine Braswell (1828–1868)
4. John Braswell (1801–1848) *m.* 1820 Elizabeth Taylor (1803–1888)
5. Zadock Braswell (1779–1852) *m.* 1800 Sally Howell (1780–1803)
6. Benjamin Braswell (1744–1792) *m.* 1765 Mary I. Mercer (1740–1792)
7. James Bracwell (1692–) *m.* ———
8. Robert Bracwell (–1696) *m.* Susannah (–1726)
9. Rev. Robert Bracwell, Sr. (1612–1688)
Service: Minister, House of Burgesses.
Reference: Braswell Family as traced by Elizabeth Braswell Pearsall; Mr. Chas. A.
      O'Connor, N. Y. City.

5866 PROPST, Mrs. Edward   Recorded 1929, Illinois
      216 Crawford Street, Paris, Illinois
1. Malina Niles *m.* Edward Propst
2. Augustus H. Niles (1848–1921) *m.* 1869 Rosa E. Colborn (1849–)
3. Stephen B. Niles (1818–1890) *m.* 1838 Malina B. Gardner (1819–1863)
4. John Gardner (1791–1835) *m.* 1816 Elizabeth Worden (1799–1859)
5. Deacon John Worden (–1802) *m.* 1772 Abigail (–1828)
6. John Worden (1746–1779) *m.* Elizabeth Babcock (1749–1808)
7. Peter Worden (1609–1681) *m.* Mary Winston (–1687)
8. Peter Worden I (1569–1639)
Service: Landed Proprietor and soldier in Indian Wars, 1648.
Reference: Worden Genealogy.

6456 PROUT, Mrs. Stephen Edward   Recorded 1944
      538 Dryden Road, Zanesville, Ohio
1. Evelyn Eberle *m.* Stephen Edward Prout
2. George W. Eberle (1863–) *m.* 1891 Elizabeth Josselyn (1866–)
3. Amos Piatt Josselyn (1820–1885) *m.* 1859 Elizabeth Handley (1831–1901)
4. Abraham Josselyn (1793–1852) *m.* 1819 Mary Piatt (1802–1891)
5. Joshua Josselyn (1761–1818) *m.* 1788 Sarah Chapman (1771–1858)
6. Nathaniel Josselyn (1722–1790) *m.* 1751 Sarah Low (1725–)
7. Nathaniel Josselyn (1686–) *m.* 1711 Frances Yellings (–1755)
8. Henry Josselyn (1652–1739) *m.* 1676 Abigail Stockbridge (1660–1743)
9. Henry Josselyn (1615–1670) *m.* 1648 Beatrice Lampson (1623–1711)
10. Thomas Josselyn (1592–1660) *m.* 1614 Rebecca Marlowe
Service: A Founder of Hanover, Mass.; subscriber to the town covenant in Lancaster,
      Mass., 1654; he died in Lancaster, will recorded at Cambridge, Mass.
Reference: D.A.R. Lin. Book, Vol. 139, pg. 288; Dean's Hist. Situate; Berries' Hist.
      Hanover, Mass.; Lincoln's Hist of Hingham, Mass.

6528 PUGH, Delia Hanford Biddle   Recorded 1946
         130 West Broad Street, Burlington, New Jersey
      1. Delia H. Biddle *m.* 1931 Hugh Pugh
      2. John C. Biddle (1859–1946) *m.* 1889 Delia H. Sturges (1865–1941)
      3. Charles J. Biddle (1819–1873) *m.* 1856 Emma Mather (1830–1918)
      4. Nicholas Biddle (1786–1844) *m.* 1811 Jane M. Craig (1793–1856)
      5. Charles Biddle (1745–1821) *m.* 1778 Hannah Shepard (1762–1825)
      6. William Biddle 3rd (1697–1756) *m.* 1730 Mary Scull (1709–1789)
      7. William Biddle 2nd (1669–1743) *m.* 1691 Lydia Wardell
      8. WILLIAM BIDDLE (1630–1712) *m.* 1665 Sarah Kempe, *d.* 1709
      Service: Proprietor of New Jersey, first purchase of land in 1676.
      Reference: Descendants of William Biddle.

5850 QUARTERMAN, Mary Brumly   Recorded 1929
         Winder, Georgia
      1. Mary Brumly (1867–) *m.* 1893 W. H. Quarterman
      2. Alexander Brevard Brumly (1831–1879) *m.* 1866 Ellen D. Robarts (1843–1911)
      3. James William Robarts (–1864) *m.* 1838 Sophia Louisa Gibson (–1847)
      4. David Robarts *m.* 1810 Eliza Greene Low (1785–1868)
      5. Philip Low (1755–1785) *m.* 1783 Mary Sharp Jones, wid. (–1793)
      6. Anthony Low *m.* 1754 Phoebe Greene (1732–1759)
      7. Philip Greene (1705–1791) *m.* 1731 Elizabeth Wicker (1706–1776)
      8. Job Greene
      9. DR. JOHN GREENE (1590–)
      Service: Dr. John Greene.
      Reference: Heitman's Historical Register Greenes of Rhode Island.

6314 QUIN, Robert Smith   Recorded 1940, Georgia
         71 Montgomery Ferry Drive N. E., Atlanta, Georgia
      1. Robert Smith Quin *m.* 1917 *Thomas Egleston Perdue*
      2. Hugh Pharr Quin (1847–1922) *m.* 1879 Louisa Toombs DuBose (1857–1931)
      3. Dr. Langdon Cheves Quin (1816–1850) *m.* 1838 Frances Jane McLaughlin
         (1821–1894)
      4. John Candor McLaughlin (1793–1838) *m.* 1814 Margaret Pharr (1792–1872)
      5. David McLaughlin *c.* (1760–1838) *m.* Jane Nicholson, *d. c.* 1816
      6. John Nicholson (1751–1818) *m.* 1770 Penelope Mann, *d. c.* 1818
      7. Robert Nicholson 5th (1725–1797) *m.* Mary Waters (1720–1793)
      8. Robert Nicholson IV *m.* Elizabeth Flood
      9. Henry Flood, *d. c.* 1740
      10. Thomas Flood, Jr., *d.* 1718, *m.* Ann, *d. c.* 1723
      11. Capt. Thomas Flood
      12. COL. JOHN FLOOD, *b. ca.* 1590, *d.* 1661, *m.* bef. 1625 Margaret Finch (widow)
      Service: Colony Interpreter, 1646; Col. of Militia, Surry Co., 1652; Colonist of Virginia,
         1610; represented James City in the Grand Assembly.
      Reference: William & Mary Quart., Vol. IX, VII, VIII, XII; Bruton Parish Register,
         Williamsburg, Va.

6753 RAINEY, Mrs. Frederick A.   Recorded 1952, Illinois
         Lincoln Drive at Johnson, Philadelphia 44, Pennsylvania
      1. Emily Maria Eaton *m.* 1922 F. A. Rainey
      2. Rev. W. W. Eaton (1862–1925) *m.* 1889 Frances Maria Sweet
      3. Simon Elon Sweet (1836–1922) *m.* 1857 Sallie Maria Noxon (1836–1930)
      4. James Pascho Noxon (1798–1876) *m.* 1833 Anna Wilkinson (1809–1892)
      5. Jeremiah Wilkinson (1771–1812) *m.* 1808 Phoebe Eldridge (abt. 1788–1814)
      6. Jeremiah Wilkinson 2nd (1741–1831) *m.* Hope Mosher (1751–1774)
      7. Jonathan Mosher, Jr. (1726–) *m.* 1749 Ann Mott (–1810)
      8. Jonathan Mosher, Sr. (1699–) *m.* 1720 Isabel Potter (1703–)
      9. Joseph Mosher (1670–1754) *m.* 1695 Lydia Taber (1673–1743)
      10. Philip Taber (–1692) *m.* abt. 1668 Mary Cooke (–1714)
      11. John Cook (–bef. 1708) *m.* Sarah Warren
      12. RICHARD WARREN, *d.* 1628, *m.* Elizabeth Jarratt
      Service: Signer of Mayflower Compact, 1620.
      Reference: Wilkinson Genealogy, pgs. 132–3, 171–3, 409–413; Mosher Genealogy,
         15; Dartmouth V. R., 167–188; The Mayflower Descendant, Vol. 10,
         pgs. 44–5; 16: 22, 228, 229, 230; Vol. 16: 22, 230, 231; Colonial Families
         of America 2: 22 (1928).

5991   RANDOLPH, Mrs. Raymond B.   Recorded 1931
           831 Carteret Avenue, Trenton, New Jersey
       1. Louise Ficht Fitz *m.* 1900 Raymond B. Randolph
       2. Ralph Ficht (1849–1930) *m.* 1874 Nellie L. Mester (1854–1890)
       3. Casimer Otto Ficht (1819–1902) *m.* 1845 Elizabeth Rebecca Hubbard (1825–1906)
       4. John Hubbard (1784–1860) *m.* Eleanor Augustine (1785–1865)
       5. Jacob Hubbard (1744–1807) *m.* 1765 Rebecca Smart (1739–1819)
       6. James Hubbard (1706–   ) *m.* 1729 Altje Ryder (1718–   )
       7. James Hubbard *m.* 1698 Rachel Bergen
       8. Sergeant James Hubbard (1613–1690) *m.* 1664 Elizabeth Bayles (–1693)
       9. Henry Hubbard *m.* Margaret
       Service: Magistrate Kings Co.
       Reference: Hubbard Gen., pages 6, 37; History of New Jersey Medicine.

6099   RANKIN, Miss Mary Burt   Recorded 1936, New York
           1234 Delaware Avenue, Buffalo, New York
       1. Mary Burt Rankin
       2. William Rankin (1838–1919) *m.* 1865 Mary Louise Wilson (1848–1904)
       3. Austin Wilson (1812–1894) *m.* 1837 Miranda Olcott (1820–1919)
       4. Abel Olcott (1793–1867) *m.* 1814 Betsey Clark (1794–1886)
       5. Abel Olcott (1768–1813) *m.* 1792 Marcy Rounds
       6. Thomas Olcott, Jr. (1722–1788) *m.* 1760 Lydia Humphrey
       7. Thomas Olcott (1697–1786) *m.* Elizabeth Ashley (1708–   )
       8. Thomas Olcott (–1712) *m.* 1695 Hannah Barnard (1662–1755)
       9. Samuel Olcott (–1704) *m.* 1654 Sarah Stocking
      10. Thomas Olcott (1609–1659) *m.* Abigail Porter (1615–1673)
       Service: Soldier in Pequot War of 1637.
       Reference: Conn. Historical Society, Vol. 14; The Colonial History of Hartford;
           Descendants of Thomas Olcott, by Goodwins.

6684   READ, Miss Mary Gaines   Recorded 1950
           187 West Garfield, Baton Rouge, Louisiana
       1. Mary Gaines Read (1923–   )
       2. Daniel W. Read, Jr. (1892–   ) *m.* 1921 Audrey Sparks (1887–   )
       3. Daniel W. Read, Sr. (1861–1918) *m.* 1891 Laura Moorman (1864–   )
       4. Granville L. Moorman (1826–   ) *m.* Mary James
       5. John C. Moorman (1796–   ) *m.* 1821 Catherine Leftwich
       6. Samuel Moorman (1772–1835) *m.* 1790 Judith Clark
       7. Zachariah Moorman *m.* 1755 Elizabeth N. Terrill (1738–1773)
       8. Henry Terrill (1690–1761) *m.* 1730 Ann Chiles
       9. John Chiles *m.* Mary Boucher
      10. Walter Chiles, Jr. *m.* Mary Page
      11. Col. John Page, Pilgrim 1627, *b.* Eng. 1601, *m.* Alise Lukins
       Service:
       Reference:

6166   REDWINE, Lucy Reagan   Recorded 1937
       1. Lucy Reagan (1889–   ) *m.* Hill Parks Redwine
       2. E. J. Reagan (1853–1926) *m.* 1876 Lula Lyon Reagan (1858–   )
       3. Joseph Reagan (1817–1904) *m.* 1843 Martha Ann Davis Reagan (1823–1896)
       4. James Reagan, Jr. (1780–1855) *m.* 1805 Mary Dandridge (Morrison) (1784–1859)
       5. Joseph Higginbotham Morrison (–1802) *m.* Frances Graves (H) Morrison
           (–179–)
       6. Capt. Aron Higginbotham *m.* Clara Graves Higginbotham
       7. Francis Graves, Jr. *m.* Ann
       8. Francis Graves, Sr. *m.* Jane
       9. Captain Thomas Graves, *d.* 1635, *m.* Katherine
       Service: Member of First Legislative Assembly in America; Sat in Smythe's Hundred
           at Jamestown, July 30, 1619.
       Reference: Hist. of Ga., Clark Howell, Vol. 4, pgs. 644–645; William & Mary Quar.,
           second series, Vol. 15, No. 4; Vol. XXVI, 3, 4; XXVII, 124; Records of
           Essex Co., Va., O. B. 1703–1708, p. 69, deeds, D. B. 12, p. 310; 13, p. 121;
           the records of the London Co. of Va., III, 121.

6400   REED, Mrs. Nelson A.   Recorded 1943
       Yonkers, New York
       1. Mary Edna Field *m.* Nelson A. Reed
       2. Alfred Frary Field (1843–1929) *m.* 1893 (2nd) Katharine Hendrick (1855–1932)
       3. Frary Field (1810–1884) *m.* 1840 Julia Ann Comins (1820–1900)
       4. Sylvanus Field (1776–1860) *m.* 1805 Cynthia Field (1787–1854)
       5. Jonathan Field (1750–1833) *m.* 1773 Sarah Kellogg (1753–1832)
       6. Capt. Jonathan Field (1697–1781) *m.* 1739 (2nd) Esther Smith (1710–1795)
       7. Capt. Joseph Field (1658–1736) *m.* 1683 Joanna Wyatt (1663–1722)
       8. ZACHARIAH FIELD (1596–1666) *m.* 1641 Mary ——— (–1670)
       Service: Pequot War; Settler Hadley, Mass. (now Hatfield).
       Reference: Field Gen., Pierce; Genealogical No. 4524, Vol. I, Vol. 2.

6073   REES, Mrs. Samuel M.   Recorded 1934, Georgia
       137 Huntington Rd. N. E., Atlanta, Georgia
       1. Margaret Caldwell *m.* 1911 Samuel M. Rees
       2. Andrew J. Caldwell (1858–1909) *m.* 1890 Rosanna McCarthy (1869–1928)
       3. Samuel B. Caldwell (1822–1901) *m.* 1849 Susan E. Roe (1826–1907)
       4. Peter Roe (1789–1877) *m.* 1819 Susan E. Williams (1793–1853)
       5. Jonas Williams (1753–1828) *m.* 1779 Abigail Brewster (1759–1804)
       6. Samuel Brewster (1718–1802) *m.* 1759 Mary Wood (1722–1807)
       7. Nathaniel Brewster (1689–1732) *m.* 1712 Phoebe Smith
       8. Timothy Brewster (1658–1743) *m.* 1685 Mary Hawkins (–1732)
       9. Nathaniel Brewster (1619–1690) *m.* 1654 Sarah Ludlow (1634–1665)
       10. ROGER LUDLOW (1590–1665) *m.* Mary Cogan (1607–)
       Service: Member of Connecticut Const. Convention; founder of Fairfield, 1651;
              First Deputy Governor of Connecticut.
       Reference: New England Register, Savage, Vol. III, p. 129; Schenk's History of
              Fairfield, Vol. I, p. 303; Stile's History of Ancient Windsor.

6466   REESE, Mrs. Alfred Irwin   Recorded 1945
       High Trees, Caversham Road, Bryn Mawr, Pennsylvania
       1. Jeanette Walton *m.* Alfred Irwin Reese
       2. John Gardener Walton (1865–1924) *m.* 1900 Clara Betts (1868–)
       3. John Brooks Betts (1836–1931) *m.* 1863 Jeanette Carter (1844–1921)
       4. Richard Kinsey Betts (1806–1890) *m.* 1835 (2nd) Ann Brooks (1807–1850)
       5. John Brooks (1772–1843) *m.* 1802 Elizabeth Baker (1784–1850)
       6. Samuel Baker (1748–1814) *m.* 1777 Elizabeth Head (1749–)
       7. Samuel Baker (1706–1760) *m.* 1741 Elizabeth Burroughs (1715–)
       8. Samuel Baker (1676–1725) *m.* 1703 Rachel Warder (1670–1760)
       9. HENRY BAKER (–1705) *m.* Margaret Hardman (–1691)
       Service: To Burlington, N. J., in 1684; took up land in Bucks Co., Pa., and is marked
              as "first purchaser" on Holme's map; Justice of the Peace, 1789.
       Reference: N. J. Archives, 1725; Col. Rec. of Pa., vol. 4; Betts & Allied Fam.; (D.A.R.
              Lib., D. C.).

6468   REESE, Gwynne Harper   Recorded 1945
       High Trees, Caversham Road, Bryn Mawr, Pennsylvania
       (JUNIOR MEMBERSHIP)
       1. Gwynne Harper Reese
       2. Alfred Irwin Reese (1896–) *m.* 1935 Jeanette Walton (1904–)
       3. John Gardener Walton (1865–1924) *m.* 1900 Clara Betts (1868–)
       4. John Brooks Betts (1836–1931) *m.* 1863 Jeanette Carter (1844–1921)
       5. Richard K. Betts (1807–1890) *m.* 1835 (2nd) Anna Brooks (1807–1850)
       6. Samuel Cary Betts (1776–1861) *m.* 1798 Grace Biles (1776–1848)
       7. William Biles (1749–1778) *m.* 1766 Hannah Kirkbride (1743–1794)
       8. Charles Biles (1702–) *m.* 1728 Anna Maria Baker (1704–1761)
       9. Samuel Baker (1676–1725) *m.* 1703 Rachel Warder (1670–1760)
       10. WILLOUGHBY WARDER (–1724) *m.* Mary ———
       Service: Came from Isle of Wight with wife and three children, to Bucks Co., Pa.,
              before 1688.
       Reference: Same as No. 6466, Henry Baker.

6348 REEVES, Mrs. T. Earle   Recorded 1941, New Jersey
      Centerton Road, Elmer, New Jersey
1. Edna V. Shaw *m.* 1911 T. Earle Reeves
2. Edward Collings Shaw (1862–1930) *m.* 1888 Elizabeth L. Veazey (1861–1929)
3. Thomas Ward Veazey (1836–1910) *m.* 1858 Mary R. Baisler (1839–1871)
4. George Clinton Veazey (1807–1854) *m.* 1834 Lydia Gilpin Hirons (1816–1877)
5. John Hirons (1785–1850) *m.* 1812 Ann Ferris Gilpin (1791–1871)
6. Edward Gilpin (1760–1844) *m.* 1788 Lydia Grubb, *d.* 1831
7. Vincent Cilpin (1732–1810) *m.* 1758 Abigail Woodward (1738–1815)
8. Joseph Gilpin (1703/4–1792) *m.* 1729 Mary Caldwell
9. Joseph Gilpin (1664–1741) *m.* 1691 Hannah Glover (1675–1757)
10. THOMAS GILPIN came to America 1695

Service: Founded first Friends' Meeting in Chester Co., Pa.
Reference: Genealogical Chart of Family of Vincent Gilpin, by George Gilpin, published 1885.

5910 REHRENDS, Cora Talbot   Recorded 1930, Texas
      4943 Victor Street, Dallas, Texas
1. John Fletcher Talbot (1827–1888) *m.* 1865 Elinor Ann Derrick (1839–1905)
2. John Derrick (1794–1858) *m.* 1831 Euphemia Eliz. Walker (1813–1866)
3. Zachariah Walker (1755–1818) *m. ca.* 1780 Ruth DuVall (1760–1844)
4. Gideon Walker (1734–1809) *m.* 1754 Priscilla DuVall (1737–1798)
5. Mareen DuVall (1702–1750) *m.* 1724 Ruth Howard (1709–1783)
6. Joseph Howard (1676–1730) *m.* 1708 Margery Keith
7. CAPT CORNELIUS HOWARD (1637–1680) *m.* 1660 Elizabeth Todd

Service: See Maryland Archives.
Reference: Welsh, Hyatt Kindred; Colonial Families, Vol. V; Col. Fam. Southern States.

6516 REPP, Mrs. John J.   Recorded 1946
      926 S. 60th Street, Philadelphia, Pennsylvania
1. Miriam Colbert *m.* 1899 John J. Repp
2. William Colbert (1824–   ) *m.* 1868 Mary Ann McGinley (1852–1897)
3. Rev. Wm. Colbert (1764–1833) *m.* 1804 Elizabeth Stroud (1784–1849)
4. Col. Jacob Stroud (1735–1806) *m.* 1761 Elizabeth McDowell (1743–1811)
5. John McDowell (1714–1779) *m.* Hannay DePuy (1719–   )
6. Nicholas DePuy (1682–1762) *m.* 1707 Wyntji Roosa (1682–   )
7. Moses DePuy (1657–1714) *m.* 1680 Marie Wynkoop (1660–1724)
8. NICHOLAS DEPUY *m.* Catalina DeVos, *d.* aft. 1691

Service: In Capt. Cornelius Steenwyck's Co., 1673.
Reference: Monroe County, Penna., History.

6249 REXFORD, Mrs. Fred A.
      Mt. Vernon Street, New Port, Vermont
1. Joyce Lottie Reed (1891–   ) *m.* 1918 Fred Albert Rexford
2. Thomas Vernon Reed (1866–   ) *m.* 1888 Mary Caroline Woodward (1869–   )
3. Oscar Daniel Woodward (1838–1878) *m.* Caroline Amelia Huntington (1829–1881)
4. Seth Huntington Esq., 1st (1796–1875) *m.* 1825 Mary Hovey (1803–1879)
5. Thomas Huntington (1767–1811) *m.* 1795 Submit Huntington (1769–1846)
6. ——— Huntington (1738–1810) *m.* 1760 Mary Dimock (1739–   )
7. Thomas Huntington (1688–1755) *m.* 1733 Mehetabel Johnson (–1740)
8. Thomas Huntington (1664–1732) *m.* 1686 Elizabeth Backus (–1728)
9. Christopher Huntington (–1691) *m.* 1652 Ruth Rockwell
10. Simon Huntington (1583–1633) *m.* 1627 Margaret Baret
11. RICHARD HUNTINGTON (1564–   ) *m.* Alice Loring

Service:
Reference: Huntington Fam. Hist.; Hist. of Norwich, Eng.; Hist. of Roxbury, Mass.; Hist. of Mansfield, Conn.; His. of Roxbury, Vt.; His. of Compton Co., by Channell.

6628 REYNOLDS, Mrs. G. D. B.   Recorded 1949
          Albemarle, North Carolina
    1. Elizabeth Parker *m.* 1913 George Dana B. Reynolds
    2. Julius C. Parker (1855–1939) *m.* 1878 Frances I. Dry (1862–1927)
    3. Arnold Parker (1824–1908) *m.* 1846 Lucinda Stokes (1826–1897)
    4. Howell Parker, Jr. (1792–1859) *m.* 1813 Nancy Newbold (1793–1861)
    5. Howell Parker, Sr. (1757–1796) *m.* Elizabeth Loftin (1756–1831)
    6. Drury Parker (1722/24–1789) *m.* Elizabeth Barham
    7. Richard Parker III (1690/1700–1751) *m.* 1721 Mrs. Judith Wyche, *d.* bef. 1731
    8. Richard Parker II, *d.* 1750, *m.* Mary ———
    9. RICHARD PARKER I, *d.* 1677, *m.* 1668 Mrs. Judith Hunt
    Service: Granted 314 acres of land on Backwater Swamp, Va., for having brought
          seven persons into the Colony.
    Reference: Recorded Wills and Deeds.

6338 RICKARD, David Thomas   Recorded 1941, New Jersey
          Judson College, Rangoon, India
                          (JUNIOR)
    1. David Thomas Rickard
    2. Samuel Harmer Rickard (1895–) *m.* 1923 Ada Pauline Thomas, *b.* 1901
    3. John Godbou Thomas (1875–) *m.* 1898 Maria Taylor Collins, *b.* 1876
    4. Richard S. Collins (1841–1919) *m.* 1867 Adaline S. Green (1841–1927)
    5. John Collins (1806–1900) *m.* 1831 Elizabeth Clark (1809–1855)
    6. Levi Collins (1772–1813) *m.* 1801 Asenath Lake (1783–1860)
    7. Daniel Lake *c.* (1740–1799) *m.* 1764 Sarah Lucas
    8. Daniel Lake *c.* (1697–1774) *m.* 1730 Gartara Steelman
    9. William Lake, *d.* 1717, *m.* Sarah
   10. John Lake, *d.* bef. 1696, *m.* Anne Spicer, *d.* aft. 1709
   11. THOMAS SPICER, *d.* 1658, *m.* Ann
    Service: Signed Compact at Newport, 1638; Treas. of Portsmouth, 1642; Original
          Proprietor of Gravesend (Brooklyn), 1645; Magistrate of Gravesend, 1658.
    Reference: "Genealogy of Lake Family," by Adams and Risley.

6337 RICKARD, Donald Collins   Recorded 1941, New Jersey
          Judson College, Rangoon, India
                          (JUNIOR)
    1. Donald Collins Rickard
    2. Samuel Harme Rickard (1895–) *m.* 1923 Ada Pauline Thomas, *b.* 1901
    3. John Godhou Thomas (1875–) *m.* 1898 Maria Taylor Collins, *b.* 1876
    4. Richard S. Collins (1841–1919) *m.* 1867 Adaline S. Green (1841–1927)
    5. John Collins (1806–1900) *m.* 1831 Elizabeth Clark (1809–1855)
    6. Levi Collins (1772–1813) *m.* 1801 Asenath Lake (1783–1860)
    7. Daniel Lake *c.* (1740–1799) *m.* 1764 Sarah Lucas
    8. Daniel Lake *c.* (1697–1774) *m.* 1730 Gartara Steelman
    9. William Lake, *d.* 1717, *m.* Sarah
   10. JOHN LAKE, *d.* bef. 1696, *m.* Anne Spicer, *d.* aft. 1709
    Service: Original Proprietor of Gravesend (now Brooklyn), 1645.
    Reference: "Genealogy of Lake Family," by Adams and Risley.

6335 RICKARD, John Godbou   Recorded 1941, New Jersey
          Judson College, Rangoon, India
                          (JUNIOR)
    1. John Godbou Rickard
    2. Samuel Harmer Rickard (1895–) *m.* 1923 Ada Pauline Thomas, *b.* 1901
    3. John Godbou Thomas (1875–) *m.* 1898 Maria Taylor Collins (1876–)
    4. Richard S. Collins (1841–1919) *m.* 1867 Adaline S. Green (1841–1927)
    5. John Collins (1806–1900) *m.* 1831 Elizabeth Clark (1809–1855)
    6. Levi Collins (1772–1813) *m.* 1801 Asenath Lake (1783–1860)
    7. Daniel Lake, *d.* 1799, *m.* 1764 Sarah Lucas
    8. Daniel Lake *c.* (1697–1774) *m.* 1730 Gartara Steelman
    9. William Lake, *d.* 1717, *m.* Sarah
   10. John Lake, *d.* bef. 1696, *m.* Anne Spicer, *d.* aft. 1709
   11. THOMAS SPICER, *d.* 1658, *m.* Ann

Service: Signed Compact at Newport, 1638; Treas. of Portsmouth, 1642; Original
    Proprietor of Gravesend (Brooklyn), 1645; Magistrate of Gravesend, 1658.
Reference: "Genealogy of the Lake Family," by Adams and Risley.

6336 RICKARD, Samuel Harmer   Recorded 1941, New Jersey
        160 S. Virginia Avenue, Atlantic City, New Jersey
                           (JUNIOR)
  1. Samuel Harmer Rickard
  2. Samuel Harmer Rickard (1895–) *m.* 1923 Ada Pauline Thomas, *b.* 1901
  3. John Godhou Thomas (1875–) *m.* 1898 Maria Taylor Collins, *b.* 1876
  4. Richard S. Collins (1841–1919) *m.* 1867 Adaline S. Green (1841–1927)
  5. John Collins (1806–1900) *m.* 1831 Elizabeth Clark (1809–1855)
  6. Levi Collins (1772–1813) *m.* 1801 Asenath Lake (1783–1860)
  7. Daniel Lake *c.* (1740–1799) *m.* 1764 Sarah Lucas
  8. Daniel Lake *c.* (1697–1774) *m.* 1730 Gartara Steelman
  9. William Lake, *d.* 1717, *m.* Sarah
10. JOHN LAKE, *d.* bef. 1696, *m.* Anne Spicer, *d.* aft. 1709
Service: Original Proprietor of Gravesend (Brooklyn), 1645.
Reference: "Genealogy of the Lake Family," by Adams and Risley.

6069 RIDER, Mrs. Robert O.   Recorded 1934, Connecticut
        Glastonbury, Connecticut
  1. Helen D. Williams *m.* 1916 Robert O. Rider
  2. James S. Williams (1859–) *m.* 1887 Katherine P. Clarke (1857–)
  3. James B. Williams (1818–1907) *m.* 1845 Jerusha M. Hubbard (1825–1866)
  4. Solomon Williams (1783–1875) *m.* 1806 Martha Baker (1786–1866)
  5. Joseph Baker, M.D. (1743–1804) *m.* 1779 Lucy Devotion (1754–1842)
  6. Samuel Baker (1706–1791) *m.* 1732 Prudence Jenkins (1711–1793)
  7. Joseph Jenkins (1669–1733) *m.* 1694 Lydia Howland (1665–)
  8. John Howland (1627–) *m.* 1651 Mary Lee
  9. JOHN HOWLAND (1592–1672) *m.* 1621 Elizabeth Tilley (–1688)
Service: Early settler in Conn.
Reference: Howland Family of America; Vital Statistics of Glastonbury, Conn.;
    Genealogy of Nicholas Baker and his Descendants; Mayflower
    Descendants.

6580 RIDDLE, Grace H.   Recorded 1948
        2340 W. 113th Place, Chicago, Illinois
  1. Grace Halbert Riddle
  2. Dr. Hamilton R. Riddle (1841–1926) *m.* 1868 Cordelia F. Constant (1849–1930)
  3. Rezin H. Constant (1809–1887) *m.* 1847 Mary L. Halbert (1817–1863)
  4. Dr. James Halbert, Jr. (1785–1858) *m.* 1816 Nancy Rennolds *ca.* (1794–1834)
  5. James Halbert, Sr. (ante 1760–1819) *m.* 1783 Sarah Shaddock, *d.* aft. 1823
  6. James Shaddock, *d.* 1795, *m.* bef. 1739 Hannah Samuel
  7. James Samuel, *d.* 1759, *m.* Sarah Boulware
  8. James Boulware, *d.* bef. 1718, *m.* Margery Gray
  9. WILLIAM GRAY, *d.* bef. 1763, *m.* Elizabeth
Service: Landed proprietor in Old Rappahannock Co., Va.
Reference: Comp. Amer. Genealogy.

6302 RIGGINS, Jane Eileen   Recorded 1940, New Jersey
        625 Colford Avenue, Collingswood, New Jersey
  1. Jane Eileen Riggins
  2. Samuel Riggins, *b.* 1891, *m.* 1915 Minnie Rickenback, *b.* 1892
  3. Francis Riggins, *b.* 1868, *m.* 1890 Jessie Patrick (1870–1928)
  4. Samuel Patrick (1822–1901) *m.* 1852 Rebecca Smith (1834–1930)
  5. William Smith (1794–1870) *m.* (2nd) 1826 Rebecca Findlay (1805–1877)
  6. Oliver Smith (1765–1803) *m.* 1787 Hannah Sims (1766–1818)
  7. Capt. William Smith (1742–1820) *m.* (2nd) 1764 Sarah Stretch (1744–1824)
  8. Bradmun Stretch (1702–1749) *m.* 1724 Sarah Hancock (1701–aft. 1749)
  9. John Hancock, *d.* 1709, *m.* 1688 Sarah Chamblen (or Chambers)
10. NATHANIEL CHAMBERS *c.* (1635–1710) *m.* Elizabeth
Service: "An eminent man in early settlement of Fenwick Colony."
Reference: Genealogy of Fenwick Colony.

6222 RIPLEY, Mrs. Thomas Jackson   Recorded 1938
         Atlanta, Georgia

1. Pauline Howard (1868–) *m.* 1890 Thomas Jackson Ripley
2. Dr. Geo. J. Howard (1831–1898) *m.* 1853 Maria Louisa Goldsmith (1833–1899)
3. Wm. Henry Howard, Jr. (1806–1891) *m.* 1831 Martha Sutton Webb (1811–1885)
4. Wm. Henry Howard, Sr. (1768–1807) *m.* 1791 Elizabeth Key (1775–1864)
5. Henry Howard (1735–1807) *m.* 1762 Priscilla Farrar (1740–1808)
6. Geo. Farrar (1695–1772) *m.* 1725 Judith Jefferson (1698–1782)
7. Thos. Jefferson (1677–1731) *m.* 1697 Mary Field (1679–1715)
8. Maj. Peter Field (1645–1702) *m.* 1678 Judith Soane (1646–1702)
9. MAJOR HENRY SOANE (1625–1702) *m.* 1645 Judith ———

Services: Speaker of the House of Burgesses; Major.
Reference: Wm. & M. Quar., Vol. 4; Valentine Papers, Vol. 4; Va. Mag. H. & B.,
         pages 10–11.

6057 RISLEY, Mrs. Walton   Recorded 1933, New Jersey
         Pleasantville, New Jersey

1. Agnes F. Leeds *m.* 1898 Walton Risley
2. Benjamin F. Leeds (1855–1927) *m.* 1878 Rejoice Penn Treen (1860–)
3. James Leeds (1818–1893) *m.* 1847 Abigail M. Webb (1827–1907)
4. Andrew Leeds (1792–1865) *m.* 1817 Armenia Lake (1797–1853)
5. John Lake (1773–1855) *m.* 1796 Abigail Adams (1775–1857)
6. Ens. John Adams (1738–1798) *m.* 1763 Margaret Garwood (1740–1826)
7. Thomas Garwood (1707–1796) *m.* 1733 Mary Ballenger (–1764)
8. Thomas Ballenger (1685–1739) *m.* 1713 Elizabeth Elkinton (1696–)
9. HENRY BALLENGER (–1733) *m.* Mary Harding

Service: Member of the Assembly of West Jersey, for Burlington Co., in 1697.
Reference: A Genealogy of the Lake Family, Adams-Risley; N. J. Archives, First
         Series, Vol. II.

6228 ROAN, Judge Augustus Morrow
         Atlanta, Georgia

1. Augustus Morrow Roan (1898–) *m.* 1926 Margaret Zattau
2. Chas. Thurston Roan (1866–1911) *m.* 1889 Issie Morrow (1870–)
3. Benj. Strickland Roan (1816–1891) *m.* 1847 Lucy Vickers (1823–1910)
4. James R. Vickers (1798–1877) *m.* 1817 Elizabeth Lassiter (1798–1889)
5. James Lassiter (1760–1828) *m.* 1782 Elizabeth Butt (1760–1798)
6. Joshua Butt (1714–1780) *m.* 1735 Mary Portlock (1715–1760)
7. Josiah Butt (1692–1763) *m.* 1713 ———
8. Robert Butt (1666–1729) *m.* 1690 Ann Armstead (1670–1698)
9. Radford Butt (1645–1701) *m.* 1664 ———
10. ROBERT BUTT (1620–1676) *m.* 1640 Ann Riddlehurst

Service:
Reference: Original Lists of Persons of Quality, by J. C. Hotten.

6220 ROAN, Bruce Jonas   Recorded 1938
         Signal Mountain, Tennessee

1. Chas. Thurston Roan (1866–1911) *m.* 1889 Issie Morrow (1870–)
2. Benj. Strickland Roan (1816–1891) *m.* 1847 Lucy Vickers (1823–1910)
3. James R. Vickers (1798–1877) *m.* 1817 Eliz. Lassiter (1798–1889)
4. James Lassiter (1760–1828) *m.* 1782 Elizabeth Butt (1760–1798)
5. Joshua Butt (1714–1780) *m.* 1735 Mary Portlock (1715–1760)
6. Josiah Butt (1692–1763) *m.* 1713 ———
7. Robert Butt (1666–1729) *m.* 1690 Ann Armstead (1670–1698)
8. Radford Butt (1645–1701) *m.* 1664 ———
9. ROBERT BUTT (1620–1676) *m.* 1640 Ann Riddlehurst

Service:
Reference: "Original Lists of Persons of Quality," by J. C. Hotten.

6269 ROAN, Charles Thurston   Recorded 1939, Georgia
       991 Oakdale Road N. E., Atlanta, Georgia
                      (JUNIOR)

1. Charles Thurston Roan
2. Augustus Morrow Roan (1898–) *m.* 1926 Margaret Zattau, *b.* 1905
3. Charles Thurston Roan (1866–1911) *m.* 1889 Issie Morrow, *b.* 1870
4. Benjamin Strickland Roan (1816–1891) *m.* 1847 Lucy Vickers (1823–1910)
5. James R. Vickers (1798–1877) *m.* 1817 Elizabeth Lassiter (1798–1889)
6. James Lassiter (Rev. War), *d.* 1828, *m.* 1782 Elizabeth Butt, *b.* 1760, *d.* aft. 1798
7. Joshua Butt (1714–1780) *m.* Mary Portlock, *d.* aft. 1760
8. Josiah Butt (1692–1763) *m.* 1713/1714 ———. She died after 1720
9. Robert Butt (1666–1729) *m. c.* 1690 Ann Armstead, *b. c.* 1670, *d.* aft. 1698
10. Radford Butt (1645–1701); wife died after 1670
11. ROBERT BUTT, *b. c.* 1620, *d.* 1676, *m.* Ann Riddlehurst, *d.* aft. 1650

Service: Came to America *c.* 1640; early settler of Lower Norfolk Co., Va.; received
     extensive land grants on Elizabeth River.
Reference: Records of Fulton Co., Ga., Clayton Co., Ga., and Walton Co., Ga.; Records
     of Halifax Co., N. C.; Records Lower Norfolk Co., Va.; Records of Captain
     Archibald Butt, U.S.N. (drowned on Titanic), Personal Aide to President
     Taft, made extensive research of this family which records are now in
     possession of his family.

6273 ROAN, Margaret Zattau   Recorded 1939, Georgia
       991 Oakdale Road N. E., Atlanta, Georgia
                      (JUNIOR)

1. Margaret Zattau Roan
2. Augustus Morrow Roan (1898–) *m.* 1926 Margaret Zattau, *b.* 1905
3. Charles Thurston Roan (1866–1911) *m.* 1889 Issie Morrow, *b.* 1870
4. Benjamin Strickland Roan (1816–1891) *m.* 1847 Lucy Vickers (1823–1910)
5. James R. Vickers (1798–1877) *m.* 1817 Elizabeth Lassiter (1798–1889)
6. James Lassiter (Rev. War), *d.* 1828, *m.* 1782 Elizabeth Butt, *b.* 1760, *d.* aft. 1798
7. Joshua Butt (1714–1780) *m.* Mary Portlock, *d.* aft. 1760
8. Josiah Butt (1692–1763) *m.* 1713/14 ———; she died after 1720
9. Robert Butt (1666–1729) *m. c.* 1690 Ann Armstead, *b. c.* 1670, *d.* aft. 1698
10. Radford Butt (1645–1701); wife died after 1670
11. ROBERT BUTT, *b. c.* 1620, *d.* 1676, *m.* Ann Riddlehurst, *d.* aft. 1650

Service: Came to America *c.* 1640; early settler of Lower Norfolk Co., Va.; received
     extensive land grants on Elizabeth River.
Reference: Records of Fulton Co., Ga., Clayton Co., Ga., and Walton Co., Ga.; Records
     of Halifax Co., N. C.; Records Lower Norfolk Co., Va.; Records of Captain
     Archibald Butt, U.S.N. (drowned on Titanic), Personal Aide to President
     Taft, made extensive research of this family which records are now in
     possession of his family.

5884 ROBERTS, Mrs. C. Wilson   Recorded 1929, Pennsylvania
       Southampton, Pennsylvania

1. Elizabeth Mercer *m.* C. Wilson Roberts
2. Henry Mercer (1839–1882) *m.* 1866 Anna M. Ervin (1839–1903)
3. James Ervin (1812–1844) *m.* 1835 Anna Hart Davis (1815–1891)
4. John Davis (1788–1878) *m.* 1813 Amy Hart (1784–1847)
5. Josiah Hart (1749–1800) *m.* 1776 Ann Watts (1759–1815)
6. Joseph Hart (1715–1788) *m.* 1740 Elizabeth Collet (1714–1788)
7. John Hart (1684–1763) *m.* 1708 Eleanor Crispin (1687–1754)
8. JOHN HART (1651–1714) *m.* 1683 Susanna Rush (–1725)

Service: Member of the First Assembly in Philadelphia; Signer of the First Charter,
     1683.
Reference: Genealogy of the Hart Family of Bucks Co., Penna., by W. W. H. Davis.

5945   ROBERTS, Mrs. Paul S.   Recorded 1930, Georgia
       Winder, Georgia

1. Cleora Eavenson *m.* Paul S. Roberts
2. John W. Eavenson (1840–   ) *m.* 1863 Josephine Oglesby (1846–1930)
3. George Eavenson (1817–1898) *m.* 1839 Sarah Thornton (1824–1863)
4. George Eavenson (1782–1842) *m.* Polly Hilly (1781–1855)
5. Eli Eavenson (1760–1829) *m.* 1781 Rachael Seal (1760–1830)
6. George Eavenson (1726–1816) *m.* 1755 Mary Williams (–1828)
7. Joseph E. Eavenson (1689–1771) *m.* 1717 Catherine George
8. Thomas E. Eavenson (1653–1726) *m.* 1677 Hannah Woodward
9. RALPH EAVENSON (1625–1655) *m.* 1650 Cicely Orton

Service:
Reference: Palmer and Trimble Genealogy.

5946   ROBERTS, Nora Pauline   Recorded 1930, Georgia
       Winder, Georgia

1. Nora Pauline Roberts
2. John W. Eavenson (1840–   ) *m.* 1863 Josephine Oglesby (1846–1930)
3. George Eavenson (1817–1898) *m.* 1839 Sarah Thornton (1824–1863)
4. George Eavenson (1782–1842) *m.* Polly Hilly (1781–1855)
5. Eli Eavenson (1760–1829) *m.* 1781 Rachael Seal (1760–1830)
6. George Eavenson (1726–1816) *m.* 1755 Mary Williams (–1828)
7. Joseph E. Eavenson (1689–1771) *m.* 1717 Catherine George
8. Thomas E. Eavenson (1653–1726) *m.* 1677 Hannah Woodward
9. RALPH EAVENSON (1625–1655) *m.* 1650 Cicely Orton

Service:
Reference: Palmer and Trimble Genealogy.

6668   ROBERTSON, Mrs. John E.   Recorded 1950
       1157 Kaufman Street, Waxahachie, Texas

1 .Margaret Templeton *m.* 1911 ———
2. Patrick Henry Templeton (1856–1921) *m.* 1881 Nannie M. Watson (1858–1946)
3. John D. Templeton (1817–1890) *m.* 1854 Alta Phoebe Lewis (1830–   )
4. James A. Templeton (1785–1830) *m.* 1811 Nancy Brevard (1791–1852)
5. Zebulon Brevard, Jr. (1769–1825) *m.* before 1790 Isabella Edminston (1773–1825)
6. Zebulon Brevard, Sr. (1724–1790) *m.* 1754 Ann Templeton (–1790)
7. JEAN BREVARD (France, *d.* Md., *m.* 1714 Agnes McKnitt

Service: Left France in Revocation of Edict of Nantes; 1685 Elder in Pres. Church.
Reference: Hunt's Sketches of Western N. C.; History of McKnitt Family.

6723   ROBISON, Mrs. Chester T.   Recorded 1951, West Virginia
       621 Second Street, Huntington, West Virginia

1. Blanche Cynthia Veazey *m.* 1921 Chester T. Robison
2. Isaac Morton Veazey (1856–1903) *m.* 1878 Effie Afton Davidson (1858–1888)
3. Jonathan C. Davidson (1829–1888) *m.* 1851 Cynthia Anne Thomas (1836–1904)
4. Joseph William Davidson (1806–   ) *m.* 1826 Jane Bryson (1809–1889)
5. William Davidson (1747–1811) *m.* 1784 Barbara McDowell (1769–1831)
6. Lewis Davidson (1712–1793) *m.* Comfort Warrington (*c.* 1716–*c.* 1749)
7. William Warrington (1690–1755) *m. c.* 1710 Comfort Tilney (*c.* 1687–1721)
8. William Tilney (1661–1695) *m.* Elizabeth Bagwell (*c.* 1666–*c.* 1720)
9. Thomas Bagwell (1642–1690) *m.* Ann Stockley (1645–1695)
10. HENRY BAGWELL (1590–*c.* 1650) *m.* 1636 Alice Hawkins Stratton (*c.* 1600–*c.* 1664)

Service: Clerk of Accomac Co., Va., 1632 until 1640.
Reference: Henry Bagwell came to Va. 1608; acct of voyage given in Davidson Genealogy, p. 99; was in House of Burgesses from Accomac Co., Va., 1629–30–32; Rector, 1636; Pat. 1639, 400 acres in Accomac Co.; Record of Henry Bagwell & Family, pgs. 99 to 105, by Elizabeth Davidson Harbaugh.

6485 ROBINSON, Miss Martha Ann   Recorded 1948
        Plain City

1. Miss Martha Ann Robinson
2. Pearl Osborne Robinson (1869–1941) *m.* 1901 Elizabeth Lane (1876–)
3. Milton Lane, M.D. (1837–1889) *m.* 1874 Sophronia McCloud (1840–1904)
4. Dr. Charles McCloud (1808–1860) *m.* 1831 Mary Jane Carpenter (1813–1911)
5. Benjamin Carpenter (1774–1855) *m.* 1793 Sarah Scovell (–1817)
6. Gilbert Carpenter (1742–1838) *m.* Sarah ——— (1744–1820)
7. Benjamin Carpenter (1697–1767) *m.* 1740 Mary Coons
8. Samuel Carpenter (1666–1745) *m.* Patience ———
9. John Carpenter (1628–1695) *m.* Hannah Hope
10. WILLIAM CARPENTER (1605–1659) *m.* 1627/8 Abigail ——— (1600–1687)

Service: 1647 made one of directors Rehoboth, Mass.; he paid 8 pounds, 17 shillings
         and 3 pence toward expense of King Philip's War; a Captain in 1642.
Reference:

6317 ROBINSON, Martha Reid   Recorded 1941, Georgia
        54 Spring Street, Newman, Georgia

1. Martha Reid Robinson
2. John E. Robinson (1847–1915) *m.* 1870 Isadore Burch (1847–1933)
3. John Evans Robinson (1807–1874) *m.* (2nd) 1835 Sarah Ann Ramey (1820–1888)
4. Daniel Ramey (1787–1852) *m.* 1818 Mary Morton (1803–1859)
5. Presley Remey (1742–1793) *m.*, *d.* aft. 1804
6. John Remey *c.* (1718–1791) *m.* 1740 Mary Linton, *d.* aft. 1791
7. William Remey (1672–1738) *m.* Catherine Asbury, *d.* aft. 1738
8. JACOB REMEY *c.* (1650–1721) *m.* Mary

Service: A Frenchman naturalized in Colony of Virginia, 1680.
Reference: Ramey (Remey) Family, by Robinson.

6621 ROCHELLE, Mrs. Zalpheus A.   Recorded 1949
        2106 University Drive, Durham, North Carolina

1. Bertha Lakey *m.* 1908 Zalpheus Aaron Rochelle
2. Hiram W. Lakey (1857–1886) *m.* 1881 Sallie Cornelius (1864–1924)
3. Abram P. Lakey (1825–1900) *m.* 1856 Carolina Foster (1837–1857)
4. Abram B. Lakey (1798–1877) *m.* 1823 Nancy Phillips (1805–1895)
5. Abram Phillips (1756–1818) *m.* 1799 Sallie C. Ridings (1780–)
6. John Ridings (1737–1811) *m.* Elizabeth Gentry, *d.* 1800
7. William Ridings (1715–1789) *m.* 1735 Ruth Parsons (1715–)
8. William Ridings (1676–aft. 1715) *m.* Sallie ———
9. Thomas Ridings (1640–aft. 1676) *m.* 1662 Rose A. Yardley (1650–)
10. Capt. Argall Yardley (1621–1655) *m.* 1649 Ann Custis
11. JOHN CUSTIS, *d.* aft. 1640, *m.* Joane ———

Service: Founder of the Custis Family of Virginia.
Reference: Lakey Bibles and cemetery records; Old Churches and Families of Va.;
         D.A.R., D.C.W., U.D.C. records.

6740 ROSSER, Mrs. Roy P.   Recorded 1952, North Carolina
        The Pines, Sanford, North Carolina

1. Sidney Matt Reinhardt *m.* 1939 Roy P. Rosser
2. Joseph Edgar Reinhard (1850–1926) *m.* 1873 Frances Anna Wilson (1854–1949)
3. Franklin M. Reinhardt (1807–1869) *m.* 1834 Sarah Smith (1816–1879)
4. Christian Reinhardt (1785–1837) *m.* 1803 Mary Forney (1785–1867)
5. Gen. Peter Forney (1756–1834) *m.* 1783 Nancy Abernathy (1766–1847)
6. David Abernathy (1720–1814) *m.* 1738 Ann ——— *ca.* (1720–af. 1814)
7. Robert Abernathy *ca.* (1685–1772) *m. c.* 1718 Mary ——— (1700–*ca.* 1772)
8. ROBERT ABERNATHY (1624–1690) *m. ca.* 1664 ———

Service: Jury service; landed proprietor, 1664.
Reference: Wm. & Mary Quarterly (I), Vol. 10, pg. 31; Va. Land Grant No. 567,
         Mar. 7, 1665; ibid., pg. 251, 7: Wm. & M., pg. 31, 251 Court Order Book,
         Charles City Co., Va., 1665; Va. Mag. of History 4, p. 274; Sherrill's
         Annals of Lincoln Co., N. C., pg. 382.

6624 ROTHROCK, Mrs. P. S.   Recorded 1949
         187 Pine Street, Mount Airy, North Carolina
   1. Jessie Martin *m.* 1903 Parmenlo S. Rothrock
   2. Leroy A. Martin (1854–1917) *m.* 1877 Cora A. Poindexter (1860–1943)
   3. Reps Martin (1826–1911) *m.* 1848 Nancy E. Poindexter (1830–1916)
   4. Denson A. Poindexter (aft. 1795–1876) *m.* 1823 Sarah Jones (1806–1862)
   5. William P. Poindexter (1766–1844) *m.* 1795 Elizabeth A. Ashburn (1778–1849)
   6. Capt. Thomas Poindexter, *d.* 1807, *m.* Elizabeth Pledge, *d.* 1816
   7. Thomas Poindexter, *d.* ca. 1774, *m.* 1691 Sarah Crawford, *d.* 1752
   8. GEORGE POINDEXTER, *d.* aft. 1698, *m.* Sussana, *d. ca.* 1698
   Service: Came to America *ca.* 1657.
   Reference: History of Poindexter (Poingdestre) Family; D.A.R. and D.A.C. records.

6504 ROWELL, Hugh Grant   Recorded 1945
         North Tarrytown, New York
   1. Hugh Grant Rowell, M.D., *m.* ——— Sept. 21, 1921
   2. George Barker Rowell (1846–1918) *m.* 1891 (2nd) Esther Rowan Grant
         (1867–)
   3. Adoniram J. Rowell (1818–1864) *m.* 1841 Lucy Ann Richardson (1818–1895)
   4. William Richardson (1794–1836) *m.* Abiah Whittier (1798–1878)
   5. William Whittier (1753–1812) *m.* Hannah Poor (1755–)
   6. Col. Thomas Poor (1732–1804) *m.* Phoebe Osgood (1735–1797)
   7. Daniel Poor (1656–1735) *m.* 1672 Mehitable Osgood
   8. DANIEL POOR (1624–1690) *m.* 1650 Mary Farnham (1629–1714)
   Service: Died in Andover, Mass., 1690; Selectman Andover, Mass., for seven years;
         Fence Viewer, Surveyor and Grand Juryman.

5883 ROWEN, Mrs. Edward   Recorded 1929, Pennsylvania
   1. Mary R. Rorer *m.* 1901 Edward Rowen
   2. David S. Rorer (1826–1912) *m.* 1849 Mary A. Woodington (1829–1901)
   3. William Woodington (1809–1877) *m.* 1827 Rebecca Dyer (1812–1880)
   4. Samuel Dyer (1783–1856) *m.* 1808 Elizabeth Keen (1790–1832)
   5. Joseph Dyer (1754–1815) *m.* 1780 Mary Ann (1756–1817)
   6. James Dyer (1727–1803) *m.* 1751 Elizabeth (–1812)
   7. Charles Dyer (1697–) *m.* 1716 Elizabeth Shuef (1698–1778)
   8. James Dyer (1669–) *m.* 1696 ———
   9. Charles Dyer (1650–1709) *m.* Mary
  10. WILLIAM DYER (–1677) *m.* Mary (–1660)
   Service: Secretary, Newport, Rhode Island, 1640; Attorney General, 1653.
   Reference: Austin's Dictionary of Rhode Island; Rhode Island Vital Statistics.

6184 ROWLAND, Frances Ohia   Recorded 1938
         558 Piedmont Avenue N. E., Atlanta, Georgia
                                 (JUNIOR)
   1. Frances Ohia Rowland (1919–)
   2. Donald A. Rowland (1875–) *m.* 1912 Frances Royal (1881–)
   3. Evans Ezekiel Royal (1840–1899) *m.* 1864 Missouri Elizabeth Patterson
         (1844–1893)
   4. Turner Dennis Patterson (1810–1875) *m.* 1829 Belerma Evangeline Rowlett
         (1810–1856)
   5. Lieut. Thomas Rowlett (1787–1841) *m.* 1809 Lucy Bruce (1791–1850)
   6. William Rowlett (abt. 1760–) *m.* 1785 Elizabeth Gill (1767–)
   7. William Rowlett (1730–1785) *m.* 1752 Sarah—Rowlett
   8. Peter Rowlett (–1749) *m.* Mary—Rowlett (–1777)
   9. PETER ROWLETT, SR. (abt. 1637–will date 1702), Va.
         Wife died before his will was made. Married in France.
   Service: Huguenot, settled south side of James River with other Huguenots.
   Reference: Peter Rowlett (Rullet, Rulleau, Rollet) came over in the "Anthony L.
         Peter" Galley of London; Henrico Co., Va., Will book 1, pg. 263; Chester-
         field Co., Va., Will book I, pg. 45, book 3, pg. 517; 622 Va. Co., Rec.,
         pg. 7; The Huguenot of the Founders of Manaken in Col. of Va.; Nat. No.
         337, Sons. & Dau. of The Pilgrims, Nat. No. 6122.

6345 RUCKER, Mrs. George N. Recorded 1941, Georgia
Roswell, Georgia

1. Edith Wing Wood *m.* 1914 George Napoleon Rucker
2. Eugene Harrison Wood (1862–1938) *m.* 1882 Annie Caroline Wing (1864–)
3. Jehu Lowery Wing (1823–1877) *m.* 1848 Mary Rebecca Johnson (1829–1882)
4. John Wing (1780–1848) *m.* 1821 Mary Tullis (1807–1877)
5. Edward Wing (1745–1804) *m.* 1775 Mary Lowery *c.* (1755–1826)
6. John Wing (1701–aft. 1745) *m.* 1727 Mary Tucker (1708–aft. 1774)
7. John Wing (1661–1728) *m.* 1685 Mary Perry, *d.* 1714
8. Edward Perry (1630–1695) *m.* 1653 Mary Freeman, *d.* aft. 1704
9. EDMUND FREEMAN (1590–1682) *m.* Elizabeth (1596–1672)

Service: Came to America 1635; Lt. Governor of Plymouth Colony with Gov. William Bradford, 1640–1646; member Council of War, 1642.
Reference: Same as Number 6343.

6334 RUNDSTROM, Mrs. Leonard G. Recorded 1941, New Jersey
Hotel Traymore, Atlantic City, New Jersey

1. Olive B. Conover
2. Harry B. Conover (1864–) *m.* 1886 Amanda B. Smith (1865–1903)
3. James A. Conover (1831–1895) *m.* 1857 Charlotte Ruth Risley (1840–1915)
4. John Conover (1808–1877) *m.* 1828 Mary Adams (1813–1847)
5. James Adams *m.* 1811 Jemina Risley, *b.* 1795
6. Morris Risley, *d.* 1802, *m.* 1772 Jemina Lake, *d.* 1802
7. Richard Risley, *d.* 1767, *m.* Rebecca
8. Richard Risley (1698–) *m. c.* 1716 Esther Couwenhoven (1698–aft. 1737)
9. Richard Risley (1648–*c.* 1716) *m.* Rebecca Adams (*c.* 1650–aft. 1716)
10. RICHARD RISLEY, *b. c.* 1614, *d.* 1648, *m.* 1640 Mary.

Service: Jan. 14, 1638, participated in adoption of the Fundamental Order, 1st Written Constitution.
Reference: Lake Family Genealogy; Risley Genealogy; New Jersey Archives.

6119 RUNYON, Mrs. James G. Recorded 1936, New York
18 Hudson Terrace, North Tarrytown, New York

1. Alice Minnerly *m.* James Garfield Runyon
2. Percy C. Minnerly (1878–) *m.* 1901 Phermetta Miller (1881–)
3. Constantine Minnerly (1845–1929) *m.* 1877 Lucy Nossiter (1851–1927)
4. Andrew J. Minnerly (1815–1894) *m.* 1835 Harriet Wicks (1811–1883)
5. William Minnerly (1781–1844) *m.* 1803 Elizabeth Lambert (1785–1845)
6. James J. Minnerly (1742–1823) *m.* 1762 Catherine Martling (1745–1826)
7. ABRAHAM MARTLING (1693–1761) *m.* 1715 ————

Service: One of the Founders of Phillipsburg Manor.
Reference: The Old Dutch Burying Ground of Sleepy Hollow; History Research Society of the Tappan Zee, 1926.

6495 RUSSELL, Mrs. Frank Elsworth Recorded 1945
Marietta, Ohio

1. Sophia McTaggart *m.* Frank Elsworth Russell
2. Archibald McTaggart (1844–) *m.* 1868 Caroline C. Kinnaird (1849–1913)
3. Rufus Kinnaird (1819–1871) *m.* 1841 Sophia S. Cook (1821–)
4. Tillinghast A. Cook (1780–) *m.* 1820 Elizabeth Russell (1799–)
5. John Russell (1764–) *m.* 1794 Elizabeth Smith (1774–)
6. Jonathan Russell (1738–) *m.* 1760 *ca.* Mary Brown
7. Daniel Russell (1713–) *m.* 1737 Phebe Roberts (1711–)
8. John Russell (1686–) *m.* 1710 Elizabeth Patton
9. Nathaniel Patton (1643–1725) *m.* 1678 Mrs Sarah (Morse) Cooper
10. WILLIAM PATTON (–1668) *m.* Mary ———— (–1673)

Service: A member of A. & H. A. Co., 1642; Proprietor of Billerico, Mass., 1688.

5879 RYAN, Mrs. John F.   Recorded 1929, New Jersey
         909 South Shore Road, Pleasantville, New Jersey
   1. Hannah Mary Ireland *m.* 1884 John Ryan
   2. James A. Ireland (1830–1908) *m.* 1862 Amelia G. Keen (1842–1899)
   3. John Ireland (1796–1850) *m.* Hannah Scull (1801–1883)
   4. Thomas Ireland (1769–1803) *m.* Hannah Steelman (1747–1796)
   5. Thomas Ireland (1721–1773) *m.* Mary Cressy
   6. Daniel Ireland (1698–1762) *m.* Ruth Williams (1699–1757)
   7. Thomas Ireland (1647–   ) *m.* Mary (–1723)
   8. Thomas Ireland (–1668) *m.* Joanna
   Service: One of the 50 Original Proprietors of Hempstead, L. I.
   Reference: Friends Records, Great Egg Harbor; Penna. Hist. Society; Hempstead
         Census, 1698; Annals of Hempstead, p. 63.

6010 SAISSLIN, Mrs. G. A.   Recorded 1932
         2644 S. Milwaukee Street, Denver, Colorado
   1. Winifred Way (1878–   ) *m.* 1901 George A. Saisslin
   2. John Franklin Way (1858–1899) *m.* Larcena Wing (1859–   )
   3. Egbert Wing (1832–1892) *m.* Elizabeth Ann Davis (1835–1930)
   4. James Wing (1804–1877) *m.* Rachel Moss Davis (–1866)
   5. Eliha Wing (1741–   ) *m.* Hesikiah Hoag
   6. Jedediah Wing (1697–   ) *m.* Deborah Gifford
   7. Elisha Wing (1668–1757) *m.* Mehitable Butler (1689–   )
   8. Stephen Wing (1621–1760) *m.* 1653 Sarah Briggs (–1689)
   9. Rev. John Wing (1584–1630) *m.* Deborah Bacheler (–1632)
   Services: Constable.
   Reference: Wing Gen.

6663 SANBORN, Mrs. Frank C.   Recorded 1949
         90 Fourteenth Avenue, Columbus 1, Ohio
   1. Elizabeth C. Hunneman *m.* 1901 Frank E. Sanborn
   2. Henry C. Hunneman (1841–1918) *m.* 1869 Abbie Twombly (1845–1937)
   3. William J. Twombly (1818–1880) *m.* 1840 Prudence J. Hood (1821–1899)
   4. James H. Twombly (–1854) *m.* 1817 Mary A. Gilman (–1831)
   5. William Gilman (1764–1862) *m.* Mary (Polly) Gilman (1771–   )
   6. Jeremiah Gilman (1740–1823) *m.* 1762 Abigail Johnson (1746–1824)
   7. Capt. Israel Gilman (–1768) *m.* (I) Deborah Thing (1708–1737)
   8. Capt. Jeremiah Gilman (1660–   ) *m.* Mary Wiggin (1668–   )
   9. Andrew Wiggin (1635–1710) *m.* 1659 Hannah Bradstreet (1643–1707)
  10. Gov. Simon Bradstreet (1603–1697) *m.* 1628 Anne Dudley (1612–1672)
  11. Gov. Thomas Dudley (1576–1654) *m.* Dorothy York (–1643)
   Service: Gov. Mass. Colony.
   Reference: Hist. of Families—Honneman, Gilman, Wiggins and Dudley.

6201 SANDERS, Emilie McCarty   Recorded 1938
         540 Eleventh Street, Huntington, West Virginia
   1. Emilie McCarty (1876–   ) *m.* 1909 Franklin Oliver Sanders
   2. William James McCarty (1842–1906) *m.* 1873 Mary Cornelia Putnam (1847–1906)
   3. Albert Brooks Putnam (1820–1896) *m.* 1842 Elizabeth McReynolds (1822–1881)
   4. Jacob Putnam (1785–1830) *m.* 1810 Lucy Brooks (1790–1868)
   5. Capt. Daniel Putnam (1755–1819) *m.* 1777 Elizabeth Oberlack (1757–1786)
   6. John Putnam (1715–1762) *m.* 1737 Sarah Maverick
   7. Samuel Putnam (1684–1753) *m.* 1709 Mary Leach (1684–   )
   8. John Putnam (1657–1722) *m.* 1678 Hannah Cutler (1655–aft. 1722)
   9. Capt. Nathaniel Putnam (1619–1700) *m.* 1651 Elizabeth Hutchinson
  10. John Putnam, bapt. 1579, *m.* 1611 Pricilla Deacon
   Service: Officer in King Philip's War; Deputy to the Gen. Court and was Selectman;
         came to America 1636.
   Reference: Carrell Gen., by Ezra Carrell, pgs. 362–544; McGinnis Hist. of Lycoming
         Co., Pa.; Putnam Lineage by Ezra Putnam (Congressional Library).

6604 SANFORD, Mrs. Donald O. Recorded 1948
5815 N. Whipple Street, Chicago 45, Illinois
1. Rose Lowenthal *m.* 1930 Donald O. Sanford
2. Julius Lowenthal (1878–1947) *m.* 1904 Emma J. Cross (1884–)
3. Eugene C. Cross (1863–) *m.* 1883 Alvina D. Green (1865–1943)
4. Wm. A. Cross (1831–1908) *m.* 1858 Jane E. Elliott (1841–1907)
5. Charles E. Elliott (1813–1892) *m.* 1837 Lucy M. Barber (1818–1891)
6. Asa Elliott (1785–1852) *m.* 1807 Betsey Williams (1788–1855)
7. Laban Elliott (1757–1830) *m.* Mehitable Harrington
8. David Elliott (1716–1798) *m.* 1739 Mehetabel Aldrich (1716–1794)
9. Peter Aldrich (1686–1748) *m.* Hannah Hayward (1680–1746)
10. Jacob Aldrich (1652–1695) *m.* 1674/5 Huldah Thayer (1657–)
11. FERDINANDO THAYER (bap. 1625–1713) *m.* 1652 Huldah Hayward, *d.* 1690
Service: In Mendon, Mass., before King Phillip's War.
Reference: Gen. Dict. of New England; New England Families; First Families of
America.

6438 SAPPINGTON, Mrs. Thomas J. Recorded 1944
301 N. Church Street, Eastman, Georgia
1. Frances Berger *m.* Thomas J. Sappington
2. James Hurt Berger (1840–1917) *m.* 1865 Frances E. Clark (1838–1898)
3. Woodson Clark (1810–1856) *m.* 1834 Dorothy Jennings (1812–1858)
4. John James Clark (1772/75–aft. 1810) *m.* 1810 ⸺
5. Capt. James Clark *m.* 1771 Sarah Woodson (1749–)
6. Charles Woodson (1710–1749) *m.* 1744 (2nd) Agnes Parsons Richardson
7. Tarleton Woodson (1691–1783) *m.* 1710 Ursula Fleming
8. John Woodson (1668–1715) *m.* Judith Tarleton
9. Robert Woodson (1634–1707) *m.* 1656 Elizabeth Ferris
10. DR. JOHN WOODSON (1586–1644) *m.* Sarah ⸺
Service: To Virginia 1619; settled at "Fleur de Hundred" on the James River near
Jamestown.
Reference: Hist. Genealogy of Woodsons and Connections (Clark); William & Mary
College Quart., Vol. 9; Cabells and Kin., Brown.

6373 SARGENT, John Henry Recorded 1942, Vermont
14 Park Street, St. Johnsbury, Vermont
1. John Henry Sargent *m.* 1917 Violet Vivian Viall
2. Harvey Adrian Sargent (1852–1938) *m.* 1879 Abbie A. Poor (1855–1928)
3. John Bailey Sargent (1819–1906) *m.* 1848 Mary W. Tucker (1826–1906)
4. Bailey Sargent (1786–1872) *m.* 1816 (Mrs.) Mary Russell, *d.* 1858
5. Timothy Sargent (1755–1836) *m.* Asenath Tillotson (1761–1801)
6. Capt. Timothy Sargent (1725–1754) *m.* 1749 Hannah Sargent (1732–1802)
7. Timothy Sargent (1698–1769) *m.* 1720 Mary Williams
8. Charles Sargent (1674–1737) *m.* Hannah Foot
9. William Sargent (1646–1712) *m.* 1668 Mary Colby, *b.* 1647
10. WILLIAM SARGENT (1602–1675) *m.* 1st and 2nd, Judith and Elizabeth, Perkins,
sisters
Service: He was one of the first settlers of Wessacucon, now Newbury, 1635; in Winna-
cusnet now, Hampton, N. H., 1638; at South Merrimac, now Salisbury,
Mass., 1639; next located at Salisbury New Town, Amesbury, 1655.
Reference: "William Sargent . . . with his Descendants," by E. E. Sargent.

6611 SAVERY, Mrs. Herbert G. Recorded 1949
Wallingford, Vermont
1. Bertha May Lane *m.* 1907 Herbert G. Savery
2. Moreland E. Lane (1837–1917) *m.* 1874 Loretta F. Atwater (1849–1933)
3. David Atwater (1821–1873) *m.* 1842 Betsey Wilder (1820–1895)
4. Daniel Atwater (1785–1861) *m.* Lois Stevens (1795–1861)
5. Simeon Atwater (1763–) *m.* ⸺
6. Daniel Atwater (1730–) *m.* 1761 Lois Mansfield
7. Daniel Atwater (1694–1765) *m.* 1717 Abigail Tuttle (1692–1769)
8. Samuel Atwater (1664–1742) *m.* 1691 Sarah Alling, *d.* 1742
9. DAVID ATWATER (bapt. 1615–1692) *m.* 1646/7 Damaris Sayre, *d.* 1691
Service: Signed Plantation Covenant 1639, for founding of Colony of New Haven.
Reference: Atwater History and Genealogy.

6098 SCHAFER, Mrs. Carl A. Recorded 1936, New Jersey
404 N. Second Street, Camden, New Jersey
1. Abigail Eastlack *m.* 1914 Carl A. Schafer
2. Oscar A. Eastlack (1868–) *m.* 1889 Marietta Taylor (1867–1909)
3. Charles F. Eastlack (1846–1928) *m.* 1867 Abigail Ann Adams (1847–1920)
4. John C. Eastlack (1808–1888) *m.* 1835 Elizabeth W. Fletcher (1812–1894)
5. Amos Eastlack (1768–1833) *m.* 1807 Rachel Cawman (1789–1871)
6. Samuel Eastlack (1740–1798) *m.* Mary Turner (1745–1801)
7. Francis Eastlack (1707–1781) *m.* 1733 Phebe Driver (1711–1779)
8. Joseph Eastlack (1674–) *m.* 1698 Ann Powell
9. FRANCIS EASTLACK (–1685)
Service: Early Settler.
Reference: First Settlers in Newton Tp., by John Clement; Records of Haddon, N. J., Meeting; History of Glouster Co., N. J., by Cushing and Sheppard; Court House Records in Woodbury, N. J.

6603 SCHLERF, Mrs. Karl F. Recorded 1948
2118 Lawrence Avenue, Chicago 25, Illinois
1. Pearl Lowenthal *m.* 1935 Karl F. Schlerf
2. Julius Lowenthal (1878–1947) *m.* 1904 Emma J. Cross (1884–)
3. Eugene C. Cross (1863–) *m.* 1883 Alvina D. Green (1865–1943)
4. Wm. A. Cross (1831–1908) *m.* 1858 Jane E. Elliott (1841–1907)
5. Charles E. Elliott (1813–1892) *m.* 1837 Lucy M. Barber (1818–1891)
6. Asa Elliott (1785–1852) *m.* 1807 Betsey Williams (1788–1855)
7. Laban Elliott (1757–1830) *m.* Mehitable Harrington
8. David Elliott (1716–1798) *m.* 1739 Mehetabel Aldrich (1716–1794)
9. Peter Aldrich (1686–1748) *m.* Hannah Hayward (1680–1746)
10. Jacob Aldrich (1652–1695) *m.* 1674/5 Huldah Thayer (1657–)
11. FERDINANDO THAYER (bap. 1625–1713) *m.* 1652 Huldah Hayward, *d.* 1690
Service: In Mendon, Mass., before King Phillip's War.
Reference: Gen. Dict. of New England; New England Families; First Families of America.

6307 SCOTT, Rev. Raymond Mathewson Recorded 1940, Vermont
111-A Grove Street, Rutland, Vermont
1. Raymond M. Scott *m.* 1939 Harriet Eunice Tracy
2. Raymond Earl Scott (1886–1918) *m.* 1908 Eunice May Mathewson, *b.* 1889
3. Harry E. Mathewson (1869–) *m.* 1888 Lena M. Douglas, *b.* 1868
4. John Mathewson (1822–1894) *m.* Eunice S. Williams (1828–1894)
5. Esek Mathewson (1794–1863) *m.* Thankful Briggs (1795–1881)
6. Oliver Mathewson (1768–) *m.* 1790 Ruth Matteson
7. John Mathewson, *b.* 1740, *m.* 1761 Elizabeth King
8. Joseph Mathewson (Matteson) (1705–1758) *m.* 1727 Martha Greene
9. THOMAS MATTESON, *d.* 1740, *m.* 1695 Martha Shipper
Service: Deputy for East Grenwich, R. I., 1717.
Reference: New England (Genealogical and Memorial) American Historical Society.

6592 SCOTT, Mrs. William E. Recorded 1948
247 S. Park Avenue, Fort Lupton, Colorado
1. Nellie M. Loftiss *m.* 1914 Wm. E. Scott
2. Gideon M. Loftiss (1855–1934) *m.* 1880 Emma A. Umphenour (1857–1926)
3. Samuel G. Umphenour (1824–1882) *m.* 1850 Martha A. Morton (1831–1873)
4. Alexander Morton, Jr. (1796–1876) *m.* 1820 Martha Anderson (1798–1881)
5. Alexander Morton (1759–1822) *m.* 1784 Ruth Strong (1762–1850)
6. Elijah Strong (1733–1774/5) *m.* 1756 Ruth Loomis (1729–)
7. Zachariah Loomis (1681–1751) *m.* 1707 Joanna Abell (1683–1759)
8. Sgt. Caleb Abell (1646/7–1731) *m.* 1669 Margaret Post (1653–1700)
9. John Post (1626–1710/1) *m.* 1652 Hester Hyde, *d.* 1703
10. WILLIAM HYDE *ca.* (1597–1681) *m.* ——
Service: Founder of Hartford, Conn., and Norwich, Conn.
Reference: Loomis Family in America, Strongs of Strongville; Desc. of Andrew Hyde.

6220 SCRUGGS, Eugenia Elizabeth   Recorded 1938
      Atlanta, Georgia
1. Anderson McLaren Scruggs (1897–1938) *m.* 1921 Leila Mae Smith (1900–1938)
2. Wm. Edgar Scruggs (1864–1931) *m.* 1888 Tallulah Eugenia Watson (1868–1938)
3. Col. Wm. Lindsay Scruggs (1836–1912) *m.* 1858 Judith Ann Potts (1837–1897)
4. Frederick Scruggs, Jr. (1807–1854) *m.* 1835 Margaret Kimbrough
5. Frederick Scruggs, Sr. (1783–1807) *m.* Rebecca Lindsay Comway
6. Rev. Gross Scruggs (1758–1822) *m.* 1782 Anne Keith Hale (1760–1787)
7. Jesse Scruggs (1736–1774) *m.* 1756 ———
8. Richard Scruggs (1689–1737) *m.* 1716 Martha ———
9. Henry Scruggs (1660–1723) *m.* 1685 Anne Gross (1665–1697)
10. RICHARD SCRUGGS (1630–1669) *m.* 1660 ———
Service: Proprietor.
Reference:

6362 SCULL, Mrs. James Gifford   Recorded 1942, New Jersey
      18 Gibbs Avenue, Somers Point, New Jersey
1. Martha Denny Robinson *m.* 1902 James Gifford Scull
2. Charles P. Robinson (1860–1929) *m.* 1881 Virginia A. Denny (1865–1933)
3. John I. A. Denny (1830–1882) *m.* 1852 Martha Hornor (1831–1875)
4. James Denny (1798–1879) *m.* 1826 Sarah Ann Dolbow (1803–1883)
5. Gideon Denny, *d.* 1824, *m.* 1782 Mary Clayton
6. Thomas Denny *m.* 1745 Elizabeth Rambo (1728–1774)
7. Peter Rambo, *b.* 1694, *m.* Christine Keen, *d.* bef. 1753
8. John Rambo (1661–1741) *m.* 1684 Brigitta Cock, *d.* bef. 1740
9. PETER RAMBO, *b. c.* 1605, *m.* Britta
Service: Member of delegation 1654/55 sent by Gov. Reping to Dutch Gov.
    Stuyvesant for terms about Christina and other forts on Delaware; in Phila-
    delphia, Pa., early in 1698; first Eng. Gov. of Delaware.
Reference: Pennsylvania Archives; Recs. of Swedesboro Church, N. J.

4764 SEGAR, Miss Minnie A.   Recorded 1921, Connecticut
      23 Mt. View Terrace, Hamden, Connecticut
1. Minnie Adams Segar
2. John D. Segar (1850–1890) *m.* 1879 Annie Grinell (1856–1931)
3. Moses Adams (1830–1882) *m.* 1852 Catherine Stevens (1831–1904)
4. John Adams II (1800–1885) *m.* 1821 Phoebe R. Chase (1799–1843)
5. Moses Adams (1773–1855) *m.* Martha Kinney (1769–1848)
6. John Adams (1747–1809) *m.* 1773 Katherine Adams (1751–1833)
7. Samuel Adams, Jr. (1710–1775) *m.* 1734 Elizabeth Young (1710–   )
8. Samuel Adams (1680–1753) *m.* Lydia Gowell (1692–   )
9. Thomas Adams (1648–1737) *m.* Hannah Parker
10. PHILIP ADAMS (1625–1692) *m.* Elizabeth (1628–1710)
Service: A Freeman in 1652. One of the Founders of the town of York.
Reference: Genealogical Dictionary of Maine and New Hampshire, by Noyes, Libby
    and Davis.

5842 SEITZ, Mrs. George E.   Recorded 1929
      18 Summit Street, East Orange, New Jersey
1. Eterline Disbrow Pedroncelli (1879–   ) *m.* 1924 George Edwin Seitz
2. Wm. Cook Disbrow (1851–   ) *m.* 1876 Elizabeth Bulger (1860–1919)
3. Wm. Cook Disbrow (1816–1893) *m.* 1848 Marg. Wessells Dill (1828–1912)
4. Sam. Warne Disbrow (1778–1873) *m.* 1811 Sarah Cook (1792–1875)
5. Benj. Disbrow (1754–1785) *m.* 1775 Deborah Robinson (1755–1785)
6. Griffin Disbrow (1712–1754) *m.* Hannah ———
7. Benj. Disbrow (1672–1733) *m.* Mary Griffin (–1737)
8. HENRY DISBROW (–1699) *m.* Margaret ———
Service: Magistrate Mamaroneck, 1673.
Reference: His. & Gen. Misc., Stillwell, Vol. 4, pg. 75; N. Y. Gen. & Biog. Rec.,
    Vol. 51, etc.; History of St. Peter's Church, Jones, pg. 246.

6646   SEVIER, Mary Jane   Recorded 1949
       Route No. 1, Asheville, North Carolina
   1. Mary Jane Sevier
   2. James V. Sevier (1847–1928) *m.* 1867 Mary S. Reynolds (1847–1915)
   3. Edward Sevier (1825–1909) *m.* 1847 Mary N. Garrett (1827–1884)
   4. Valentine Sevier III (1780–1854) *m.* 1804 Nancy Dinwiddie (1786–1844)
   5. Capt. Robert Sevier (1750–1780) *m.* 1777 Keziah Robertson
   6. Valentine Sevier II (1702–1803) *m.* 1744 Joanna Goade *ca.* (1718–1773)
   7. John Goade II *ca.* (1665–   ) *m. ca.* 1700 ———
   8. JOHN GOADE I *ca.* (1629–   ) *m.* ———
Service: Came to America by way of the Barbados in 1650 and settled in Balti-
       more, Md.
Reference: "The Sevier Family."

6124   SEYMOUR, Miss Ann   Recorded 1937, Connecticut
       Hartford, Connecticut
   1. Miss Ann Seymour
   2. Moses E. Seymour (1856–1936) *m.* 1884 Marion Bachaus (1859–1931)
   3. Chester Seymour (1823–1895) *m.* 1849 Sabra T. Ensign (1826–1901)
   4. Moses Ensign (1794–1864) *m.* 1816 Martha T. Whiting (1797–1853)
   5. Elijah Whiting (1769–1840) *m.* 1793 Sabra Hart (1770–1821)
   6. Allyn Whiting (1740–1818) *m.* Elizabeth Merry (1738–   )
   7. Col. John Whiting (1693–1766) *m.* Jerusha Lord (1699–1776)
   8. Capt. Joseph Whiting (1645–1717) *m.* 1676 Anna Allyn (1654–1735)
   9. Col. John Allyn (–1696) *m.* 1653 Anna Smith
  10. Judge Henry Smith (–1681) *m.* Ann Pynchon
  11. HON. WILLIAM PYNCHON (–1661)
Service: An incorporator named by the King in the Mass. Bay Charter, 1636.
Reference: Genealogical Notes of the Whiting Family, by A. F. Whiting.

6503   SHAUCK, Mrs. Robert Lee   Recorded 1945
       Mansfield, Ohio
   1. Janet McKitrick *m.* Robert Lee Shauck
   2. Donald Kent McKitrick (1891–   ) *m.* 1916 Nellie Merle Jones (1894–   )
   3. Dr. Austin S. McKitrick (1863–1941) *m.* 1889 Mary Eliza Donaldson (1866–1928)
   4. John H. Donaldson (1834–1919) *m.* 1860 Lura Permelia Barker (1836–1897)
   5. Daniel Gilbert Barker (1803–1887) *m.* 1829 Eliza Baker (1800–1865)
   6. Marshall Baker (1774–1848) *m.* 1795 Elizabeth Ward (1776–1849)
   7. Sylvanius Ward (1753–1834) *m.* 1775 Hannah Goddard (1753–1812)
   8. Robert Goddard (1723–1807) *m.* 1752 Hannah Stone (1726–1757)
   9. Edward Goddard (1697–1777) *m.* 1722 Hepzibah Hapgood (1704–1763)
  10. Thomas Hapgood (1669–1763) *m.* 1690/93 Judith Barker (1671–1759)
  11. John Barker (1646–1718) *m.* 1668 Judith Simonds (1646–   )
  12. WILLIAM SIMONDS (1611–1672) *m.* 1644 Judith Phippen (1619–1689/90)
Service: Early settler Concord, Mass.; Landed Proprietor of Woburn, Mass., 1645.
Reference:

6327   SHEA, Mrs. Edward H.   Recorded 1941, Maryland
       15 South Third East, Salt Lake City, Utah
   1. Jean Glenn *m.* 1905 Edward H. Shea
   2. Robert Lee Glenn (1863–1931) *m.* 1883 Quintie Thomas (1862–1938)
   3. Charles Quincy Thomas (1827–1862) *m.* 1853 Sallie Linthicum (1835–1886)
   4. Charles Wms. Linthicum (1813–1866) *m.* 1833 Mary Eliza Slaughter (1819–1852)
   5. Thomas Prather Linthicum (1771–1859) *m.* 1793 Anne Nancy Williams
       (1776–1843)
   6. Charles Williams (1743–1826) *m.* 1765 Anne Beckwith (1748–1824)
   7. Basil Beckwith (1703–1780) *m.* 1741 Volinda Clagett, *b.* 1705
   8. Charles Beckwith (1669–   ) *m.* 1702 Margaret Ann Banks, *b.* 1672
   9. GEORGE BECKWITH (1606–1675) *m.* Frances Hervey, *d.* 1676
Service: Member of House of Burgesses; merchant and planter.
Reference: "Gen. of Linthicum and Allied Families," Badger; "Sidelights on Mary-
       land Hist.," Richardson; "The Beckwith's," Paul Beckwith.

6465 SHELDON, Miss Ruth Recorded 1945
  5907 Washington Blvd., Milwaukee, Wisconsin
  1. Miss Ruth Bradley Sheldon (deceased) (State Regent, Philippine, Dar.)
  2. Benjamin Olcott Sheldon (1839–1920) *m.* 1867 Henrietta E. Foster (1848–1897)
  3. Nehemiah Foster (1819–1877) *m.* 1842 Nancy Day (1822–1890)
  4. Wyllis David Foster (1783–1834) *m.* 1806 Abigail Chaffee (1786–1861)
  5. Calvin Chaffee (1760–1817) *m.* 1786 Ruth Everden (1768–)
  6. James Chaffee (1713–) *m.* 1759 Rhoda Cady (–1799)
  7. Joseph Chaffee (1671–1750) *m.* 1712 (2nd) Jemima Chadwick
  8. Joseph Chaffee (1639–1746) *m.* 1670 Annis Martin (–1729/30)
  9. Thomas Chaffee (–1683) *m.* ———
  Service: Resident Hingham, Hull, Rehoboth and Swansea, Mass.
  Reference: First Fam. of America, Virkus; Compendium, V. R. Wallingford, Vol. 23;
    Conn. V. R. 1670–1850; Mass. Gen., Cutler.

6637 SHELTON, Mrs. Elbert M. Recorded 1949
  122 North Mulberry Street, Statesville, North Carolina
  1. Ivetta Cain *m.* 1927 Elbert M. Shelton
  2. Cary T. Cain (1860–1921) *m.* 1885 Lula E. Coffey (1866–1933)
  3. William E. Coffey (1839–1912) *m.* 1880 Margaret A. Kincaid (1845–1921)
  4. Milton Kincaid (1821–1903) *m.* 1833 Abigail Bristol (1816–1894)
  5. Benedict Bristol (1780–1868) *m.* 1810 Jessie McCall (1790–1820)
  6. Robert McCall (1752–1820) *m.* 1780 Elizabeth Sitkin (1760–1828)
  7. John McCall (1698–1781) *m.* 1742 Helen Moore (1721–1786)
  8. George McCall (1662–1740) *m.* 1696 Martha Moore (1673–1718)
  9. John McCall (1630–1690) *m.* 1660 Mary Smith (1640–1672)
  10. John McCall (1591–1669) *m.* 1620 Jane Sirkins (1602–1650)
  Service: Mayflower passenger. His first wife died in childbirth and was buried at
    sea from the Mayflower.
  Reference: Bristol Genealogy, by Victor G. Bristol; McCall Genealogy, by Victor G.
    Bristol; D.A.R.; D.A.C.

6091 SHEPARD, Mrs. Finley J. Recorded 1935, New York
  579 Fifth Avenue, New York City
  1. Helen Gould *m.* 1913 Finley J. Shepard
  2. Jay Gould (1836–1892) *m.* 1863 Helen Day Miller (1838–1889)
  3. John Burr Gould (1792–1866) *m.* 1827 Mary More (1798–1841)
  4. Abraham Gould (1766–1823) *m.* 1789 Anna Osborn (1764–1847)
  5. Eleazer Osborn (1739–) *m.* 1764 Sarah Burr (1743–)
  6. Ephraim Burr (1700–1776) *m.* 1725 Abigail Burr (1702–1780)
  7. Major Peter Burr (1668–1724)
  8. John Burr, Jr. (1625–1692) *m.* Elizabeth Prudden (1643–)
  9. John (Jehu) Burr (1600–1670)
  Service: One of the Pilgrims who came with Winthrop's famous fleet in 1630 and
    settled in Roxbury, Mass.
  Reference: Burr Genealogy; Genealogical Charts of Donald Jacobus; Colonial Dames
    of New York.

6623 SHIPP, Mrs. Connie H. Recorded 1949
  1104 Watts Street, Durham, North Carolina
  1. Ada Cates *m.* 1900 Connie H. Shipp
  2. Headen M. Cates (1858–1930) *m.* 1880 Mary Couch (1865–1916)
  3. Isaiah Cates (1824–1892) *m.* 1852 Rhoda E. Ray (1828–1896)
  4. David Ray (1794–aft. 1812) *m.* 1824 Annie Hatch (1796–1885)
  5. John Ray (1762–aft. 1827) *m.* Sallie Clark *ca.* (1775–1835)
  6. James Ray, *d.* aft. 1800, *m.* Ann Latta, *d.* 1812
  7. James Ray (bef. 1716–aft. 1775) *m.* 1761 Abigail Conner *ca.* (1730–)
  8. William Conner *ca.* (1700–) *m.* Sarah Rogers (–aft 1700)
  9. William Conner (aft. 1660–aft. 1716) *m. ca.* 1700 Abigail
  10. Phillip Conner (1613–aft. 1703) *m.* aft. 1634 Mary
  Service: Came to this country 1634; located first in Kent Island, Md.
  Reference: Va. Historical Magazine, U.D.C., 1812, D.C.W. records.

6082 SHOVER, Mrs. H. C.   Recorded 1935, Georgia
        14 Ridgeland Way, Atlanta, Georgia
  1. Eliza Crosby Gibbes *m.* 1897 Hayden C. Shover
  2. Washington A. Gibbes (1841–1927) *m.* 1869 Elizabeth F. Hunt (1851–1890)
  3. Robert Wilson Gibbes (1809–1866) *m.* 1827 Caroline E. Guignard (1811–1865)
  4. William H. Gibbes (1754–1834) *m.* 1808 Mary P. Wilson (1772–1844)
  5. William Gibbes (1722–1780) *m.* 1748 Elizabeth Hasell (1725–1762)
  6. William Gibbes (1689–1733) *m.* 1716 Alice Culcheth (1700–1739)
  7. Robert Gibbes (1644–1715) *m.* Mary E. Donne
  Service: Member of Assembly 1699.
  Reference: Appleton's Cyclopedia of American Biography, Vol. II; South Carolina
        Historical & Genealogical Magazine, Vol. XII.

6488 SHREWDER, Mrs. Roy Valentine   Recorded 1945
        Ashland, Kansas
  1. Dorothy Berryman *m.* Roy Valentine Shrewder
  2. Jerome Woods Berryman (1870–1940) *m.* 1898 Nancy Annette McNickle (1871–)
  3. Gerard Q. Berryman (1835–1895) *m.* 1869 Minerva Anderson Woods (1843–1892)
  4. James Harris Woods (1810–1845) *m.* 1835 Martha Jane Stone (1815–1868)
  5. Anderson Woods (1788–1841) *m.* 1809 Elizabeth Harris (1791–1868)
  6. James Woods (1748–1822) *m.* 1779 Mary Garland (1760–1833)
  7. John Woods (1712–1791) *m.* 1742 Susannah Anderson (1725–)
  8. Rev. James Anderson (1678–1740) *m.* 1712/3 Suit Garland (1694–1736)
  9. Sylvester Garland (1670–) *m.* ———
  10. John Garland (–1673) *m.* Susannah VerPlanck (1642–)
  11. Abraham Isaacson Ver Planck (–1672) *m.* 1635 Maria DeVigne (–1671)
  Service: Member of the Representative Body of Nieuw Netherlands, known as "The
        Twelve Men," 1641–2.

5886 SHROY, Mrs. Letitia S.   Recorded 1929, Pennsylvania
  1. Letitia-Starkweather *m.* 1915 ——— Shroy
  2. Emilius T. Starkweather (1846–1924) *m.* 1870 Elizabeth A. Donat (1843–1923)
  3. George A. Starkweather (1821–1904) *m.* 1844 Rumanda Lee (1821–1896)
  4. Horace Lee (1794–1867) *m.* 1817 Catherine Hamlin (1792–1867)
  5. Harris Hamlin (1776–1854) *m.* 1787 Ruey Easton (1770–1833)
  6. William Hamlin (1726–1821) *m.* 1750 Hannah Allen (1728–1807)
  7. Nathaniel Hamlin (1699–1731) *m.* 1725 Sarah Harris (1703–)
  8. William Hamlin (1668–1733) *m.* 1692 Susanna Collins (1669–1721)
  9. Giles Hamlin (1622–1689) *m.* 1655 Hester Crow (1628–1700)
  Service: Deputy to General Assembly from 1666 to 1784.
  Reference: The Hamlin Family Genealogy of Capt. Giles Hamlin, by Hon. H.
        Franklin Andrews (1900), pages 14, 15, 19, 23.

6319 SIMPSON, Hon. Wilder Arthur   Recorded 1941, Vermont
        Lyndonville, Vermont
  1. Wilder Arthur Simpson *m.* 1912 ———
  2. James E. Simpson (1863–1900) *m.* 1885 Mabel A. Wilder (1865–1921)
  3. Elias Wilder (1833–1925) *m.* Elvira ——— (1833–1916)
  4. Levi Wilder (1792/3–1876) *m.* Sophronia Hartwell (1803–1876)
  5. Oliver Hartwell (1756–1812) *m.* Hannah Kelly, *b.* 1763
  6. Joseph Hartwell (1722–1803) *m.* Sarah ———
  7. William Hartwell, *b.* 1671, *m.* Ruth ———, *d.* 1751/2
  8. Samuel Hartwell (1645–1725) *m.* 1665 Ruth Wheeler
  9. William Hartwell (1613–1690) *m.* ———, *d.* 1695
  Service: Town Official, Concord, Mass., 1672; an Overseer of Concord, 1654; on
        Committee of Seven.
  Reference: Shattuck's "Hist. of Concord, Mass.;" Hemenway's "Hist. of Vermont;"
        Hartwell Family History; V. R. of Bedford, Mass.; Brown's "Hist. of
        Bedford, Mass."

6455   SLOAN, Mrs. Clarence Reuben   Recorded 1944
       215 Fourth Street, Marietta, Ohio

1. Helen Cornwall Hill *m.* Dr. Clarence R. Sloan
2. Willis Edgar Hill (1857–1918) *m.* 1882 Emma Elizabeth Oglevee (1859–1888)
3. Harvey Dale Hill (1828–1867) *m.* 1855 Angeline Sheets Dye (1833–1910)
4. Capt. Ira Hill (War 1812) (1787–1866) *m.* 1816 Welthes Little (1795–1870)
5. Nathaniel Little (Rev. War) (1759–1808) *m.* 1792 Pamela Bradford (1764–1823)
6. Paybody Bradford (1735–1782) *m.* 1760 Welthea Delano (1741–1783)
7. Gamaliel Bradford (1704–1778) *m.* 1728 Abigail Bartlett (1703–1776)
8. Samuel Bradford (1668–1714) *m.* 1689 Hannah Rogers (1668–)
9. John Rogers (1641–1732) *m.* 1666 Elizabeth Paybody (1647–1707) ca.
10. John Rogers *m.* Ann Churchman
11. THOMAS ROGERS (–1621)

Service: Mayflower passenger, died first year.
Reference: No. 162941 D. A. R. Reg. of Colonial Dames of America, Mass., 1927,
       pp. 353–353.

6054   SLUSSER, Mrs. C. R.   Recorded 1933, Colorado
       1342 Columbine Street, Denver, Colorado

1. Harriet E. Turner *m.* 1898 Charles R. Slusser
2. George K. Turner (1832–1908) *m.* 1871 Jennie A. Baird (1846–1921)
3. Paine Turner (1780–1847) *m.* 1826 Lucy M. Griswold (1792–1861)
4. Paine Turner *m.* Abigail Tracy
5. Jonathan Turner (1748–1815) *m.* Bridget McArthur
6. Paine Turner (1713–) *m.* 1745 Eleanor Haines
7. Lt. Jonathan Turner *m.* 1709 Elizabeth Paine
8. Jonathan Turner (1678–1757) *m.* Martha Busbidge
9. John Turner *m.* 1645 Mary Brewster (1627–)
10. HUMPHREY TURNER (–1673) *m.* Lydia Garner

Service:
Reference: Turner Family Bible; Mayflower Descendants, Vols. X-XVII.

5849   SMITH, Denta Watson   Recorded 1929
       111 Church Street, Winder, Georgia

1. Denta Watson (1892–) *m.* 1916 Herschel Willoughby Smith
2. James William Watson (1850–1919) *m.* 1874 Georgia England (1858–)
3. Marion Watson (1823–1903) *m.* 1848 Emily Ann Norton (1823–1902)
4. William Norton (1765–1843) *m.* 1810 Mary Landrum (1791–1862)
5. Thomas Norton (1736–1802) *m.* 1757 Mary
6. William Norton (1677–1751)
7. Capt. John Norton *m.* Elizabeth Thaxter
8. Rev. John Norton *m.* 1674 Mary Mason
9. REV. WILLIAM NORTON (1610–1694) *m.* Lucy Downing

5916   SMITH, Edward Luther   Recorded 1930, Pennsylvania
       363 York Avenue, Towanda, Pennsylvania

1. Edward Luther Smith *m.* Mildred Louise Rahn
2. Myron Smith (1831–1908) *m.* 1861 Frances Marion Scott (1840–1922)
3. Jesse Smith (–1871) *m.* 1828 Anna Lent (1811–1850)
4. Joseph Lent (1786–1869) *m.* Mary Ann Johnson (1785–1855)
5. John Johnson (1755–1819) *m.* 1779 Anna Hinman (1759–)
6. Samuel Hinman (1730–1791) *m.* 1757 Amy Twichel (1741–)
7. Wait Hinman (1706–1775) *m.* 1729 Ann Hurd (1706–1785)
8. Benjamin Hinman (1662–1713) *m.* 1684 Elizabeth Lum
9. EDWARD HINMAN (–1681) *m.* 1652 Hannah Stiles

Service: Edward Hinman was a Sergeant of Stratford, Conn.
Reference: Gen. Stiles Ancient Windsor, Vol. II.

6239	SMITH, Mrs. Edward T.					Recorded 1939
		7171 Kingsbury Blvd., St. Louis, Missouri
	1.	Mellcene Thurman *m.* Edward T. Smith
	2.	John William Thurman (1850–1931) *m.* 1869 Cecelia Marion Woodward (1851–1918)
	3.	Manson Jesse Woodward (1821–1898) *m.* 1849 Fanny Belinda Abell (1826–1903)
	4.	David Woodward (1781–1832) *m.* 1814 Diedema Hare (1796–1845)
	5.	Elisha Woodward (1754–1841) *m.* 1778 Lucy Manson (–1791)
	6.	Benajah Woodward (1712–1792) *m.* 1742 Abigail Harvey
	7.	Israel Woodward (1681–1766) *m.* Elizabeth Gilmore (1683–1765)
	8.	John Woodward (1654–1688) *m.* 1675 Sarah Crossman (1653–1692)
	9.	Nathaniel Woodward, Jr. (1609–1694) *m.* 1642 Mary Jackson
	10.	NATHANIEL WOODWARD, SR. (–1667) *m.* Margaret
	Service: Founder of Boston and Dedham, Mass.; Surveyor.
	Reference: Daughter of Am. Colonists No. 346; Enc. of Biography, Vol. 45, p. 203; His. of D.A.C. in Mo., by Mellcene T. Smith.

6439	SMITH, Gilbert Pennoyer					Recorded 1944
		30 Putnam Cir., Springfield 4, Massachusetts
	1.	Gilbert Pennoyer Smith *m.* Elizabeth May Cheshire
	2.	Henry Harland Smith (1868–1935) *m.* 1908 Genevra M. Pennoyer (1882–)
	3.	Henry J. B. Pennoyer (1835–1911) *m.* 1867 Mary Emma Huntington (1842–1896)
	4.	Seth Huntington *m.* Mary Hovey
	5.	Chester Hovey (1778–) *m.* Olive Rexford (–1833)
	6.	Capt. Ebenezer Hovey (1752–1838) *m.* Rebecca Simmons
	7.	Nathaniel Hovey (1717–1784) *m.* 1747 Ruth Parker
	8.	Nathaniel Hovey (1691–1761) *m.* 1712 Abigail Gennings (–1773)
	9.	Nathaniel Hovey (1657–1692) *m.* 1679 Sarah Fuller
	10.	DANIEL HOVEY (1618–1692) *m.* Abigail Andrews (–1676/83)
	Service: Early settler Ipswich, Mass.; 1659 Selectman, Ipswich; Surveyor of Highways, 1648–9 and 50; Constable, 1658; Juror, 1649.
	Reference: S. & D. of Pilgrims No. 6349; Hist. Compton Family, Channel; "Hovey Nook" No. 354, etc.

6264	SMITH, Mrs. Irving Bell				Recorded 1939, New Jersey
		Madison Avenue, Fort Washington, Montgomery Co., Pennsylvania
	1.	Helen Walton *m.* 1929 Irving Bell Smith, Jr.
	2.	John Gardner Walton (1865–1924) *m.* 1900 Clara R. G. Betts, *b.* 1868
	3.	John Brooks Betts (1836–1931) *m.* 1863 Jeanette Carter (1844–1921)
	4.	Richard Kinsey Betts (1807–1890) *m.* 1835 Anna Brooks (1807–1850)
	5.	Samuel Cary Betts (1776–1861) *m.* 1798 Grace Biles (1776–1848)
	6.	William Biles (1749–1778) *m.* 1766 Hannah Kirkbride (1743–1794)
	7.	Thomas Kirkbride (1712–1747) *m.* 1738 Grace Woolston, *b.* 1715
	8.	THOMAS KIRKBRIDE, *d.* 1724, *m.* 1707 Elizabeth Banner Darby
	Service: Came to America about 1690.
	Reference: Presby. Ch., Churchville, Pa.; Lancaster Co., Pa., Rec., 1807; Wills, Camden, N. J.; St. Paul's P. Ch. Rec., Camden, N. J., 1900; 1st Unitarian Ch., Phila., Pa., 1863; Penna. Statistics, 1909; Ch. of Good Shepherd, Rosemont, Pa., 1929.

5983	SMITH, Mrs. James F.					Recorded 1931
	1.	Anna Thompson Rorer (1890–) *m.* 1915 James Fisher Smith
	2.	Francis C. W. Rorer (1863–) *m.* 1886 Ella Applegate Herbert (1864–)
	3.	David Simmons Rorer (1826–1912) *m.* 1849 Mary Ann Woodington (1829–1901)
	4.	William Woodington (1809–1877) *m.* 1827 Rebecca Dyer (1812–1880)
	5.	Samuel Dyer (1783–1855) *m.* 1808 Elizabeth Keen (1790–1832)
	6.	Joseph Dyer (1754–1815) *m.* 1780 Mary Ann
	7.	James Dyer (1728–1803) *m.* 1751 Elizabeth
	8.	Charles Dyer (1697–) *m.* 1716 Elizabeth Shrief (1698–1778)
	9.	James Dyer (1669–) *m.* 1696 ———
	10.	Charles Dyer (1650–1709) *m.* Mary
	11.	WILLIAM DYER (–1677) *m.* Mary (–1660)
	Service: Sec. for Portsmouth and Newport, R. I., 1640; Gen. Recorder, 1650–1653; Atty. Gen.
	Reference: William Dyer Gen. Directory of R. I., by Austin.

6232 SMITH, Mrs. James Sebritt   Recorded 1938
      Gov. Albert C. Ritchie Highway, Brooklyn, Baltimore, Maryland
1. Olivia C. Tubbs (1865–) *m.* 1885 James Sebritt Smith
2. John Tubbs (1827–1898) *m.* 1858 Olivia Anne Stewart (1835–1877)
3. Joshua Steward (1790–1873) *m.* 1816 Caroline Cromwell (1796–1879)
4. John Giles Cromwell (1769–1823) *m.* 1793 Elizabeth Jacob Rowles
5. Thomas Ireton Cromwell (–1799) *m.* Hannah Henrietta Smith
6. Oliver Cromwell (1708–1786) *m.* Anna Maria Giles
7. Thomas Cromwell (1679–1723) *m.* 1705 Jemina Morgan Murray
8. WILLIAM CROMWELL (–1684) *m.* Elizabeth Treherne
Service:
Reference: Newman's Anne Arundel Co. Gen., pg. 600; Eng. Hist., Vol. 1, 2, 3, 4, by
     J. R. Green.

6218 SMITH, Jan Clare   Recorded 1938
      Madison Avenue, Fort Washington, Pennsylvania
1. Jan Clare Smith
2. Irving Bell Smith, Jr. (1904–) *m.* 1929 Helen Walton (1909–)
3. John Gardener Walton (1865–1924) *m.* 1900 Clara R. G. Betts (1868–)
4. John Brooks Betts (1836–1931) *m.* 1863 Jeanette Carter (1844–1921)
5. Richard Kinsey Betts (1807–1890) *m.* 1835 Anna Brooks (1807–1850)
6. Samuel Cary (1776–1861) *m.* 1798 Grace Biles (–1848)
7. Zacheriah Betts (1736–1808) *m.* 1770 Bethula Cary (1748–1777)
8. Thomas Betts (1689–1747) *m.* 1725 Susanna Field (1704–)
9. Thomas Betts (1660–1709) *m.* 1688 Mercy Whitehead
10. RICHARD BETTS (1613–1713) *m.* Joanna ———
Service: Member Provincial Assembly; Magistrate; Justice of Peace; Captain.
Reference: Riker's Annals of Newborough, L. I., p. 74.

6523 SMITH, Julia Gloria   Recorded 1946
      Madison Avenue, Fort Washington, Pennsylvania
             (JUNIOR)
1. Julia Gloria Smith
2. Irving B. Smith, Jr. (1904–) *m.* 1929 Helen Walton (1909–)
3. John G. Walton (1865–1924) *m.* 1900 Clara R. G. Betts (1868–)
4. John B. Betts (1836–1931) *m.* 1863 Jeanette Carter (1844–1921)
5. Richard K. Betts (1807–1890) *m.* 1835 Anna Brooks (1807–1850)
6. John Brooks (1772–1843) *m.* 1802 Elizabeth Baker (1784–)
7. Samuel Baker III (1748–1814/16) *m.* 1777/8 Elizabeth Head (Scattergood)
   (1749–1836)
8. Samuel Baker II (1706–1760) *m.* 1741 Elizabeth Burroughs (1715–)
9. Samuel Baker (1676–1725) *m.* 1703 Rachel Warder (1670–1760)
10. HENRY BAKER, *d.* 1705, *m.* Margaret Hardman, *d.* 1691
Service: Justice of Peace, 1689; member Provincial Assembly; "First Purchaser"
   on Holme's Map.
Reference: Betts and Allied Families.

6477 SMITH, Mrs. Lloyd DeWitt   Recorded 1945
      Grosse Point, Michigan
1. Mabel E. Gale *m.* Lloyd DeWitt Smith
2. Theodore Gale (1846–1904) *m.* 1867 Laura Ann Beardsley (1846–1932)
3. Hiram Beardsley (1819–1908) *m.* 1845 Mary Howell Clarke (1822–1908)
4. Philip Beardsley *m.* 1818 Laura Ingham (1796–)
5. Benjamin Ingham (1756–1810) *m.* Anna Steele (1764–1826)
6. James Steele (1719–1766) *m.* Lois ———
7. Thomas Steele (1681–1757) *m.* 1709 Susannah Webster (1686–1757)
8. Samuel Steele (1652–1710) *m.* 1680 Mercy Bradford (1660–1720)
9. Major William Bradford (1624–1704) *m.* Alice Richards (1627–1670)
10. Gov. WILLIAM BRADFORD (1590–1657) *m.* Alice C. Southworth (1590–1690)
Service: Governor of Plymouth Colony, 1621, for 12 years; Deputy Governor for two
   years; Chief Justice; Minister of Foreign Affairs; Speaker of the General
   Court, 1653.

6365   SMITH, Margaret Foster   Recorded 1942, New York
            1032 Warburton, Yonkers, New York
       1. Margaret Foster *m.* 1912 Franklin Howell Smith
       2. Charles Humphrey Foster (1858–1919) *m.* 1887 Ellinor Gibbs (1864–   )
       3. Charles Foster (1816–1901) *m.* 1847 Sarah Robilson Baird (1826–1882)
       4. Jacob Baird (1800–1851) *m.* 1882 Joanna Cobb Barrows (1798–1877)
       5. Andrew Barrows (1775–1824) *m.* 1797 Mary Shurtleff (1775–1866)
       6. Andrew Barrows (1748–1809) *m.* 1771 Sarah Perkins (1753–1835)
       7. Joshua Perkins (1729–1797) *m.* 1749 Hannah Samson (1730–1797)
       8. George Sampson (1690–1774) *m.* 1718 Hannah Soule (1696–1776)
       9. Benjamin Soule, *d.* 1729, *m.* Sarah Standish, *d.* 1740
      10. Alexander Standish, *d.* 1702, *m.* Sarah Alden, *b.* 1629
      11. JOHN ALDEN, *d.* 1687, *m.* Priscilla Mullins
      Service: Mayflower passenger.
      Reference: Mayflower Descendants; "Plymouth Landmarks;" Appleton's Amer.
            Cyclopedia, Vol. I; Descendants of Wm. Shurtluff; Carver V. R.; Plympton
            V. R.

6554   SMITH, Mrs. Morris Horatio   Recorded 1947
            1710 Lakewood Avenue, Lima, Ohio
       1. Helen O. Longsworth *m.* 1927 Morris Horatio Smith
       2. Ira R. Longsworth (1859–1932) *m.* 1882 Mary E. Methany (1860–1939)
       3. Dr. Wm. N. Longsworth (1818–1903) *m.* 1856 Olivia Richie (1836–1931)
       4. Mirabeau F. Richey (1807–1892) *m.* 1835 Sarah Eaton (1808–1900)
       5. Samuel Richey (1782–1839) *m.* bef. 1807 Olivia Ferree (1788–1831)
       6. Jacob Ferree (1750–1807) *m.* 1783 Alice Powell (1761–1846)
       7. Isaac Ferree, *d.* 1782, *m.* Elizabeth
       8. Philip Ferree (1687–1753) *m.* 1713 Leah DuBois (1687–1758)
       9. Abraham Du Bois (1657–1731) *m.* 1681 Margaret D'Oyaeux
      10. Louis Du Bois (1627–1696) *m.* 1655 Catherine Blanchan, *d.* 1713
      11. Matthys Blanchan *m.* Madeline J. de Rapalje
      12. JORIS JANSEN DE RAPALJE (1572–1661) *m.* Catalyntie Tricault (Trico) (1605–1689)
      Service: Came to New Amsterdam 1623; was a leading citizen and served as Magis-
            trate of Brooklyn.
      Reference: Hist. of Allen and Van Wert Counties, Ohio; Hist. of Allegheny and Lan-
            caster Counties, Penna.

6114   SMITH, Richard Bell   Recorded 1936, New Jersey
            1704 Hillcrest Road, Philadelphia, Pennsylvania
       1. Richard Bell Smith
       2. Irving Bell Smith (1904–   ) *m.* 1929 Helen Walton (1909–   )
       3. John G. Walton (1865–1924) *m.* 1900 Clara R. Betts (1868–   )
       4. John B. Betts (1836–1931) *m.* 1863 Jeanette Carter (1839–1921)
       5. James T. Carter (1812–1882) *m.* 1838 Sarah Dauphin (1806–1880)
       6. Joshua Carter (1766–1816) *m.* 1792 Ann Liston (1776–1838)
       7. John Carter (1736–   ) *m.* Margaret Carter
       8. William Carter (1717–1781) *m.* 1735 Ann Haile
       9. Sparrow Carter (–1721) *m.* 1716 Elizabeth Saunders (–1722)
      10. Edward Carter *m.* ——— Sparrow
      11. EDWARD CARTER (–1682) *m.* Ann
      Service: Burgess of Virginia, 1657.
      Reference: Maryland Historical Magazine, Vol. 5.

5918   SMITH, Rosina Farrell   Recorded 1930, Pennsylvania
            826 W. Main Street, Norristown, Pennsylvania
       1. Rosina Farrell *m.* Ira Armsby Smith
       2. John Barry Farrell II (1820–1884) *m.* 1866 Caroline Barton Davis (1832–1887)
       3. William Barton (1794–1855) *m.* 1817 Rachel Supplee (1794–1879)
       4. Jacob Supplee (1759–1825) *m.* 1782 Rebecca Ramsey (1760–1823)
       5. Josiah Supplee (–1823)
       6. Jacob Supplee (1727–   ) *m.* 1746 Margaret Yocum (1726–   )
       7. Jacob Supplee (1690–1749) *m.* 1720 Elizabeth Enoch (1698–1748)
       8. ANDREAS SUPPLEE (1634–1726) *m.* Gertrude
      Service: Andreas Supplee was the first Sheriff, Germantown, Pa.
      Reference: Watson's Annals; Stapleton's "Memorials of the Huguenots;" History of
            Germantown.

6143 SMITH, Mrs. Samuel F. Recorded 1937, Georgia
      2087 Ridgewood Dr. N. E., Atlanta, Georgia
1. Emmie Durden *m.* 1925 Samuel F. Smith, Jr.
2. William M. Durden (1853–1918) *m.* 1883 Emma Kennedy (1863–1915)
3. Albert N. Durden (1828–1904) *m.* 1851 Eliza L. Brinson (1833–1911)
4. Benjamin E. Brinson (1800–1861) *m.* 1825 Mary Lewis (1804–1870)
5. Adam Brinson II (1751–1825) *m.* 1786 Mary Sheppard (1760–1820)
6. ADAM BRINSON I (1689–1769) *m.* 1715 Sara Sterring (1693–1774)
Service: Fought in the Colonial Wars in North Carolina.
Reference: "Men of Mark in Georgia;" Northern Colonial Records of North Carolina,
      Vol. 22.

6379 SMITH, Mrs. Therne V. Recorded 1942, West Virginia
      1012 Eighth Street, Huntington, West Virginia
1. Lois Headly Keeler *m.* 1913 Therne V. Smith
2. Heister Harrison Keeler (1853–) *m.* 1882 Esther Franklin Headly (1856–1937)
3. Heister Keeler (1821–) *m.* 1851 Lois Adeline Sharpe (1827–1896)
4. Asa Keeler (1780–1867) *m.* 1807 Betty Newman (1785–1849)
5. Paul Keeler, Jr. (1756–1812) *m.* 1775 Sarah Burt Cornwall, *d.* 1826
6. Paul Keeler, *d.* 1787, *m.* ——— Smith
7. Joseph Keeler (1683–1757) *m.* Elizabeth Whitney, *d.* 1763
8. Samuel Keeler (1656–1713) *m.* 1682 Sarah Senton (St. John) (1659–1714)
9. RALPH KEELER (1613–1672) *m.* (2nd) 1653 Sarah Whelpley
Service: One of the first settlers of Norwalk, Conn., 1651; owned a lot in Hartford,
      Conn., 1640.
Reference: Rockwell & Keeler Genealogy, by James Boughton.

6426 SMITH, Valerie Ann Recorded 1943
      Fort Washington, Pennsylvania
          (JUNIOR)
1. Valerie Ann Smith
2. Irving Ball Smith (1904–) *m.* 1929 Helen Walton (1909–)
3. John Gardener Walton (1865–1924) *m.* 1900 Clara R. G. Betts (1868–)
4. John Brooks Betts (1836–1931) *m.* 1863 Jeanette Carter (1844–1921)
5. James Tilton Carter (1812–1882) *m.* 1838 Sarah Ann ——— (1806–1880)
6. Joshua Carter (1766–1816) *m.* 1792/3 Ann Liston (1776–1836)
7. William Liston (1752–1789) *m.* 1775 Mary Allee (1755–)
8. Edmund Liston (1725–1769) *m.* 1753 Rachel Farson (1726–)
9. Edmund Liston (1694–1760) *m.* bef. 1718 Sarah Richardson, *b.* 1696–)
10. MORRIS LISTON (–1709) *m.* 1685 Jane Greaves
Service: Landowner Delaware, 1675.
Reference: Betts and Allied Fam., Mather; D.A.R., Wash.

6443 SMITH, Mrs. Wilbur Richard C. Recorded 1944
      15 Inman Circle N. E., Ansley Pk., Atlanta, Georgia
1. Mary Edna Pope *m.* Wilbur Richard C. Smith
2. David Winfield Pope (1850–1896) *m.* 1874 Laura Jane Campbell (1854–1930)
3. John Pope (1826–1890) *m.* 1844 Martha Allen (1826–1895)
4. David Pope (1807–1880/85) *m.* 1825 Matilda Bruce (1809–)
5. John Pope (1778–1849) *m.* 1804 Susannah ——— (1780–1844)
6. Henry Pope (1748–1778) *m. ca.* 1775 Charity Hinton (1747–)
7. William Pope (1725–1748) *m. ca.* 1746 Mary ——— (1727–)
8. John Pope (1697–1735) *m.* 1723 Elizabeth Pope (cousins) 1699–)
9. Nathaniel Pope (1654–1719) *m. ca.* 1690 Jane Brown (–1752)
10. Nathaniel Pope (–aft. 1665) *m.* 1654 Mary Sisson
11. COL. NATHANIEL POPE (1610–1660) *m. ca.* 1631 Luce ———
Service: Comm. Lieut. Col. of Westmoreland Co., Va., troops, April 4, 1655; appointed
      agent to Kent Island, 1647; came to America before 1637, settled first in
      Md., later in Va.
Reference: Georgia Desc. of Nathaniel Pope, John D. Humphries; Wm. & Mary
      Quart., (I), Vol. 12.

6245   SMYTH, Miss Helen Agnes
            Brookside Drive, Greenwich, Connecticut
    1. Helen Conrad Smyth (1866–1934) *m.* 1893 Wm. J. Smyth (1857–1918)
    2. John Hicks Conrad (1827–1896) *m.* 1857 Almeda Tomlin (1832–1914)
    3. John Conrad (1785–1871) *m.* 1814 Hannah Kettler
    4. Benjamin Conrad (1758–   ) *m.* Sarah Allowar
    5. John Cunrads (–1793) *m.* Ann Rogers
    6. Henry Cunreds (1688–1758) *m.* 1710 Katherine Streeper
    7. THOMAS KUNDERS (–1729) *m.* Elin Streypers
    Service: Burgess of Germantown, Pa., 1691.
    Reference: Thos. Kunders and his children; Hen Cunreds "of Whitpair."

6625   SNAPP, Mrs. Howard M., Jr.   Recorded 1949
            321 Richards Street, Joliet, Illinois
    1. Althea Ruth Mecham *m.* 1918 Howard M. Snapp, Jr.
    2. John B. Mecham (1858–1930) *m.* 1892 Frances M. Hill (1869–   )
    3. John C. Mecham (1832–1918) *m.* 1855 Anna E. H. Faylor (1829–1901)
    4. Caleb Mecham (1810–1852) *m.* 1830 Mary Currier (1813–1892)
    5. Joshua Meachem (1773–1846) *m.* Pamela Chapman (1777–1856)
    6. Samuel Meacham, Jr. (1739–1811) *m.* 1763 Phebe Main (1747–   )
    7. Samuel Meacham (1712–   ) *m.* 1734 Bethia Pease
    8. Jeremiah Meacham (1673–   ) *m.* Deborah Brown
    9. Jeremiah Meachem *m.* 1672 Mary Trask
    10. JEREMIAH MEACHAM (1613–1696) *m.* Alice Dorne (1622–1696)
    Service: Served the town of Salem, Mass., as Constable, Highway Surveyor and other
            offices.
    Reference: Babcock and Main Gen.; History of Salem, Mass.; D.F.P.A. Records.

6535   SOUERS, Mrs. Loren E.   Recorded 1946
            221 Eighteenth Street N. W., Canton 3, Ohio
    1. Ilka Gaskell *m.* Loren E. Souers
    2. Silas S. C. Gaskell (1859–1929) *m.* 1887 Esther K. Danner (1863–1936)
    3. John Danner (1823–1918) *m.* 1847 Terressa A. Millard (1828–1914)
    4. William J. Millard (1796–1877) *m.* 1816 Betsy J. Ball (1800–1891)
    5. Willoughby Millard (1770–1857) *m.* 1792 Esther Kellogg (1772–   )
    6. Jehoiada Millard (1740–   ) *m.* 1761 Mary Willoughby
    7. Rev. Robert Millard (1702–1784) *m.* 1725 Hannah Eddy (1710–   )
    8. Nehemiah Millard (1668–1751) *m.* 1696 Phebe Share (Shoar), *d.* 1717
    9. Robert Millard (1632–1699) *m.* 1663 Elizabeth Saben (1642–1717)
    10. JOHN MILLARD, JR., *d.* 1668, *m.* Elizabeth, *d.* 1680
    Service: Landed proprietor and served in the defense of Rehoboth, Aug. 25, 1675.
    Reference: History of Stark County, N. Y.; Gen. and Biogra. Record.

6441   SOULE, John Edward   Recorded 1944
            2327 Shenandoah Avenue N. E., Atlanta, Georgia
    1. John Edward Soule *m.* Adelia Elsa Rosasco
    2. Fayette Fletcher Soule (1877–   ) *m.* 1901 Isabel Atkinson (1880–   )
    3. Charles Edward Soule (1841–1925) *m.* 1867 Lucinda Saxton Hall (1842–1926)
    4. Ambrose Latten Soule (1801–1857) *m.* 1824 Ruth (Paddock) Brown (1804–1851)
    5. Aaron Paddock (1773–1860) *m.* 1796 Sarah Benjamin (1779–   )
    6. David Paddock (1734–1794) *m.* 1762 Miriam Belden (1744–1828)
    7. David Paddock (1705–1771/2) *m.* 1727 Mary Foster (1709–   )
    8. Chillingsworth Foster (1680–1764) *m.* 1705 Mercy Freeman (1687–1720)
    9. John Freeman (1651–1721) *m.* 1676 Sarah Merrick (1654–1696)
    10. Maj. John Freeman (1622–1719) *m.* 1650 Marcy Prence (1631–1711)
    11. Gov. Thomas Prence (1601–1673) *m.* 1624 Patience Brewster (–1634)
    12. ELDER WILLIAM BREWSTER (1563–1643) *m.* Mary ———
    Service: Signer Mayflower Compact.
    Reference: Mayflower Index, 4, 7, 11; Soul & Soulis Hist. Rev. Ridlon.

6524 SOUTHWORTH, Mrs. Louise Hendee   Recorded 1946
        Woodstock Avenue, Rutland, Vermont
   1. Louise Hendee *m.* Dr. John Deane Southworth
   2. Caleb R. Hendee, Jr. (1842–1922) *m.* Sabrina A. Jackson (1850–   )
   3. Caleb R. Hendee (1808–1842) *m.* 1836 Mary A. Granger (1812–   )
   4. Dea. Caleb Hendee, Jr. (1768–1854) *m.* 1789 Lydia Rich (1768–1835)
   5. Caleb Hendee 1st (1745–1823) *m.* 1767 Caroline Ellsworth (1748–1791)
   6. Jonathan Hendee (1720–1775) *m.* Martha Millington
   7. Ensign Richard Hendee (1666–1742/3) *m.* 1695 Elizabeth Conant (Connaut)
   8. RICHARD HENDEE, *d.* 1670, *m.* ———
Service: Settled in Boston, Mass.
Reference: History of Pittsford, Vt.

5894 SPEER, Mrs. Charles A.   Recorded 1930, Iowa
        415 W. Jefferson Street, Washington, Iowa
   1. Myrtle Morton *m.* (1) Fred Bragg, (2) Charles A. Speer
   2. John Wesley Morton (1842–1926) *m.* 1874 Alice Rogers (1855–1917)
   3. Thomas Edgar Rogers (1828–1879) *m.* 1851 Susan Maria Curtis (1831–1889)
   4. Almond Curtis (1792–1861) *m.* 1812 Elizabeth Sanborn (1794–1834)
   5. Moses Sanborn (1766–1804) *m.* 1789 Hannah Fitts (1769–   )
   6. John Sanborn (1741–1797) *m.* 1759 Elizabeth Sargent (1738–1828)
   7. Abraham Sanborn (1717–1780) *m.* 1737 Abigail Clifford (1713–1797)
   8. Tristam Sanborn (1684–1771) *m.* 1711 Margaret Taylor (1688–1771)
   9. John Sanborn (1649–1727) *m.* 1674 Judith Coffin (1653–1724)
  10. Tristam Coffin (1632–1704) *m.* 1652 Judith Greenleaf (1625–1705)
  11. EDMUND GREENLEAF (1574–1670) *m.* 1612 Sarah Dote (–1663)
Service: 1637, Command Co. against Indians; 1639, Ensign at Newbury, Mass.; 1642,
        Lieut., Mass. Provincial Forces.
Reference: Town Records.

6072 SPEER, Mrs. John M.   Recorded 1934, Georgia
        216 Twelfth Street N. E., Atlanta, Georgia
   1. Maude Roach *m.* 1895 John Moreland Speer
   2. Elisha J. Roach (1833–1890) *m.* 1855 Ellen Mitchell (1835–1910)
   3. William Roach (1800–1839) *m.* 1823 Eliza Gunby (1804–1861)
   4. Elisha Gunby (1765–1848) *m.* 1797 Elizabeth Whittington (1772–1825)
   5. Southey Whittington (1723–1786) *m.* 1749 Esther Nairne (1730–1806)
   6. Southey Whittington (1686–1769) *m.* 1723 Mary Fassett (1699–1740)
   7. William Fassett (1662–1735) *m.* 1696 Mary Harrison (1673–1744)
   8. JOHN FAWSETT (1629–1673) *m.* 1661 Rhoda Lamberton (–1672)
Service: Attorney for Accomac County, Va., 1664–1671.
Reference: History of Atlanta, by Reed; Deeds and Wills, Accomac County, Va.;
        by Stratton Nottingham.

5927 SPELLMAN, Miss Harriet Waring   Recorded 1930, Texas
        Stoneleigh Court, Dallas, Texas
   1. Harriet Waring Spellman
   2. John M. Spellman (1877–   ) *m.* 1908 Mabel Heafer (1881–   )
   3. James H. Heafer (1848–1930) *m.* 1870 Nancy M. Waring (1853–1925)
   4. Francis Waring (1826–1908) *m.* 1850 Harriet W. Williams (1827–1866)
   5. William Williams (1787–1875) *m.* 1826 Maria Denny (1797–1883)
   6. Isaac Denny (1765–1813) *m.* 1793 Grace Tibb (–1859)
   7. Samuel Denny (1731–1817) *m.* 1757 Elizabeth Henshaw (1737–1787)
   8. Daniel Henshaw (1701–1781) *m.* 1724 Elizabeth Bass
   9. Joseph Bass *m.* Mary Belcher
  10. John Bass *m.* Ruth Alden (1627–   )
  11. JOHN ALDEN (1599–1687) *m.* Priscilla Mullins (–1650)
Service:
Reference: Denny Genealogy; Vital Records of Massachusetts.

5926   SPELLMAN, Miss Mabel Fulton   Recorded 1930, Texas
             Stoneleigh Court, Dallas, Texas
   1. Mabel Fulton Spellman
   2. John M. Spellman (1877–) *m.* 1908 Mabel Heafer (1881–)
   3. James Henry Heafer (1848–1930) *m.* 1870 Nancy Marie Waring (1853–1925)
   4. Frances Waring (1826–1908) *m.* 1850 Harriet W. Williams (1827–1866)
   5. William Williams (1787–1875) *m.* 1826 Maria Denny (1797–1883)
   6. Isaac Denny (1765–1813) *m.* 1793 Grace Tibb (–1859)
   7. Samuel Denny (1731–1817) *m.* 1757 Elizabeth Henshaw (1737–1787)
   8. Daniel Henshaw (1701–1781) *m.* 1724 Elizabeth Bass
   9. Joseph Bass *m.* Mary Belcher
  10. John Bass *m.* Ruth Alden (1627–)
  11. JOHN ALDEN (1599–1687) *m.* Priscilla Mullins (–1650)
   Service:
   Reference: Denny Genealogy; Vital Records of Massachusetts.

6081   SPEESE, Mrs. Claude M.   Recorded 1935, Virginia
             504 Avenham Avenue, Roanoke, Virginia
   1. Annie Enfield *m.* 1901 Claude M. Speese
   2. David Enfield (1844–1927) *m.* 1872 Amanda Westover (1844–1921)
   3. Enos Westover (1816–1908) *m.* 1836 Mary Kimmerling (1818–1899)
   4. Oliver Westover, Jr. (1775–1855) *m.* 1797 Elizabeth Webster (1778–1849)
   5. Oliver Westover (1739–) *m.* 1775 Jerusha (1739–)
   6. Nathaniel Westover (1707–1755) *m.* 1727 Mary Enno (1712–1760)
   7. Jonas Westover (1664–1714) *m.* 1701 Abigail Case (–1728)
   8. Nathaniel Westover (1642–1708) *m.* 1663 Hannah Griswold (1642–1714)
   9. EDWARD GRISWOLD (1607–1689) *m.* 1637 Margaret (1607–1685)
   Service: One of the founders of Windsor, Conn.
   Reference: Stiles' History of Windsor, Conn.; Simsbury Vital Records; Glimpses
             of Ancient Windsor, Barbour.

6300   SPENCER, Mrs. Herbert   Recorded 1940, Connecticut
             1039 Asylum Avenue, Hartford, Connecticut
   1. Ruth Ensign *m.* Herbert Spencer
   2. Milton E. Ensign (1860–1897) *m.* 1882 Anna Tracy Comstock (1863–1938)
   3. Franklin Greene Comstock (1838–1922) *m.* 1862 Antoinette Deming (1832–1883)
   4. William Greene Comstock (1810–1899) *m.* 1837 Adeline Strong (1812–1880)
   5. Franklin G. Comstock (1790–1845) *m.* Tryphenia Tracy (1791–1874)
   6. Gamaliel Tracy (1759–1853) *m.* 1789 Sarah Lewis (1770–1853)
   7. Nehemiah Tracy (1723–1776) *m.* 1744 Susannah Mack Smith, *d.* 1806
   8. Winslow Tracy, *b.* 1689, *m.* 1714 Rachel Ripley
   9. John Tracy (1642–1702) *m.* Mary Winslow (1646–1721)
  10. THOMAS TRACY, *b.* 1610, *m.* 1641 Mrs. Mary Mason
   Service: Lt. in War against Dutch and Indians.
   Reference: Mack Genealogy.

6748   SQUIRES, Mrs. Irvin Rudy   Recorded 1952, North Carolina
             3049 Country Club Drive, Greensboro, North Carolina
   1. Frances Rothrock *m.* 1924 I. R. Squires
   2. Parmenio S. Rothrock (1873–) *m.* 1903 Jessie Martin (1879–1951)
   3. Leroy A. Martin (1854–1917) *m.* 1877 Cora A. Poindexter (1860–1943)
   4. Elizabeth Poindexter (1830–1916) *m.* 1848 Reps Martin (1826–1911)
   5. Denson Ashburn Poindexter (1809–1876) *m.* 1822 Sarah Jones (1806–1862)
   6. Wm. Pledge Poindexter (1766–1844) *m.* 1796 Elizabeth A. Ashburn (1777–1849)
   7. Capt. Thomas Poindexter (abt. 1737–1807) *m.* 1760 Elizabeth Pledge (abt.
             1740–1816)
   8. Thomas Poindexter (abt. 1705–1773/4) *m.* Sarah ———, living after 1747
   9. Thomas Poindexter (abt. 1670–1744) *m.* 1691 Sarah Crawford (1670–1752)
  10. GEORGE POINDEXTER (–aft. 1698) *m.* Susanna (–1698)
   Service: George Poindexter came from Isle of Jersey to America, 1657; he died after
             1698; his mother was Elizabeth Efford, whose brother Peter Efford had come
             to America and living in York Co., Va.
   Reference: Complete history of the Poindexter and Crawford families were submitted
             with the mother's application papers. Mother's National Number in
             S. & D. of Pilgrims 6624.

6546 STAPLETON, Mrs. L. L.   Recorded 1947
        115 West Benson Street, Decatur, Georgia
   1. Addie Alford *m.* 1909 Luther Linwood Stapleton
   2. Drewry C. Alford (1856–   ) *m.* 1878 Sarah Thornton (1854–1924)
   3. Benjamin C. Thornton (1827–1881) *m.* 1851 Priscilla Teasley, *d.* 1896
   4. Rev. Benj. Thornton (1801–1878) *m.* 1817 Nancy Payne (1802–1864)
   5. Benj. Thornton (1781–1854) *m.* 1800 Sarah Upshaw (1782–1805)
   6. Dozier Thornton (1755–1843) *m.* 1773 Lucy Hill (1760–1836)
   7. Mark Thornton (1725–   ) *m.* Susannah Dozier (1739–1782)
   8. William Thornton (*ca.* 1705–   ) *m.* Elizabeth Fitzhugh
   9. Col. Francis Thornton (1682–   ) *m.* Mary Taliaferro
  10. Francis Thornton (1651–1726) *m.* Alice Savage
  11. WILLIAM THORNTON, *d.* 1708
Service: Eavenson-Strickland and Allied Families.

6088 STARKE, Mrs. William W.   Recorded 1935, Georgia
        75 S. Elm Street, Commerce, Georgia
   1. Arabella Brown *m.* 1888 Judge William Starke
   2. Andrew F. Brown (1830–1912) *m.* 1856 Alice M. Maley (1838–1907)
   3. Sidney Maley (1813–1893) *m.* 1835 Alice A. Deadwyler (1810–1881)
   4. John Maley (1765–1831) *m.* 1799 Sarah Rice (–1832)
   5. James Maley (1725–1788) *m.* 1760 Winifred Haynie (1735–1818)
   6. Hezekiah Haynie (1705–1788) *m.* 1730 Hannah Christopher
   7. John Haynie, Jr. (1665–1738) *m.* 1700 Hannah Neale (1684–1711)
   8. CAPT. JOHN HAYNIE (1624–1697) *m.* 1650 Jane Morris (1630–1682)
Service: Member of Virginia House of Burgesses, 1657–8; an officer in the Indian
        Wars, 1675–77.
Reference: Northumberland County Records; Va. Colonial Militia, Crozier; Colonial
        Va., Register, Stanard.

6169 STARKWEATHER, Miss Esther   Recorded 1937
        36 Forest Street, Hartford, Connecticut
   1. Esther Starkweather (1903–   )
   2. Charles Merrick Starkweather (1864–1924) *m.* 1894 Lucy Williston (1866–   )
   3. A. Lyman Williston (1834–1915) *m.* 1861 Sarah Tappan Stoddard (1839–1912)
   4. John Payson Williston (1803–1872) *m.* 1827 Cecelia Lyman (1805–1890)
   5. Asabel Lyman (1776–1864) *m.* 1804 Lucy Parsons (1782–1874)
   6. Elias Lyman (1740–1816) *m.* 1764 Hannah Clapp (1742–1813)
   7. Elias Lyman (1710–1790) *m.* 1736 Hannah Allen (1754–1770)
   8. Lieut. John Lyman 2nd (1660–1740) *m.* 1687 Mindwell Sheldon (1660–1735)
   9. Lieut. John Lyman (1623–1690) *m.* Dorcas Plumb (–1725)
  10. RICHARD LYMAN (bapt. 1580–1640) *m.* in Eng. Sarah Osborne, born in Eng.
Service: Richard Lyman was one of the original proprietors of Hartford, Conn.
Reference: Hartford Rec., Vol. of births, 1903, pg. 438; Starkweather Gen.; Williston
        Gen., pg. 17; Lyman Gen., pgs. 36, 39, 40, 265, 266, 247, 248, 243, 244, 263.

6284 STEARNS, Mrs. Wilbur Watkins   Recorded 1939, New York
        43 Jordan Drive, Willoughby, Ohio
   1. Marian Christine Johnson *m.* 1918 Wilbur Watkins Stearns, M.D.
   2. George H. Johnson (1850–   ) *m.* 1879 Clara M. Crocker (1856–1921)
   3. Henry F. Johnson (1813–1877) *m.* 1842 Eunice Sophia Fay (1824–1891)
   4. Elisha Johnson, Jr. (1783–1854) *m.* 1808 Sophia Loomis (1787–1840)
   5. Elisha Johnson (1753–1838) *m.* (2nd) 1778 Sarah Perry (1752–1847)
   6. Isaac Johnson (1713–1801) *m.* 1733 Rachel Thomas, *d.* 1794
   7. William Johnson (1665–1754) *m.* (2nd) 1699 Hannah Rider (1678–1757)
   8. Jonathan Johnson (1641–1712) *m.* 1663 Mary Newton (1644–1728)
   9. WILLIAM JOHNSON (1630–1677) *m.* Elizabeth Story, *d.* 1684
Service:
Reference: "Johnson, Our Family Record," by George H. Johnson; Genealogical
        Record, Vol. 33.

6151 STEBBINS, Agnes Newell   Recorded 1937
        347 Adelphi Street, Brooklyn, New York
  1. Agnes Newell Stebbins (1880–)
  2. William Newell Stebbins (1850–) *m.* 1874 Agnes Kennedy Perry (1850–1920)
  3. Samuel Newell Stebbins (1819–1929) *m.* 1845 Fanny Bryant (1816–1880)
  4. William Stebbins (1789–1881) *m.* 1815 Eliza Bowker
  5. William Stebbins (1768–) *m.* 1788 Margaret Newell (–1825)
  6. Ezra Stebbins (1731–1796) *m.* 1757 Margaret Chapin (1743–1808)
  7. Samuel Chapin (1699–1779) *m.* 1757 Anna Horton (1700–1808)
  8. Samuel Chapin (1665–1729) *m.* 1690 Hannah Sheldon (1670–)
  9. Japhet Chapin (1642–1712) *m.* 1664 Abilenah Cooley (1642–1710)
  10. Dea. Samuel Chapin (1598–1675) *m.* 1632 Cicely Penny (1601–1682)
  Service: Founder of Springfield, Mass.
  Reference: Stebbins Gen., Vol. I, pgs. 372, 373, 248, 180 (Greenlea); Chapin Book,
        2, 3, 9, 21, 131.

5921 STEPHEN, Mrs. J. A.   Recorded 1930, Texas
        Sealy, Texas
  1. Elizabeth Burch Darden *m.* Jos. A. Stephen
  2. William B. Darden (1824–1911) *m.* 1853 Anna Eliza Fuller (1832–1910)
  3. Lemuel Darden (1790–1826) *m.* 1814 Rebecca Weaver (1792–1830)
  4. George Darden, Jr. (1763–1844) *m.* 1783 Elizabeth Strowshour (1766–1840)
  5. George Darden, Sr. (1738–1800) *m.* 1759 Martha Burch (1742–1790)
  6. John Burch *m.* 1741 Elizabeth Lanier (1725–)
  7. Samson Lanier *m.* 1682 Elizabeth Washington (–1757)
  8. Richard Washington (1660–1738) *m.* 1678 Elizabeth Jordan
  9. John Washington *m.* Mary Blount, nee Lord (–1756)
  Service: John Washington of Surry Co., Va., a Patriot.
  Reference: Tyler's Quarterly, Vol. III.

6453 STEVENS, Mrs. Ralph Townsend   Recorded 1944
        Cape May, New Jersey
  1. Charlotte Kimball *m.* Ralph Townsend Stevens
  2. James D. Kimball (1861–1921) *m.* 1889 Lottie M. Manrose (1860–1936)
  3. James Parker Kimball (1828–1882) *m.* 1858 Mary Barton Dickinson (1834–1873)
  4. James Kimball (1797–1861) *m.* 1825 Emily Parker (1800–1874)
  5. James Kimball (1758–1829) *m.* 1793 (3rd) Ruth Kimball (1761–1832)
  6. Richard Kimball (1732–1780) *m.* 1755 Sarah Harriman (1731–1797)
  7. Benjamin Kimball (1698–1752) *m.* 1719 Priscilla Hazen (1699–1783)
  8. Richard Kimball (1665–1711) *m.* 1692 Mehitable Day (1669–1733)
  9. Benjamin Kimball (1637–1690) *m.* 1661 Mercy Hazelton (1642–1708)
  Service: Land owner Bradford, Rowley and Haverhill, Mass.; Cornet of Horse
        Troops; soldier 1683–84 under Capt. Appleton.
  Reference: History Kimball Family in America, Morrison & Sharpless, Boston, 1897.

6219 STEVICK, Shirley Carol   Recorded 1938
        8111 Flower Avenue, Silver Spring, Maryland
  1. Shirley Carol Stevick
  2. Floyd W. Stevick (1897–) *m.* 1932 Emma Decatur (1907–)
  3. Elizabeth ——— (1876–) *m.* 1895 Floyd J. Willard (1866–1897)
  4. John Huntsinger (1842–1919) *m.* 1865 Katurah Jones (1843–1884)
  5. Geo. Jones (1814–1851) *m.* 1836 Elizabeth Joslin (1816–1889)
  6. Elial Joslin (1792–1864) *m.* 1813 Sarah Hewett (1792–1861)
  7. Isaac Joslin (1759–1804) *m.* Mary ——— (1764–1828)
  8. William Joslin (1701–1771)
  9. Thomas Joslin (1659–1722) *m.* ———
  10. Abraham Joslin (1615–1669) *m.* Beatrice Lampson (1623–1712)
  11. Thomas Joslin (1592–1660) *m.* 1614 Rebecca Marlow
  Service:
  Reference: N. J. Col. Doc., Vol. 22.

5990 STEWARD, Miss Rose McMullen   Recorded 1931
        Green Gables, Oradell, New Jersey
1. Miss Rose McMullen
2. James Porter Stewart (1838–1902) *m.* 1870 Jane Johnston Fulton (1841–1917)
3. James Stewart (1813–1896) *m.* 1830 Rosanna McMullen (1804–1846)
4. Stewart McMullen (–1822) *m.* 1798 Jane Higgins (1781–)
5. James Higgins (1760–) *m.* 1779 Rosanna Archer
6. James Higgins (1733–1779) *m.* 1759 Sarah Stout
7. Jediah Higgins (1691–1772) *m.* 1715 Hannah Stout (1694–)
8. Jediah Higgins (1656–1715) *m.* 1684 ———
9. RICHARD HIGGINS (1613–1675) *m.* 1651 Mary Yates
Service: Founder, Selectman, Deputy of Gen. Court.
Reference: Richard Higgins and His Desc., p. 91.

5974 STEWART, Mrs. Adele K.   Recorded 1930, Iowa
        422 Avenue E., Fort Madison, Iowa
1. Adele Kretsinger *m.* 1889 ——— Stewart
2. William H. Kretsinger (1816–1895) *m.* 1859 Maria Ramsdale (1827–1914)
3. Henry Ramsdale (1790–1850) *m.* 1821 Lovena Sweet (1801–1873)
4. Benjamin Sweet (1778–1861) *m.* 1799 Hannah Stanton (1778–1861)
5. Ebenezer Stanton (1746–1811) *m.* 1773 Mary Palmer (1757–1778)
6. Joseph Stanton (1710–1778) *m.* Abigail Freeman (1720–)
7. John Stanton (1665–) *m.* 1705 Mary Starkweather (1666–)
8. John Stanton (1641–1713) *m.* 1664 Hannah Thompson (1641–)
9. THOMAS STANTON (1610–1677) *m.* 1637 Anna Lord (1621–)
Service: Interpreter to the Colonial Authorities.
Reference: De Forest's History of the Indians of Conn.; Mass. Historical Collection,
        Vol. 18; Roger Williams' Letters, R. I. Historical Collection, Vol. III.

6573 STEWART, Mrs. Walter E.   Recorded 1948
        1603 S. College Street, Tyler, Texas
1. Lela Marshall *m.* 1901 Walter E. Stewart
2. William O. Marshall (1849–1931) *m.* 1872 Margaret L. Bolin (1848–1891)
3. William Bolin (1819–1887) *m.* 1846 Mary P. McLean (1820–1888)
4. Hugh McLean (1772–1852) *m.* 1810 Margaret Peabody (1791–1861)
5. John T. Peabody (1756–1822) *m.* 1789 Catherine Jessup
6. Asa Peabody (1717–1788) *m.* 1742 Mary Prentice (1725–)
7. Rev. Nathaniel Prentice (1698–1737) *m.* 1724 Mary Tyng, *d.* 1739
8. William Tyng (1679–) *m.* Lucy Clarke
9. Jonathan Ting (1642–1724) *m.* Sarah Usher
10. Edward Ting *m.* Mary Sears
11. RICHARD SEARS (SARES) *ca.* (1590–1676) *m.* 1632 Dorothy Thatcher
Service: On tax list of Plymouth, Mass.; awarded grant of land at Salem, Mass.;
        Founder of Yarmouth, Mass.
Reference: Gen. Paige's Hist. of Cambridge; Gen. Prentice Genealogy.

6601 STINER, Mrs. Frederick M.   Recorded 1948
        N. E. Cor. Bellona and Berwick Avenues, Rixton 4, Maryland
1. Bertha M. Kidd *m.* 1942 Frederick M. Stiner
2. Francis H. W. Kidd (1878–) *m.* 1913 Bertha Moulton (1878–)
3. Charles Henry Kidd (1833–1920) *m.* 1859 Eliza M. Weeks (1840–1885)
4. Henry A. C. Weeks (1801–1842) *m.* 1827 Sarah A. MacLaMar (1799–1884)
5. Maj. Lemuel Weeks, Jr. *ca.* (1757–) *m.* 1780 Sarah Crabtree (1763–)
6. Lemuel Weeks *ca.* (1727–) *m.* 1750 Peggy Gooding
7. William Weeks (1690–1749/50) *m.* 1724 Sarah Tukekee (Tukey)
8. Ebenezer Weeks (1665–) *m.* 1689 Deliverance Sumner (1669–1711/2)
9. William Sumner, Jr., *d.* 1675, *m.* Elizabeth Clement
10. WILLIAM SUMNER (1607/5–1688) *m.* 1625 Mary West, *d.* 1676
Service: Selectman of Dorchester, Mass., for more than 20 years; Commissioner;
        Clerk in Trained Band; Deputy to Gen. Court.
Reference: Gen. of George Weekes of Dorchester, Mass.; Record of Desc. of William
        Sumner.

6172   STOLL, Mazie Smith   Recorded 1938
          Brooklyn, R. F. D. 9, Baltimore, Maryland
    1. Mazie Smith (1866–) *m.* 1916 Frederick Conrad Stoll
    2. James Sebrit Smith (1861–1931) *m.* 1885 Olivia Cordelia Tubbs (1865–)
    3. John Tubbs (1827–1898) *m.* 1858 Olivia Ann Stewart (1835–1877)
    4. Joshua Stewart (1790–1873) *m.* 1816 Caroline Cromwell (1796–1879)
    5. John Giles Cromwell (1769–) *m.* 1793 Elizabeth Jacob
    6. Samuel Jacob (1734–bef. 1793) *m.* Bethia Oley (1739–1774)
    7. Richard Jacob, Sr. (1697/8–1779) *m.* 1709 Hannah Howard (1707–ante 1751)
    8. Joseph Howard *c.* (1676–1736) *m.* (I) Hannah Dorsey (1678–*c.* 1705)
    9. Capt. Cornelius Howard (–1680) *m.* Elizabeth
    10. Matthew Howard, Sr. (1609–bef. 1659) *m.* Ann (Hall?)
    11. LORD THOMAS ARUNDEL HOWARD (2nd) wife Ann Philipson
    Service: In 1638 Matthew, Sr., was granted by Charles 1st, 150 acres of land in Va.,
          also patented land in Md. His rights by his own emigration and the trans-
          portation of wife Ann and two servants, 650 A. on the Severn.
    Reference: Newman's A. A. Gentry, pg. 600, 445, 448, 449; Warfield Founders of A. A.
          and Howard Cos. of Md.

6579   STOLLMAN, Mrs. Almon Winfield   Recorded 1948
          1001 S. Third Street, Champaign, Illinois
    1. Lois Gertrude Franklin *m.* 1909 Almon W. Stoolman
    2. William L. Franklin (1830–1913) *m.* 1860 Caroline E. Morton (1843–1922)
    3. Alexander Morton, Jr. (1796–1876) *m.* 1820 Martha Anderson (1798–1881)
    4. Alexander Morton, Sr. (1759–1822) *m.* 1784 Ruth Strong (1762–1850)
    5. Elijah Strong (1733–1774/5) *m.* 1756 Ruth Loomis (1729–)
    6. Zachariah Loomis (1681–1751) *m.* 1707 Joanna Abell (1683–1759)
    7. Sgt. Caleb Abell (1646/7–1731) *m.* 1669 Margaret Post (1653–1700)
    8. John Post (1626–1710/1) *m.* 1652 Hester Hyde, *d.* 1703
    9. WILLIAM HYDE *ca.* (1597–1681) *m.* ——
    Service: Founder of Hartford, Conn., and Norwich, Conn.
    Reference: Desc. of John Strong; Loomis Fam. in America; Desc. of Andrew Hyde.

6037   STORMFELTZ, Mrs. William L.   Recorded 1932
          502 Harrison Street, Ridley Park, Pennsylvania
    1. Elvira Keffer (1864–) *m.* 1892 William Luther Stormfeltz
    2. Washington Keffer (1830–1884) *m.* 1856 Elizabeth A. Moss (1834–1884)
    3. Hosia Moss (1807–1853) *m.* 1833 Elvira E. Franklin (1810–)
    4. Sylvancous Franklin (1782–) *m.* 1804 Elizabeth Buell (1788–1814)
    5. Asa Buell (1760–1827) *m.* 1784 Mercy Porter
    6. Nathaniel Buell (1728–1770) *m.* 1751 Thankful Griffen (1731–)
    7. Daniel Buell (1689–1782) *m.* 1720 Eliz. Post (1695–)
    8. Samuel Buell 2nd (1663–1732) *m.* 1686 Judith Stevens (1668–1732)
    9. Samuel Buell 1st (1641–1720) *m.* 1662 Deborah Griswold (1646–1719)
    10. WILLIAM BUELL (1610–1681) *m.* 1640 Mary Goggin
    Service:
    Reference: Gen. of the Moss Fam., by J. Howard Moss; Buell Gen., Wells; Styles
          Hist. of Windsor.

5899   STOUT, Frances Farnam   Recorded 1930, New Jersey
          28 Morningside Drive, Trenton, New Jersey
    1. Frances Farnam Stout (1873–) *m.* 1901 Charles F. Stout
    2. George Farnam (1846–1925) *m.* 1873 Elizabeth J. Lippincott (1852–)
    3. Daniel H. Farnam (1810–1887) *m.* 1838 Lucy M. Knapp (1806–1879)
    4. Joseph Farnam (1779–1843) *m.* 1803 Miriam Hickcox (1781–1820)
    5. Seth Farnam (1733–1820) *m.* 1766 Dinah Gibbs (1741–1816)
    6. John Farnam (1702–) *m.* 1725 Hannah Crittenden
    7. Peter Farnam (–1703) *m.* 1686 Hannah Wilcoxon
    8. HENRY FARNAM (1636–1700) *m.* Johanna Ruttke (–1689)
    Service: Deacon and joiner in Windsor and Killingworth.
    Reference: American Ancestry, Vol. VII.

5971 STRICKLAND, John Glen   Recorded 1930, Georgia
      Forsyth, Georgia
   1. John Glen Strickland *m.* 1921 Marie Sutton
   2. Alexander H. Strickland (1855–1921) *m.* 1889 Sexta Eavenson (1868–)
   3. John W. Eavenson (1840–1930) *m.* 1865 (2nd) Josephine Oglesby (1846–)
   4. George Eavenson (1817–1898) *m.* 1839 Sarah Thornton (1824–1863)
   5. George Eavenson (1782–1842) *m.* Polly Hilly (1781–1855)
   6. Eli Eavenson (1761–1829) *m.* 1781 Rachel Seal (1760–1830)
   7. George Eavenson (1726–1816) *m.* 1755 Mary Williamson (1727–1828)
   8. Daniel Williamson, Jr. (1688–) *m.* Hannah Malin
   9. DANIEL WILLIAMSON, SR. (1660–1727) *m.* 1685 Mary Smith
   Service: Early settler.
   Reference: Penna. Society, Colonial Dames, p. 191; 1922 Roster of the Society of
      Colonial Wars.

6567 STUARD, Annie L.   Recorded 1947
      104 Cricket Avenue, Ardmore, Pennsylvania
   1. Annie L. Hickey *m.* 1900 ——— Stuard
   2. George F. Hickey (1851–1936) *m.* 1872 Catherine Oliver (1853–1936)
   3. Joseph B. Oliver, *d.* 1884, *m.* 1851 Lovanda P. Smith (1835–1897)
   4. William W. Smith (1809–1844) *m.* 1832 Elizabeth Schellinger (1812–1903)
   5. Aaron Schellinger (1785–1872) *m.* 1811 Sophia Bennett (1792–1876)
   6. William Schellinger (1746–1827) *m.* 1770 Philomelia Stites (1752–1793)
   7. Richard Stites (1725–1772) *m.* 1748 Zeuriah Stillwell (1729–)
   8. Richard Stites (1696–1739) *m.* 1718 Abigail Garlick (1698–)
   9. Henry Stites (1662–1748) *m.* 1693 Hannah Garlick (1664–)
  10. Richard Stites (1640–1702) *m.* ———
  11. JOHN STITES, M.D. (1595–)
   Service: Pilgrim to Plymouth, then to Hempstead, N. Y.; Surgeon to Colonists in
      time of Cromwell.
   Reference: N. J. Archives; Epitaphs from Long Island; Records of town of Hempstead,
      N. Y., Gen. and Biog. Rec.

6511 SUMMERS, Mrs. Thomas J.   Recorded 1945
      Marietta, Ohio
   1. Grace Newton *m.* Thomas Jefferson Summers
   2. Aaron Newton (1836–1878) *m.* 1857 Emily Ayers Stickney (1837–1918)
   3. Marcus Stickney (1805–1855) *m.* 1827 Sarah Ellison (1810–1846)
   4. Samuel Belnap Stickney (1770–1832) *m. ca.* 1795 Mary Schults (1777–1830)
   5. James Stickney (1742–1823) *m.* 1768 Mary Belnap (1740–1820)
   6. Abraham Stickney (1703–1783) *m.* 1728 Abigail Hall (1702–1785)
   7. Samuel Stickney (1663–1714) *m.* 1689 *ca.* Mary Hazeltine (1672–1731)
   8. Samuel Stickney *ca.* (1633–1704) *m. ca.* 1653 Julian Swan
   9. RICHARD SWAN *ca.* (1607–1678) *m.* Ann ——— (–1658)
   Service: Dismissed from Church in Boston to form a church at Rowley, Mass., 1639;
      King Philip's War and Expedition to Canada; Deputy 1666–1667; Deputy
      General Court 1666–73, 1675, 1677.

6064 SUTHERLAND, Mrs. James B.   Recorded 1934, Minnesota
      1819 Dupont Avenue S., Minneapolis, Minnesota
   1. Myra Lee *m.* 1886 James B. Sutherland
   2. Mylo Lee (1828–1902) *m.* 1855 Margaret R. Conklin (1835–1909)
   3. Elisha Lee (1794–1849) *m.* 1820 Almyra Scoville (1797–1879)
   4. Milo Lee (1760–1829) *m.* 1782 Ruth Camp (1760–1833)
   5. Jonathan Lee (1718–1788) *m.* 1744 Elizabeth Metcalf (1716–1762)
   6. Joseph Metcalf (1682–1723) *m.* 1707 Abiel Adams (1685–)
   7. William Adams (1650–1685) *m.* 1680 Alice Bradford (1661–1745)
   8. William Bradford (1624–1704) *m.* 1652 Alice Richards (–1671)
   9. WILLIAM BRADFORD (1588–1657) *m.* 1623 Alice Carpenter Southworth (–1670)
   Service: Governor of Plymouth Colony.
   Reference: John Lee and His Descendants; N. E. Hist. and Gen. Register; Mayflower
      Descendants.

6012 SWAYNE, Mrs. Theodore   Recorded 1932
         2581 Dexter Street, Denver, Colorado
    1. Gertrude Eaton (1862–) *m.* 1888 Theodore Swayne
    2. Allen Smith Eaton (1829–1914) *m.* 1857 Martha Adelia Smith (1836–1914)
    3. William Eaton (1792–1866) *m.* 1819 Rebecca Sherman (1799–1848)
    4. Luther Eaton (1758–1829) *m.* 1782 Sally Rice (–1842)
    5. Nathaniel Eaton (1728–1804) *m.* 1755 Sarah Johnson
    6. Nathaniel Eaton (1704–1785) *m.* 1727 Esther Parry (1710–1769)
    7. Thomas Eaton (1675–1748) *m.* 1697 Lydia Starr Gay (1670–1748)
    8. John Eaton (1636–1694) *m.* Alice ——— (–1694)
    9. JOHN EATON (–1658) *m.* Abigail Damat
    Service: Surveyor.
    Reference: Nathanael Eaton, "Hist. Gen. & Biog. of Eaton Families;" John Eaton,
         by Nellie Z. R. Molyneux.

6363 SWALLOW, Hon. Lewis Garfield   Recorded 1942, Vermont
         29 Pine Street, Bellows Falls, Vermont
    1. Lewis Garfield Swallow *m.* 1907 M. Ethelyn Mowry
    2. Joseph Swallow (1841–1912) *m.* 1868 Adelaide Eliza Olney (1848–1927)
    3. Jerry Angell Olney (1812–1888) *m.* 1835 Eliza Sherman (1809–1883)
    4. John Sherman (1775–1842) *m.* 1797 Polly Skinner (1775–1842)
    5. Job Sherman (1746–1837) *m.* 1768 Elizabeth Holmes (1746–1817)
    6. Experience Holmes (1716–) *m.* 1737 Hannah Samson, *d.* 1797
    7. Abraham Samson (1686–1775) *m.* Penelope
    8. Abraham Samson (1658–1729) *m.* Lorah Sarah Standish
    9. Alexander Standish, *d.* 1702, *m.* Sarah Alden
    10. MYLES STANDISH (1584–1656) *m.* Barbara, *d.* aft. 1656
    Service: Captain of Plymouth Colony
    Reference: "Genealogy of Descendants of Thomas Olney," T. H. Olney; "Rhode
         Island Representative Men and Families," Vol. II; V. R. Foxborough,
         Mass.; V. R. of Rochester, Mass., Vol. II; "Ancient Landmarks of
         Plymouth," by Wm. T. Davis; Hist. of Town of Duxbury, Mass.

6767 SWEENEY, Mrs. William J.   Recorded 1952, Illinois
         816 Twentieth Street, Rock Island, Illinois
    1. Bessie Cleveland *m.* William Jackson Sweeney
    2. Henry Clay Cleveland (1844–1899) *m.* 1866 Olivia Sophia Hayes (1848–1909)
    3. Alonzo William Cleveland, *b.* and *d.* Woodstock, Vt., *m.* 1832 Betsy S. Pratt
         (1811–1863)
    4. Timothy Pratt (1787–1869) *m.* 1810 Judith Mason (1787–1873)
    5. Asa Pratt (1757–aft. 1833) *m.* 1782 Betty Stanford (1760–1787)
    6. Moses Pratt (1729–1795) *m.* 1752 Jemima Alden (1729/30–1786)
    7. John Alden (1705–1783) *m.* 1728 Thankful Parker (1704–1790)
    8. Henry Alden (abt. 1671–1728/9) *m.* 1693 Deborah ———
    9. David Alden (1646–1719) *m.* abt. 1670 Mary Southworth (abt. 1650–1719)
    10. JOHN ALDEN (abt. 1599–1687) *m.* bef. 1624 Priscilla Mullins (–aft. 1650)
    Service: Signer of Mayflower Compact Act; Gov. of Mass.
    Reference: Pg. 131, Mayflower Descd., III, 1947; Cleveland Genealogy, by E. J. &
         H. J. Cleveland, Vol. 3, pgs. 2331–2; Alden Memorial, by Ebenezer Alden,
         pg. 6.

6358 SWEET, Hon. Harold Edward   Recorded 1941, Massachusetts
         N. Main Street, Attleboro, Massachusetts
    1. Harold Edward Sweet *m.* 1900 Gertrude O. Hunton
    2. Joseph Lyman Sweet (1852–1932) *m.* 1876 Florence May Hayward, *b.* 1855
    3. Eldridge Sweet (1811–1876) *m.* 1837 Dorothy Sulloway (1812–1885)
    4. Otis Sweet (1783–1855) *m.* 1806 Wealthy Wheeler (1788–1860)
    5. Benjamin Sweet (Rev. War) (1738–1819) *m.* 1761 Susannah Foster (1742–1811)
    6. John Sweet (1695–) *m.* 1730 Sarah Maclaflen
    7. HENRY SWEET *m.* Elizabeth
    Service:
    Reference: Vital Records of Mansfield, Mass.; Vital Records of Attleboro Mass.

5953 SWEET, Mrs. Robert C.   Recorded 1930, West Virginia
        St. Albans, West Virginia
    1. Edith Mohler *m.* 1911 Robert C. Sweet
    2. Thomas H. Mohler (1863–   ) *m.* 1884 Lavinia E. Campbell (1864–   )
    3. John W. Campbell (1841–1876) *m.* 1863 Adaline Calvert (1843–   )
    4. John Lewis Calvert (1803–1863) *m.* 1825 Elizabeth A. Slack (1807–1882)
    5. Francis Calvert (1751–1823) *m.* 1791 Elizabeth Witt (1772–1806)
    6. Jacob Calvert (1720–1772) *m.* 1750 Sarah Crupper (1730–1789)
    7. John Calvert (1690–1735) *m.* 1710 Elizabeth Harrison
    8. George Calvert (1664–1740) *m.* 1688 Elizabeth Doyne
    9. William Calvert (1642–1682) *m.* 1660 Elizabeth Stone
   10. Gov. LEONARD CALVERT (1606–1647) *m.* 1641 Anne Brent
   Service: Colonizer and Founder of the Province of Maryland.
   Reference: Maryland Historical Magazine, Vol. 16, p. 196; Vol. 25, p. 30.

6522 SYNNOT, Mrs. Clayton E.   Recorded 1946
        189 Delaware Street, Woodbury, New Jersey
    1. Faith Botsford *m.* 1897 Clayton Eldridge Synnott
    2. Alfred P. Botsford (1827–1925) *m.* 1856 Mary A. Pardee (1832–1907)
    3. Edmund W. Botsford (bapt. 1798–1836) *m.* 1821 Mary A. Clark (1802–1892)
    4. Ephraim Botsford, Jr. (1750–1821) *m.* 1772 Marib Bounds
    5. Ephraim Botsford, Sr. (1720–1795) *m.* 1741 Sarah Hawley
    6. Joseph Botsford (1688–1774) *m.* 1718 Mary Bennett
    7. Elnathan Botsford (bapt. 1641–1691) *m.* 1667 Hannah Baldwin (bapt. 1644–1706)
    8. HENRY BOTSFORD (bapt. 1608–1685/6) *m.* 1640 Elizabeth
    9. Edward Botsford (bapt. 1579–   ) *m.* 1606 Alice Prior
   10. Richard Botsford (bapt. 1545–1607) *m.* 1569 Neyle
   Service: Original Proprietor of Milford, Conn., 1639; Corp. for Expedition against
       Dutch, 1654.
   Reference: Adventures in Ancestors—Botsford Family and Botsford-Marble Ancestral
       Lines.

6645 TALBOT, Mrs. W. O.   Recorded 1949
        Texas Hotel, Fort Worth, Texas
    1. Rose Dale A. Andrews *m.* 1901 William O. Talbot, M.D.
    2. Daniel Andrews (1810–1878) *m.* 1874 Marie A. (Morbach) West (1847–1941)
    3. Peter Andrews (1781–1857) *m.* 1803 Elizabeth Mory (1786–1837)
    4. Thomas Mory (1760–1829) *m.* Margaret Montgomeries (1761–1846)
    5. Jonathan Mory (1730–1796) *m.* 1758 Lydia Campbell (1730–1806)
    6. Jonathan Mory (1699–   ) *m.* Elizabeth Swift
    7. Jonathan Morey *m.* 1689 Hannah Bourne
    8. Jonathan Mowry (1637–   ) *m.* Mary Bartlett
    9. Robert Bartlett (1711/2–   ) *m.* Mary Warren
   10. RICHARD WARREN, *d.* 1628, *m.* Elizabeth Jonatt, *d.* 1673
   Service: Twelfth signer of Mayflower Compact, Nov. 11/2, 1620; in first encounter with
       Indians at Great Meadow Creek, Dec. 8, 1620 (D S), three days before landing
       at Plymouth.
   Reference:

5844 TAYLOR, Mrs. Annie L. F.   Recorded 1929
        Linthicum Hgts., Maryland
    1. Annie Louise Fretwell (1881–   ) *m.* 1904 —— Taylor
    2. James Burlington Fretwell (1853–1918) *m.* 1880 Katie Linthicum Pearson
       (1856–1893)
    3. Rev. Charles Garland Linthicum (1822–1903) *m.* 1849 Ann Louise Pearre
       (1830–1900)
    4. Amasa Linthicum (1765–1823) *m.* Sarah Johnson
    5. Hezekiah Linthicum (1723–1767) *m.* Sarah Bateman (1713–   )
    6. Thomas Linthicum, Jr. (1660–   ) *m.* 1698 Deborah Wayman
    7. THOMAS LINTHICUM, SR. (1630–1701) *m.* Jane ——
   Service:
   Reference:

6662   TAYLOR, Margaret Elizabeth Kennemur   Recorded 1949
       4314 Trellis Court, Dallas, Texas
   1. Margaret Elizabeth Kennemur *m.* 1906 Haden C. Taylor
   2. Isaac George Kennemur (1862–1944) *m.* 1885 Lela May Rose (1863–1909)
   3. David Harvey Kennemur (1815–1893) *m.* 1838 Malinda Miller (1819–1913)
   4. Isaac Miller (1797–1865) *m.* 1818 Mary (Polly) Allgood (1802–1865)
   5. Barnett H. Allgood (1779–1861) *m.* 1801 Frances Dean (1783–1840)
   6. Joel Dean (1755–1842) *m.* 1775 Mary Brockman (1759–1825)
   7. John Brockman (1725–1801) *m.* 1754 Amelia Martin
   8. John Brockman (1700–1755) *m.* Mary Collins
   9. Thomas Brockman *m.* Amy ———
   Service: Pilgrim, England to Virginia via Barbadoes.
   Reference: Early American History (Brockman), Vol. 2, pg. 2.

6159   TAYLOR, Mabel Pettit   Recorded 1937
       619 Coleman Place, Westfield, New Jersey
   1. Mabel Pettit (1889–   ) *m.* 1917 Harry D. Taylor
   2. H. Frank Pettit (1859–1935) *m.* 1887 Anna M. Weber (1868–   )
   3. William H. Pettit (1834–1885) *m.* 1858 Abigail Ward (1837–1900)
   4. William Tatum Ward (1793–1858) *m.* 1818 Abigail M. Howey (1799–1840)
   5. Isaiah Ward (1762–1834) *m.* 1791 Abigail Tatem (1770–aft. 1833)
   6. James Ward (1729–1795) *m.* 1755 Margaret Hopper
   7. Moses Ward (1707–1774) *m.* 1728 Mary Clark
   8. James Ward (–W.P. 1728) *m.* 1698 Hannah Unit
   Service:
   Reference: Biographical Review of Camden and Burlington Counties, N. J., Vol. XIX,
       pp. 265, 266; Ward Family Bible; Photostatic Copy in D. A. R. Library,
       Washington, D. C.; Abstract of will of James Ward is given New Jersey
       Archives (First Series), Vol. XXIII, p. 489; Abstracts of Wills,
       1670–1730.

6494   TEALL, Mrs. Russell F.   Recorded 1945
       Toledo, Ohio
   1. Blanche L. Dunbar *m.* Russell F. Teall
   2. William Dunbar (1858–1932) *m.* 1879 Minnie L. Crippen (1857–1943)
   3. Roger Gale Crippen (1824–1912) *m.* 1854 Ann Eliza Crane (1833–1912)
   4. Daniel Crippen (1794–1876) *m.* 1816 Charlotte Gale (1795–1888)
   5. Deborah Crippen (1765–1828) *m.* 1783 Mary Whiting (1765–   )
   6. John Crippen (1743–   ) *m.* ———
   7. John Crippen (1720–1785) *m.* 1741 Mary Richmond
   8. Jabez Crippen (1680–1785) *m.* 1707 Thankful Fuller (1689–   )
   9. John Fuller (1656–1726) *m.* 1678 Mehitable Rowley (1661–1732) *ca.*
  10. Samuel Fuller *m.* Jane Lothrop
   Service:
   Reference:

5867   TEBO, Mrs. Clarence D.   Recorded 1930, Georgia
       12 E. Shadow Lawn Avenue, Atlanta, Georgia
   1. Alma Patterson *m.* 1905 Clarence D. Tebo
   2. LeRoy F. Patterson (1853–1924) *m.* 1877 Isabelle Gremmer (1857–1917)
   3. Turner D. Patterson (1810–1875) *m.* 1829 Selerma E. Rowlett (1810–1856)
   4. Turner Patterson *m.* 1800 Cecelia Dennis
   5. Turner Patterson (1730–1779) *m.* Susanna
   6. Capt. Thomas Patterson
   Service: None given.
   Reference: Heitman's Register; History of the Scotch-Irish, by Hanna, Vol. II.

6122   TEBO, Heyl G.   Recorded 1936, Georgia
       12 E. Shadow Lawn Avenue, Atlanta, Georgia
   1. Heyl Gremmer Tebo
   2. Clarence D. Tebo (1878–1933) *m.* 1905 Alma Patterson (1879–   )

3. LeRoy F. Patterson (1853–1924) *m.* 1877 Isabelle T. Gremmer (1857–1917)
4. Turner D. Patterson (1810–1875) *m.* 1829 Belerma Rowlett (1810–1856)
5. Lt. Thomas Rowlett (1787–1841) *m.* 1809 Lucy Bruce (1791–1850)
6. William Rowlett (1760–   ) *m.* 1785 Elizabeth Gill (1767–   )
7. William Rowlett (1730–1785) *m.* 1752 Sarah
8. Peter Rowlett (–1749) *m.* Mary (–1777)
9. PETER ROWLETT (1637–1702)
Service: Early settler; Huguenot.
Reference:

6236   TEBO, Olna Patricia   Recorded 1939
       12 E. Shadow Lawn Avenue, Atlanta, Georgia
                         (JUNIOR)
1. Olna Patricia Tebo
2. LeRoy Patterson Tebo (1907–1938) *m.* 1931 Clara Lucille Hall (1910–   )
3. Clarence Decker Tebo (1878–1933) *m.* 1905 Olna Maudest Patterson (1879–   )
4. Senator Leroy Fillmore Patterson (1853–1925) *m.* 1877 Isabelle Teel Gremmer
   (1857–1917)
5. Turner Dennis Patterson (1810–1875) *m.* 1829 Belerma Evangeline Rowlett
   (1810–1856)
6. Lt. Thomas Rowlett (1787–1841) *m.* 1809 Lucy Bruce (1790–1850)
7. Wm. Rowlett (1760–   ) *m.* 1785 Elizabeth Gill (1767–   )
8. William Rowlett (1730–1785) *m.* 1752 Sarah ———
9. Peter Rowlett (–1749) *m.* Mary ———
10. PETER ROWLETT (1637–1702)
Service: Early settler; Huguenot.
Reference:

6235   TEBO, Kathryn Isabel   Recorded 1939
       12 E. Shadow Lawn Avenue, Atlanta, Georgia
                         (JUNIOR)
1. Kathryn Isabel Tebo
2. Leroy Patterson Tebo (1907–1938) *m.* 1931 Clara Lucille Hall (1910–   )
3. Clarence Decker Tebo (1878–1933) *m.* 1905 Olna Maudest Patterson (1879–   )
4. Senator Leroy Fillmore Patterson (1853–1925) *m.* 1877 Isabelle Teel Gremmer
   (1857–1917)
5. Turner Dennis Patterson (1810–1875) *m.* 1829 Belerma Evangeline Rowlett
   (1810–1856)
6. Lt. Thomas Rowlett (1787–1841) *m.* 1809 Lucy Bruce (1790–1850)
7. William Rowlett (1760–   ) *m.* 1785 Elizabeth Gill (1767–   )
8. William Rowlett (1730–1785) *m.* 1752 Sarah ———
9. Peter Rowlett (–1749) *m.* Mary ———
10. PETER ROWLETT (1637–1702)
Service: Early settler; Huguenot.
Reference:

5848   TEFFT, Mrs. Charles Eugene   Recorded 1929
       Guilford, R. 2, Maine
1. Mary Foote Burt (1871–   ) *m.* 1899 Charles Eugene Tefft
2. Arthur Seymour Burt (1848–1929) *m.* 1869 Alice Augusta Rice (1844–1913)
3. Daniel Rice, Jr. (1818–   ) *m.* 1842 Fanny Dean Tobey (1820–   )
4. Daniel Rice (1777–1867) *m.* Sarah Brown (1778–1867)
5. Joel Rice (1752–1834) *m.* Lydia Farnsworth (1742–   )
6. Jonas Rice (1732–1824) *m.* 1751 Bathsheta Parmentier (–1817)
7. Jonas Rice (1707–1793) *m.* Jane Hall
8. Jonas Rice (1672–1753) *m.* 1701 Mary Stone (1677–   )
9. Thomas Rice (1622–1681) *m.* Mary King (1630–1715)
10. DEACON EDMUND RICE (–1663) *m.* Tamazine Hosmer (–1654)
Service: Founder of Sudbury, 1639; Magistrate, 1641.
Reference:

5848   TEFFT, Mrs. Charles Eugene   Recorded 1929
              Guilford, R. 2, Maine
   1. Mary Foote Burt (1871–   ) *m.* 1889 Charles Eugene Tefft
   2. Arthur Seymour Burt (1848–1929) *m.* 1869 Alice Augusta Rice (1844–1913)
   3. Daniel Rice, Jr. (1818–   ) *m.* 1842 Fanny Tobey (1820–   )
   4. Williams Tobey (1773–1852) *m.* 1804 Zilpha Hall (1780–   )
   5. Isaac Tobey (1749–1845) *m.* 1772 Lydia Williams
   6. Rev. Samuel Tobey (1715–   ) *m.* 1738 ——— Crocker (1717–   )
   7. Timothy Crocker (1681–1737) *m.* 1709 Melatiah Crocker (1681–1737)
   8. Josiah Crocker (1647–   ) *m.* 1668 Meletiah Hinckley (1648–1714)
   9. GOVERNOR THOMAS HINCKLEY (–1705) *m.* 1641 Mary Richards
   Service: Governor.
   Reference: Lives of Governors of Plymouth Colony, by Moore; Whey Gen., Pope;
              Gen. of Burt Family, Burt.

5848   TEFFT, Mrs. Charles Eugene   Recorded 1929
              Guilford, R. 2, Maine
   1. Mary Foote Burt (1871–   ) *m.* 1899 Charles Eugene Tefft
   2. Arthur Seymour Burt (1848–1929) *m.* 1869 Alice Augusta Rice (1844–1913)
   3. Daniel Rice, Jr. (1818–   ) *m.* 1843 Fanny Tobey (1820–   )
   4. Williams Tobey (1773–1852) *m.* 1804 Zilpha Hall (1780–   )
   5. Isaac Tobey (1749–1845) *m.* 1772 Lydia Williams (1753–1773)
   6. Col. Geo. Williams (1717–1803) *m.* 1736 Sarah Leonard Hodges (1714–1771)
   7. Richards Williams (1671–   ) *m.* Ann Wilbore
   8. Joseph Williams *m.* Mary Fuller
   9. RICHARDS WILLIAMS (1606–1692) *m.* 1632 Frances Higleton (1611–1701)
  10. William Williams (–1618) *m.* 1663 Jane Woodward (–1614)
  11. John Williams (–1579)
  12. Richard Williams (1487–1559) *m.* Christian
  13. John Williams (–1502) *m.* Margaret Smyth (–1501)
   Service: One of the original founders of Taunton, Mass.
   Reference: Williams Gen., by Williams; Company Rolls, Taunton; Tobey Gen., by
              Pope; Pope's Pioneers of Mass.

4966   *TELLER, Judge Harvey   Recorded 1931
              1660 Gaylord Street, Denver, Colorado
   1. Harvey Teller *m.* Frances L. Wheelock
   2. John Teller (1800–1870) *m.* 1827 Charlotte Chapin Moore (1808–1901)
   3. John Teller (1760–   ) *m.* Catherine McDonald
   4. Isaac Teller (–1776 *m.* Rebecca Remsen
   5. William Teller IV (–1714) *m.* ———
   6. William Teller III (1689–   ) *m.* 1706 Maria Van Trickt
   7. William Teller II (1651–   ) *m.* Rachel Kiersted
   8. WILLIAM TELLER I (1620–1701) *m.* Margaret Deuchson; *m.* (2nd) Maria Varleth
   Service: Trustee land tracts in Ft. Orange.
   Reference: "First Settlers of Ancient Co. Albany, 1630–1800," Prof. Jonathan
              Pearson.
   *Omitted in Vol. I.

6669   TEMPLETON, Miss Nancy Brevard   Recorded 1950
              115 Kauffman Street, Waxahachie, Texas
   1. Nancy Brevard Templeton
   2. Patrick Henry Templeton (1856–1921) *m.* 1881 Nannie Watson (1858–1946)
   3. John D. Templeton (1817–1890) *m.* 1854 Alta Phoebe Lewis (1830–1852)
   4. James A. Templeton (1785–1830) *m.* 1811 Nancy Brevard (1791–1852)
   5. Zebulon Brevard, Jr. (1769–1825) *m.* bef. 1790 Isabella Edminston (1773–1825)
   6. Zebulon Brevard, Sr. (1724–1790) *m.* 1754 Ann Templeton (1773–1790)
   7. JEAN BREVARD (*b* France, *d.* Md.) *m.* 1714 Agnes McKnitt.
   Service: Left France in Revocation of Edict of Nates; 1685 Elder in Pres. Church.
   Reference: Hunt's sketches of Western N. C.; History of McKnitt Family.

6277 THOMAS, Col. Fred B.   Recorded 1939
        Randolph, Vermont
1. Fred B. Thomas *m.* 1899 Etta M. Goodale
2. Henry A. Thomas (1845–1923) *m.* 1868 Elvira Barnes, *b.* 1850
3. Adrian Thomas (1810–*c.* 1848) *m.* 1838 Hannah Barrows (1814–1896)
4. Gardner Thomas, *b. c.* 1775, *m.* ——
5. Capt. Andrew Thomas *b. c.* 1745, *m.* ——
6. Israel Thomas (1712/3–1778) *m.* 1742 Phebe Lyon (1723/4–1795)
7. William Thomas *c.* (1660–1734) *m.* 1704/5 Sarah Barden
8. DAVID THOMAS
Service: Was in Marblehead from 1645–1668; settled in Thomaston in Middle-
        borough, Mass., after 1668.
Reference: New England Families, by William Richard Cutter; Middleborough Vital
        Records; Mayflower Descendants.

5869 THOMAS, Mrs. William B.   Recorded 1929, Colorado
        1351 Grant Street, Denver, Colorado
1. Henrietta Averill *m.* William Burton Thomas
2. George P. Averill (1832–1908) *m.* 1858 Maria A. Coltrin
3. Calvin K. Averill (1800–1881) *m.* 1825 Emily A. Coit (1801–1866)
4. Nathan Averill, Jr. (1774–1865) *m.* 1794 Polly Ketchum (1778–1865)
5. Nathan Averill, Sr. (1745–1820) *m.* Rosanna Noble (1752–1812)
6. Daniel Averill (1716–1785) *m.* Lucy Cogswell (1726–   )
7. Isaac Averill (1680–   ) *m.* Esther Walker (1687–   )
8. William Averill, Jr. *m.* 1661 Hannah Jackson (–1691)
9. WILLIAM AVERILL, SR. (1603–1653) *m.* Abigail (–1653)
Service: Selectman, Surveyor, 1638.
Reference: Connecticut Vital Records.

6060 THOMPSON, Miss Eliza Scott   Recorded 1934, New Jersey
        3411 Winchester Avenue, Atlantic City, New Jersey
1. Eliza Scott Thompson
2. William W. Thompson (1830–1865) *m.* 1857 Hester T. Pennington (1825–1910)
3. John Pennington (1791–1858) *m.* 1812 Elizabeth Taylor (1793–1875)
4. Nathan Pennington (1758–1810) *m.* 1783 Margaret W. Leonard (1765–1853)
5. Samuel Pennington (1725–1791) *m.* 1745 Mary Sandford (1725–1805)
6. William Sandford (1696–1750) *m.* 1720 Mary Van Emburgh (1698–1728)
7. William Sandford (1670–1732) *m.* 1696 Mary Smith (1672–1732)
8. Lt. Michael Smith (–1685) *m.* 1669 Francina Berry (1643–1737)
9. MAJOR JOHN BERRY (1619–1714) *m.* 1640 Francina (1620–1683)
Service: Deputy Governor of East Jersey in 1672; member of Council under Carteret,
        1669–1682.
Reference: Smith's History of the Colony of Nova Caesaria or New Jersey; East
        Jersey under the Proprietors, by Whitehead.

5871 THOMPSON, Miss Jean A.   Recorded 1929, Colorado
        2263 Bellaire Street, Denver, Colorado
1. Jean A. Thompson
2. J. Arthur Thompson (1897–   ) *m.* 1923 Myra Hough (1899–   )
3. Lawrence P. Hough (1842–   ) *m.* 1895 Emma T. Price (1861–   )
4. George M. Price (1829–1902) *m.* 1861 Myra A. Kelsey (1844–1906)
5. Levi Kelsey III (1807–1879) *m.* 1828 Emma Stevens (1807–1883)
6. Benjamin Stevens (1779–1826) *m.* 1805 Esther Kelsey (1780–1872)
7. William Stevens (1750–1803) *m.* 1777 Anne Hollister (1754–1832)
8. Joseph Hollister (1732–1793) *m.* 1751 Rebecca Treat (1733–1768)
9. Isaac Treat (1701–   ) *m.* 1730 Rebecca Bulkeley (1709–   )
10. Capt. Edward Bulkeley (1673–1748) *m.* 1702 Dorothy Prescott (1681–1760)
11. Gersham Bulkeley (1636–1713) *m.* 1659 Sarah Chauncey (1630–1699)
12. REV. CHARLES CHAUNCEY (1592–1672) *m.* 1630 Catherine Eyre (–1667)
Service: Second President of Harvard.
Reference: N. E. Historical & Genealogical Register, Vol. X; Hollister Genealogy.

5872 THOMPSON, Miss Mildred M.   Recorded 1929, Colorado
        2263 Bellaire Street, Denver, Colorado
    1. Mildred M. Thompson
    2. J. Arthur Thompson (1897-) *m.* 1923 Myra Hough (1899-)
    3. Lawrence P. Hough (1842-) *m.* 1895 Emma Price (1861-)
    4. George M. Price (1829-1902) *m.* 1861 Myra Kelsey (1844-1906)
    5. Levi Kelsey III (1807-1879) *m.* 1828 Emma Stevens (1807-1883)
    6. Benjamin Stevens (1779-1826) *m.* 1805 Esther Kelsey (1780-1872)
    7. William Stevens (-1803) *m.* 1777 Anne Hollister (1754-1832)
    8. Joseph Hollister (1732-1793) *m.* 1751 Rebecca Treat (1733-1768)
    9. Isaac Treat (1701-) *m.* 1730 Rebecca Bulkeley (1709-)
   10. Capt. Edward Bulkeley (1673-1748) *m.* 1702 Dorothy Prescott (1681-1760)
   11. JONATHAN PRESCOTT (1631-1709) *m.* 1675 Elizabeth Hoar (-1689)
    Service: Early settler, 1640.
    Reference:

6437 THOMPSON, Mrs. Helen M.   Recorded 1944
        53 Daniel Avenue, Providence, Rhode Island
    1. Helen M. Grant *m.* ——— Thompson
    2. Edgar Weston Grant (1864-1940) *m.* 1889 (2nd) Ellen M. Horton (1869-1932)
    3. Daniel M. Horton (1827-1890) *m.* 1855 Josephine M. Slater (1835-1929)
    4. Brayton Slater (1808-) *m.* Patience Millard
    5. Silas Slater (1777-1865) *m.* Susan Burgess
    6. Silas Slater *m.* Beriah Adams
    7. Joseph Slater (1608-1787) *m.* ———
    8. JOHN SLATER *m.* ———
    Service: Settled at Lynn, Mass.; came from Wales, 1680.
    Reference: Memorial of John Slater, Rev. Edmond Slater, Vol. I.

6140 THORNLEY, Miss Harriet   Recorded 1937, Georgia
        Decatur, Georgia
    1. Harriet L. Thornley
    2. Ernest S. Thornley (1856-1904) *m.* 1877 Elizabeth Thornley (1861-1893)
    3. John Louis Thornley, Jr. (1828-1900) *m.* 1855 Elizabeth T. McFall (1829-1863)
    4. John L. Thornley, Sr. (1800-1833) *m.* 1826 Louisa (Chollet) Hutchinson
        (1800-1871)
    5. Alexander P. Chollet (-1799) *m.* 1787 Elizabeth Ripault (1765-1800)
    6. John Ripault (1729-1805) *m.* 1755 ———
    7. Dr. James Ripault (1690-1743) *m.* 1720 Elizabeth Colleton (1695-1750)
    8. MAJOR JAMES COLLETON (1665-1727) *m.* 1690 Anne (Mrs. Henry Russell) (-1735)
    Service: Major in the Provincial Forces.
    Reference: History of South Carolina under Proprietory Government.

6666 THORNTON, Mrs. John W.   Recorded 1950
        310 South Wilson Avenue, Dunn, North Carolina
    1. Julia Forbes *m.* John W. Thornton
    2. Cleveland O. Forbes *m.* 1885 Mary Louise Jones (1856-1947)
    3. Louis Dibrell Jones *m.* 1859 Louise T. Flippen (1840-1915)
    4. William D. Jones *m.* 1817 Judith B. Legrand (1798-1884)
    5. Michael Jones (1750-1821) *m.* 1777 Leanna Dibrell (1759-)
    6. Anthony Dibrell (1728-1800) *m.* 1756 Elizabeth Lee (1734-1770)
    7. Thomas Lee (1679-1735) *m.* 1700 Elizabeth Keene
    8. Charles Lee (1656-1702) *m.* 1676 Elizabeth Medstand
    9. COL. RICHARD LEE (1619-1664) *m.* Anna ———
    Service:
    Reference:

6361 TILLMAN, Charles Thomas   Recorded 1941, Georgia
        606 North Court Street, Quinton, Georgia
    1. Charles Thomas Tillman *m.* 1896 Eugenie Paul Pillot

2. John Tillman (1845–1899) *m.* 1868 Mary Lawson Wyche (1844–1871)
3. John Scott Wyche (1810–1855) *m.* (2nd) 1837 Hannah Lawson McIntyre (1819–1889)
4. Batte Wyche (1767–1819) *m.* 1789 Mary Jarrett (1771–1817)
5. George Wyche (1746–1809) *m.* Mary Peterson, *d.* aft. 1772
6. Peter Wyche, *d.* aft. 1756, *m.* Alice Scott, *d.* aft. 1756
7. George Wyche, *d.* 1757, *m.* Sarah ———, *d.* aft. 1753
8. HENRY WYCHE (1648–1714) *m.* ———

Service: Resident Surry Co., Va., 1679; named as foot-soldier of Surry Co., 1687.
Reference: Court Records of Tattnall Co., Ga.; Recs. of Richmond Co., Ga.; Recs. of Brunswick Co., Va.; Recs. of Sussex Co., Va.

6370 TILLMAN, Mrs. Charles T.   Recorded 1942, Georgia
          606 North Court Street, Quitman, Georgia

1. Eugenie Paul Pillot *m.* 1896 Charles Thomas Tillman
2. Edward Nicholas Pillot (1839–1892) *m.* 1865 Victoria Bellamy (1838–1891)
3. Col. Abram Bellamy (1800–1839) *m.* 1825 Eliza Ann Williams (1807–1871)
4. Samuel Williams, *d. c.* 1809, *m.* Ann Hill (1787–1849)
5. Theophilus Hill *m.* 1762 Teresa Thomas, *d.* aft. 1787
6. Abraham Hill, *d.* 1760, *m.* Judith, *d.* aft. 1760
7. HENRY HILL, *d.* 1719/20 *m.* Mary ———

Service: Land owner and resident of Nansemond Co., Va., prior to 1700; removed to Chowan Co., N. C., 1700.
Reference: "Hills of Wilkes Co., Ga., and Allied Families," by L. J. Hill; Recs. St. Augustine, Fla.; Archives of N. C. Historical Commission, Raleigh, N. C.; Clemens' "North and South Carolina Marriages;" Recs. Chowan Co., N. C.; Land patents in Land Office at Richmond, Va.

6372 TILNEY, Bradford Sargent   Recorded 1942, Connecticut
          Sperry Road, Cheshire, Connecticut

1. Bradford Sargent Tilney *m.* 1938 Josephine Toy Collins
2. Robert Fingland Tilney (1882–1934) *m.* 1907 Rhoda Miles Sargent (1883–)
3. Henry Bradford Sargent (1851–1927) *m.* 1879 Harriet Amelia Oaks (1854–1942)
4. Clark Henry Oaks (1819–1882) *m.* 1850 Rhoda Miles (1818–1884)
5. August Miles (1788–1864) *m.* 1811 Roxanna Norton (1792–1875)
6. Alexander Norton (1763–1848) *m.* 1786 Rhoda Collins (1766–1855)
7. Cyprian Collins (1733–1807) *m.* 1756 Axubah Gibbs (1734–1823)
8. Rev. Timothy Collins (1699–1776/7) *m.* 1723 Elizabeth Hyde, bap. 1703
9. John Collins (1665–1751) *m.* 1691 Anna Leete (1702–1724)
10. John Leete (1639–1692) *m.* 1670 Mary Chittenden (1647–1712)
11. Gov. WILLIAM LEETE, *d.* 1683, *m.* Ann Payne, *d.* 1668

Service: Governor of Connecticut, 1661–1664)
Reference: "Sargent Genealogy," Sargent; "Norton Genealogy," W. W. Norton; "Collins Genealogy;" "Hyde Genealogy;" "Leete Family."

6242 TILSON, Mrs. P. S.   Recorded 1939
          1516 McGowan, Houston, Texas

1. Frances Parker (1879–) *m.* 1902 P. S. Tilson
2. Milton Parker (1840–1906) *m.* 1864 Millie Johnson (1844–1923)
3. Samuel Parker (1798–1857) *m.* 1825 Mary B. Dunn (1801–1852)
4. Thos. G. Parker (1775–1826) *m.* 1795 Frances Grisham (1770–1846)
5. John Parker (1755–1801) *m.* 1775 Elizabeth Muse (1759–1801)
6. Richard Parker (1729–1813) *m.* 1751 Elizabeth Beale (1730–)
7. Col. William Beale (1705–1778) *m.* 1729 Anna Harmar (1709–)
8. Thos. Beale (1675–1729) *m.* 1704 Elizabeth Taverner
7. Capt. Thos. Beale, Jr. (1647–1679) *m.* Arm Gooch (1674–)
8. COL. THOMAS BEALE (1629–) *m.* Alice ———

Service: Member King's Council, 1662; Colonel.
Reference: Va. His. Mag., Vol. 5; Beall & Ball Fam., by Beall.

6050 TOLLERTON, Mrs. William James   Recorded 1933
          10502 S. Seeley Avenue, Chicago, Illinois

1. Clara Horsely (1876–   ) *m.* 1906 William James Tollerton
2. Louis Langley Horsley (1846–1883) *m.* 1866 Florentine Gunn (1850–1926)
3. Wm. Carroll Gunn (1814–1855) *m.* 1849 Eliz Susan Moreland (1831–1917)
4. Andrew Moreland (1782–1859) *m.* 1811 Eliz Lee Rucker (1796–1868)
5. John Rucker (1766–1812) *m.* 1788 Nancy Shelton (1767–1860)
6. Isaac Rucker (1740–1799) *m.* 1861 Mildred Hawkins Plunkett
7. Capt. John Rucker (–1742) *m.* 1707 Susanna
8. PETER RUCKER (1670–1743) *m.* Elizabeth (1670–1752)

Service: Capt. Col. Militia.
Reference: Am. Gen.; Rucker Gen., by Sudie Rucker Wood; Hening's Statute,
          Vol. 11, page 202.

6103 TOMPKINS, Mrs. F. J.   Recorded 1936, New York
          560 N. Broadway, Yonkers, New York

1. Zula Smith *m.* 1891 Frederick J. Tompkins
2. Harvey S. Smith (1840–1922) *m.* 1868 Leah L. Polhemus (1846–1933)
3. Caleb H. Smith (1808–1890) *m.* 1829 Aurelia C. Boardman (1807–1866)
4. Timothy Boardman (1764–1825) *m.* 1789 Ruth Elliott (1771–1844)
5. John Boardman (1735–1817) *m.* 1760 Lydia Dean (1746–1772)
6. John Dean (1713–   ) *m.* 1743 Sarah Douglass (1715–   )
7. John Dean (1678–   ) *m.* 1710 Lydia Thatcher (1680–   )
8. James Dean (1648–1725) *m.* 1673 Sarah Tisdale (1651–1726)
9. WALTER DEAN (1615–1693) *m.* 1635 Eleanor Strong (1614–   )

Service: Freeman at Taunton, Mass., 1637.
Reference:

5913 TOZIER, Kathleen Seaman   Recorded 1910, Ohio
          11322 Hessler Road, Cleveland, Ohio

1. Kathleen Seaman *m.* 1887 Chas. Burt Tozier
2. Benjamin Daniel Seaman (1833–1902) *m.* 1863 Estelle J. Cobb (1838–1871)
3. Justus Cobb (1815–1897) *m.* 1837 Eliza J. Morgan (1821–1874)
4. George Morgan (1784–1879) *m.* 1815 Deborah Headley (wid.) (1790–1834)
5. Jesse Morgan (1758–1846) *m.* 1783 Matilda Fish (1756–1837)
6. Timothy Morgan (1722–1795) *m.* Deborah (1729–1794)
7. Samuel Morgan (1669–1734) *m.* 1708 Hannah Avery (1685–   )
8. Capt. James Avery (1646–1728) *m.* 1669 Deborah Stallyon (–1729)
9. Capt. James Avery (1620–1700) *m.* 1643 Joanne Greenslade
10. CHRISTOPHER AVERY *m.* 1616 Margery Stevens

Service: Capt. James Avery served in King Philip's War; Deputy to General Court,
          1659.
Reference: The Groton-Avery Clan, Vol. I; Connecticut Colonial Records.

6572 TRIMBLE, Mrs. R. H.   Recorded 1948
          27 East Columbus Street, Mt. Sterling, Ohio

1. Florence Lohr *m.* Dr. Robert Henry Trimble
2. James M. Lohr (1840–1904) *m.* 1865 Mary C. Pringle (1845–1936)
3. George W. Lohr (1813–1897) *m.* 1837 Sarah F. Reeder (1817–1875)
4. Jacob Reeder, Jr. (1782–1848) *m.* 1804 Sarah Truesdale (1786–1855)
5. John Truesdale (1737–aft. 1808) *m.* 1760 Mary Whitney (1742–aft. 1808)
6. Daniel Whitney (1720–1809) *m.* 1741 Thankful Burt (1721–   )
7. Henry Whitney (1680–1728) *m.* 1710 Elizabeth Olmsted (1690–   )
8. Ensign Jno. Olmsted (bapt. 1649–1704) *m.* 1670 Mary Benedict
9. CAPT. RICHARD OLMSTED (1612–aft. 1686) *m.* bef. 1640 ———

Service: Pequot War, 1637; King Philip's War, 1675; one of the founders of Hartford,
          Conn.
Reference: Whitney Genealogy of Conn.; Olmsted Gen.

6331 TRIPP, Mrs. Frank   Recorded 1941, Vermont
       33 North Avenue, Orleans, Vermont
   1. Myra Wolcott *m.* 1883 Frank Tripp
   2. Hiram Alonzo Wolcott (1827–1888) *m.* 1855 Savilla Spaulding (1832–1916/7)
   3. Emerson Wolcott, Jr. (1777–1861) *m.* 1810 Hannah Morse (1793–1861)
   4. Emerson Wolcott (1738–   ) *m.* 1767 Mary Adams
   5. Capt. Nathaniel Wolcott, *d.* 1771 *m.* 1723 Deborah Walker
   6. John Woolcott III (1660–1747) *m.* 1684/5 Joanna Emerson, *d.* aft. 1747
   7. John Woolcott, Jr. *c.* (1632–1696) *m.* 1653 Mary Thurlow
   8. JOHN WOOLCOTT
   Service: Sold property in Salem, Mass., 1635.
   Reference: "Hist. of North Brookfield, Mass.," Temple; Hemenway's Vt. Gazeteer,
           Vol. III; V. R. of Vermont; Genealogical Register.

6079 TROTTI, Mrs. Hugh H.   Recorded 1935, Georgia
       230 Wilton Dr., Decatur, Georgia
   1. Mary L. Haygood *m.* 1914 Hugh H. Trotti
   2. Wilbur F. Haygood (1864–   ) *m.* 1887 Mary R. Rogers (1864–   )
   3. Osborn T. Rogers (1824–1896) *m.* 1861 Mary (Wood) Stokes (1832–1920)
   4. Cary Wood (1795–1857) *m.* 1823 Mary R. Billups (1803–1873)
   5. William Billups (1763–1817) *m.* 1787 Mary Richardson (1763–1803)
   6. Richard Richardson, Jr. (1741–1818) *m.* 1761 Dorcas Nelson (1741–1836)
   7. Richard Richardson (1704–1780) *m.* 1738 Mary Cantey (1720–1767)
   8. William Cantey (1680–1729) *m.* 1702 Arabella Oldys (1685–1724)
   9. GEORGE CANTEY (1650–1716) *m.* 1670 Martha
   Service: A member of the Jury; Assessor; Vestryman of St. James, South Carolina.
   Reference: South Carolina Historical Society Magazine, Vol. 11, p. 204; South Carolina
           Collections, Vol. 5.

6655 TURNER, Mrs. M. J.   Recorded 1949
       4328 Stanford, Dallas, Texas
   1. Virginia McKinney, *m.* 1944 ———
   2. Dr. Eugene P. McKinney (1869–1926) *m.* 1898 Mary Massengale (1869–   )
   3. Alfred M. Massengale (1814–1874) *m.* 1867 Caroline Lovelace (1838–1873)
   4. Dr. Wm. R. Lovelace (1815–1901) *m.* 1837 Martha Atkinson (1821–1876)
   5. James Lovelace (1779–1860) *m.* 1805 Mary Stapler (1783–1803)
   6. William Lovelace (1750–1815) *m.* 1773 Margery Beall (1741–1803)
   7. James Beall (1698–1783) *m.* 1724 Margaret Edmonston (1708–   )
   8. Col. Archibald Edmonston (1670–1734) *m.* 1700 Jane Beall (1685–   )
   9. COL. NINIAN BEALL (1625–1717) *m.* 1668 Ruth Moore (1652–1707)
   Service: Commissioned Lt., 1668, Capt., 1681, Lt. Col., 1694, Co. and Chief of all
           His Majesty's Forces, 1694; member Gen. Assembly, 1697–1701, Md.;
           Gen. Assembly passed "Act of Gratitude" for Distinguished Indian Service,
           1699.
   Reference: Tombstones in Texas; Wm. Lovelace Family Bible; Wills in Hall of
           Records, Annapolis, Md.; "Founding of Maryland," by Andrews.

6078 UMBERGER, Mrs. Benjamin   Recorded 1935, Pennsylvania
       Duncannon, Pennsylvania
   1. Nellie Deming *m.* 1899 Benjamin F. Umberger
   2. John H. Deming (1835–1919) *m.* 1868 Sarah E. McCoy (1844–1915)
   3. Horace Deming (1788–1845) *m.* 1820 Emily Rising (1798–1866)
   4. John Deming (1769–1800) *m.* Roxy Galpin (1769–1844)
   5. Moses Deming (1720–1795) *m.* 1746 Sarah Norton (1726–1809)
   6. Jacob Deming (1689–1771) *m.* 1709 Dinah Churchill (–1751)
   7. Jonathan Deming (1639–1700) *m.* 1673 Elizabeth Gilbert (1654–1714)
   8. JOHN DEMING (–1692) *m.* Honor Treat
   Service: Among the first settlers of Wethersfield, Conn., in 1635; a constable and
           court deputy.
   Reference: Genealogy of the Descendants of Hon. John Deming of Wethersfield,
           Conn., by Judson Keith Deming, 1904.

6568   VAN METRE, Grace Applegate   Recorded 1947
          515 Fifth Street, Marietta, Ohio
   1. Grace Applegate *m.* 1895 Wyllis V. Van Metre
   2. Robert M. Applegate (1838–1896) *m.* 1861 Julia M. Russell (1839–1913)
   3. Charles Russell (1807–1841) *m.* 1838 Clarinda J. Clark (1811–1902)
   4. John Russell (1764–1829) *m.* 1794 Elizabeth (Betsy) Smith (1774–1864)
   5. Jonathan Russell (1738–1809) *m.* abt. 1760 Mary Brown
   6. Daniel Russell (1713–1776) *m.* 1737 Phebe Roberts (1711–)
   7. David Roberts (1684–) *m.* Rachel Pierce (1681–)
   8. Thomas Pierce (1645–1717) *m.* 1680 Rachel Bacon (1652–)
   9. Daniel Bacon *ca.* (1615–) *m.* Mary Reed
   10. MICHAEL BACON, *d.* 1648, *m.* ———
   Service: Was one of the signers of the Church Covenant of Dedham.
   Reference: Michael Bacon of Dedham and His Descendants.

6038   VERDERY, Mrs. Horace M.   Recorded 1933
          4925 Larchwood Avenue, Philadelphia, Pennsylvania
   1. Mary Helen Rutherford *m.* 1887 ——— Verdery
   2. Wm. John Rutherford (1832–1906) *m.* 1856 Constantia Louisa Rich (1840–1879)
   3. Chas. Thomas Rich (1804–1886) *m.* 1827 Mary Hasson (–1891)
   4. Aquila Rich (1759–1813) *m.* 1793 Hannah Thomas (1773–1835)
   5. Obadiah Rich (1730–1760) *m.* 1754 Priscilla Rich (1734–1807)
   6. Richard Rich (1698–1742) *m.* 1720 Hannah Doane (1702–1754)
   7. Isaac Doane (1670–1755) *m.* 1700 Margaret Wood
   8. John Doane (1635–1708) *m.* Hannah Bangs (1644–1677)
   9. DEACON JOHN DOANE (–1685)
   Service: Deacon first church in Plymouth; Deputy Colony Ct.; Asst. to Governor.
   Reference: N. Eng. Gen. Hist. Register; Desc. of Deacon John Doane.

6367   VERNER, Mrs. John Clark   Recorded 1942, Georgia
          93 South Elm Street, Commerce, Georgia
   1. Ruth Stark *m.* 1911 Dr. John Claude Verner
   2. William Weldon Stark (1864–) *m.* 1888 Arabella Brown (1871–1939)
   3. Andrew Franklin Brown (1830–1912) *m.* 1856 Alice Mildred Maley (1838–1907)
   4. Sidney Maley (1813–1893) *m.* 1835 Alice Arrena Deadwyler (1810–1881)
   5. John Maley, *d.* 1831, *m.* 1799 Sarah Rice, *d.* bef. 1832
   6. James Maley, *d.* 1788/9, *m.* Winnefred Haynie, *d.* 1818
   7. Hezekiah Haynie, *d.* 1788, *m.* Hannah Christopher
   8. John Haynie, *d.* 1738, *m.* Hannah Neale (1684–aft. 1711)
   9. CAPTAIN JOHN HAYNIE (1624–1697) *m.* 1650 Jane Morris, *d.* aft. 1682
   Service: Member Va. House of Burgesses, 1657–1658; Justice; Surveyor; King's
       Attorney; Officer in Susquehannough Indian Wars, 1675–1677.
   Reference: Records Elbert Co., Ga., Northumberland Co., Va.; Tyler's Quarterly,
       Vol. 22; Wm. & Mary Quart., Vol. 124; Crozier's "Va. Colonial Militia;"
       Hening's Statutes, I; Colonial Va. Register; Journals of H. of Burgesses,
       1619–1659.

6749   WADE, Mrs. J. L.   Recorded 1952, North Carolina
          408 South Orange Avenue, Dunn, North Carolina
   1. Helena Morris *m.* 1912 J. L. Wade
   2. Capt. Wm. G. B. Morris (1842–1892) *m.* 1870 Elizabeth King (1852–1947)
   3. Richard Morris (1797–1879) *m.* 1832 Lucinda MacLean (1801–1885)
   4. Charles MacLean, Jr. (1772–1858) *m.* 1797 Elizabeth Hughes (1778–1863)
   5. John Hughes (1728–1803) *m.* 1764 Martha Moore (1735–1799)
   6. Leander Hughes (abt. 1704–) *m.* Elizabeth ——— (abt. 1707–1775)
   7. ORLANDA HUGHES (1677 in Wales–1768 in Va.) *m.* Elizabeth
   Service:
   Reference: Orlanda Hughes Will, 1768; Leander Hughes Will, 1775; Land Grants in
       Powhatan and Goochland Co., Va.; Family History, by Lucy Henderson
       Horton, Vol. 2, pgs. 8, 10; American Ancestry, Vol. IV, 1889, pgs. 77, 78;
       Pittman's "Americans of Gentle Birth and Their Ancestors," Vol. 2,
       pg. 81.
   Orlanda Hughes came to America prior to 1697 with two older brothers.

6517 WAGNER, Charles Arthur Recorded 1946
46 Main Street, Irvington, New York

1. Charles A. Wagner
2. George Louis Wagner (1885–) *m.* 1914 Charlotte White (1874–)
3. Charles A. White (1842–1920) *m.* 1873 Anna W. Nichols (1841–1929)
4. Abner White (1802–1883) *m.* 1835 Charlotte Harvey (1803–1854)
5. Rufus Harvey (1758–1807) *m.* 1790 Sarah Jones, *d.* 1803
6. Jonathan Harvey (1712–1797) *m.* 1740 Freelove Hicks
7. William Harvey (1680–1733) *m.* bef. 1702 Hopestill Briggs
8. Thomas Harvey (1641–1728) *m.* 1679 Elizabeth Willis, *d.* 1719
9. WILLIAM HARVEY (1614–1691) *m.* Joane Hucker, *d.* 1649

Service: Was at Dorchester, Mass., 1636; Deputy Mass., 1664, 1677.
Reference: Harvey Genealogy; History of Milford, Conn.; Colonial Ancestry of the Family of John Green Briggs and Isabel Gibbs de Groff.

6208 WAGNER, Mrs. George Louis Recorded 1938
Irvington-on-Hudson, New York

1. Charlotte White (1874–) *m.* George Louis Wagner
2. Chas. Abner White (1842–1920) *m.* 1873 Anna Williamson Nichols (1841–1929)
3. Abner White (1802–1883) *m.* 1835 Charlotte Harvey (1803–1854)
4. Joseph White (1773–1826) *m.* 1800 Hannah Habeltine (1781–1866)
5. Peter White (1738–1805) *m.* 1759 Deborah Fish (1741–1825)
6. Peter White (1714–) *m.* 1736 Jamima Taft
7. Joseph White, Jr. (1661–1757) *m.* 1682 Lydia Copeland (1661–1727)
8. Capt. Joseph White (1640–1706) *m.* 1660 Lydia Rogers (1642–1727)
9. CAPT. THOMAS WHITE (1599–1679)

Service: Lawyer; Founder of Weymouth, Mass.; Rep. Colonial Legislature.
Reference: Comp. of Am. Gen., Vol. III, p. 631; Hazeltine Gen.; The Rawson Family, by S. S. Rawson.

6014 WAITE, Mrs. Daniel M. Recorded 1932
3429 Stuart Street, Denver, Colorado

1. Anna R. —— (1867–) *m.* 1886 Daniel M. Waite
2. Hannah Eliz. Fairchild (1829–1920) *m.* 1849 Nelson Fairchild (1823–1908)
3. Lyman Alden (1806–1886) *m.* Nancy Doran (–1887)
4. John Adams Alden (1762–1843) *m.* 1787 Hannah Daniels (1768–)
5. John Alden *m.* —— Adams
6. John Needham Alden (1731–) *m.* ——
7. John Alden (1663–1729) *m.* 1684 Eliz. Phelps (–1719)
8. John Alden (1622–1702) *m.* Elizabeth ——
9. JOHN ALDEN (1589–1687) *m.* 1620 Priscilla Mullen

Service:
Reference:

6635 WAITT, Mrs. E. B. Recorded 1949
1089 Blue Ridge Ave. N. E., Atlanta, Georgia

1. Laura Haynes *m.* 1902 E. B. Waitt
2. Benjamin Haynes (1848–) *m.* 1878 Rebecca T. Alexander (1841–1912)
3. John D. Alexander (1813–1870) *m.* 1837 Mary R. Baird (1816–1851)
4. William D. Baird (1780–1843) *m.* 1803 Abigail Martin (1784–1853)
5. Josiah Martin (1756–1852) *m.* 1783 Mary McClary (1765–1852)
6. Robert McClary *m.* Abigail McDowell, *b.* 1740
7. John McDowell *m.* Mary —— (1709–1789)
8. EPHRAIM MCDOWELL (1672–1774) *m.* Margaret Irwin

Service:
Reference: Genealogical Histories of Families, by N. W. McConnell; Compendium of American Genealogy First Families of America, F. A. Virkus.

6582 WALES, Marion Porter   Recorded 1948
          500 Diversey Parkway, Chicago 14, Illinois
      1. Marion Porter Wales
      2. Dr. Royal P. Wales (1838–1907) *m.* 1863 Anna Belding (1845–1908)
      3. Horatio Wales (1810–1890) *m.* 1833 Mary E. Williams (1811–1892)
      4. Ebenezer Williams (1777–1856) *m.* 1808 Elizabeth Whitwell (1778–1827)
      5. Rev. Nehemiah Williams (1749–1796) *m.* 1775 Persia Keyes (1749–1827)
      6. Rev. Chester Williams (1718–1755) *m.* 1744 Sarah Porter (1726–1774)
      7. Rev. Ebenezer Williams (1690–1753) *m.* 1711 Penelope Chester (1693–1764)
      8. Samuel Williams (1656–1735) *m.* 1679 Sarah May (1659–1712)
      9. Samuel Williams (1632–1698) *m.* 1653 Theoda Parke (1637–1718)
     10. Dea. William Parke *ca.* (1604–1683) *m.* 1636 Martha Holgrave *ca.* (1614–1708)
     11. ROBERT PARKE (1580–1665) *m.* 1601 Martha Chaplyn (bapt. 1583–bef. 1630)
     Service: Sect. to Gov. Winthrop, Mass.
     Reference: Hist. Brimfield, Mass.; Hist. Pomfert, Conn.; Hist. Roxbury, Mass.

6660 WALKER, Flora Ann B.   Recorded 1949
          3133 Connecticut Avenue N. W., Washington 8, D. C.
      1. Flora Ann Bredes *m.* 1909 Wm. Sherman Walker
      2. Henry T. Bredes (1852–1912) *m.* 1873 Ella M. King (1853–1940)
      3. Orris A. King (1822–1870) *m.* 1847 Susan B. Glasier (1826–1906)
      4. Elisha King (1795–   ) *m.* 1818 Zurviah Green (1797–1870)
      5. Gemaliel King (abt. 1771–1837) *m.* 1794 Priscilla Bosworth
      6. Zadoc Bosworth (1735–1810) *m.* Joanna Raymond, *d.* 1819
      7. David Bosworth (1699–aft. 1746) *m.* 1720 Priscilla Shaw (1702–aft. 1743)
      8. David Bosworth (1669–1747) *m.* 1698 Mercy Sturtevant (1676–1707)
      9. Jonathan Bosworth *m.* Hannah Howland
     10. JOHN HOWLAND
     Service: Mayflower passenger.
     Reference: Bosworth Gen., Swansea Records, Mayflower Desc.

6089 WALKER, Mrs. Florence J.   Recorded 1935, Pennsylvania
          Greene Manor, Germantown, Pennsylvania
      1. Florence Jepson *m.* ——— Walker
      2. George E. Jepson (1842–1916) *m.* 1871 Emma E. Fitch (1843–1915)
      3. Austin G. Fitch (1813–1891) *m.* 1840 Mary C. March (1816–1911)
      4. Jacob March (1786–1823) *m.* 1814 Mary L. Monroe (1791–1869)
      5. Stephen Monro(e) (1758–1826) *m.* 1790 Susannah LeBaron (1767–1811)
      6. Lazarus LeBaron (1744–1827) *m.* 1767 Susannah Johonnot (1738–1774)
      7. Lazarus LeBaron (1721–1784) *m.* 1743 Margaret Newsome
      8. Lazarus LeBaron (1698–1773) *m.* 1720 Lydia Bartlett (1697–1742)
      9. Joseph Bartlett (1665–1703) *m.* 1692 Lydia Griswold (1672–1752)
     10. Joseph Bartlett (1639–1711) *m.* Hannah Pope (1638–1710)
     11. Robert Bartlett *m.* 1628 Mary Warren
     12. RICHARD WARREN
     Service: Signer of Compact on Mayflower.
     Reference: The Mayflower Descendants; Sutton Vital Records.

6678 WALLACE, Mrs. George M.   Recorded 1950
          2229 Ovid Street, Baton Rouge, Louisiana
      1. Eleanor R. Murphy *m.* 1929 George M. Wallace
      2. John Barrett Murphy (1868–   ) *m.* 1899 Eleanor Prescott (1879–   )
      3. Capt. Lewis D. Prescott (1837–1900) *m.* 1856 Lucy G. Offutt
      4. William M. Prescott (1808–1854) *m.* 1830 Evelina S. Moore (1812–1875)
      5. Judge John Moore (1788–1867) *m.* 1810 Symphrose A. Demarest (1791–   )
      6. Major Lewis Moore *m.* Retecka Heushaw (1770–   )
      7. Capt. William Heushaw (1736–1799) *m.* 1768 Agnes Anderson (1735–1806)
      8. Nicholas Heushaw *m.* Rebecka Smith
      9. John Heushaw (1701–   ) *m.* Mary Stubman
     10. Jacob Neushaw (1661–1719) *m.* 1682 Elizabeth Sumner (–1728)
     11. William Sumner, Jr. (1636–   ) *m.* 1660 Elizabeth Clement
     12. WILLIAM SUMNER, SR. (–Eng. 1688) *m.* 1635 Mary Nest (–Eng. 1676)
     Service:
     Reference: Gen. Sumner Family, by Mrs. B. Trash.

5992 WALTHEN, John Bernard, Jr. Recorded 1931
      Mocking Bird Valley, Jefferson Co., Kentucky
1. John Bernard Walthen, Jr. (1880–) *m.* 1903 ———
2. John Bernard Walthen (1844–1919) *m.* 1867 Margaret Adams (1844–1930)
3. James Adams (1802–1881) *m.* 1827 Ann Pamelia Hill (1807–1845)
4. Clement Hill (1776–1832) *m.* 1798 Mary Hamilton (1782–1833)
5. Rev. Thomas Hamilton (1745–1807) *m.* 1781 Ann Hodgkins (1757–1819)
6. Capt. James Hamilton (1715–1785) *m.* Mary Ann Coombs (1718?–)
7. Thomas Coombs (–1753) *m.* Elizabeth Wharton (–1772)
8. Dr. Jesse Wharton (–1676) *m.* Elizabeth Sewall
9. Secty Henry Sewall (–1665) *m.* 1654? Lady Jane Lowe (–1701)
Service: Secretary.
Reference: Gen. Thomas Hill and Desc.; Gen. McKinzies, Col. Fam. Vol. 1, page 291.

5896 WALTHEN, Richard Eugene Recorded 1930, Kentucky
      1397 South Third Avenue, Louisville, Kentucky
1. Richard E. Walthen (1877–) *m.* 1910 Ada Marie Walsh
2. John Bernard Walthen (1884–1919) *m.* 1867 Margaret Adams (1844–)
3. James Adams (1802–1881) *m.* 1827 Ann Pamelia Hill (1807–1845)
4. Clement Hill (1776–1832) *m.* 1798 Mary Hamilton (1782–1833)
5. Thomas Hamilton (1733–1807) *m.* 1781 Ann Hodgkins (1757–1819)
6. James Hamilton (1715–1785) *m.* Mary Ann Coombs (–1785)
7. Thomas Coombs (–1753) *m.* Elizabeth Wharton (–1772)
8. Dr. Jesse Wharton (–1676) *m.* 1672 Elizabeth Sewall (–1710)
Service: Deputy Governor, Maryland, 1676.
Reference: Maryland Archives, Vol. II, Vol. V.

6393 WALTON, Mrs. Wycliff Recorded 1942
      1215 Wendover, Rosemont, Pennsylvania
1. Carolyn M. Lewis *m.* W. Wycliff Walton
2. Edwin O. Lewis (1879–) *m.* 1905 Eleanor A. Lord (1878–1935)
3. Louis Lewis (1848–1926) *m.* 1875 Jane Elizabeth Owen (1859–1940)
4. Arthur Benjamin Owen (1820–1896) *m.* 1853 Mary S. (Taylor) Hall (wid.) (1822–1912)
5. John Owen (1781–) *m.* 1817 Catherine Montague
6. William Montague (1758–) *m.* 1790 Elizabeth Valentine
7. William Montague (1730–1764) *m.* 1754 Catherine ——— (1736–)
8. Thomas Montague (169?–1756) *m.* 1727 Penelope ———
9. Peter Montague (1666–) *m.* abt. 1693 ———
10. Peter Montague (1631–1702) *m.* 1663 Mary ——— (–1682)
11. Peter Montague (1603–1659) *m.* 1633 Cicely ———
Service: Member House of Burgesses, Nansemond, Va.; member House of Burgesses, Lancaster Co.
Reference: Stanard's Col. Va. Reg.; Lewis, Moody, Pa. Hist. Soc.; Montague Gen., G. M. Montague; Hist. So. Pa.

6387 WALTON, W. Wycliff Recorded 1942
      Rosemont, Pennsylvania
1. W. Wycliff Walton *m.* Carolyn M. Lewis
2. John Gardener Walton (1865–1924) *m.* 1900 Clara Betts (1868–)
3. John Brooks Betts (1836–1931) *m.* 1863 Jeanette Carter (1844–1921)
4. Richard Kinsey Betts (1807–1890) *m.* 1835 Anna Brooks (1807–1850)
5. Samuel Cary Betts (1776–1861) *m.* 1798 Grace Biles (1776–1848)
6. Zachariah Betts (1736–1808) *m.* 1770 Bethula Cary (1748–1777)
7. Thomas Betts (1689–1747) *m.* 1724 Susannah Field (1704–1771)
8. Thomas Betts (1660–1709) *m.* 1688 Mercy Whitehead (1674–)
9. Richard Betts (1613–1713) *m.* Joanna
Service: Member Provincial Assembly; High Sheriff; member High Court; Magistrate; Captain; Justice. Long Island.
Reference: Annals of Newton, Pa., Ricker; Abington Friends Rec., 1835; Betts Allied Fam.

6388 WALTON, Stephanie Lord   Recorded 1942
         Rosemont, Pennsylvania
                              (JUNIOR)
   1. Stephanie Lord Walton
   2. Wm. Wycliff Walton (1902–   ) *m.* 1932 Carolyn Lewis (1907–   )
   3. John Gardener Walton (1865–1924) *m.* 1900 Clara Betts (1868–   )
   4. John Brooks Betts (1836–1931) *m.* 1863 Jeanette Carter (1844–1921)
   5. Richard Kinsey Betts (1807–1890) *m.* 1835 Anna Brooks (1807–1850)
   6. John Brooks (1772–1843) *m.* 1802 Elizabeth Baker (1784–1856)
   7. Samuel Baker (1748–1814) *m.* 1778 Elizabeth (Head) Scattergood (1749–1836)
   8. John Head (1723–1792) *m.* 1746 Mary Hudson (1724–1757)
   9. Samuel Hudson (1690–1726) *m.* 1715 Mary Holton (1698–1795)
  10. WILLIAM HUDSON (1664–1742) *m.* 1688 Mary Richardson (1668–1708)

Service: Mayor of Philadelphia, Pa., 1725–6; Alderman, 1715; Original Councilman.
Reference: Wills in Philadelphia, Liber G, Vol. 9; Abington Friends Rec., 1835 to 1863.

5897 WALTON, Kenneth Betts   Recorded 1930, New Jersey
         1214 Atlantic Avenue, Atlantic City, New Jersey
   1. Kenneth Betts Walton
   2. John Gardener Walton (1865–1924) *m.* 1900 Clara R. Betts (1868–   )
   3. John Brooks Betts (1836–   ) *m.* 1863 Jeanette Carter (1844–1921)
   4. Richard Kinsey Betts (1807–1890) *m.* 1835 Anna Brooks (1807–1850)
   5. Samuel Cary Betts (1776–1861) *m.* 1798 Grace Biles (1776–1848)
   6. Zachariah Betts (1736–1808) *m.* 1770 Bethula Cary (1748–1777)
   7. Thomas Betts (1689–1747) *m.* 1724 Susannah Field (1704–   )
   8. Thomas Betts (1660–1709) *m.* 1683 Mercy Whitehead (1662–   )
   9. CAPTAIN RICHARD BETTS *ca.* (1613–1713) *m.* Joanna

Service: Member Provincial Assembly, Newton, L. I., 1665; High Sheriff of York-
         shire, 1678.
Reference:

6467 WALTON, Geoffrey Lewis Brooks   Recorded 1945
         Rosemont, Pennsylvania
                              (JUNIOR)
   1. Geoffrey Lewis Brooks Walton
   2. Lt. Wm. Wycliff Walton (1902–   ) *m.* 1932 Carolyn Montague Lewis (1907–   )
   3. John Gardener Walton (1865–1924) *m.* 1900 Clara Betts (1868–   )
   4. John Brooks Betts (1836–1931) *m.* 1863 Jeanette Carter (1844–1921)
   5. Richard K. Betts (1806–1890) *m.* 1835 (2nd) Anna Brooks (1807–1850)
   6. John Brooks (1772–1843) *m.* 1802 Elizabeth Baker (1784–1850)
   7. Samuel Baker (1748–1814) *m.* 1777 Elizabeth Head (1749–1836)
   8. Samuel Baker (1706–1760) *m.* 1741 Elizabeth Burroughs (1715–   )
   9. Samuel Baker (1676–1725) *m.* 1703 Rachel Warder (1670–1760)
  10. HENRY BAKER (–1705) *m.* Margaret Hardman (–1691)

Service: Came to Burlington, N. J., 1684; took up land in Bucks Co., Pa.; is marked
         as "first purchaser" on Holme's map; Justice of the Peace, 1689.
Reference: Same as No. 6466 (Henry Baker).

6113 WALTON, John G.   Recorded 1936, New Jersey
         309 Twenty-first Street, Brigantine, New Jersey
                              (JUNIOR)
   1. John Gardener Walton
   2. Kenneth B. Walton (1901–   ) *m.* 1930 Jessie Sellars (1906–   )
   3. John G. Walton (1865–1924) *m.* 1900 Clara R. Betts (1868–   )
   4. John B. Betts (1836–1931) *m.* 1863 Jeanette Carter (1844–1921)
   5. Richard K. Betts (1807–1890) *m.* 1835 Anna Brooks (1807–1850)
   6. John Brooks (1772–1843) *m.* 1802 Elizabeth Baker (1784–1855)

7. Samuel Baker (1748–1814) *m.* 1777 Elizabeth Head (1749–1836)
8. John Head (1723–1792) *m.* 1746 Mary Hudson (1724–1757)
9. Samuel Hudson (1690–1726) *m.* 1715 Mary Holton (1699–1795)
10. William Hudson (1664–1742) *m.* 1688 Mary Richardson (1668–1708)
11. SAMUEL RICHARDSON (1645–1719) *m.* 1667 Elliner Richardson (–1703)

Service: Member Proprietary Council, 1688.
Reference: Watson's Annals.

6164 WALTON, David Sellers   Recorded 1937
       Brigantine, New Jersey

(JUNIOR)
1. David Sellers Walton (1934–)
2. Kenneth Betts Walton (1901–) *m.* 1930 Jessie Sellers (1906–)
3. John Gardner Walton (1865–1924) *m.* 1900 Clara R. G. B. Walton (1868–)
4. John Brooks Betts (1836–1931) *m.* 1863 Jeanette Carter Betts (1844–1921)
5. Richard Kinsey Betts (1807–1890) *m.* (2nd) 1935 Anna Brooks Betts (1807–1850)
6. Samuel Cary Betts (1776–1861) *m.* 1798 Grace Biles Betts (1776–1848)
7. Zachariah Betts (1736–1808) *m.* (2nd) 1770 Bethula Cary Betts (1748–1777)
8. Thomas Betts 2nd (1689–1747) *m.* (2nd) 1724 Susannah Field Betts
9. Thomas Betts (1660–1709) *m.* 1668 Mercy Whitehead Betts
10. CAPTAIN RICHARD BETTS (1613–1713) *m.* Joanna

Service: Came to New England in 1648; member High Court of Assize; member
      Provincial Assembly, 1665; High Sheriff of Yorkshire, 1678–81.
Reference: Chesterfield, Buck Co., Pa., Monthly Meeting Rec., 4–17–1730; Pa.
      Monthly Meet., 1835, pg. 92; Riker's Annals of Newton, L. I.; Will of
      Thomas Betts, Newton, L. I., 1747; Rec. First Unitarian Ch., Phila., Pa.,
      1863.

6251 WARNOCK, Mrs. Henry C.
       The Manse, Marlboro Town, Vermont

1. Una Winchester (1883–) *m.* 1905 Henry Childs Warnock
2. Reuben Clark Winchester (1857–1913) *m.* 1890 Mary Cole (1861–1911)
3. Reuben Winchester (1825–1906) *m.* 1850 Hannah Kimball Brown (1829–1878)
4. Samuel Whitney Brown (1795–1863) *m.* 1819 Phila Mather (1797–1871)
5. Timothy Mather, Jr. (1757–1818) *m.* 1779 Hannah Church (1756–1827)
6. Timothy Mather (1722–1827) *m.* 1748 Hannah Fuller (1722–1757)
7. William Mather (1698–1747) *m.* 1721 Silence Buttolph (1701–1747)
8. Atherton Mather (1663–1734) *m.* 1694 Rebecca Stoughton (1673–)
9. Timothy Mather (1628–1684) *m.* Catherine Atherton
10. REV. RICHARD MATHER (1596–1669) *m.* 1624 Catherine Holt (–1655)

Service: Minister.
Reference: Mather Gen.; Hist. and Gen., Reg. 1925 for Winchester.

6565 WATTS, Mrs. H. A.   Recorded 1947
       266 Kent Road, Upper Darby, Pennsylvania

1. Wanda A. Keeler *m.* 1931 H. A. Watts
2. Heister H. Keeler (1853–1921) *m.* 1882 Esther F. Headley (1856–1937)
3. Heister Keeler (1821–1887) *m.* 1851 Lois A. Sharpe (1827–1897)
4. Elisha Sharpe (1805–1870) *m.* 1827 Mary Bixby (1805–1859)
5. Samuel Bixby (1774–1857) *m.* 1800 Lois Moss (1776–1852)
6. Samuel Bixby (1739–1820) *m.* 1762 Hannah Powers (1739–1819)
7. Samuel Bixby (1716–1800) *m.* 1737 Mary Buck (1712–)
8. Mephibosheth Bixby (1690–1767) *m.* 1713 Mary Emmons (1683–)
9. Daniel Bixby (1651–1717) *m.* 1674 Hannah Chandler, *d.* 1730
10. JOSEPH BIXBY (1620–1701) *m.* 1647 Sarah Heard (widow)

Service: Sergeant of the "soldiery of Topsfield and the villages adjoining thereto."
Reference: Bixby Genealogy.

6454   WEATHERILL, Mrs. Robert Thomas   Recorded 1944
            189 Delaware Street, Woodbury, New Jersey
    1. Marion B. Synnott *m*. Robert Thomas Weatherill
    2. Clayton E. Synnott (1876–1941) *m*. 1897 Alice Faith Botsford (1872–   )
    3. Alfred P. Botsford (1827–1925) *m*. 1856 Mary Abigail Pardee (1832–1907)
    4. Edmond Ward Botsford (1798–1833) *m*. 1821 Mary Ann Clark (1802–1892)
    5. Ephraim Botsford (1750–1821) *m*. 1772 Merib Dowd (1754–   )
    6. Ephraim Botsford (1720–1795) *m*. 1741 Sarah Hawley (1721–   )
    7. Joseph Botsford (1688–1774) *m*. 1718 Mary Bennett
    8. Elnathan Botsford (1641–1691) *m*. 1677 Hannah Baldwin (1644–1706)
    9. HENRY BOTSFORD (1608–1686) *m. ca.* 1640 Elizabeth ———
    Service: Original proprietor of Milford, Conn., 1639; Corporal for expedition against
            the Dutch, June, 1654.
    Reference: Adventures in Ancestors—Botsford Fam. Gen., Vol. 2; An American
            Family—Botsford lines. (These Gen. found). Hist. Soc. Pa.; D. A. R.
            Lib., Wash.; N. Y. Pub. Lib.

5932   WEATHERS, Mrs. Nell Gray   Recorded 1930, Georgia
            Graysville, Georgia
    1. Nell Gray *m*. ——— Weathers
    2. Arthur H. Gray (1850–1885) *m*. 1882 Cora Linthicum (1864–   )
    3. George Linthicum (1837–1912) *m*. 1860 Catherine Linthicum (1837–1911)
    4. Philip Linthicum (1805–   ) *m*. Eleanor McElfresh (1805–   )
    5. Frederick Linthicum (1774–   )
    6. Zachariah Linthicum (1735–   ) *m*. Sarah Prather
    7. John Linthicum (1700–   )
    8. Thomas Linthicum, Jr. (1660–   ) *m*. 1698 Jane
    9. THOMAS LINTHICUM, SR. (1630–1701) *m*. Deborah Wayman
    Service:
    Reference: All Hallows Records, Md.

6599   WEAVER, Mrs. F. D.   Recorded 1949
            Elm Tree Farm, Salem, N. J.
    1. Katherine B. Krewson *m*. 1890 Francis D. Weaver
    2. Rev. Jacob B. Krewson (1838–1922) *m*. 1869 Mary A. Ward (1840–1920)
    3. John Krewson (1809–1882) *m*. 1831 Sarah A. Barnes (1809–1900)
    4. Jacob Barnes (1786–1824) *m*. 1809 Mary Irwin (1787–1829)
    5. Robert Barnes (1756–1815) *m*. 1781 Rachel Billew (1759–1862)
    6. Isaac Billew (1722–1803) *m*. 1747 Rachel Brittain (1724–1814)
    7. Jacob Billew (1685–1747) *m*. Ann S. VanPelt (*ca.* 1682–*ca.* 1753)
    8. Isaac Billew (1661–1709) *m*. 1684 Ida Suebring (1664–   )
    9. PIERRE BILLEW, *d*. 1702, *m*. 1649 Francoise du Bois
    Service: Member of Assembly in New Amsterdam, 1664; was Schoute in Staten
            Island, 1673.
    Reference: Wilson and Allied Families.

6112   WEBB, Miss Katherine L.   Recorded 1936, Nebraska
            403 North Sixth Street, Beatrice, Nebraska
    1. Miss Katherine L. Webb
    2. Joseph L. Webb (1837–1912) *m*. 1873 Katie Sheppard (1854–1934)
    3. Luther H. Webb (1799–1847) *m*. 1823 Martha B. Bates (1799–1890)
    4. Luther Webb (1763–1860) *m*. 1792 Dorothy Wheelock (1769–1856)
    5. Joshua Webb (1722–1808) *m*. 1744 Hannah Abbe (1724–1815)
    6. Samuel Webb (1690–1779) *m*. 1711 Hannah B. Ripley (1685–1751)
    7. Samuel Webb (1660–1738) *m*. 1686 Mary Adams (1664–1744)
    8. CHRISTOPHER WEBB (1630–1694) *m*. 1654 Hannah Scott (1638–1718)
    Service: Town Clerk of Braintree, Mass., 1678.
    Reference: History of Rockingham, Vt.; Savage Genealogical Dictionary, Vol. 4.

6499 WEBBER, Mrs. John D.   Recorded 1945
         Bridgeport, New Jersey
   1. Mary Hess Higgins *m*. John D. Webber
   2. Lewis S. Higgins (1846–1913) *m*. 1864 Judith Meloney (1846–1927)
   3. Robert Meloney (1819–1887) *m*. 1844 Submitte Scull (1825–1885)
   4. John Scull (–1807) *m*. Judith Steelman (–1864)
   5. Frederick Steelman (1752–1809) *m*. 1773 Naomi Edwards (1755–1847)
   6. Andrew Steelman (1719–1772) *m*. 1747 Hannah Ingersoll
   7. Andrew Steelman (1690–1737) *m*. 1715 Judith ——— (1695–)
   8. JAMES STEELMAN (–1734) *m*. Susannah Toy
   Service: Died 1734, Great Egg Harbor, N. J.; Justice of Atlantic Co., N. J.; Court,
         1694, and for several years after.

6094 WEBER, Mrs. O. F.   Recorded 1936, Illinois
         22 East 82nd Street, New York City
   1. Clara Harding *m*. 1915 Orlando F. Weber
   2. John C. Harding (1862–) *m*. 1884 Amelia J. Thomas (1864–1894)
   3. John R. Harding (1829–1919) *m*. 1856 Mary M. Sturtevant (1828–1915)
   4. Jared Harding (1804–1881) *m*. 1826 Cynthia Roundy (1807–)
   5. Freeman Harden (1783–1870) *m*. 1800 Thankful Stetson (1779–1868)
   6. Perry Harden (1748–1825) *m*. 1779 Molly Keen (1761–1831)
   7. Snow Keen (1734–1811) *m*. 1756 Rebecca Burbank (1736–1777)
   8. Nathaniel Keen (1692–1737) *m*. 1725 Thankful Winslow (1696–1737)
   9. Nathaniel Winslow (1667–1736) *m*. 1692 Lydia Snow (1672–1716)
   10. Josiah Snow (–1692) *m*. 1669 Rebecca Baker (–1711)
   11. Anthony Snow (–1692) *m*. 1639 Abigail Warren (–1692)
   12. RICHARD WARREN (–1628) *m*. 1611 Elizabeth (1583–1673)
   Service: Mayflower Compact Signer.
   Reference: Mayflower Descendants, Vols. IV, VIII, XXV, XXXI; Savage, IV; Pem-
         broke Vital Records.

5860 WEBER, Mrs. Robert M.   Recorded 1929, New Jersey
         118 Jackson Street, Trenton, New Jersey
   1. Elizabeth Ogden *m*. 1910 Robert M. Weber
   2. Edward C. Ogden (1861–) *m*. 1886 Elizabeth B. Holdcraft (1869–)
   3. Elmer Ogden (1832–1886) *m*. Mary Ann Duffy (1837–1886)
   4. Capt. Jason Ogden (1777–1845) *m*. 1822 (2nd) Elizabeth Taylor (1800–1875)
   5. Jason Ogden, Sr. *m*. Joanna Davis
   6. David Ogden (1707–1760) *m*. Hannah Dayton
   7. Lt. John Ogden (1670–1745) *m*. Mary Dimon
   8. RICHARD OGDEN IV (1610–1689) *m*. 1639 Mary Hall
   Service: Assisted in building the second Reformed Church, known as St. Nicholas
         Church, in 1642, at Stamford, Conn.
   Reference: The Ogden Family; Records of Officers and Men of New Jersey in Wars,
         1791; "South Jersey Ogdens;" Colonial Wars.

6350 WEIS, Rev. Robert Lewis   Recorded 1941, Massachusetts
         Universalist General Convention, 16 Beacon St., Boston, Massachusetts
   1. Robert Lewis Weis *m*. 1925 Mary Lilian Dawson Collett
   2. John Peter Carl Weis (1866–1945) *m*. 1891 Georgina Lewis (1868–1937)
   3. Abiel Smith Lewis (1814–1895) *m*. 1865 Harriett Phipps Richardson (1841–1865)
   4. Thomas Lewis 3rd (1771–1824) *m*. 1813 Polly Clapp (1780–1865)
   5. William Clapp (1733–1805) *m*. Priscilla Otis (1742–1836)
   6. Dr. Ephraim Otis (1708–1794) *m*. 1733 Rachel Hersey (1714–1793)
   7. Job Otis (1667–1758) *m*. Mercy Little (1678–1755)
   8. Ephraim Little (1650–1717) *m*. 1672 Mary Sturtevant (1651–1717)
   9. Thomas Little, *d*. 1671, *m*. 1633 Ann Warren
   10. RICHARD WARREN, *d*. 1628, *m*. Elizabeth, *d*. 1673
   Service: Original Mayflower passenger.
   Reference: Dexter Genealogy; "Edmund Lewis of Lynn and Some of His Descendants;"
         Dean's "Hist. of Scituate, Mass."; "Hist. of Hingham, Mass."; "Colonial
         Families of U. S.," Vol. IV; Mayflower Descendants; Bradford's "Hist. of
         Plymouth Plantation."

5958 WELCHER, Miss Eleanor B.   Recorded 1930, New Jersey
      80 Farley Avenue, Newark, New Jersey

1. Eleanor Bruen Welcher
2. John W. Welcher (1842–) *m.* 1867 Anne E. Powers (1838–1913)
3. Jacob Powers (1802–1880) *m.* 1825 Mary Fairchild (1807–1882)
4. Jeremiah Fairchild (1773–1842) *m.* 1800 Phebe Carmichael (1771–1849)
5. Caleb Fairchild (1743–1807) *m.* 1763 Phebe Gard (1744–1817)
6. Matthew Fairchild (1720–1790) *m.* 1742 Sarah (1717–1750)
7. Caleb Fairchild (1693–1777) *m.* 1716 Ann Trowbridge (1701–1777)
8. Zachariah Fairchild (1651–1703) *m.* 1681 Hannah Beach (1665–1730)
9. JOHN BEACH (1623–1677) *m.* 1650 Mary

Service: Early settler in New Haven Colony, 1643.
Reference: Morristown Church Records, pp. 30, 134; History of the Willis Family,
      pp. 191, 192; Descendants of Rev. John Beech, p. 143; Crayon's Rockaway
      Records.

5959 WELCHER, Harold A.   Recorded 1930, New Jersey
      143 Johnson Avenue, Newark, New Jersey

1. Harold A. Welcher, Jr.
2. Harold A. Welcher, Sr., *m.* 1902 Fanny B. Halstead
3. John W. Welcher (1842–) *m.* 1867 Anne E. Powers (1838–1913)
4. Jacob Powers (1802–1880) *m.* 1825 Mary Fairchild (1807–1882)
5. Jeremiah Fairchild (1773–1842) *m.* 1800 Phebe Carmichael (1772–1849)
6. Caleb Fairchild (1743–1808) *m.* 1763 Phebe Gard (1744–1817)
7. Matthew Fairchild (1720–1790) *m.* 1742 Sarah
8. Caleb Fairchild (1693–1777) *m.* 1716 Ann Trowbridge (–1777)
9. Zachariah Fairchild (1651–1703) *m.* 1681 Hannah Beach (1665–)
10. THOMAS FAIRCHILD (1610–1670) *m.* Sarah Seabrook

Service: Representative in 1659; Deputy appointed by the General Court in 1654.
Reference: Crayon's Rockaway Records; History of the Willis Family.

6473 WENDELKEN, Mrs. Charles W.   Recorded 1945
      Portsmouth, Ohio

1. Goldie Lantz *m.* Dr. Charles W. Wendelken
2. Henry Clay Lantz (1863–) *m.* 1892 Emma Jane Samson (1875–)
3. Henry Lantz (1831–1915) *m.* 1856 Lovina Bennett (1833–1913)
4. Joseph Bennett (1794–1863) *m.* 1814 Elizabeth Mills (wid.) (1792–1862)
5. Thaddeus Bennett (1764–1834) *m.* 1782 Eunice Bently (1761–1794)
6. Ephraim Bennett (1714–) *m.* 1758 Mary Stafford
7. Samuel Bennett (1690–) *m.* 1712 Mary
8. Samuel Bennett (–1745) *m.* 1689 Sarah Fordham (–1697)
9. SAMUEL BENNETT (–1684) *m.* Anna ——— (–1705)

Service: Died 1684, Coventry, R. I.
Reference:

5912 WEST, Jessie Cook   Recorded 1930, Colorado
      Price, Utah

1. Jessie Cook *m.* George R. West
2. Philip Barnes Cook (1832–1907) *m.* 1865 Emma F. Langworthy (1843–1892)
3. Joel Cook (1791–1886) *m.* 1814 Polly Russell (1794–1861)
4. Joel Cook (1746–1836) *m.* 1768 Dinah Dunbar (1751–1830)
5. John Dunbar (1724–1786) *m.* 1743 Temperance Hall (1727–1770)
6. Jonathan Hall (1679–1760) *m.* 1703 Dinah Andrews (1684–1763)
7. Samuel Andrews (1635–1704) *m.* 1661 Elizabeth Peck
8. WILLIAM PECK (–1694) *m.* Elizabeth (–1683)

Service: William Peck came to America 1637; signed the first compact for New
      Haven in 1639; he was an Original Proprietor and a deacon from 1659 to 1694.
Reference: Savage, Vol. 3; New Haven Collections; Register of Mass. Colonial Dames.

6199 WESTENIUS, Chattie Coleman   Recorded 1938
Stromsburg, Nebraska
1. Chattie Coleman (1871–   ) *m.* 1922 John A. Westenius
2. Jacob Hesser Coleman (1841–1922) *m.* 1867 Nicy Lavonia Farmer (1849–1892)
3. Henry Downey Farmer (1821–1886) *m.* 1843 Mary Elizabeth Gooch (1821–1905)
4. James Gooch (1780–1853) *m.* 1802 Sarah Porter (1783–1844)
5. James Gooch (bef. 1750–   ) *m.* Ann Hart (bef. 1755–   )
6. William Gooch *a.* (1675–   ) *m.* Ursula Claiborne
7. Rev. John Gooch, *d.* 1683/4, (1) wife
Service: Minister in Jamestown, Va., before 1700.
Reference: The Kohlman Family, 1937, pgs. 22, 118, 119, 120, 121, 122; Wm. & Mary
Quart., Ser. 1, Vol. 5, pg. 111; D.A.R. Nat. No. 104959.

6555 WHITAKER, Rev. Fenelon Brown   Recorded 1947
Penns Grove, New Jersey
1. Fenelon Brown Whitaker *m.* 1913 ———
2. Hudson J. Whitaker (1867–   ) *m.* 1890 Josephine Brown (1861–   )
3. Henry M. Brown (1824–1905) *m.* 1856 Margaret Nicholl (1826–1919)
4. John Nicholl (1771–1861) *m.* 1824 Eliza Stewart (1797–1880)
5. James Stewart (1772–1834) *m.* 1796 Elizabeth Culver (1776–1826)
6. Robert Culver (1740–1814) *m.* 1763 Martha
7. Robert Culver, Sr. (1715–1783) *m.* Anne Clark (1717–1783)
8. John Culver (1670–1760) *m.* Sarah Winthrop (1683–1766)
9. John Culver, Sr. (1640–1725) *m.* Mary Winthrop
10. Edward Culver, *d.* 1685, *m.* 1638 Anna Ellica, *d.* 1678
Service:
Reference: N. Y. Gen. and Biol. Society—Culver, by Cathering Stewart Kulling.

6642 WHITAKER, Mrs. Ralph O.   Recorded 1949
199 North Main Street, London, Ohio
1. F. Edythe Horney *m.* 1909 Ralph Oral Whitaker
2. Frank A. Horney (1859–1930) *m.* 1883 Catherine M. Brown (1861–1925)
3. Forris Horney (1833–1912) *m.* 1858 Esther Williams (1838–1911)
4. Jefferson E. Horney (1810–1884) *m.* 1832 Margaret Griffith (1812–1876)
5. Daniel Horney (1786–1865) *m.* 1808 Margaret Calloway (1790–1855)
6. Rev. William Horney (1750–1829) *m.* 1772 Hannah Chipman (1753–aft. 1804)
7. Perez Chipman, *d.* 1801, *m.* 1751 Margaret Manlove, *d.* 1803
8. Perez Chipman (1702–1781) *m.* Judith Draper
9. Hon. John Chipman (1670–1756) *m.* 1691 Mary Skiff (1671–1711)
10. Capt. Stephen Skiff (1641–1710) *m.* Lydia Snow
11. Anthony Snow, *d.* 1692, *m.* 1639 Abigail Warren, *d.* 1692
12. Richard Warren, *d.* 1628, *m.* 1611 Elizabeth March Pratt (1583–1673)
Service: Signer of Mayflower Compact; settler at Plymouth.
Reference: Gravestones at Jeffersonville, Ohio; Mayflower Planters, by Hills, Vol. II,
p. 150–2.

6146 WHITSEL, Mrs. Henrietta S.   Recorded 1937, West Virginia
1125 Eleventh Street, Huntington, West Virginia
1. Henrietta Stafford *m.* 1893 ——— Whitsel
2. Courtlandt Stafford (1833–1892) *m.* 1863 Gabriela Ayer (1833–1868)
3. Cornelius Stafford (1806–1894) *m.* 1830 Harriet Danforth (1808–1847)
4. Luther Danforth (1781–1857) *m.* 1807 Henrietta Ellsworth (1786–1841)
5. Jonathan Danforth (1745–1840) *m.* Hannah Leman
6. Jonathan Danforth (1714–1747) *m.* 1743 Anna Blanchard (1722–   )
7. Lt. Jonathan Danforth (1688–1761) *m.* 1713 Elizabeth Manning
8. Ens. Jonathan Danforth (1659–1710) *m.* 1682 Rebecca Parker (1661–1754)
9. Capt. Jonathan Danforth (1627–1710) *m.* 1654 Elizabeth Powter
Service: Captain of Militia; Surveyor; Town Clerk.
Reference: Five Colonial Families, by Poole & Treman; Danforth Genealogy.

6619 WHITTEKIN, Mrs. Edna Coggeshall   Recorded 1949
      4309 Fairfax Avenue, Dallas, Texas
      1. Edna Coggeshall *m.* 1918 ———— Whittekin
      2. William A. Coggeshall (1861–1936) *m.* 1886 Elva D. Williams (1868–1941)
      3. Lindley Coggeshall (1835–1916) *m.* 1857 Hannah Lane (1835–1911)
      4. Edward Coggeshall (1791–1863) *m.* 1820 Sophia Baldwin (1796–1850)
      5. Tristram Coggeshall (1762–1850) *m.* 1790 Lucy Terrell (1775–1807)
      6. Job Coggeshall (1733–) *m.* 1758 Deborah Starbuck (1739–1781)
      7. Caleb Coggeshall (1709–1740) *m.* 1732 Marcy Mitchell (1712–1744)
      8. John Coggeshall (1659–1727) *m.* Mary Stanton (1668–1747)
      9. Joshua Coggeshall (1623–1688) *m.* 1652 Joan West (1631–1676)
      10. JOHN COGGESHALL (1601–1647) *m.* Mary ———— *ca.* (1604–1684)
      Service: First President of Rhode Island.
      Reference: Beaumont's History of Coggeshall; Lynchburg's Pioneer Quakers.

6247 WILCOX, Mrs. Henry R.   Recorded 1939
      Windsor County, Stockbridge, Vermont
      (P. O. address, Bethel, Vermont)
      1. Josie Harriet Mills (1889–) *m.* 1922 Henry R. Wilcox
      2. Geo. T. N. Mills (1860–1935) *m.* 1887 Minnie Jane Grant (1865–1935)
      3. Nelson M. Grant (1840–1926) *m.* 1863 Harriet B. Pierce (1846–1912)
      4. William Pierce (1801–1892) *m.* 1840 Hannah Brockway (1819–1907)
      5. William Pierce (1770–1854) *m.* 1796 Hannah Baker (1777–1863)
      6. Jedediah Pierce (1740–1826) *m.* 1764 Susanna Eaton (1744–1831)
      7. Nathaniel Pierce (1701–1775) *m.* 1723 Elizabeth Stevens (1707–1748)
      8. Timothy Pierce (1673–1748) *m.* 1696 Lydia Spaulding (–1705)
      9. Thomas Pierce, Jr. (1645–1717) *m.* Elizabeth ————
      10. Thomas Pierce (1608–1683) *m.* 1635 Elizabeth Cole (–1688)
      11. THOMAS PIERCE (1583–1666) *m.* Elizabeth (1595–)
      Service:
      Reference: Pierce Gen., by F. B. Pierce of Boston.

6633 WILHELM, Mrs. W. Bright   Recorded 1949
      1340 West 106th Street, Cleveland 2, Ohio
      1. Evalina Longshore *m.* 1906 Wm. Bright Wilhelm
      2. Clarence S. Longshore (1841–1905) *m.* 1872 Frances E. Mepledoram (1849–1934)
      3. Dr. Ashbel B. Longshore (1813–1875) *m.* 1835 Maria J. Righter (1816–1883)
      4. Lt. Isaiah Longshore (1791–1836) *m.* 1811 Ann J. Wilson (1784–1875)
      5. Lt. Wm. Wilson (1746–1837) *m.* 1777 Sarah Billew (1755–1839)
      6. Isaac Billew (1722–1803) *m.* 1747 Rachel Brittain (1724–1814)
      7. Jacob Billew (1685–1747) *m.* Ann (Stillwell) Van Pelt (1682–1753)
      8. Lt. Thomas Stillwell (bapt. 1651–1705) *m.* 1670 Martha Billew (1652–)
      9. NICHOLAS STILLWELL (1612–1671) *m.* Anne Van Dyke
      Service: Ensign against Indians at Massacre at Hurley, 1663; Lt. of an English
      Troop Ship; Magistrate at Gravesend, L. I., 1649–56.
      Reference: Penna. Arch. Ser.; Penna. Gen. Soc.

6195 WILLE, Louisa Dawson Mather   Recorded 1938
      6531 Irving Avenue, Merchantville, New Jersey
      1. Louisa Dawson Mather (1867–) *m.* 1891 George A. Wille
      2. John Atkinson Mather (1837–1921) *m.* Louisa Wallace Dawson (1842–1923)
      3. James Carr Dawson (1815–1872) *m.* 1838 Elizabeth B. Cade (1818–1895)
      4. Isaac Cade (1780–1823) *m.* 1804 Judith A. Hendrickson (1784–1867)
      5. Andrew Henricsson (1748–) *m.* 1770 Judy Jones (1751–1793)
      6. Peter Henricsson (1718–) *m.* bef. 1748 Catherine Lock(e) (1725 or 1729–)
      7. ANDERS HENRICSSON *m.* bef. 1713 Beaba, *d.* 1722
      Service: A Swedish settler of West New Jersey, before 1700.
      Reference: Church Recs., Church of the Ascension, Philadelphia; St. Peter's P. E.
      Church, Clarksboro, N. J.; Trinity Church, Swedesboro, N. J., pgs.
      343, 204, 376, 203, 310–11; spelling of the name Henricsson, Henricksson,
      Hendrickson, Henrixon, all occur in the records of the Swedish Church at
      Swedesboro, N. J. That it is all one family is shown by dates and
      Christian names, as may be seen on the translated copy in the Penna.
      Hist. Soc., 13th and Locust Sts., Phila., Pa.

6115 WILLETS, Mrs. Clarence   Recorded 1936, New Jersey
       1432 W. State Street, Trenton, New Jersey

1. Clara Doane *m.* Clarence Willets
2. Frank Doane (1847–) *m.* 1874 Rebecca Levins (1847–1904)
3. George P. Doane (1807–1888) *m.* Mary V. ——— (1813–1882)
4. Thomas Doane (–1823) *m.* Jane
5. Israel Doane *m.* Rachel V. ———
6. Israel Doane (1699–1797) *m.* Esther ———
7. Daniel Doane (–1743) *m.* Mehitable ———
8. Daniel Doane (1636–1712)
9. DEACON JOHN DOANE (1590–1685)

Service: Early settler Plymouth Colony, 1629.
Reference: The Doane Family, by Alfred A. Doane.

6371 WILLIAMS, Eugenie   Recorded 1942, Connecticut
       47 Fernwood Road, West Hartford, Connecticut

1. Eugenie Williams
2. Almeron Newberry Williams (1862–1929) *m.* 1899 Alice Eugenie Burr (1873–1941)
3. Elisha Williams (1819–1895) *m.* 1860 Mary Ann Newberry (1828–1873)
4. Joseph Moseley Newberry (1804–1870) *m.* 1826 Jane Elizabeth Mills (1805–1886)
5. John Newberry (1756–1825) *m.* 1784 Elizabeth Ellsworth (1765–1816)
6. Joseph Newberry (1709–1797) *m.* 1749 Sybil Stoughton (1730–1794)
7. Sergt. Joseph Newberry (1684–1751) *m.* 1708 Sarah Loomis (1689–1771)
8. Thomas Newberry (1657–1688) *m.* 1676 Anna Ford
9. Major Benjamin Newberry (1624–1689) *m.* 1646 Mary Allyn (1628–1703)
10. THOMAS NEWBERRY (1594–1635) *m.* 1619 Joane Dabinott (1600–1629)

Service: An active leader in settling Windsor, Conn.
Reference: Newberry Genealogy, by J. Gardner Bartlett.

6002 WILLIAMS, Dr. Henry Lane   Recorded 1931
       Hampshire Arms Hotel, Minneapolis, Minnesota

1. Henry Lane Williams (1869–) *m.* Nina Meadows Boyd
2. Job Williams (1842–1914) *m.* 1868 Catherine Stone (1845–1909)
3. Giles Williams (1807–1869) *m.* 1833 Fannie M. Gallup (1814–1863)
4. Zephania Williams (1778–1853) *m.* Olive Howe (1776–1855)
5. Seth Williams (1746–1818) *m.* 1765 Mary Snow (1747–1818)
6. Nathaniel Williams 3rd (1711–1775) *m.* 1737 Mary Atherton (–1778)
7. Nathaniel Williams 2nd (1679–1726) *m.* 1709 Lydia King (1688–1749)
8. Nathaniel Williams 1st (1639–1692) *m.* 1668 Elizabeth Rogers (–1724)
9. RICHARD WILLIAMS (1606–1693) *m.* 1632 Frances Dighton (1611–1706)

Service: Deputy, Selectman.
Reference: Mayflower Desc., Vol. 23, pages 1–7; Reg. Order of Founders & Pat. of
     America, Vol. I, page 212.

6620 WILLIAMS, Mrs. J. M.   Recorded 1949
       214 Cameron Ave., Chapel Hill, North Carolina

1. Lena Stone *m.* James Malachi Williams
2. Robert S. Stone (1848–1882) *m.* 1876 Elizabeth A. Markham (1853–1940)
3. William A. Markham (1819–1895) *m.* 1842 Nancy Mason (1823–1913)
4. Edmund Markham (1798–1829) *m.* 1815 Nancy Mason (1802–1862)
5. Thomas Markham (1750–1838) *m.* 1773 Frances Herndon (1754–1839)
6. Edmund Herndon *ca.* (1708–1760) *m.* 1730 Elizabeth Williams, *d.* 1756
7. Edward Herndon (1678–1745) *m.* 1698 Mary Waller (1669–*ca.* 1720)
8. William Herndon (1649–1722) *m.* 1677 Catherine Digges (1654–1727)
9. EDWARD DIGGES (1620–1675) *m.* Elizabeth Page, *d. ca.* 1691

Service: Introduced culture of the silkworm into the colony near Yorktown, Va.;
     Gov. of Va., 1655–58; Auditor-General of Va., 1670–75.
Reference: Herndon Family of Virginia; Herndon-Hunt and Allied Families.

6632 WILLIAMS, Miss Lena Mae   Recorded 1949
          214 Cameron Ave., Chapel Hill, North Carolina
      1. Lena Mae Williams
      2. James M. Williams (1877–1917) *m.* 1902 Lena Stone (1878–   )
      3. Robert S. Stone (1848–1882) *m.* 1878 Elizabeth A. Markham (1853–1940)
      4. William A. Markham (1819–1895) *m.* 1842 Nancy Mason (1823–1913)
      5. Edmund Markham (1798–1829) *m.* 1820 Nancy Mason (1802–1862)
      6. Thomas Markham (Marcum), *d.* 1838, *m.* 1773 Fanny Herndon (1754–1839)
      7. Edmund Herndon *ca.* (1708–1769) *m.* 1730 Elizabeth Williams, *d.* 1750
      8. Edward Herndon (1678–1745) *m.* 1698 Mary Waller (1669–1720)
      9. William Herndon (1649–1722) *m.* 1677 Catherine Digges (1654–1727)
     10. EDWARD DIGGES (1620–1675) *m.* Elizabeth Page, *d. ca.* 1691
      Service: Governor of Virginia, 1655–1658; Auditor-General of Virginia, 1670–1675.
      Reference: Wood and Nesbitt, Herndon-Hunt and Allied Families.

6672 WILLIAMS, Lester James, M.D.   Recorded 1950
          739 Convention Street, Baton Rouge, Louisiana
      1. Lester James Williams
      2. Austria D. Williams (1858–1902) *m.* 1878 Margery C. Porter (1860–1906)
      3. Josiah Pitts Williams (–1891) *m.* 1836 Maria A. Bushnell (–1891)
      4. Charles Bushnell (1782–1835) *m.* 1812 Ann O'Brien Jones
      5. Samuel Bushnell, Jr. (1746–1830) *m.* 1767 Elsie Kelsey (1746–   )
      6. Samuel Bushnell 2nd (1724–1793) *m.* Hannah Dennison
      7. Capt. Samuel Bushnell (1682–1752) *m.* 1709 Hannah Hill (1689–   )
      8. Samuel Bushnell (1655–1727) *m.* 1675 Patience Rudd
      9. Lieut. William Bushnell (1610–1683) *m.* Rebecca Chapman
     10. FRANCIS BUSHNELL (1580–1646)
      Service:
      Reference: Chapman Family, Bushnell Family Genealogy, by George E. Bushnell,
          1945.

6610 WILLIAMS, Mrs. Roy H.   Recorded 1948
          1415 Columbus Avenue, Sandusky, Ohio
      1. Verna Lockwood *m.* 1898 Judge Roy H. Williams
      2. Ralph M. Lockwood (1851–1906) *m.* 1874 Emma Montgomery (1853–1923)
      3. Usher Montgomery (1830–1863) *m.* 1849 Sarah E. Fowler (1833–1919)
      4. Frederick W. Fowler (1789–1868) *m.* 1826 Mary Inman (1800–1849)
      5. William Fowler (1748–1815) *m.* Olive Coan
      6. Ebenezer Fowler (1719–1800) *m.* 1743 Desire Bristol
      7. Ebenezer Fowler (1684–1768) *m.* 1718 Elizabeth Starr
      8. Abraham Fowler (1652–1719) *m.* 1677 Elizabeth Bartlett
      9. John Fowler *m.* 1647 Mary Hubbard
     10. WILLIAM FOWLER *d.* 1661
      Service: One of founders of New Haven Colony, and Milford, Conn.
      Reference: Fowler Genealogy.

6306 WILLIAMS, Susan Montgomery   Recorded 1940, Georgia
      1. Susan Montgomery Williams
      2. Milton Wells Williams (1870–1939) *m.* 1913 Margaret Rhind Hill (1886–   )
      3. Wm. Meriwether Hill (1856–   ) *m.* 1884 Susan Montgomery Stokes (1861–1934)
      4. William Wylie Hill (1826–1909) *m.* 1851 Emma Eugenie Anthony (1829–1892)
      5. Col. Ledewick M. Hill (1804–1883) *m.* 1824 Nancy H. Johnson (1808–1846)
      6. Wylie Hill (1775–1844) *m.* 1799 Martha (Patsey) Pope (1782–1853)
      7. Burwell Pope (1751–1800) *m.* 1772 Priscilla Wooten (1756–1806)
      8. Henry Pope, *d.* 1764, *m.* 1748 Tabitha ———, *d.* 1808
      9. John Pope (1698/9–1745) *m.* 1721/2 Mourning McKinnie (*c.* 1704–*c.* 1750)
     10. Col. Barnaby McKinnie *c.* (1673–1740) *m.* 1703 Mary Exum Ricke (widow)
     11. MICHAEL MACKQUINNEY, *d.* 1686, *m.* Elizabeth, *d.* aft. 1704
      Service: Landed Proprietor in Isle of Wight Co., Va., before 1673.
      Reference: "Hills of Wilkes Co., Ga., and Allied Families," by L. J. Hill; Chapman's
          "Abstracts of Wills and Administrations of Isle of Wight Co., Va.

6671 WILLS, Elsie Beattie   Recorded 1950
       5415 Bryan Street, Dallas, Texas

1. Elsie Beattie Wills
2. Albert Gallatin Wills (1858–1917) *m.* 1885 Nannie Newell (1867–1945)
3. Albert Gallatin Wills (1824–1870) *m.* 1853 Martha Hatcher (1834–1902)
4. Samuel Hatcher (1790–1867) *m.* 1832 Martha L. C. Watkins (widow) (1798–1857)
5. Lt. John Hatcher (1757–1837) *m.* 1780 Nancy Geutry (1798–1857)
6. Frederick Hatcher (1743/6–1783) *m.* 1756 Sarah Woodson (1738–1813)
7. John Woodson (1696–1789) *m.* 1731 Mary Miller
8. Benjamin Woodson (1666–1723) *m.* 1688 Larale Porter (1672–)
9. Col. Robert Woodson (1634–1707) *m.* 1656 Elizabeth Ferris
10. Dr. John Woodson (1586–1644) *m.* 1619 Sarah Winston

Service:
Reference: Woodson Family, Henry Woodson.

6423 WILLS, Hon. William Henry   Recorded 1943
       Old Bennington, Vermont

1. Hon. William Henry Wills *m.* Hazel McLeod
2. James Henry Wills (1850–1893) *m.* 1871 Alzina Wheeler Foster (1846–1911)
3. Harry Aldridge Wills (–1893) *m.* Julia Bigelow
4. Jacob Wills (1764–) *m.* 1792 Penelope (Nelly) ———
5. John Wills (1721–) *m.* 1746 Elizabeth Dodge (1726–)
6. Jacob Wills (1693–1750) *m.* 1720 Dinah Peck (1700–)
7. Lieut. Joshua Welles (abt. 1637–1721) *m.* 1681 (2nd) Hannah Buckland (1654–1694)

Service: Church Collector, 1706, 1709; was at Windsor, Conn., 1647.
Reference: Town Rec. of Bennington, Keeseville, Vergennes, Chelsea, Trunbridge of Vermont; Town Rec. and Vital Rec., Norwich, Windsor and New Haven, Conn.; Gen. of Ancient Windsors (Stiles).

6049 WILSON, Mr. Frank Taylor   Recorded 1933
       4641 Penn Street, Philadelphia, Pennsylvania

1. Frank Taylor Wilson
2. Frank Warren Wilson (1845–1922) *m.* 1871 Miraim H. Taylor (1843–1912)
3. Chas. H. Wilson (1814–1899) *m.* 1840 Marg. English (1815–1893)
4. Isaac English (1776–1843) *m.* 1805 Susannah Thomas (1776–1858)
5. Timothy Thomas (1746–1832) *m.* 1774 Bathsheba Gardiner (1749–)
6. David Thomas (–1770) *m.* 1745 Margaret Lucas (1719–1782)
7. Robt. Lucas, Jr. (–1740) *m.* 1703 Eliz. Scott (1681–)
8. Robert Lucas (–1688) *m.* Elizabeth ———

Service:
Reference: White Gen. in Penna.

6520 WILSON, Mrs. Grace Goodwin Bacon   Recorded 1946
       Chelsea, Vermont

1. Grace Goodwin Bacon *m.* Hon. Stanley Calef Wilson (1909–)
2. Erdix N. Bacon (1844–1934) *m.* 1870 Mary M. Goodwin (1847–1935)
3. George D. Bacon (1807–1882) *m.* 1838 Harriet A. Hovey (1815–1895)
4. Dr. Ebenezer Bacon (1776–1847) *m.* Betsy Austin (1785–1863)
5. Asa Bacon (1738–1807) *m.* Rhoda Dunham (1742–1833)
6. John Bacon (1710–) *m.* Sarah
7. Thomas Bacon (1667–1749) *m.* 1691 Hannah F. Fales
8. John Bacon (bef. 1630–1683) *m.* 1651 Rebecca Hall, *d.* 1694
9. Capt. Michael Bacon, *d.* 1688, *m.* Mary, *d.* 1655

Service: Came to America about 1630; one of the Planters of Dedham, Mass.; one of those to subscribe to Town of Woburn, Mass., 12–18–1640.
Reference: Asa Bacon Genealogy.

6153   WILSON, Lavinia Rose   Recorded 1937
       208 Kenyon Street, Hartford, Connecticut

1. Lavinia Rose (1875–   ) *m.* 1909 Albion Benjamin Wilson
2. Miles Jeptha Rose (1839–1915) *m.* 1864 Sophia Lucinda Beach (1843–1928)
3. Jeptha Rose (1804–1884) *m.* (I) Polly Gillet (1808–1843)
4. Peter Rose (1761–1823) *m.* (2) 1801 Hannah Wilcox (1773–1853)
5. Sharon Rose (1731–1821) *m.* 1758 Mercy Fowler (1737–1821)
6. Jonathan Rose (1679–1768) *m.* 1707 Abigail Hale
7. Daniel Rose (1631–aft. 6–16–1711) *m.* 1664 Elizabeth Goodrich (1645–aft 6–1711)
8. ROBERT ROSE (1594–1665) *m.* (I) Margery (1594–*d.* bef. 1664)

Service: Sharon Rose, Pvt. in Col. Tolen Moreley's Regiment, Mass. Troops; Peter
       Rose, Pvt. Col. Elisha Porter's Regiment, Hampshire Co., Mass., Troops.
Reference: D.A.R. Nat. No. 142723–142895. Savage, Gen. Dict., Vol. 3, pgs. 575,
       576; Vol. 2, pg. 274; also Stiles Weth., Vol. 2, pgs. 590, 371.

6145   WILSON, Mrs. Otis G.   Recorded 1937, West Virginia
       1555 Fifth Avenue, Huntington, West Virginia

1. Helen Vance *m.* 1913 Otis Guy Wilson
2. William Ball Vance (1852–1933) *m.* 1881 Anna Fairbairn (1852–1925)
3. Joseph Vance (1806–1897) *m.* 1844 Hannah Ball (1816–1897)
4. Joseph Ball (1777–   ) *m.* Eunice Harrison (1781–1847)
5. Joseph Ball (1742–1808) *m.* Rachel Tompkins (–1783)
6. Aaron Ball (–1752) *m.* Hannah (Camp) Johnson (–1790)
7. Thomas Ball (1687–1744) *m.* 1710 Sarah Davis (–1778)
8. EDWARD BALL (1642–1724) *m.* 1664 Abigail Blatchley

Service: Sheriff, Committeeman on Boundaries.
Reference:

6405   WILSON, Mrs. Richard Wayne   Recorded 1943
       Atlanta, Georgia

1. Elenora Rembert McCandless *m.* Richard Wayne Wilson
2. Alexander L. McCandless (1820–1898) *m.* 1847 Frances A. Coleman (1820–1889)
3. Erastus Coleman (1775–1846) *m.* 1796 Cornelia Billings (1777–1858)
4. Elijah Coleman (1745–1818) *m.* 1772 Tabitha Meekin (1747–1818)
5. Elijah Coleman (1714–1745) *m.* 1744 Mary Smith.
6. Nathaniel Coleman (1684–1755) *m.* 1705 Mary Ely
7. Dea. John Coleman (abt. 1633–1711) *m.* (2nd) 1679 Mehitable (?) ———
8. THOMAS COLEMAN (1598–1674) *m.* 1630/32 ——— (–aft. 1635)

Service: At Weathersfield, Conn., 1639; Representative 1652 and 1656; removed to
       Hadley, Mass., and was made Freeman, 1661.
Reference: Gen. Dict. N. E., Vol. I; Rec. Wetherfield, Conn.; Hist and Early Settlers,
       Hadley, Mass., Judd.

6521   WILSON, Hon. Stanley Calef   Recorded 1946
       Chelsea, Vermont

1. Stanley Calef Wilson *m.* 1909 Grace Goodwin Bacon
2. William W. Wilson (1835–1912) *m.* 1863 Lydia Browning (1841–   )
3. Alfred Browning (1808–1886) *m.* Lucia French (1810–1892)
4. Joseph Browning (1760–1831) *m.* 1786 Lucy Sherman (1766–1851)
5. Asaph Sherman (1741–   ) *m.* 1762 Lucy Whitney (1744–   )
6. Col. Nathaniel Sherman (1696–   ) *m.* 1726 Mary Livermore (1702–   )
7. Joseph Sherman (1650–1730/1) *m.* 1673 Elizabeth Winship (1652–1730)
8. CAPT. JOHN SHERMAN (1612–1690/1) *m.* Martha Palmer, *d.* 1700

Service: Selectman, Town Clerk, Surveyor, Schoolmaster, Clerk of Writs, Com-
       missioner, Rep. in Gen. Court, Sergeant of Train Band, Captain, Steward of
       Harvard College.
Reference: Sherman Genealogy.

6657 **WINDSOR, Mrs. Herbert T.** Recorded 1949
Box 447, "Mid-Oaks," Geneva, Illinois
1. Jessie H. Wheeler *m.* (2) 1934 Herbert T. Windsor
2. James A. Wheeler (1842–1911) *m.* 1869 Mary C. Hoselton (1849–1900)
3. Benjamin Wheeler (1803–1875) *m.* 1828 Dorcas Havens (1810–1892)
4. Jesse Havens, Jr. (1781–1862) *m.* 1805 Rebecca Henthorn (1785–1864)
5. Jesse Havens, Sr. *ca.* (1750–1812) *m.* bef. 1781 Content *ca.* (1760–aft. 1783)
6. John Havens *ca.* (1720–1788) *m.* 1745 Anna Davis *ca.* (1720–1788)
7. Daniel Havens *ca.* (1680–1740) *m.* 1720 Christiana ——— *ca.* (1680–1739)
8. John Havens, *d.* 1687, *m. ca.* 1680 Anna Stannard, *d.* aft. 1687
9. WILLIAM HAVENS *ca.* (1618–1685) *m.* 1640 Dennis (Dionis) *ca.* (1618–aft. 1692)
Service: One of the first settlers of Portsmouth, R. I.; signed Compact, signed oath of allegiance.
Reference: Wheeler Gen., Havens Family.

6343 **WING, Rosa Florence** Recorded 1941, Georgia
341 Ponce de Leon Avenue N. E., Atlanta, Georgia
1. Rosa Florence Wing
2. Jehu Lowery Wing (1823–1877) *m.* 1848 Mary Rebecca Johnson (1829–1882)
3. John Wing (1780–1848) *m.* 1821 Mary Tullis (1807–1877)
4. Edward Wing (1745–1804) *m.* 1775 Mary Lowery (1755–1826)
5. John Wing (1701–aft. 1745) *m.* 1727 Mary Tucker (1708–1774)
6. John Wing (1661–1728) *m.* 1685 Mary Perry, *d.* 1714
7. Edward Perry (1630–1695) *m.* 1653 Mary Freeman (*b.* aft. 1635–1704)
8. EDMUND FREEMAN (1590–1682) *m.* Elizabeth (1596–1672)
Service: Lt. Governor of Plymouth Colony with Gov. William Bradford (1640–1646; member Council of War, 1642.
Reference: "First 100 years of Cobb Co., Ga.," by Temple; Austin's Vital Statistics of Rhode Island; Friends' Records at Spring Hill, Sandwich, Mass.; Quaker Records at Dartmouth, Mass.; "The Perrys of Rhode Island," by C. B. Perry.

6036 **WINSEMIUS, Mrs. Harry** Recorded 1932
1. Anna Kent (1900–) *m.* 1923 Harry Thomas Winsemius
2. Geo. Layton Kent (1876–) *m.* 1897 Mollie Emma Thompson (1870–)
3. James Kent (1841–1887) *m.* 1873 Martha Emma Hopkins (1846–1914)
4. Geo. Clarke Hopkins (1811–1886) *m.* 1832 Eliz Ann Salisbury (1812–1882)
5. Samuel Hopkins (1783–1854) *m.* 1806 Mary Luther (1782–1843)
6. Jabez Luther (1759–1818) *m.* 1782 Lydia Browne (1760–)
7. Esek Browne (1712–1784) *m.* 1751 Rachel Cole (–1785)
8. Esek Browne (1679–1772) *m.* 1705 Mercy Carr (1683–1776)
9. Caleb Carr (1657–1700) *m.* Deborah Sales (–1700)
10. John Sales (1633–1681) *m.* 1650 Mary Williams (1633–1681)
11. ROGER WILLIAMS (1599–1683) *m.* Mary Barnard
Service: Founded city of Providence, R. I.
Reference: Gen. of his Descendants, by W. B. Browne; Gen. Dic. of R. I., by Austin; Ancestry of 33 Rhode Islanders, by Osborne Austin.

6385 **WISE, Mrs. William Oliver** Recorded 1942
St. Albans, Vermont
1. Anna Hale Ellis *m.* William O. Wise
2. Fred Orin Ellis (1836–1929) *m.* 1874 Emma Jane Hale (1852–1896)
3. John Waldron Hale (1804–1878) *m.* 1839 Betsy Evans (1820–1901)
4. Stephen Hale (1779–1855) *m.* 1802 Susan Waldron (abt. 1781–1835)
5. Col. John Waldron (1740–1827) *m.* Mrs. Margaret (Frost) Wentworth
6. Richard Waldron *m.* ——— Smith
7. JOHN WALDRON *m.* 1698 Mary (Ham) Horne, (wid.) (1668–1706)
Service: Immigrant Pioneer.
Reference: Hist. Royalston, Mass., Caswell; Dover, N. H. Scales; N. E. H. Reg., Vols. 5, 18, 26, 32, etc.

6142   WOFFORD, Mrs. Henry R.   Recorded 1937, Texas
       234 Mistletoe Avenue, San Antonio, Texas

1. Simona Broadbent *m.* 1905 Henry R. Wofford
2. Charles S. Broadbent (1842–1931) *m.* 1884 Cordelia V. Fiske (1857–1900)
3. James N. Fiske (1815–1876) *m.* 1849 Simona Smith (1829–1890)
4. Hon. James Fiske (1763–1844) *m.* 1786 Priscilla West (1763–1840)
5. Stephen Fisk (1714–1764) *m.* 1751 Anna (Bradish) Green (1729–1826)
6. William Fiske (1678–1750) *m.* 1708 Eunice Jennings (1686–   )
7. LIEUT. NATHAN FISKE (1642–1694) *m.* Elizabeth Fry (–1696)

Service: Lieut. of a Watertown, Mass., Company in 1692.
Reference: Fiske Genealogy, by Frederick Clifton Pierce.

6570   WOLF, Mrs. Daniel D.   Recorded 1948
       309 Jericho Road, Abington, Pennsylvania

1. Edna Kempton *m.* Daniel Dorsey Wolf
2. Chas. C. Kempton, Jr. (1861–1947) *m.* 1885 Anna M. Mintzer (1863–1942)
3. Chas. C. Kempton (1834–1893) *m.* 1859 Margaret Bishop (1838–1903)
4. James Kempton (1803–1867) *m.* 1830 Mary Antrim (1803–   )
5. Stacy Antrim (1765/6–1823) *m.* 1783 Mary Knight (1759–1847)
6. Ebenezer Antrim *m.* 1755/6 Elizabeth Fenton
7. James Antrim, Jr., *m.* 1725 Mary Mulcher
8. James Antrim, *d.* 1736, *m.* 1696 Mary Hance (1670–   )
9. JOHN HANCE *ca.* (1635–1710) *m.* 1666 Elizabeth Hanson (1645–1732)

Service: Original settler; Justice; member of Assembly; Captain, Monmouth C.,
       N. J.
Reference: Enc. of American Quakers; Antrim Gen.

6714   WOLFE, Miss Evelyn Frazier   Recorded 1951, West Virginia
       1111 Virginia Street, Martins Ferry, Ohio

1. Miss Evelyn Frazier Wolfe
2. George Francis Wolfe (1863–1916) *m.* 1894 Florence Morrell (1873–   )
3. Thomas R. Morrell (1832–1909) *m.* 1856 Evaline Flint (1836–1917)
4. Jacob Flint (1804–1886) *m.* 1833 Eliza Aplin (1803–1883)
5. Porter Flint (1763–   ) *m.* 1790 Lucy Farewell (1771–   )
6. Joseph Flint (1737–1815) *m.* 1762 Hannah Herrick
7. Thomas Flint (1705–1775) *m.* 1732 Priscilla Porter (bap. 1712–1774)
8. Thomas Flint (1678–   ) *m.* 1703 Lydia Putnam (1684–1711)
9. Capt. Thomas Flint (1645–1721) *m.* 1674 Mary Doughton
10. THOMAS FLINT (1603–1663) *m.* Ann ———

Service:
Reference: Births and marriages in Belmont Court House; Genealogical Reg. of Desc.
       of Thomas Flint, by John Flint; Andover, Warren F. Draper, pgs. 7, 13,
       19, 32; Putnams Lineage, by Eben Putnam, pg. 64.

6065   WOLFE, Mrs. Grace Coit   Recorded 1934, Nebraska
       404 Washington Avenue, Beatrice, Nebraska

1. Grace H. Coit *m.* 1890 ——— Wolfe
2. Dwight S. Coit (1824–1887) *m.* 1850 Lucy A. Parsons (1827–1912)
3. Maurice Parsons (1797–1890) *m.* 1819 Amanda Clark (1800–1842)
4. Elias Parsons (1722–1842) *m.* Mary Stetson (1) (1769–1823); *m.* 1796 Lois Strong
       (2) (1776–1842)
5. Josiah Parsons (1682–1768) *m.* 1719 Sarah Sheldon
6. Josiah Parsons, Esq. (1647–1729) *m.* 1669 Elizabeth Strong
7. CORNET JOSEPH PARSONS (1617–1683) *m.* Mary Bliss

Service: An original proprietor of Northampton, and a first settler in 1655.
Reference: Parsons Family, by Henry Parsons, Vols. 1 and 2.

6596 WOLFE, Mrs. James W.   Recorded 1948
        7647 North Bosworth Avenue, Chicago 26, Illinois

1. Frances Cora Ward *m.* 1917 James W. Wolfe
2. Frank E. Ward (1868–) *m.* 1895 Cora B. Sutcliffe (1871–1947)
3. William J. Ward (1833–1899) *m.* 1864 Marietta E. McBane (1843–1921)
4. Dr. Angus M. McBane (1808–1860) *m.* 1836 Ellen E. Willard (1815–1860)
5. Rev. Joseph Willard, Jr. (1770–1823) *m.* 1797 Elizabeth Turner (1776–bef. 1823)
6. Rev. Joseph Willard (1741–1828) *m.* 1769 Hannah Parker (1746–1833)
7. Benjamin Willard (1716–1798) *m.* 1739 Sarah Brooks
8. Joseph Willard (1693–1774) *m.* 1715 Martha Clarke (1694–1794)
9. Benjamin Willard (1664/5–1732) *m.* Sarah Lakin
10. MAJOR SIMON WILLARD (1605–1676) *m.* 1664 Mary Dunster (bapt. 1630–1715)

Service: Clerk of Writs, Concord, Mass., 19 years; Deputy to Gen. Court 18 years;
        Com. in Chief of British forces in King Phillip's War, 1654.
Reference: Willard Memoirs.

5997 WOOD, Mrs. J. A.   Recorded 1931
        7 West Andrews Dr., Atlanta, Georgia

1. Virginia E. Willington (1887–) *m.* 1929 Dr. James Augustine Wood
2. Broadus E. Willingham (1863–) *m.* 1885 Annie Lewis Rushen (1866–)
3. James K. Rushen (1830–1898) *m.* 1855 Virginia Thomas (1837–1915)
4. John Hughes Thomas (1797–1870) *m.* 1827 Sarah A. Hunter (1813–1867)
5. Alex. Hunter *m.* Elizabeth Haughton (1787–)
6. James Haughton *m.* Sallie Burke
7. William Haughton (1684–1739) *m.* Mary Luten
8. MAJOR THOMAS LUTEN (–1729) *m.* 1684 Mary ———

Service: Major, Justice for Chowan Precinct; Provost Marshal; Deputy Surveyor.
Reference: Hathaway's N. C. Register, Vol. 1.

6523 WOODBURY, Mrs. William S.   Recorded 1939
        28 Vine Street, Northfield, Vermont

1. Inez Julia Rich (1861–) *m.* 1878 Wm. Stebbins Woodbury
2. Alden Rich (1827–1909) *m.* 1853 Marcella Cram (1835–1915)
3. Martin Cram (1802–1840) *m.* 1828 Louisa Steele (1807–1876)
4. Robert Cram (1776–1854) *m.* 1801 Hannah Webster (1775–1863)
5. David Cram (1737–1825) *m.* Mary Badger (1740–1825)
6. Jonathan Cram (1708–1790) *m.* 1732 Mary Chamberlain (1706–1776)
7. John Cram (1685–1758) *m.* 1707 Sarah Hold (1678–1757)
8. Thomas Cram (1660–) *m.* 1681 Elizabeth Weare
9. JOHN CRAM (1617–) *m.* Hester ———
Service:
Reference: Hist. of Lyndeborough; Holts Fam. in U.S.A., by Durrie.

6283 WOODWARD, Phyllis Harriet   Recorded 1939, Georgia
        215 N. Candler Street, Decatur, Georgia
                        (JUNIOR)
1. Phyllis Harriet Woodward
2. Douglas Lawley Woodward, *b.* 1901, *m.* 1922 Adeline Milledge, *b.* 1894
3. Richard Habersham Milledge (1841–1916) *m.* 1875 Rosa Gresham (1852–1899)
4. John Milledge (1814–1872) *m.* 1836 Catherine Habersham (1816–1904)
5. Richard Wyth Habersham (1786–1842) *m.* 1808 Sarah Hazzard Elliott
6. Capt. Barnard Elliott *m.* 1785 Catherine Hazzard (1763–1843)
7. Thomas Elliott *m.* Sarah Harvey
8. Thomas Elliott, *d. c.* 1739, *m.* 1723 Isabella West, *d.* bef. 1738
9. WILLIAM ELLIOTT (1660–1738) *m.* Katherine Schenckingh *c.* (1671–1722)

Service: Elected to Commons House, Assembly of South Carolina, 1698, 1700, 1707.
Reference: History and Genealogy of Habersham Family, by Bullock; S. C. His-
        torical and Genealogical Mag., Vols. XII, XIII, XV, XXIII.

5874   WRIGHT, Mrs. Frank W.   Recorded 1929, Colorado
          525 S. Rustin Street, Sioux City, Iowa
   1. Winnifred H. Livermore *m.* Frank W. Wright
   2. Charles H. Livermore (1856–1909) *m.* 1884 Margaret A. Griffin (1853–   )
   3. Zalmon Livermore (1820–1886) *m.* 1848 Olive C. Hall (1830–1915)
   4. Asahel Hall (1799–1877) *m.* 1816 Betsey W. Ripley (1799–1858)
   5. Hezekiah Ripley (1771–1846) *m.* 1795 Priscilla Wood (1776–1843)
   6. Ephraim Wood III (1744–1831) *m.* 1773 Sarah French (1753–   )
   7. Ephraim Wood, Jr. (1715–1781) *m.* 1742 Mary Lazell (–1752)
   8. Dea. Ephraim Wood, Sr. (1679–1744). *m.* 1710 Susannah Howland (1690–1743)
   9. Isaac Howland (1659–1723) *m.* 1677 Elizabeth Vaughn (1653–1727)
  10. JOHN HOWLAND (1592–1672) *m.* 1624 Elizabeth Tilley (1609–1687)
   Service: A Mayflower passenger.
   Reference:

6282   WRIGHT, Mrs. Jesse Edgar   Recorded 1939, Georgia
          324 College Street, Macon, Georgia
   1. Alline Lowe *m.* 1905 Jesse Edgar Wright
   2. William Sterling Lowe (1851–1906) *m.* 1877 Clifford Maud Lockhart (1859–1930)
   3. John Holman Lowe (1797–1880) *m.* 1831 Mary Freeman Hardin (1811–1887)
   4. James Hardin (1770–1820) *m.* 1801 Nancy Morgan (1775–1842)
   5. Mark Hardin *c.* (1738–1817) *m.* 1760 Mary Hunter *c.* (1740–*c.* 1780)
   6. Henry Hardin (1710–1796) *m.* Judith Lynch, *b. c.* 1712
   7. MARK HARDIN (Hardouin) (1660–1732) *m.* 1690 Mary Hogue
   Service: A Huguenot, fled France after Edict 1685; went to England, Canada, Penn-
          sylvania, Virginia.
   Reference: "Huguenot Emigration to Virginia," by R. A. Brock; "Historic Georgia
          Families," by L. W. Rigeby.

6031   WRIGHT, Mrs. Vernon   Recorded 1932
          121 Clifton Avenue, Minneapolis, Minnesota
   1. Grace Tileston Clarke (1874–   ) *m.* 1899 Vernon Ames Wright
   2. Thos. William Clarke (1834–1895) *m.* 1868 Eliz. Ann Raymond (1845–1895)
   3. Calvin Whiting Clarke (1796–1878) *m.* 1832 Ann Kettell Townsend (1796–1879)
   4. Dr. David Townsend (1753–1829) *m.* 1785 Eliz. Wendell Davis (1758–1833)
   5. Solomon Davis (1715–1791) *m.* Eliz. Wendell (1729–1777)
   6. John Wendell (1703–1762) *m.* 1724 Eliz. Quincy (1704–1769)
   7. HON. EDMUND QUINCY (1681–1737) *m.* 1701 Dorothy Flynt
   Service: Councillor; Judge of Superior Court; Agent to Court of St. James.
   Reference: Wendell in Salisbury Fam., 465.

5855   WYATT, Mrs. Charles   Recorded 1929, Pennsylvania
          106 Tenth Avenue, Haddon Heights, Camden, New Jersey
   1. Mabel C. Knox *m.* 1888 Charles Wyatt
   2. Joseph Brewster Knox (1828–1905) *m.* 1850 Adelaide Bailey (1826–1900)
   3. Curtis Knox *m.* Rowena Brewster (1793–1865)
   4. Oliver Brewster II (1760–1812) *m.* 1781 Jerusha Badger
   5. Wadsworth Brewster (1737–1812) *m.* Jerusha Newcomb (–1813)
   6. Oliver Brewster I (1708–   ) *m.* Martha Wadsworth
   7. William Brewster III (1681–1768) *m.* Hopestill Wadsworth
   8. William Brewster II (1640–1723) *m.* Lydia Partridge
   9. Love Brewster (–1650) *m.* 1634 Sarah Collier
  10. ELDER WILLIAM BREWSTER (1560–1644) *m.* Mary
   Service: Passenger on the Mayflower; early settler of Plymouth.

6545   WYMAN, William Levi   Recorded 1947
          11040 122nd Street, Edmonton, Alberta, Canada
   1. William L. Wyman *m.* (1st) 1899 Helen A. Johnston; (2nd) 1935, Florence G.
      Lyons

2. Levi Wm. Wyman (1833–1901) *m.* 1860 Hannah S. Salls (1829–1913)
3. Uriah Wyman (1806–1884) *m.* 1828 Lois T. Fisk (1807–1879)
4. Levi Wyman (1761–1844) *m.* Dorothy Wells (1760–1847)
5. Levi Wyman (1732–1768) *m.* 1760 Patience Webber
6. Joseph Wyman (1695–1772) *m.* Ruth Baldwin (1701/2–1778)
7. Timothy Wyman (1661–1709) *m.* Hannah
8. Francis Wyman (1617–1699) *m.* 1650 Abigail Reed, *d.* 1688

Service: Signed orders agreed upon for making Woburn, Mass., a town, 1640.
Reference: The Wyman Family.

6630 YARBROUGH, Josephine M.   Recorded 1949
     1907 Vail Avenue, Charlotte, North Carolina

1. Josephine McDonald *m.* Joel A. Yarbrough
2. James M. McDonald (1826–1884) *m.* 1877 Emma J. Cornwell (1844–1900)
3. Joseph F. Cornwell (1814–1849) *m.* 1838 Frances M. Prather (1820–1876)
4. Leonard D. Prather (1776–1830) *m.* 1799 Frances Williamson (1781–1867)
5. John S. Prather II (1753–1778) *m.* 1775 Jane Deakins (1706–1794)
6. Josiah Prather (1727–1755) *m.* 1751 Jane Deakins (1730–1755)
7. John S. Prather I (1706–1763) *m.* 1727 Elizabeth Nuthall (1709–)
8. Thomas Prather (1673–1712) *m.* 1698 Martha Sprigg (1677–1742)
9. Thomas Sprigg (1630–1704) *m.* 1652 Eleanor Nuthall (1635–aft. 1696)

Service: Justice of Calvert County, Md.; member of the Quorum.
Reference: Recorded wills.

5836 YOUNG, Mrs. Frank H.   Recorded 1929
     2265 Elm Street, Denver, Colorado

1. Eleanor Nickerson Baxter (1857–) *m.* 1881 Frank Herbert Young
2. John Baxter (1825–1864) *m.* 1850 Eleanor Landford Nickerson (1826–1858)
3. Ohea Baxter (1772–) *m.* Bertha Eldridge
4. David Baxter (1745–) *m.* Winifred ———
5. Isaac Baxter *m.* Abigail Taylor
6. John Baxter *m.* Desire Gorham
7. Lieut. Thomas Baxter *m.* Temperance Gorham
8. Capt. John Gorham (1620–1645) *m.* Desire Howland (1621–1683)
9. John Howland (1593–1673) *m.* Elizabeth Tilly (1607–1687)
10. Theophilus Nickerson (1793–1875) *m.* Mary Sandford (1804–1893)
11. Joseph Sandford (1761–1835) *m.* Eleanor Macomber (1763–1844)
12. George Sandford (1726–1820) *m.* Mercy Phillips (1733–1793)
13. John Sandford *m.* Abigail Pitts (1689–1713)

Service:
Reference: 4th Vol. American Ancestry, page 178; Savage's Gen. Dictionary of N. E.,
     Vol. I, page 207, under Babbitt.

6614 YOUNG, Mrs. Frederick W.   Recorded 1949
     42 Washington Street, Stoneham, Massachusetts

1. Ada May Ellis *m.* 1897 Frederick W. Young
2. Joseph D. Ellis (1832–1908) *m.* 1875 Mary N. Wood (1844–1883)
3. Hervey Wood (1804–) *m.* 1827 Mary Duncklee (1807–1885)
4. Abel Duncklee (1776–1867) *m.* 1803 Ruth Wright (1776–1867)
5. Thaddeus Duncklee (1753–1837) *m.* 1774 Sarah Prince (1754–1826)
6. Hezekiah Duncklee (bapt. 1708–1772) *m.* 1734 Damaris Wilson (1710–)
7. Nathaniel Duncklee *m.* Mary French (1670–1729)
8. Lt. William French (1604–1681) *m.* 1669 Mary Stearns (widow) (1640–aft. 1735)

Service: One of the first settlers of Billerica, Mass.
Reference: History of Billerica, Mass.; Hist. of Amherst, N. H.; Genealogies of
     Watertown, Mass.

6548   YUTZLER, Mrs. Harry A.   Recorded 1947
         6958 Ogontz Avenue, Philadelphia, Pennsylvania

   1. Martha Loy *m.* 1920 Harry A. Yutzler
   2. George W. Loy (1855–1924) *m.* 1878 Ida C. Evinger (1858–1943)
   3. Andrew Loy (1816–1898) *m.* 1835 Maria Wormley (1815–1858)
   4. Nicholas Loy (1770–1848) *m.* 1815 Mary Kuhn (1772–1844)
   5. Michael Loy (1740–1823) *m.* 1769 Margaret Lambert (1749–1809)
   6. Thomas G. Lambert (1707–1784) *m.* Anna ——— (1678–)
   7. Thomas Lambert, Jr. (1672–1733) *m.* 1695 Margaret A. Scott (1678–)
   8. THOMAS LAMBERT *m.* Joane Terry

   Service: Signer of Grants and Concessions; member of early Courts of Burlington;
         member of General Assembly.
   Reference: General Rodgers Collection; History of Trenton.

6013   ZIRKLE, Mrs. Homer William   Recorded 1932
         357 Lincoln Street, Denver, Colorado

   1. Grace Scrafford (1875–) *m.* 1910 Homer W. Zirkle
   2. Geo. Lester Scrafford (1852–1924) *m.* 1874 Elnora Stelle (1855–)
   3. Arnold Freeman Stelle (1829–1905) *m.* 1852 Garafelia Fitz Randolph (1833–1916)
   4. Azariah Fitz Randolph (1805–1868) *m.* 1828 Lucy Crandell Maxson (1807–1888)
   5. Abel Fitz Randolph (1773–) *m.* 1802 Ruth Ayars (1780–)
   6. James Fitz Randolph (1748–1791) *m.* 1772 Phoebe Ayars (1755–)
   7. Jos. Fitz Randolph (1713–) *m.* ———
   8. David Fitz Randolph (1690–) *m.* Sarah Malloson
   9. Thomas Fitz Randolph (1659–) *m.* 1686 Elizabeth Manning
  10. EDWARD FITZ RANDOLPH (1613–1675) *m.* 1637 Elizabeth Blossom (1620–1713)

   Service:
   Reference: Gen. Rec. Geo. F. Randolph, Nortonville, Ka.; Gen. Rec. Micah Ayers,
         Paulsboro, N. J.; Pioneers of Mass., page 169.

5835   ZOOK, Dr. Erle Will   Recorded 1929
         Peoria State Hospital, Peoria, Illinois

   1. Erle Will Zook, M.D. (1873–) *m.* 1897 Florence E. Edwards
   2. Joseph Zook, Jr. (1846–1890) *m.* 1872 Elizabeth Emmaline Will (1848–1873)
   3. Joseph Zook, Sr. (1816–1874) *m.* 1839 Matilda Sell (1819–1875)
   4. David Zook (1791–1875) *m.* Susannah LeFevre (1794–1838)
   5. Joseph LeFevre (1765–1835) *m.* Suzanna Bowman (1769–1840)
   6. Benjamin Bowman *m.* Elizabeth Ferree
   7. Isaac Ferree *m.* Elizabeth Ferree
   8. Philip Ferree (1687–1753) *m.* 1713 Leah DuBois (1687–1758)
   9. Abraham DuBois (1657–1731) *m.* 1681 Margaret Deyo
  10. Louis DuBois (1626–1696) *m.* Catherine Blaushan
  11. MATHESE BLAUCHAN *m.* Madeline Jorisse

   Service: Founder of New Paltz, New York.
   Reference: History of New Paltz, N. Y., pages 289, 509, 515, 253, and appendix,
         page 84; Mast Family History, pages 187, 190.

BROWN (cont.)
  Rachel 132
  Rachel Barber 126
  Ruth (Mrs.) 196
  Samuel Whitney 219
  Sara Rowe 96, 97
  Sarah 49, 207
  Thomas 141
BROWNE, Chad (Rev.) 158
  Esek 229
  Lydia 229
  Martha 159
  W. B. 229
  William B. 158
BROWNELL, Francis E. 30
  Francis E. (Mrs.) 30
BROWNING, (?) 145
  Alfred 228
  C. H. 122
  Joseph 228
  Lydia 228
BROWNINGS, (?) 114
BROYE, Jeanne 38
BRUBAKER, George 13
  Georgianna 13
BRUCE, (?) 58
  Lucy 164, 165, 207
  Margaret 158
BRUEN, Hannah 5
  Obadiah 5
  Sarah (Mrs.) 5
BRUISON, Adam (I) 34
  Adam (II) 34
  Benjamin E. 34
  Eliza L. 34
BRUMLY, Alexander
    Brevard 172
  Mary 172
BRUNDAGE, Mary 159
BRUSLE, Ophelia 39
BRYAM, George 11
  Sarah 11
BRYAN, (?) 37
  Clark W. 33
  Lillian W. 171
  Lydia 159
  Mary 102, 170
  Rachel 42
  William Alden 159
  William B. 159
BRYANT, E. Sumner 9
  Ebenezer 9
  Fanny 200
  Minnie 9
BRYSON, Jane 90, 180
BUCK, (?) 31
  Elizabeth 166
  Jessica Williams
    (Mrs.) 31
  Mary 25, 219
  Richard (Rev.) 59, 166
BUCKINGHAM, Elizabeth 96
BUCKLAND, Hannah 227
BUCKLEY, William G. 31
  William G. (Mrs.) 31
BUCKLIN, Jeremiah 26
  John 26
  John (Maj.) 26
  Joseph 26
  Susan Eliza 26
  Susannah (Mrs.) 26
BUCKMINISTER, Sarah 148
BUELL, (?) 202
  Asa 202
  Daniel 202
  Elizabeth 202
  Elmina 132
  Nathaniel 202

BUELL (cont.)
  Samuel (I) 202
  Samuel (II) 202
  William 202
BUFFINGTON, Charlotte
    Temple 131
  Hannah 8
  Jesse 131
  Joseph 83
  May 83
  Richard (I) 131
  Richard (II) 131
  Richard (III) 131
  Richard (IV) 131
BULGER, Elizabeth 59,
    87, 134, 166, 187
BULIS, Hester Ann 113
BULKELEY, (?) 113
  Edward (Cpt.) 209, 210
  Gersham 209
  Peter 23
  Peter (Rev.) 23, 113
  Rebecca 209, 210
  Sarah 23, 113
  Thomas 23, 113
BULKELY, Dorothy 118
  Peter (Dr.) 118
  Peter (Rev.) 118
BULKLEY, (?) 23, 118
BULL, Charles A. 31
  Jacob Edmund 31
  Mary Ellen 31
  Peace 14
BULLARD, Daniel O. 31
  Dexter (Rev.) 31
  Dorothy 94
  Irene B. 31
BULLOCH, (?) 170
  J. G. B. 170
BULLOCK, (?) 32, 231
  Eliza 85
  Helena Mercy Smith
    (Mrs.) 32
  Sarah 21
BUMPUS, Elizabeth 94
BUNCE, Allen (Mrs.) 32
  Allen H. 32
BUNKER, Hussey 133
  Rachel 133
BUNTING, Catherine M. 42
  Job 42
  John 42
  Joseph (Jr.) 42
  Samuel 42
  Solomon 42
BURBANK, Rebecca 55, 221
BURBEE, Frances
    Elizabeth 30
  James E. 30
BURCH, Isadore 181
  John 200
  Martha 200
BURCHAM, Norma 98
BURGESS, Alice 88
  Priscilla 42
  Ruth 9
  Susan 210
  William 9
BURKE, Sallie 231
BURNELL, John Patrick
    (Mrs.) 32
  John Phillips 32
  Polly Ann 32
BURNETT, Adda M. 148
  Frances 142
  Ralph P. 142
BURNEY, Estelle 39
  John F. 39

BURNEY (cont.)
  Julius A. 39
  Minnie Melton 33
  William B. 33
BURNHAM, Abigail 92
  Adelaide L. 1
  George S. (Col.) 89
  Mary A. 89
  Roderick H. 33
  Simon P. 1
BURNLEY, Mary 141
  Richmond 141
BURR, (?) 162, 189
  Abigail 189
  Alice Eugenie 225
  Daniel 162
  Elizabeth (Mrs.) 162
  Ephraim 189
  Ezekiel 162
  Jabez 162
  Jehu 162, 189
  John (Jr.) 189
  Louise W. 162
  Peter (Maj.) 189
  Sarah 189
  William E. 162
BURRELL, Alexander 123
  Elizabeth 9
  Sarah 123
BURRILL, Eunice 61
  Samuel 61
BURROUGHS, Elizabeth
    174, 193, 218
BURRUS, Edmund 4
  Mildred 4
BURT, (?) 208
  Alonzo Fremont 33
  Arthur Seymour 207,
    208
  Gertrude Leone 33
  Henry 25, 33
  James 33
  John 33
  John (Cpt.) 33
  Jonathan (Dea.) 33
  Mary 25
  Mary Foote 207, 208
  Rix 33
  Sarah A. 71
  Thankful 212
  Thomas 25
  Ulalia (Mrs.) 25
BURTON, (?) 91
  Sarah 84
  Susannah 133
BURTS, Martha E. 33
  Ransom 33
BURWELL, John 33
  John S. 33
  Lena A. 33
  Lena Almira 33
BUSBIDGE, Martha 191
BUSH, Grace 112
BUSHNELL, (?) 226
  Anna 67
  Charles 226
  Francis 226
  George E. 226
  Maria A. 226
  Samuel 226
  Samuel (II) 226
  Samuel (Cpt.) 226
  Samuel (Jr.) 226
  William (Lt.) 226
BUSHROD, Apphia 145
BUSSENIUS, Frederick W.
    34
  Frederick W. (Mrs.) 34

257

FRETWELL (cont.)
Charles B. 78
Charles Burlington 78
James 78
James Burlington 205
FRICK, Rosanna 5
FRISBEE, Katherine 126
FROST, (?) 26
Edmund 26
Ellen Sophia 26
Josephine 3
Josiah 26
Margaret 229
Noah 26
Robert 26
Samuel 26
Thomasine (Mrs.) 26
FRUEAUFF, Frank
Wheatcroft 77
Margaret Hall 77
FRY, Elizabeth 230
Mary 15
FRYE, (?) 86
Harley E. 77
Harley E. (Mrs.) 77
Jeffrey A. 86
Mary 121
Olney 86
Roxy 86
Thomas 86
FRYER, Evalena G. 96
John P. 96
FULLER, (?) 21, 110
Abial 24
Alexander Lemuel 78
Ann (Mrs.) 110
Anna Eliza 200
Anna M. 21
Asenath 110
Damon 78
Edward 110
Edwin M. 78
Edwin M. (Mrs.) 78
Eliz. 158
Emma Elnora 66
Frances (Mrs.) 78
George Washington 24
Hannah 89, 219
Irad 110
Isaac (Dr.) 21
Jabez 21
Jabez (Dr.) 21
Jane 34
Jehiel (Cpt.) 110
John 24, 110, 206
Jonathan (Dr.) 21
Judah 78
Lemuel 78
Martha 69
Mary 30, 208
Mary (Mrs.) 78
Mathew 78
Matthew (Cpt.) 78
Maud Elizabeth 167
Myrta D. 71
Nathan 24
Samuel 78, 110, 206
Samuel (Dr.) 21
Samuel (Rev.) 21
Sarah 158, 192
Sarah Viola 24
Susanna 105
Susannah 7, 32
Thankful 206
Thomas 110
FULTON, Jane Johnson 201
FURBEE, Frances
Elizabeth 29

FURBEE (cont.)
James 130
James S. 29, 130, 131
Sarah Louise 130
GAERTNER, Herman 79
Herman J. 79
Herman J. (Mrs.) 79
Herman Julius (Jr.) 79
Nellie Jane 79
GAGE, Jane 113
GAGER, Hannah 15, 28
GAGES, Lucy Peck 132
GAINER, Ann 8
GAINES, (?) 17, 19
Annie Lee 85, 146
Daniel (Cpt.) 17, 19,
85, 146
Elizabeth 17, 19, 56,
85, 146
Heirom 17
Heirome 17, 19
Heirome (Jr.) 17, 19,
56, 85, 146
Heirome (Sr.) 56, 85,
146
James H. 19, 56
James Henry 85, 146
James R. 19, 56
James Ralph 85, 146
Margaret (Mrs.) 19,
146
Margaret Cunningham 17
Mary 139
Mattie B. 56
Mttie B. 19
Thomas 17, 19, 146
GAINS, Margaret (Mrs.)
146
Thomas 146
GAJER, Hannah 15
GALE, (?) 80
Abraham 80
Amos Curtis 80
Charlotte 206
Dinah 46
Elisha (Lt.) 80
Frank Gilbert 80
George 80
Hannah 121
Isaac (Cpt.) 80
Jacob 79
Lydia Hammond 79
Mabel E. 193
Richard 80
Royce Larebee 80
Stephen 121
Theodore 193
William Bradford 79
GALLOP, (?) 101
Christobel (Mrs.) 101
John 101
John (Jr.) (Cpt.) 101
John (Sr.) 101
Martha 101
GALLUP, (?) 119
Benadam 80
Christobel (Mrs.) 80
Elisha Swan 80
Esther 119
Fannie M. 225
John 80, 119
John (Cpt.) 80, 119
Joseph (Cpt.) 80
Joseph Adam 80
Walter Palmer 80
Walter Palmer (Jr.) 80
William 80
GALPIN, Roxy 213

GANNAWAY, Sarah 2
GANSERROTT, Elizabeth 86
Leonard 86
GANTT, Charles Alfred
(Dr.) 140
Irene 140
Pleasant Jordan 140
GANZHORN, Sophia 8
GARD, Phebe 222
GARDINER, Bathsheba 227
Lydia 45
GARDNER, John 171
Julia 50
Malina B. 171
Sarah J. 6
GARILION, Madeleine 86
GARLAND, John 190
Mary 190
Suit 190
Sylvester 190
GARLICK, Abigail 203
Hannah 203
GARLINGTON, Christopher
146, 147
Elizabeth H. 146
Sara (Mrs.) 147
GARMAN, Helen
Sonnenschein 80
LeRoy C. 80
GARNER, Lydia 191
GARNSEY, Helen 25
Oscar N. 25, 80
Winora Hanchett 80
GARR, (?) 95
GARRETT, John W. (Dr.)
19, 56
John Wilkinson 85, 146
Lillie Corinne 146
Louka Adele 56
Loula A. 19
Mary N. 188
Sallie Lee 85
GARRISON, Ann 29, 30,
130, 131, 143
Sarah P. 72
GARVIN, Ella L. 96
James B. 96
GARWOOD, Margaret 1, 47,
119, 120, 178
Thomas 47, 178
GARY, Claire 64
Clare 132
GASKELL, Ilka 196
Silas S. C. 196
GASKILL, Hannah 42
Sarah 167
Zerubbabel 42
GATES, Caleb 1
Damalis 12
Ephraim 1
Janet D. 1
Johnathan 1
Rebecca 43
GATLETT, Mary 17
GAWTHROPE, Sarah 90
GAY, Kydia Starr 66
Lydia 66
Lydia Starr 204
GEAR, Amos 39
George 39
Robert (Cpt.) 39
Robert (Jr.) 39
Sally Ann 39
GEBBS, Mary C. 7, 32
GEER, (?) 39
Walter 39
GEISE, Reuben 62
Susie Bright 62

GOULD, (?) 153
  Abraham 189
  Alvira 153
  Elizabeth (Mrs.) 83
  Elvira 83
  Gideon 153
  Godeon 83
  Helen 189
  Jay 189
  John Burr 189
  Joseph 83, 153
  Nathan 83, 153
  Samuel 83, 153
GOVE, Mary 121
GOWDY, Nellie Peters 83
  Willis 83
GOWELL, Lydia 187
GOWER, James 75
  Susan Norton 75
GRAF, J. A. (Mrs.) 83
  John A. 83
GRAFF, J. A. (Mrs.) 83
  John A. 83
GRAHAM, John Lincoln 84
  John Lincoln (Mrs.) 84
  Sarah G. 67
GRANADE, Martha A. 168
GRANGER, Dorothy 89
  Lancelot 89
  Mary A. 197
GRANT, Edgar Weston 210
  Esther Rowan 182
  Helen M. 210
  Minnie Jane 224
  Nelson M. 224
  R. J. (Mrs.) 84
  Robert J. 84
GRAVES, Ann (Mrs.) 173
  Francis 37
  Francis (Jr.) 173
  Francis (Sr.) 173
  Hannah 145
  Jane (Mrs.) 173
  Katherine 37
  Katherine (Mrs.) 173
  Mary 37
  Richard 37
  Thomas (Cpt.) 37, 173
GRAY, Anna 18
  Ardis 53, 97
  Arthur H. 220
  Charles A. 53, 84, 97
  Elisie Maud 16
  Elizabeth 99
  Elizabeth (Mrs.) 37,
    91, 177
  Faith 160
  Hannah 96, 97
  Harry L. 84
  Henrietta M. 38
  Henrietta Montgomery
    38
  Inez 97
  J. E. 84
  J. E. (Mrs.) 84
  Margery 37, 91, 177
  Mary 155
  Nell 220
  Ninian Edwards 38
  Parnell 128
  William 37, 91, 177
GREANLEAF, Elizabeth 9
GREAVES, Hannah 8
  Jane 195
GREEN, Adaline S. 176,
    177
  Adeline S. 137
  Alvina D. 54, 136,

GREEN (cont.)
    185, 186
  Anna 128
  Anna (Mrs.) 230
  Harry C. (Mrs.) 84
  Harry Clifford (Dr.)
    84
  Henrietta 14
  J. R. 193
  Jane 42
  Lucius Felton (Mrs.)
    85
  Lucy 92
  Mary 66
  Mary Sayles (Wid.) 125
  Richard H. 14
  Zurviah 216
GREENE, (?) 172
  Amanda 133
  Audrey 15
  Job 172
  John 15
  John (Dr.) 15, 172
  John (Maj.) 15
  Julia E. 15
  Martha 186
  Mary 45
  Philip 172
  Phoebe 172
  Ransom J. 15, 133
  Warren 45
  William 45
GREENFIELD, Martha 95
GREENHAUGH, Elizabeth 6
GREENHILL, Rebecca 120,
    135
  Rebecca (Mrs.) 1
  Rebecca (Wid.) 119
  Sam'l. 1
  Samuel 119
GREENLEAF, Edmund 197
  Elizabeth 41, 155
  Judith 197
  Stephen (Cpt.) 155
  Stephen (Jr.) (Cpt.)
    155
GREENMAN, Abigail 39, 45
GREENSLADE, Joanne 212
GREENWOOD, Elizabeth 36
  Nancy 111
GREGG, Cordelia Matilda
    69
GREGORIE, Charles
    Colcock 68
  Emily 68
  Grace 68
  Henry Hutson 68
  James 68
GREMMER, Isabelle 206
  Isabelle T. 207
  Isabelle Teel 207
GRESHAM, Rosa 231
  Vicotira 8
GRIFFIN, Florrie L. 38
  Florrie Lewis 38
  Henry C. 38
  Henry Clay 38
  Jane M. 36, 37
  Katherine 145
  Margaret A. 232
  Mary 59, 87, 134, 166,
    187
  Thankful 202
GRIFFITH, Anna M. 98
  Margaret 223
GRIFFITTS, Hester 38
  William 38
GRIGGS, John F. 85

GRIGGS (cont.)
  Wilkinson Garrett 85
GRIMSLEY, G. Reed 85
  G. Reed (Mrs.) 85
GRINELL, Annie 187
GRINNELL, Daniel 112
  Sarah 112
GRISHAM, Frances 211
GRISWOLD, Albert C. 86
  Alma L. 86
  Anna (Mrs.) 86
  Deborah 202
  Edward 198
  Hannah 198
  Jacob 86
  James 86
  Josiah (Maj.) 86
  Julius E. 86
  Julius E. (Mrs.) 86
  Lucy M. 191
  Lydia 110, 216
  Margaret (Mrs.) 198
  Michael 86
  Ozias 86
GROESBECK, Jacob 20
  Nicholas 20
  Rachel 20
GROO, Edward 159
  Isaac 159
GROOM, Avery Burr 86
  Avery Burr (Mrs.) 86
GROSE, Anne 143
GROSS, Anne 143, 187
  Elizabeth 41
GROSVENAR, (?) 57
GROSVENOR, (?) 51, 62
GROTON, (?) 212
GROUT, Sarah 11
GROW, (?) 159
  Edward 159
  Isaac 159
  John 159
  Melissa A. 159
  Rebecca 159
GRUBB, (?) 73, 141
  Charity 141
  Elizabeth 165
  Frances 131
  Lydia 175
  Phoebe 131
  Rebecca 73
  Samuel 73
GUERNSEY, Susanna 45
GUEST, Phoebe 38
GUIGNARD, Caroline E.
    190
GUILFORD, Electa 25
  Paul 25
GUMBART, George C. 86
  George C. (Mrs.) 86
GUNBY, Elisha 197
  Eliza 197
  Mary 58
GUNN, Edgar R. (Mrs.) 86
  Edgar Ross 86
  Florentine 77, 212
  William C. 77
  Wm. Carroll 212
GUNTHER, (?) 87
  Beatrice 134
  Charles (Mrs.) 87
  Charles O. 87, 134
  Jack Disbrow 87
GWALTNEY, Oceana W. 138
HABELTINE, Hannah 215
HABERSHAM, (?) 170, 231
  Catherine 231
  Richard Wyth 231

LORING, Alice 175
  Bezaleel 101
  John Mason 101
  Rachel Cutter 101
LOTHROP, Anna (Mrs.) 136
  Barnabas 136
  Chester H. 136
  David 136
  Donald G. (Rev.) 136
  Henry Allen 136
  Hornell 20
  Jane 206
  John (Cpt.) 136
  John (Rev.) 136
  Jonathan 136
  Jonathan (Dea.) 20
  Lucy 20
  Mark 20
  Sarah (Mrs.) 136
  Soloman 20
LOUGHEAD, Mary 19
LOUKE, E. H. 35
LOUW, Janneken 79
LOVE, Elizabeth May 26
  John Wesley 26
LOVELACE, Caroline 213
  James 213
  William 213
  Wm. 213
  Wm. R. (Dr.) 213
LOVELL, Deborah 94
LOW, Anthony 172
  Eliza Greene 172
  Jane (Lady) 68
  Johanna 21
  Philip 172
  Sarah 171
LOWDEN, Hannah S. 20
LOWE, Alline 232
  Jane (Lady) 217
  John Holman 232
  William Sterling 232
LOWELL, Dorcas 122
LOWENTHAL, Fay 54
  Julius 185, 186
  Julius L. 54, 136
  Julius L. (Mrs.) 136
  Pearl 186
  Rose 185
LOWERY, Mary 101, 183,
  229
LOWNSDALE, Agnes 121
  Thomas N. 121
LOWTHER, Catherine 87
LOY, Andrew 234
  George W. 234
  Martha 234
  Michael 234
  Nicholas 234
LOYSEE, Dorothea 161
LUBBERTS, Marie 53
LUBBERTSEN, Frederick 49
  Rebecca 49
LUCAS, Elizabeth (Mrs.)
  227
  Margaret 227
  Robert 227
  Robt. (Jr.) 227
  Sarah 23, 137, 176,
  177
  Susannah 84
LUDINGTON, Clarissa 110
LUDLOW, Roger 174
  Sarah 174
LUDWIG, Rosanna 67
LUKINS, Alise 173
LUKOMSKA, Helena 136
LULL, Adeline 76

LUM, Elizabeth 191
LUNDIE, Eliz. Bland 51
  Elizabeth Bland 57, 62
  Ida Clara 7
  Thomas (Rev.) 51, 57,
  62
LUNDY, Mary Earle 143
LUPTON, Alfred H. (Mrs.)
  137
  Alfred Holmes 137
  B. Frank 137
  B. Frank (Mrs.) 137
LUSE, Hariette E. 99
  Jacob 99
LUTEN, Mary 231
  Mary (Mrs.) 231
  Thomas (Maj.) 231
LUTHER, (?) 158
  Caleb 158
  George H. 158
  Jabez 158, 229
  John (Cpt.) 158
  Leviette J. 158
  Mary 229
  Samuel 158
  Samuel (Jr.) 158
  Sarah (Mrs.) 158
LYDDALL, Ann 22
  George (Col.) 22
LYE, John 61
  Joseph (Jr.) 61
  Sarah 61
LYERLY, Mary Lunda 16,
  17
LYLE, Albert F. (Rev.)
  129
  Rosa Marian 129
LYMAN, (?) 199
  Asabel 199
  Cecelia 199
  Elias 199
  John (II) (Lt.) 199
  John (Lt.) 199
  Lydia Marsh 154
  Phillis 100
  Richard 199
LYNCH, Judith 232
LYNCHBURG, (?) 224
LYNDE, Elizabeth 82
  Nathaniel (Jdg.) 82
LYNN, (?) 155
LYON, Andrew 14
  Jessie 14
  Mary 75
  Phebe 209
LYONS, (?) 19, 32, 54,
  170
  Edwin James 137
  Edwin James (Jr.) 137
  Florence G. 232
  Mary 86
  Polly 86
MABEE, Mary J. 36
MABEN, John 79
  Mary Lucinda 79
MABRY, Benjamin Seawell
  121
  Elizabeth Gilliam 121
  Frances 121
  Francis 121
  Henshaw 121
  Henshaw (Jr.) 121
  Henshaw (Sr.) 121
  Indiana Seawell 121
  Seth 121
MACBETH, Sabrina Ann 156
MACCOURN, Isabel 24
MACK, (?) 74, 145, 198

MACK (cont.)
  Alonzo Shaw 74
  Benjamin 74
  Diadema 145
  Ebenezer 145
  Elisha (Jr.) 145
  Elisha (Sr.) 145
  Eunice (Mrs.) 74
  Jack 145
  John 74
  Nehemiah 74
MACKEEL, (?) 64
MACKEELE, (?) 64
  (?) (Mrs.) 64
  John 64
  John (Cpt.) 64
  Mary 64
  Thomas 64
  Thomas (Cpt.) 64
MACKENZIE, (?) 47, 57
  N. (Gen.) 129
MACKERNESS, Frances 29
MACKIE, Eliza 24
MACKILWEAN, Anne 37
  Francis 37
MACKQUINNEY, (?) 226
  Elizabeth (Mrs.) 102,
  111, 226
  L. J. 226
  Michael 102, 111, 226
MACLAFLEN, Sarah 204
MACLAMAR, Sarah A. 201
MACLEAN, Charles (Jr.)
  214
  Lucinda 214
MACOMBER, Eleanor 233
MACON, Ann 111
MACPHAIL, D. R. 142
  D. R. (Mrs.) 142
MACPHERSON, Ronald 143
  Ronald (Mrs.) 143
MADDUX, Lizzie R. 20
MAHIEU, Hester 94
MAHON, Charles L. (Rev.)
  143
  Charles LeDow (Rev.)
  131
  Chas. LeDow (Dr.) 29
  Chas. LeDow (Rev.) 29,
  130
  Chas. Ledow (Dr.) 30
  Chas. Ledow (Rev.) 30
  Harriette W. 143
  Harriette Warrick 143
  James (Cpt.) 30
  John (Cpt.) 29, 130,
  131, 143
  Louise Christian 130
  Louise Christine 29,
  30, 131
MAHONEY, Mary 9
MAIN, Phebe 196
MALEY, Alice M. 199
  Alice Mildred 214
  James 199, 214
  John 199, 214
  Sidney 199, 214
MALIN, Hannah 203
MALLORY, Lina 144
MALLOSON, Sarah 234
MALONE, Chaste Alberta
  143
  E. P. 143
  E. P. (Mrs.) 143
  Frank Nettles 143
MALTBY, Emily (Mrs.) 17
  Harrison 17
  Mary 17